CAMBRIDGE GREEK AND LATIN CLASSICS

GENERAL EDITORS

P. E. EASTERLING
Regius Professor Emeritus of Greek, University of Cambridge

PHILIP HARDIE
Senior Research Fellow, Trinity College, and Honorary Professor of Latin, University of Cambridge

NEIL HOPKINSON
Fellow, Trinity College, University of Cambridge

RICHARD HUNTER
Regius Professor of Greek, University of Cambridge

E. J. KENNEY
Kennedy Professor Emeritus of Latin, University of Cambridge

S. P. OAKLEY
Kennedy Professor of Latin, University of Cambridge

SENECA
SELECTED LETTERS

EDITED BY
CATHARINE EDWARDS
Birkbeck, University of London

CAMBRIDGE
UNIVERSITY PRESS

University Printing House, Cambridge CB2 8BS, United Kingdom

One Liberty Plaza, 20th Floor, New York, NY 10006, USA

477 Williamstown Road, Port Melbourne, VIC 3207, Australia

314–321, 3rd Floor, Plot 3, Splendor Forum, Jasola District Centre,
New Delhi – 110025, India

79 Anson Road, #06-04/06, Singapore 079906

Cambridge University Press is part of the University of Cambridge.

It furthers the University's mission by disseminating knowledge in the pursuit of education, learning, and research at the highest international levels of excellence.

www.cambridge.org
Information on this title: www.cambridge.org/9780521460118
DOI: 10.1017/9781139048637

© Cambridge University Press 2019

This publication is in copyright. Subject to statutory exception and to the provisions of relevant collective licensing agreements, no reproduction of any part may take place without the written permission of Cambridge University Press.

First published 2019

Printed and bound in Great Britain by Clays Ltd, Elcograf S.p.A.

A catalogue record for this publication is available from the British Library.

Library of Congress Cataloging-in-Publication Data
NAMES: Seneca, Lucius Annaeus, approximately 4 B.C.–65 A.D., author. | Edwards, Catharine, editor.
TITLE: Seneca: selected letters / edited by Catharine Edwards.
OTHER TITLES: Correspondence | Cambridge Greek and Latin classics.
DESCRIPTION: Cambridge : Cambridge University Press, 2019. | Series: Cambridge Greek and Latin classics
IDENTIFIERS: LCCN 2018058449 | ISBN 9780521460118
SUBJECTS: LCSH: Seneca, Lucius Annaeus, approximately 4 B.C.–65 A.D. – Correspondence. | Seneca, Lucius Annaeus, approximately 4 B.C.–65 A.D.
CLASSIFICATION: LCC PA6661.E7 A2 2019 | DDC 876/.01–dc23
LC record available at https://lccn.loc.gov/2018058449

ISBN 978-0-521-46011-8 Hardback
ISBN 978-0-521-46583-0 Paperback

Cambridge University Press has no responsibility for the persistence or accuracy of URLs for external or third-party internet websites referred to in this publication and does not guarantee that any content on such websites is, or will remain, accurate or appropriate.

CONTENTS

Acknowledgements	*page* vii
List of Abbreviations	ix
Introduction	1
1 *Seneca's Life and Works*	1
2 *The* Epistulae morales *and their Addressee*	3
3 *Letters as a Genre*	6
4 *Stoic Terms and Concepts*	9
5 *Stoic Background*	12
6 *Other Philosophical Influences*	15
7 *Ethical Focus and Techniques of the Self*	18
8 *Seneca and Earlier Latin Poetic Authors*	22
9 *Senecan Style*	23
10 Clausulae *in Seneca*	27
11 *Reception of the Letters*	29
12 *The Selection*	32
13 *The Text*	32
SENECA: SELECTED LETTERS	35
Letter 1	37
Letter 7	37
Letter 12	39
Letter 18	41
Letter 21	42
Letter 24	44
Letter 33	48
Letter 34	49
Letter 46	50

Letter 47	50
Letter 53	53
Letter 64	54
Letter 70	56
Letter 86	59
Letter 90	62
Letter 114	69
Commentary	75
Bibliography	306
Index of Latin Words	334
General Index	340

ACKNOWLEDGEMENTS

This commentary has been a remarkably long time in gestation and numerous debts have been incurred along the way, which it is a great pleasure to acknowledge.

In Bristol Christopher Rowe first prompted me to consider writing a commentary on the Letters (though the seeds were surely sown in Cambridge undergraduate supervisions with that doyen of Green & Yellow commentators, Neil Hopkinson). Other Bristol colleagues, Duncan Kennedy, Charles Martindale and the late Thomas Wiedemann, offered important advice at an early stage, as did series editor Ted Kenney. In more recent years, the support of Shadi Bartsch, Mary Beard, Susanna Morton Braund, all, in their different ways, exemplary models of scholarship, has been invaluable. Mike Trapp very kindly offered detail comments in relation to Letter 90 and I am most grateful for his philosophical expertise. I have also benefitted immensely from exchanges (sometimes themselves epistolary) with a number of other distinguished Latinists, Mireille Armisen-Marchetti, Francesca Romana Berno, Rita Degl'Innocenti Pierini, Barbara Del Giovane, Alex Dressler, William Fitzgerald, James Ker, Roland Mayer, Janja Soldo, several of whom have generously shared their work in advance of publication. Chris Whitton kindly offered patient guidance on the intricacies of Latin prose rhythm. Rebecca Langlands and Marden Nichols were kind enough to let me read preliminary versions of their splendid books. I owe much to Emily Gowers (my friend since the days of those undergraduate supervisions), herself a model commentator.

As series editors, Stephen Oakley and Philip Hardie have been unfailingly patient and exceptionally generous with their time and their phenomenal expertise. I am hugely grateful to them for spurring me to think further about a whole range of issues and to strive for the kind of precision a commentary owes its readers. Michael Sharp, Classics Editor at CUP, and Lisa Sinclair, Senior Content Manager, have provided much help along the way, while Iveta Adams has been an eagle-eyed and judicious copy editor. Naturally all remaining errors are my own.

The department of History, Classics and Archaeology at Birkbeck has been a hugely stimulating and supportive environment in which to work (my friends and colleagues Christy Constantakopoulou, Serafina Cuomo and Jen Baird deserve particular mention). The Institute of Classical Studies/Hellenic and Roman library, with its supremely helpful and expert librarians – and virtually all its books on open shelves – is the commentator's dream. Some crucial work was also done in the wonderful surroundings of the British School at Rome. I was very fortunate to be awarded a Leverhulme Research Fellowship for 2015–16, which played a critical role in enabling me to bring this project to a conclusion.

This book is dedicated to my magnificent and much loved daughters, Isabel and Miranda, who, having refused to study Latin beyond GCSE, will probably never read it.

ABBREVIATIONS

CIL	*Corpus Inscriptionum Latinarum*, Berlin 1863–
DK	H. Diels and W. Kranz, *Fragmente der Vorsokratiker*, 6th edn, Berlin 1952
G–L	G. L. Gildersleeve and G. Lodge, *Latin grammar*, 3rd edn, London 1895
KRS	G. Kirk, J. E. Raven and M. Schofield, *The pre-Socratic philosophers: a critical history with a selection of texts*, 2nd edn, Cambridge 1983
K–S	R Kühner and C. Stegmann, *Ausführliche Grammatik der lateinishen Sprache*, Hanover 1955
LSJ	H. G. Liddell and R. Scott, *A Greek–English lexicon*, 9th edn, rev. H. S. Jones, Oxford 1940
NLG	Allen and Greenough's *New Latin grammar*, rev. edn, Boston 1903
NLS	E. C. Woodcock, *A new Latin syntax*, London 1959
NP	H. Gärtner, *Paulys Realencyclopädie der Altertumswissenschaft, neue Bearbeitung*, Munich 1980–
OCD[4]	S. Hornblower, A. Spawforth and E. Eidinow (eds.), *Oxford classical dictionary*, 4th edn, Oxford 2012
OLD	P. W. Glare, *Oxford Latin dictionary*, Oxford 1968–82
ORF[4]	E. Malcovati (ed.), *Oratorum Romanorum fragmenta liberae rei publicae*, 4th edn, 2 vols., Turin 1976–9
PIR[2]	E. Groag, A. Stein *et al.*, *Prosopographia imperii Romani*, 2nd edn, Berlin 1933–
RE	A. F. von Pauly, *Paulys Realencyclopädie der Altertumswissenschaft*, Stuttgart 1893
Schanz–Hosius	M. Schanz, *Geschichte der römischen Litteratur bis zum Gesetzgebungwerk des Kaisers Justinian*, rev. vols. I[4] (1927) and II[4] (1935) by C. Hosius; III[3] (1922) by G. Krüger; IV.1[2] (1914) and IV.2 (1920) by Schanz, Hosius and Krüger, Munich
SVF	H. von Arnim and M. Adler, *Stoicorum veterum fragmenta*, Leipzig 1903–24
Tab. Vindol. II	A. K. Bowman and J. D. Thomas, *The Vindolanda Writing-Tablets (Tabulae Vindolandenses II)*, London 1994
TLL	*Thesaurus linguae Latinae*, Munich 1900–

Journal titles are abbreviated in accordance with *L'Année philologique*. The names and titles of classical authors and texts are generally abbreviated in accordance with *OLD* for Latin and *OCD* for Greek. Latin authors and works not included in *OLD* are cited according to the conventions in *OCD*. In addition, the following abbreviations are used for works of Seneca (S):

Brev.	*De breuitate uitae*
Clem.	*De clementia*
EM	*Epistulae morales*
Marc.	*Consolatio ad Marciam*
Polyb.	*Consolatio ad Polybium*
VB	*De uita beata*

INTRODUCTION

1 SENECA'S LIFE AND WORKS

Born at Corduba (modern Córdoba in southern Spain) between 4 BCE and 1 CE into a wealthy equestrian family, Seneca the Younger (hereafter S) was the second son of Seneca the Elder, an acclaimed rhetorician who wrote treatises on declamation, and of Helvia (addressee of *Ad Heluiam matrem*, written during S's exile). Though little is known of his life before 41 CE, he studied rhetoric at Rome and claims to have been attracted to philosophy at an early age, citing as his teachers the Stoic Attalus, as well as Sotion and Papirius Fabianus. After a period in Egypt, S returned to Rome in 31 CE, where some time later he secured election to the quaestorship (thus entering the senate), and established a reputation as a brilliant orator. After eight years in exile on the island of Corsica for alleged involvement in the adultery of Gaius' sister Livilla (Dio 60.8), he was recalled to Rome on the initiative of Claudius' new wife Agrippina to serve as tutor to her 12-year-old son, the future emperor Nero.[1]

S was closely associated with Nero for more than a decade, going on to serve, when Nero succeeded Claudius in 54 CE, as his adviser and speechwriter. S's treatise *De clementia*, addressed to the new emperor, dates from soon after his accession and offers the young emperor a philosophically informed model of the proper relationship between ruler and subjects.[2] A powerful figure at the imperial court, S held the suffect consulship in 56 CE. The relatively benign rule of Nero's earlier years was attributed to S's influence, along with that of the praetorian prefect Burrus (Tac. *Ann.* 13.2, 13.4–5, 14.52 and Dio 61.4). But he was also implicated in murkier aspects of Nero's regime, allegedly confecting the emperor's defensive speech to the senate, after the emperor had ordered the murder of his mother Agrippina in 59 CE. Tacitus attributes to S a remarkable ability to conceal his true feelings in his dealings with Nero (*Ann.* 14.56).

S acquired extensive property, including magnificent estates, much of it as gifts from the emperor (Tac. *Ann.* 14.52).[3] He is characterised by both Juvenal (10.16) and Tacitus (*Ann.* 15.64) as *praediues* and, unsurprisingly, had his detractors; the accusations of Suillius (a close associate of Nero's

---

[1] On S's first fifty years see Griffin 1992: 29–66. Her biography remains the most comprehensive, but see also Grimal 1978, Sørensen 1984, Wilson 2014.

[2] See Braund.

[3] For the metaphorical significance of allusions to his property holdings see below, intro. to *Ep.* 12.

predecessor), alleging self-enrichment through extortionate money-lending, are cited by Tacitus (*Ann.* 13.42) and Dio (61.33.9); Dio, indeed (61.10.3), also describes S as debauched. Martial celebrates his generosity as a patron (12.36). In view of his often repeated insistence on the unimportance of wealth (e.g. 4.10–11,19.4, 42.10–11, 66.22, 98.13) and the salutary effects of poverty (e.g. *Ep.* 17), Seneca has frequently been termed a hypocrite.[4] Economic relations (ownership, loans, prodigality) certainly play a key role in his writing but these potent concepts are redeployed to operate on a metaphorical level; the economic associations of that key Stoic term *ratio*, for instance, are often in play.[5] Nero himself is never referred to explicitly in the *EM*, which date from the final years of S's life, after he had fallen out of favour with the emperor (following the death of the praetorian prefect Burrus in 62 CE). The *EM* often urge those who would focus on philosophy to withdraw from the distractions of public office.[6]

S was a prolific author; Quintilian (*Inst.* 10.1.128–9) comments on the variety of his output.[7] Though the dating of much of his work remains disputed,[8] he wrote tragedies (of which *Thyestes* and *Phoenissae* are likely to be Neronian),[9] numerous philosophical treatises[10] and the *Naturales quaestiones* on meteorology and related matters.[11] Further works (including the *libri moralis philosophiae*, as well as treatises on marriage and on friendship) survive only in fragments.[12]

The *EM*, a series of letters addressed to a single addressee, Lucilius, constitute S's most substantial surviving work. They offer advice and teaching addressed to an individual friend progressing towards more advanced engagement with Stoic philosophy. Exhortative, apparently confessional, these self-reflexive letters, often presenting S himself as a fallible moral

---

[4] Griffin 1992: 286–314, though as she notes, elsewhere S discusses the opportunities for virtue offered by wealth (*De uita beata* 22.3). The motif of hypocrisy is nicely analysed by Jones 2014; S often draws attention to his own failure to live up to expectations (e.g. 75.4, 15–16).

[5] Von Albrecht 2004: 34–52, Bartsch 2009: 204–5, Habinek 2014: 4.

[6] E.g. *Epp.* 19, 22, 55, 68; cf. *De otio*, with Williams, arguing that lack of participation may be the right course, if the regime is corrupt, Griffin 1992: 315–66, Bartsch 2017.

[7] On his range see Volk and Williams 2006: Introduction, Ker 2006, Braund 2015. Graver 2016b offers an analytic bibliography of scholarship on S and his works.

[8] Griffin 1992: 395–411, Marshall 2014.

[9] Fitch 1981. On the philosophical relationship between the tragedies and the prose works see Rosenmeyer 1989.

[10] Including *De otio*, *De breuitate uitae*, on which see Williams, as well as *De ira* and *De beneficiis*, on which see Griffin 2015.

[11] Williams 2012.

[12] Vottero. The interrelationships between S's works are suggestively discussed by Ker 2006.

exemplum, have been described as 'tricksily autobiographical'.[13] While their focus is for the most part on the ethical disposition of the individual, they also offer piecemeal treatment of topics in physics, as well as reflection on how philosophy should be taught.[14]

Death, in particular the fear of death and how it is to be tackled, is a dominant theme (*Epp.* 4, 24, 54, 70, 71, 77, 82, 120).[15] The imperial instruction to commit suicide (which, according to Tac. *Ann.* 15.60–4, came in the aftermath of the unsuccessful conspiracy to replace Nero with Piso in April 65 CE) cannot have been unexpected. Tacitus' detailed account of S's death offers a complement to and an implicit comment on S's own reflections in the letters on the prospect of death.[16]

2 THE *EPISTULAE MORALES* AND THEIR ADDRESSEE

The title *Epistulae morales* first appears with reference to S's letters in Aulus Gellius (12.2.3) but may well be S's own. The precise dating remains disputed (the letters contain only one reference to a datable event, the fire at Lyons of July 64 CE in *Ep.* 91, and even references to the seasons are few). Some scholars argue for a period of composition over two years, 62–4 CE;[17] others take the view that S embarked on the project only in 63 (so that the spring of 23.1 and the spring of 67.1 refer to the same year).[18]

124 letters survive. The extant MSS preserve twenty books of variable length but book divisions are unclear for a substantial section of the text. The known divisions are as follows:

Book 1: *Epp.* 1–12
Book 2: *Epp.* 13–21
Book 3: *Epp.* 22–9
Book 4: *Epp.* 30–41
Book 5: *Epp.* 42–52
Book 6: *Epp.* 53–62
Book 7: *Epp.* 63–9
Book 8: *Epp.* 70–4
Book 9: *Epp.* 75–80
Book 10: *Epp.* 81–3

Book 11 begins with *Ep.* 84. The openings of Books 12 and 13 are not known.

---

[13] Jones 2014: 395.
[14] Hadot 2014a: 210 on their combination of ethics, physics and paraenesis.
[15] Edwards 2007, Ker 2009a.
[16] Ker 2009a: 257–79.
[17] Mazzoli 1989: 1850–3, Grimal 1991: 219–39, 443–56.
[18] Griffin 1992: 400.

Book 14: *Epp.* 89–92
Book 15: *Epp.* 93–5
Book 16: *Epp.* 96–100
Book 17 begins with *Ep.* 101. The opening of Book 18 is not known.
Book 19: *Epp.* 110–17
Book 20: *Epp.* 118–24

Gellius (*NA* 12.2.3) quotes from what he refers to as Book 22 of the *EM*.[19] It seems, then, that we do not have the complete text as S wrote it. It is also possible that there have been losses from the first twenty books.[20] As regards publication, individual books may have circulated separately. The last letter of Book 3 (29.10) refers to Lucilius' expectation of a quotation from Epicurus as *ultimam . . . pensionem*, perhaps suggesting the conclusion of this section of the collection (see also 33.1 and note); some have inferred that Books 1–3 were published together.[21] Others suppose rather that at least the first seven books (*Epp.* 1–69) appeared as a group.[22]

The collection develops from offering practical advice for managing one's emotional stability and ethical disposition in the first letters to a dominant focus on the exploration of more abstract and technical philosophical issues later in the collection (a development against which Lucilius is presented as occasionally protesting, e.g. 121.1: *hoc quid ad mores?*).[23] With the implication that his addressee has attained a more advanced grasp of Stoic thought, this progression itself serves to demonstrate the success of S's teaching.[24] Yet the trajectory is not linear; an issue explored in one letter will be repeatedly returned to in later ones. As John Henderson observes, 'the topics handled in separate compositions thicken, trouble and reconceptualise one another'.[25] While earlier letters tend to be more recognisably epistolary in articulation and dimensions, a number in later books are decidedly bulky (with 66, 90, 94, 95 coming in at 2,993, 2,919, 4,164 and 4,106 words respectively; S reflects on this at 95.3). The last two extant books, however, return to a format closer to that of the earlier ones.[26]

---

[19] Though Hachmann (1995: 237) suggests that *Ep.* 124 marks a logical end point and notes that the letter quoted by Gellius could fit earlier in the collection, e.g. Book 17 or 18.

[20] In late antiquity the collection circulated in at least two volumes. Reynolds 17 suggests the possibility that an entire volume of letters may have been lost at an early stage. This is disputed by Cancik 1967: 8–12, but see further Spallone 1995 and Malaspina 2018.

[21] Russell 1974: 78, Lana 1991: 280–1, Fedeli 2004: 203–4.

[22] Griffin 1992: 349.

[23] On the latter part of the collection see Inwood.

[24] Cf. Maurach 1970: 199–206.

[25] Henderson 2004: 5.

[26] Lana 1991: 292–304 gives full details; see also Mazzoli 1989: 1823–5 and the insightful comments of Henderson 2004: 28–9.

2 THE *EPISTULAE MORALES* AND THEIR ADDRESSEE

The *EM* (in this respect analogous to Cicero's *Ad Atticum*) have a single addressee, Lucilius Junior. Lucilius (hereafter L), an equestrian (44.2), appears to be a few years younger than S (26.7) but a friend of long standing. Brought up in Campania (49.1) and currently procurator of Sicily (45.1), he himself has literary ambitions (8.10, 19.5, 24.19–21, 46.1, 79).[27] L, also the addressee of *De providentia* and *Naturales quaestiones*, is known only from S's own work; his historical reality has occasionally been questioned.[28] Outside titles, L is named fifty-seven times in *Epp.* 1–69 and thirty-five times in *Epp.* 70–124. S often refers to questions L has asked him or to L's responses to his advice,[29] though, as Griffin notes, the 'you' and the 'I' of the letters cannot always be assumed to be biographical.[30] Some of the letters appear to have been written from Campania (see intro. to *Ep.* 53), while others (e.g. 104, 110) are apparently written from one of S's villas. According to Tacitus (*Ann.* 15.45, 60), S spent most of his time in Rome after 62, after 64 rarely leaving his house. Miriam Griffin suggests the majority of the letters were probably written in Rome,[31] though Rome as a place barely features in them.[32] As Donald Russell underlines, the correspondence is certainly intended to appear chronological.[33]

The studies of Hildegard Cancik (1967) and Gregor Maurach (1970) both underline the importance of appreciating the collection as a whole. The question as to whether this is a 'real' correspondence has prompted much debate.[34] Giancarlo Mazzoli summarises different views and suggests the collection is a selection of 'genuine' letters.[35] The letters of Pliny (reworked versions of 'real' letters, artfully disposed within individual books) are invoked by Paolo Cugusi as a parallel.[36] For Griffin and others, by contrast, the letters are 'a literary fiction'.[37] As Marcus Wilson observes, it is perhaps unhelpful to think in terms of a sharp division between

---

[27] *PIR*² L388, Pflaum 1960–1: 1.70 no. 30 and III.961–2. L's portrayal in the letters and elsewhere is discussed by Griffin 1992: 91, 347–53.

[28] E.g. by Bourgery 1911: 51; see Gowers 2011. For Schafer 2011: 44, 'Lucilius is Seneca writ small'. Henderson 2004: 42 terms him a 'belittled catachresis for the father of free speech [i.e. the satirist Lucilius] in Latin letters'.

[29] 3.1, 19.1, 40.1, 48.1, 50.1, 59.4. See further intro. to *Ep.* 34. Wilson 1987: 112.

[30] Griffin 1992: 347.

[31] Griffin 1992: 93, 358 n. 1.

[32] See further intro. to *Ep.* 86.

[33] Russell 1974: 72. He also suggests the possibility (p. 79) that some of later letters were written earlier.

[34] Cf. Wilson 1987: 119, Grimal 1978: esp. 441–3.

[35] Mazzoli 1989: 1846–50, though Mazzoli 1991 highlights the deftness with which they are often structured. Albertini 1923 also regards the letters as 'real'.

[36] Cugusi 1983: 200–3.

[37] Griffin 1992: 519. Cf. Bourgery 1911, Cancik 1967, Maurach 1970.

'literary' and 'real' letters,[38] though certainly the *EM* are, as Henderson puts it,[39] 'scrubbed scrupulously bare of referents and ambient presence' (of the kind one might expect in 'genuine' correspondence) – and thus the more accessible and appealing for later readers.

The degree to which book divisions are important has also provoked disagreement. Cancik highlights their significance, at least in relation to earlier books (1967: 138–51). Most scholars agree in seeing Book 1 as a clearly demarcated introduction.[40] Some books have been read as showcasing particular themes (e.g. Book 4 focusing on the role of *uirtus*,[41] and Book 6 scrutinising S's own deficiencies).[42] Yet in a number of other books it is harder to trace a potentially unifying thread (contrast, in this respect, the letter collections of both Cicero and Pliny).[43] Maurach and others have tracked a wide range of thematic patterns cutting across or linking books, which offer alternative ways of structuring the collection. Maurach emphasises sequences (such as *Epp.* 1–10, 12–15, 16–32) and terms a number of letters situated mid-book 'division letters'.[44] Cancik and Maurach both stress the thematic coherence of the collection, regarding it as close in conception to Horace's *Epistles* (on which see below).[45] For some, notably Cugusi, the organising features of the collection have been generated retrospectively through editing.[46] The overall artistry of the *EM* has received increasing attention in recent years; Schönegg, for instance, characterises the collection as a 'philosophical work of art'.[47]

3 LETTERS AS A GENRE

Although some readers have been inclined to view the *EM* as essentially a series of essays rather than letters,[48] much recent scholarship focuses on their epistolary form (while it remains true that some of them, e.g.

---

[38] Wilson 1987: 119.
[39] Henderson 2004: 43. Cf. Russell 1974: 77.
[40] See the editions of Scarpat (b) and Richardson-Hay (who takes issue with the 'cycles' perceived by Maurach) (2006: 22–3), and the suggestive comments of Henderson (2004: 6–29).
[41] Maso 1999: 84, Davies.
[42] On which see Berno (see further intro. to *Ep.* 53).
[43] On the book structure of Cic. *Fam.* and *Att.* see Beard 2002. On the book structure of Pliny's letters see Gibson and Morello 2012: 234–64.
[44] Maurach 1970: esp. 128–9, 199–206. Hachmann adopts a similar approach, while highlighting somewhat different cycles and points of transition.
[45] Cancik 1967: 54–8, Maurach 1970: 196–7.
[46] Cugusi 1983: 200–3.
[47] 'Philosophisches Kunstwerk', Schönegg 1999.
[48] Following the lead of Francis Bacon (see further below). Influential has been the view of Williamson, 'Seneca's practice of writing essays as epistles' (1951: 194).

Ep. 47, have relatively few epistolary markers, others are strongly epistolary, e.g. *Epp.* 34, 46).[49] This form already had a philosophical pedigree.[50] Though the dating of the letters attributed to Plato remains disputed,[51] Cicero was already familiar with the Platonic *Epistles* 5, 7 and 9, as well as Aristotle's *symbouleutikon* addressed to Alexander.[52] Diogenes Laertius draws on the letters of numerous philosophers in his account of their views and includes three treatise-like letters by Epicurus on philosophical themes (10.35–135). Epicurus was a celebrated letter-writer, to whom are attributed over ninety extant letter fragments (more occasionally come to light from the Herculaneum archive and among the Oxyrhynchus papyri).[53] Pamela Gordon argues that, while most of these fragments are probably not authentic, their currency attests to the key role played by letters in characterisations of Epicurus by followers and detractors alike. It seems that the correspondence of the early Epicureans circulated widely, sometimes in the form of anthologies, apparently put together in the second century BCE.[54] These letters functioned as a medium for philosophical discourse, a crucial mechanism in the development of an Epicurean diaspora;[55] Plutarch explicitly connects Epicurus' letter-writing with the desire to secure converts, δοξοκοπίας (*Mor.* 1101B). S refers to Epicurus' letters on numerous occasions.[56] Epicurean quotations are, for Tom Habinek, 'a way of signalling generic competition with antiquity's most famous writer of philosophical letters'.[57]

As for precedents in Latin epistolography, Horace's verse *Epistles* explore philosophical questions with a distinctively Roman inflection.[58] The degree to which Cicero's letters engage (if allusively) with philosophical ideas has recently been highlighted.[59] S was familiar with his letters (as well as with his philosophical treatises; cf. e.g. 100.9),[60] comparing his own epistolary project with the letters to Atticus, which were evidently well

---

[49] Wilson 2001 stresses their protean form. See also Inwood 2007, Edwards 2018a. On the history of epistolography see Cugusi 1983.
[50] See Inwood 2007: 136.
[51] There are good reasons to suppose the collection was familiar in its current form by the early first century CE (see Morrison 2013: 111–12).
[52] McConnell 2014: 27, 35–44.
[53] See e.g. *P.Oxy.* lxxvi.5077, with Obbink and Schorn *ibid.*, pp. 37–50.
[54] Gordon 2013.
[55] See Graver 2016: 199.
[56] 9.1, 21.3–6. For Inwood (2007: esp. 142–8), Epicurus is a key influence on S's choice of the letter form.
[57] Habinek 1992: 189–90, n. 10. Cf. Henderson 2004: 29–31, Inwood 2007, Wildberger 2014.
[58] De Pretis 2002 (exploring their concern with temporality), Morrison 2007. On S's engagement with Horace see further below.
[59] Griffin 1995, McConnell 2014.
[60] Setaioli 2003.

known by S's time.[61] Though S himself highlights the contrast between his own philosophically urgent letters and the allegedly mundane concerns of Cicero (118.1–4 with Inwood *ad loc.*),[62] his letters, like those of Cicero, combine intimacy, humour, self-reproach, emotional intensity and mercurial shifts of tone, if with a much greater degree of self-awareness and a sustained concern with self-transformation.[63] All the same, Wilson is surely right to regard S as establishing 'a new branch of epistolography'.[64] The influence of S's *EM* has recently been tracked in the more worldly correspondence of Pliny.[65]

The potential of epistolary form to convey meaning, brilliantly analysed in Janet Altman's classic study (1982), has fed into much recent work on epistolarity in classical literature.[66] Texts may gesture towards epistolarity through the deployment of a range of epistolary markers (such as opening greetings or references to letters received).[67] Particular features of the epistolary structure of the *EM* are fundamental to S's philosophical project. Ancient literary theorists regarded letter-writing as the literary equivalent of informal conversation (e.g. Demetrius, *On style* 225).[68] Letters, particularly between friends, were distinguished for their colloquial language (see Cic. *Fam.* 9.21 *cottidianis uerbis texere solemus*).[69] S himself makes much of his conversational style of writing (esp. *Ep.* 75; cf. 22.8, 38.1 *plurime proficit sermo quia minutatim irrepit animo*, 40.1, 65.2, 67.2). This insistence is surely to be related to his assertion at 6.5 of the superiority of personal encounters to written text in inculcating sound ethical practice. If the letter comes closest to oral exchange, the letter collection instantiates the relationship of habitual familiarity, which is the most efficacious for philosophical teaching.[70] The potency of S's first-person voice, in part at least a function of the epistolary genre, gives this text a compelling urgency.[71] If a prime function of letters, as Cicero notes, is to express friendship, this does not imply that they are of interest only to the author and addressee. Occasionally indeed S refers explicitly to

---

[61] *Pace* Shackleton Bailey 1965: 60–76. See Setaioli 1976, Cugusi 1983: 168–73 and *Ep.* 21.
[62] On Cicero's letters as an 'anti-model' see Lana 1991: 261.
[63] On the texture of Cicero's letters see Beard 2002, Hall 2009, White 2010.
[64] Wilson 2001: 187. Cf. von Albrecht 2004: 2.
[65] Henderson 2002: 84–5, Marchesi 2008: 14–15.
[66] Trapp 2003, De Pretis 2003, Morello and Morrison 2007, Marchesi 2008, Gibson and Morello 2012, Whitton 2013, Martelli 2016, Leach 2017.
[67] On epistolary *formulae* see Trapp 2003: 34–8.
[68] Russell and Winterbottom 1972: 211. Cf. Cic. *Q. fr.* 1.1.45 = SB 1 *quia cum tua lego, te audire, et quia, cum ad te scribo, tecum loqui uideor*.
[69] Coleman 1974: 277. On epistolary style see further below.
[70] Edwards 2018a: 336–7.
[71] Inwood 2005: 346–7. Cf. Nussbaum 1994: 337–8.

readers of the future, as at 8.2 *posterorum negotium ago; illis aliqua quae possint prodesse conscribo*;[72] any reader may choose to assume the role of Lucilius, to feel herself interpellated.[73]

Epistolary form is particularly suited to enhancing the reader's awareness of her relationship to time.[74] 'Each new epistle re-situates the author differently in a new time, a new mood, sometimes in a new place', as Wilson observes.[75] The discontinuity of the series, each letter ostensibly anchored in a particular (if unspecified) day, focuses attention on the importance of the present moment,[76] while repetition renders explicit the extension of the series in time.[77]

How long should a letter be? S asks (45.13), toying with his epistolary form. The issue of how and when an individual letter should draw to a close is often raised, e.g. 11.8, 22.13, 26.8. These playful questions echo on a formal level one of the collection's most profound concerns, what might be an appropriate *clausula* for the individual human life (77.20).[78] While the disappearance of the final books (see above) is probably an accident of fate, S (no doubt expecting Nero's fatal instruction) anticipated this would be an open-ended text (61.1–2): *hanc epistulam scribo, tamquam me cum maxime scribentem mors euocatura sit.*

4 STOIC TERMS AND CONCEPTS

Particularly in the earlier letters Epicurus figures prominently, while the term 'Stoic' does not occur until 9.19 (where, indeed, S emphasises a view common to both Stoics and Epicureans). Yet the *EM* constitute an important (and enormously influential) document of Stoic philosophy. The elements of philosophy (analysed and discussed at 89.9–13, for instance) comprise physics (including metaphysics, theology and psychology, as well as the workings of the physical world), logic (including epistemology and linguistics, as well as reasoning and argument) and ethics. While later letters are more concerned than are earlier ones with the theoretical framework of Stoic teaching and the exploration of technical philosophical questions,[79] all the letters are firmly underpinned by Stoic thinking.[80]

---

[72] Cf. 21.5(n.), 22.2, 64.7–8.
[73] Edwards 2018a.
[74] Sangalli 1988: 53. On time in S see further Lévy 2003, Edwards 2014.
[75] Wilson 2001: 167.
[76] Ker 2009a: 175.
[77] Armisen-Marchetti 1995: 547.
[78] See Ker 2009a: 118–19.
[79] See Inwood, Scarpat (a) on 65, Hachmann on 66, Stückelberger on 88, Schafer 2009 on 94 and 95.
[80] Stoic concepts and terminology in the *EM* are systematically analysed by Wildberger 2006.

Even for a reader of the earlier letters, some familiarity with key Stoic terms and concepts will be useful.[81]

For Stoics, human happiness is wholly contingent on virtue, *uirtus*. Philosophy, serving as the framework through which to actualise virtue consistently, is essential if we are to live fulfilled lives (see 90.1). Insofar as they share in reason, *ratio*, humans are united in community with the divine (76.9–10, 92.27); S senses the divine primarily through natural phenomena (see e.g. *Epp.* 41, 90.28).[82] *Ratio* is sometimes qualified as right reason, *recta ratio*, to distinguish it from more practical forms of understanding.[83] Philosophy, *philosophia*, is the pursuit of right reason (89.6).[84] Through the use of perfected reason, humans are able to live in accordance with nature, *natura*, thus achieving a happy life, *uita beata* or *beatus status* (*natura* in turn is informed by divine *ratio*, 90.16). This is the highest good, *summum bonum*. We must understand that ultimately only virtue, *uirtus*, matters (cf. e.g. 74.24, 92.24), only the pursuit of virtue is morally good, *honestum*, and everything else (e.g. status, wealth, health, family or any other matters beyond our control) is a matter of indifference; we must learn to set aside the errant judgements of other people (*Ep.* 7).[85] Yet it is in choosing between indifferents, *indifferentia*, that we exercise virtue; some indifferents, such as health, food, shelter, are naturally preferred, *commoda* or *petenda* (i.e. they accord with a life according to nature; cf. e.g. 74.17), while others, e.g. illness, are dispreferred, *incommoda* or *fugienda*, so that we are right to avoid them (see *Epp.* 66 and 67). At the same time actions are to be judged virtuous not by their results but purely in terms of the intentions motivating them (14.6).

The would-be philosopher strives to attain the right mental disposition, *bona mens* (110.1). For Stoics the mind, *animus*, is wholly corporeal.[86] Yet the body itself is liable to be a distraction from the pursuit of virtue, if we place too much importance on its pains and pleasures (65.16–22).[87] The would-be philosopher pursues mental tranquillity, *securitas*, by working to overcome the turbulent force of the emotions, *affectus* (sometimes translated as the passions), e.g. desire for riches, which derive from incorrect judgements, in particular by training impulse, *impetus*, so that is in

---

[81] An excellent recent introduction to Stoic thought is Reydams-Schils 2005. See also Long's lucid analysis (1996) and the essays in Inwood 2003. For a comprehensive analysis of Stoic concepts in the *EM* see Wildberger 2006.
[82] See Setaioli 2014b.
[83] Wildberger 2006: 249–52.
[84] The term *sapientia* is often treated as equivalent but see the distinction drawn at 89.4.
[85] Cf. 75.15, 94.52 on repelling the *populi praecepta*, 99.16–17, 123.6.
[86] Long and Sedley 1987: passage 45 C–D, Long 1996: 224–49.
[87] On the suffering body in the *EM* see Edwards 1999, 2005b and Chambert 2002.

4 STOIC TERMS AND CONCEPTS

accord with the true value of objects (89.15).[88] Thus it is in learning to regard objects commonly pursued or avoided as matters of indifference that we enable ourselves to overcome the emotions.[89] The Stoic ideal is the wise man, *sapiens* (42.1–2, 120.10–14), who first appears in *Ep.* 9. Though even the *sapiens* will experience involuntary reactions to certain experiences, his self-mastery and sound judgement will prevent these from developing into full-blown emotions, since he will not assent to them.[90] True virtue is shown in consistently sound judgement (71.32). In the *EM*, S is particularly concerned to vanquish the chaotic forces of fear, anger, desire (especially for material possessions) and grief, which cause disturbance to the spirit; self-mastery is critical (75.18). Such self-mastery will bring us immunity from whatever *fortuna*, chance, brings;[91] indeed it will enable us to understand and welcome whatever befalls us as fated, *fatum*, something whose occurrence is in accordance with the nature of the universe more generally (19.6, 77.12, 107.11).[92]

S makes no claims to come close to being a *sapiens* himself (116.5); indeed such a perfect man is rare as the phoenix (42.1), though Cato the Younger may be a specimen (cf. *Constant.* 7.1). The *sapiens*, embodying true enlightenment, is a sublime point of reference.[93] Those making progress towards virtue may be termed *proficientes*.[94] S conveys a strong sense of the stages of progress towards perfection (75.8–10).

While a general sense of what is according to nature for all humans is important in Stoicism, each individual also needs to develop a sense of goals which are to be pursued because they are right for his or her individual nature (*De otio* 3.4–5; cf. *Ep.* 11.8–10 on choosing an appropriate mentor) or stage of life (*Ep.* 121.15–16). In his *De officiis* (1.107–21), Cicero gives an account of Panaetius' four *personae* theory, which offered an attractive model for those seeking to accommodate a commitment to Stoicism with an active involvement in Roman political life.[95] Each individual should take account of four aspects or 'roles' in determining how he ought to behave, what is fitting (τὸ πρέπον): the demands of universal human nature, his own individual strengths and weaknesses, the lot in

---

[88] Cf. *Ep.* 24. On Stoic theory concerning the emotions see Graver 2007. For emotions in S see Konstan 2015.
[89] Nussbaum 1994, Trapp 2007: 65–9.
[90] 75.12 *affectus sunt motus animi improbabiles*; cf. *De ira* 2.3.4.
[91] On the combative nature of encounters with *fortuna* in S (e.g. at 64.4) see Asmis 2009. This is a feature of the diatribe tradition, as Del Giovane (2015b: 21) notes.
[92] Cf. *Ben.* 4.7.2, Wildberger 2006: 42–5.
[93] Williams 2016. On the sage in earlier Stoic thought, see Brouwer 2014.
[94] 35.4, 71.30, 75.8–10, 94.50, 109.15, *Ben.* 7.2.1.
[95] Brunt 2013: 108–50, 275–309.

life allocated by chance (health, wealth) and the career path chosen by himself. The idea of the fourth *persona* entails a recognition that different ways of behaving are appropriate to different occupations.[96] A sense of appropriate actions or duties, *officia*, also determines one's dealings with other people.[97]

At the same time, there is also a sense in which for S, each contains within herself a trace of the *deus* (41.1; cf. 31.11). As Pierre Hadot puts it, 'the feeling of belonging to the whole is an essential element'.[98] We should aspire to feel ourselves a part of the universe (e.g. 66.6 *toti se inserens mundo*). This is a rapturous state, perhaps most readily achieved by contemplating the grandeur of the natural world (e.g. 102.28–9); the sublime, in this sense, is an insistent presence in the *EM*.[99]

5 STOIC BACKGROUND

Zeno of Citium, considered the founder of Stoicism, lived in Athens in the late fourth and early third centuries BCE. Much influenced by Socratic and Cynic thought, he developed his own philosophical system, which he taught in the Stoa Poikile in the Agora (hence the term 'Stoic'). S's references to Zeno are often critical (e.g. 83.9). Cleanthes, one of his pupils, succeeded him as head of what had become a Stoic school. Later in the third century, Chrysippus succeeded Cleanthes. His elaboration of Stoic doctrine was rapidly accepted as orthodoxy (though S does not refer to him often in the letters). The teachings of the earliest Stoics survive only in fragmentary form.[100] They seem to have focused on the perfection of the Stoic wise man, compared to whom all others are equally wanting, no matter their degree of progress.[101]

Panaetius of Rhodes, a later head of the school (from 129 to 110 BCE), spent a considerable amount of time in Rome and played an important part in introducing leading Romans to Stoicism (he is referred to by S only rarely, e.g. 33.4, 116.5–6). Posidonius, sent as representative of Rhodes to Rome in 87 BCE and closely associated with many leading Romans, appears (like Panaetius) to have modified Stoic doctrines in ways

---

[96] Gill 1988, 2008: 35–45. Setaioli 2000: 130–6, 162–91 persuasively suggests this principle is extended by S to literary style. See further on *Ep.* 114.
[97] This is analysed at length in *De beneficiis*; see Griffin 2015.
[98] Hadot 1995: 208.
[99] See Williams 2016 (cf. Williams 2012 on the *Naturales quaestiones*). On the sublime generally in S see Gunderson 2015.
[100] Long and Sedley 1987. See also Inwood 1985, Boys-Stones 2001, Reydams-Schils 2005, Graver 2007. On the ideal community of the early Stoics see Schofield 1999.
[101] Brouwer 2014.

which made them more appealing to the Roman elite (as well as emphasising common ground with Platonism).[102] S quotes him frequently (e.g. 87.31–8, 90 *passim*, 113.28, *Nat.* 7.20.2), generally with approval.[103] Their work (which included discussion of historical, geographical and mathematical questions) also survives only in fragments but, as regards ethics, seems to have been primarily concerned with the struggles of those on the road to virtue, the careful use of external advantages and how the virtuous individual might deploy his talents and assets to the benefit of the community.[104]

This version of Stoicism was taken up by numerous elite Romans of the late republic and principate, Cato the Younger figuring among its most notable adherents.[105] Cicero, much influenced by the teaching of Panaetius and Posidonius, though he did not consider himself a Stoic, remains an important source for reconstructing their views.[106] His extensive philosophical writings also played a critical role in the development of a Roman philosophical vocabulary (though S does not always defer to his usage).[107]

Given the fragmentary state of the evidence relating to earlier Stoics, it is sometimes difficult to determine the degree to which S follows Stoic authorities. Indeed, though most now accept his Stoic orthodoxy, some have questioned the extent to which S was even familiar with their works.[108] Nevertheless S regularly asserts his independence; I am not a slave to my predecessors, he underlines (80.1). He also expresses an apparent hostility to syllogisms and technical questions of a kind which were considered characteristic of Stoic logic (45.5, 83.8–17, 85, 108.12).[109] This should be seen as a rhetorical move (elsewhere, e.g. *Ep.* 65, S shows himself adept at analysing technical matters).[110] S is assertive in forging a new literary

---

[102] See Sedley 2003: 20–4.
[103] On S's references to Panaetius and Posidonius see further Setaioli 1988: 307–8, 316–57 and below, intro. to *Ep.* 90.
[104] Gill 1988: 170–1. On Posidonius, Kidd 1999: 1–28.
[105] Griffin 1989, Rawson 1989, Reydams-Schils 2005, Trapp 2007, Brunt 2013: 108–50, 275–309.
[106] In *Tusc.*, *Fin.* and *Off.* particularly; see Dyck 1996: 17–29.
[107] S expresses approval of Cicero's translation choices at 58.6 and 111.1 but his usage often differs from Cicero's (Setaioli 1988: 36–7, 2003: 68–9, Grimal 1992b). Inwood 2005: 18–22 underlines the difficulty of mapping S's terminology back on to that of Greek texts.
[108] Following Rist 1989. See further Cooper 2004, Inwood 2005: 18, Wildberger 2006. Setaioli 1988: 257–374.
[109] Barnes 1997; see also Inwood's commentary on *Ep.* 85. This has led some to dismiss S as a serious philosopher. See e.g. Cooper 2004: 310–1: 'he does not write as an expert philosopher or an expert in philosophical truth ... He is ... a philosophical amateur.'
[110] See also *Constant.* for his use of syllogisms.

form for philosophy.[111] He is thinking in Latin, using it as a medium to develop new ideas.[112] The later letters in particular (to which Inwood provides a magisterial guide) tend towards the exploration of more technical philosophical questions, which show S fully in command of a wide range of philosophical arguments. It is precisely as a Stoic that S feels impelled to add something new to established doctrines (45.4; see further intro. to *Ep.* 33). The degree to which S was an innovator with regard to the substance of Stoic doctrine is disputed. Inwood's assessment is relatively cautious, though he does see S as making an important contribution in his reflections on mental causation, self-control and self-awareness.[113]

Stoicism under the Roman empire (often dismissed by earlier scholars as stale) is now considered to have undergone significant developments, with S himself a key contributor, along with Epictetus and Marcus Aurelius. Though his work survives mainly in fragments, Cornutus also seems to have been an influential teacher.[114] For Gretchen Reydams-Schils, the importance placed on friendship and all types of relationships among rational beings is a particular feature of Roman Stoicism, informing the Stoics' fundamental commitment to community.[115] The *EM*, written in final phase of S's life, after his retirement, highlight active involvement less strongly than some of his earlier works (while making clear that philosophy has value only when it is shared, 6.4, 73.7). Yet attachment to other people remains important.[116] Human beings have by nature an attachment to themselves (the premise of **oikeiōsis, conciliatio**; cf. 14.1) and they are by nature inclined to come together in social groups: *hoc primum philosophia promittit, sensum communem, humanitatem et congregationem* (5.4; cf. 48.2, 95.52).[117] Although the *sapiens* is not reliant on others (since his virtue does not depend on them), friendship offers opportunities for the

---

[111] Griffin 1992: 7.
[112] Inwood 2005: 20. Cf. Grimal 1992b.
[113] Inwood 2005: 132–56. His comments at e.g. 2005: 344 are more circumspect. See also Asmis 2015 and Gloyn 2017 (arguing for S's innovations in thinking on the family).
[114] For an excellent survey of philosophy in the Roman empire see Trapp 2007. Hadot emphasises the vibrant diversity of Stoic writing in this period (2014a: 181–8). The essays in Williams and Volk 2016 focus particularly on philosophical writing in Latin. On Epictetus see Long 2002, on Marcus Aurelius, Gill 2013. On the ethical dimension of Cornutus' work see Boys-Stones 2007. Another important Stoic figure is Musonius Rufus, on whose fragmentary work see Nussbaum 2002 and Whitmarsh 2001: 141–55.
[115] She notes particularly the concise formulation offered by Marcus Aurelius, 'to be rational is to be social' (Reydams-Schils 2005: 74).
[116] See e.g. 121.14–15 on *societas* emphasised by Habinek 2014.
[117] See Cic. *Fin.* 3.62–3, Engberg-Pedersen 1986, Trapp 2007: 42–5, Gill 2009. This aspect of S's thought is played down by Veyne 2003: 31–4, following Foucault, as Hadot stresses (2014a: 188–90).

exercise of virtue and is prompted by nature (3.2–3, 6.2–3, 9.17 *naturalis irritatio*, 109.1–13).[118] S also attributes an important ethical role to his relationship with his wife (104.2–5). The would-be Stoic must negotiate, in Reydams-Schils' words, 'the delicate equilibrium . . . between affection for loved ones and not being devastated by loss; between being connected to one's external circumstances and being detached and independent at the same time'.[119]

6 OTHER PHILOSOPHICAL INFLUENCES

Few scholars would now characterise S as philosophically eclectic in a strong sense.[120] Inwood, notably, plays down the degree to which S draws on non-Stoic philosophical predecessors.[121] Nevertheless S, in forging his distinctive version of Stoicism, frequently appropriates for his own project features of the teaching of other philosophical schools.[122]

Epicureans advocated a quiet life, ideally among other followers of **Epicurus**, with a close focus on the demands of nature.[123] Epicurean philosophy, particularly as mediated through the writings of Philodemus, exercised a strong following in Rome, especially in the late republic.[124] L is presented as having Epicurean leanings (23.9 refers to 'your Epicurus'). S himself favoured Epicurus' own writings and claims to be reading them at the time he writes his earlier letters (8.7 *adhuc Epicurum complicamus, cuius hanc uocem hodierno die legi*).[125] Margaret Graver (2016) teases out a number of distinct and sometimes contradictory strands in S's engagement

---

[118] Graver 2007: 180–1.
[119] Reydams-Schils 2005: 171. On this passage see further Dressler 2016: 33–4.
[120] Against eclecticism Hadot 2014a: 186–8. Indeed the notion of 'eclecticism' is rarely invoked in recent analyses of ancient philosophical thought, as Gill notes (2003: 44–50; see further Dillon and Long 1988). For S as 'eclectic' see e.g. Wilson 2015.
[121] Inwood 2005: esp. ch. 2, though ch. 5 'Seneca and psychological dualism' does highlight Platonic influence (see, however, the critique by Hadot 2014b = 2014a: 373–414).
[122] In this respect taking a leaf out of Chrysippus' book, suggests Hadot 2014a: 188.
[123] Though recent scholarship has challenged the idea that Epicureanism required individuals to abandon their occupations or to withdraw into isolated alternative communities (Asmis 2004: 134–42).
[124] Lucretius appears to be unusual in engaging directly with the writings of Epicurus. Recent discoveries from the Villa dei Papiri, owned by Piso, a close associate of Philodemus, have vastly increased our knowledge of the latter's reworking of Epicurean doctrines (see e.g. Konstan *et al.* 1998, Asmis 2004). On the reputation of Epicurus in Rome see Gordon 2012.
[125] Gigante 2000 explores the possibility that S was familiar with Philodemus' work.

with Epicurus.[126] Although Epicureanism was notorious for the emphasis it placed on pleasure as a key criterion for decision-making (explicitly deplored by S, e.g. *VB* 7.1–8.2),[127] several other features of Epicurus' teaching exercised considerable appeal for S, in particular the abstemious personal habits of Epicurus (indeed S readily acknowledges the ascetic understanding of pleasure in Epicurus' own writings; see 18.9–11, 21.10), his observations about the experience of pain and his focus on companionship.[128] S acknowledges the psychological efficacy of Epicurus' teaching methods, including letter-writing and in particular daily reflection, as a way to inculcate sound philosophical habits;[129] he also notes approvingly Epicurus' stress on personalised advice (52.3–4).[130]

Epicurus is introduced at 2.5; he, Metrodorus and other Epicurean authors are between them quoted on twenty-seven occasions in *Epp.* 2–29.[131] Asserting that wisdom is available to all, S (2.5) excuses his forays into the enemy camp (*in aliena castra*; cf. 12.11, 16.7). Yet Epicurean precepts take on a different significance in a new context, argues Wildberger, noting the shift from a focus on control of appetite in terms of quantity for Epicureans, to the Stoic concern with a qualitative transformation (cf. 16.9, 15.11).[132] As Hadot observes, 'the spiritual exercise of trying to live in the present moment is very different for Stoics and Epicureans. For the former, it means mental tension and constant wakefulness of the moral conscience; for the latter, it is ... an invitation to relaxation and security.'[133] S first underlines in *Ep.* 33 the superiority of the Stoic approach, whose distinctive benefits come more clearly into focus from this point; in the last six books (*Epp.* 89–124), Epicurus is referred to only three times (89.11, 92.25, 97.13–15), though his follower Metrodorus also features in other letters (98.9, 99.25) and S refers critically to Epicurean doctrine at e.g. 90.35.[134]

S only occasionally invokes **Plato** as a paradigmatic philosopher (6.6, 44.3, 64.10, 108.38). Socrates, however, central to Plato's dialogues, features frequently in the *EM*. A distinctive version of Socrates had been

---

[126] See also Wildberger 2014, Schiesaro 2015.
[127] See further Gordon 2012: 109–38.
[128] Graver 2016.
[129] Cf. Epicurus, *Ep. Men.* 135 'rehearse these and the related precepts day and night'.
[130] Cf. Philodemus' *On frank criticism*; see Konstan *et al.* 1998: 8.
[131] Epicurus is cited more often by S than by any other ancient philosopher, aside from Lucretius (Lana 1991: 263). On the quotations see Setaioli 1988: 171–256, Hachmann 1995: 220–30.
[132] She notes a 'conscious misrepresentation' of Epicurean ideas in earlier letters (Wildberger 2014: 432).
[133] Hadot 1995: 88.
[134] Schiesaro 2015.

6 OTHER PHILOSOPHICAL INFLUENCES

appropriated as an exemplary figure by earlier Stoics,[135] though it seems to be S himself who gives him such particular prominence (for S's engagement with the *Apology* and *Phaedo* see 24.4–6nn.).[136] In places S chooses to interrogate and criticise features of Plato's work (e.g. the discussion of Platonic ontology in *Ep.* 58, with Inwood *ad loc.*; cf. 65.7–14, 85.31, 87.12).[137] Certain other features of Platonic thought occasionally inform S's treatment of e.g. body and soul.[138]

Although **Cynic** thought was little concerned with logic or physics, its arresting ethical precepts offered inspiration to Stoics generally and to S in particular, for whom the pared-down figure of Diogenes, determined to exemplify human life in accordance with the barest requirements of nature, was a source of compelling fascination, a pertinent object of reflection, particularly for one seeking to overcome the fear of poverty (cf. 90.14).[139] Indeed the Cynic's position on living according to nature might be seen as an extreme version of the Stoic; S observes (*Brev.* 14.1) that we may choose *hominis naturam cum Stoicis uincere, cum Cynicis excedere*, 'to overcome human nature with the Stoics or to go beyond it with the Cynics'.

Among other philosophical influences should be noted **Pythagoreanism**, whose later adherents at least also seem to have advocated some form of daily self-scrutiny, as well as the close regulation of diet.[140] S mentions among his teachers Sotion (49.2, 108.17–21) from whom he acquired familiarity with the teachings of Pythagoras. From Sotion, too, S became acquainted with the teachings of **Quintus Sextius** (who lived under Julius Caesar and Augustus); his writings are celebrated in 64.2–5. Though he wrote in Greek, Sextius was regarded as founder of the one philosophical school originating in Rome (according to *Nat.* 7.32.2, no longer extant in S's day).[141] Sextius and his associates (among them Celsus) had a particular interest in physics and in medicine. Sextian teachings seem to have focused on the details of day-to-day life, such as diet; he is credited

---

[135] Döring 1979, Long 1996: 1–34, Reydams-Schils 2005: 3, Brouwer 2014: 136–66.

[136] Isnardi Parente 2000: 219.

[137] See further Wildberger 2010, Boys-Stones 2013.

[138] Reydams-Schils 2010.

[139] S also expresses admiration for the Cynic Demetrius, his contemporary (20.9, 62.3, 91.13, *Ben.* 7.1.3). See Griffin 1996 and, on cynicism more generally, Goulet-Cazé 1990.

[140] Cf. Cic. *Sen.* 38, Iamblichus, *On the life of Pythagoras* 165, Porphyry, *Life of Pythagoras* 40, Ker 2009b: 168–76. On Pythagorean influence in Rome see Volk 2016.

[141] *uirum acrem, Graecis uerbis Romanis moribus philosophantem* (59.7). On Sextius see Lana 1973: 339–84, 1992, Griffin 1992: 37–41, Hadot 2007, 2014a: 191–2, Di Paola 2014.

with the particular form of daily self-examination described by S in *De ira* 3.36.1.¹⁴²

At 59.7, in the course of a discussion of similes, S chooses from the work of Sextius a vivid and extended image, comparing the *sapiens* to a military leader deploying his virtues in square formation in readiness for an attack from any quarter; though the emphasis on courage as a philosophical virtue may be traced back to Plato (e.g. *Laches* 190e), the celebration of quasi-military courage as the supreme virtue is perhaps (as Omar Di Paola 2014 argues) where the novelty of the Sextian school lies (cf. *Nat.* 7.32.2). Sextius is again cited at 73.15, where, quoting Virgil (*A.* 9.641), as S himself often does, he urges frugality, moderation and courage.¹⁴³ The pervasiveness of medical analogies and metaphors in the *EM* perhaps owes something to the Sextian tradition (see e.g. 53.3–8, 68.7–9, 75.11–12).¹⁴⁴

7 ETHICAL FOCUS AND TECHNIQUES OF THE SELF

Like other Stoics of the principate, S is closely focused on ethics and concerned, particularly in the *EM*, with practices of self-scrutiny and self-transformation.¹⁴⁵ Tony Long characterises this process in terms of the repeated invocation of a normative self (the best possible version of oneself) to which one should aim to make one's error-prone occurrent self conform.¹⁴⁶ Indeed, noting the prominence of the sage in S's *EM*, Long suggests reading this figure here 'as a way of concretising the normative selfhood that is central to his project'.¹⁴⁷ Self-consistency is a key objective in the *EM* (20.3, 34.3–4, 92.3). The letters' multivocal texture, at first sight paradoxical, could be read as conveying the difficult nature of the ongoing struggle to achieve this self-consistency; at 120.22, S observes, 'how hard it is to play the part of one man'.¹⁴⁸

In the course of one of his more sustained accounts of the nature of philosophical teaching, S divides philosophy into *scientia* and *habitus animi* (94.48).¹⁴⁹ It is the latter, philosophy as practice, which is the

---

[142] Ker 2009b, Hadot 2014a: 293–7.
[143] See, too, 98.13, *De ira* 2.36.1, Plin. *Nat.* 18.274.
[144] Though, as Nussbaum notes (1994: 316–17), Cicero criticises the excessive use of medical analogies on the part of Stoic writers (*Tusc.* 4.23).
[145] Foucault 1986 (following Veyne), Hadot 1995. Trapp 2007 provides an excellent recent overview. On S in particular see Edwards 1997a, Bartsch 2006: 191–207, Hadot 2014a.
[146] Long 2009: 26–34.
[147] Long 2009: 32.
[148] On the tension between consistency and the plurality of voices in the *EM* see Edwards 1997a, Gill 2009.
[149] On *Epp.* 94 and 95 see Schafer 2009.

primary concern of the *EM* (even if technical discussions become increasingly prominent in later letters). This kind of philosophical expertise is to be mastered through embodied habit, *exercitatio* (71.31, 78.16, 84.47, 90.46, 94.3). While the value of habituation had long been recognised, it is championed with particular insistence in philosophical discourse of this period.[150] A variety of mental exercises and strategies are showcased in the letters.[151]

Some letters include an account of how S has spent his day, apparently in response to a request from L (65.1–2, 83.1–7). The relentless vigilance over one's own behaviour advocated in the *EM* involves a particular focus on daily routine, to include time set aside for close reflection on one's behaviour and disposition over the course of the day;[152] the importance of such an exercise is described at length in S's *De ira*[153] and regularly reaffirmed in the *EM* (e.g. 4.5 *cotidie meditari*, 16.1 *cotidiana meditatio*, 59.7–8, 83.1–2, 101.8). Repetition is crucial to the efficacy of this exercise.[154] The serial nature of letters as a collection (as noted above) makes them an especially suitable medium for actualising regular self-scrutiny over an extended period.

Letter-writing thus serves as a meditative practice, which has benefits for the author as well as the addressee; indeed for S, 'conversation' can be envisaged as taking place within the self.[155] He advises L (89.23): 'Say these things to others, so that you hear yourself while you speak.' While Michel Foucault suggestively explores the *EM*'s concern with 'self-scripting', constructing a 'better' self through writing,[156] this practice should be understood, as Graver emphasises, as essentially a route to transcending the self.[157]

This process of self-improvement is not envisaged as a solitary activity;[158] the epistolary relationship itself, as noted above, makes it intrinsically collaborative. As Altman comments, 'the epistolary experience, as

[150] Trapp 2007: 55–62.
[151] Newman 1989. Cf. Trapp 2007: 59–60 (citing Epictetus).
[152] S associates this with Sextius (*De ira* 3.36). For Hadot (2014a: 296–7) the practice is widespread among philosophical schools.
[153] *De ira* 3.36; see Ker 2009b. Inwood 2005: 344 notes 'the stunning vividness of Seneca's self-exemplification'.
[154] Hadot 2014a: 221–2.
[155] Grimal 1978: 229 on *EM* as interior dialogue, Edwards 1997a, Ker 2009b.
[156] Foucault 1997: 207–22.
[157] Graver 2014: 276. Cf. Hadot 1995: 211.
[158] Cf. Trapp, who also notes the salience of this element in the Stoicising guidance of Plutarch and Galen (2007: 58). In this respect, as he observes, the *mise en scène* of the *EM* can be compared with that of Arrian's *Discourses of Epictetus* (2007: 83–4).

distinguished from the autobiographical, is a reciprocal one'.[159] Foucault stresses the inter-subjectivity specific to epistolography, which involves the calibration of the gaze of the other and the gaze to which one subjects oneself in scrutinising one's everyday actions.[160] S differentiates insistently (29.1–3, 38, 40.2–4) between moralising aimed at a larger audience and advice targeted at a specific individual. Strategies for self-improvement need to be tailored to the individual (cf. 22.1, 64).

S's addressee (particularly in the early stages of his Stoic education) is also encouraged to imagine a suitable witness to his activities to spur himself on to virtue (11.10, 25.5–6) and to spend time with good men (52.8, 94.39–40). Conversely one should avoid those whose influence could be deleterious; to liberate oneself from contamination by the emotions of others, S advocates withdrawal, *secessio* (*Ep.* 7, 8.2, 19.10–11).[161]

The regulation of appetite, for food, drink and material possessions, features, particularly in the earlier letters, as a daily struggle of critical importance in the quest for *securitas*. The need to overcome the fear of poverty is introduced in *Ep.* 2; strategies to achieve this include the cultivation of ascetic habits (4.10–11, *Ep.* 18).[162] The would-be philosopher should aim to be satisfied with little and must endeavour to avoid attachment to any possessions. Fighting against the seductiveness of things, S proposes conscious redescription to reflect their true value, so that, for instance, L's promising career prospects, his litter, his escort are to be seen as nothing more than baggage weighing him down (22.9–12).[163] Social status, wealth and office have no bearing on an individual's true value (76.32).

Other philosophical techniques are also set out; cognitive strategies include *praemeditatio* (introduced at *Ep.* 4), mentally rehearsing precisely those events which one most fears may happen.[164] This exercise is particularly associated with learning to overcome the fear of pain and of death (see further on *Epp.* 24 and 70). Only thus can true mental freedom be attained (4.3–9, 8.7, 17.6, 85.28).[165]

In the course of his quest for self-improvement, the would-be philosopher is urged to reflect on the characteristics and imagine the behaviour of exemplary figures (6.5, 84.11). These include philosophical role models, such as Socrates (24.4) and Diogenes (90.14), but also more

---

[159] Altman 1982: 88 – even if the reciprocity may sometimes be fictive.
[160] Foucault 1997: 221.
[161] See Bartsch 2006: 194–8.
[162] On the preoccupation with poverty in Book 2 see Soldo.
[163] Cf. Trapp 2007: 85 quoting Epictetus.
[164] Cf. 76.34, 77.34, 78.16, Armisen-Marchetti 2008, Bartsch 2007.
[165] Inwood 2005: 302–21.

7 ETHICAL FOCUS AND TECHNIQUES OF THE SELF

traditional Roman exemplars, such as Mucius Scaevola (24.5) or Scipio Africanus (86.1–13).[166] Cato the Elder and Laelius, both held up as models by Cicero, also appear (11.10), while Cato the Younger, a professed Stoic, occupies a particularly prominent place (see on 24.6–8).[167] Traditional Roman concern with the standards of the *maiores* (figures of authority introduced at 1.5) acquires a distinctively Stoic inflection, while everyday exemplary discourse is itself subjected to a Stoic critique in later letters (94.61–9, 120.1–8).[168] Slaves and humbler figures also feature *ex maiore* as *exempla* (24.11, 24.14, 70.23, 70.26, 77.14–15). To be most effective, such examples need to be repeatedly visualised (78.18). But exemplarity is not a one-way process; a later letter exhorts Lucilius: 'let us too be among the *exempla*' (98.13).

Much is also to be learned from reading, but S makes clear that different reading strategies are appropriate depending on the stage reached by the would-be philosopher.[169] Selections are suitable for beginners, and may be drawn from Epicurean, as well as Stoic, texts (2.2–6, 6.4–5). For more advanced students, it is better to focus on Stoic works and to read them in their entirety (see further on 33.3–8, 39.1–2).[170] With his satiric vignette of Calvisius Sabinus (27.5–8), S mocks those who recognise only the display value of learning.[171] He also warns against reading uncritically; *Ep.* 84 discusses at length how to digest one's reading matter, to make it one's own.[172] At 67.2 he characterises his own reading as like conversation, *sermo*, not passive but interactive.[173]

Certainly the letters sometimes 'challenge and contradict one another'.[174] S sometimes appears inconsistent in the positions he adopts; his pedagogy has been characterised as opportunistic, the practical effect he is pursuing at a particular point being paramount.[175] Griffin stresses rather the dynamic nature of the teaching and learning experience in the *EM*, as L makes progress, becoming capable of engaging with more

---

[166] Castagna 1991, Mayer 1991, Maso 1999: 43–81, Langlands 2018.
[167] Though, as Gowing 2005: 75–6 notes, S makes less frequent use of traditional Roman exemplars in the *EM* than in his earlier work.
[168] Roller 2016; on the operation of traditional Roman exemplary discourse see Roller 2004, Langlands 2018.
[169] Hadot 2014a: 116–17 detects three distinct stages.
[170] Much Stoic teaching seems to have taken the form of writing commentaries on authoritative texts. On the ethical dimension of Cornutus' commentaries see Boys-Stones 2007.
[171] Wilson 2001: 175.
[172] See Graver 2014.
[173] See Edwards 2018a.
[174] Richardson-Hay: 54.
[175] Chaumartin 1985: 292–3.

complex and theoretical philosophical issues.[176] The apparently chronological ordering of the letters attests to L's philosophical development, even if the chronological span implied seems relatively brief for such a thoroughgoing transformation.[177] Earlier letters exhort L to retire from his official duties (19, 22, 36), while later ones focus on how to spend one's time after retirement (68.6–14, 82.1–4). L's concerns or episodes from S's daily life feature less often as ostensible prompts in later letters (though cf. e.g. 87.2–4, 123.1–5). *Epp.* 94 and 95 reflect extensively and self-consciously on pedagogic method.[178]

8 SENECA AND EARLIER LATIN POETIC AUTHORS

S (as is also evident from his tragedies) was intimately familiar with the works of Lucretius, Virgil, Horace and Ovid, as well as other Roman tragedians.[179] His letters shimmer with quotations from or allusions to works from a wide range of literary genres.[180] In the *EM* Seneca quotes extensively and explicitly from Virgil (particularly *G.* 1 and 3, *A.* 6 and 1), to a significantly greater degree than in his own earlier work. There are sixty-nine Virgilian citations in forty-two letters, of which only twenty-seven occur in the first half of the collection (*Epp.* 1–80), while forty-two come in the last forty odd letters.[181] Such quotations might have an important paraenetic function, as S notes (94.28–9, 108.8–10). His deployment of Virgil has sometimes been read as allegorical.[182] The teleological force of the poem at times lends both momentum and grandeur to the Stoic project of the letters, though elsewhere S chooses rather to read against Virgil's grain.[183] At 21.5, indeed, he sets himself up in competition with the epic poet.

---

[176] Griffin 2007: 90. Cf. Maurach 1970, who dismisses the suggestion made by Leeman 1953 that the more technical content of later letters is a consequence rather of S's simultaneous work on his *philosophia moralis*.

[177] Griffin 1992: 350–1, Trapp 2007: 83.

[178] Schafer 2009: 67–77.

[179] *Ep.* 79 touches on the challenge of writing poetry as a late-comer.

[180] Tischer 2017. In this respect they are comparable to Cicero's letters (particularly those to Atticus), which are studded with quotations from Homer and other authors. The early Stoic Chrysippus appears to have made extensive use of quotations from poetry in his writings (Diog. Laert. 7.180; see Nussbaum 1994: ch. 10, 447). On quotations generally in S see also Mazzoli 1970: 157–264, Dueck 2009.

[181] *Vergilius noster*: 21.5, 28.1, 28.3, 56.12, 59.3, 70.2, 84.3, 86.15, 92.9, 95.69, 104.25 (Mazzoli 1970: 215–32). See also Auvray 1987.

[182] Mazzoli 1970: 224–5.

[183] As Berno 2004: 9 notes. Cf. Setaioli 1965 (discussing particularly *Epp.* 66, 18, 82, 108).

The thoroughly literary nature of the letters is also manifest in more oblique engagements with earlier texts. Verbal echoes of Horace's *Odes* may be detected in a number of passages (e.g. 12.9).[184] Thematically, however, the *EM* resonate more closely with the *Epistles* and *Satires*.[185] The *EM* themselves offer vignettes with a distinctly satiric colouring (the pretentious Calvisius Sabinus of 27, the luxurious dinner of 47.2–8, the noisy baths of 56.1–2), while their often conversational mode is reminiscent of satire;[186] Horace's *Satires* indeed were also referred to as *Sermones*.[187] Both Horace and S deploy what Horace terms *Bioneis sermonibus et sale nigro* (*Ep.* 2.2.60), a reference to the Cynic Bion of Borysthenes.[188] S evokes Bion's diatribes (which seem to have featured baroque attacks on luxurious eating, for instance) both directly and through the medium of Horace's work.[189] Yet Horace's ironic treatment of Stoic philosophy (following on from Lucilius, it seems)[190] perhaps finds a riposte in S.

9 SENECAN STYLE

S himself reflects explicitly on the relationship between style and ethical purpose.[191] The term *compositio*, for instance, has both ethical and literary connotations, though the language of truth, S asserts paradoxically, should be *oratio incomposita . . . et simplex* (40.4).[192] Yet stylistic variety also has its place in the pursuit of ethical progress. Criticising the pedestrian style of the moralist Fabianus (a contemporary of his father), S exhorts: 'Let him show us the keenness of oratory, the loftiness of tragedy, the subtlety of comedy' (100.10). He himself deploys all these modes and more in the *EM*, whose style is both varied and distinctive.[193] The letters' dramatic, multivocal qualities are well delineated by Alfonso Traina, who

---

[184] Berthet 1979, Vogt-Spira 2017.
[185] Gowers 2011, Berno 2017b, Del Giovane 2017 and Edwards 2017a.
[186] Wilson 2001: 175. S was himself the author of the satirical *Apocolocyntosis*. Ker 2006: 31 comments on S's tendency to embed one genre in another.
[187] Gowers 2012: 12.
[188] On Bion see Kindstrand 1976.
[189] S quotes Bion at 36.3, 115.8, *Tranq.* 8.1–9, 15.4. See Del Giovane (who offers, at 2015a: 28–36, a judicious account of the problematic term 'diatribe'); S's teacher Attalus may have favoured a Cynic style (Del Giovane 2015b). See also Griffin 1992: 508–9.
[190] Mayer 2005.
[191] See further intro. to *Ep.* 114, also *Epp.* 40, 75.
[192] He praises the signs of *mens composita* in L (2.1); cf. 115.2, discussed by Coleman 1974: 276–7. See Lee Too 1994: 217.
[193] Summers' comprehensive analysis (xlii–xcv) illustrates key features. See also Bourgery 1922, Coleman 1974, Wilson 1987, Setaioli 2000: 111–217, von Albrecht 2004: 9–52. Also valuable are the more recent accounts by von Albrecht 2014 (particularly 741–4 discussing S's reflections on style) and by Williams 2015.

underlines in particular the contrast S himself articulates (38.1) between the more intimate mode of *sermo* and the rousing, hortatory mode of *disputatio*.[194]

The style of the *EM* is often colloquial, prosaic indeed;[195] S explicitly eschews (e.g. 114.13) what he terms excessive poeticisms in prose writing.[196] Strings of questions are common, as are imagined interjections (introduced by *inquis* or *inquit*), sometimes attributed to L but at other times apparently from a more hostile interlocutor (a feature of the diatribe tradition). Buttonholing imperatives abound (e.g. the opening of 1.1, *Ita fac*), as do first- and second-person verbs (intensely clustered in e.g. *Epp.* 34, 46). As S directs attention inwards, the reflexive adjective comes to be identified not with one's material possession but with the *se* itself; the formulation *suus/meus/tuus esse* conveys the sense of being one's own master (e.g. 12.9: the *sapiens* is *securus sui possessor*).[197]

S favours compressed modes of expression, employing the future participle, for instance, to express attribution or purpose (e.g. 7.4 *interfecturis*, 18.9 *uisurus*, 70.11 *nauigaturus*).[198] Stoic literary theory apparently emphasised brevity[199] (though S, like Cicero, stresses the limitations of the unadorned style associated with the Stoics);[200] this quality (though uncharacteristic of his project as a whole) is sometimes exemplified in individual letters. Sentences are often short (there is relatively little subordination), or composed of short units, generating a choppiness and unpredictability inimical to complacent reading. Words are placed to achieve maximum effect. S makes extensive use of anaphora, antithesis, repetition (sometimes of entire sentences, as at 24.9–10 *'imperator', inquit, 'se bene habet'*, or 47.1 *'serui sunt!'*). Fond of alliteration, he is generally alert to acoustic effects, often deploying similar-sounding words, sometimes in polysyllabic pairs, such as *leuis est, si ferre possum, breuis est, si ferre non possum* (24.14), sometimes in pairs where one word is longer than the other, such as *uerborum ... uerberibus* (47.19). Frequent, too, are cases where the pair consists of two forms of the same word or cognate words, e.g. *cum crescimus, uita descrescit* (24.20).

---

[194] Traina 1987: 9–41. See also Hijmans 1966, Lotito 2001. According to Fronto (*Ant.* 2.14, pp. 141–2 van den Hout = *SVF* II.27), Chrysippus' style appears to have been dramatic, introducing characters, putting words into people's mouths, though it is not clear to what degree S was familiar with his writings.
[195] Setaioli 2000: 9–95.
[196] Hine 2005.
[197] Traina 1987: 12. See also Lotito 2001.
[198] Coleman 1974: 279.
[199] Moretti 1995: 52–7, Protopapas-Marneli 2002: 50–2, Hadot 2014a: 206.
[200] Cic. *Orat.* 62–4, *De orat.* 1.229, Sen. *Ep.* 82.8–9.

9 SENECAN STYLE

S's taste for maxims (e.g. 94.27–8) and the sentential epigram (a form designed to lodge in the memory) was notorious. Even Quintilian admires many of his *sententiae* (10.1.129).[201] Such *sententiae* gain their energy from paradox, oxymoron and wordplay, e.g. *inhumanior redeo quia inter homines fui* (7.3), *philosophiae seruire libertas est* (8.8), *imperare sibi maximum imperium est* (113.30).[202] S contrasts radically different conceptual orders, the everyday and the philosophically elevated in the two elements of a formulation.[203] Indeed, as Williams puts it, 'paradox is not so much a feature of Senecan style as a precondition of it'.[204]

Particularly in the first half of the collection (the focus of this selection), moral exhortation, paraenesis (characterised at 95.1), is a favoured mode.[205] Quintilian describes S as *egregius uitiorum insectator* (10.1.129). S's own observations on a weakness in the writings of the moralist Fabianus are revealing; he looks in vain for 'any rugged denunciation of vice, any courageous words in the face of danger, any proud defiance of fortune, any scornful threats against self-seeking. I wish to see luxury rebuked, lust condemned, waywardness crushed out' (100.10). No one could criticise S for such an omission; this mode works to rouse the addressee to virtue (e.g. 82.22–4), to channel feelings of contempt for the vice-prone (evident particularly in e.g. 47.2–8, 86.6–7) – but also, we should not forget, to entertain.

One of the chief pleasures of reading the *EM* is the play of image and metaphor as S's language swoops, swerves and flips between literal and metaphorical, between the granular quotidian, the rousing hortatory and the meditative sublime. S conveys his meaning through homespun analogies with wool-dyeing (71.31–2) or seed-sowing (73.16), through memorably graphic evocations of suppurating sores (8.2, 14.6) or vomiting voluptuaries (47.5), through to exalted personifications of philosophy (53.8–12).[206]

In some respects, S may be following Stoic tradition in his use of imagery; Zeno is said to have favoured memorable images.[207] The Stoic-educated Ariston of Chios was admired for his use of vividly conceived analogies, *Homoiomata* (the sage, for instance, is compared to a talented

---

[201] Though he deplores their excessive influence on the style of others (8.5.31): *nec multas plerasque sententias dicunt, sed omnia tamquam sententias.*

[202] On use of the *sententia* in Latin prose more generally see Sinclair 1995. Bloomer 2011: 139–69 offers insightful analysis of the moral *sententia* in Roman education. On *sententiae* in S's tragedies see Dinter 2014, on their occurrence in the *EM*, Mindt 2017: esp. 327–30.

[203] Traina 1987: 19–22.

[204] Williams 2015: 147.

[205] See also e.g. 108.12, 121.4.

[206] Catalogued and analysed by Armisen-Marchetti 1989 and 2015.

[207] Moretti 1995: 38.

actor).²⁰⁸ S himself appears notably alert to what can be seen as the essentially figural properties of language,²⁰⁹ defending his use of metaphors and similes, on the grounds that they serve to bring both speaker and listener 'face to face with the subject at issue' (59.6, *in rem praesentem adducant*).²¹⁰ The precise operation of image and metaphor in his work, particularly their role in articulating philosophical argument, has received increasing attention.²¹¹ Bartsch (2009) notes the significant tensions between the images S often selects and the Stoic orthodoxies he is apparently trying to convey. Yet, as she argues, S's images are not to be dismissed as purely ornamental, nor are they a manifestation of philosophical confusion on his part.²¹² Rather they have a critical role to play, a cognitive and communicative force, as S himself underlines (59.6). S, as Bartsch observes, 'constantly asks us to *refigure* our self-understanding as an essential step on the path to self-improvement'.²¹³

The processes of Roman political life are thus turned inwards in the *EM* (118.1–4). The economic preoccupations so prominent in Cicero's philosophical writing are redeployed by S as metaphor so that ownership remains important, but the Stoic's only true possession is himself; his material trappings, no matter what their critical role in determining social and political status, are of no relevance to his philosophical project.²¹⁴ Pervasive military metaphors enable S to present the would-be philosopher's struggle to withstand the potentially disturbing blows of fortune in terms of heroic martial conflict.²¹⁵ This strategy, as Bartsch comments, enables the 'refiguring of an essentially passive and intellectual practice on the part of the Stoic student as an act of martial resistance and self-defense'.²¹⁶ S's version of Stoicism is thus assimilated in important respects to traditional Roman ideals of manliness.²¹⁷

Some scholars have found S's inclination to deploy in metaphorical form iniquitous institutions of Roman life, such as slavery (in *Ep.* 47) or

---

²⁰⁸ *SVF* III.383–403. See Moretti 1995: 120–3, Protopapas-Marneli 2002: 70–5.
²⁰⁹ Coleman 1974: 277–8. On the pervasiveness and potency of metaphorical language in general see Lakoff and Johnson 1980.
²¹⁰ Nicely analysed by Dressler 2012. See also Sjöblad 2015.
²¹¹ Armisen-Marchetti 1991, Grimal 1992b, Bartsch 2009, Edwards 2009 (on slavery as metaphor), Dressler 2012, Riggbsy 2016 (on metaphor in the *De ira*).
²¹² As is suggested by Inwood 2005: 31–3.
²¹³ Bartsch 2009: 195; cf. Dressler 2012.
²¹⁴ For S's use of economic imagery in relation to time, a pervasive feature of the *EM*, see Armisen-Marchetti 1995.
²¹⁵ On S's military imagery see Lavery 1980, Armisen-Marchetti 1989: 94–6, Galimberti 2001, Sommer 2001, Edwards 2007: 93. Examples are many, e.g. 13.1, 3 (*multum enim adicit sibi uirtus lacessita*), 30.4, 49.6, 51.10, 67.15, 99.32, 104.2, 109.8; cf. *VB* 15.5.
²¹⁶ Bartsch 2009: 203–4.
²¹⁷ See also Roller 2001: 22–6, 99–108 and Edwards 2007: 90–8 for the gap between traditional ideas of *uirtus* and the term as deployed by S.

gladiatorial spectacle (in *Ep.* 7), a disappointing evasion.[218] Certainly the *EM* offer little encouragement to change the world (perhaps unsurprising at this stage in S's career). Instead his focus is on changing one's own disposition towards the world.

Physical pain is an insidious and persistent presence in the *EM*. S, in Platonising mode, urges his reader to transcend the experiences of the body and focus rather on the health of the mind (e.g. 23.6, 53.5–7, 54.7, 78.27).[219] Yet few Roman writers convey the experience of physical pain in such gripping and graphic detail.[220] S has often been characterised as a valetudinarian, his obsession with illness and ailments (e.g. *Epp.* 54, 78, 108) compared to that of Aelius Aristides or Fronto.[221] Yet rather than diagnosing references to agonising joints or breathing difficulties as autobiographical traces, modern readers would do better to reflect on the haunting power of physical pain in a world without effective analgesia and to appreciate the metaphorical dynamics of this domain in S's writing. While the idea of philosophy as a therapy analogous to medicine is pervasive in Hellenistic thought,[222] the urgency of afflictions of the mind, their desperate need for a cure, acquires a distinctive energy in S's writing (see e.g. 7.1). Sometimes contrasting the domains of the mental and the physical, sometimes eliding them, S repeatedly underlines his own frailty, poignantly reminding his reader that he himself is a sick man (27.1, 68.7–9) who has sometimes struggled to find the reserves of endurance needed to carry on living (78.1–5, 104.3–5).[223]

10 *CLAUSULAE* IN SENECA

Seneca is among the many writers of Latin prose who articulated their prose with rhythmical *clausulae* (inherited ultimately from Hellenistic oratory).[224] The ends of his sentences much more often than not are marked by these rhythmical *clausulae*; they occur very frequently at pauses inside a sentence, although at such points unrhythmical cadences are also common. This practice may be discerned first on a large scale in the writings of Cicero and the rhetorical treatise *Ad Herennium*, but it spread much more widely during the principate; for example, Mela, Petronius, Curtius

---

[218] E.g. Joshel 2011.
[219] Though see Reydams-Schils 2010 for S's significant adaptations of Platonic thought.
[220] Courtouil 2014, 2015.
[221] E.g. Russell 1974: 80.
[222] As Nussbaum 1994 compellingly demonstrates. Particularly associated with the Stoics (Long and Sedley 1987: 1.385), the connection is also prominent in the diatribe tradition of popular philosophy.
[223] Edwards 1999.
[224] This section in particular is heavily endebted to Stephen Oakley.

Rufus, Quintilian, Pliny the Younger, and Suetonius also employ similar rhythmical *clausulae*.

Broadly speaking, all these writers used rhythms based on the metrical 'feet' known as the cretic (— ⏑ —) and the trochee (— ⏑ — ×). Scansion follows the rules of verse, with elision and prodelision observed in midphrase but not over a pause. Resolution of a heavy syllable into two light syllables is common. Rhythms favoured by S (as by others) and some of the resolutions found with them may be tabulated as follows:

(1) — ⏑ — — × = cretic + spondee
(1a) ⏑⏑ ⏑ — — ×
(1b) — ⏑ ⏑⏑ — ×
(1c) — ⏑ — ⏑⏑ ×
(2) — ⏑ — — ⏑ × = double cretic
(2a) ⏑⏑ ⏑ — — ⏑ ×
(3) — ⏑ — × = double trochee or trochee + spondee (often preceded by a cretic)
(3a) — ⏑ ⏑⏑ ×
(4) — — — — ⏑ × = molossus + cretic
(4a) — — — — ⏑ ⏑×
(4b) — — ⏑⏑ — ⏑ ×
(4c) — ⏑⏑ — — ⏑ ×
(5) — ⏑ — ⏑ × = trochee + cretic (hypodochmiac)
(5a) ⏑⏑ ⏑ — ⏑ ×
(6) — — — × = double spondee

The cretic spondee and molossus cretic are also frequent in Ciceronian epistolography.[225] Seneca particularly favours the double cretic (less common in Cicero).[226] Conversely some rhythms such as — ⏑ ⏑ — × (the so-called 'heroic' clausula) and — ⏑ — ⏑ — × (the so-called 'triple trochee') tend to be avoided. As for the double spondee (— — — ×), in writers of rhythmical prose it is statistically less common than one might expect in a writer paying no attention to prose-rhythm: to impart a lift to the rhythm at least the third or fourth from last syllable needs to be light. But it is not avoided entirely. Indeed in the opening passage of *Ep.* 1 it is employed repeatedly, and sometimes one may suspect that it has

---

[225] On Cicero see Hutchinson 1998: 9–12. Whitton 2013: 28–32 provides a lucid and insightful guide to prose rhythm in Pliny's letters.

[226] Russell 1974: 74. S's prose rhythm is analysed by Bourgery 1910 (with statistics on his preferred *clausulae*), Axelson 1933 and 1939, Hijmans 1976 and 1991, Soubiran 1991 and, briefly but clearly, Ker 2011: 130–2.

been employed to impart a weighty and sonorous close (see e.g. 53.8 *expērgīscāmŭr*).

To illustrate this the opening of *Ep.* 1 has been scanned.[227] A | marks a point at which it seems likely that there was a pause (in places a different marking may be possible).[228] Neither 1c nor 3a appear in this passage, but see e.g. 26.2 *partem oneñs sūī pŏsŭ̍it* for the former, 26.5 *uerbis ēxhĭbŭĭmŭs* for the latter.

Ita fac, mī Lūcīlī: |⁶ uīndĭcā tē tĭ̍bi, |² et tempus quod adhuc aut aūfĕrēbātŭr |¹ aut subripiebātŭr (|?) aūt ēxcĭdēbăt |³ cōllĭg(e) ēt sēruā. |¹ persuade tibi hoc sic ēss(e) ūt scrībō |⁶: quaedam tempora eripiūntūr nōbīs, |⁶ quaedam subducūntūr, | quaēd(am) ēfflŭūnt. |⁴ turpissima tamen est iactura quae per neglegēntĭām fĭ̍t. |³ et si uolŭĕrĭ̍s āttēndĕrĕ̆, |²ᵃ magna pars uitae elabitur male agentibus, | maxima nĭ̍hĭl ăgēntĭ̍bŭs, |⁵ᵃ tota uita alĭŭd ăgēntĭ̍bŭs. |⁵ᵃ [2] quem mihi dabis qui aliquod pretium tēmpŏrī pōnat, |¹ quī dĭ̍(em) aestĭ̍mĕt, |⁵ qui intellegat sē cōtĭdĭē mŏrī? |⁴ᵇ in hōc ĕnīm fāllĭmŭ̆r, |² quōd mōrtēm prōspĭ̍cĭmŭs: |⁴ᵃ magna pars eīūs iām praētĕrĭt; |⁴ quidquid aetatīs rētrō (e)st (|?) mōrs tĕ̆nĕt. |⁴ fac ergo, mī Lūcīlī, |⁶ quod făcĕrĕ̆ tē scrībis, |¹ᵃ omnes hōrās cōmplēctĕrĕ̆; |⁴ sic fiet ut minus ex crāstīnō pēndĕas, |⁴ si hodiērnō măn(um) ĭniēcĕ̆rĭs. |⁴ᵇ [3] dum differtur |⁶ uītă trānscūrrit. |¹ omnia, Lūcīl(i), ălĭĕnă sūnt, |⁴ᵇ tempus tāntūm nōstrūm (e)st; |⁶ in huius rei unius fugācĭs āc lūbrĭcāe |² possessiōnem natŭrā nōs mīsit, |¹ ex qua expēllĭt quīcūmquĕ uŭlt. |⁴ et tanta stultĭtĭ̆ă mōrtālĭ̆ūm (e)st |²ᵃ ut quae minima et uilissima sunt, | cērtē rĕ̆părābĭlĭ̆(a), |⁴ᵇ imputari sibi cum impetrauērĕ̆ pătĭăntŭ̆r, |¹ᵇ nemo se iudicet quicquam debere qui tēmpŭs āccēpit, |¹ cum interim hoc unum est quod ne gratus quidēm pŏtēst rēddĕrĕ̆. |²

11 RECEPTION OF THE LETTERS

S was evidently a key player in the literary landscape of Neronian Rome. Tacitus, rather disparagingly, comments (*Ann.* 13.3) that his talent was particularly suited to his age, *ingenium . . . temporis eius auribus accommodatum*, though among some of his contemporaries, S's style excited violent dislike; Caligula (Suet. *Cal.* 53.2) described it as 'sand without lime', if also *lenius comptiusque*.[229] Later literary critics are on the whole, like Tacitus, unenthusiastic. Quintilian, a fully paid up Ciceronian, acknowledges S's merit but also highlights the pernicious consequences of his extraordinary influence as a stylist;[230] in S there is much to admire, he

---

[227] For an alternative approach to the same passage see Hijmans 1976: 1–11.
[228] For the division of Latin prose into cola see Nisbet 1995: 312–24.
[229] Wilson 1987: 107–8, 120 nn. 9–11.
[230] Dominik 1997b, Ker 2006: 21–2.

notes (*Inst.* 10.1.131), but one needs to be selective. Archaisers of the Antonine age were also inclined to frown upon S's prose. Fronto (pp. 153.11–154.13 van den Hout) deplores S's 'soft, feverish plums', *mollibus et febriculosis prunuleis*, and complains about repetitiveness; the occasional well-turned witticisms to be found in S are like the silver coins that sometimes turn up in sewers. While allowing for some stylistic skill, Gellius, too, affronted particularly by S's criticism of Cicero, makes plain his disapproval (12.2.1, 12.2.8, 11,14).[231] The pungency of these critiques is itself a reflection of S's status as 'the second founder of Roman prose', in Guillemin's phrase.[232]

Macrobius liked the *EM* enough to plagiarise *Epp*. 84 and 47 at some length (in his introduction and at 1.11.7–16).[233] They also found favour with at least some early Christian writers; Tertullian (*A treatise on the soul* 20.1) terms S *saepe noster*. S's ethical commitment is celebrated by Jerome, who includes him in the catalogue of saints (*De viris illustribus* 12). The affinity felt by many Christians for his writing (particularly the *EM*) is especially evident in the widespread circulation in the early medieval period of the spurious letters of Paul and Seneca, whose existence served to legitimate S as a trustworthy authority on ethics (though their style bears little obvious resemblance to that of the *EM*).[234]

In twelfth-century France, as interest in classical literature gained new vigour, the content and the style of the *EM* themselves were praised and imitated by leading Christian scholars, notably Peter Abelard.[235] By the thirteenth century, manuscripts of the *EM* were circulating in Italy and Spain.[236] Petrarch owned a copy of the *EM* and drew inspiration from them in composing his own letters (the *Seniles*, in particular, exhibit a strain of Senecan Stoicism).[237] The *EM* first appeared in print in 1470 and commanded widespread admiration among Italian humanists.[238] Erasmus revered S as a moralist and celebrated his prose style, which, while terming it 'silver' in comparison with the 'gold' of Ciceronian Latin, he deemed particularly suitable for more informal purposes.[239] His editorial

---

[231] On the letters' reception in antiquity see Trillitzsch 1971.
[232] Guillemin 1957.
[233] Setaioli 2015.
[234] Torre 2015. They are cited with approval by Augustine, for instance (e.g. *Epist.* 153.14). See further Trillitzsch 1971, von Albrecht 2004: 130–72.
[235] Reynolds: 112–24, Ker 2009a: 187–97, Mayer 2015. Colish 1985 documents the influence of Stoic ideas more generally.
[236] Fohlen 2000, De Robertis and Resta 2004, Mayer 2015.
[237] Ascoli 2015, Zak 2015.
[238] Panizza 1983.
[239] Mayer 2015: 284.

work (notably his 1529 edition of S's collected prose) did much to strip the text of medieval accretions.[240]

In the late sixteenth and seventeenth centuries, the *EM* were appreciated for their philosophical content, as well as their distinctive style. Interest in Stoicism flourished, with Antoine Muret, Henri Estienne and above all Justus Lipsius championing S's work. For Lipsius, S's Stoicism offered an appealing refuge amid the religious conflicts of the late sixteenth century (indeed neo-Stoicism struck a chord across Europe).[241] Lipsius' prefatory essay to his 1605 edition of the letters celebrated S's style as especially appropriate to epistolography. Elsewhere he comments approvingly on the structure of S's prose that 'all is arranged for the battle or the arena, not for pleasure or theatrical display', *pugnae atque arenae omnia, non delectationi aut scaenae parata*.[242]

S's *EM* also played a significant role in the emergence of the essay as a genre. While he was no Stoic, Montaigne admired S's psychological acuity; his essays (1580–92) are notably Senecan in both approach and texture.[243] As William Fitzgerald notes, the term 'essay' 'returned to bite [Seneca] in the many modern characterisations of his moral epistles as essays rather than letters'.[244] Francis Bacon (himself influenced in his essay-writing by both S and Montaigne) comments: 'For Senecaes Epistles to Lucilius, yf one marke them well, are but essaies; That is dispersed Meditiacions, though conveyed in the form of Epistles.'[245]

S's influence declined in the eighteenth century (though the *EM* found enthusiasts in David Hume, Denis Diderot and Jean-Jacques Rousseau, among others).[246] Nietzsche memorably described S as a 'toreador of virtue' but S's approach to ethics was out of tune with that of most moral philosophers of the nineteenth century.[247] Nineteenth- and twentieth-century critics of S's style have often resorted to bizarre and vivid similes in a paradoxically Senecan vein; T. B. Macaulay, for instance, compared reading S's concentrated, motto-studded prose to 'dining on

---

[240] Panizza 1987.
[241] Morford 1991. Other neo-Stoics were less keen on S, preferring Marcus Aurelius (Brooke 2012: 96–100).
[242] 1604 essay cited by Williamson 1951: 111.
[243] See Cancik 1967: 91–101, von Albrecht 2004: 173–92, Kraye 2007, Mayer 2015: 286–7.
[244] Fitzgerald 2015: 281.
[245] M. Kiernan, ed. *Sir Francis Bacon: the Essaies or Counsels civill and morall* (Oxford 1985) p. 317.
[246] Citti 2015.
[247] F. Nietzsche, *Twilight of the idols* in *The antichrist, Ecce homo and Twilight of the idols and other writings*, ed. A. Ridley and J. Norman (Cambridge 2005) p. 191. Citti 2015: 306.

nothing but anchovy sauce'.²⁴⁸ Yet, while S was widely disparaged, particularly in the English-speaking world, for much of the nineteenth and twentieth centuries, he has returned to popularity in more recent decades, a reassessment spurred in part by the attention he receives in Foucault's *History of sexuality*,²⁴⁹ but also by renewed appreciation of his supple thinking, linguistic bravura and poignant self-awareness.

12 THE SELECTION

This selection aims to convey the range and variety of the letters, with a bias towards letters from the earlier part of the collection, which tend to be less philosophically technical (thus complementing Inwood). Individual letters are not self-sufficient; one aim of the commentary is to highlight the complex ways in which the letters included relate to those which immediately precede and follow them, those in the same book (where the book divisions are known) and, more broadly, to others in the collection. It is essential to understand the letters in relation to the trajectory of moral and intellectual progress in which both S and L are involved.

Summers' venerable edition of the letters has received criticism for including only the most essay-like (while some more polythematic letters are significantly cut).²⁵⁰ The current selection overlaps considerably with that of Summers but also includes a number of shorter, more obviously 'epistolary' letters.

13 THE TEXT

The manuscript tradition is expertly discussed in Reynolds, with further observations in Reynolds 1983.²⁵¹ Additional insights are offered by Malaspina (2018). The 124 surviving letters have been preserved in two distinct *corpora* (*Epp.* 1–88 and 89–124) with differing manuscript traditions, very rich in the case of 1–88, much less so for 89–124.²⁵² Samples of the manuscripts are illustrated and discussed in De Robertis and Resta.²⁵³

---

[248] Letter to T. F. Ellis, 30 May 1836 (Macaulay 1976: 178).
[249] Vol. III (1986). On Foucault's reading of the *EM* see Long 2009: 21–4.
[250] Wilson 2001: 165, and on Summers: 'his selection gives a very distorted picture of the *Epistles to Lucilius*' (1987: 120).
[251] See further Fohlen 2000 on the medieval tradition.
[252] *Epp.* 1–52 and 53–88 were at some stage before the ninth century also preserved independently from one another (Spallone 1995: 186, Malaspina 2018: 86).
[253] De Robertis and Resta 2004: 210–25.

This edition follows L. D. Reynolds' Oxford Classical Text with the following modifications: (i) capitalisation is standard only at the start of letters; (ii) orthography is regularised to follow the spelling of *lemmata* in the *OLD*, so that prefixes are assimilated (e.g. *imb-* for *inb-*) and *-es* replaces *-is* in the third declension acc. plur. The present text departs from Reynolds' in the following places:

12.7	dixit enim alius parem
	plura facit ista, non alia. alias contractior, alias productior uita
18.1	publicae
21.10	†et inscriptum hortulis† legeris
34.3	aliud
47.5	\<toro\> *omitted*
53.6	exercitatione *OCT misprint*
90.7	et cauis tectos
114.5	comantibus? uide ut alueum

SENECA

SELECTED LETTERS

SENECA
SELECTED LETTERS

Letter 1

SENECA LVCILIO SVO SALVTEM

Ita fac, mi Lucili: uindica te tibi, et tempus quod adhuc aut auferebatur 1
aut surripiebatur aut excidebat collige et serua. persuade tibi hoc sic esse
ut scribo: quaedam tempora eripiuntur nobis, quaedam subducuntur,
quaedam effluunt. turpissima tamen est iactura quae per neglegentiam
fit. et si uolueris attendere, magna pars uitae elabitur male agentibus,
maxima nihil agentibus, tota uita aliud agentibus. quem mihi dabis qui 2
aliquod pretium tempori ponat, qui diem aestimet, qui intellegat se
cotidie mori? in hoc enim fallimur, quod mortem prospicimus: magna
pars eius iam praeterît; quidquid aetatis retro est mors tenet. fac ergo,
mi Lucili, quod facere te scribis, omnes horas complectere; sic fiet ut
minus ex crastino pendeas, si hodierno manum inieceris. dum differtur
uita transcurrit. omnia, Lucili, aliena sunt, tempus tantum nostrum est; in 3
huius rei unius fugacis ac lubricae possessionem natura nos misit, ex qua
expellit quicumque uult. et tanta stultitia mortalium est ut quae minima
et uilissima sunt, certe reparabilia, imputari sibi cum impetrauere patiantur, nemo se iudicet quicquam debere qui tempus accepit, cum interim
hoc unum est quod ne gratus quidem potest reddere.

    interrogabis fortasse quid ego faciam qui tibi ista praecipio. fatebor 4
ingenue: quod apud luxuriosum sed diligentem euenit, ratio mihi constat
impensae. non possum dicere nihil perdere, sed quid perdam et quare
et quemadmodum dicam; causas paupertatis meae reddam. sed euenit
mihi quod plerisque non suo uitio ad inopiam redactis: omnes ignoscunt,
nemo succurrit. quid ergo est? non puto pauperem cui quantulumcum- 5
que superest sat est; tu tamen malo serues tua, et bono tempore incipies.
nam ut uisum est maioribus nostris, 'sera parsimonia in fundo est'; non
enim tantum minimum in imo sed pessimum remanet. uale.

Letter 7

SENECA LVCILIO SVO SALVTEM

Quid tibi uitandum praecipue existimes quaeris? turbam. nondum illi 1
tuto committeris. ego certe confitebor imbecillitatem meam: numquam
mores quos extuli refero; aliquid ex eo quod composui turbatur, aliquid

ex iis quae fugaui redit. quod aegris euenit quos longa imbecillitas usque eo adfecit ut nusquam sine offensa proferantur, hoc accidit nobis quorum animi ex longo morbo reficiuntur. inimica est multorum conuersatio: nemo non aliquod nobis uitium aut commendat aut imprimit aut nescientibus allinit. utique quo maior est populus cui miscemur, hoc periculi plus est. nihil uero tam damnosum bonis moribus quam in aliquo spectaculo desidere; tunc enim per uoluptatem facilius uitia surrepunt.

3 quid me existimas dicere? auarior redeo, ambitiosior, luxuriosior? immo uero crudelior et inhumanior, quia inter homines fui. casu in meridianum spectaculum incidi, lusus expectans et sales et aliquid laxamenti quo hominum oculi ab humano cruore acquiescant. contra est: quidquid ante pugnatum est misericordia fuit; nunc omissis nugis mera homicidia sunt. nihil habent quo tegantur; ad ictum totis corporibus expositi numquam

4 frustra manum mittunt. hoc plerique ordinariis paribus et postulaticiis praeferunt. quidni praeferant? non galea, non scuto repellitur ferrum. quo munimenta? quo artes? omnia ista mortis morae sunt. mane leonibus et ursis homines, meridie spectatoribus suis obiciuntur. interfectores interfecturis iubent obici et uictorem in aliam detinent caedem;

5 exitus pugnantium mors est. ferro et igne res geritur. haec fiunt dum uacat harena. 'sed latrocinium fecit aliquis, occidit hominem.' quid ergo? quia occidit, ille meruit ut hoc pateretur: tu quid meruisti miser ut hoc spectes? 'occide, uerbera, ure! quare tam timide incurrit in ferrum? quare parum audacter occidit? quare parum libenter moritur? plagis agatur in uulnera, mutuos ictus nudis et obuiis pectoribus excipiant.' intermissum est spectaculum: 'interim iugulentur homines, ne nihil agatur.' age, ne hoc quidem intellegitis, mala exempla in eos redundare qui faciunt? agite dis immortalibus gratias quod eum docetis esse crudelem qui non potest discere.

6 subducendus populo est tener animus et parum tenax recti: facile transitur ad plures. Socrati et Catoni et Laelio excutere morem suum dissimilis multitudo potuisset: adeo nemo nostrum, qui cum maxime concinnamus ingenium, ferre impetum uitiorum tam magno comitatu uenientium

7 potest. unum exemplum luxuriae aut auaritiae multum mali facit: conuictor delicatus paulatim eneruat et mollit, uicinus diues cupiditatem irritat, malignus comes quamuis candido et simplici rubiginem suam affricuit: quid tu accidere his moribus credis in quos publice factus est impetus?

8 necesse est aut imiteris aut oderis. utrumque autem deuitandum est: neue similis malis fias, quia multi sunt, neue inimicus multis, quia dissimiles sunt. recede in te ipse quantum potes; cum his uersare qui te meliorem facturi sunt, illos admitte quos tu potes facere meliores. mutuo ista fiunt,

9 et homines dum docent discunt. non est quod te gloria publicandi ingenii producat in medium, ut recitare istis uelis aut disputare; quod facere te

uellem, si haberes isti populo idoneam mercem: nemo est qui intellegere te possit. aliquis fortasse, unus aut alter incidet, et hic ipse formandus tibi erit instituendusque ad intellectum tui. 'cui ergo ista didici?' non est quod timeas ne operam perdideris, si tibi didicisti.

sed ne soli mihi hodie didicerim, communicabo tecum quae occurrunt mihi egregie dicta circa eundem fere sensum tria, ex quibus unum haec epistula in debitum soluet, duo in antecessum accipe. Democritus ait, 'unus mihi pro populo est, et populus pro uno.' bene et ille, quisquis fuit (ambigitur enim de auctore), cum quaereretur ab illo quo tanta diligentia artis spectaret ad paucissimos peruenturae, 'satis sunt' inquit 'mihi pauci, satis est unus, satis est nullus.' egregie hoc tertium Epicurus, cum uni ex consortibus studiorum suorum scriberet: 'haec' inquit 'ego non multis, sed tibi; satis enim magnum alter alteri theatrum sumus.' ista, mi Lucili, condenda in animum sunt, ut contemnas uoluptatem ex plurium assensione uenientem. multi te laudant: ecquid habes cur placeas tibi, si is es quem intellegant multi? introrsus bona tua spectent. uale.

Letter 12

SENECA LVCILIO SVO SALVTEM

Quocumque me uerti, argumenta senectutis meae uideo. ueneram in suburbanum meum et querebar de impensis aedificii dilabentis. ait uilicus mihi non esse neglegentiae suae uitium, omnia se facere, sed uillam ueterem esse. haec uilla inter manus meas creuit: quid mihi futurum est, si tam putria sunt aetatis meae saxa? iratus illi proximam occasionem stomachandi arripio. 'apparet' inquam 'has platanos neglegi: nullas habent frondes. quam nodosi sunt et retorridi rami, quam tristes et squalidi trunci! hoc non accideret si quis has circumfoderet, si irrigaret.' iurat per genium meum se omnia facere, in nulla re cessare curam suam, sed illas uetulas esse. quod intra nos sit, ego illas posueram, ego illarum primum uideram folium. conuersus ad ianuam 'quis est iste?' inquam 'iste decrepitus et merito ad ostium admotus? foras enim spectat. unde istunc nanctus es? quid te delectauit alienum mortuum tollere?' at ille 'non cognoscis me?' inquit 'ego sum Felicio, cui solebas sigillaria adferre; ego sum Philositi uilici filius, deliciolum tuum.' 'perfecte' inquam 'iste delirat: pupulus, etiam delicium meum factus est? prorsus potest fieri: dentes illi cum maxime cadunt.'

debeo hoc suburbano meo, quod mihi senectus mea quocumque aduerteram apparuit. complectamur illam et amemus; plena <est> uoluptatis, si illa scias uti. gratissima sunt poma cum fugiunt; pueritiae maximus in exitu decor est; deditos uino potio extrema delectat, illa quae mergit, quae ebrietati summam manum imponit; quod in se iucundissimum omnis

uoluptas habet in finem sui differt. iucundissima est aetas deuexa iam, non tamen praeceps, et illam quoque in extrema tegula stantem iudico habere suas uoluptates; aut hoc ipsum succedit in locum uoluptatium,
6 nullis egere. quam dulce est cupiditates fatigasse ac reliquisse! 'molestum est' inquis 'mortem ante oculos habere.' primum ista tam seni ante oculos debet esse quam iuueni (non enim citamur ex censu); deinde nemo tam senex est ut improbe unum diem speret. unus autem dies gradus uitae est. tota aetas partibus constat et orbes habet circumductos maiores minoribus: est aliquis qui omnis complectatur et cingat (hic pertinet a natali ad diem extremum); est alter qui annos adulescentiae excludit; est qui totam pueritiam ambitu suo asstringit; est deinde per se annus in se omnia continens tempora, quorum multiplicatione uita componitur; mensis artiore praecingitur circulo; angustissimum habet dies gyrum, sed et hic ab ini-
7 tio ad exitum uenit, ab ortu ad occasum. ideo Heraclitus, cui cognomen fecit orationis obscuritas, 'unus inquit 'dies par omni est.' hoc alius aliter excepit. dixit enim alius parem esse horis, nec mentitur; nam si dies est tempus uiginti et quattuor horarum, necesse est omnes inter se dies pares esse, quia nox habet quod dies perdidit. alius ait parem esse unum diem omnibus similitudine; nihil enim habet longissimi temporis spatium quod non et in uno die inuenias, lucem et noctem, et in alternas mundi uices
8 plura facit ista, non alia. alias contractior, alias productior uita. itaque sic ordinandus est dies omnis tamquam cogat agmen et consummet atque expleat uitam. Pacuuius, qui Syriam usu suam fecit, cum uino et illis funebribus epulis sibi parentauerat, sic in cubiculum ferebatur a cena ut inter plausus exoletorum hoc ad symphoniam caneretur: βεβίωται, βεβίωται.
9 nullo non se die extulit. hoc quod ille ex mala conscientia faciebat nos ex bona faciamus, et in somnum ituri laeti hilaresque dicamus,

> uixi et quem dederat cursum fortuna peregi.

crastinum si adiecerit deus, laeti recipiamus. ille beatissimus est et securus sui possessor qui crastinum sine sollicitudine expectat; quisquis dixit 'uixi' cotidie ad lucrum surgit.
10 sed iam debeo epistulam includere. 'sic' inquis 'sine ullo ad me peculio ueniet?' noli timere: aliquid secum fert. quare aliquid dixi? multum. quid enim hac uoce praeclarius quam illi trado ad te perferendam? 'malum est in necessitate uiuere, sed in necessitate uiuere necessitas nulla est.' quidni nulla sit? patent undique ad libertatem uiae multae, breues faciles. agamus deo gratias quod nemo in uita teneri potest: calcare ipsas necessitates licet.
11 'Epicurus' inquis 'dixit: quid tibi cum alieno?' quod uerum est meum est; perseuerabo Epicurum tibi ingerere, ut isti qui in uerba iurant nec quid dicatur aestimant, sed a quo, sciant quae optima sunt esse communia. uale.

Letter 18

SENECA LVCILIO SVO SALVTEM

December est mensis: cum maxime ciuitas sudat. ius luxuriae publicae 1
datum est; ingenti apparatu sonant omnia, tamquam quicquam inter
Saturnalia intersit et dies rerum agendarum; adeo nihil interest ut non
uideatur mihi errasse qui dixit olim mensem Decembrem fuisse, nunc
annum. si te hic haberem, libenter tecum conferrem quid existimares 2
esse faciendum, utrum nihil ex cotidiana consuetudine mouendum an,
ne dissidere uideremur cum publicis moribus, et hilarius cenandum et
exuendam togam. nam quod fieri nisi in tumultu et tristi tempore ciuitatis non solebat, uoluptatis causa ac festorum dierum uestem mutauimus.
si te bene noui, arbitri partibus functus nec per omnia nos similes esse 3
pilleatae turbae uoluisses nec per omnia dissimiles; nisi forte his maxime
diebus animo imperandum est, ut tunc uoluptatibus solus abstineat cum
in illas omnis turba procubuit; certissimum enim argumentum firmitatis
suae capit, si ad blanda et in luxuriam trahentia nec it nec abducitur.
hoc multo fortius est, ebrio ac uomitante populo siccum ac sobrium esse, 4
illud temperantius, non excerpere se nec insignire nec misceri omnibus
et eadem sed non eodem modo facere; licet enim sine luxuria agere festum diem.

ceterum adeo mihi placet temptare animi tui firmitatem ut ex praecepto magnorum uirorum tibi quoque praecipiam: interponas aliquot 5
dies quibus contentus minimo ac uilissimo cibo, dura atque horrida ueste,
dicas tibi 'hoc est quod timebatur?' in ipsa securitate animus ad difficilia 6
se praeparet et contra iniurias fortunae inter beneficia firmetur. miles in
media pace decurrit, sine ullo hoste uallum iacit, et superuacuo labore
lassatur ut sufficere necessario possit; quem in ipsa re trepidare nolueris,
ante rem exerceas. hoc secuti sunt qui omnibus mensibus paupertatem
imitati prope ad inopiam accesserunt, ne umquam expauescerent quod
saepe didicissent. non est nunc quod existimes me dicere Timoneas cenas 7
et pauperum cellas et quidquid aliud est per quod luxuria diuitiarum
taedio ludit: grabattus ille uerus sit et sagum et panis durus ac sordidus.
hoc triduo et quatriduo fer, interdum pluribus diebus, ut non lusus sit
sed experimentum: tunc, mihi crede, Lucili, exultabis dipondio satur et
intelleges ad securitatem non opus esse fortuna; hoc enim quod necessitati sat est dabit et irata. non est tamen quare tu multum tibi facere 8
uidearis (facies enim quod multa milia seruorum, multa milia pauperum
faciunt): illo nomine te suspice, quod facies non coactus, quod tam facile erit tibi illud pati semper quam aliquando experiri. exerceamur ad
palum, et ne imparatos fortuna deprehendat, fiat nobis paupertas familiaris; securius diuites erimus si scierimus quam non sit graue pauperes

9 esse. certos habebat dies ille magister uoluptatis Epicurus quibus maligne famem extingueret, uisurus an aliquid deesset ex plena et consummata uoluptate, uel quantum deesset, et an dignum quod quis magno labore pensaret. hoc certe in iis epistulis ait quas scripsit Charino magistratu ad Polyaenum; et quidem gloriatur non toto asse se pasci, Metrodorum, qui
10 nondum tantum profecerit, toto. in hoc tu uictu saturitatem putas esse? et uoluptas est; uoluptas autem non illa leuis et fugax et subinde reficienda, sed stabilis et certa. non enim iucunda res est aqua et polenta aut frustum hordeacii panis, sed summa uoluptas est posse capere etiam ex his uoluptatem et ad id se deduxisse quod eripere nulla fortunae iniquitas possit.
11 liberaliora alimenta sunt carceris, sepositos ad capitale supplicium non tam anguste qui occisurus est pascit: quanta est animi magnitudo ad id sua sponte descendere quod ne ad extrema quidem decretis timendum sit!
12 hoc est praeoccupare tela fortunae. incipe ergo, mi Lucili, sequi horum consuetudinem et aliquos dies destina quibus secedas a tuis rebus minimoque te facias familiarem; incipe cum paupertate habere commercium;

      aude, hospes, contemnere opes et te quoque dignum finge deo.

13 nemo alius est deo dignus quam qui opes contempsit; quarum possessionem tibi non interdico, sed efficere uolo ut illas intrepide possideas; quod uno consequeris modo, si te etiam sine illis beate uicturum persuaseris tibi, si illas tamquam exituras semper aspexeris.
14   sed iam incipiamus epistulam complicare. 'prius' inquis 'redde quod debes.' delegabo te ad Epicurum, ab illo fiet numeratio: 'inmodica ira gignit insaniam.' hoc quam uerum sit necesse est scias, cum habueris et
15 seruum et inimicum. in omnes personas hic exardescit affectus; tam ex amore nascitur quam ex odio, non minus inter seria quam inter lusus et iocos; nec interest ex quam magna causa nascatur sed in qualem perueniat animum. sic ignis non refert quam magnus sed quo incidat; nam etiam maximum solida non receperunt, rursus arida et corripi facilia scintillam quoque fouent usque in incendium. ita est, mi Lucili: ingentis irae exitus furor est, et ideo ira uitanda est non moderationis causa sed sanitatis. uale.

Letter 21

SENECA LVCILIO SVO SALVTEM

1 Cum istis tibi esse negotium iudicas de quibus scripseras? maximum negotium tecum habes, tu tibi molestus es. quid uelis nescis, melius probas honesta quam sequeris, uides ubi sit posita felicitas sed ad illam peruenire non audes. quid sit autem quod te impediat, quia parum ipse dispicis, dicam: magna esse haec existimas quae relicturus es, et cum proposuisti

tibi illam securitatem ad quam transiturus es, retinet te huius uitae a
qua recessurus es fulgor tamquam in sordida et obscura casurum. erras, 2
Lucili: ex hac uita ad illam ascenditur. quod interest inter splendorem
et lucem, cum haec certam originem habeat ac suam, ille niteat alieno,
hoc inter hanc uitam et illam: haec fulgore extrinsecus ueniente percussa
est, crassam illi statim umbram faciet quisquis obstiterit: illa suo lumine
illustris est. studia te tua clarum et nobilem efficient. exemplum Epicuri 3
referam. cum Idomeneo scriberet et illum a uita speciosa ad fidelem stabilemque gloriam reuocaret, regiae tunc potentiae ministrum et magna
tractantem, 'si gloria' inquit 'tangeris, notiorem te epistulae meae facient
quam omnia ista quae colis et propter quae coleris.' numquid ergo men- 4
titus est? quis Idomenea nosset nisi Epicurus illum litteris suis incidisset?
omnes illos megistanas et satrapas et regem ipsum ex quo Idomenei titulus petebatur obliuio alta suppressit. nomen Attici perire Ciceronis epistulae non sinunt. nihil illi profuisset gener Agrippa et Tiberius progener
et Drusus Caesar pronepos; inter tam magna nomina taceretur nisi sibi
Cicero illum applicuisset. profunda super nos altitudo temporis ueniet, 5
pauca ingenia caput exerent et in idem quandoque silentium abitura
obliuioni resistent ac se diu uindicabunt. quod Epicurus amico suo potuit
promittere, hoc tibi promitto, Lucili: habebo apud posteros gratiam, possum mecum duratura nomina educere. Vergilius noster duobus memoriam aeternam promisit et praestat:

> fortunati ambo! si quid mea carmina possunt,
> nulla dies umquam memori uos eximet aeuo,
> dum domus Aeneae Capitoli immobile saxum
> accolet imperiumque pater Romanus habebit.

quoscumque in medium fortuna protulit, quicumque membra ac partes 6
alienae potentiae fuerant, horum gratia uiguit, domus frequentata est,
dum ipsi steterunt: post ipsos cito memoria defecit. ingeniorum crescit
dignatio nec ipsis tantum honor habetur, sed quidquid illorum memoriae
adhaesit excipitur.
    ne gratis Idomeneus in epistulam meam uenerit, ipse eam de suo red- 7
imet. ad hunc Epicurus illam nobilem sententiam scripsit qua hortatur
ut Pythoclea locupletem non publica nec ancipiti uia faciat. 'si uis' inquit
'Pythoclea diuitem facere, non pecuniae adiciendum sed cupiditati detrahendum est.' et apertior ista sententia est quam ut interpretanda sit, 8
et disertior quam ut adiuuanda. hoc unum te admoneo, ne istud tantum existimes de diuitiîs dictum: quocumque transtuleris, idem poterit.
si uis Pythoclea honestum facere, non honoribus adiciendum est sed
cupiditatibus detrahendum; si uis Pythoclea esse in perpetua uoluptate,
non uoluptatibus adiciendum est sed cupiditatibus detrahendum; si uis

Pythoclea senem facere et implere uitam, non annis adiciendum est sed
9 cupiditatibus detrahendum. has uoces non est quod Epicuri esse iudices:
publicae sunt. quod fieri in senatu solet faciendum ego in philosophia
quoque existimo: cum censuit aliquis quod ex parte mihi placeat, iubeo
illum diuidere sententiam et sequor quod probo.

eo libentius Epicuri egregia dicta commemoro, ut istis qui ad illum
confugiunt spe mala inducti, qui uelamentum ipsos uitiorum suorum
habituros existimant, probent quocumque ierint honeste esse uiuendum.
10 cum adieris eius hortulos †et inscriptum hortulis† legeris 'hospes, hic
bene manebis, hic summum bonum uoluptas est', paratus erit istius domi-
cilii custos hospitalis, humanus, et te polenta excipiet et aquam quoque
large ministrabit et dicet, 'ecquid bene acceptus es?' 'non irritant' inquit
'hi hortuli famem sed extinguunt, nec maiorem ipsis potionibus sitim
faciunt, sed naturali et gratuito remedio sedant; in hac uoluptate con-
11 senui.' de his tecum desideriis loquor quae consolationem non recipiunt,
quibus dandum est aliquid ut desinant. nam de illis extraordinariis quae
licet differre, licet castigare et opprimere, hoc unum commonefaciam:
ista uoluptas naturalis est, non necessaria. huic nihil debes; si quid impen-
dis, uoluntarium est. uenter praecepta non audit: poscit, appellat. non est
tamen molestus creditor: paruo dimittitur, si modo das illi quod debes,
non quod potes. uale.

Letter 24

SENECA LVCILIO SVO SALVTEM

1 Sollicitum esse te scribis de iudicî euentu quod tibi furor inimici denuntiat; existimas me suasurum ut meliora tibi ipse proponas et acquiescas
spei blandae. quid enim necesse est mala accersere, satis cito patienda
cum uenerint praesumere, ac praesens tempus futuri metu perdere? est
sine dubio stultum, quia quandoque sis futurus miser, esse iam miserum.
2 sed ego alia te ad securitatem uia ducam: si uis omnem sollicitudinem
exuere, quidquid uereris ne eueniat euenturum utique propone, et
quodcumque est illud malum, tecum ipse metire ac timorem tuum taxa:
intelleges profecto aut non magnum aut non longum esse quod metuis.
3 nec diu exempla quibus confirmeris colligenda sunt: omnis illa aetas tulit.
in quamcumque partem rerum uel ciuilium uel externarum memoriam
miseris, occurrent tibi ingenia aut profectus aut impetus magni. numquid
accidere tibi, si damnaris, potest durius quam ut mittaris in exilium, ut
ducaris in carcerem? numquid ultra quicquam ulli timendum est quam
ut uratur, quam ut pereat? singula ista constitue et contemptores eorum
4 cita, qui non quaerendi sed eligendi sunt. damnationem suam Rutilius sic
tulit tamquam nihil illi molestum aliud esset quam quod male iudicare-
tur. exilium Metellus fortiter tulit, Rutilius etiam libenter; alter ut rediret

rei publicae praestitit, alter reditum suum Sullae negauit, cui nihil tunc negabatur. in carcere Socrates disputauit et exire, cum essent qui promitterent fugam, noluit remansitque, ut duarum rerum grauissimarum hominibus metum demeret, mortis et carceris. Mucius ignibus manum 5 imposuit. acerbum est uri: quanto acerbius si id te faciente patiaris! uides hominem non eruditum nec ullis praeceptis contra mortem aut dolorem subornatum, militari tantum robore instructum, poenas a se irriti conatus exigentem; spectator destillantis in hostili foculo dexterae stetit nec ante remouit nudis ossibus fluentem manum quam ignis illi ab hoste subductus est. facere aliquid in illis castris felicius potuit, nihil fortius. uide quanto acrior sit ad occupanda pericula uirtus quam crudelitas ad irroganda: facilius Porsina Mucio ignouit quod uoluerat occidere quam sibi Mucius quod non occiderat.

'decantatae' inquis 'in omnibus scholis fabulae istae sunt; iam mihi, 6 cum ad contemnendam mortem uentum fuerit, Catonem narrabis.' quidni ego narrem ultima illa nocte Platonis librum legentem posito ad caput gladio? duo haec in rebus extremis instrumenta prospexerat, alterum ut uellet mori, alterum ut posset. compositis ergo rebus, utcumque componi fractae atque ultimae poterant, id agendum existimauit ne cui Catonem aut occidere liceret aut seruare contingeret; et stricto gladio 7 quem usque in illum diem ab omni caede purum seruauerat, 'nihil' inquit 'egisti, fortuna, omnibus conatibus meis obstando. non pro mea adhuc sed pro patriae libertate pugnaui, nec agebam tanta pertinacia ut liber, sed ut inter liberos, uiuerem: nunc quoniam deploratae sunt res generis humani, Cato deducatur in tutum.' impressit deinde mortiferum corpori 8 uulnus; quo obligato a medicis cum minus sanguinis haberet, minus uirium, animi idem, iam non tantum Caesari sed sibi iratus nudas in uulnus manus egit et generosum illum contemptoremque omnis potentiae spiritum non emisit sed eiecit.

non in hoc exempla nunc congero ut ingenium exerceam, sed ut 9 te aduersus id quod maxime terribile uidetur exhorter; facilius autem exhortabor, si ostendero non fortes tantum uiros hoc momentum efflandae animae contempsisse sed quosdam ad alia ignauos in hac re aequasse animum fortissimorum, sicut illum Cn. Pompei socerum Scipionem, qui contrario in Africam uento relatus cum teneri nauem suam uidisset ab hostibus, ferro se transuerberauit et quaerentibus ubi imperator esset, 'imperator' inquit 'se bene habet.' uox haec illum parem maioribus fecit 10 et fatalem Scipionibus in Africa gloriam non est interrumpi passa. multum fuit Carthaginem uincere, sed amplius mortem. 'imperator' inquit 'se bene habet': an aliter debebat imperator, et quidem Catonis, mori? non reuoco te ad historias nec ex omnibus saeculis contemptores mortis, 11 qui sunt plurimi, colligo; respice ad haec nostra tempora, de quorum languore ac delicîs querimur: omnis ordinis homines suggerent, omnis fortunae, omnis aetatis, qui mala sua morte praeciderint. mihi crede, Lucili, adeo mors timenda non est ut beneficio eius nihil timendum sit.

12 securus itaque inimici minas audi; et quamuis conscientia tibi tua fiduciam faciat, tamen, quia multa extra causam ualent, et quod aequissimum est spera et ad id te quod est iniquissimum compara. illud autem ante omnia memento, demere rebus tumultum ac uidere quid in quaque re

13 sit: scies nihil esse in istis terribile nisi ipsum timorem. quod uides accidere pueris, hoc nobis quoque maiusculis pueris euenit: illi quos amant, quibus adsueuerunt, cum quibus ludunt, si personatos uident, expauescunt: non hominibus tantum sed rebus persona demenda est et reddenda

14 facies sua. quid mihi gladios et ignes ostendis et turbam carnificum circa te frementem? tolle istam pompam sub qua lates et stultos territas: mors es, quam nuper seruus meus, quam ancilla contempsit. quid tu rursus mihi flagella et eculeos magno apparatu explicas? quid singulis articulis singula machinamenta quibus extorqueantur aptata et mille alia instrumenta excarnificandi particulatim hominis? pone ista quae nos obstupefaciunt; iube conticiscere gemitus et exclamationes et uocum inter lacerationem elisarum acerbitatem: nempe dolor es, quem podagricus ille contemnit, quem stomachicus ille in ipsis delicîs perfert, quem in puerperio puella perpetitur. leuis es si ferre possum; breuis es si ferre non possum.

15 haec in animo uoluta, quae saepe audisti, saepe dixisti; sed an uere audieris, an uere dixeris, effectu proba; hoc enim turpissimum est quod nobis obici solet, uerba nos philosophiae, non opera tractare. quid? tu nunc primum tibi mortem imminere scisti, nunc exilium, nunc dolorem?

16 in haec natus es; quidquid fieri potest quasi futurum cogitemus. quod facere te moneo scio certe fecisse: nunc admoneo ut animum tuum non mergas in istam sollicitudinem; hebetabitur enim et minus habebit uigoris cum exurgendum erit. abduc illum a priuata causa ad publicam; dic mortale tibi et fragile corpusculum esse, cui non ex iniuria tantum aut ex potentioribus uiribus denuntiabitur dolor: ipsae uoluptates in tormenta uertuntur, epulae cruditatem afferunt, ebrietates neruorum torporem tremoremque, libidines pedum, manuum, articulorum omnium deprauat-

17 tiones. pauper fiam: inter plures ero. exul fiam: ibi me natum putabo quo mittar. alligabor: quid enim? nunc solutus sum? ad hoc me natura graue corporis mei pondus adstrinxit. moriar: hoc dicis, desinam aegrotare posse, desinam alligari posse, desinam mori posse.

18 non sum tam ineptus ut Epicuream cantilenam hoc loco persequar et dicam uanos esse inferorum metus, nec Ixionem rota uolui nec saxum umeris Sisyphi trudi in aduersum nec ullius uiscera et renasci posse cotidie et carpi: nemo tam puer est ut Cerberum timeat et tenebras et larualem habitum nudis ossibus cohaerentium. mors nos aut consumit aut exuit; emissis meliora restant onere detracto, consumptis nihil restat, bona

pariter malaque summota sunt. permitte mihi hoc loco referre uersum 19
tuum, si prius admonuero ut te iudices non aliis scripsisse ista sed etiam
tibi. turpe est aliud loqui, aliud sentire: quanto turpius aliud scribere, aliud
sentire! memini te illum locum aliquando tractasse, non repente nos in
mortem incidere sed minutatim procedere. cotidie morimur; cotidie enim 20
demitur aliqua pars uitae, et tunc quoque cum crescimus uita decrescit.
infantiam amisimus, deinde pueritiam, deinde adulescentiam. usque ad
hesternum quidquid transît temporis perît; hunc ipsum quem agimus diem
cum morte diuidimus. quemadmodum clepsydram non extremum stilicidium exhaurit sed quidquid ante defluxit, sic ultima hora qua esse desinimus
non sola mortem facit sed sola consummat; tunc ad illam peruenimus, sed
diu uenimus. haec cum descripsisses quo soles ore, semper quidem mag- 21
nus, numquam tamen acrior quam ubi ueritati commodas uerba, dixisti,

> mors non una uenit, sed quae rapit ultima mors est.

malo te legas quam epistulam meam; apparebit enim tibi hanc quam
timemus mortem extremam esse, non solam. uideo quo spectes: quaeris 22
quid huic epistulae infulserim, quod dictum alicuius animosum, quod
praeceptum utile. ex hac ipsa materia quae in manibus fuit mittetur aliquid. obiurgat Epicurus non minus eos qui mortem concupiscunt quam
eos qui timent, et ait: 'ridiculum est currere ad mortem taedio uitae, cum
genere uitae ut currendum ad mortem esset effeceris.' item alio loco 23
dicit: 'quid tam ridiculum quam appetere mortem, cum uitam inquietam
tibi feceris metu mortis?' his adicias et illud eiusdem notae licet, tan-
tam hominum imprudentiam esse, immo dementiam, ut quidam timore
mortis cogantur ad mortem. quidquid horum tractaueris, confirmabis 24
animum uel ad mortis uel ad uitae patientiam; at in utrumque enim
monendi ac firmandi sumus, et ne nimis amemus uitam et ne nimis oderimus. etiam cum ratio suadet finire se, non temere nec cum procursu
capiendus est impetus. uir fortis ac sapiens non fugere debet e uita sed 25
exire; et ante omnia ille quoque uitetur affectus qui multos occupauit,
libido moriendi. est enim, mi Lucili, ut ad alia, sic etiam ad moriendum
inconsulta animi inclinatio, quae saepe generosos atque acerrimae ind-
olis uiros corripit, saepe ignauos iacentesque: illi contemnunt uitam, hi
grauantur. quosdam subit eadem faciendi uidendique satietas et uitae 26
non odium sed fastidium, in quod prolabimur ipsa impellente philosophia, dum dicimus 'quousque eadem? nempe expergiscar dormiam,
<edam> esuriam, algebo aestuabo. nullius rei finis est, sed in orbem nexa
sunt omnia, fugiunt ac sequuntur; diem nox premit, dies noctem, aestas
in autumnum desinit, autumno hiemps instat, quae uere compescitur;
omnia sic transeunt ut reuertantur. nihil noui facio, nihil noui uideo:
fit aliquando et huius rei nausia.' multi sunt qui non acerbum iudicent
uiuere sed superuacuum. uale.

Letter 33

SENECA LVCILIO SVO SALVTEM

1 Desideras his quoque epistulis sicut prioribus adscribi aliquas uoces nostrorum procerum. non fuerunt circa flosculos occupati: totus contextus illorum uirilis est. inaequalitatem scias esse ubi quae eminent notabilia sunt: non est admirationi una arbor ubi in eandem altitudinem tota silua 2 surrexit. eiusmodi uocibus referta sunt carmina, refertae historiae. itaque nolo illas Epicuri existimes esse: publicae sunt et maxime nostrae, sed in illo magis adnotantur quia rarae interim interueniunt, quia inexpectatae, quia mirum est fortiter aliquid dici ab homine mollitiam professo. ita enim plerique iudicant: apud me Epicurus est et fortis, licet manuleatus sit; fortitudo et industria et ad bellum prompta mens tam in Persas 3 quam in alte cinctos cadit. non est ergo quod exigas excerpta et repetita: continuum est apud nostros quidquid apud alios excerpitur. non habemus itaque ista ocliferia nec emptorem decipimus nihil inuenturum cum intrauerit praeter illa quae in fronte suspensa sunt: ipsis permittimus 4 unde uelint sumere exemplar. iam puta nos uelle singulares sententias ex turba separare: cui illas assignabimus? Zenoni an Cleanthi an Chrysippo an Panaetio an Posidonio? non sumus sub rege: sibi quisque se uindicat. apud istos quidquid Hermarchus dixit, quidquid Metrodorus, ad unum refertur; omnia quae quisquam in illo contubernio locutus est unius ductu et auspiciis dicta sunt. non possumus, inquam, licet temptemus, educere aliquid ex tanta rerum aequalium multitudine:

> pauperis est numerare pecus.

quocumque miseris oculum, id tibi occurret quod eminere posset nisi inter 5 paria legeretur. quare depone istam spem posse te summatim degustare ingenia maximorum uirorum: tota tibi inspicienda sunt, tota tractanda. <continuando> res geritur et per lineamenta sua ingenii opus nectitur ex quo nihil subduci sine ruina potest. nec recuso quominus singula membra, dummodo in ipso homine, considere: non est formonsa cuius crus laudatur aut brachium, sed illa cuius uniuersa facies admirationem par6 tibus singulis abstulit. si tamen exegeris, non tam mendice tecum agam, sed plena manu fiet; ingens eorum turba est passim iacentium; sumenda erunt, non colligenda. non enim excidunt sed fluunt; perpetua et inter se contexta sunt. nec dubito quin multum conferant rudibus adhuc et extrinsecus auscultantibus; facilius enim singula insidunt circumscripta 7 et carminis modo inclusa. ideo pueris et sententias ediscendas damus et has quas Graeci chrias uocant, quia complecti illas puerilis animus potest, qui plus adhuc non capit. certi profectus uiro captare flosculos turpe est et fulcire se notissimis ac paucissimis uocibus et memoria stare: sibi iam innitatur. dicat ista, non teneat; turpe est enim seni aut prospicienti senectutem ex commentario sapere. 'hoc Zenon dixit': tu quid? 'hoc Cleanthes': tu quid? quousque sub alio moueris? impera et dic quod memoriae tradatur, aliquid et de tuo profer. omnes itaque istos, numquam 8 auctores, semper interpretes, sub aliena umbra latentes, nihil existimo habere generosi, numquam ausos aliquando facere quod diu didicerant. memoriam in alienis exercuerunt; aliud autem est meminisse, aliud scire. meminisse est rem commissam memoriae custodire; at contra scire est et sua facere quaeque nec ad exemplar pendere et totiens respicere ad magistrum. 'hoc dixit Zenon, hoc Cleanthes.' aliquid inter te intersit et 9 librum. quousque disces? iam et praecipe. quid est quare audiam quod legere possum? 'multum' inquit 'uiua uox facit.' non quidem haec quae alienis uerbis commodatur et actuari uice fungitur. adice nunc quod isti 10 qui numquam tutelae suae fiunt primum in ea re sequuntur priores in qua nemo non a priore desciuit; deinde in ea re sequuntur quae adhuc quaeritur. numquam autem inuenietur, si contenti fuerimus inuentis. praeterea qui alium sequitur nihil inuenit, immo nec quaerit. quid ergo? 11 non ibo per priorum uestigia? ego uero utar uia uetere, sed si propiorem planioremque inuenero, hanc muniam. qui ante nos ista mouerunt non domini nostri sed duces sunt. patet omnibus ueritas; nondum est occupata; multum ex illa etiam futuris relictum est. uale.

Letter 34

SENECA LVCILIO SVO SALVTEM

Cresco et exulto et discussa senectute recalesco quotiens ex iis quae 1 agis ac scribis intellego quantum te ipse – nam turbam olim reliqueras – superieceris. si agricolam arbor ad fructum perducta delectat, si pastor ex fetu gregis sui capit uoluptatem, si alumnum suum nemo aliter intuetur quam ut adulescentiam illius suam iudicet, quid euenire credis iis qui ingenia educauerunt et quae tenera formauerunt adulta subito uident? assero te mihi; meum opus es. ego cum uidissem indolem tuam, 2 inieci manum, exhortatus sum, addidi stimulos nec lente ire passus sum sed subinde incitaui; et nunc idem facio, sed iam currentem hortor et inuicem hortantem. 'quid aliud?' inquis 'adhuc uolo.' in hoc plurimum 3 est, non sic quomodo principia totius operis dimidium occupare dicuntur. ista res animo constat; itaque pars magna bonitatis est uelle fieri bonum. scis quem bonum dicam? perfectum, absolutum, quem malum facere nulla uis, nulla necessitas possit. hunc te prospicio, si perseuerans et 4 incubueris et id egeris ut omnia facta dictaque tua inter se congruant ac respondeant sibi et una forma percussa sint. non est huius animus in recto cuius acta discordant. uale.

Letter 46

SENECA LVCILIO SVO SALVTEM

1 Librum tuum quem mihi promiseras accepi et tamquam lecturus ex commodo adaperui ac tantum degustare uolui; deinde blanditus est ipse ut procederem longius. qui quam disertus fuerit ex hoc intellegas licet: leuis mihi uisus est, cum esset nec mei nec tui corporis, sed qui primo aspectu aut Titi Liuii aut Epicuri posset uideri. tanta autem dulcedine me tenuit et traxit ut illum sine ulla dilatione perlegerim. sol me inuitabat,
2 fames admonebat, nubes minabantur; tamen exhausi totum. non tantum delectatus sed gauisus sum. quid ingenii iste habuit, quid animi! dicerem 'quid impetus!', si interquieuisset, si ex interuallo surrexisset; nunc non fuit impetus sed tenor. compositio uirilis et sancta; nihilominus interueniebat dulce illud et loco lene. grandis, erectus es: hoc te uolo tenere, sic ire. fecit aliquid et materia; ideo eligenda est fertilis, quae capiat inge-
3 nium, quae incitet. de libro plura scribam cum illum retractauero; nunc parum mihi sedet iudicium, tamquam audierim illa, non legerim. sine me et inquirere. non est quod uerearis: uerum audies. o te hominem felicem, quod nihil habes propter quod quisquam tibi tam longe mentiatur! nisi quod iam etiam ubi causa sublata est mentimur consuetudinis causa. uale.

Letter 47

SENECA LVCILIO SVO SALVTEM

1 Libenter ex iis qui a te ueniunt cognoui familiariter te cum seruis tuis uiuere: hoc prudentiam tuam, hoc eruditionem decet. 'serui sunt.' immo homines. 'serui sunt.' immo contubernales. 'serui sunt.' immo humiles amici. 'serui sunt.' immo conserui, si cogitaueris tantundem in utrosque
2 licere fortunae. itaque rideo istos qui turpe existimant cum seruo suo cenare: quare, nisi quia superbissima consuetudo cenanti domino stantium seruorum turbam circumdedit? est ille plus quam capit, et ingenti auiditate onerat distentum uentrem ac desuetum iam uentris officio, ut
3 maiore opera omnia egerat quam ingessit. at infelicibus seruis mouere labra ne in hoc quidem, ut loquantur, licet; uirga murmur omne compescitur, et ne fortuita quidem uerberibus excepta sunt, tussis, sternumenta, singultus; magno malo ulla uoce interpellatum silentium luitur; nocte
4 tota ieiuni mutique perstant. sic fit ut isti de domino loquantur quibus coram domino loqui non licet. at illi quibus non tantum coram dominis sed cum ipsis erat sermo, quorum os non consuebatur, parati erant pro domino porrigere ceruicem, periculum imminens in caput suum auer-
5 tere; in conuiuîs loquebantur, sed in tormentis tacebant. deinde eiusdem

arrogantiae prouerbium iactatur, totidem hostes esse quot seruos: non habemus illos hostes sed facimus. alia interim crudelia, inhumana praetereo, quod ne tamquam hominibus quidem sed tamquam iumentis abutimur. cum ad cenandum discubuimus, alius sputa deterget, alius reliquias temulentorum subditus colligit. alius pretiosas aues scindit; per pectus et clunes certis ductibus circumferens eruditam manum frusta excutit, infelix, qui huic uni rei uiuit, ut altilia decenter secet, nisi quod miserior est qui hoc uoluptatis causa docet quam qui necessitatis discit. alius uini minister in muliebrem modum ornatus cum aetate luctatur: non potest effugere pueritiam, retrahitur, iamque militari habitu glaber retritis pilis aut penitus euulsis tota nocte peruigilat, quam inter ebrietatem domini ac libidinem diuidit et in cubiculo uir, in conuiuio puer est. alius, cui conuiuarum censura permissa est, perstat infelix et expectat quos adulatio et intemperantia aut gulae aut linguae reuocet in crastinum. adice obsonatores quibus dominici palati notitia subtilis est, qui sciunt cuius illum rei sapor excitet, cuius delectet aspectus, cuius nouitate nauseabundus erigi possit, quid iam ipsa satietate fastidiat, quid illo die esuriat. cum his cenare non sustinet et maiestatis suae deminutionem putat ad eandem mensam cum seruo suo accedere. di melius! quot ex istis dominos habet! stare ante limen Callisti dominum suum uidi et eum qui illi impegerat titulum, qui inter reicula manicipia produxerat, aliis intrantibus excludi. rettulit illi gratiam seruus ille in primam decuriam coniectus, in qua uocem praeco experitur: et ipse illum inuicem apologauit, et ipse non iudicauit domo sua dignum. dominus Callistum uendidit: sed domino quam multa Callistus!

uis tu cogitare istum quem seruum tuum uocas ex isdem seminibus ortum eodem frui caelo, aeque spirare, aeque uiuere, aeque mori! tam tu illum uidere ingenuum potes quam ille te seruum. Variana clade multos splendidissime natos, senatorium per militiam auspicantes gradum, fortuna depressit: alium ex illis pastorem, alium custodem casae fecit. contemne nunc eius fortunae hominem in quam transire dum contemnis potes.

nolo in ingentem me locum immittere et de usu seruorum disputare, in quos superbissimi, crudelissimi, contumeliosissimi sumus. haec tamen praecepti mei summa est: sic cum inferiore uiuas quemadmodum tecum superiorem uelis uiuere. quotiens in mentem uenerit quantum tibi in seruum tuum liceat, ueniat in mentem tantundem in te domino tuo licere. 'at ego' inquis 'nullum habeo dominum.' bona aetas est: forsitan habebis. nescis qua aetate Hecuba seruire coeperit, qua Croesus, qua Darei mater, qua Platon, qua Diogenes? uiue cum seruo clementer, comiter quoque, et in sermonem illum admitte et in consilium et in conuictum.

hoc loco acclamabit mihi tota manus delicatorum 'nihil hac re humilius, nihil turpius.' hos ego eosdem deprehendam alienorum seruorum
14 osculantes manum. ne illud quidem uidetis, quam omnem inuidiam maiores nostri dominis, omnem contumeliam seruis detraxerint? dominum patrem familiae appellauerunt, seruos, quod etiam in mimis adhuc durat, familiares; instituerunt diem festum, non quo solo cum seruis domini uescerentur, sed quo utique; honores illis in domo gerere, ius dicere permiserunt et domum pusillam rem publicam esse iudicauerunt.
15 'quid ergo? omnes seruos admouebo mensae meae?' non magis quam omnes liberos. erras si existimas me quosdam quasi sordidioris operae reiecturum, ut puta illum mulionem et illum bubulcum. non ministeriis illos aestimabo sed moribus: sibi quisque dat mores, ministeria casus assignat. quidam cenent tecum quia digni sunt, quidam ut sint; si quid enim in illis ex sordida conuersatione seruile est, honestiorum conuictus excutiet.
16 non est, mi Lucili, quod amicum tantum in foro et in curia quaeras: si diligenter attenderis, et domi inuenies. saepe bona materia cessat sine artifice: tempta et experire. quemadmodum stultus est qui equum empturus non ipsum inspicit sed stratum eius ac frenos, sic stultissimus est qui hominem aut ex ueste aut ex condicione, quae uestis modo nobis circum-
17 data est, aestimat. 'seruus est.' sed fortasse liber animo. 'seruus est.' hoc illi nocebit? ostende quis non sit: alius libidini seruit, alius auaritiae, alius ambitioni, omnes spei, omnes timori. dabo consularem aniculae seruientem, dabo ancillulae diuitem, ostendam nobilissimos iuuenes mancipia pantomimorum: nulla seruitus turpior est quam uoluntaria. quare non est quod fastidiosi isti te deterreant quominus seruis tuis hilarem te praestes et non superbe superiorem: colant potius te quam timeant.
18 dicet aliquis nunc me uocare ad pilleum seruos et dominos de fastigio suo deicere, quod dixi, 'colant potius dominum quam timeant.' 'ita' inquit 'prorsus? colant tamquam clientes, tamquam salutatores?' hoc qui dixerit obliuiscetur id dominis parum non esse quod deo sat est. qui
19 colitur, et amatur: non potest amor cum timore misceri. rectissime ergo facere te iudico quod timeri a seruis tuis non uis, quod uerborum castigatione uteris: uerberibus muta admonentur. non quidquid nos offendit et laedit; sed ad rabiem cogunt peruenire deliciae, ut quidquid non ex
20 uoluntate respondit iram euocet. regum nobis induimus animos; nam illi quoque obliti et suarum uirium et imbecillitatis alienae sic excandescunt, sic saeuiunt, quasi iniuriam acceperint, a cuius rei periculo illos fortunae suae magnitudo tutissimos praestat. nec hoc ignorant, sed occasionem nocendi captant querendo; acceperunt iniuriam ut facerent.
21 diutius te morari nolo; non est enim tibi exhortatione opus. hoc habent inter cetera boni mores: placent sibi, permanent. leuis est malitia, saepe mutatur, non in melius sed in aliud. uale.

Letter 53

SENECA LVCILIO SVO SALVTEM

Quid non potest mihi persuaderi, cui persuasum est ut nauigarem? solui mari languido; erat sine dubio caelum graue sordidis nubibus, quae fere aut in aquam aut in uentum resoluuntur, sed putaui tam pauca milia a Parthenope tua usque Puteolos surripi posse, quamuis dubio et impendente caelo. itaque quo celerius euaderem, protinus per altum ad Nesida derexi praecisurus omnes sinus. cum iam eo processissem ut mea nihil interesset utrum irem an redirem, primum aequalitas illa quae me corruperat periit; nondum erat tempestas, sed iam inclinatio maris ac subinde crebrior fluctus. coepi gubernatorem rogare ut me in aliquo litore exponeret: aiebat ille aspera esse et importuosa nec quicquam se aeque in tempestate timere quam terram. peius autem uexabar quam ut mihi periculum succurreret; nausia enim me segnis haec et sine exitu torquebat, quae bilem mouet nec effundit. institi itaque gubernatori et illum, uellet nollet, coegi, peteret litus. cuius ut uiciniam attigimus, non expecto ut quicquam ex praeceptis Vergilii fiat,

            obuertunt pelago proras

aut

            ancora de prora iacitur:

memor artificii mei uetus frigidae cultor mitto me in mare, quomodo psychrolutam decet, gausapatus. quae putas me passum dum per aspera erepo, dum uiam quaero, dum facio? intellexi non immerito nautis terram timeri. incredibilia sunt quae tulerim, cum me ferre non possem: illud scito, Ulixem non fuisse tam irato mari natum ut ubique naufragia faceret: nausiator erat. et ego quocumque nauigare debuero uicensimo anno perueniam.

ut primum stomachum, quem scis non cum mari nausiam effugere, collegi, ut corpus unctione recreaui, hoc coepi mecum cogitare, quanta nos uitiorum nostrorum sequeretur obliuio, etiam corporalium, quae subinde admonent sui, nedum illorum quae eo magis latent quo maiora sunt. leuis aliquem motiuncula decipit; sed cum creuit et uera febris exarsit, etiam duro et perpessicio confessionem exprimit. pedes dolent, articuli punctiunculas sentiunt: adhuc dissimulamus et aut talum extorsisse dicimus nos aut in exercitatione aliqua laborasse. dubio et incipiente morbo quaeritur nomen, qui ubi ut talaria coepit intendere et utrosque distortos pedes fecit, necesse est podagram fateri.

contra euenit in his morbis quibus afficiuntur animi: quo quis peius se habet, minus sentit. non est quod mireris, Lucili carissime; nam qui

leuiter dormit, et species secundum quietem capit et aliquando dormire
se dormiens cogitat: grauis sopor etiam somnia extinguit animumque
8 altius mergit quam ut in ullo intellectu sui sit. quare uitia sua nemo confitetur? quia etiamnunc in illis est: somnium narrare uigilantis est, et
uitia sua confiteri sanitatis indicium est. expergiscamur ergo, ut errores
nostros coarguere possimus. sola autem nos philosophia excitabit, sola
somnum excutiet grauem: illi te totum dedica. dignus illa es, illa digna te
est: ite in complexum alter alterius. omnibus aliis rebus te nega, fortiter,
9 aperte; non est quod precario philosopheris. si aeger esses, curam intermisisses rei familiaris et forensia tibi negotia excidissent nec quemquam
tanti putares cui aduocatus in remissione descenderes; toto animo id
ageres ut quam primum morbo liberareris. quid ergo? non et nunc idem
facies? omnia inpedimenta dimitte et uaca bonae menti: nemo ad illam
peruenit occupatus. exercet philosophia regnum suum; dat tempus, non
accipit; non est res subsiciua; ordinaria est, domina est, adest et iubet.
10 Alexander cuidam ciuitati partem agrorum et dimidium rerum omnium
promittenti 'eo' inquit 'proposito in Asiam ueni, ut non id acciperem
quod dedissetis, sed ut id haberetis quod reliquissem.' idem philosophia
rebus omnibus: 'non sum hoc tempus acceptura quod uobis superfuerit,
11 sed id uos habebitis quod ipsa reiecero.' totam huc conuerte mentem,
huic asside, hanc cole: ingens interuallum inter te et ceteros fiet; omnes
mortales multo antecedes, non multo te di antecedent. quaeris quid inter
te et illos interfuturum sit? diutius erunt. at mehercules magni artificis est
clusisse totum in exiguo; tantum sapienti sua quantum deo omnis aetas
patet. est aliquid quo sapiens antecedat deum: ille naturae beneficio non
12 timet, suo sapiens. ecce res magna, habere inbecillitatem hominis, securitatem dei. incredibilis philosophiae uis est ad omnem fortuitam uim
retundendam. nullum telum in corpore eius sedet; munita est, solida;
quaedam defetigat et uelut leuia tela laxo sinu eludit, quaedam discutit et
in eum usque qui miserat respuit. uale.

Letter 64

SENECA LVCILIO SVO SALVTEM

1 Fuisti here nobiscum. potes queri, si here tantum; ideo adieci 'nobiscum';
mecum enim semper es. interuenerant quidam amici propter quos maior
fumus fieret, non hic qui erumpere ex lautorum culinis et terrere uigiles
2 solet, sed hic modicus qui hospites uenisse significet. uarius nobis fuit
sermo, ut in conuiuio, nullam rem usque ad exitum adducens sed aliunde
alio transiliens. lectus est deinde liber Quinti Sextii patris, magni, si quid
3 mihi credis, uiri, et licet neget Stoici. quantus in illo, di boni, uigor est,
quantum animi! hoc non in omnibus philosophis inuenies: quorundam

scripta clarum habentium nomen exanguia sunt. instituunt, disputant, cauillantur, non faciunt animum quia non habent: cum legeris Sextium, dices, 'uiuit, uiget, liber est, supra hominem est, dimittit me plenum ingentis fiduciae.' in qua positione mentis sim cum hunc lego fatebor tibi: 4 libet omnis casus prouocare, libet exclamare, 'quid cessas, fortuna? congredere: paratum uides.' illius animum induo qui quaerit ubi se experiatur, ubi uirtutem suam ostendat,

> spumantemque dari pecora inter inertia uotis
> optat aprum aut fuluum descendere monte leonem.

libet aliquid habere quod uincam, cuius patientia exercear. nam hoc 5 quoque egregium Sextius habet, quod et ostendet tibi beatae uitae magnitudinem et desperationem eius non faciet: scies esse illam in excelso, sed uolenti penetrabilem. hoc idem uirtus tibi ipsa praestabit, 6 ut illam admireris et tamen speres. mihi certe multum auferre temporis solet contemplatio ipsa sapientiae; non aliter illam intueor obstupefactus quam ipsum interim mundum, quem saepe tamquam spectator nouus uideo. ueneror itaque inuenta sapientiae inuentoresque; adire 7 tamquam multorum hereditatem iuuat. mihi ista acquisita, mihi laborata sunt. sed agamus bonum patrem familiae, faciamus ampliora quae accepimus; maior ista hereditas a me ad posteros transeat. multum adhuc restat operis multumque restabit, nec ulli nato post mille saecula praecludetur occasio aliquid adhuc adiciendi. sed etiam si omnia 8 a ueteribus inuenta sunt, hoc semper nouum erit, usus et inuentorum ab aliis scientia ac dispositio. puta relicta nobis medicamenta quibus sanarentur oculi: non opus est mihi alia quaerere, sed haec tamen morbis et temporibus aptanda sunt. hoc asperitas oculorum colleuatur; hoc palpebrarum crassitudo tenuatur; hoc uis subita et umor auertitur; hoc acuetur uisus: teras ista oportet et eligas tempus, adhibeas singulis modum. animi remedia inuenta sunt ab antiquis; quomodo autem admoueantur aut quando nostri operis est quaerere. multum egerunt 9 qui ante nos fuerunt, sed non peregerunt. suspiciendi tamen sunt et ritu deorum colendi. quidni ego magnorum uirorum et imagines habeam incitamenta animi et natales celebrem? quidni ego illos honoris causa semper appellem? quam uenerationem praeceptoribus meis debeo, eandem illis praeceptoribus generis humani, a quibus tanti boni initia fluxerunt. si consulem uidero aut praetorem, omnia quibus honor 10 haberi honori solet faciam: equo desiliam, caput adaperiam, semita cedam. quid ergo? Marcum Catonem utrumque et Laelium Sapientem et Socraten cum Platone et Zenonem Cleanthenque in animum meum sine dignatione summa recipiam? ego uero illos ueneror et tantis nominibus semper assurgo. uale.

Letter 70

SENECA LVCILIO SVO SALVTEM

1   Post longum interuallum Pompeios tuos uidi. in conspectum adulescentiae meae reductus sum; quidquid illic iuuenis feceram uidebar mihi fac-
2   ere adhuc posse et paulo ante fecisse. praenauigauimus, Lucili, uitam et quemadmodum in mari, ut ait Vergilius noster,

> terraeque urbesque recedunt,

sic in hoc cursu rapidissimi temporis primum pueritiam abscondimus, deinde adulescentiam, deinde quidquid est illud inter iuuenem et senem medium, in utriusque confinio positum, deinde ipsius senectutis optimos
3   annos; nouissime incipit ostendi publicus finis generis humani. scopulum esse illum putamus dementissimi: portus est, aliquando petendus, numquam recusandus, in quem si quis intra primos annos delatus est, non magis queri debet quam qui cito nauigauit. alium enim, ut scis, uenti segnes ludunt ac detinent et tranquillitatis lentissimae taedio lassant,
4   alium pertinax flatus celerrime perfert. idem euenire nobis puta: alios uita uelocissime adduxit quo ueniendum erat etiam cunctantibus, alios macerauit et coxit. quae, ut scis, non semper retinenda est; non enim uiuere bonum est, sed bene uiuere. itaque sapiens uiuet quantum debet,
5   non quantum potest. uidebit ubi uicturus sit, cum quibus, quomodo, quid acturus. cogitat semper qualis uita, non quanta sit. si multa occurrunt molesta et tranquillitatem turbantia, emittit se; nec hoc tantum in necessitate ultima facit, sed cum primum illi coepit suspecta esse fortuna, diligenter circumspicit numquid illic desinendum sit. nihil existimat sua referre, faciat finem an accipiat, tardius fiat an citius: non tamquam de magno
6   detrimento timet; nemo multum ex stilicidio potest perdere. citius mori aut tardius ad rem non pertinet, bene mori aut male ad rem pertinet; bene autem mori est effugere male uiuendi periculum. itaque effeminatissimam uocem illius Rhodii existimo, qui cum in caueam coniectus esset a tyranno et tamquam ferum aliquod animal aleretur, suadenti cuidam ut
7   abstineret cibo, 'omnia' inquit 'homini, dum uiuit, speranda sunt.' ut sit hoc uerum, non omni pretio uita emenda est. quaedam licet magna, licet certa sint, tamen ad illa turpi infirmitatis confessione non ueniam: ego cogitem in eo qui uiuit omnia posse fortunam, potius quam cogitem in eo qui scit mori nil posse fortunam?
8   aliquando tamen, etiam si certa mors instabit et destinatum sibi supplicium sciet, non commodabit poenae suae manum: sibi commodaret. stultitia est timore mortis mori: uenit qui occidat, expecta. quid occupas? quare suscipis alienae crudelitatis procurationem? utrum inuides carnif-
9   ici tuo an parcis? Socrates potuit abstinentia finire uitam et inedia potius quam ueneno mori; triginta tamen dies in carcere et in expectatione

mortis exegit, non hoc animo tamquam omnia fieri possent, tamquam multas spes tam longum tempus reciperet, sed ut praeberet se legibus, ut fruendum amicis extremum Socraten daret. quid erat stultius quam mortem contemnere, uenenum timere? Scribonia, grauis femina, amita Drusi 10 Libonis fuit, adulescentis tam stolidi quam nobilis, maiora sperantis quam illo saeculo quisquam sperare poterat aut ipse ullo. cum aeger a senatu in lectica relatus esset non sane frequentibus exsequîs (omnes enim necessarii deseruerant impie iam non reum sed funus), habere coepit consilium utrum conscisceret mortem an expectaret. cui Scribonia 'quid te' inquit 'delectat alienum negotium agere?' non persuasit illi: manus sibi attulit, nec sine causa. nam post diem tertium aut quartum inimici moriturus arbitrio si uiuit, alienum negotium agit. non possis itaque de re in 11 uniuersum pronuntiare, cum mortem uis externa denuntiat, occupanda sit an expectanda; multa enim sunt quae in utramque partem trahere possunt. si altera mors cum tormento, altera simplex et facilis est, quidni huic inicienda sit manus? quemadmodum nauem eligam nauigaturus et domum habitaturus, sic mortem exiturus e uita. praeterea quemad- 12 modum non utique melior est longior uita, sic peior est utique mors longior. in nulla re magis quam in morte morem animo gerere debemus. exeat qua impetum cepit: siue ferrum appetit siue laqueum siue aliquam potionem uenas occupantem, pergat et uincula seruitutis abrumpat. uitam et aliis approbare quisque debet, mortem sibi: optima est quae placet. stulte haec cogitantur: 'aliquis dicet me parum fortiter fecisse, ali- 13 quis nimis temere, aliquis fuisse aliquod genus mortis animosius.' uis tu cogitare id in manibus esse consilium ad quod fama non pertinet! hoc unum intuere, ut te fortunae quam celerrime eripias; alioquin aderunt qui de facto tuo male existiment. inuenies etiam professos sapientiam 14 qui uim afferendam uitae suae negent et nefas iudicent ipsum interemptorem sui fieri: expectandum esse exitum quem natura decreuit. hoc qui dicit non uidet se libertatis uiam cludere: nihil melius aeterna lex fecit quam quod unum introitum nobis ad uitam dedit, exitus multos. ego 15 expectem uel morbi crudelitatem uel hominis, cum possim per media exire tormenta et aduersa discutere? hoc est unum cur de uita non possimus queri: neminem tenet. bono loco res humanae sunt, quod nemo nisi uitio suo miser est. placet? uiue: non placet? licet eo reuerti unde 16 uenisti. ut dolorem capitis leuares, sanguinem saepe misisti; ad extenuandum corpus uena percutitur. non opus est uasto uulnere diuidere praecordia: scalpello aperitur ad illam magnam libertatem uia et puncto securitas constat. quid ergo est quod nos facit pigros inertesque? nemo nostrum cogitat quandoque sibi ex hoc domicilio exeundum; sic ueteres inquilinos indulgentia loci et consuetudo etiam inter iniurias detinet. uis 17 aduersus hoc corpus liber esse? tamquam migraturus habita. propone tibi quandoque hoc contubernio carendum: fortior eris ad necessitatem

exeundi. sed quemadmodum suus finis ueniet in mentem omnia sine
18 fine concupiscentibus? nullius rei meditatio tam necessaria est; alia enim
fortasse exercentur in superuacuum. aduersus paupertatem praeparatus
est animus: permansere diuitiae. ad contemptum nos doloris armauimus: numquam a nobis exegit huius uirtutis experimentum integri ac
sani felicitas corporis. ut fortiter amissorum desideria pateremur prae-
19 cepimus nobis: omnes quos amabamus superstites fortuna seruauit. huius
unius rei usum qui exigat dies ueniet. non est quod existimes magnis
tantum uiris hoc robur fuisse quo seruitutis humanae claustra perrumperent; non est quod iudices hoc fieri nisi a Catone non posse, qui quam
ferro non emiserat animam manu extraxit: uilissimae sortis homines
ingenti impetu in tutum euaserunt, cumque e commodo mori non licu-
isset nec ad arbitrium suum instrumenta mortis eligere, obuia quaeque
20 rapuerunt et quae natura non erant noxia ui sua tela fecerunt. nuper in
ludo bestiariorum unus e Germanis, cum ad matutina spectacula parare-
tur, secessit ad exonerandum corpus – nullum aliud illi dabatur sine cus-
tode secretum; ibi lignum id quod ad emundanda obscena adhaerente
spongia positum est totum in gulam farsit et interclusis faucibus spiritum
elisit. hoc fuit morti contumeliam facere. ita prorsus, parum munde et
21 parum decenter: quid est stultius quam fastidiose mori? o uirum fortem,
o dignum cui fati daretur electio! quam fortiter ille gladio usus esset,
quam animose in profundam se altitudinem maris aut abscisae rupis
immisisset! undique destitutus inuenit quemadmodum et mortem sibi
deberet et telum, ut scias ad moriendum nihil aliud in mora esse quam
uelle. existimetur de facto hominis acerrimi ut cuique uisum erit, dum
hoc constet, praeferendam esse spurcissimam mortem seruituti mun-
22 dissimae. quoniam coepi sordidis exemplis uti, perseuerabo; plus enim
a se quisque exiget, si uiderit hanc rem etiam a contemptissimis posse
contemni. Catones Scipionesque et alios quos audire cum admiratione
consueuimus supra imitationem positos putamus: iam ego istam uirtutem
habere tam multa exempla in ludo bestiario quam in ducibus belli ciuilis
23 ostendam. cum adueheretur nuper inter custodias quidam ad matutinum
spectaculum missus, tamquam somno premente nutaret, caput usque eo
demisit donec radiis insereret, et tamdiu se in sedili suo tenuit donec
ceruicem circumactu rotae frangeret; eodem uehiculo quo ad poenam
24 ferebatur effugit. nihil obstat erumpere et exire cupienti: in aperto nos
natura custodit. cui permittit necessitas sua, circumspiciat exitum mollem; cui ad manum plura sunt per quae sese asserat, is dilectum agat et
qua potissimum liberetur consideret: cui difficilis occasio est, is proximam quamque pro optima arripiat, sit licet inaudita, sit noua. non deerit
25 ad mortem ingenium cui non defuerit animus. uides quemadmodum
extrema quoque mancipia, ubi illis stimulos adegit dolor, excitentur et
intentissimas custodias fallant? ille uir magnus est qui mortem sibi non

tantum imperauit sed inuenit. ex eodem tibi munere plura exempla promisi. secundo naumachiae spectaculo unus e barbaris lanceam quam in aduersarios acceperat totam iugulo suo mersit. 'quare, quare' inquit 'non omne tormentum, omne ludibrium iamdudum effugio? quare ego mortem armatus expecto?' tanto hoc speciosius spectaculum fuit quanto honestius mori discunt homines quam occidere. quid ergo? quod animi perditi quoque noxiosi habent non habebunt illi quos aduersus hos casus instruxit longa meditatio et magistra rerum omnium ratio? illa nos docet fati uarios esse accessus, finem eundem, nihil autem interesse unde incipiat quod uenit. eadem illa ratio monet ut si licet moriaris <quemadmodum placet, si minus> quemadmodum potes, et quidquid obuenerit ad uim afferendam tibi inuadas. iniuriosum est rapto uiuere, at contra pulcherrimum mori rapto. uale.

Letter 86

SENECA LVCILIO SVO SALVTEM

In ipsa Scipionis Africani uilla iacens haec tibi scribo, adoratis manibus eius et ara, quam sepulchrum esse tanti uiri suspicor. animum quidem eius in caelum ex quo erat redisse persuadeo mihi, non quia magnos exercitus duxit (hos enim et Cambyses furiosus ac furore feliciter usus habuit), sed ob egregiam moderationem pietatemque, quam magis in illo admirabilem iudico cum reliquit patriam quam cum defendit. aut Scipio Romae esse debebat aut Roma in libertate. 'nihil' inquit 'uolo derogare legibus, nihil institutis; aequum inter omnes ciues ius sit. utere sine me beneficio meo, patria. causa tibi libertatis fui, ero et argumentum: exeo, si plus quam tibi expedit creui.' quidni ego admirer hanc magnitudinem animi, qua in exilium uoluntarium secessit et ciuitatem exonerauit? eo perducta res erat ut aut libertas Scipioni aut Scipio libertati faceret iniuriam. neutrum fas erat; itaque locum dedit legibus et se Liternum recepit tam suum exilium rei publicae imputaturus quam Hannibalis.

uidi uillam extructam lapide quadrato, murum circumdatum siluae, turres quoque in propugnaculum uillae utrimque surrectas, cisternam aedificiis ac uiridibus subditam quae sufficere in usum uel exercitus posset, balneolum angustum, tenebricosum ex consuetudine antiqua: non uidebatur maioribus nostris caldum nisi obscurum. magna ergo me uoluptas subiit contemplantem mores Scipionis ac nostros: in hoc angulo ille 'Carthaginis horror', cui Roma debet quod tantum semel capta est, abluebat corpus laboribus rusticis fessum. exercebat enim opere se terramque (ut mos fuit priscis) ipse subigebat. sub hoc ille tecto tam sordido stetit, hoc illum pauimentum tam uile sustinuit: at nunc quis est qui sic lauari sustineat? pauper sibi uidetur ac sordidus nisi parietes magnis et pretiosis orbibus refulserunt, nisi Alexandrina marmora Numidicis

crustis distincta sunt, nisi illis undique operosa et in picturae modum uariata circumlitio praetexitur, nisi uitro absconditur camera, nisi Thasius lapis, quondam rarum in aliquo spectaculum templo, piscinas nostras circumdedit, in quas multa sudatione corpora exaniata demittimus, nisi
7 aquam argentea epitonia fuderunt. et adhuc plebeias fistulas loquor: quid cum ad balnea libertinorum peruenero? quantum statuarum, quantum columnarum est nihil sustinentium sed in ornamentum positarum impensae causa! quantum aquarum per gradus cum fragore labentium! eo deliciarum peruenimus ut nisi gemmas calcare nolimus.
8 in hoc balneo Scipionis minimae sunt rimae magis quam fenestrae muro lapideo exsectae, ut sine iniuria munimenti lumen admitterent; at nunc blattaria uocant balnea, si qua non ita aptata sunt ut totius diei solem fenestris amplissimis recipiant, nisi et lauantur simul et colorantur, nisi ex solio agros ac maria prospiciunt. itaque quae concursum et admirationem habuerant cum dedicarentur, ea in antiquorum numerum reiciuntur cum aliquid noui luxuria commenta est quo ipsa se obrueret. at
9 olim et pauca erant balnea nec ullo cultu exornata: cur enim exornaretur res quadrantaria et in usum, non in oblectamentum reperta? non suffundebatur aqua nec recens semper uelut ex calido fonte currebat, nec
10 referre credebant in quam pellucida sordes deponerent. sed, di boni, quam iuuat illa balinea intrare obscura et gregali tectorio inducta, quae scires Catonem tibi aedilem aut Fabium Maximum aut ex Corneliis aliquem manu sua temperasse! nam hoc quoque nobilissimi aediles fungebantur officio intrandi ea loca quae populum receptabant exigendique munditias et utilem ac salubrem temperaturam, non hanc quae nuper inuenta est similis incendio, adeo quidem ut conuictum in aliquo scelere seruum uiuum lauari oporteat. nihil mihi uidetur iam interesse, ardeat
11 balineum an caleat. quantae nunc aliqui rusticitatis damnant Scipionem quod non in caldarium suum latis specularibus diem admiserat, quod non in multa luce decoquebatur et expectabat ut in balneo concoqueret! o hominem calamitosum! nesciit uiuere. non saccata aqua lauabatur sed saepe turbida et, cum plueret uehementius, paene lutulenta. nec multum eius intererat an sic lauaretur; ueniebat enim ut sudorem illic abl-
12 eret, non ut unguentum. quas nunc quorundam uoces futuras credis? 'non inuideo Scipioni: uere in exilio uixit qui sic lauabatur.' immo, si scias, non cotidie lauabatur; nam, ut aiunt qui priscos mores urbis tradiderunt, brachia et crura cotidie abluebant, quae scilicet sordes opere collegerant, ceterum toti nundinis lauabantur. hoc loco dicet aliquis: 'liquet mihi immundissimos fuisse.' quid putas illos oluisse? militiam, laborem, uirum. postquam munda balnea inuenta sunt, spurciores sunt.
13 descripturus infamem et nimiis notabilem deliciis Horatius Flaccus quid ait?

> pastillos Buccillus olet.

dares nunc Buccillum: proinde esset ac si hircum oleret, Gargonii loco esset, quem idem Horatius Buccillo opposuit. parum est sumere unguentum nisi bis die terque renouatur, ne euanescat in corpore. quid quod hoc odore tamquam suo gloriantur?

haec si tibi nimium tristia uidebuntur, uillae imputabis, in qua didici ab Aegialo, diligentissimo patre familiae (is enim nunc huius agri possessor est) quamuis uetus arbustum posse transferri. hoc nobis senibus discere necessarium est, quorum nemo non oliuetum alteri ponit, †quod uidi illud arborum trimum et quadrimum fastidiendi fructus aut deponere.† te quoque proteget illa quae

> tarda uenit seris factura nepotibus umbram,

ut ait Vergilius noster, qui non quid uerissime sed quid decentissime diceretur aspexit, nec agricolas docere uoluit sed legentes delectare. nam, ut alia omnia transeam, hoc quod mihi hodie necesse fuit deprehendere, adscribam:

> uere fabis satio est; tunc te quoque, medica, putres
> accipiunt sulci, et milio uenit annua cura.

an uno tempore ista ponenda sint et an utriusque uerna sit satio, hinc aestimes licet: Iunius mensis est quo tibi scribo, iam procliuis in Iulium: eodem die uidi fabam metentes, milium serentes.

ad oliuetum reuertar, quod uidi duobus modis positum: magnarum arborum truncos circumcisis ramis et ad unum redactis pedem cum rapo suo transtulit, amputatis radicibus, relicto tantum capite ipso ex quo illae pependerant. hoc fimo tinctum in scrobem demisit, deinde terram non adgessit tantum, sed calcauit et pressit. negat quicquam esse hac, ut ait, pisatione efficacius. uidelicet frigus excludit et uentum; minus praeterea mouetur et ob hoc nascentes radices prodire patitur ac solum apprendere, quas necesse est cereas adhuc et precario haerentes leuis quoque reuellat agitatio. rapum autem arboris antequam obruat radit; ex omni enim materia quae nudata est, ut ait, radices exeunt nouae. non plures autem super terram eminere debet truncus quam tres aut quattuor pedes; statim enim ab imo uestietur nec magna pars eius quemadmodum in oliuetis ueteribus arida et retorrida erit. alter ponendi modus hic fuit: ramos fortes nec corticis duri, quales esse nouellarum arborum solent, eodem genere deposuit. hi paulo tardius surgunt, sed cum tamquam a planta processerint, nihil habent in se abhorridum aut triste. illud etiamnunc uidi, uitem ex arbusto suo annosam transferri; huius capillamenta quoque, si fieri potest, colligenda sunt, deinde liberalius sternenda uitis, ut etiam ex corpore radicescat. et uidi non tantum mense Februario positas sed etiam Martio exacto; tenent et complexae sunt non suas ulmos. omnes autem istas arbores quae, ut ita dicam, grandiscapiae sunt, ait aqua adiuuandas cisternina; quae si prodest, habemus pluuiam in nostra potestate.

plura te docere non cogito, ne quemadmodum Aegialus me sibi aduersarium parauit, sic ego parem te mihi. uale.

Letter 90

SENECA LVCILIO SVO SALVTEM

1 Quis dubitare, mi Lucili, potest quin deorum immortalium munus sit quod uiuimus, philosophiae quod bene uiuimus? itaque tanto plus huic nos debere quam dis quanto maius beneficium est bona uita quam uita pro certo haberetur, nisi ipsam philosophiam di tribuissent; cuius scien-
2 tiam nulli dederunt, facultatem omnibus. nam si hanc quoque bonum uulgare fecissent et prudentes nasceremur, sapientia quod in se optimum habet perdidisset, inter fortuita non esse. nunc enim hoc in illa pretiosum atque magnificum est, quod non obuenit, quod illam sibi quisque debet, quod non ab alio petitur. quid haberes quod in philosophia sus-
3 piceres si beneficiaria res esset? huius opus unum est de diuinis humanisque uerum inuenire; ab hac numquam recedit religio, pietas, iustitia et omnis alius comitatus uirtutum consertarum et inter se cohaerentium. haec docuit colere diuina, humana diligere, et penes deos imperium esse, inter homines consortium. quod aliquamdiu inuiolatum mansit, antequam societatem auaritia distraxit et paupertatis causa etiam iis quos fecit locupletissimos fuit; desierunt enim omnia possidere, dum uolunt
4 propria. sed primi mortalium quique ex his geniti naturam incorrupti sequebantur eundem habebant et ducem et legem, commissi melioris arbitrio; natura est enim potioribus deteriora summittere. mutis quidem gregibus aut maxima corpora praesunt aut uehementissima: non praecedit armenta degener taurus, sed qui magnitudine ac toris ceteros mares uicit; elephantorum gregem excelsissimus ducit: inter homines pro maximo est optimum. animo itaque rector eligebatur, ideoque summa felicitas erat gentium in quibus non poterat potentior esse nisi melior; tuto enim quantum uult potest qui se nisi quod debet non putat posse.
5 illo ergo saeculo quod aureum perhibent penes sapientes fuisse regnum Posidonius iudicat. hi continebant manus et infirmiorem a ualidioribus tuebantur, suadebant dissuadebantque et utilia atque inutilia monstrabant; horum prudentia ne quid deesset suis prouidebat, fortitudo pericula arcebat, beneficentia augebat ornabatque subiectos. officium erat imperare, non regnum. nemo quantum posset aduersus eos experiebatur per quos coeperat posse, nec erat cuiquam aut animus in iniuriam aut causa, cum bene imperanti bene pareretur, nihilque rex maius minari
6 male parentibus posset quam ut abiret e regno. sed postquam surrepentibus uitiis in tyrannidem regna conuersa sunt, opus esse legibus coepit,

quas et ipsas inter initia tulere sapientes. Solon, qui Athenas aequo iure fundauit, inter septem fuit sapientia notos; Lycurgum si eadem aetas tulisset, sacro illi numero accessisset octauus. Zaleuci leges Charondaeque laudantur; hi non in foro nec in consultorum atrio, sed in Pythagorae tacito illo sanctoque secessu didicerunt iura quae florenti tunc Siciliae et per Italiam Graeciae ponerent.

hactenus Posidonio adsentior: artes quidem a philosophia inuentas quibus in cotidiano uita utitur non concesserim, nec illi fabricae adseram gloriam. 'illa' inquit 'sparsos et cauis tectos aut aliqua rupe suffossa aut exesae arboris trunco docuit tecta moliri.' ego uero philosophiam iudico non magis excogitasse has machinationes tectorum supra tecta surgentium et urbium urbes prementium quam uiuaria piscium in hoc clausa ut tempestatum periculum non adiret gula et quamuis acerrime pelago saeuiente haberet luxuria portus suos in quibus distinctos piscium greges saginaret. quid ais? philosophia homines docuit habere clauem et seram? quid aliud erat auaritiae signum dare? philosophia haec cum tanto habitantium periculo imminentia tecta suspendit? parum enim erat fortuitis tegi et sine arte et sine difficultate naturale inuenire sibi aliquod receptaculum. mihi crede, felix illud saeculum ante architectos fuit, ante tectores. ista nata sunt iam nascente luxuria, in quadratum tigna decidere et serra per designata currente certa manu trabem scindere;

> nam primi cuneis scindebant fissile lignum.

non enim tecta cenationi epulum recepturae parabantur, nec in hunc usum pinus aut abies deferebatur longo uehiculorum ordine uicis intrementibus, ut ex illa lacunaria auro grauia penderent. furcae utrimque suspensae fulciebant casam; spissatis ramalibus ac fronde congesta et in procliue disposita decursus imbribus quamuis magnis erat. sub his tectis habitauere sed securi: culmus liberos texit, sub marmore atque auro seruitus habitat.

in illo quoque dissentio a Posidonio, quod ferramenta fabrilia excogitata a sapientibus uiris iudicat; isto enim modo dicat licet sapientes fuisse per quos

> tunc laqueis captare feras et fallere uisco
> inuentum et magnos canibus circumdare saltus.

omnia enim ista sagacitas hominum, non sapientia inuenit. in hoc quoque dissentio, sapientes fuisse qui ferri metalla et aeris inuenerint, cum incendio siluarum adusta tellus in summo uenas iacentis liquefacta fudisset: ista tales inueniunt quales colunt. ne illa quidem tam subtilis mihi quaestio uidetur quam Posidonio, utrum malleus in usu esse prius an forcipes coeperint. utraque inuenit aliquis excitati ingenii, acuti, non magni nec elati, et quidquid aliud corpore incuruato et animo humum spectante quaerendum est. sapiens facili uictu fuit. quidni? cum hoc quoque saeculo esse quam expeditissimus cupiat. quomodo, oro te, conuenit ut et Diogenen

mireris et Daedalum? uter ex his sapiens tibi uidetur? qui serram commentus est, an ille qui, cum uidisset puerum caua manu bibentem aquam, fregit protinus exemptum e perula calicem <cum> hac obiurgatione sui: 'quamdiu homo stultus superuacuas sarcinas habui!', qui se complicuit
15 in dolio et in eo cubitauit? hodie utrum tandem sapientiorem putas qui inuenit quemadmodum in immensam altitudinem crocum latentibus fistulis exprimat, qui euripos subito aquarum impetu implet aut siccat et uersatilia cenationum laquearia ita coagmentat ut subinde alia facies atque alia succedat et totiens tecta quotiens fericula mutentur, an eum qui et aliis et sibi hoc monstrat, quam nihil nobis natura durum ac difficile imperauerit, posse nos habitare sine marmorario ac fabro, posse nos uestitos esse sine commercio sericorum, posse nos habere usibus nostris necessaria si contenti fuerimus iis quae terra posuit in summo? quem si audire humanum genus uoluerit, tam superuacuum sciet sibi cocum esse quam militem.
16 illi sapientes fuerunt aut certe sapientibus similes quibus expedita erat tutela corporis. simplici cura constant necessaria: in delicias laboratur. non desiderabis artifices: sequere naturam. illa noluit esse districtos; ad quaecumque nos cogebat instruxit. 'frigus intolerabilest corpori nudo.' quid ergo? non pelles ferarum et aliorum animalium a frigore satis abundeque defendere queunt? non corticibus arborum pleraeque gentes tegunt corpora? non auium plumae in usum uestis conseruntur? non hodieque magna Scytharum pars tergis uulpium induitur ac murum, quae tactu mollia et impenetrabilia uentis sunt? quid ergo? non quilibet uirgeam cratem texuerunt manu et uili obliuerunt luto, deinde de stipula aliisque siluestribus operuere fastigium et pluuiis per deuexa labentibus hiemem
17 transiere securi? 'opus est tamen calorem solis aestiui umbra crassiore propellere.' quid ergo? non uetustas multa abdidit loca quae uel iniuria temporis uel alio quolibet casu excauata in specum recesserunt? quid ergo? non in defosso latent Syrticae gentes quibusque propter nimios solis ardores nullum tegimentum satis repellendis caloribus solidum est nisi
18 ipsa arens humus? non fuit tam iniqua natura ut, cum omnibus aliis animalibus facilem actum uitae daret, homo solus non posset sine tot artibus uiuere; nihil durum ab illa nobis imperatum est, nihil aegre quaerendum, ut possit uita produci. ad parata nati sumus: nos omnia nobis difficilia facilium fastidio fecimus. tecta tegimentaque et fomenta corporum et cibi et quae nunc ingens negotium facta sunt obuia erant et gratuita et opera leui parabilia; modus enim omnium prout necessitas erat: nos ista pretiosa, nos mira, nos magnis multisque conquirenda artibus fecimus. sufficit
19 ad id natura quod poscit. a natura luxuria desciuit, quae cotidie se ipsa incitat et tot saeculis crescit et ingenio adiuuat uitia. primo superuacua coepit concupiscere, inde contraria, nouissime animum corpori addixit et illius deseruire libidini iussit. omnes istae artes quibus aut circitatur

ciuitas aut strepit corpori negotium gerunt, cui omnia olim tamquam seruo praestabantur, nunc tamquam domino parantur. itaque hinc textorum, hinc fabrorum officinae sunt, hinc odores coquentium, hinc molles corporis motus docentium mollesque cantus et infractos. recessit enim ille naturalis modus desideria ope necessaria finiens; iam rusticitatis et miseriae est uelle quantum sat est.

incredibilest, mi Lucili, quam facile etiam magnos uiros dulcedo orationis abducat a uero. ecce Posidonius, ut mea fert opinio, ex iis qui plurimum philosophiae contulerunt, dum uult describere primum quemadmodum alia torqueantur fila, alia ex molli solutoque ducantur, deinde quemadmodum tela suspensis ponderibus rectum stamen extendat, quemadmodum subtemen insertum, quod duritiam utrimque comprimentis tramae remolliat, spatha coire cogatur et iungi, textrini quoque artem a sapientibus dixit inuentam, oblitus postea repertum hoc subtilius genus in quo

> tela iugo uincta est, stamen secernit harundo,
> inseritur medium radiis subtemen acutis,
> quod lato pauiunt insecti pectine dentes.

quid si contigisset illi uidere has nostri temporis telas, in quibus uestis nihil celatura conficitur, in qua non dico nullum corpori auxilium, sed nullum pudori est? transit deinde ad agricolas nec minus facunde describit proscissum aratro solum et iteratum quo solutior terra facilius pateat radicibus, tunc sparsa semina et collectas manu herbas ne quid fortuitum et agreste succrescat quod necet segetem. hoc quoque opus ait esse sapientium, tamquam non nunc quoque plurima cultores agrorum noua inueniant per quae fertilitas augeatur. deinde non est contentus his artibus, sed in pistrinum sapientem summittit; narrat enim quemadmodum rerum naturam imitatus panem coeperit facere. 'receptas' inquit 'in os fruges concurrens inter se duritia dentium frangit, et quidquid excidit ad eosdem dentes lingua refertur; tunc umore miscetur ut facilius per fauces lubricas transeat; cum peruenit in uentrem, aequali eius feruore concoquitur; tunc demum corpori accedit. hoc aliquis secutus exemplar lapidem asperum aspero imposuit ad similitudinem dentium, quorum pars immobilis motum alterius expectat; deinde utriusque attritu grana franguntur et saepius regeruntur donec ad minutiam frequenter trita redigantur; tum farinam aqua sparsit et assidua tractatione perdomuit finxitque panem, quem primo cinis calidus et feruens testa percoxit, deinde furni paulatim reperti et alia genera quorum feruor seruiret arbitrio.' non multum afuit quin sutrinum quoque inuentum a sapientibus diceret.

omnia ista ratio quidem, sed non recta ratio commenta est. hominis enim, non sapientis inuenta sunt, tam mehercules quam nauigia quibus amnes quibusque maria transimus, aptatis ad excipiendum uentorum

impetum uelis et additis a tergo gubernaculis quae huc atque illuc cursum nauigii torqueant. exemplum a piscibus tractum est, qui cauda reguntur
25 et leui eius in utrumque momento uelocitatem suam flectunt. 'omnia' inquit 'haec sapiens quidem inuenit, sed minora quam ut ipse tractaret sordidioribus ministris dedit.' immo non aliis excogitata ista sunt quam quibus hodieque curantur. quaedam nostra demum prodisse memoria scimus, ut speculariorum usum perlucente testa clarum transmittentium lumen, ut suspensuras balneorum et impressos parietibus tubos per quos circumfunderetur calor qui ima simul ac summa foueret aequaliter. quid loquar marmora quibus templa, quibus domus fulgent? quid lapideas moles in rotundum ac leue formatas quibus porticus et capacia populorum tecta suscipimus? quid uerborum notas quibus quamuis citata excipitur oratio et celeritatem linguae manus sequitur? uilissimorum
26 mancipiorum ista commenta sunt: sapientia altius sedet nec manus edocet: animorum magistra est. uis scire quid illa eruerit, quid effecerit? non decoros corporis motus nec uarios per tubam ac tibiam cantus, quibus exceptus spiritus aut in exitu aut in transitu formatur in uocem. non arma nec muros nec bello utilia molitur: paci fauet et genus humanum ad
27 concordiam uocat. non est, inquam, instrumentorum ad usus necessarios opifex. quid illi tam paruola assignas? artificem uides uitae. alias quidem artes sub dominio habet; nam cui uita, illi uitae quoque ornantia seruiunt:
28 ceterum ad beatum statum tendit, illo ducit, illo uias aperit. quae sint mala, quae uideantur ostendit; uanitatem exuit mentibus, dat magnitudinem solidam, inflatam uero et ex inani speciosam reprimit, nec ignorari sinit inter magna quid intersit et tumida; totius naturae notitiam ac sui tradit. quid sint di qualesque declarat, quid inferi, quid lares et genii, quid in secundam numinum formam animae perpetitae, ubi consistant, quid agant, quid possint, quid uelint. haec eius initiamenta sunt, per quae non municipale sacrum sed ingens deorum omnium templum, mundus ipse, reseratur, cuius uera simulacra uerasque facies cernendas mentibus
29 protulit; nam ad spectacula tam magna hebes uisus est. ad initia deinde rerum redit aeternamque rationem toti inditam et uim omnium seminum singula proprie figurantem. tum de animo coepit inquirere, unde esset, ubi, quamdiu, in quot membra diuisus. deinde a corporibus se ad incorporalia transtulit ueritatemque et argumenta eius excussit; post haec quemadmodum discernerentur uitae aut uocis ambigua; in utraque enim falsa ueris immixta sunt.
30 non abduxit, inquam, se (ut Posidonio uidetur) ab istis artibus sapiens, sed ad illas omnino non uenit. nihil enim dignum inuentu iudicasset quod non erat dignum perpetuo usu iudicaturus; ponenda non sumeret.
31 'Anacharsis' inquit 'inuenit rotam figuli, cuius circuitu uasa formantur.' deinde quia apud Homerum inuenitur figuli rota, maluit uideri uersus

falsos esse quam fabulam. ego nec Anacharsim auctorem huius rei fuisse contendo et, si fuit, sapiens quidem hoc inuenit, sed non tamquam sapiens, sicut multa sapientes faciunt qua homines sunt, non qua sapientes. puta uelocissimum esse sapientem: cursu omnes anteibit qua uelox est, non qua sapiens. cuperem Posidonio aliquem uitrearium ostendere, qui spiritu uitrum in habitus plurimos format qui uix diligenti manu effingerentur. haec inuenta sunt postquam sapientem inuenire desîmus. 'Democritus' inquit 'inuenisse dicitur fornicem, ut lapidum curuatura paulatim inclinatorum medio saxo alligaretur.' hoc dicam falsum esse; necesse est enim ante Democritum et pontes et portas fuisse, quarum fere summa curuantur. excidit porro uobis eundem Democritum inuenisse quemadmodum ebur molliretur, quemadmodum decoctus calculus in zmaragdum conuerteretur, qua hodieque coctura inuenti lapides in hoc utiles colorantur. ista sapiens licet inuenerit, non qua sapiens erat inuenit; multa enim facit quae ab imprudentissimis aut aeque fieri uidemus aut peritius atque exercitatius.

quid sapiens inuestigauerit, quid in lucem protraxerit quaeris? primum uerum naturamque, quam non ut cetera animalia oculis secutus est, tardis ad diuina; deinde uitae legem, quam ad uniuersa derexit, nec nosse tantum sed sequi deos docuit et accidentia non aliter excipere quam imperata. uetuit parere opinionibus falsis et quanti quidque esset uera aestimatione perpendit; damnauit mixtas paenitentia uoluptates et bona semper placitura laudauit et palam fecit felicissimum esse cui felicitate non opus est, potentissimum esse qui se habet in potestate. non de ea philosophia loquor quae ciuem extra patriam posuit, extra mundum deos, quae uirtutem donauit uoluptati, sed de illa quae nullum bonum putat nisi quod honestum est, quae nec hominis nec fortunae muneribus deleniri potest, cuius hoc pretium est, non posse pretio capi.

hanc philosophiam fuisse illo rudi saeculo quo adhuc artificia deerant et ipso usu discebantur utilia non credo. †sicut aut† fortunata tempora, cum in medio iacerent beneficia naturae promiscue utenda, antequam auaritia atque luxuria dissociauere mortales et ad rapinam ex consortio <docuere> discurrere: non erant illi sapientes uiri, etiam si faciebant facienda sapientibus. statum quidem generis humani non alium quisquam suspexerit magis, nec si cui permittat deus terrena formare et dare gentibus mores, aliud probauerit quam quod apud illos fuisse memoratur apud quos

> nulli subigebant arua coloni;
> ne signare quidem aut partiri limite campum
> fas erat: in medium quaerebant, ipsaque tellus
> omnia liberius nullo poscente ferebat.

38 quid hominum illo genere felicius? in commune rerum natura fruebantur; sufficiebat illa ut parens in tutelam omnium; haec erat publicarum opum secura possessio. quidni ego illud locupletissimum mortalium genus dixerim in quo pauperem inuenire non posses? irrupit in res optime positas auaritia et, dum seducere aliquid cupit atque in suum uertere, omnia fecit aliena et in angustum se ex immenso redegit. auaritia paupertatem intulit
39 et multa concupiscendo omnia amisit. licet itaque nunc conetur reparare quod perdidit, licet agros agris adiciat uicinum uel pretio pellens uel iniuria, licet in prouinciarum spatium rura dilatet et possessionem uocet per sua longam peregrinationem: nulla nos finium propagatio eo reducet unde discessimus. cum omnia fecerimus, multum habebimus: uniuersum
40 habebamus. terra ipsa fertilior erat illaborata et in usus populorum non diripientium larga. quidquid natura protulerat, id non minus inuenisse quam inuentum monstrare alteri uoluptas erat; nec ulli aut superesse poterat aut deesse: inter concordes diuidebatur. nondum ualentior imposuerat infirmiori manum, nondum auarus abscondendo quod sibi iaceret
41 alium necessariis quoque excluserat: par erat alterius ac sui cura. arma cessabant incruentaeque humano sanguine manus odium omne in feras uerterant. illi quos aliquod nemus densum a sole protexerat, qui aduersus saeuitiam hiemis aut imbris uili receptaculo tuti sub fronde uiuebant, placidas transigebant sine suspirio noctes. sollicitudo nos in nostra purpura uersat et acerrimis excitat stimulis: at quam mollem somnum
42 illis dura tellus dabat! non impendebant caelata laquearia, sed in aperto iacentis sidera superlabebantur et, insigne spectaculum noctium, mundus in praeceps agebatur, silentio tantum opus ducens. tam interdiu illis quam nocte patebant prospectus huius pulcherrimae domus; libebat intueri signa ex media caeli parte uergentia, rursus ex occulto alia surgen-
43 tia. quidni iuuaret uagari inter tam late sparsa miracula? at uos ad omnem tectorum pauetis sonum et inter picturas uestras, si quid increpuit, fugitis attoniti. non habebant domos instar urbium: spiritus ac liber inter aperta perflatus et leuis umbra rupis aut arboris et pellucidi fontes riuique non opere nec fistula nec ullo coacto itinere obsolefacti sed sponte currentes et prata sine arte formosa, inter haec agreste domicilium rustica politum manu – haec erat secundum naturam domus, in qua libebat habitare nec ipsam nec pro ipsa timentem: nunc magna pars nostri metus tecta sunt.
44   sed quamuis egregia illis uita fuerit et carens fraude, non fuere sapientes, quando hoc iam in opere maximo nomen est. non tamen negauerim fuisse alti spiritus uiros et, ut ita dicam, a dis recentes; neque enim dubium est quin meliora mundus nondum effetus ediderit. quemadmodum autem omnibus indoles fortior fuit et ad labores paratior, ita non erant ingenia omnibus consummata. non enim dat natura uirtutem:
45 ars est bonum fieri. illi quidem non aurum nec argentum nec pellucidos <lapides in> ima terrarum faece quaerebant parcebantque adhuc etiam

mutis animalibus: tantum aberat ut homo hominem non iratus, non timens, tantum spectaturus occideret. nondum uestis illis erat picta, nondum texebatur aurum, adhuc nec eruebatur. quid ergo est? ignorantia 46 rerum innocentes erant; multum autem interest utrum peccare aliquis nolit an nesciat. deerat illis iustitia, deerat prudentia, deerat temperantia ac fortitudo. omnibus his uirtutibus habebat similia quaedam rudis uita: uirtus non contingit animo nisi instituto et edocto et ad summum assidua exercitatione perducto. ad hoc quidem, sed sine hoc nascimur, et in optimis quoque, antequam erudias, uirtutis materia, non uirtus est. uale.

Letter 114

SENECA LVCILIO SVO SALVTEM

Quare quibusdam temporibus prouenerit corrupti generis oratio quaeris 1 et quomodo in quaedam uitia inclinatio ingeniorum facta sit, ut aliquando inflata explicatio uigeret, aliquando infracta et in morem cantici ducta; quare alias sensus audaces et fidem egressi placuerint, alias abruptae sententiae et suspiciosae, in quibus plus intellegendum esset quam audiendum; quare aliqua aetas fuerit quae translationis iure uteretur inuerecunde. hoc quod audire uulgo soles, quod apud Graecos in prouerbium cessit: talis hominibus fuit oratio qualis uita. quemadmo- 2 dum autem uniuscuiusque actio †dicendi† similis est, sic genus dicendi aliquando imitatur publicos mores, si disciplina ciuitatis laborauit et se in delicias dedit. argumentum est luxuriae publicae orationis lasciuia, si modo non in uno aut in altero fuit, sed approbata est et recepta. non 3 potest alius esse ingenio, alius animo color. si ille sanus est, si compositus, grauis, temperans, ingenium quoque siccum ac sobrium est: illo uitiato hoc quoque afflatur. non uides, si animus elanguit, trahi membra et pigre moueri pedes? si ille effeminatus est, in ipso incessu apparere mollitiam? si ille acer est et ferox, concitari gradum? si furit aut, quod furori simile est, irascitur, turbatum esse corporis motum nec ire sed ferri? quanto hoc magis accidere ingenio putas, quod totum animo permixtum est, ab illo fingitur, illi paret, inde legem petit?

quomodo Maecenas uixerit notius est quam ut narrari nunc debeat 4 quomodo ambulauerit, quam delicatus fuerit, quam cupierit uideri, quam uitia sua latere noluerit. quid ergo? non oratio eius aeque soluta est quam ipse discinctus? non tam insignita illius uerba sunt quam cultus, quam comitatus, quam domus, quam uxor? magni uir ingenii fuerat si illud egisset uia rectiore, si non uitasset intellegi, si non etiam in oratione diffluere. uidebis itaque eloquentiam ebrii hominis inuolutam et errantem et licentiae plenam. quid turpius 'amne siluisque ripa comantibus'? 5 'uide ut alueum lyntribus arent uersoque uado remittant hortos.' quid?

si quis 'feminae cinno crispat et labris columbatur incipitque suspirans, ut ceruice lassa fanantur nemoris tyranni.' 'irremediabilis factio rimantur epulis lagonaque temptant domos et spe mortem exigunt.' 'genium festo uix suo testem.' 'tenuisue cerei fila et crepacem molam.' 'focum mater
6 aut uxor inuestiunt.' non statim cum haec legeris hoc tibi occurret, hunc esse qui solutis tunicis in urbe semper incesserit (nam etiam cum absentis Caesaris partibus fungeretur, signum a discincto petebatur); hunc esse qui in tribunali, in rostris, in omni publico coetu sic apparuerit ut pallio uelaretur caput exclusis utrimque auribus, non aliter quam in mimo fugitiui diuitis solent; hunc esse cui tunc maxime ciuilibus bellis strepentibus et sollicita urbe et armata comitatus hic fuerit in publico, spadones duo, magis tamen uiri quam ipse; hunc esse qui uxorem milliens duxit,
7 cum unam habuerit? haec uerba tam improbe structa, tam neglegenter abiecta, tam contra consuetudinem omnium posita ostendunt mores quoque non minus nouos et prauos et singulares fuisse. maxima laus illi tribuitur mansuetudinis: pepercit gladio, sanguine abstinuit, nec ulla alia re quid posset quam licentia ostendit. hanc ipsam laudem suam corrupit istis orationis portentosissimae delicîs; apparet enim mollem fuisse, non
8 mitem. hoc istae ambages compositionis, hoc uerba trauersa, hoc sensus miri, magni quidem saepe sed eneruati dum exeunt, cuiuis manifestum facient: motum illi felicitate nimia caput. quod uitium hominis esse inter-
9 dum, interdum temporis solet. ubi luxuriam late felicitas fudit, cultus primum corporum esse diligentior incipit; deinde supellectili laboratur; deinde in ipsas domos impenditur cura ut in laxitatem ruris excurrant, ut parietes aduectis trans maria marmoribus fulgeant, ut tecta uarientur auro, ut lacunaribus pauimentorum respondeat nitor; deinde ad cenas lautitia transfertur et illic commendatio ex nouitate et soliti ordinis commutatione captatur, ut ea quae includere solent cenam prima ponantur,
10 ut quae aduenientibus dabantur exeuntibus dentur. cum assueuit animus fastidire quae ex more sunt et illi pro sordidis solita sunt, etiam in oratione quod nouum est quaerit et modo antiqua uerba atque exoleta reuocat ac profert, modo fingit et nota deflectit, modo, id quod nuper
11 increbruit, pro cultu habetur audax translatio ac frequens. sunt qui sensus praecidant et hoc gratiam sperent, si sententia pependerit et audienti suspicionem sui fecerit; sunt qui illos detineant et porrigant; sunt qui non usque ad uitium accedant (necesse est enim hoc facere aliquid grande temptanti) sed qui ipsum uitium ament.

itaque ubicumque uideris orationem corruptam placere, ibi mores quoque a recto desciuisse non erit dubium. quomodo conuiuiorum luxuria, quomodo uestium aegrae ciuitatis indicia sunt, sic orationis licentia, si modo frequens est, ostendit animos quoque a quibus uerba exeunt pro-
12 cidisse. mirari quidem non debes corrupta excipi non tantum a corona sordidiore sed ab hac quoque turba cultiore; togis enim inter se isti, non

iudicîs distant. hoc magis mirari potes, quod non tantum uitiosa sed uitia laudentur. nam illud semper factum est: nullum sine uenia placuit ingenium. da mihi quemcumque uis magni nominis uirum: dicam quid illi aetas sua ignouerit, quid in illo sciens dissimulauerit. multos tibi dabo quibus uitia non nocuerint, quosdam quibus profuerint. dabo, inquam, maximae famae et inter admiranda propositos, quos si quis corrigit, delet; sic enim uitia uirtutibus immixta sunt ut illas secum tractura sint.

adice nunc quod oratio certam regulam non habet: consuetudo illam 13 ciuitatis, quae numquam in eodem diu stetit, uersat. multi ex alieno saeculo petunt uerba, duodecim tabulas loquuntur; Gracchus illis et Crassus et Curio nimis culti et recentes sunt, ad Appium usque et Coruncanium redeunt. quidam contra, dum nihil nisi tritum et usitatum uolunt, in sordes incidunt. utrumque diuerso genere corruptum est, tam mehercules 14 quam nolle nisi splendidis uti ac sonantibus et poeticis, necessaria atque in usu posita uitare. tam hunc dicam peccare quam illum: alter se plus iusto colit, alter plus iusto neglegit; ille et crura, hic ne alas quidem uellit.

ad compositionem transeamus. quot genera tibi in hac dabo quibus 15 peccetur? quidam praefractam et asperam probant; disturbant de industria si quid placidius effluxit; nolunt sine salebra esse iuncturam; uirilem putant et fortem quae aurem inaequalitate percutiat. quorundam non est compositio, modulatio est; adeo blanditur et molliter labitur. quid 16 de illa loquar in qua uerba differuntur et diu expectata uix ad clausulas redeunt? quid illa in exitu lenta, qualis Ciceronis est, deuexa et molliter detinens nec aliter quam solet ad morem suum pedemque respondens? non tantum uno in genere sententiarum uitium est, si aut pusillae sunt et pueriles aut improbae et plus ausae quam pudore saluo licet, si floridae sunt et nimis dulces, si in uanum exeunt et sine effectu nihil amplius quam sonant. haec uitia unus aliquis inducit, sub quo tunc eloquentia est, 17 ceteri imitantur et alter alteri tradunt. sic Sallustio uigente amputatae sententiae et uerba ante expectatum cadentia et obscura breuitas fuere pro cultu. L. Arruntius, uir rarae frugalitatis, qui historias belli Punici scripsit, fuit Sallustianus et in illud genus nitens. est apud Sallustium 'exercitum argento fecit', id est, pecunia parauit. hoc Arruntius amare coepit; posuit illud omnibus paginis. dicit quodam loco 'fugam nostris fecere', alio loco 'Hiero rex Syracusanorum bellum fecit', et alio loco 'quae audita Panhormitanos dedere Romanis fecere.' gustum tibi dare uolui: totus his 18 contexitur liber. quae apud Sallustium rara fuerunt apud hunc crebra sunt et paene continua, nec sine causa; ille enim in haec incidebat, at hic illa quaerebat. uides autem quid sequatur ubi alicui uitium pro exemplo est. dixit Sallustius 'aquis hiemantibus'. Arruntius in primo libro belli 19 Punici ait 'repente hiemauit tempestas', et alio loco cum dicere uellet frigidum annum fuisse ait 'totus hiemauit annus', et alio loco 'inde sexaginta onerarias leues praeter militem et necessarios nautarum hiemante aquilone misit.' non desinit omnibus locis hoc uerbum infulcire. quodam loco dicit Sallustius 'dum inter arma ciuilia aequi bonique famas petit'. Arruntius non temperauit quominus primo statim libro poneret ingentes esse 'famas' de Regulo. haec ergo et eiusmodi uitia, quae alicui impressit imitatio, non sunt indicia luxuriae nec animi corrupti; propria enim esse debent et ex ipso nata ex quibus tu aestimes alicuius affectus: iracundi hominis iracunda oratio est, commoti nimis incitata, delicati tenera et fluxa. quod uides istos sequi qui aut uellunt barbam aut interuellunt, qui labra pressius tondent et arradunt seruata et summissa cetera parte, qui lacernas coloris improbi sumunt, qui perlucentem togam, qui nolunt facere quicquam quod hominum oculis transire liceat: irritant illos et in se auertunt, uolunt uel reprehendi dum conspici. talis est oratio Maecenatis omniumque aliorum qui non casu errant sed scientes uolentesque. hoc a magno animi malo oritur: quomodo in uino non ante lingua titubat quam mens cessit oneri et inclinata uel prodita est, ita ista orationis quid aliud quam ebrietas nulli molesta est nisi animus labat. ideo ille curetur: ab illo sensus, ab illo uerba exeunt, ab illo nobis est habitus, uultus, incessus. illo sano ac ualente oratio quoque robusta, fortis, uirilis est: si ille procubuit, et cetera ruinam sequuntur.

       rege incolumi mens omnibus una est:
  amisso rupere fidem.

rex noster est animus; hoc incolumi cetera manent in officio, parent, obtemperant: cum ille paulum uacillauit, simul dubitant. cum uero cessit uoluptati, artes quoque eius actusque marcent et omnis ex languido fluidoque conatus est. quoniam hac similitudine usus sum, perseuerabo. animus noster modo rex est, modo tyrannus: rex cum honesta intuetur, salutem commissi sibi corporis curat et illi nihil imperat turpe, nihil sordidum; ubi uero impotens, cupidus, delicatus est, transit in nomen detestabile ac dirum et fit tyrannus. tunc illum excipiunt affectus impotentes et instant; qui initio quidem gaudet, ut solet populus largitione nocitura frustra plenus et quae non potest haurire contrectans; cum uero magis ac magis uires morbus exedit et in medullas neruosque descendere deliciae, conspectu eorum quibus se nimia auiditate inutilem reddidit laetus, pro suis uoluptatibus habet alienarum spectaculum, sumministrator libidinum testisque, quarum usum sibi ingerendo abstulit. nec illi tam gratum est abundare iucundis quam acerbum quod non omnem illum apparatum per gulam uentremque transmittit, quod non cum omni exoletorum feminarumque turba conuolutatur, maeretque quod magna pars suae felicitatis exclusa corporis angustiis cessat. numquid enim, mi Lucili, non in hoc furor est, quod nemo nostrum mortalem se cogitat, quod nemo imbecillum? immo quod nemo nostrum unum esse se cogitat? aspice culinas nostras et concursantis inter tot ignes cocos: unum uideri putas uentrem cui tanto tumultu comparatur cibus? aspice ueteraria nostra et plena multorum saeculorum uindemiis horrea: unum putas uideri uentrem cui tot consulum regionumque uina cluduntur? aspice quot locis terra uertatur, quot millia colonorum arent, fodiant: unum uideri putas uentrem cui et in Sicilia et in Africa seritur? sani erimus et modica concupiscemus si unusquisque se numeret, metiatur simul corpus, sciat quam nec multum capere nec diu possit. nihil tamen aeque tibi profuerit ad temperantiam omnium rerum quam frequens cogitatio breuis aeui et huius incerti: quidquid facies, respice ad mortem. uale.

COMMENTARY

LETTER 1

The programmatic opening letter invites its reader to embark on a process of self-scrutiny and self-improvement, its epistolary greeting signalling the genre of the work. *Ep.* 1 begins on a note of urgency (there are four imperatives in the first sentence alone), which will characterise many in the series. Lucilius must assert his ownership of himself and take control of his time. That S and his addressee are close friends is clear from the first sentence, though otherwise we learn from this pared-down letter almost nothing specific about either man. While *Ep.* 1, apparently responding to one from L (§2 *scribis*), seems to plunge the reader *in medias res*, it is also marked as the start of the collection (§5 *incipies*).

Time (specifically present time) is personal in this letter and turns out to be the only thing, fugitive though it is, that one can properly possess. The legal language of ownership which runs through the first half of the letter (§1 *uindica*, §2 *manum inieceris*, §3 *possessionem*) is thus richly ironic; the grandest Roman senator, it implies, can possess no more than the humblest slave. For Stoics, only that which is fully in our control is truly our own. Nothing else, whether it be riches, position, friends, family, bodily health, can be depended on. To achieve mental equanimity (*securitas*), we must regard all such things as *aliena* (§3). As S will make clear later (e.g. 9.18–19), one's own *uirtus* is all that is necessary for happiness. Inasmuch as we are only able to exercise our *uirtus* in the present moment, that is the only portion of time we may truly possess (cf. 77.11), and only when we make time ours by using it correctly do we gain possession of ourselves. The haptic dimension of the legal imagery adds a further irony, given the Stoic emphasis on the incorporeality of time (on the metaphysical understanding of time in Stoic thought see Goldschmidt 1977: esp. 37–45, Sangalli 1988, Armisen-Marchetti 1995, Reydams-Schils 2005: 29–34). S does not generally stress time's incorporeality, although, as he notes elsewhere (*Brev.* 8.1, *quia res incorporalis est . . . ideoque uilissima aestimatur*), it is perhaps this characteristic which misleads people into regarding it of no value.

In §§2, 4 and 5 of the letter, S deploys financial imagery to articulate a better approach to personal time (*pretium, aestimat, imputari, ratio, constat, impensae, perdere, reddam*; see Armisen-Marchetti 1995). The effort usually spent on scrutinising one's accounts, he implies, is better devoted to keeping track of how one spends one's time. As in the case of money, we might worry about whether we have enough. The letters in Book 2, in particular, return repeatedly to economic anxieties, reflecting on our disposition towards material wealth (see Soldo). Our inability to be satisfied is a recurrent concern (e.g. 2.6, 16.7–9); if we cultivate the right attitude, S argues, we can be happy with the barest minimum to keep body and soul together (e.g. 4.10–11, 17.9). The claim made in *Ep.* 1 in relation to time is in some respects similar. While time should not be wasted, even the smallest amount of time may suffice for the exercise of virtue (and thus the achievement of happiness). Yet S's financial imagery also throws into relief the incommensurability of time and money; only time has true worth, so that the usual concerns of 'economic' thinking have no significance.

Ep. 1 resumes a number of themes S had explored in earlier works, most particularly *De breuitate uitae* (15.5–16.1; cf. Scarpat (b): 21 and Williams: intro. to *Brev.*), where the value of time is also considered from a moral (rather than a metaphysical) perspective, with a particular stress on the contrast between how time is used by the *occupati* (those caught up in pointless activities) and by the wise (Armisen-Marchetti 1995: esp. 552–3). The concern not only with the ethical disposition of the addressee but also with that of the author (§4 *fatebor ingenue*) is a distinctive feature of the *EM* (foreshadowed to a degree in the *Ad Heluiam matrem*). Recognising one's own need for self-improvement is a crucial first step (Trapp 2007: 55), here modelled by S himself.

In this opening letter, S presents a proper understanding of death as the key to making good use of one's time. The reader is reminded *se cotidie mori*, 'that he dies each day' (§2), a paradoxical message which, as Ker (2009a: 161) notes, will be elaborated in relation both to the importance of the individual day (e.g. 12.6, 65.1–2, 74.27, 78.28, 83.1–7, 101.8–9) and to the perpetual presence of death (e.g. 4.7–8, 24.20, 49.11, 54.7, 63.15, *Ep.* 93, 101.10). Earlier Stoics do not seem to have emphasised death as S does (Rist 1969: ch. 13). Some key concerns of the Stoic tradition are introduced in this letter, such as the role of nature, the value of time, happiness as independent of external circumstances, but S makes no explicit mention of philosophy in general, let alone the doctrines of specific schools. This is an introduction to living well; technicalities and abstractions will appear later (Maurach 1970: 25–9, Hachmann 1995: 19–123).

This letter's complementary relationship to *Ep.* 2, the two together forming a proem, is stressed by Maurach 1970: 25–9; *Ep.* 2's emphasis on the insignificance of place (a change of location will do nothing to improve one's mental state) balances *Ep.* 1's stress on the importance of time. *Ep.* 2 also pursues the theme of poverty, adumbrated metaphorically at the end of *Ep.* 1, and introduces Epicurus, who will figure in *Epp.* 2–29 more prominently than any Stoic authority. Book 1 (*Epp.* 1–12) more generally serves as an introduction to the collection (Hachmann 1995: 19–123, Henderson 2004: 6–27, Richardson-Hay: 13).

Later letters will revisit and elaborate several points made in *Ep.* 1. In particular, *Ep.* 62 (the last in Book 6) invites the reader to look back to *Ep.* 1 and consider the progress made in the interim: *uaco, Lucili, uaco, et ubicumque sum, ibi meus sum* (62.1; Motto, Clark 1993: 105–14). *Ep.* 101 offers a more expansive reprise, illustrated with the cases of Senecio and Maecenas.

The style of the opening letter is deceptively simple in some places, in others more elaborately articulated (with particular use of the tricolon) and characterised by repetition with variation and antithesis. While the language (with its imagery drawn from law and accounting) sometimes borders on the colloquial, there are also subtle echoes of Horatian lyric (esp. *Carm.* 2.14; see Berthet 1979).

Henderson (2002: 84–5) notes echoes of S's opening letter in Pliny's correspondence (*Ep.* 3.1.2, 3.5.12). *Ep.* 1, as the opening of an especially esteemed work, received particular attention from Renaissance humanists (Panizza 1983).

Commentaries: Scarpat (b), Motto, Richardson-Hay.

Further reading: Guillemin 1957: 280–1, Maurach 1970: 25–9, Hijmans 1976: 7–11, 134–7, Panizza 1983, von Albrecht 1989, Mazzoli 1991, Armisen-Marchetti 1995, Gagliardi 1998: 51–68, Lotito 2001: 131–75, Henderson 2004: 7, Ker 2009a: 155–61, Long 2009.

Seneca . . . salutem 'Seneca greets his Lucilius' (understand *dicit*). Standard form of opening for letters between close friends and family members (cf. Cic. *Att., Fam.* esp. Book XIV, *Q. fr.*; Dickey 2002: 36–7).

1 The first sentence opens and closes with imperatives, conveying a sense of urgency as well as familiarity. **Ita fac** 'Carry on thus'. Insofar as *ita* seems to refer to L's current behaviour, at least as he reports it (cf. §2 *fac . . . quod facere te scribis*), we are at once given the sense of the letters as the product of an established friendship, though it can also be read as referring forward to the advice which follows. The phrase recurs, recalling this opening letter, at 19.1. The rhythmic *clausulae* of this first sentence, the double cretic *uindica te tibi,* and the cretic spondee, *collig(e) et serua,* make clear from the outset that this prose is carefully wrought (von Albrecht 1989: 114). **mi Lucili:** *mi* (historically the genitive or dative form of the pronoun *ego,* treated as a vocative from 2nd cent. BCE) is particularly associated with the epistolary genre; in Cicero it occurs with every vocative address to Q. Cicero and the majority of those to Atticus, as well as when Cicero is seeking to give the impression of closeness in addressing others (Dickey 2002: 214–20, Hall 2009: 67–8). Vocative address itself is used infrequently in the letters (after *Ep.* 1 it next occurs only at 5.7) though more often than in e.g. Cicero's correspondence. Its use three times in the opening letter (see also §2, §3) underlines the identity of the addressee; cf. the vocatives which often occur in the opening lines of S's prose treatises (e.g. *Brev.* 1.1).   **uindica te tibi** 'claim yourself for yourself' or 'set yourself free'. The idea of acquiring possession of oneself is to be found in Epicurus: ὅλοι γενώμεθα ἑαυτῶν ('Let us become entirely our own', Arrighetti 1973: no. 237). *uindicare* has specific legal overtones, meaning 'to assert one's title' to something, 'to claim as one's property what is in the possession of another' (*OLD* 1). *uindicare* is often used, too, as short-hand for *uindicare in libertatem*, 'to claim as free one who asserts he is wrongly held in slavery' (*OLD* 3). Thus it is perhaps implied that L is enslaved to everyday concerns or similar (the theme of metaphorical enslavement recurs frequently later in the collection, cf. e.g. 37.4, 47.17, Edwards 2009). The phrase is emphatically self-reflexive (on linguistic reflexivity in S see Traina 1987: 14–19, 52–65, Bartsch 2006: 246–52). This vivid formulation recurs at 33.4 (a letter which marks a new phase in the collection; cf. intro. to *Ep.* 33 and note *ad loc.*). Cf. 82.5 *in insuperabili loco stat animus qui . . . arce se sua uindicat. se sibi uindicare* occurs too at *Brev.* 2.4 after a catalogue of pointless activities by which individuals involved in the tussles of the law courts are distracted from what should be their true purpose (*hic aduocat, hic adest, ille periclitatur, ille defendit, ille iudicat, nemo se sibi uindicat*). On the significance of the phrase in S see Lotito 2001: 131–75, Ker 2009a: 157–8. On S's use of legal language more generally see Traina 1987: 11–12, 52–3. Cicero anticipates S's moralising use of *uindicare: sapientiam esse solam, quae nos a libidinum impetu et a formidinum terrore uindicet* (*Fin.* 1.46).   **tempus . . . collige**: the self, *te*, and time, *tempus,* are treated as parallel (this is a pairing which recurs often, e.g. 71.36). This sentence and two of the three following are dominated by triads. Each has three divisions, describing in various ways how time slips away. *auferebatur* (cf. *eripiuntur* later in the text) suggests that time is taken away openly, *surripiebatur* (cf. *subducuntur* later) surreptitiously, and *excidebat* (cf. *effluunt,* below) that it slips away unnoticed (Panizza 1983: 41; cf. Scarpat (b): 25–33).   **persuade tibi:** already here S evokes the kind of interiorised dialogue which figures so frequently in the letters (cf. Edwards 1997a).   **quaedam tempora eripiuntur nobis . . . effluunt:** tricolon. *nobis*: S, too, is susceptible to wasting time, as he emphasises in §§4–5.   **turpissima** 'most shameful' (*OLD* 3): because this loss at least is subject to the individual's control.   **iactura** 'squandering' (*OLD* 3; cf. in similar context *Brev.* 9.1).   **si uolueris attendere:** fut. pf., sc. *animum,* 'if you will pay proper attention'.   **magna pars . . . aliud agentibus:** sc. *nobis.* Another tricolon. *magna . . . maxima . . . tota*: favoured by Erasmus (1529), the rarer MS reading (most have *maxima . . .*

magna ... *tota* ...), which accords with the rhetorical figure of *gradatio*, is preferred by Reynolds. This sentence attracted particular attention from Renaissance commentators, who took the paradox for obscurity. How can a large part, the largest part and all our life pass away in three different ways? Several read this sentence as referring to three different groups of people (Panizza 1983), though S's third category can surely subsume the first two; *aliud* 'something different from what we ought to be doing' suggests displacement activity (cf. *Brev.* 1.3). For the thought cf. also *Brev.* 2.1–2, Hor. *Carm.* 2.14.1–2 (the latter echoed also in the wording of §3 below); *elabitur* echoes Hor. *Ep.* 1.2.41–4: *uiuendi qui recte prorogat horam, | rusticus exspectat dum defluat amnis; at ille | labitur et labetur in omne uolubilis aeuum.* How exactly one is to make the right use of time is not spelled out, though this is something S will return to again and again in later letters (e.g. 15.4, 17.5, 49.5–11).

2 S now turns from the time we lose to the time that we possess but do not value sufficiently. **quem mihi dabis** 'What person can you show me ...?' (*OLD do* 14) Rhetorical questions are a frequent feature of the letters. The threefold anaphora (here of the relative pronoun *qui*), often with a crescendo, is a distinctive characteristic of S's writing (Traina 1987: 33–4). **pretium ... ponat** 'places due value on' (*OLD pretium* 3). **se cotidie mori** 'that every day he dies'. A paradoxical thought, which will recur repeatedly in the letters (e.g. 24.20 *cotidie morimur*, 58.24), with the implication that death is not a future prospect but an incremental process, always already present in our lives (Ker 2009a: 155–61). This is the first mention of death (reinforced by *mortem* and *mors* in the two following sentences), one of the predominant themes of the collection and (within Book 1) a particular focus of *Ep.* 4. **praeterît**: pf. (contracted form). Printed thus (following Reynolds) it gives a molossus + cretic *clausula*. **fac ergo, mi Lucili:** a virtual reprise of the opening phrase. The rest of the sentence, too, is close to the corresponding part of the first sentence. **omnes horas:** a more specific equivalent to the opening sentence's *tempus*. **complectere:** 2nd pers. sing. imp. of *complecti* 'to grasp' (*OLD* 3). This verb introduces the notion of time as reified (cf. below). It is used in a similar sense at 12.4(n.). **sic fiet, ut minus ex crastino pendeas, si hodierno manum inieceris:** *ut ... pendeas* 'that you are less reliant on what tomorrow brings' (*OLD pendeo* 13b); *manum inieceris* continues the imagery of Roman legal procedure suggested by *uindica te tibi* in the opening sentence (though here it is present time rather than L himself which is the object). See *OLD manus*[1] 15b, *manum inicere* 'to seize (property claimed as one's own)'. For the thought cf. *Brev.* 9.1 *expectatio, quae pendet ex crastino, perdit hodiernum.* The importance of the present day is frequently reiterated. The term *hodiernum* recurs repeatedly, esp. to characterise the 'daily' quotations from Epicurus and others with which letters 2 to 29 conclude (e.g. 2.5).

3 omnia . . . aliena sunt 'all other things are outside our control' (*OLD alienus* 1).   **tempus tantum nostrum est** 'time alone belongs to us' – specifically present time (future time is always beyond our control); cf. *Brev.* 10.2. *tempus* is the central term of this letter (as Hijmans 1976: 136 notes in his analysis of *Ep.* 1's structure).   **in huius rei unius fugacis ac lubricae possessionem natura nos misit** 'nature has put us in possession of this fleeting and slippery thing alone'. *natura*, 'nature', first mentioned here, is a key concept in Stoic thought (see main intro. section 4). *possessio* in the sense of 'the factual physical control of corporeal things' (*OLD* 1a) also has legal overtones, though it is often used for the enjoyment of immaterial goods (*OLD* 1c). With *fugacis* cf. Hor. *Carm.* 2.14.1–2 *Eheu fugaces, Postume, Postume, | labuntur anni* (Berthet 1979). See also 1.1n. on *elabitur*.   **ex qua expellit quicumque uult** 'from which [possession] anyone who wishes evicts us'. How is not here specified but the phrase hints at the arbitrary nature of death, which may come at any time and at the hands of even the humblest slave (cf. 4.8 *nemo non seruus habet in te uitae necisque arbitrium*).   **mortalium:** the term highlights human transience.   **ut quae minima et uilissima sunt, certe reparabilia, imputari sibi cum impetrauere patiantur** 'that whatever things are most trivial and insignificant (and certainly replaceable), when they have acquired them, they allow to be charged to their account'. *reparabilia* (as Lotito 2001: 167 notes) evokes Virgil's contrasting characterisation of time (*G.* 3.284 *fugit irreparabile tempus, A.* 10.467–8 *stat sua cuique dies, breue et irreparabile tempus | omnibus est uitae*). *imputari sibi*: in a semi-technical accounting sense (*OLD* 1b).   **qui tempus accepit** 'one who has taken over another's time' (*OLD accipio* 4).   **ne gratus quidem** 'not even one who acknowledges the debt'.

4 interrogabis fortasse 'You will perhaps ask'. S frequently includes an imagined objection or question, which his correspondent might pose, thus reinforcing the sense of an ongoing dialogue between friends (the interjections need not always be attributed to L himself, though here *tibi* later in the sentence suggests it is L who is being addressed).   **quid ego faciam** 'how I behave'. The letter's stylistic register now shifts from paraenesis to confession, as its focus moves to the author. Does he practise what he preaches? S is quick to admit, in a self-deprecating manner, that he does not always manage this.   **ratio . . . impensae:** another semi-technical accounting term. 'The reckoning of my expenditure is correct.' Cf. also in relation to time: *Brev.* 17.5, *Tranq.* 3.8, Plin. *Ep.* 1.9.1 *singulis diebus in urbe ratio aut constet aut constare uideatur* (perhaps influenced by

S). Later letters offer occasional illustrations of exactly how S spends his time (e.g. 83.1 *Singulos dies tibi meos et quidem totos indicari iubes*, apparently in response to a specific request).   **non possum dicere nihil perdere:** sc. *me.*   **quid... quare... quemadmodum:** compressed tricolon. Though S still wastes time, he at least keeps a detailed account of how he spends it. This sentence offers an abbreviated, time-focused, version of the process of daily self-scrutiny, which S repeatedly advocates (in greatest detail in *De ira* 3.36; Ker 2009b).   **paupertatis:** here invoked metaphorically in relation to time, with *reddam* continuing the financial imagery of *ratio, constat, impensae, perdere.*   **omnes ignoscunt, nemo succurrit**: characteristically gnomic use of asyndeton.

5 quid ergo est? A rhetorical question introducing the letter's summation and conclusion (*OLD ergo* 2).   **non puto pauperem... sat est:** poverty recurs repeatedly as a concern in the letters (see intro. to *Ep.* 18), often with the admonishment to be satisfied with what you have (e.g. 2.5–6), a common theme esp. in Horace (e.g. *Ep.* 1.12.3–4 *tolle querellas | pauper enim non est, cui rerum suppetit usus*). **quantulumcumque**: colloquial (cf. 77.3 in relation to time).   **serues tua** 'keep what is your own'. *serues*: subj. following *malo*, sc. *ut. tua*: cf. *Ep.* 7 end *introrsus bona tua spectent* (Maurach 1970: 28–9).   **bono tempore** 'in good time', an expression otherwise unattested.   **incipies** perhaps echoes Hor. *Ep.* 1.2.40–1, *sapere aude | incipe*. Cf. Maurach 1970: 25.   **maioribus nostris** 'to our ancestors'. The phrase (invariably positive) is often deployed by Cicero to emphasise the wisdom of long-established Roman practice (or to present a practice as long established). Sallust and Livy also make speakers invoke *maiores* in a positive sense, generally in relation to the preservation of institutions and practices (e.g. Sal. *Cat.* 12.3, Liv. 5.52.8). In some contexts the ways of the *maiores* are specifically contrasted with the teachings of Greek philosophers (Cic. *N.D.* 3.6, *Div.* 1.84). A Roman reader with reservations about philosophy and its Greek antecedents would perhaps find S's initial deference to the wisdom of earlier Romans reassuring. S often uses individual Romans of earlier generations as *exempla* (see e.g. *Ep.* 24 on Cato, *Ep.* 86 on Scipio). At 44.3, however, S will urge L to claim earlier philosophers such as Socrates, Cleanthes and Plato as his *maiores*, by acting in a manner worthy of them (*omnes hi maiores tui sunt, si te illis geris dignum*).   **sera parsimonia in fundo est** 'It is late to be sparing when you're at the bottom of the barrel.' This concluding thought is suggestively ambiguous (is it already too late for S? Henderson 2004: 7). For the thought cf. 108.26, Persius 2.51 *nequiquam fundo suspiret nummus in imo*. A version of the same proverb occurs in Hes. *Op.* 369 (presumably known to S). S is happy (at least in the earlier letters where he regularly quotes Epicurus) to appropriate any writer's insights for his own purposes, claiming them as common property (cf. e.g. 8.8, 12.11 *quod uerum est, meum est*, 21.9). As Wilson (2001: 176) comments, 'the voice of philosophical authority is displaced from Seneca onto the broad philosophical tradition'. **non... tantum... sed:** this corrective form recurs often in the letters, e.g. 5.1, 8.2, 24.8, 46.2. **pessimum:** that the final part of one's life is the least valuable is, however, contradicted by 12.4–6(nn.). **uale:** standard epistolary close.

LETTER 7

The issue of the relationship between the would-be philosopher and the mass of humanity is first introduced in *Ep.* 5, where S advises L not to cut himself off from the rest of society by adopting the ostentatiously austere lifestyle often associated with philosophers. Only by exhibiting *sensus communis, humanitas* and *congregatio* can one hope to persuade others to follow one's own example (5.4). *Ep.* 6, too, stressed the importance of community, of sharing the goods of philosophy, at least with those who can value them; contact with individuals such as Zeno or Socrates conferred great benefit on their followers. However, *Ep.* 7 opens by warning L of the dangers of mixing with crowds of people and thus coming to share their vices (a concern of *VB* 1.4–5, as well as later letters, 32.2, 103.1–2, 123.6). To drive home his point, S conjures up the first narrative episode in the letters, a trip to the arena – a shocking and intense scene of taunts, screams and bloodshed.

For all the letters' vividness, only a few tantalising glimpses of urban life are offered (cf. e.g. *Ep.* 56 evoking the noises of the bathhouse). Rome itself is scarcely mentioned, its absence sometimes conspicuous, as in *Ep.* 91, which, opening with a friend's grief at a terrible conflagration in Lugdunum, goes on to other instances of devastated cities, without any explicit reference to Rome – despite the massive fire of 64, which took place shortly before the Lugdunum disaster (Tac. *Ann.* 16.13.3). For Henderson (2004: 13) *Ep.* 7 'is as close as we come to Rome'.

In *Ep.* 7, S advises that the would-be philosopher should avoid mixing with the crowd (§§1–2), associating instead with the philosophically inclined few or even avoiding company altogether to concentrate on his own philosophical health (§§8–12). S is highly critical of these public executions and of those who derive pleasure from them (§§3–4). However, his main concern is not the suffering of those who are forced to fight one another to the death but the effect on the spectator, whose mental composure is disturbed (§5). Bad company corrupts even those most disposed towards virtue (§§6–7). In §2 S associates the games in general with *uoluptas*, dangerous because it is often the means by which *uitia* may infect the unwary. Such is the power of the reprehensible pleasure experienced by the crowd, warns S, that it may undermine the resolve even of those (such as Socrates or Cato) noted for their moral strength (§6). Thus, while it is the horror of these spectacles which receives more explicit emphasis here, the pleasure associated with them is also acknowledged. The subject of the *turba* is continued immediately in *Ep.* 8, where S ostensibly tackles L's concern that the advice to withdraw offered in *Ep.* 7 goes against the Stoic advocacy of public service.

Powerful images serve to structure *Ep.* 7. As often in the letters, S compares moral weakness to physical illness at §1. The analogy acquires greater significance in the light of S's repeated and detailed reference to his own poor physical health in later letters (e.g. 54, 78). The spreading of vices as if by contagion at §2 and §7 continues this physical imagery (for the contagious nature of vice cf. *De ira* 3.8.1–2 *sumuntur a conuersantibus mores et ut quaedam in contactos corporis uitia transiliunt, ita animus mala sua proximis tradit, Tranq.* 7.3 *serpunt enim uitia et in proximum quemque transiliunt et contactu nocent*). The imagery of physical sores is picked up by *ulceribus meis* in the next letter (8.2).

Another important set of images relates to the idea of spectacle (S often uses imagery derived from the games; see Solimano 1991: 64–91). The dangers posed by visual pleasure are a particular concern of ancient critics (cf. e.g. Var. *L.* 8.80, Pl. *Resp.* 439e–440a on Leontius' desire to look at corpses, Fredrick 2002: 1–30, Bartsch 2006: 162). S contrasts the position of the audience at the games, changed for the worse by what they see, with the philosopher observing his own philosophical state or that of his peers (cf. §4 *spectatoribus*, §5 *ut hoc spectes*, §11 *quo . . . spectaret* and *haec . . . theatrum sumus*, §12 *introrsus bona tua spectent*). We move from the dehumanising jeers and slaughter of the arena to the intense and edifying communion of philosophical dialogue – or indeed introspection. Here, the gaze may be metaphorical (Armisen-Marchetti 1989: 258 on the 'théâtre intérieure' of the letters). This kind of oscillating perspective is characteristic of S's writing (cf. the contrast drawn at 118.1–4 between the struggle for political advancement in the hurly burly of the *comitia* in Cicero's time and the quest for philosophical advancement pursued in the internalised *comitium* of the would-be wise man).

S's emphatic disapproval of the gruesome entertainment described in *Ep.* 7 has often been taken to show that at least some Romans shared modern feelings of revulsion at the arena games generally (see e.g. Gibbon 1994: II.139). It is important to distinguish, however, between those condemned to die in the arena, *noxii*, who might be forced to fight, though without training – and sometimes without weapons (on *noxii* see Kyle 1998: 91–5) – on the one hand and, on the other, spectacles involving trained gladiators (a category which includes those condemned *ad ludos*, the gladiatorial training schools). As Wistrand stresses, it is the former spectacle which is the subject of S's discussion (1990: 42; cf. Kyle 1998: 3–4). Elsewhere S often uses the trained gladiator (esp. as regards his disposition towards the prospect of death) as a model for the would-be wise man (see e.g. 30.8, 93.12, Gunderson 1996; though, as Bartsch (2006: 161) notes, his comment at 95.33 *quem erudiri ad inferenda accipiendaque uulnera nefas erat* remains puzzling). It is striking that he (and other elite writers, notably Cicero) tend to identify rather with the gladiator facing death than with the one inflicting it (e.g. 30.8, Edwards 2007: 66–77). Observing death in *Ep.* 7, however (in contrast to many other letters, e.g. 24, 30, 77), is no source of edification; unlike trained gladiators, the victims show no bravery in meeting their end.

Other Roman writers recommend that enjoyment of games of any sort (including the theatre and the circus) be avoided as not consonant with the dignity proper to members of the Roman elite (e.g. Cic. *Fam.* 7.1.3 = 24 SB, Plin. *Ep.* 9.6, disdaining circus games; see Wiedemann 1992: 141, Gunderson 1996). Such a concern is less evident here; but, despite S's frequent Stoic stress on the irrelevance of social status to the good life (e.g. *Ep.* 44), one might argue, along the lines of Habinek 1998: 141, that in urging displays of philosophic impassivity towards popular entertainments S may not be immune to considerations of social distinction (cf. the concerns expressed by Cicero in *Fam.* 7.1.1–3 = SB 24 to M. Marius contrasting public games with more valuable ways of spending time).

This letter, with its vivid evocation of the public slaughter of criminals in the arena, may be compared with August. *Conf.* 6.8, which describes how Alypius, at first repulsed by the horrors of gladiatorial combat, is, when he watches as part of an enthusiastic crowd, overcome by the *uoluptas* of the spectacle (*percussus est grauiore uulnere in anima quam ille in corpore*). Indeed, S's letter may perhaps have influenced the critiques of the games articulated by a number of early Christian writers, such as Tertullian and Lactantius. See below §4n. (citing Lactant. *Div. inst.*) and also e.g. Tert. *De spect.* 15.3, 5 'There is no spectacle without disturbance to the spirit ... For even if a man enjoys spectacles modestly and uprightly, in accordance with his status or age or even natural disposition, his soul is not unstirred and he is not without a silent rousing of the spirit.'

Commentaries: Summers, Scarpat (b), Motto, Costa, Richardson-Hay.
For pagan Roman attitudes to the spectacle of slaughter in the arena see the discussions by Wiedemann 1992, Barton 1993, Gunderson 1996, Hopkins and Beard 2005, Futrell 2006, Edwards 2007 ch. 2. Fagan 2011 uses a social–psychological approach to explore the responses of spectators. On executions as spectacles see particularly Coleman 1990, Kyle 1998.

1 Quid...quaeris? as often, S implies that his letter has been occasioned by a question posed by his correspondent, apparently asking what, in his quest for mental tranquillity, he should avoid. *tibi* can also be the reader (see further main intro. section 7). **existimes** 'you should think'. Some manuscripts have *existimem*, thus 'what *I* think ought to be avoided by you'. The latter reading would imply a greater degree of authority on the part of S as adviser, the former a greater degree of independence on the part of L as pupil. **turbam:** the single-word sentence makes a striking answer to S's opening. S regularly opens letters with short, sharp sentences, cf. e.g. *Ep.* 18, 19, 27, 45, 61. As well as 'crowd', *turba* can mean 'disorder' or 'confusion'; cf. *Marc.* 22.1 *in tanta inconstantia turbaque rerum nihil nisi quod praeterit certum est.* The crowd will be S's primary concern in this letter. For philosophical advice to avoid the crowd cf. Cic. *Tusc.* 2.4 *philosophia... multitudinem consulto ipsa fugiens.* **nondum illi tuto committeris** 'you are not yet entrusted to it safely'. S emphasises the dynamic nature of L's philosophical condition; he is not yet ready to face the test of mixing with a crowd but may become so. For the invulnerability of the *sapiens* cf. *Constant.* 2.3 *tutus est sapiens nec ulla affici aut iniuria aut contumelia potest.* **ego... imbecillitatem meam:** S does not present his own state as perfect. Though more philosophically advanced than L, he too is still a *proficiens*, and susceptible to the dangers of mixing with the morally reprobate (cf. e.g. *Ep.* 56). S's own weakness (touched on in 1.1) is here more prominent. For the Stoic view of philosophical progress as well as S's presentation of his own level of development see main intro. section 4. **mores** 'moral character', here that of the individual. The previous letter stressed the beneficial influence one might derive from spending time with men of great virtue (6.6 *Plato... plus ex moribus quam ex uerbis Socratis traxit*). **refero** 'bring home', balancing *extuli*, the first in a series of three antitheses. **ex eo quod composui** 'from the mental calm I have achieved'. *componere* is often used by S for the process by which philosophical exercise produces a state of mental calm (cf. e.g. 2.1, 4.1, 23.7, 71.19–20, 95.57, 120.11). **turbatur:** S emphasises the association between the crowd and mental disturbance through verbal echo, *turba... turbatur.* The words are etymologically linked (*OLD turbo* [*turba* + *-o*]). **quod aegris euenit... hoc accidit nobis:** medical metaphors and images, first introduced at 6.1, occur extensively throughout the letters (cf. e.g. 53.5–9nn., 95.15–29, Armisen-Marchetti 1989: 133–5; see further main intro. section 9). Note the repetition of *imbecillitas.* **proferantur** 'are taken out in public' *OLD* 6b.

2 conuersatio 'association', 'familiarity' (*OLD* 2). **nemo non** 'there is no one who does not', i.e. everyone (Traina 1987: 29–30). **allinit** 'besmears'. The third verb in this tricolon is especially vivid. In its literal sense it is used pejoratively of substances such as mud (e.g. *Nat.* 3.20.4). The image of vice being physically transferred reappears at §7 *rubiginem affricuit*. The notion of unpleasant physical contact fits well with S's evocation of the crush of public spectacles.   **quo maior ... est, hoc ... plus est** 'the greater is the crowd with whom we mix, the greater is the danger'.   **bonis moribus:** at 5.5 there is a clear distinction between *bonos mores et publicos*, where the former are the ways of *sapiens*.   **in aliquo spectaculo:** S here refers to the dangerous pleasures associated with all games, not just gladiatorial combats (*spectacula* include the circus and the theatre, as well as wild-beast fights and gladiatorial shows).   **desidere** 'to sit', 'to linger', with connotations of idleness (cf. *deses* 'idle', 'inactive', 'sluggish').   **per uoluptatem:** the nature of the *spectaculum* here has not yet been made clear, but on the pleasure of watching murderous games cf. 95.33 (where, as part of a general attack on the power of *uoluptas*, S deplores that *homo, res sacra homini, iam per lusum ac iocum occiditur*) and more generally Edwards 2007: 62–6.   **uitia ... surrepunt** 'vices creep up', 'attack stealthily' (*OLD surripio* 2). As often in S, vices are personified, or rather, presented in bestial form, cf. 45.7 *uitia ... obrepunt*, 90.6 *surrepentibus uitiis*. The spectators themselves are associated with animals in §4.

3 quid me existimas dicere? such rhetorical questions are associated with the so-called diatribe tradition (see main intro. section 8).   **auarior ... luxuriosior?** L is imagined suggesting possible vices, here vices which characteristically feature in Roman accounts of moral decline. See e.g. Sal. *Cat.* 5.8 *incitabant praeterea corrupti ciuitatis mores, quos pessuma ac diuorsa inter se mala, luxuria atque auaritia uexabant*.   **immo uero:** S often uses the corrective *immo* (Traina 1987: 32); cruelty is presented as a worse vice.   **crudelior:** cf. *Clem.* 1.25.1 *crudelitas minime humanum malum*.   **inhumanior, quia inter homines fui** 'more inhuman because I have been among human beings'. *inhumanus* in the sense of lacking in human feeling (*OLD* 2); cf. 5.4 *hoc primum philosophia promittit, sensum communem, humanitatem et congregationem*. The paradox (highlighted here by *figura etymologica*) is emphasised throughout *Ep.* 7 by repetition of *homines* and cognate words.   **casu ... incidi** 'by chance ... I happened upon'. S often organises a letter around what he presents as a chance incident from everyday life; cf. e.g. *Ep.* 12, ostensibly provoked by a visit to S's villa (see below), and *Ep.* 55, presented as inspired by a ride in a litter.   **meridianum spectaculum:** on the basis of this passage and another from Tertullian (*Apol.* 15.5 *risimus et inter ludicras meridianorum crudelitates*), it is often inferred that the standard programme for gladiatorial games involved a morning of fights between trained men and wild beasts (*uenationes*; Sen. *Ep.* 70.20 refers to a beast fighter in the *matutina spectacula*, cf. §4 below *mane ... leonibus*), a midday slot used for fights between convicted criminals, then combats of fully armed professional gladiators later in the afternoon (cf. Wiedemann 1992: 55, Kyle 1998: 91–2, Futrell 2006: 84–119, Fagan 2011: 5–6). Suetonius refers to lunchtime combats as if they were generally regarded as trivial – though not by Claudius, who watched while others went off to eat (*Claud.* 34.2). Elsewhere, however, executions appear as a significant attraction (Fagan 2011: 184–5). S's apparent surprise at discovering the nature of the show might suggest that comedy interludes were the usual lunchtime fare (cf. Hopkins and Beard 2005: 70–3). But perhaps 'it is . . . dangerous to attempt to reconstruct a "typical" *munus*', as Edmondson (1996: 77) comments. **lusus . . . et sales** 'light-hearted amusements'. **aliquid laxamenti** 'some respite'. *laxamenti* (*OLD* 2) is partitive gen. (G-L §369). **quo . . . acquiescant** 'with which human eyes might take a holiday from the sight of human blood' (final subj.). The repetition of cognate terms *hominum . . . humano* ironically reinforces the emphasis on *inhumanior* in the previous sentence. **contra est:** a characteristically terse corrective preliminary to the mordant description of the midday scene of slaughter. **misericordia:** ironic. Cf. *Med.* 904–5 *quidquid admissum est adhuc,* | *pietas uocetur.* **omissis nugis** 'trifling put aside', abl. abs. **mera homicidia** 'unadulterated murder'. The echo of *meridianum* might be read as reinforcing the association. The word *merus* is normally used of undiluted liquids, esp. wine (*OLD* 2). The intoxicating effect of watching such spectacles may be hinted at; cf. Augustine's description of the effects of the show on Alypius (*Conf.* 6.8) *cruenta uoluptate inebriebatur.* **numquam frustra manum mittunt** 'no blow falls without effect'. The use of *frustra* implicates the reader in the crowd's desire for blood (cf. note on §4 *spectatoribus*). For similar expressions see Liv. 21.8.9 *nullo inter arma corporaque uano intercidente telo,* Luc. 6.190 *nulla fuit non certa manus.*

4 ordinariis paribus et postulaticiis: *ordinarii pares* are the regular pairs of trained gladiators. The *postulaticii* (a term rarely attested) are presumably men shown by special request (from *postulo* 'demand', 'request'). Cf. Suet. *Dom.* 4.1 'he even granted the people the privilege of calling for (*postulandi*) two pairs of gladiators from his own school'. **quidni praeferant?** 'And why shouldn't they prefer it?' Subjunctive following *quidni* (*OLD*) is potential. An ironical question – as if the point of the show was to have people killed as quickly as possible. Note the series of short statements and questions, without conjunction. The tone is harsh. **quo munimenta?** 'What is the point of armour?' *quo* = 'for what purpose', with a verb (e.g. *habeant*) understood. For fighting untaught and unarmed see also 95.33 *quem erudiri ad inferenda accipiendaque uulnera nefas est, is iam nudus inermisque producitur satisque spectaculi ex homine mors est.* **artes:** i.e. the skills of the trained gladiator to attack and defend (and to welcome death when necessary), skills which these *noxii* are without.   **mortis morae:** sarcastic paronomasia.   **spectatoribus:** grammatically parallel to *leonibus et ursis* (the phrases nicely balanced by *mane* and *meridie*), the spectators are assimilated to them and presented as equally responsible for human deaths (cf. *De ira* 1.2.4, where spectators of gladiatorial games are compared to enemies in war). The late third-/early fourth-century Christian writer Lactantius deploys a similar paradox in stressing the guilt of those who watch in the arena deaths of condemned criminals (*Div. inst.* 6.20.10) *nam qui hominem quamuis ob merita damnatum in conspectu suo iugulari pro uoluptate computat conscientiam suam polluit, tam scilicet quam si homicidii quod fit spectator et particeps fiat.*   **interfectores ... caedem** 'they order that those who have killed be exposed to those who will kill them and they keep the winner for further slaughter'. In regular gladiatorial combat, by contrast, the victorious member of a pair would, it seems, normally be granted a respite from fighting at least until the next day (Ville 1981: 324–5, 396–7). *interfectores interfecturis:* use of the fut. partic. makes this phrase characteristically compressed (cf. e.g. 36.11, 70.11, *Brev.* 3.4).   **ferro et igne res geritur** 'Fire and the sword keep things going.' Participants were apparently compelled to continue fighting by guards armed with swords and brands, cf. §5 *occide, uerbera, ure!*, Mart. *Sp.* 19.1 *qui modo per totam flammis stimulatus arenam* and Tert. *De spect.* 21 *gladiatorem ad homicidium flagellis et uirgis compellat inuitum*. These words also evoke the oath sworn by professional gladiators who undertook to suffer branding, being bound in chains or death by the sword, an oath invoked by S at 37.1, 71.2–3, also Petr. 117.5 (cf. Ville 1981: 47, 246–55, Barton 1993: 14–17).   **dum uacat harena** 'in the interval', i.e. before the trained gladiators return. Little importance is attributed to these human deaths by the spectators; cf. §5 *interim iugulentur homines ne nihil agatur*.

5 '**sed latrocinium fecit aliquis . . .**': the imagined objection is a characteristic associated with the diatribe tradition and often to be found in S's letters (see main intro. section 8).   **ille meruit ut hoc pateretur:** it is not clear whether *quia occidit . . . pateretur* is spoken by S or by his imagined interlocutor. If by S, then he seems to concede the justice of the punishment, though his words might be read ironically. Summers *ad loc.* offers a supplement (*'sed latrocinium fecit aliquis' quid ergo? occidit hominem? 'occidit hominem.' quia occidit ille meruit ut hoc pateretur . . .*) which would give sarcastic emphasis to the interlocutor's self-righteous assertion that the criminal deserves to die because he has killed a man.   **tu quid meruisti miser ut hoc spectes?** 'What have you done, you wretch, to deserve looking at this?' An unusual use of *mereo* (cf. *OLD* 4b; *TLL* VIII.808.34–50). Elsewhere S offers a somewhat more sympathetic articulation of the viewer's response (*De ira* 2.2.4): *mouet mentes et atrox pictura et iustissimorum*

suppliciorum tristis aspectus 'our minds are also moved by the dreadful image and sad spectacle of even justified torments'. Christian Lactantius, when warning against the pleasures of watching people killed (*Div. inst.* 6.20.10), feels obliged to add, *quamuis ob meritum* 'no matter how justly condemned'. **'occide . . . excipiant':** three imperatives (*occide, uerbera, ure*, directed at the armed guards, cf. §4 *ferro et igne*), followed by three brief rhetorical questions (all starting *quare*), culminate in two jussive subjunctives (*agatur, excipiant*) and, echoing the spectators' staccato shouts, serve to convey their obtuse cruelty. The heated violence of the writing is typical of S. On the psychology of the spectators in relation to these executions, see Fagan 2011: 133–5, 252–3, citing similar exclamations in martyr acts (cf. Euseb. *Hist. eccl.* 5.138–60). **parum audacter occidit:** presumably *ocādit* 'he kills' rather than *occidit* 'he dies'. **parum libenter moritur:** Roman audiences admired those who died bravely in the arena (cf. e.g. Cic. *Mil.* 92). S himself elsewhere invokes the brave death of a gladiator as a source of edification (30.8). Here, those criticising the *noxii* for their cowardice in dying are presented as lacking all humanity; cf. S's criticism (*De ira* 1.2.4) of the anger of the *populus* which feels it an injury when gladiators *non libenter pereunt*. **intermissum est spectaculum** 'there's a break in the main show'. **iugulentur:** regularly used in this sense, 'to kill by cutting the throat' (*OLD* 1), for arena killings. **age . . . intellegitis:** *age*, commonly used in colloquial Latin to mean 'come now' (cf. *OLD* 24), remains in the singular, while *intellegitis* refers to the crowd in the plural. **mala exempla in eos redundare qui faciunt** 'bad examples rebound on those who set them'. Cf. *Thy.* 311 *saepe in magistratum scelera redierunt sua*. Here the sense is that those who set no value on human life may find their own lives held equally cheap. **eum docetis esse crudelem qui non potest discere** 'you are teaching cruelty to one who cannot learn it', presumably the fighter who *parum audacter occidit*. His imminent death makes learning lessons of any kind an impossibility.

6 subducendus populo est tener animus et parum tenax recti 'a vulnerable mind, insufficiently committed to what is right, is to be kept away from the crowd'. For a similar use of *subduco* see 119.11. *populus* here is, in a sense, equivalent (*OLD* 4) to *turba*, but there has been a subtle shift from the literal sense of 'crowd' to the idea of 'the common herd' (*OLD* 3b). Cf. 8.3 *uitate quaecumque uulgo placent*. The verbal similarity between *tener* 'susceptible' and *tenax recti* 'committed to the right way' draws attention to their contrasting meanings. For the latter cf. Hor. *Carm.* 3.3.1–2 *Iustum et tenacem | propositi uirum* 'the man who is just and adheres to his course'. S's response to the moral damage caused by the games is not that they should be abolished but that the would-be philosopher should absent himself from them. Only the true *sapiens* can withstand the trials of mixing with the crowd. **facile transitur ad plures** 'it is easy to become one of the many'. *transitur* is impersonal. **Socrati et Catoni et Laelio:** these three names are all used regularly by S to represent figures of outstanding virtue (that of Cato the most frequently, see 24.6(n.)). Socrates (first mentioned at 6.6) is the fifth-century BCE Athenian philosopher, best known from the works of Plato. Cato (first mentioned here) could be either Cato the Censor (who flourished in the early second century BCE) or his descendant, Cato the Younger (a noted Stoic who flourished in the late republic); both were admired for their upright morals (on the Censor see the intro. to *Ep.* 86 below; Cato the Younger appears with particular frequency in the letters, see 24.6n.). Laelius is presumably Gaius Laelius, used by Cicero as one of the major protagonists in his philosophical dialogues *Laelius de amicitia* and *De republica* (and nicknamed *sapiens*; Cic. *Off.* 2.40). Laelius, too, appears repeatedly (cf. e.g. 11.10, 25.6, 64.10n.). S regularly cites both Greeks and Romans as moral *exempla* (see intro. to *Ep.* 24). **excutere** 'to expel' (lit. 'shake out'), a word with violent connotations (*OLD* 3; Foucault 1986: 61–2, Rimell 2015a: 137-47). **dissimilis** 'of different moral character'. **qui cum maxime concinnamus ingenium** 'we who are even now in the process of ordering our minds'. A very striking expression (*concinno* is elsewhere used only of objects or physical features, though cf. Tert. *Cult. fem.* 2.5.3). For the thought cf. *componere* (§1n.). *cum maxime* 'at that very moment' (*OLD maxime* 6b), emphatic, is a common phrase in S; cf. e.g. 12.6, 18.1, 23.10. On *ingenium* see Graver 2014: 281–4. **impetum uitiorum:** *impetus* is regularly used of violent mental impulses in philosophical Latin, though it retains its military overtones, particularly here where S speaks of the vices' great retinue. S often uses military metaphors to convey the dangers posed by vices and the courage needed to oppose them (see main intro. section 9). The metaphor is continued in §7.

7 S now switches his focus to the moral damage which may be caused even by a single corrupt companion. **unum exemplum ... multum mali facit:** Roman writers (e.g. Quint. *Inst.* 12.2.30) were especially sensitive to the persuasive power of example (often presented as more effective than speech). At 6.7 S contends that Plato and Aristotle derived more benefit from Socrates' deeds than from his words. The vices of luxury and avarice were often represented as corroding Roman society generally (see above §3 *auarior ... luxuriosior?*). **eneruat et mollit:** as often in S, luxury is presented as undermining manhood (cf. e.g. 82.2, 90.19). **rubiginem suam affricuit** 'rubs his sores against', again the imagery of contagion (cf. §2 *allinit*). *rubigo*, originally 'rust', came also to mean foul deposits in the mouth or corroding sores. Here it is used metaphorically for 'malice' (*OLD* 3b; cf. 95.36 at *illis ... mala consuetudine obsessis diu rubigo animorum* *effricanda est*). The imagery is vividly physical; cf. e.g. Col. 7.5.6 of sheep with scabies: *uitiosum locum pecudes . . . arbori affricant*. S often uses the perfect tense in illustrations. **publice:** thus inflicting more extensive damage than those private encounters (*conuictor . . . uicinus . . . comes*).

8 necesse est aut imiteris aut oderis 'You must either imitate them or loathe them.' S characteristically offers exclusive alternatives only to reject both. The point is made neater through homoeoteleuton: *imiteris* pres. subj. (dep.), *oderis* pf. subj. with present meaning. S elsewhere (*De ira* 1.14.2, 2.28.8) urges rather that we should not hate those who err, since we ourselves are in this category. **neue similis . . . dissimiles sunt:** the balanced structure of the sentence (*neue . . . quia . . . neue . . . quia . . .*) is emphasised by the use of parallel terms in a typically Senecan manner. Perhaps a return to the sentiment expressed at 5.1–3 (and echoed, with later qualification, at 18.3) that one should avoid marking oneself out as ostentatiously different from the crowd. **recede in te ipse:** S advises L to turn inwards. He should keep company only with those who are disposed to help him towards his philosophical goals or who are at least disposed to pursue such goals themselves (cf. 19.11, 21). This advocacy of withdrawal (even if only partial) is very close to the position set out in *De otio* which may have been written at around the time S was composing the letters (see Williams for discussion of the dating of *De otio*). **mutuo:** the positive interchange here balances the vicious *mutuos ictus* in §5. **homines:** here those who are truly human rather than the inhuman crowd of §3. **dum docent discunt:** this emphasis on interdependence of pupil and teacher has implications for relations between S and L (cf. 6.4 *gaudeo discere, ut doceam*). Contrast the failed attempt to impart a lesson in cruelty with which §5 ends.

9 non est quod . . . 'there is no reason why'. The commonest construction used by S in the letters for second-person prohibitions (cf. e.g. 21.9, 33.3, 46.3, Hine 2005: 225; cf. K–S II.278–9). **gloria publicandi ingenii** 'the glory of making known your abilities'. *gloria* is an ambivalent term in S. See 21.3(n.) (Newman 2008, Edwards 2017b). On *ingenium* in S see Graver 1998, 2014 (cf. *Epp.* 21, 114). **producat in medium** 'should bring before the public' (*OLD medium* 3b). There is an idea of ostentation here. **recitare** 'to make a public reading of one's work' (*OLD* 1). **disputare** 'to lecture', 'to engage in public philosophical debate' (*OLD* 1). **mercem** 'wares'. A commercial image anticipating the treatment of the *sententiae* offered by S in settlement of a 'debt' to L (§10). Cf. 1.4(n.). **aliquis . . . formandus . . . ad intellectum tui:** other parallels (esp. that noted under §10 *mihi hodie didicerim*) encourage the reader to see this as an implicit comment on S's relationship with L, who is being formed as an intelligent reader of S's writings. S makes extensive use of the gerundive in preference to more periphrastic ways of expressing obligation.   **si tibi didicisti:** this emphasis on learning for oneself rather than to impress others (cf. §12 *introrsus bona tua spectent*) has numerous philosophical precedents but is contrary to (or perhaps an internalisation of) the traditional Roman practice of seeing oneself in others' eyes (cf. §11 *theatrum sumus*).

10 mihi hodie didicerim: the verbal parallel with §9 *tibi didicisti* confirms the impression that S's advice should be seen as applying as much to himself as to L; he now wants to share with L what he has learned. *hodie*: S often refers to his concluding quotations as a daily offering (e.g. 2.5, 4.10, 6.7). Though the letters are not written daily, each is anchored to a particular (if unspecified) day.   **egregie dicta . . . tria:** as in all the letters in the early part of the collection (1–29), S concludes with *sententiae* taken from a variety of sources (most often the writings of Epicurus). Usually only one is offered.   **sensum** 'meaning'.   **ex quibus . . . in debitum** 'one of which this letter dispatches in payment of its debt'. *in debitum* here in the sense (*OLD in* 14) of 'as far as' (in contrast to more usual *debitum* as object of *soluere*, 102.19, *Ben.* 4.32.4 and often in Justinian's *Digesta*, e.g. 4.4.25. pr. 2). S often presents L as claiming the final *sententia* of a letter as something owed (6.7, 9.20, 12.10). Numerous variants on this financial image are explored in the first part of the collection (cf. e.g. 5.7 *huius . . . diei lucellum*, 8.10 *hoc non imputo in solutum*, 15.9 *una mercedula*).   **in antecessum** 'in advance' (the word *antecessus* occurs only in this phrase, *OLD*).   **Democritus:** fifth-century BCE Greek cosmologist from Abdera, best known for his view that the world is composed of atoms (in this a precursor of Epicurus). He reappears at 79.14 and 90.32(n.). S's quotation = fr. 302a Diels–Kranz.   **unus . . . pro uno:** cf. Cic. *Att.* 2.5.1 = 50 SB (on Cato) *qui mihi unus est pro centum milibus*. Democritus was perhaps echoing Heraclitus (fr. 49 Diels) 'one man is to me worth tens of thousands, if he is the best'. A similar anecdote is attributed to Antimachus (Cic. *Brut.* 191), who, deserted by the rest of his audience, commented that Plato alone was as good as a hundred thousand.

11 bene et ille, quisquis fuit . . . , cum quaereretur ab illo . . . , inquit: 'he, too, whoever it was . . . , when someone asked him . . . , said rightly'.   **quo tanta diligentia . . . spectaret** 'what was the purpose of such conscientiousness . . .'   **uni ex consortibus:** S locates Epicurus' observation in the context of a correspondence with one of his followers, parallel to his own with L.   **'haec . . . theatrum sumus':** each in turn plays the role of spectator and performer. This quotation from Epicurus (fr. 208 Usener = 129 Arrighetti) revives the theme of spectacles, now to constructive effect.

Epicurus, like S, invokes the theatrical metaphor through the medium of correspondence. Henderson (2004: 13) comments: 'the spectacle of Epistolarity is itself a scene where "Three's a crowd"'; cf. 102.11, the judgement of one good man is sufficient. We might compare Persius' comments at the start of *Sat.* 1, preferring *aut duo aut nemo* appreciative readers to undiscerning crowds.

12 condenda 'to be stored up'.   **contemnas uoluptatem** emphasises again that it is pleasure which poses the most insidious threat to the *proficiens* who associates with the crowd.   **assensione:** according to Stoic understanding, emotions (which are necessarily disturbing) are the consequence of assenting (an act of judgement) to an impression that something actually indifferent is good or bad (see e.g. 113.18, *De ira* 2.3.1–4, Inwood 2005: ch. 3, Graver 2007: 94–9). The *sapiens*, understanding that only virtue is good, and only its absence bad, has learned not to assent to such impressions. Here, S advises L not to be misled by the crowd's mistaken understanding of this spectacle as a source of pleasure.   **introrsus bona tua spectent:** the final word plays upon a recurrent theme of the letter (cf. §5 *ut hoc spectes* and §11 *quo spectaret*).

LETTER 12

Ep. 12 concludes Book 1, developing further the concern with *securitas* evident particularly in *Epp.* 9 and 10. Returning to some themes of the first letter, notably death and time, it frames the book (though Maurach 1970: 74 sees *Ep.* 12 as opening a new phase in the letters, comprising 12–15). While *Ep.* 11 offered an optimistic picture of a younger man intent on making philosophical progress, *Ep.* 12 opens with the image of an old man who has not fully absorbed the lessons of philosophy. 11.8–10 advised L to choose a model 'good man' under whose scrutiny he should imagine himself at all times, as an incentive to becoming good himself; in *Ep.* 12 S himself figures as *exemplum* (as he promised he would in 1.4) but not a wholly positive one. Unlike most of the other letters in Book 1 (7 is another exception here), 12 offers the reader a strikingly vivid vignette. S is a landowner inspecting his country estate. *Ep.* 12's scenario evokes the kind of situation envisaged in Cato the Elder's treatise on estate management, *De agricultura*, e.g. at 2.1. In the final section of *Ep.* 11 Cato (the Elder we may infer from the contrast with his contemporary Laelius) was suggested as the kind of 'good man' who might serve as imagined observer for the would-be philosopher.

After an opening sentence summing up the significance of the scene which is about to unfold, S at 12.1 steps into the *persona* of an elderly man, who, at least at first, fails to recognise his own condition. But as he acknowledges his relationship to the decaying house, the ailing trees and finally the aged slave, he is forced to admit that he too is old (§§1–3). While the farm-manager's responses to his master are indirect, S himself shifts from indirect to direct speech. His encounter with Felicio is comic (Grant 2000 detects an echo of Plautine encounters between the irascible elderly master and his slave) but also disturbing for the reader (we wince at the master's frank critique of the slave's uselessness and decrepitude) and of course for S also. Felicio is, in Henderson's words, 'his abjected reflection' (2004: 25; the ambivalence of master–slave relationships is explored further in *Ep.* 47).

S changes role, his gaze turning inwards, as the letter modulates into a celebration of old age (§4). The analogies of §§4–5 evoke Horatian admonishments to seize ephemeral pleasures before old age supervenes; S's concern, however, is rather with savouring the pleasures particular to old age. In §§5–6, S draws on Plato's *Republic* (esp. 328d) and Cicero's *Cato maior de senectute*, though with a focus which appears more personal (and S is much less concerned here with the disadvantages of old age). In particular S can be seen as responding to two of the complaints against old age set out (and answered) in Cic. *Sen.* 15 *quod priuet fere omnibus uoluptatibus . . . quod haud procul absit a morte* (see Scarpat (b) *ad loc.* for a fuller discussion of the relationship). Old age is to be relished, even, or especially, while mortality is recognised. The topic of old age is developed further in *Epp.* 26, 45, 58, 67, 78, 83 and 104 (on S's philosophical deployment of his own ageing body see Edwards 2005b). Pliny's later treatment of old age in Book 3 of his letters also offers an interesting point of comparison (Henderson 2002: 27–30).

The discussion of human life in terms of circles, which follows (§§6–8), is not easy to interpret (the text itself is problematic, esp. in §7). S seems to propose one set of circles relating to the individual life. Of these a larger one encloses the entire period from birth to death, while smaller circles enclose different phases of life, such as childhood or adolescence. Intersecting with this set is another set of circles corresponding to different units of time, the year, the month, the day (while these may be imagined as concentric, S also emphasises the repetition of individual units). The day constitutes the crucial unit, fulfilling multiple functions; for S, the single day is the unit of time on which a philosophical approach to life should focus (cf. 4.5, 16.1, 101.8 *qui cotidie uitae suae summam manum imposuit, non indiget tempore*). Indeed, Armisen-Marchetti 1995: 563 suggests that, although S does not make explicit what he understands by 'present' time, the present day, *dies*, sometimes seems to have this sense. A well-used day, S contends at 61.1–2, is of equivalent value to a well-used life: *id agar ut mihi instar totius uitae dies sit* (cf. 74.27). Thus the smallest of the chronological circles in *Ep.* 12, the day, can on another level be equated to the largest of circles relating to the individual life.

The predictability and regularity of sunrise and sunset serve to underline the resemblance of one day to another; no day brings anything fundamentally new. At the same time, insofar as the day serves as an analogy for the life of an individual, the inevitable nature of its beginning and end works to bring acceptance of the individual's death as equally immutable (and also perhaps cyclic in some sense). The image of the circle elides birth and death. 'Change becomes continuity', as Richardson-Hay (363) comments. We might compare 102.28, where S presents an existence after death in terms of the experience of continuous light, in contrast to the alternating light and darkness associated with mortal existence. Also relevant here is the cosmic model of time invoked at *Brev.* 10.6, where S declares that the passage of present time can no more suffer delay 'than the universe or the stars, whose perpetual unceasing motion never lets them rest in the same position'.

As often, S proposes a range of strategies for facing up to and living with the certainty of death. Seneca's prime concern here is with human time, lived time, rather than cosmic time (Armisen-Marchetti 1995: 548; cf. Rist 1969: 287). The rational conception of the cycles of time is to be reinforced by the daily practice of calling death to mind. S exploits two models (§§8–9), one comic (or perhaps satiric) and one tragic (or rather epic). Neither is in itself sufficient; that of Pacuvius is presented as an explicit manifestation of his perverse moral disposition. Indeed the motives of both exemplars are problematic; their spectacular performances are not to be imitated – but they function as iconic enactments of the awareness of mortality even while, in the degree to which they differ from it, they highlight the distinctiveness of the interiorised practice commended to the would-be philosopher. The following letter, *Ep.* 13, concludes by inviting the reader to think more specifically about the manner of his or her own death and offering the edifying deaths of Cato and Socrates by way of example.

S's choice of setting in *Ep.* 12 is significant. One of the opening observations of Cato the Elder's *De agricultura* posits an equivalence between a man and his property (1.6 *idem agrum quod hominem*). Cicero's correspondence frequently articulates his concern that his properties should be fitted out in a manner becoming to his sense of self (e.g. *Att.* 1.4.3 = 9 SB, 1.8.2 = 4 SB). Also relevant to *Ep.* 12 is Horace's relationship with his Sabine farm, esp. as figured in *Ep.* 1.14 and 16 (as well as *S.* 2.6, which itself draws on Cicero's portrait (*Sen.* 46) of Cato on his Sabine estate; see Leach 1993: 285). For the villa estate as, in a sense, representing its owner, esp. in an epistolary context, see Whitton 2013 on Plin. *Ep.* 2.17 and Riggsby 2003. S in *Ep.* 12 self-consciously exploits what is already an established trope (for the fundamentally literary character of the estate described in *Ep.* 12 see Watson and Watson 2009).

Leach refers to the Sabine farm as Horace's 'ostensible sign of privacy and interior self-sufficiency'. In this respect S's evocation of his estate is similar. Horace (*Ep.* 1.14) addresses the *uilicus* of his estate. The poem offers a challenge: *certemus, spinas animone ego fortius an tu | euellas agro, et melior sit Horatius an res* (1.14.4–5). The *uilicus* is responsible for the state of the farm, Horace himself for the state of his own *animus* (though, like S, he also offers advice to remedy the moral weaknesses of others). S too interrogates his *uilicus*, taking the man to task for failing to do his job. Yet, in Hor. *Ep.* 1.14 and elsewhere, the Sabine farm figures as a place of productivity, both literary and agricultural, of relaxation and a sociability, which includes philosophical conversation; see e.g. *S.* 2.6.73–4 *utrumne | diuitiis homines an sint uirtute beati*. In Horace's case, allusions to the farm serve to suggest 'the intensity of his social bonds', reflecting the complex network of relationships which feature in these poetic letters (Leach 1993: 289; on the interrelationship between city and countryside in the *Epistles* see also De Pretis 2002: 120–2). S's villa, by contrast, at least in the first part of *Ep.* 12, offers only disturbing evidence of barrenness and decrepitude. For the moralising exploitation of a country villa compare *Ep.* 55 on Vatia's villa and *Ep.* 86 on Scipio's villa (with the acute discussion of all three in Henderson 2004).

The latter part of this letter offers a suggestive illustration of S's complex relationship with Virgil and Horace. A line from Virgil (*A.* 4.653), radically decontextualised, is quoted (12.9), so that the words of grief-stricken, frenzied Dido appear as sentiments proper to one who has achieved philosophical calm and accepts that life is complete. S transforms Dido's words from the expression of a victim of unhappy love, one who is *furens* – an emblematic instance, we might think, of the negative effects of passion – to an articulation of contentment. At the same time, numerous subtle verbal echoes recall Horace's *Odes* (a text never quoted in the letters) whose purport seems much closer to that of *Ep.* 12. Berthet's suggestion (1979) that S was reluctant to quote the *Odes* because of their Epicurean associations seems implausible given his willingness to quote Epicurus. As Berno (2014: 135) suggests, Horace's *Odes* may have been less appealing because their language is too philosophical; Virgil's emotionally potent and familiar line can serve an effective mnemonic function precisely because its recontextualisation is so drastic.

Commentaries: Summers, Scarpat (b), Costa, Richardson-Hay, (on §§1–3) Adams 2016: 227–36.

Further reading: Delatte 1950, Habinek 1982, Ronnick 1999, Viparelli 2000: 33–41, Henderson 2004: 1–17, Mann 2006, Ker 2009a: 333–41, Watson and Watson 2009, Berno 2014, Vogt-Spira 2017.

1 Quocumque me uerti 'Wherever I turn' (pf. of iterative action, G–L §567). The verb *uerti* is picked up by *conuersus* in §3 and *aduerteram* in § 4. **senectutis meae** recalls the subtitle of Cicero's *Cato maior, de senectute*, but also plays on S's name. **uideo:** while the letter offers a scene filled with memorable visual detail, what S perceives in the opening sentence is a series of prompts to a moral lesson. **in suburbanum meum:** a *villa suburbana* was located outside, but not too far distant from, Rome. Wealthy Roman aristocrats commonly possessed several country properties (the letters of Cicero and, particularly, Pliny make detailed reference to their authors' villas, e.g. Plin. *Ep.* 2.17 (with Whitton 2013), 5.6, Rawson 1976). L, it emerges (105.1), has a villa at Ardea (on whose resonance see Henderson 2004: 42). Characteristically S does not specify further which villa might feature in *Ep.* 12 (though he is known to have had properties at Nomentum, 104.1, 110.1, and Alba/Albanum, 123.1, both a few miles from the city). S also presents himself in the role of landed proprietor at 112.1–2. Watson and Watson (2009), stressing the intensely literary character of the description, argue that the villa in *Ep.* 12 is essentially fictitious, the first of three metaphors for senescence. **uilicus:** the farm manager whose responsibilities are described in Columella Book 11. **uitium** 'fault' (*OLD* 2a). **omnia:** emphasised by its position. **creuit:** a verb more usually used of organic growth than the construction of a building, thus highlighting the parallel between man and villa. **quid mihi futurum est** 'what will happen to me/what is my future': colloquial; see *OLD sum*[1] 5d. **putria:** see *OLD* 2 of buildings and other inorganic things (cf. Plin. *Ep.* 10.48 in relation to *lapis*), also used (*OLD* 1) of living things which can putrefy (e.g. *Ep.* 120.17 *corpus putre*). For the analogy between an old body and a crumbling building cf. of the elderly Bassus, 30.2 *tamquam in putri aedificio*, *De ira* 2.28.4 *domicilium putre*. 52.5–6 uses a similar analogy to stress the importance of good philosophical foundations to ensure an individual's long-term spiritual stability. **aetatis meae saxa** 'stones of my own age', gen. of description.

2 iratus illi: the would-be philosopher should fight to extirpate anger as one of the passions (cf. S's treatise *De ira*). A later letter (47.17, cf. 18.14–15) particularly counsels masters not to be angry with their slaves. S's anger towards the *uilicus* is unjustified, as he already makes clear; he is, we may infer, angry rather at having to confront signs of his own old age. It is perhaps a sign of S's philosophical progress that he later presents himself (123.1–2) as uncomplaining when confronted with a lapse by the staff at his Alban villa (Watson and Watson 2009: 224). **stomachandi** 'showing my irritation'. This term, derived from *stomachus* ('stomach' *OLD* 1, also 'vexation' *OLD* 4), and its cognates appear frequently in Cicero's letters, where, for Hoffer (2007), noting the colloquial and medical flavour of *stomachus*, its consequent jocularity serves to soften references to anger. Cicero writes (*Att.* 14.21.3 = 375 SB) *legendus mihi saepius est 'Cato maior' ad te missus. amariorem enim me senectus facit. stomachor omnia. sed mihi quidem* βεβίωται; *uiderint iuuenes*. There are echoes of this passage in *Ep.* 12 (cf. §8n. on βεβίωται), which may perhaps be read as offering retrospective advice to Cicero (cf. *Ep.* 24 with intro.). **platanos:** the type of tree is significant. As Ronnick (1999) stresses, plane trees have a philosophical pedigree. They figure prominently in the setting of Plato's *Phaedrus* (indeed the species name, derived from the Greek πλατύς 'broad', might be read as echoing Plato's name; cf. 58.30). As the dialogue opens, Socrates declares ironically that 'country places and trees don't teach me anything' (230d) – an assertion countered by the development of the dialogue. Cicero's *De oratore* self-consciously evokes Plato's plane trees when Cotta asks (1.28) *cur non imitamur, Crasse, Socratem illum, qui est in Phaedro Platonis? nam me haec tua platanus admonuit, quae non minus ad opacandum hunc locum patulis diffusa ramis quam illa, cuius umbram secutus est Socrates*. In contrast to Plato and Cicero, S describes plane trees without leaves which 'do not provide the utility of shade, but instead stand out as stark symbols of something all living creatures have in common, namely their mortality' (Ronnick 1999: 227). **quam nodosi sunt et retorridi rami, quam tristes et squalidi trunci!** 'How gnarled and shrivelled are the branches, how wretched and scaly the trunks!' the adjectives can be applied as readily to humans as to trees, *nodosus* perhaps suggesting the arthritic joints which often afflict the elderly (cf. e.g. Prudent. *Perist.* 10.495). *retorridus* is otherwise largely confined to the technical works of Varro and Columella on agriculture and Pliny the Elder. For the term applied to trees cf. 86.18(n.), to human flesh, see 66.51 *retorridam manum Mucii* and 95.16, on the afflictions brought on by luxurious living (*retorridi digiti articulis obrigescentibus*). We might also compare the *arbor breuis, retorrida, infelix*, invoked as one of many possible avenues to self-inflicted death in *De ira* 3.15.4, a passage echoed in §10 below. That plane trees are noteworthy for their longevity (Mart. 9.61, Watson and Watson 2009: 215) makes S's observation the more pointed. On the symbolic significance of these trees see further Watson and Watson 2009: 216–18. **si ... si:** the emphatic anaphora is reproachful. **circumfoderet** 'dug around them', a semi-technical term, found primarily in the agricultural writers and Pliny the Elder. **iurat per genium meum** 'he swears on my genius'. A man's genius or guardian spirit (frequently associated with the *Lares*), the most important of his household divinities, was appealed to in entreaties or in support of strong assertions (see also 110.1–2, 114.5); see e.g. Hor. *Ep.* 1.7.94, 2.2.187–9, Petr. 75.2.   **se omnia facere ... sed illas uetulas:** the emphatically placed pronouns stress the conscientiousness of the *uilicus*; it is the superannuated trees themselves that are the problem. *uetulus* (as Watson and Watson 2009: 218 point out) is a term much more often applied to elderly humans than to trees (e.g. Plaut. *Merc.* 314 *uetulus decrepitus senex*).   **quod intra nos sit** 'may this be between ourselves'. On *intra* see Traina 1987: 73; the emphasis is on what can be shared by close friends (here in the context of epistolary intimacy) in contrast to what one allows to be known more broadly. One of the few epistolary touches in this letter.   **ego ... ego:** emphatic anaphora balances *si ... si*.

3 decrepitus 'worn out'. Cf. *Brev.* 11.1 *decrepiti senes*. S uses this colloquial term of himself in 26.1 (perhaps suggesting his developing self-awareness). It occurs repeatedly in contemptuous characterisations of the elderly in comedy; see e.g. Pl. *Mer.* 291, *As.* 833, Ter. *Eu.* 231. Cicero uses it only of animals (*Tusc.* 1.94). S's usage is paralleled by Isid. *Orig.* 10.74 *decrepitus quod morti sit propior et quasi ad mortis tenebras uertat sicut crepusculum tempus noctis*.   **merito ad ostium admotus** 'with good reason put by the door'. The slave apparently serves as janitor, the lowest of the low in the household (cf. McKeown on Ov. *Am.* 1.6 intro. note citing this passage and *De ira* 3.37.2 *ostiario ... extremo mancipio*). He is thus conveniently positioned for being carried out for burial.   **istunc:** this form of acc. sing. masc., which otherwise only occurs in Plautus and Terence (*TLL* IV.2.496.46), is perhaps a contemptuous colloquialism (Adams 2016: 233–4).   **quid te delectauit** 'why were you pleased to ...?' (with inf., see *OLD* 3b). Sarcastic. Ironically foreshadows *deliciolum* in Felicio's response.   **alienum mortuum tollere:** lit. 'pick up someone else's corpse', i.e. take on the trouble and expense of disposing of someone's remains (the phrase seems to be a variant on a proverb; cf. *Clem.* 2.6.4, Petr. 54 *alienum mortuum plorare*). The slave's proximity to death is brutally underlined. There is perhaps a suggestion, too, of the dead-weight burden of maintaining a slave no longer fit for work.   **ego ... ego:** the slave's words, echoing those S used with reference to himself in §2, underline his role as 'abjected reflection' (see intro. above).   **Felicio:** a name characteristically used of slaves (with some irony here), and particularly suited to a favourite (twenty-three instances of slaves or freedmen so named are listed by Solin 1996: 1.93). An ex-slave *delicium* called Felicio is commemorated in an inscription (Ebner 1970: 266–7; cf. *CIL* IV.2013, 3163, 3164, Setaioli 2000: 331–3). Epictetus (1.19.19–23) describes a Felicio, sold by his master as useless, who eventually becomes a slave of Caesar and is sedulously cultivated by the same former master. As Watson and Watson (2009: 212) note, the pathetic figure of Felicio in *Ep.* 12 is often misleadingly discussed out of context by historians of slavery, to illustrate Roman attitudes to elderly slaves.   **sigillaria:** figurines (usually of terracotta) often given to children at the Saturnalia in December (cf. Macr. 1.11.1, *RE* IIA², col. 2278). The Saturnalia was a time when distinctions between masters and slaves were blurred or inverted, as they are here between S and Felicio. S uses the Saturnalia as a rich analogy for the disorder of ordinary life in *Ep.* 18 (see below).   **Philositi:** a Greek name characterically used of slaves (though relatively uncommon; Solin 1996: II.235 lists only seven instances), its significance 'food-lover' denoting a 'slavish' quality. The majority of known Roman slave names are Greek, in many instances bearing no relation to their place of origin.   **deliciolum** 'your little playmate', diminutive (otherwise unattested, though cf. Cic. *Att.* 1.8.3 = 4 SB *deliciolae*, used of his young daughter) of *delicium*, a term which (esp. in pl. *deliciae*) often, though not necessarily, has a sexual connotation. Cf. rather perhaps the pet boy slave in Trimalchio's household, Petr. 67.9.   **perfecte ... iste delirat** 'he's thoroughly gaga'. On *perfecte* (a term generally found in technical or academic, rather than colloquial, prose) see Adams 2016: 235.   **pupulus ... factus est?** 'he's become a boy, even a playmate?'   **dentes illi cum maxime cadunt:** as a consequence of old age, his teeth are falling out just as a child's milk teeth would (the phrase *dentes cadunt* is normally used only for the latter). The same parallel is stressed in 83.4 (where again there is a comparison between S and one of his slaves). 'His aged body has ... come "full circle"', foreshadowing the circular imagery which will dominate the latter part of the letter (Ronnick 1999: 221). For the perception of old age as a second childhood see Parkin 2003 index s.v. 'Second childhood'. For *cum maxime* see 7.6n.

4 debeo ... aduerteram apparuit: picking up the terms of the letter's opening two sentences.   **complectamur illam et amemus** 'let us embrace and love it', i.e. old age. *complectamur illam* echoes the exhortation in 1.2 *omnes horas complectere*. All one's allocation of time should be fully exploited.   **plena <est> uoluptatis:** *est* was missing in the archetype but is needed to complete the sense and is supplied in some MSS. *uoluptas*, which often has the meaning 'sensual pleasure' (e.g. 7.2(n.), 23.5), is an ambivalent term in S's writing. Here (as in e.g. 86.5) it has a positive meaning. The analogies he goes on to set out relate to the pleasures of the senses, in contrast to the more serious nature of the *uoluptas* S has in mind here (which is more fully developed in the following sentences).   **poma cum fugiunt** 'apples when they are on the point of going off' (*OLD fugere* 8b). Cf. Ovid (stressing the attractions of a mature lover) in *Ars* 3.576 *quae fugiunt, celeri carpite poma manu!*, *Ep.* 18.181 *uelle* *quid est aliud fugientia prendere poma?* Cic. *Sen.* 71 has Cato compare dying in old age to the ripe apple falling from the tree, *quasi poma ex arboribus.* **pueritiae maximus in exitu decor** 'youth is most attractive in its final phase'. Young men were considered especially attractive as objects of desire to older males (and women) when they were on the cusp of transition from boyhood to maturity, *flos aetatis* (Cic. *Cael.* 9, Virg. *Ecl.* 7.4, Williams 2010: 78–9). **deditos uino ... quae mergit** 'the final drink, the one that drowns them, delights the devotees of wine'. Cf. *Tranq.* 17.8 *non numquam ... usque ad ebrietatem ueniendum, non ut mergat nos, sed ut deprimat; eluit enim curas.* At 58.32, S uses immoderate drinking as an analogy for those overfond of clinging on to life (cf. 1.5(n.)). He comments at length on the inadvisability of drunkenness for the would-be philosopher at 83.17–27. **summam manum imponit** 'adds the finishing touch' (*OLD manus*[1] 20). At 101.8, S comments, *qui cotidie uitae suae summam manum imposuit non indiget tempore.* Cf. Cic. *Brut.* 126 *manus extrema non accessit operibus eius.*

5 deuexa iam, non tamen praeceps 'in decline now, though not headlong' (*OLD praeceps* 1f). Henderson (2004: 22) nicely paraphrases this as 'over the hill, yes – but not off a cliff'. Cf. Cic. *Att.* 9.10.3 = 177 SB *aetas iam a diuturnis laboribus deuexa ad otium.* **illam** sc. *aetatem.* **in extrema tegula stantem** 'poised on the edge of the tile'. The image seems to be of a drop of water poised to fall off the edge of a roof, having dripped down its slope. Scarpat compares 83.4 *iam aetas nostra non descendit sed cadit.* Some editors have preferred *regula* to *tegula.* The metaphor might thus relate to racing (in Stat. *Theb.* 6.593, *regula* is the bolt whose fall allows racehorses to start, *OLD* 3c) or else to astronomy ('borderline', 'horizon', favoured by Summers), though this is very speculative. **suas uoluptates ... nullis egere:** the true nature of the *uoluptas* celebrated by S in this letter now becomes apparent. It is the pleasure of no longer craving pleasures. Cf. *VB* 4.2 *uera uoluptas erit uoluptatum contemptio.* The muting of appetites in old age is also celebrated in Cic. *Sen.* 46–7, where Cato is made to comment on his reduced appetite for food and drink and his loss of interest in sexual pleasure and remarks, *quamquam non caret is qui non desiderat; ergo non desiderare dico esse iucundius,* citing Pl. *Resp.* 329b in support of this. Diogenes Laertius attributes a similar thought to Diogenes (6.71): 'just as those who are accustomed to a life of pleasure feel disgust when they pass over to the opposite experience, so those whose training has been of the opposite kind derive more pleasure from despising pleasure than from the pleasures themselves' (trs. R. D. Hicks). **quam dulce ... reliquisse!** cf. 10.5 *omnibus cupiditatibus solutum.* This state is explicitly associated by S with *tranquillitas animi* in *Tranq.* 2.4.

6 'molestum est' inquis: here the addressee (though we need not see these words as necessarily uttered by L) is imagined interjecting a common complaint about old age; cf. 4.4, Cic. *Sen.* 66.   **tam seni ... quam iuueni:** the order is the reverse of what might be expected, reinforcing the point S goes on to make. S makes use of such reversals elsewhere also, e.g. 77.7.   **non ... citamur ex censu** 'we are not summoned in the order we appear in the census'. The census allocated men *classes* and *centuriae* (of seniors and of juniors). The list recorded the age of each man (cf. Cic. *Leg.* 3.44). For the thought cf. 26.7, 63.14, 93.6, *Marc.* 21.7.   **ut improbe unum diem speret** 'that it would be presumptuous to wish for one more day'. One more day of life is a realistic hope even for the very old (this is a significant variant on the thought expressed in Cic. *Sen.* 24 *nemo... est tam senex, qui se annum non putet posse uiuere*). The single day as a unit of time has a particular potency in S's writing (see further below, as well as main intro. section 7, on the practice of daily self-scrutiny).   **gradus uitae:** the day as a 'step' could be read in terms of the metaphor of life as a journey which recurs often in the letters (cf. Lavery 1980, Armisen-Marchetti 1989: 86–9, Richardson-Hay: 98). For the stages of life as *gradus* cf. 49.3.   **tota aetas partibus constat et orbes habet circumductos maiores minoribus** 'Our whole life is divided into parts; it consists of larger circles enclosing smaller.' Here S shifts to a description of time couched in spatial terms (but with moral implications). The conceptualisation of human life in terms of concentric circles is not paralleled in extant classical texts (Habinek 1982: 66) and contrasts with the linear sense of life as a journey more frequently found in S (cf. e.g. 70.1–3). Lévy (2003), noting the ambiguity of *gradus* (which can also mean stair), argues that these concentric circles should be seen in three dimensions, forming a sort of graduated cone, with the day of one's birth at the apex, though it is hard to see how the circle of each individual day could then be accommodated. S often considers time in spatial terms (Armisen-Marchetti 1995: 550–3).   **aliquis:** sc. *orbis*. The idea of the individual human life as a circle serves to render its ending as one with its beginning (S often stresses that to die is to return to the state we were in before birth; see e.g. 54.6, 74.34).   **excludit** 'separates' (used of geographical space, *OLD* 2).   **per se annus ... tempora** 'the year in its own right which includes all the units of time in itself'. The idea of the year as a circle can be traced back to Homer, e.g. *Il.* 23.833 (Habinek 1982: 66). Maltby (1991) s.v. *annus* cites Var. *L.* 6.8 *uocatur annus quod ut parui circuli anuli, sic magni dicebantur circites ani, unde annus.*   **quorum multiplicatione uita componitur** 'from the repetition of which human life is made up'. The idea that life is made up of the same elements repeated will be developed further.   **angustissimum ... ad occasum** 'the day has the smallest circle, but this too has its beginning and its end, its sunrise and sunset'. For the daily round conceived in cyclic terms cf. 24.26 *in orbem nexa sunt omnia,* 77.6 *cibus, somnus, libido – per hunc circulum curritur.*

7 Heraclitus . . . obscuritas: the philosopher Heraclitus of Ephesus, who flourished *c.* 500 BCE (KRS 184). Cicero refers to his *cognomen* ὁ σκοτεινός 'the obscure' and suggests he deliberately sought to be hard to understand (*Fin.* 2.15). S also cites him at 58.23, *De ira* 2.10.5, *Nat.* 2.56.1. For the influence of Heraclitus on Stoic thought generally see Long 1986: 145–7.   **'unus . . . est'** 'One day is equal to every [other] day', fr. 106 DK. The saying is also attributed to Heraclitus by Plut. *Cam.* 19.3.   **alius aliter excepit** 'interpreters have understood this in a number of different ways'.   **dixit enim alius parem esse horis:** the text must be lacunose here (possibly the name of an authority is missing: '*X* says that . . .', more likely just *alius*, Gemoll's conjecture, adopted here). According to this first interpretation of Heraclitus, each day is the same length, and made up of the same number of hours as any other. *horis* is an abl. of respect ('in terms of its hours').   **nox . . . perdidit:** i.e. when the day is shorter, the night is correspondingly longer.   **parem esse unum diem omnibus similitudine; nihil enim habet longissimi temporis spatium, quod non et in uno die inuenias, lucem et noctem** 'One day is equal to all days in terms of resemblance, because the very longest space of time possesses no element which you could not find in a single day, as regards light and darkness.' *parem . . . similitudine* is parallel to *parem . . . horis. lucem et noctem,* acc. of respect. According to the second interpretation, each day is like the sum of all days, in terms of the alternation of light and dark.   **in alternas mundi uices** 'as the cosmos alternates'. One might see this as a reference specifically to the alternation of night and day or, possibly, to the succession of seasons. Cf. 24.26 (see below), 102.28 *dies et nox aeris infimi uices sunt.*   **plura facit ista, non alia. alias contractior, alias productior uita** 'makes them [the days and nights] more numerous, not different in nature. Life is sometimes shorter, sometimes longer.' Again the text is problematic (the OCT reads: *plura facit ista non <alia>: *** alias contractior alias productior*). Summers' supplement *uita* (1908a: 24), with altered punctuation (adopted here), and understanding *est,* has particular merits, preparing the way for the following *itaque.* Numerous other suggestions have been made (helpfully discussed by Stégen 1972; see also Malaspina 2018: 93–4).

8 sic . . . expleat uitam 'every day should be regulated as if it concluded the series, as if it consummated and filled out our life'. *cogat agmen* a military metaphor, 'brings up the rear' (*OLD cogo* 2b); *consummet* 'rounds out' is a term which recurs a number of times in this sense (cf. 32.3 *quam pulchra res sit consummare uitam ante mortem,* 74.20, 92.2, *De ira* 3.36.1).

Another implication of the resemblance seems to be that because each day of your life is *like* the last day of your life, it should not be too onerous to treat it as if it *were* the last day of your life (this thought recurs repeatedly; cf. *Brev.* 7.9 *qui omnes dies tamquam uitam ordinat, nec optat crastinum, nec timet, Epp.* 61.1–2, 93.6, 101.8). An individual life seen as a circle may be experienced as complete, perfect, whenever it comes to an end. The idea (though not preceded by a structured argument) is to be found in Hor. *Ep.* 1.4.13–4 *omnem crede diem tibi diluxisse supremum. | grata superuenies quae non sperabitur hora.* **Pacuuius qui . . . fecit:** when Aelius Lamia, appointed governor of Syria by Tiberius, was not permitted to take up his appointment (see Tac. *Ann.* 6.27.2, 2.79.2), Pacuvius, his *legatus legionis*, functioned as *de facto* governor (*RE* xviii.2, cols. 2158–9). Pacuvius, 'who played a dead unRoman while he still lived', is the first Roman subject of an anecdote in the letters (and the only one in Book 1), while Syria is the only geographical referent in the book (Henderson 2004: 6–7). In Roman law *usus*, the use of something, e.g. a property, over a period of time gave one a certain claim to it (see e.g. Ulpian in *Dig.* 8.5.10). In relation to a province this is merely a figure of speech; cf. 88.12, Liv. 22.44.6 *Hannibal iam uelut usu cepisset Italiam.* **cum . . . sibi parentauerat** 'whenever he had celebrated the day of his own death'. The verb (used only by S with the reflexive pronoun to refer to the living) is cognate with Parentalia, the festival (13–21 February) dedicated to celebrating the memory of dead ancestors. Cf. 122.3. Rites were also performed on the anniversary of the individual's birth or death. This often involved 'sharing' a meal with the dead (cf. Tert. *De resurrectione carnis* 1.2, Dunbabin 2003: 125–32). Grotanelli (1995: 66–7) takes S to suggest that the ritual is a Syrian practice and explores a parallel with Lucian, *On grief* 21. **illis** 'the well known'. **exoletorum:** *exoletus* is pf. partic. of *exolescere*, 'having grown up', in contrast to *adolescens* 'growing up'. *Pace OLD* and Williams 2010: 90–3, these are not usually male prostitutes but attractive male slaves, generally post-adolescent (in contrast to younger *delicati*), whose particular role was to provide sexual services (Butrica 2005: 223–31). They are often, as here, invoked to characterise negatively someone who associates with them (cf. 66.53, 95.24, 114.25(n.), Tac. *Ann.* 16.19, Suet. *Tib.* 43.1, *Gal.* 22.1). **ad symphoniam** 'to the sound of a chorus'. **βεβίωται, βεβίωται:** 'he has lived, he has lived!' (pf. pass., impers., of βιοῦν, 'to pass one's life', *sc.* αὐτῷ), i.e. his life is complete. Cicero uses the same term to lament that his own life is effectively over in *Att.* 14.21.3 = 375 SB (quoted above, §2n.). Another letter implies that this was an Epicurean maxim: *Att.* 12.2.2 = 238 SB and Shackleton Bailey 1966 *ad loc.* Cicero comments sarcastically that Balbus can forget about political and military problems and enjoy life, following Epicurean principles: *uerum si quaeris, homini non recta sed uoluptaria quaerenti nonne* βεβίωται? (cf. also Plin. *Ep.* 5.5.4 *qui uoluptatibus dediti quasi in diem uiuunt, uiuendi causas cotidie finiunt*). S rarely uses Greek terms (here further emphasised by the Grecising *symphoniam*).

9 nullo non se die extulit: Pacuvius performs his perverse mock funeral every day, adding a frisson of extra pleasure to his evening meal by treating it as his last. The freedman Trimalchio orchestrates a similar anticipation of his own funeral at the dinner table in Petr. 71–8, exhorting his guests: '*putate uos ad parentalia mea inuitatos esse!*' His slaves, too, are obliged to lament their master (see Dunbabin 2003: 132–40, Edwards 2007: 167–78). S in satiric mode several times compares the lives of the luxurious to living death (see 60.4, 82.24, 122.2–3, *VB* 7.3, 11.4, *Brev.* 12.7–9). See further Delatte 1950, Berno 2017b.   **ex mala conscientia:** why should *mala conscientia* provoke Pacuvius to rehearse his own funeral? It is tempting to link this with a comment S makes at 122.14 *grauis malae conscientiae lux est*; cf. 43.5, 105.7 and Delatte 1950. The decadent Pacuvius has an inkling he may be better off dead but cannot go beyond the compulsion to act out his funeral, in his case a symptom of despair (cf. *Brev.* 16.2, *Tranq.* 2.15).   **nos ex bona faciamus:** with *bona* sc. *conscientia*. The would-be philosopher is encouraged to rehearse his own death – but not in terms of the physical enactment devised by Pacuvius. The rehearsal should be interiorised (cf. S's praise for Bassus in *Ep.* 30: he has prepared himself so well for death by imagining it in anticipation that (30.3) *eo animo uultuque finem suum spectat, quo alienum spectare nimis securi putares*). Pacuvius' *exemplum* is thus radically refigured by the ethically opportunistic S (Dressler 2012: 159–60).   **laeti hilaresque:** for the joy of the wise man cf. 59.14 *sapiens . . . plenus est gaudio, hilaris et placidus, inconcussus.*   **uixi . . . peregi:** Virg. *A.* 4.653. This first quotation from Virgil in the letters comes from the speech made by Dido just before she kills herself, devastated by the departure of Aeneas. While the would-be philosopher was discouraged from imitating Pacuvius too closely, he is here invited to impersonate Dido. Dido's state of extreme emotion might not be thought an ideal model for the would-be philosopher (though the reader's knowledge of her suicide foreshadows the explicit mention of suicide later in the letter). See further Gill 2003, 2006: 447–8, arguing that this part of Dido's speech has a strong Stoic/Epicurean resonance, and Mann 2006. The word *fatum*, fate, of critical importance in Stoic thinking, is used by Virgil shortly before Dido's exclamation (4.651). S quotes the *Aeneid* passage also in *VB* 19.1 (where the words are put in the mouth of the Epicurean philosopher Diodorus before he kills himself) and *Ben.* 5.17.5 (where the words model a properly accepting attitude, albeit with an Epicurean flavour, to the end of life). For a perceptive comparison of the different ways S uses the quotation see Berno 2014.   **peregi:** *peragere* (*OLD* 6b) is used elsewhere by S to characterise a life lived to completion; cf. the final sentence of *Ep.* 32 *ille demum necessitates supergressus est et exauctoratus ac liber qui uiuit uita peracta*, 77.3 and 77.8 *peracta uita* (both the latter referring to circumstances when suicide may be appropriate). The pairing with *uita* in these passages itself recalls *uixi . . . peregi* in the Virgil quotation here (Berno 2014: 126). Similar phrases are also to be found in the context of funerary epigraphy, e.g. *CIL* x.1309.8–9 *per|acto tempore uitae* (Berno 2014: 136). Pease (*ad A.* 4) reads Dido's words in the context of Virgil's poem as themselves epigraphic in tone. Thus both Virgil and Seneca might be re-elaborating funerary formulae, while the epitaph of the *seuir* L. Carullius Epaphroditus, *CIL* xiv.316.5–10 *hic sum positus qui | semper sine cri|mine uixi | et quem mi dederat | cursum fortuna, | peregit* clearly alludes to Virgil (Berno 2014: 136). **beatissimus . . . securus sui possessor:** contrast with *usu* in §8. Cf. the exhortation of 1.1: *uindica te tibi.* The term *beatus* here suggests a specifically philosophical well-being (cf. e.g. Cic. *Fin.* 1.61 *neque stultorum quisquam beatus neque sapientium non beatus*). On the Stoic significance of *securitas* see main intro., section 4. **crastinum . . . lucrum:** here, too, Horace has apparently shaped S's phrasing; see *Carm.* 1.9.13–15 *quid sit futurum cras, fuge quaerere, et | quem Fors dierum cumque dabit lucro | appone* (though Horace goes on to urge his addressee to enjoy love and dancing before old age constrains him). *ad lucrum* also recalls *Ben.* 5.17.5, where, quoting the same *Aeneid* passage, S complains how few, nearing the end of life, utter such words of acceptance. **'uixi'** 'I have lived.' The one-word utterance, recognising that life is complete, is suggestively echoed in 61.4, where S declares that he himself has lived enough (*uixi . . . quantum satis erat*). With *laeti recipiamus* in the previous sentence, there is an echo here of Hor. *Carm.* 3.29.41–3 *ille potens sui | laetusque deget, cui licet in diem | dixisse 'uixi.'* (Berthet 1979, Görler 1996: 163–9, Berno 2014; see also Mazzoli 1970: 233–6, who regards the parallel as superficial). For Vogt-Spira (2017), *Ep.* 12.9 echoes the advice of Hor. *Carm.* 3.29.41–8 that one should make oneself independent of the flow of time, but while Horace's Sabine farm offers both owner and guest a refuge from *rapax tempus*, S's property figures rather as a vivid demonstration of time's ravages. **cotidie ad lucrum surgit:** *cotidie* 'every day' is an especially resonant term in the letters (see intro. above). Each new day is a bonus, not something to which one should feel an entitlement (cf. Hor. *Ep.* 1.4.14, quoted in §8n.). This may well have been a commonplace (cf. Pl. *Mer.* 553–4 *id iam lucrumst | quod uiuis*, Cic. *Fam.* 9.17.1 = 195 SB *de lucro prope iam quadriennium uiuimus*).

10 includere 'seal up' or 'close off' (*OLD* 6), echoing the closing off of the circles of time in §6 (cf. esp. *qui annos adulescentiae excludit*). There is perhaps an analogy between letter and day.   **peculio:** *peculium* was pocket money or an allowance for children, slaves or others who could not legally own property (an allusion to S's encounter with the slave Felicio in §3). S favours humble terms for the 'gifts' of Epicurean sayings with which he concludes the early letters, cf. e.g. *lucellum* (5.7), *munusculum* (10.5, 16.7).   **uoce . . . quam illi trado ad te perferendam:** S entrusts this vital message (*OLD uox* 7b) to the personified letter who is to convey it to L.   **'malum . . . nulla est':** Epicurus fr. 487. Quotations from Epicurus round off most of the letters up to 29. See 7.11n. and intro. to *Ep.* 33.   **quidni nulla sit?** 'Why should there be no need?' For *quidni* see 7.4n. Here *sit* picks up *est*, with a change of mood following *quidni*.   **patent undique ad libertatem uiae multae, breues faciles:** S elaborates the quotation, reading it as a reminder that no one is obliged to go on living, for suicide can always offer a way out. *uiae multae*: a metaphor regularly used in relation to suicide (its earliest appearance is Ar. *Ran.* 117–18). S repeatedly celebrates the possibility of suicide as a source of freedom, *libertas*; cf. e.g. 22.5–6, 24.7 (discussed below), 26.10, 70.14 (discussed below), *Prov.* 6.7, *De ira* 3.15.4 (which elaborates at length on *breues, faciles*), Inwood 2005: ch. 11. Though S's readiness to contemplate suicide is marked, he is by no means alone in seeing suicide in such positive terms; cf. Plin. *Nat.* 2.5.27, where the possibility of suicide, *sibi mortem consciscere*, constitutes the greatest gift to man amid life's sufferings, *optimum in tantis uitae poenis* (Beagon 2005). Cicero at *Fin.* 1.49 makes the Epicurean Torquatus assert that the individual may leave life whenever he chooses, though S writes as if Epicureans did not generally endorse suicide (*VB* 19.1).   **agamus deo gratias** 'Let us give thanks to god'.   **nemo in uita teneri potest:** cf. *Phoen.* 152–3 *eripere uitam nemo non homini potest,* | *at nemo mortem . . .*

11 quid tibi cum alieno? 'What are you doing with someone else's words?' For this common idiom (*TLL* IV.1374.2–32) cf. e.g. Liv. 8.25.3 and Oakley 1998 *ad loc*. *alieno* here echoes *alienum mortuum* in §3. In 2.5, S characterised the practice of reading Epicurus as *ad aliena castra transire*, going over to the enemy camp (cf. 14.18). In 4.10 he offers a saying, *ex alienis hortulis*. The term also functions as a comment on 1.3 *omnia aliena sunt*. We might contrast 108.38 *omnia quae dicunt . . . aliena sunt*, where S complains rather of those who offer philosophical advice but do not live by it.   **tibi ingerere** 'to din into your ears' (*OLD ingero* 4).   **in uerba iurant** 'swear absolute allegiance'. Cf. Hor. *Ep.* 1.1.14 *addictus iurare in uerba magistri*.   **quae optima sunt esse communia:** for the thought cf. 14.18, 16.7, 21.9, 33.2.   **isti . . . a quo:** this whole phrase is the subject of *sciant*.

LETTER 18

The letters which comprise Book 2 (13–21) return repeatedly to the question of how to overcome the fear of poverty, since this fear often causes individuals, intent on achieving the security of material wealth, to defer their commitment to philosophy. *Ep.* 17 argues at length that poverty, *expedita* and *secura* (17.3), could actually be desirable, if one is seeking to attain *mens bona*, the right disposition towards philosophy (another key concern of this book; cf. 16.1 and Soldo). If not *pauper* (17.5), the would-be wise man should practise a *frugalitas*, which is *paupertas uoluntaria*. *Ep.* 18 opens with a dyspeptic outburst at the frenzied festivities associated with the annual celebration of the Saturnalia but moves on to contemplate a very different kind of change to one's daily routine, advocating the regular episodic practice of extreme frugality – exemplifying the *paupertas uoluntaria* proposed in the previous letter. In *Ep.* 20, which develops further a number of concerns explored in *Ep.* 18, S argues that the rehearsal of poverty can even make experiencing the real thing *iucundum* (20.12).

The Saturnalia, a festival celebrated over a number of days in December, was associated with feasting, drinking, jokes, gift-giving (cf. 12.3n. on *sigillaria*), distinctive dress (abandonment of the toga for the Greek-style *synthesis* and wearing the *pilleus*, a cap associated with newly freed slaves), and the removal of normal restrictions on behaviour (dice-playing and gambling, for instance, were permitted), including a particular licence for slaves (Macr. 1.7.26 *Saturnalibus tota seruis licentia permittitur*). While the festival was associated with the temporary suspension of social distinction, its carnivalesque aspect has been overemphasised, e.g. by Versnel 1993; see Beard 2014: 62–5. Pliny the Younger, influenced perhaps by S, makes much of his solitary, bookish retirement to a remote apartment during the festival, so that his household may be uninhibited in their merry-making (*Ep.* 2.17.24 with Whitton 2013 *ad loc.*). But at least some Roman aristocrats (and members of the imperial family) took part in seasonal revelry: Tacitus describes in darkly symbolic terms Saturnalian party games in which the young emperor Nero sought to humiliate his adoptive brother Britannicus (*Ann.* 13.15). The festival often involved the transgression of normal practice with regard to eating (joke food, for instance); it also had a particular association with the literary genre of satire (Freudenburg 1993: 211–35, 2001: 114, Gowers 1993: 117, 133–6, 159–60).

While S's earlier *Apocolocyntosis* has affinities with Menippean satire, a significant point of reference for the letters, *Ep.* 18 in particular, is Horace's satiric *Sermones* (whose title underlines their varied, conversational nature). Letters were described by ancient critics as the literary form closest to conversation; Libanius, for instance, comments (*De forma epistolari* 2): 'a letter, then, is a kind of written conversation (ὁμιλία τις)' (cf. Demetrios, *De elocutione* 225, C. Julius Victor, *Ars rhetorica* 27). S himself comments (75.1) that he wants his letters to be like his conversation, *sermo*. *Variatio* of tone and matter characterises both Horatian satire and S's letters (Fitzgerald 2016: 116–17, 132–7 on Horace and satire). Horace, like S, claims to use examples to highlight vices – and to be addressing his advice to himself as much as anyone (*S.* 1.4.106, 137–9). For the satiric mode in the letters see Wilson 2001: 175–9 *ad Ep.* 27, Del Giovane 2016. In exploiting the Saturnalia as an occasion for the Stoic critique of excess, S echoes particularly Hor. *S.* 2.3 (where Damasippus' Stoic rant is set during the Saturnalia) and 2.7 (which also has a Saturnalian theme). For the implications of this association see further Edwards 2017a.

The satirically indignant tone with which *Ep.* 18 opens is thus highly appropriate to the Saturnalian setting. S explores two possible options for the would-be wise man during the festival (§§2–4). L is imagined advocating a middle ground ('If I know you well, *you* would advise that we should neither resemble the crowd in all things nor mark ourselves out as different in every respect...'). This course of action, praised as indicative of *temperantia*, echoes 5.1 (*illud... te admoneo... ne facias aliqua, quae in habitu tuo aut genere uitae notabilia sint*) and coheres with the acknowledgement offered in several earlier letters that extreme withdrawal can have its dangers (the wise man should avoid novel ways of living, *nouitate uitae*, 14.14). Philosophy is not for show (5.2, 16.3; cf. 19.2, 29.2). We might perhaps see here an allusion to a Horatian preference for the mean (e.g. *S.* 1.1–3).

In *Ep.* 18, however, S goes on to suggest (§5) that it would be a surer sign of *firmitas* (a quality he esteems highly, cf. 20.1) if one were to adopt a course of action *opposite* to that of others, embracing a life of extreme abstinence. S apparently intends (§3 *his maxime diebus*) that this period of abstinence coincide with the festival of the Saturnalia; given that the Saturnalia is often associated with reversals, this would itself be a Saturnalian move. To overcome one's fear of poverty by accustoming oneself to little is to win *securitas*, a key goal for the would-be wise man (cf. e.g. 17.9, 20.12, 92.3 *quid est beata uita? securitas*). The impression one makes on others is no longer a concern here (there is a real contrast with *Ep.* 5). The practice of poverty, neither a game (§7), nor a heroic feat (§8), should be seen as a form of training; a striking feature of *Ep.* 18 is the vivid use of military metaphor (§§6, 8); the figure of the soldier as a model for the *proficiens* recurs frequently in the letters (e.g. *Ep.* 36; see further main intro. section 9). Though the practice advocated here is episodic rather then permanent, there are echoes of Cynic discourse (Del Giovane 2015a: 247–8).

In taking as an example Epicurus' experiments with basic diet (§§9–10), the letter returns us to the question of pleasure, *uoluptas*. In strong contrast to those seeking gross pleasure in the messy excesses of Saturnalian revelry alluded to earlier in the letter, Epicurus extracts finely calibrated pleasure from the minimal satisfaction of bodily needs. Indeed the phrase *siccum et sobrium* (§4) echoes S's *VB* 12.4, where the same adjectives are used to characterise Epicurus' austere conception of *uoluptas* (sadly perverted by many who claim to follow him but pursue much grosser pleasures, 12.3 *uitiis dediti luxuriam suam in philosophiae sinu abscondunt*). S is less concerned here than in later letters to explore differences between Stoic and Epicurean appetite (Wildberger 2014 argues for the pervasive influence of Epicurus in *Ep.* 18). While the quotation from Virgil at §12 (Evander invites Aeneas into his simple home) lends authoritative epic endorsement to frugal living and marks another shift of register, satiric concerns also remain in play (the moderation of appetite and the provision of humble hospitality are frequent themes of Horatian satire).

The conclusion of *Ep.* 18 (§§14–15) focuses rather on the dangers of anger and the importance of mental *sanitas* (a return to the concern with the health of the *animus* which dominates the opening of *Ep.* 15; cf. 17.7). We have moved from the sweaty bustle of the Saturnalia via the competitive asceticism of Epicurus to the torrid heat of the passions. Temporal patterns are significant in this letter; the monthly practice of the inverse Saturnalia advocated for the *proficiens* is a mirror image in miniature of the annual celebration of the traditional festival, which itself is translated from an overblown month of celebration into a metaphor for licentious living all year round. Yet just as the Saturnalia may become a permanent state, so too may extreme poverty.

For S, the basic circumstances of the slave's life offer a model the would-be wise man can embrace as a philosophical exercise (§8 *facies . . . quod multa milia seruorum . . . faciunt*), while the issue of relations between masters and slaves, often characterised by uncontrolled anger, surfaces briefly at the end of the letter. Allusions to slavery (a theme which recurs in a number of letters, most obviously *Ep.* 47) have a particular role to play in *Ep.* 18. 14.1–2 presents the relation between mind and body as properly that of master and slave, thus emphasising how wrong it is to be enslaved to one's bodily appetites; the pursuit of bodily *uoluptas* associated with the Saturnalia can itself be seen as a manifestation of slavishness. This is an issue explored at length in Hor. *S.* 2.7, where the slave Davus, taking advantage of Saturnalian licence to speak freely, is allegedly using the arguments of a Stoic philosopher, Crispinus, to criticise his master's enslavement to pleasure (see Freudenburg 1993: 211–23).

An earlier Horatian satire (*S.* 2.2) explores the advantages of accustoming oneself to a simple diet, with strenuous exercise as stimulus to the appetite; in *Ep.* 18, however, the diet has *become* the exercise. Horace's farmer Ofellius praises the economical and health-giving properties of simple, home-grown food (as opposed to imported luxury), noting that the practice of restraint may be enlivened by occasional indulgence when holidays come. Yet the rustic philosopher also criticises those who live too meanly, 2.2.53 *sordidus a tenui uictu distabit*; his *sapiens* will be (2.2.66) *in neutram partem cultus miser*. Wealth is a good, which may be spent well (or badly) or saved to serve as security for the future. In *Ep.* 18, by contrast, a middle way is mooted but a more strenuous path preferred. The material security of even a modest estate is presented as ultimately unnecessary to the would-be wise man. Horace (*S.* 1.1.119) compares the wise man, who understands how life should be lived, to the satisfied dinner guest, *conuiua satur* (cf. Lucr. 3.938–9, where personified Nature chides: *cur non ut plenus uitae conuiua recedes | aequo animoque capis securam, stulte, quietem?* Berno 2008). In S's letters, where gastronomic excess is often pilloried in repellent detail (e.g. 47.2, 78.23–4, 83.24, 95.23–9, 122.3–4), the pleasures of the table offer not a satisfying analogy for, but an insidious threat to, the would-be philosopher's mental tranquillity.

S several times explores the practice of poverty in later letters: 87.1–7 (a letter which opens with a development of several elements of *Ep.* 18, before proceeding to a dialectical discussion of wealth as a preferred indifferent; see Inwood's commentary), 110.18, 123 (with Inwood's commentary) and the discussion of *Epp.* 87 and 123 at Del Giovane 2015a: 248–65; cf. *Helv.* 12.3 (with Griffin 1992: 299–300).

Commentaries: Summers, Motto, Soldo.
Further reading: Wildberger 2014, Del Giovane 2015a: 246–8, Edwards 2017a.

1 December est mensis: a deceptively simple opening. References to specific times of the year are relatively rare in the letters (for another instance see 67.1) and always have a moral point (as S comments explicitly at 23.1).   **cum maxime:** see 7.6n.   **sudat:** lit. 'sweats' (paradoxically for Rome in winter), emphatically placed to balance *December*. *sudor* often has a positive connotation in S; cf. e.g. 31.7 *non est uiri timere sudorem*, 86.11(n.); colloquially the term *sudare* could mean 'to work very hard'. In this case the emphasis is on frantic bustle, cf. 4.11 *ad superuacua sudatur* (for the idea of pointless activity as heated cf. 13.13 *aestuare ac discurrere*), and the literal meaning (*OLD* 1) is in paradoxical tension with the winter season (Cic. *Orat.* 2.223 makes a similar play).   **ius luxuriae publicae datum est** 'licence is given to public luxury'. *luxuria* (a particular focus of *Epp.* 90 and 122) always has negative connotations in S. *publicae:* cf. (as

Soldo notes) 114.2 *argumentum publicae*. **ingenti apparatu:** the phrase echoes S's evocation of the army's terrifying approach in 14.6; cf. also 24.14 (personified pain appears *magno apparatu*). **sonant:** S elsewhere stresses the annoyance occasioned by noise (while emphasising that the would-be philosopher should seek to rise above such distractions). See e.g. 56.1 *ecce undique me uarius clamor circumsonat*, 80.1. **tamquam** 'as if' (*OLD* 5); sarcastic. **Saturnalia:** in religious terms, 17 December was the important day of the Saturnalia (founded in 496 BCE according to Liv. 2.21) but the festivities extended over a number of subsequent days. For details of the celebration see Stat. *Silv.* 1.6, Scullard 1981: 205–9, Versnel 1993 (also 12.3(n.)). **olim mensem ... nunc annum:** Augustus had responded to complaints about the increasing number of days devoted to the Saturnalia by limiting the festivities to three days, a restriction which was short-lived (Macr. 1.10.23–4). Claudius extended the limit to five days (Dio Cass. 60.25.8), again failing to contain the celebrations. S uses the idea of perpetual Saturnalia to characterise the reign of Claudius himself at *Apoc.* 8 (*Saturno . . . cuius mensem toto anno celebrauit Saturnalicius princeps*), a passage echoed here. This was an especially appropriate metaphor given that Claudius was considered subservient to his own freedmen (Dickison 1977). See also Petr. 44.4, where the complaint is voiced that the wealthy, whose appetites are always indulged, observe a perpetual Saturnalia.

2 si te hic haberem: we are reminded of L's absence. While the letter can be deemed equivalent to conversation (see main intro. section 3), absence makes dialogue concerning immediate circumstances impossible. **quid existimares esse faciendum:** indirect question following *conferrem* (here with the sense of 'discuss', *OLD* 13), the main verb in the apodosis. As Soldo notes, this is the first occasion in the *EM* on which S asks L for his opinion. **utrum ... togam:** this clause, offering two alternatives, expands on *quid ... esse faciendum*. The characteristically Roman *toga*, the garment worn for public and private business, is set aside. **publicis moribus:** while *mores* (*OLD* 2) *maiorum* 'ancestral customs' are invariably positive, *mores publici* are more neutral; cf. the contrast *inter bonos mores et publicos* articulated in 5.5, though there S advocates rather a middle way (more achievable for the fledgling *proficiens*). **ex cotidiana consuetudine:** the daily routine of the philosopher's way of life is already established as a key preoccupation in the *EM* (4.5, 16.1; cf. *De ira* 3.36.1–3). **nisi in tumultu et tristi tempore:** *tumultus* (*OLD* 2) 'military crisis' has a quasi-technical sense here (cf. e.g. *Dig.* 16.3.1.1 from the praetor's edict, where *tumultus* is included alongside fire as a mitigating circumstance when property owed has not been deposited). In such a crisis, when there was no opportunity for the usual recruitment procedure, citizens were summarily called to arms, exchanging the toga for a military cloak, as for instance in Cic. *Phil.* 6.16.10 *ut mihi senatus adsentiens tumultum decerneret, saga sumi iuberet.* This foreshadows the military imagery of §6 below. It had also been customary in times of public mourning (e.g. following a major military defeat) for all citizens to dress in dark clothing; cf. e.g. Liv. 43.16.14, Cic. *Pis.* 17; see Edmondson 2008: esp. 26–32.   **uoluptatis causa:** *uoluptas* is a key term in this letter, esp. §10.   **uestem mutauimus:** although this particular phrase generally refers to mourning dress, particularly when assumed as a public protest (cf. e.g. Cic. *Sest.* 26.3, Liv. 6.16.4), it was usual during the Saturnalia for togas to be laid aside in favour of the costume normally worn for evenings known as a *synthesis* (Mart. 6.14, 14.1). The costume worn for seasonal celebration is thus assimilated to a sign of public unhappiness.

3 si te bene noui: colloquial, 'if I know you well'; cf. 16.7, Ov. *Am.* 1.2.43, Mart. 1.115.7. We should also understand here a second protasis, 'if you had been here'.   **arbitri partibus functus** 'performing the role of a judge' (*OLD fungor* 1b).   **pilleatae turbae:** the *pilleus* was a cap specifically associated with slaves who had won their freedom (cf. e.g. V. Max. 5.2.63). It seems to have been widely worn during the Saturnalia as a symbol of the temporary blurring of distinctions between slave and free. Martial invokes *pilleata Roma* in laying claim to Saturnalian licence (11.6.4; cf. 14.1). According to Suet. *Nero* 57.1, the public sense of liberation following Nero's death was such that *plebs pilleata tota urbe discurreret.* The term *turba* recalls *Ep.* 7.1, where S insisted that it was *uitandum praecipue.*   **nisi forte ... procubuit:** S politely offers an alternative possibility – that it might be right for the would-be philosopher to exercise particular abstinence just when most people are abasing themselves (*OLD procumbo* 3c) to pleasures; cf. *Ben.* 4.26.3.   **animo imperandum est:** an instance of the language of self-command (cf. Inwood 2005: 147, Star 2012: 36–41 on psychological *imperium*). The *animus* (which often has the sense of 'oneself' in Latin) is the subject of the *ut* clause.   **blanda ... trahentia:** these beguiling neuter plural forces are sinisterly vague.

4 siccum ac sobrium: S uses these adjectives at 114.3 to characterise the proper state of an individual's literary talent, *ingenium*, which must correspond to his *animus* (see 114.3nn. on *animo* and *siccum ac sobrium*), while at *VB* 12.4 the same phrase is used of Epicurus' experience of pleasure (in contrast to that of some of those who claim to follow him). For the paradox of sobriety during the Saturnalia cf. Hor. *S.* 2.3.4 *ab ipsis | Saturnalibus huc fugisti sobrius.*   **illud temperantius:** the virtue of *temperantia* 'self-control' (*OLD* 1) is of central importance in Academic (Cic. *Tusc.* 3.16), as well as Stoic, philosophy (this approach, indeed, seems quite consonant with the moderate pleasures celebrated in Horace's *Satires*, e.g. 2.2.66). *firmitas* 'tenacity' (*OLD* 3) is a more specifically Stoic virtue; cf. Sen. *Ep.* 63.1, 78.16, *Polyb.* 17.1 (to be linked with the Stoic emphasis on consistency, *aequalis animi tenor*; cf. *Ep.* 59.14).   **se … insignire** 'to make oneself noteworthy' (*OLD* 4).   **licet enim sine luxuria agere festum diem** 'for it is permissible to observe a feast day without luxury', revisiting *ius luxuriae* of §1.

5 temptare animi tui firmitatem: the focus is now on testing L's philosophical progress. L's continuing philosophical development (already remarked on at 13.1, the opening of Book 2) will turn out to be a condition of the continuing friendship between S and L (35.1).   **ex praecepto … praecipiam:** emphatic use of cognate terms. In *Epp.* 94–5, S explores at length the value (and limitations) of teaching by *praecepta*, which can be understood as moral guidance tailored to specific circumstances (see Schafer 2009, Roller 2016). 'Great men' is presumably a reference to Epicurus and Metrodorus (see §9), though others too (e.g. 108.17, Sextius) advocated accustoming oneself to a frugal diet. As Soldo notes, the idea of the monthly poverty experiment is not otherwise attested.   **interponas aliquot dies:** *interponere* 'introduce' (*OLD* 4a). The subjunctive here (as with the following *dicas, praeparet, firmetur*) expresses the indirect command following *praecipiam*. As will become clear in §6, this is envisaged as a monthly practice.   **minimo … ueste** balances §2 *hilarius cenandum et exuendam togam. ueste* picks up the costume change in the following sentence. The focus of the next few sections is, however, primarily on diet.

6 in ipsa securitate … firmetur 'Particularly in untroubled times, let the spirit prepare itself to face difficulties and, amid fortune's blessings, be hardened against her injuries.' *firmetur* underlines the importance of *firmitatis* in §3 and *firmitatem* in §5. The need to prepare oneself to endure misfortune is a central concern of the *EM* (cf. e.g. 78.29, 91.7, 107.4).   **miles:** military metaphors feature prominently in the *EM* (see main intro. section 9). The preceding letter, highlighting the need to train oneself to endure poverty (17.4 stomachs must be *bene institutos*), offers as illustration (17.7) the soldier's ability to endure deprivation. Horace's satires also characterise the Stoic *sapiens* in military terms (*S.* 2.2.111); by practising moderation when wealthy, one prepares oneself for leaner times: *in pace, ut sapiens, aptarit idonea bello* (Del Giovane 2015a: 246).   **decurrit** 'performs manoeuvres' (*OLD* 7), regularly used in this sense by Livy, e.g. 23.35.6 *crebro decurrere milites cogebat ut tirones … assuescerent signa sequi et in acie agnoscere ordines suos*.   **uallum iacit** 'throws up a rampart', which, together with a ditch, was the usual means of fortifying an army camp (cf. e.g. Liv. 3.28.3). **superuacuo** 'unnecessary'. **sufficere** 'to be able to withstand' (*OLD* 4a) **necessario:** sc. *labori*. **quem ... exerceas** 'he whom you would not wish to be fearful when the crisis comes, you should train before it comes'. **omnibus mensibus:** the practice of poverty should be undertaken every month (contrast the opening reference to the single month of December). **quod ... didicissent:** subj. in relative clause in final sentence: G–L §628. S stresses the importance of repeating exercises on a regular basis to derive full benefit from them (cf. 24.15).

7 non est ... quod : see 7.9n. **Timoneas cenas:** Timon of Athens was notoriously cynical about the motives of his would-be friends and withdrew from society to live a proto-Cynic life in the woods (referred to by Phrynichus, fr. 18 Kassel–Austin, his story appears in greater detail in Lucian, *Timon, or the misanthrope*). Strabo refers to Mark Antony constructing a Timoneion when his friends had abandoned him after his defeat at Actium (17.794; cf. Plut. *Ant.* 69–70). *Timoneas* (Turnebus' conjecture) is not otherwise attested. **pauperum cellas** 'poor men's cabins'. At 100.6 *pauperis cella et quicquid aliud luxuria non contenta decore simplici miscet*, S uses the idea of playing at poverty figuratively to convey certain characteristics of literary composition; cf. Mart. 3.48, Gowers 1993: 18. One might also see here a parallel with another affectation criticised by S, the mock funeral practised by Pacuvius (see 12.8–9(nn.)). **per quod luxuria diuitiarum taedio ludit** 'through which luxury, bored by riches, amuses itself'. *taedio*: causal abl. (*NLS* 32). Similar diversions, again prompted by *diuitiarum taedium*, are criticised at *Helv.* 12.3. **grabattus:** a basic pallet or camp-bed (cf. Petr. 92.3, Mart. 1.92.5). 87.2 describes an experiment in plain living S himself claims to have undertaken, a journey of two days during which he slept on a mattress on the ground (*culcita in terra iacet, ego in culcita*). Cf. 90.41 on the *securitas* of earlier generations, who slept on the hard ground rather than soft beds. **sagum** 'a rough cloak'. Cf. 20.9–11, where a saying of Epicurus, *'magnificentior, mihi crede, sermo tuus in grabatto uidebitur et in panno. non enim dicentur tantum illa, sed probantur'*, is taken as point of departure. Here, too, humble bedding and rough clothes may be read as symbols of an individual's commitment to philosophy. **panis durus ac sordidus:** *sordidus* 'coarse' (*OLD* 4), in contrast to the affected simplicity of the luxurious at their *Timoneae cenae*. Again in 87.3, S's deliberately plain journey involves the simplest fare: *de prandio nihil detrahi potuit*. **triduo et quatriduo** 'for three or four days'. As often, S uses the colloquial abl. (rather than acc.) for duration of time. **non lusus ... sed experimentum:** persistence will mark the difference between the dilettante, playing at poverty, and the would-be wise man who is making a test of himself (cf. 16.3, where he comments of philosophy: *nec in hoc adhibetur, ut cum aliqua oblectatione consumatur dies, ut dematur otio nausia*). For *experimentum* cf. 20.1   **dipondio satur** 'when you're full for just a copper'. If he practises the monthly inverse Saturnalia advocated by S, L will rejoice in being *dipondio satur*. *dipondium* or *dupondium* (two asses) was proverbial for a trivial sum of money; cf. Petr. 58.4. In §9 S quotes Epicurus' boast that he could satisfy himself spending less than one as.   **dabit et:** the MS tradition has *debet* here but the emphasis should rather be on what will be forthcoming under any circumstances. I thus follow Reynolds in accepting Haupt's emendation to *dabit et*.   **irata:** even those whose circumstances make clear that fortune is angry with them (such as slaves or, later, those awaiting execution) still receive a sufficiency to sustain themselves.

8 non est tamen quare multum tibi facere uidearis 'there's no reason you should imagine you're doing a big thing'; cf. 110.12 and 7.9(n.) *non est quod*. The phrase, introducing a comparison with the poor, balances §7 *non est nunc*, introducing a comparison with the pretentious rich.   **multa milia ... multa milia:** the repetition hammers home the number (cf. Traina 1987: 32).   **seruorum:** frequently in the letters (e.g. 80.10) S presents the material conditions of the slave, but also the slave's total lack of social and political capital, as a bracing image of pared-down human possibility.   **illo nomine** 'under the following heading': an accounting metaphor (*OLD nomen* 24).   **te suspice** 'respect yourself' (*OLD suscipio* 2).   **exerceamur ad palum** elaborates the military imagery of §6. Roman soldiers learned to fight by attacking a stake (*palus*) set in the ground (Veg. *Mil.* 1.11 *quemadmodum ad scuta uiminea uel ad palos antiqui exercebant tirones*).   **familiaris:** here 'customary' but the sense of 'friend' is perhaps also relevant, as is the phrase *res familiaris* 'personal property', concern for which is noted as a distraction in 17.1.   **securius diuites erimus si scierimus** 'we shall be wealthy with less anxiety if we have learned ...'; cf. *VB* 26.1 *sapiens tunc maxime paupertatem meditatur cum in mediis diuitiis constitit*. While the fear of losing wealth may endanger his mental tranquillity, S does not see wealth as intrinsically a hindrance to the would-be wise man; cf. 5.6 *magnus ille est qui fictilibus sic utitur quemadmodum argento, nec ille minor est qui sic argento utitur quemadmodum fictilibus*. See in general Griffin 1992: 286–314.

9 ille magister uoluptatis Epicurus: in the earlier letters, S stresses with approval the pared-down nature of Epicurus' notion of pleasure (here in contrast to the excessive pleasures of the crowd in §3). Later letters are more concerned to identify problems in the Epicurean approach (e.g. 85.18–19). See main intro. section 6.   **maligne famem extingueret**

'he would satisfy his hunger grudgingly'. Epicurus fr. 158 Usener (= 83 Arrighetti). Cf. Diog. Laert. 10.131 (= Epicurus, *Ep. Men.* 131): 'To habituate oneself, therefore, to a simple and inexpensive diet supplies all that is needful for health and enables a man to meet the necessary requirements of life without shrinking.' At 21.10 this appears to be habitual Epicurean practice rather than, as here (*certos dies*), a periodic exercise. Avotins (1977) connects the periodic exercise of extreme frugality with Diog. Laert. 10.130 (= Epicurus, *Ep. Men.* 130), where self-sufficiency, *autarkeia* (a key goal in Epicurean teaching), is defined as the *ability* to subsist on little. S describes his own experiment in simple living at 87.2–4 (cf. 123.1–3). **uisurus... pensaret:** Epicurus sought to determine whether there was any difference between the pleasure achieved by satisfying hunger in the most basic way and the greatest possible pleasure and, if such a difference existed, whether it was worth the additional trouble to secure the greatest possible pleasure. S often emphasises the contrast between the untroubled life which merely satisfies the minimum requirements of nature and the far more stressful life which aims at wealth, fame and power (e.g. 4.10). On the potential difficulties associated with Epicurean arguments identifying pleasure as the only good (Cic. *Tusc.* 3.18.41–2, Diog. Laert. 10.129–30 = Epicurus, *Ep. Men.* 129–30) and claiming that pleasures do not increase beyond a certain point (cf. Diog. Laert. 10.133 = Epicurus, *Ep. Men.* 133, Epicurus, *Kuriai doxai* 18, also §10 of this letter, *summa uoluptas*...) see Woolf 2009. **dignum** [sc. *esset*] **quod quis magno labore pensaret:** *dignum* = adj. followed by generic relative clause in subj. *pensaret* 'exchange', 'pay for with' (*OLD* 3b). **epistulis:** that Epicurus communicated philosophical advice in letters to his friends is highly significant (see further intro. above and 21.3(nn.)). S seems to have had a Greek text of collected Epicurean letters. At 99.25 he quotes in Greek from Metrodorus' letter to his sister. **Charino magistratu:** Epicurus apparently dated his letters by reference to the archon for the year in Athens, in this case 291/290 BCE (Meritt 1957: 53–4). By this time, Epicurus had been teaching philosophy for around two decades (Avotins 1977). **Polyaenum:** a close associate of Epicurus, known for his work on mathematics as well as philosophy (cf. 6.6, Cic. *Fin.* 1.20, Diog. Laert. 10.24). Several fragments are extant of letters addressed to him (frr. 156–60 Usener = 83–7 Arrighetti). **gloriatur:** the competitiveness suggested by Epicurus' boasting about his frugality reintroduces an element of game-playing characteristic of the Roman Saturnalia. On playing games with the satisfaction of appetite as a satiric trope see Gowers 1993: 130. **non toto asse:** for the as as a proverbially small sum of money cf. Catul. 5.3 and *OLD* 2. **Metrodorum:** Metrodorus of Lampsacus was another close associate of Epicurus (cf. 6.6, 52.3, Cic. *Fin.* 1.25, 2.7, Diog. Laert. 10.18, 22–4). Surviving fragments of Epicurus' *On* *nature* record a dialogue between Epicurus and Metrodorus on problems of language (Long 1986: 16–17).   **profecerit** 'made philosophical progress'.

10 in hoc . . . uoluptas est 'Do you think there is satiety in such a diet? There is even pleasure.' *saturitas* 'fullness', 'satiety' (*OLD* 1a). For Epicureans pleasure was defined in terms of the absence of pain, for instance that of hunger (a position set out clearly by Torquatus in Cic. *Fin.* 1.37–9. See also Gosling and Taylor 1982: 345–413, Woolf 2009). The satisfaction of hunger, even in the most basic way, brings pleasure. S occasionally uses *saturitas* elsewhere (e.g. 19.7, 119.14 of the luxurious), but the term, relatively rare, also evokes the Saturnalia and indeed the discourse of *satura* (a connection noted, for instance, by Isidore of Seville, 20.1.8), which significantly colours this letter. S's pointed use of questions draws his reader into imagining Epicurus' experience.   **uoluptas non illa leuis et fugax . . . sed stabilis et certa:** the distinction here is between kinetic pleasure (associated with change of condition) and static pleasure (associated with stability of condition) in accordance with the categories of Epicureanism (Diog. Laert. 10.136, Long and Sedley 1987: 1.112–25). Gosling and Taylor (1982: 365–96, esp. 387) argue that the significance of the distinction is not critical to Epicurean thought but is exaggerated by Cicero (esp. *Fin.* 2). S may be influenced by Cicero here.   **aqua et polenta:** the pairing of water and barley porridge (porridge, requiring no oven for its preparation, being lowlier than bread) as the most basic means of sustaining life recurs at 21.10 and 110.18 and has an Epicurean pedigree (Epicurus, *Ep. Men.* 131); cf. the pairing of bread with the salt of satire in Hor. *S.* 2.2.17–18 *cum sale panis | latrantem stomachum bene leniet.*   **hordeacii** 'made from barley', a term common in the work of technical writers (Cato, Varro, Columella and Scribonius Largus) as well as Pliny the Elder's *Natural history.*

11 alimenta . . . carceris: in subsisting on a diet more basic than that offered to those in prison or awaiting execution, S implicitly suggests that one may thus prepare oneself to withstand those threats also.   **sepositos . . . pascit** 'He who is going to kill those set aside for execution does not feed them so meanly.'   **quanta est animi magnitudo . . . timendum sit!** 'How great is the nobility of spirit to lower oneself of one's own accord to that which even for those who have been condemned to death is not be feared!' The syntax is compressed, with the infinitive *descendere* explaining *magnitudo animi.* The fear of death which might be thought rather more disturbing to mental tranquillity under such circumstances than even the most wretched food is tackled in numerous later letters, e.g. 24, 54, 70.   **praeoccupare tela fortunae** 'to pre-empt the weapons of fortune'.

The substantival use of the infinitive is very common in S. *tela* continues the imagery of military conflict. S repeatedly urges L to prepare himself against future troubles of all kinds by rehearsing them in the present; cf. e.g. *Ep.* 24(nn.), 78.29, *Ep.* 107. On S's deployment of *praemeditatio* see Armisen-Marchetti 2008.

12 incipe: repeated in the next phrase, this imperative reminds the reader that L is still at an early stage in his philosophical journey. **secedas:** subj. of purpose following imp. *destina* + rel. *quibus. secessio* in the sense of philosophical withdrawal from public life (equivalent to ἀναχώρησις, Rutherford 1989: 29–30) is a particular preoccupation in Book 2 (see Soldo). In *Ep.* 21 (see below), S advises L to withdraw altogether from public life (cf. 8.1–2, 19.11, 68.6, 73.4, 82.4, *Brev.* 3.5, *De otio* 1.1). **te facias familiarem** 'make yourself at home' with the bare minimum (echoes *fiat nobis paupertas familiaris* in §8). **incipe . . . commercium** 'begin to have dealings with poverty'. The quotidian financial metaphor is ironically juxtaposed with the high-flown words of Virgil's Evander. **aude hospes. . . finge deo:** a quotation from the *Aeneid* (8.364–5), where these words are spoken on the site of future Rome by the exile Evander welcoming Aeneas to his humble dwelling (which, he has emphasised, Hercules did not disdain to enter). As Setaioli (1965: 140) notes, Stoics often invoke Hercules as an exemplar (cf. e.g. *Constant.* 2.1, Epict. *Diss.* 3.24, Galinsky 1972: 106–7, 146–9, Sedley 1999: 150). S quotes part of these lines again in 31.11, having urged his reader to understand *deus* as equivalent to an *animus* which is *rectus, bonus, magnus: quid aliud uoces hunc quam deum in corpore humano hospitantem?*

13 qui opes contempsit: 31.11, glossing this same passage, makes the point that in earlier times, when the gods were propitious towards Rome, their images were made of earthenware rather than gold. Cf. the passage from 5.6 quoted above in relation to §8, *securius diuites.* **quod . . . aspexeris** 'this you will achieve in one way only, if you have persuaded yourself that even without them you can live happily, if you have always regarded them as being liable to disappear'.

14 incipiamus epistulam complicare 'let us begin to close the letter'. After the exhortative anaphora, *incipe . . . incipe* of §12, S shifts to a more playful register. The phrase *epistulam complicare* is also used by Cicero, e.g. *Q. fr.* 3.1.17 = 21 SB, *Att.* 12.1.2 = 248 SB. S refers far less often than Cicero to the physical processes associated with letter-writing (though cf. 45.13). **'redde quod debes':** phrase characteristic of the ritual of *flagitatio*, when a creditor, often with associates, publicly demanded the repayment of a debt. See Lintott 1999: ch. 1. Cf. Petr. 57.5 *nemo mihi in foro dixit* '*redde quod debes*'. The ritual already has a literary form in Pl. *Mos.* 603–4, Catul. 42 and Cic. *Brut.* 17–18.   **delegabo:** a technical expression for paying a creditor through a third party (*OLD* 1c). S treats Epicurus as his banker, who will make good S's obligation to L (cf. 26.8 *scis cuius arca utar*).   **Epicurum:** this is Epicurus' second appearance in this letter.   '**immodica ira . . . insaniam':** fr. 484 Usener (= 246 Arrighetti). Epicurus advises against *uncontrolled* anger. S usually endorses the more orthodox Stoic position that all anger is a form of madness. While all the passions were to be extirpated by the would-be philosopher, S often treats anger, which becomes the focus of this letter's conclusion, as the most dangerous (cf. his lengthy treatise *De ira*, composed some years previously). The reference to anger also picks up on S's characterisation of *fortuna* as *irata* in §7.   **cum habueris et seruum et inimicum:** the master's relationship to his slaves is often seen by ancient authors as offering the greatest scope for the exercise of unrestrained anger (Fitzgerald 2000: 32–41). The festival of the Saturnalia with which this letter opens was especially associated with slaves (cf. Hor. *S.* 2.7, Macr. 1.7.26).

15 hic exardescit affectus: the appetites whose indulgence is associated with the Saturnalia have perhaps been serving as proxy for more dangerous passions, notably anger.   **lusus et iocos:** evoking the jokes and games associated with the Saturnalia but also the activities of the luxurious of §7 who play at being poor (rather than taking the rehearsal of poverty seriously).   **ignis:** nom., subject of *incidat*, displaced (emphasising parallel with *affectus*).   **non refert** 'it does not matter'   **quam magnus:** sc. *sit*.   **maximum:** sc. *ignem*.   **receperunt** 'catch' (*OLD* 4c). Perfect as often in S's similes.   **ita est, mi Lucili:** closely echoing the opening words of *Ep.* 1.   **furor:** passion as madness. The previous letter specifically links the endurance of poverty with the overcoming of passions: *dubitabit aliquis ferre paupertatem, ut animum furoribus liberet?* (17.7).   **non moderationis causa sed sanitatis** revisits the contrast between *temperantia* and *firmitas* which informs §§3–4.

LETTER 21

Ep. 21, concluding the second book, probes further L's imagined ambivalence to the withdrawal from public life advocated by S in numerous earlier letters (esp. 5, 8, 14, 18, 19). Yet L is apparently still an official in Sicily when S writes *Ep.* 43, remaining there at least until *Ep.* 79; thereafter he is apparently retired (see Griffin 1992: 347–53). The focus on withdrawal links *Ep.* 21 to *Ep.* 22, the first of Book 3, where S advises L at least not to seek further advancement, again citing the letters of Epicurus in support (§§5–6, 13–14).

Ep. 21 opens with a staccato series of reprimands, which appear to spring from the subject matter of L's own correspondence ('Do you think your trouble is with those people?'). Yet though S's advice (with its string of second-person verbs) is ostensibly directed at L, there are reasons for seeing S himself as his own principal target, as he counterposes the powerful attractions of public life (particularly Roman public life, though parallels are also drawn with other societies), the fame and glory it can bring, to the more lasting benefits associated with literary and philosophical achievement.

Elsewhere, S stresses inner security and calm as the prizes which await the would-be philosopher and at 19.2 comments, *neque ego suaserim tibi nomen ex otio petere*. While *Ep.* 21 emphasises *securitas* (§1) as the goal, L is consoled for the obscurity withdrawal from the public eye may bring him by the prospect of the fame he will secure as S's correspondent; he will be celebrated far into the future like Idomeneus (correspondent of Epicurus), Atticus (addressee of many of Cicero's letters) and even Nisus and Euryalus, whose heroic early deaths are celebrated in Virgil's *Aeneid*. These examples (§§3–5) take us from philosophical letters, to the letters of a leading Roman politician (also known for his philosophical writing), to the national epic of Rome. S explicitly engages here (as he did briefly in *Ep.* 8) with the question of his wider readership and positions himself as a writer, comparing himself not only with Epicurus, but also Cicero (particularly as letter-writer, though S also expresses admiration for Cicero's philosophical writing, 100.9) and, strikingly, Virgil, who, in the passage quoted, implies the power of his own poem to last as long as Rome itself (Virgil, explicitly quoted in *Epp.* 12 and 18, has already been established as the most prominent literary presence in the *EM*; cf. Mazzoli 1970, Berthet 1979 and, specifically on this letter, Cermatori 2010). The spheres in which these three figures excel (philosophy, statesmanship, poetry) reflect the range of S's own achievements (Schönegg 1999: 175–6). Ker (2011: xxxiv) comments in relation to S's invocation of Virgil here: 'in an important sense, the *EM* are as ambitious and poetic as Virgil's epic'. The comparison drawn by Virgil (cf. Hor. *Carm.* 3.3 *exegi monumentum*) between the durability of a monument and that of a work of literature (a nexus of ideas deftly explored by Fowler 2000: 193–217) is suggestively alluded to here through the figurative use of a series of terms associated with commemorative structures (Cermatori 2010).

We cannot help but be aware that lasting fame accrues to these writers themselves far more than to those they write to or about. S, then, consoles himself for the loss of temporal power (he had been, as Nero's adviser, one of the most influential men in Rome) with the prospect of the greater and more lasting glory his writing will bring him. The value traditionally placed on *nobilitas, honores, gloria* is here appropriated for the would-be philosopher – more particularly for one who articulates the life of the would-be philosopher in writing. Soldo too notes suggestive parallels with assertions in Roman poetry of the author's power to transcend the destructive effects of time (e.g. Hor. *Carm.* 3.30); certainly this letter brings Book 2 to a confident conclusion.

After this invocation of elevated precedents, the tone of the letter changes, with the jocular deployment of financial imagery at §7. Although S has been celebrating the intrinsic splendour of the philosophical life, elevating it above the borrowed lustre enjoyed by the political adviser, the letter concludes (§§10–11) with a visit to a place celebrated for its shade, *umbra*, the garden (κῆπος) of Epicurus in Athens. Here S teases out in somewhat more technical language the important Epicurean distinction between necessary pleasures and unnecessary ones, aspects of which align with Stoic teaching on bringing one's desires under control. The topic of old age re-emerges in the latter part of the letter (§§ 8–10), which has a number of correspondences with *Ep.* 12, the concluding letter of Book 1.

There are some significant parallels in *Ep.* 21 with *De otio* where S comments on the benefit to future generations Zeno and Chrysippus brought precisely by retiring from public life to devote themselves to philosophy. *quo animo ad otium sapiens secedit? ut sciat se tum quoque ea acturum, per quae posteris prosit* (*De otio* 6.4 with Williams *ad loc.*). The divergence between Stoics and Epicureans on when withdrawal from public life might be appropriate (discussed at length in *De otio*, esp. 3) is, however, not touched on here.

On the recognition the philosopher may gain from posterity, *Ep.* 21 is foreshadowed by *Ep.* 8, where (§6) S also compares the Roman politician with the philosopher to the latter's advantage (Schönegg 1999: 171; on the prefatory qualities of *Ep.* 8 see Ker 2004: 229–32). A concern with bringing benefits to posterity is articulated in a number of later letters; S comments 64.7 *maior ista hereditas a me ad posteros transeat* (see note). Although the literary renown the letters will bring S is not explicitly revisited, *Ep.* 79 combines a discussion of literary work (ostensibly in relation to a poetic project of Lucilius) with a consideration of the *gloria* which attends philosophical achievement (§13), again invoking the example of Epicurus (§§15–16). On future fame we might note 79.13 *gloria . . . aliquando in auerso est maiorque quo serior, ubi inuidia secessit* (cf. Newman 2008).

Success in Roman public life is rejected as a goal in *Ep.* 21. Nevertheless S appropriates some key terms of Roman political discourse. With its focus on overcoming the threat of silence and oblivion, 21.5 echoes the proem of Sallust's *Bellum Catilinae*, whose opening sentence exhorts humans *ne uitam silentio transeant ueluti pecora*. Sallust is defensive (more so than is S) about his own withdrawal from active engagement in public life (*Cat.*

3–4) but his proem goes on to highlight the comparable *gloria* which may be won from writing in the service of the *res publica* (cf. *Jug.* 4). In the contrast it articulates between true glory and glory as commonly conceived, *Ep.* 21 deploys to Stoic ends the terms of the speech which Sallust puts in the mouth of Marius (*Jug.* 85.25), contrasting the inherited reputation of those commonly termed *nobiles* (who claim glory for themselves on the basis of their ancestors' achievements, *ex alieni uirtute sibi arrogant*) with his own authentic *nobilitas*, derived from his own military *uirtus* (the sometimes paradoxical ambiguity of *nobilitas* and its relationship to *uirtus*, and *gloria* is also invoked by Cicero in a fragmentary letter to Hirtius, Non. 437.29 = fr. VI.3 in Watt's OCT of *Q. fr.*, *cum enim nobilitas nihil aliud sit quam cognita uirtus, quis in eo, quem inueterascentem uideat ad gloriam, generis antiquitatem desideret?* 'Since nobility is nothing other than *uirtus* made known, who would require a long family tree from one whom he sees to be of well-established glory?'). At *Ep.* 114.17–19, S criticises those who ape Sallustian style but this need not imply criticism of the historian himself; S at *Ep.* 94.46 quotes approvingly Sallust, *Jug.* 10.6 and at *Ep.* 60.4 *Cat.* 1.1 (see Traina 1987: 159–64 for Sallustian influence on the opening of *De breuitate uitae*). It is intriguing, however, that S elsewhere suggests it may be appropriate to prefer those with distinguished ancestors to others of greater merit in awarding public offices (*Ben.* 4.30; see Griffin 2013: 251–4).

Martial (7.44.7–10) may be borrowing from the language of *Ep.* 21 when he characterises S's own fame (Ker 2009a: 154). Pliny's letter to Tacitus (7.20) appears to be influenced by S in its interweaving of *gloria*, *fama* and literary friendship (see also *Ep.* 46). The speech Tacitus puts in S's mouth in a confrontation with Nero (*Ann.* 14.53.4) highlights the *claritudo* which comes from *studia* (cf. *Ep.* 21.2 *studia te tua clarum et nobilem efficient*), while S himself is celebrated *ob claritudinem studiorum* (*Ann.* 12.8.2).

Commentaries: Summers, Motto, Soldo.
Further reading: Maurach 1970: 88–90, Schönegg 1999: esp. 171–8, Habinek 2000, Newman 2008, Cermatori 2010, Edwards 2017b.

1 cum istis tibi esse negotium iudicas de quibus scripseras? presented as a response to a letter of L (the plpf. *scripseras* suggests a letter previous to the one just received), S's question, reproving in tone, mimics the vividness of actual correspondence. *negotium*: trouble (*OLD* 3); frequently used in this sense in Cicero's letters (e.g. *Fam.* 3.10.1 = 73 SB). **maximum negotium tecum habes:** again S exhorts L to focus his attention inwards. The problem is not other people but L himself. *Ep.* 21 thus balances the apparent optimism of *Ep.* 20. **quid uelis nescis** personalises the generalisation of 20.6, *nesciunt... homines quid uelint* (Maurach 1970: 88–9)   **melius probas honesta quam sequeris:** L has made sufficient philosophical progress to value what is right – but not yet to do it; cf. Ov. *Met.* 7.20–1 *uideo meliora proboque: | deteriora sequor.*   **peruenire** 'to get through to' (*OLD* 2).   **dispicis** 'discern' (*OLD* 3).   **magna esse... quae relicturus es:** L places too high a value on the things which S is asking him to forego (L has been procurator, financial official in an imperial province, on which basis he might hope for further advancement, cf. 19.5–7, also *Nat.* 4a.pr.1). The sequence of four periphrastic future verbs in this sentence, with L as their subject, positions him on the brink of a major life change (though one which turns out to be endlessly deferred). On S's predilection for the periphrastic future see Traina 1987: 28–9.   **securitatem:** the key to *uita beata*; cf. 24.2, 92.3.   **fulgor** 'splendour' (*OLD* 5); cf. Tac. *Ann.* 4.39 *neque fulgorem honorum umquam precatum.* The easily disrupted nature of the transmission of *fulgor* is emphasised in the following section. For *fulgor* as specious see also *Ep.* 120.5.   **tamquam in sordida et obscura casurum:** L is afraid the life of philosophical withdrawal he is about to embark on will mean a descent into lowly obscurity. *casurum* agrees with *te* earlier.

2 erras sustains the metaphor of travelling (cf. 59.14 on L's faltering progress: *ad hoc cupis peruenire, sed erras*).   **ascenditur:** impers. The philosophical life is a step up, not a step down, from the political.   **quod... cum... illam** 'What the difference is between brilliance and light, since the latter possesses its own certain source and the former shines with that which is borrowed, this is [the difference] between the latter life [the philosophical] and the former [the political]'.   **crassam illi statim umbram faciet quisquis obstiterit:** *obstiterit* = fut. pf. of *obstare* 'block the path of' (*OLD* 2). Since the light which renders the statesman brilliant comes from an external source, it may be blocked out by anyone who stands in the way. The thickness of the shadow is a vividly sinister detail. For Schönegg (1999: 172–3) the imagery is Platonic in flavour, evoking the figure of the cave, Pl. *Resp.* 514a–520a. On the characteristically Senecan use of *facere* with *umbram* (and cf. §10 *sitim faciunt*) see Setaioli 2000: 15.   **studia te tua clarum et nobilem efficient** 'Your studies will bring you fame and renown.' *studia* here covers both philosophical and literary endeavour. Despite the emphatic *tua* in this assertion, later sections of the letter concentrate not on L's own literary achievements (though his writing is the subject of *Epp.* 46 and 79) but on his role as addressee. The term *nobilis* (derived from *nosco* 'I know'), while suggesting moral distinction (*OLD* 4), was often used in a more precise sense in Roman social and political life, to denote those whose ancestors had achieved high senatorial office (L is an equestrian). Though scholars disagree as to the degree to which the term was applied consistently, even when used in a relatively technical sense the quality of *nobilitas* is regularly associated with ancestral *uirtus*; see Cic. *Sest.* 21, *Planc.* 18, Badian in *OCD*[4] s.v. *nobilitas*. S stresses philosophy's ability to confer *nobilitas*; cf. 44.5 *non facit nobilem atrium plenum fumosis imaginibus . . . animus facit nobilem* (discussed by Nussbaum 1994: 354–7), *Brev.* 15.3 (great philosophers offer their readers the chance to become part of a truly noble family) *nobilissimorum ingeniorum familiae sunt; elige in quam adscisci uelis, Ben.* 3.28.1 *nemo altero nobilior, nisi cui rectius ingenium et artibus bonis aptius.* Juvenal (8.20) asserts that *nobilitas sola est atque unica uirtus* (for *uirtus* subject and *nobilitas* predicate see Henderson 1997: 61), 8.224 (Habinek 2000: 292). Gellius describes the poet Archilochus as *poematis clarum et nobilem* (17.21.8). *Clarus* too has political connotations; Cicero terms leading senators *clarissimi* (Gelzer 1969: 40–4).

3 exemplum Epicuri: in this letter, as in *Ep.* 18, Epicurus occurs both as example and as the source of concluding moral maxims. Here Epicurus serves to highlight S's own role as philosopher and teacher of philosophy through letters. While Epicurus has featured in virtually every letter so far, in *Ep.* 21 he appears particularly as a writer of letters (cf. 18.9). **Idomeneo:** Idomeneus of Lampsacus (*c.* 325–*c.* 270 BCE), friend and biographer of Epicurus (cf. frr. 128–38 Usener, 52–61 Arrighetti). The letters of Epicurus to Idomeneus are quoted at §7 and 22.5. According to Diog. Laert. 10.22, Idomeneus was the addressee of Epicurus' famous deathbed letter (though according to Cic. *Fin.* 2.96, it was Hermarchus). **uita speciosa:** a life of superficial splendour, outwardly impressive. The difficulty of withdrawing from this life is the focus of 22.9. The pejorative flavour of the adjective is esp. evident at 22.1 *occupationibus speciosis et malis*. At 22.3 S advises either to leave that life or to withdraw from life itself. **ad fidelem stabilemque gloriam:** the philosophical life is here described as embodying 'trustworthy and stable glory' (in contrast to the *gloria* of political life whose attractions are conceded in the following clause); cf. 82.12 and at 79.13 the discussion of *gloria* as the *umbra uirtutis*. In Roman political life, *gloria* was particularly associated with the achievement of great military commanders (cf. Sal. *Jug.* 85.34, Cic. *Off.* 1.121, Tac. *Ag.* 8.3, Earl 1967: 30, Lendon 1997: 108–9, Habinek 2000). In the opening sentence of the previous letter (20.1), S commented, *mea enim gloria erit, si te istinc ubi sine spe exeundi fluctuaris extraxero*. At 102.17, more cautious about *gloria*, S contrasts the usual form of *gloria* valued by the many with *claritas* valued by the good. **regiae . . . potentiae ministrum:** gen. of quality; *regiae* is emphatically placed. **si gloria . . . tangeris:** *tango* here in an almost erotic sense, 'if you are turned on by glory'. Epicurus declares that his letters will make their recipient famous (fr. 132 Usener = 55 Arrighetti). Another of his letters to Idomeneus is quoted at 22.5.   **notiorem:** compar. of *notus* *OLD* 6b 'well known'; it picks up §2 *nobilem*.

4 incidisset 'had inscribed' (*OLD* 3b). The term, here used figuratively, evokes funerary monuments (Cermatori 2010: 448–9); cf. *titulus* in the next sentence.   **megistanas et satrapas et regem ipsum** 'the grandees, provincial governors and king himself' of Persia; cf. Tac. *Ann.* 15.27.3 *megistanas Armenios*.   **titulus:** here in the sense of 'position' but often (as Cermatori 2010: 449–51 notes) used for the honorific inscription on a funerary monument (cf. *Brev.* 20.2 *titulum sepulcri*) or associated with an ancestral portrait (of the kind evoked at 44.5, quoted in §2n. on *studia te tua clarum et nobilem efficient*).   **obliuio alta suppressit:** *suppressit* (*OLD* 3) 'to press down so as to remove from sight'. S repeatedly uses the word in this sense (e.g. *Marc.* 26.6). *alta* + *obliuio* seems to be unique in this passage in classical Latin, though the image of the deep waters of oblivion is echoed by Tac. *Ag.* 46.4 *nam multos ueterum uelut inglorios et ignobiles obliuio obruet* (cf. Habinek 2000: 274), while *altum* is elsewhere used to characterise *silentium* in similar expressions (e.g. Ov. *Met.* 1.349); cf. §5 *silentium*.   **Attici:** a close friend of Cicero and addressee of a collection of his letters, Titus Pomponius Atticus (110–32 BCE) was a wealthy equestrian who chose not to seek senatorial office and lived for many years in Athens. From here he assisted Cicero with the conduct of his business affairs and acted as intermediary. Like L (as he emerges from S's letters), Atticus had a strong interest in literature and philosophy, especially Epicureanism (Cic. *Fin.* 5.1–3, *Att.* 5.19 = 112 SB, *RE* 102, suppl. 8, Rawson 1985: esp. 100–4).   **Ciceronis:** the range of Cicero's achievements, as statesman (cos. 63), transmitter of Greek philosophical thought and letter-writer, makes him an especially apt point of comparison for S. Sixteen books of his letters to Atticus survive; this is the first reference to them in the *EM* (see main intro. section 3).   **nihil illi profuisset** 'They would have benefited him nothing' (sing. vb. agreeing with Agrippa as nearest subject).   **gener Agrippa . . . Drusus Caesar pronepos:** Marcus Agrippa, Augustus' close associate, married Atticus' daughter Attica. They had a daughter, Vipsania Agrippina, to whom the future emperor Tiberius was briefly married. Tiberius' son Drusus Caesar was thus Atticus' great-grandson. Suetonius (*Tib.* 7) seems to confirm S's judgement.   **sibi . . . applicuisset** 'had attached to him by ties of friendship' (*OLD applico* 8).

5 profunda super nos altitudo temporis ueniet: a vivid reprise of the image of the depths of oblivion in §4, this time with the specific mention of *nos*, the words *super . . . ueniet* suggesting a flood. *altitudo temporis* (*OLD altitudo* 7d), though close to 99.10 (*temporis profundi uastitatem*), is not paralleled elsewhere but cf. the words put in the mouth of Scipio Africanus at Cic. *Rep.* 6.23 *propter eluuiones exustionesque terrarum, quas accidere tempore certo necesse est, non modo non aeternam sed ne diuturnam quidem gloriam assequi possumus* (cf. 6.25, Schönegg 1999: 175). **ingenia** 'those endowed with literary or philosophical gifts' (*OLD* 5b). The ambiguity of this term (in Graver's words 'mediating between the strictly psychic realm and the external products of talent', 1998: 628) is useful for S (see further Graver 2014). **caput exerent** 'will make themselves stand out' (*OLD ex(s)ero* 1b). As Ker (2015: 119) notes, S here supplements the Virgil quotation with an allusion to Ovid's *Fasti* 1.300, *Altius . . . exseruisse caput*, where poets who have set forth the motions of heavenly bodies are immortalised through cosmic sublimation. **in idem quandoque silentium abitura:** for *silentium* 'obscurity' (*OLD* 5) cf. Sal. *Cat.* 1.1, Cic. *Orat.* 2.7, Plin. *Ep.* 9.14.1. **se diu uindicabunt:** S concedes that even these *ingenia* will perish in the long run but they will for a long while resist oblivion. The unusual phrase *se uindicare* returns us to the opening of S's first letter, where L was enjoined *uindica te tibi* (see 1.1n.), but with the sense 'they will protect themselves' (from oblivion; cf. Cic. *de Orat.* 2.7 *ut laudem eorum . . . ab obliuione hominum atque a silentio uindicarem*). Even after death these few great minds will still have some kind of existence, though in fame and memory only (here S seems to give no credence to the idea of life after death as such; cf. 24.18). **amico suo:** letters were regarded as playing a key role in sustaining friendships (cf. Cicero on the letter as *confirmatio amicitiae, Fam.* 15.14 = 106 SB, Edwards 2018a). Epicurus also placed a high premium on friendship (*Sent. Vat.* 52, *Kuriai doxai* 27). **habebo apud posteros gratiam:** S explicitly includes himself among the great who will be remembered. The tone here is far removed from the self-deprecating manner with which S often handles his own philosophical progress. For the idea of posterity as his audience cf. 22.2 *tale consilium non tantum absentibus, etiam posteris datur,* as well as 8.6. For the orientation towards posterity see also *Ep.* 64, discussed below. **educere** 'to lead away to safety' (*OLD* 3a); cf. 22.1 *educendum esse te ex istis occupationibus*. Also relevant (as Cermatori 2010: 453–4 notes) is the sense (*OLD* 7b) 'to set up as a monument' (cf. *Polyb.* 18.2 *tumulos in magnam eductos altitudinem*). **Vergilius noster:** S repeatedly characterises Virgil thus (e.g. 28.1, 56.12, 86.15). As Mazzoli (1970: 216) notes, *noster* appears with *Vergilius* only in those works of S addressed/dedicated to Lucilius, the *EM* and *Naturales quaestiones*. The use of *noster* in relation to Cicero in *Ep.* 40 stresses his identity as Roman; while S also uses *noster* of major Stoic thinkers, applied to Virgil the term highlights his Roman identity rather than implying an adherence to Stoicism (cf. esp. 58.1–5, *De ira* 2.35.6 *uates nostri*). On S's use of Virgil see further Setaioli 1965: 133–56, Berno 2004, 2011, 2014. **memoriam aeternam:** the passage promises remembrance as long as the poem continues to be read; the Capitol was especially associated with references to Rome as the eternal city (see further below). **promisit et praestat:** *promisit* echoes the promise made by Epicurus, *promittere*, and that made by S, *promitto*, in the preceding sentence. For Virgil's standing cf. *Brev.* 9.2 *maximus uates.* **fortunati ambo ... Romanus habebit:** Virg. *A.* 9.446–9. Nisus and Euryalus (whose names S does not include in his letter) were young Trojans who met heroic deaths in the conflict between Aeneas' followers and the native inhabitants of Italy. Virgil's apostrophe links their memory to the continued life of his own poem, the cults of the Capitoline and the Roman empire itself (the Capitol often stands as a symbol of the eternity of Rome; see Edwards 1996: 87–8). As exemplars of devoted friendship and of bravery in the face of death they resonate with a number of themes in the letters. For Henderson (2004: 31) they signify here as 'eternally acclaimed for the inspirational lessons of losers and loss'; is L being cast in this mould? The verse citation shifts the tone of the letter, the fictive poetic third example in tension with the historically attested individuals featured in the first two (Schönegg 1999: 176–7).

6 in medium 'before the public'. **quicumque ... defecit:** *membra ac partes* 'ministers and agents' (cf., of client kings, Suet. *Aug.* 48 *membra partesque imperii*). *dum ipsi steterunt* 'for as long as they themselves stood firm'. *post ipsos* 'after their deaths'. S's comment on those whose position is dependent on the power of another (use of the past tense here gives an air of greater specificity) focuses on the transience of their fame; they will have no lasting *memoria*. Cf. Tacitus' comments on the fall of Nero's mother Agrippina (*Ann.* 13.19.1 *nihil rerum mortalium tam instabile et fluxum est quam fama potentiae non sua ui nixae*), an event which took place during the period of S's own ascendancy at the imperial court. **ingeniorum crescit dignatio:** word order stresses the importance of *ingenia* (on which see §5n.). *dignatio* 'esteem' (*OLD* 1); cf. 25.6, 64.10. **nec ... tantum honor habetur:** while those prominent in political life may aspire to and achieve honour, great minds will secure more than this. **quidquid illorum memoriae inhaesit excipitur** 'whatever has fixed itself to their memory is taken up'. See *OLD excipio* 8; cf. 114.12 *mirari quidem non debes corrupta excipi*, Cic. *Rep.* 4.8.

7 ne gratis Idomeneus ... redimet 'So that Idomeneus did not come for nothing into my letter, he will now pay for it at his own expense.' Idomeneus has profited (securing increased fame) from his appearance in S's work. *de suo* 'at his own expense' (*OLD* 5b). Once again (cf. 7.10n.) S uses a financial metaphor in relation to his practice of including in his letters quotations from Epicurus. **nobilem sententiam:** for the resonance of *nobilis* see §2n. **ut Pythoclea ... faciat** 'to make

Pythocles a rich man by means neither ordinary nor perilous'. *Pythoclea*: Gk acc. Pythocles is the addressee of a letter of Epicurus (Diog. Laert. 10.83–116). **non pecuniae . . . est**: fr. 135 Usener. True wealth is to be achieved not by adding money but by limiting the desire for it. Riches and poverty are measured only in relation to the wants of the individual, for Epicureans as for Stoics (cf. Epicurus, *Kuriai doxai* 25). Cf. 62.3 *breuissima ad diuitias per contemptum diuitiarum uia est*, 87.3 *fecit sibi diuitias nihil concupiscendo, Ep.* 119 (and Inwood *ad loc.*).

8 apertior . . . adiuuanda 'this pronouncement is too clear to need to be explained and too clever to need to be reinforced'. For the comparative with the second term introduced by *quam ut* see *NLS* §166, §252 n. iii. Cf. 24.3, 53.3, 90.25, 114.4.   **ne istud tantum existimes de diuitis dictum**: sc. *esse*, 'lest you should suppose this only applies to riches'.   **quocumque transtuleris, idem poterit** 'wherever you apply it, it will be equally true'.   **honoribus adiciendum**: the *honestas* at issue here is that accruing from marks of public esteem such as magistracies, *honores* (which would be the object of Pythocles' desires). *honestas* in the sense of moral rectitude is not to be treated as relative.   **si uis . . . detrahendum**: emerging here is the more technical notion of pleasure as used by Epicureans, explored further in the concluding section of the letter.   **si uis Pythoclea senem facere et implere uitam**: S treats the desire for long life in the same way as the desire for riches and the desire for pleasures (the threefold repetition of the frame *si uis Pythoclea . . . sed cupiditatibus detrahendum* hammers home the message). The would-be wise man must learn not to expect more. Here, unusually, Pythocles (object of *facere* but subject of *implere*) is not only encouraged to fill out his life, in the sense of making best use of the time he has, but to see himself as a *senex*, i.e. as having attained the completeness implied by old age, so that there is nothing further he wishes to achieve (cf. Lucr. 3.938 *ut plenus uitae conuiua . . .*).

9 has uoces non est quod Epicuri esse iudices 'you are not to think that these sayings are the property of Epicurus'. On *non est quod* see 7.9n.   **publicae sunt**: for the idea cf. 8.8, 12.11. As Fantham comments *ad* 21.9, S adopts the language of a civil arbitrator who assigns private property to one party or another, in this case declaring the property common to all.   **quod fieri in senatu solet**: in the Roman senate a senior magistrate would make a proposal with which other senators might individually indicate their agreement or disagreement (Talbert 1984: 279–85). S uses this analogy to make a related point in *De otio* 3.1, where he expresses a view at variance with Stoic orthodoxy: *si quis semper unius sequitur* [sc. *sententiam*] *non in curia sed in factione est*.   **censuit** 'has made a proposal', a term often used in relation to senatorial procedure (*OLD* 4a).   **diuidere**

sententiam 'to divide his proposal'. A semi-technical usage of *sententia* (more generally used by S to denote a pithy philosophical maxim, cf. §7) in the senate; cf. e.g. Cic. *Fam.* 1.2.1 = 13 SB *postulatum est ut Bibuli sententia diuideretur*, following which one section of the proposal is approved, the other rejected. S makes clear that he does not fully subscribe to Epicurus' position.   **quod ex parte mihi placeat** 'which I would approve of in part' (*OLD pars* 3c).   **sequor quod probo** echoes *melius probas honesta quam sequeris* in §1.   **egregia dicta commemoro:** S himself helps to perpetuate the memory of Epicurus' great writings (cf. §6). *commemoro* echoes *memoria* which occurs twice in §6.   **ut istis ... probent quocumque ierint honeste esse uiuendum** (sc. *egregia dicta*) 'so that [the notable sayings] will be proof to those people ... that wherever they go they must live honorably'. *probent*: *OLD* 7.   **qui ad illum ... existimant:** for the idea of *uelamentum uitiorum* cf. *VB* 12.5 *libidinibus suis patrocinium aliquod ac uelamentum* (again on the misuse of Epicureanism). Epicureanism had a reputation for attracting those who wished to exploit the prominent place it gave to pleasure as a justification for their own self-indulgence; cf. Cic. *Cael.* 40–1, *Pis.* 68–70 (though in *Fin.* 1.25, 29–39 Cicero is careful to convey the austerity of Epicurean pleasure). S has already made clear through his own careful treatment of Epicurus' notion of pleasure (§8) that this by no means required a life of self-indulgence (for his other criticisms of Epicureanism, which emerge later in the letters, see main intro. section 6). Nevertheless there is a distinction between Epicurean *uoluptas* and the Stoic *gaudium* which, by-product rather than a goal of the good life, is described as *res seuera* at 23.4.

10 cum adieris eius hortulos 'When you shall have come to his little garden'. On the garden of Epicurus see intro. above; cf. 4.10, 33.4(n.). While Cicero at *N.D.* 1.93 seems to use garden in a derogatory sense, elsewhere (*Leg.* 1.54) he puts the term *hortuli* in the mouth of Atticus, who was known for his Epicurean sympathies: *me ex nostris paene conuellit hortulis.*   †**et inscriptum hortulis**†: the text is corrupt at this point and no satisfactory emendations have been proposed. *legeris* has been supplied here (following Bücheler).   '**hospes, hic bene manebis, hic summum bonum uoluptas est**': *hospes* echoes Evander's address to Aeneas in the passage from *A.* 8 S quoted at 18.12(n.), reinforcing *Ep.* 21's Virgilian colouring. *manebis* 'you shall lodge' (*OLD* 2). *hic summum bonum uoluptas est* can be translated either as 'here pleasure is the supreme good' or 'here the supreme good is a pleasure'. The formulation *summum bonum uoluptas* is also attributed to the Epicureans by Cicero (*Fin.* 2.23.7), Seneca the Elder (*Con.* 2.6.2) and Quintilian (*Decl.* 268.10).   **polenta ... aquam:** Epicurus is quoted by Stobaeus: 'I revel in the pleasure of my poor body, employing water and bread, and I spit upon the pleasures of extravagance, not for their own sake, but because of the difficulties which follow from them' (3.17.33 = fr. 181 Usener, 124 Arrighetti, trs. Inwood and Gerson). The role of water and barley meal in the exercises in poverty advocated by S in 18.10 is also symbolic (cf. too 110.18). *polenta* is termed a basic necessity at 45.10.   **ecquid** 'is it not the case that?' (*OLD* 1b).   **non irritant ... sedant:** while luxuries stimulate the appetite unnecessarily (cf. 95.15, 108.15), the basic supplies provided in the gardens of Epicurus alleviate natural needs simply.   **in hac uoluptate consenui:** Epicurus' own writings repeatedly emphasise the pleasure of satisfying one's basic needs in a basic way; cf. e.g. Diog. Laert. 10.131 (= Epicurus, *Ep. Men.* 131). *consenui* 'I have grown old' echoes *senem* in §8.

11 his ... desideriis ... quae consolationem non recipiunt: i.e. those desires which correspond to the body's basic needs for food, water and shelter, as well as freedom from physical pain, and cannot be entirely allayed by philosophical argument. For *consolationem recipiunt* 'are amenable to alleviation' cf. *B. Alex.* 8 *suorum timorem consolatione et ratione minuebat*.   **ista uoluptas naturalis est, non necessaria:** *ista uoluptas* 'pleasure of that kind'. Epicurus distinguished between pleasures which were natural and necessary (those of satisfying the need for food, water and shelter), those which were natural but unnecessary, e.g. sex, and those which were both unnatural and unnecessary, such as the desire for crowns and statues (Diog. Laert. 10.127–32 = Epicurus, *Ep. Men.* 127–32, scholion on Epicurus, *Kuriai doxai* 29, Long and Sedley 1987: 1.121–5). S has very little to say in the *EM* about the desire for sexual pleasure and how it may be controlled. Desire for future fame is legitimate, since fame enhances the would-be wise man's ability to serve as an *exemplum* (Edwards 2017b).   **uenter praecepta non audit: poscit, appellat:** the stomach is personified. *appellat*: technical term for pressing a debtor (*OLD* 5).   **non est tamen molestus creditor:** again a financial metaphor. *molestus* picks up *tu tibi molestus es* in §1.   **dimittitur** 'is satisfied', another term with financial overtones; see *OLD* 3b.

LETTER 24

Ep. 24, by some way the longest so far (at over 1,500 words, roughly twice the length of most letters in the first three books), makes more complex demands on its addressee, as S sets out in detail the strategy of *praemeditatio* (a practice whose importance is already noted at 4.5 in relation to preparation for death; see Armisen-Marchetti 2008). S here stresses that L should always be prepared for the worst, advising him of the benefits to be had from rehearsing for himself the most dreadful experiences he can imagine.

Ep. 22 (the first in Book 3), in its conclusion, raises the fear of death as a concern (22.14), and death is a major focus of other letters in this book (esp. *Ep.* 26, stressing the significance of the manner of an individual's death in an assessment of character: §6 *mors de te pronuntiatura est*, and advising how to die well: §9 *egregia res est mortem condiscere*). While *Ep.* 23 advised against tormenting oneself with hope (which may not be realised), *Ep.* 24 is primarily concerned with relieving oneself of anxieties about the future. The opening section purports to respond to a letter from L, in which he sets out his fear (in the face of a forthcoming lawsuit) and anticipates a reassuring response from S (cf. e.g. 13.4 *ne sis miser ante tempus*). But this is not to be the main thrust of *Ep.* 24, which instead will offer an alternative route to security from *all* worries. The focus is not L's personal affairs. Rather his fears are treated by S as typical of fears in general. L's courage (and that of every reader) is to be fortified by the thought of others who have borne bravely exile, imprisonment, death and pain.

S invokes several famous names, drawing on the tradition of *exempla* familiar from historians, such as Livy, as well as orators (see Mayer 1991, Langlands 2018). The first (§4) are distinguished Romans who endured exile (Metellus, Rutilius). There is also an implicit counter-*exemplum* at this point in the letter, the third in Book 3. It is not irrelevant that Book 3 of Cic. *Ad Atticum* is made up of his letters from exile, written in the aftermath of the bill initiated by Publius Clodius in 58 BCE, re-enacting the law that anyone who had executed a citizen without trial (as Cicero had done following the defeat of the Catilinarian conspiracy in 63) should be banished. Cicero was away from Rome for eighteen months (he was formally recalled in August 57). The letters written during his absence are characterised by tears and solipsistic lament (Hutchinson 1998: ch. 2). Those to Atticus are thoroughly informed by *miseria*, e.g. 3.5.1 (= 50 SB) *ego uiuo miserrimus et maximo dolore conficior*, 3.6.1 (= SB 51) *me uix misereque sustento*. At 3.7.2. (= 52 SB) his despair is such that he threatens suicide. At 21.4–5, S explicitly invokes Cicero's letters to Atticus as a model. Echoes of Cicero's letters in *Ep.* 24 are noted below. Yet Cicero's response to exile, as he describes it in his own correspondence, could hardly be further from the recommended response to exile, as it is modelled in *Ep.* 24 by Rutilius and Metellus (at *Brev.* 5.1, in a passage which goes on to quote a letter, lost now or imaginary, to Atticus, S characterises Cicero as *nec aduersarum* [sc. *rerum*] *patiens* and contrasts his behaviour with that of the *sapiens*; see Williams *ad loc.*). It has, however, been argued that Cicero in his letters (and in *De domo sua*, a speech delivered on his return to Rome) is deliberately taking issue with the traditional motifs of Stoic *consolatio* on the subject of exile (Narducci 1997).

Ep. 24 now moves on to tackle the fear of death and imprisonment; next comes Socrates, rational in the face of execution, often invoked as an *exemplum* in S's work (see main intro. section 6). S then names Mucius Scaevola (§5), celebrated in Liv. 2.12.1–16 for his display of bravery in burning off his own right hand after he had failed to assassinate the enemy king. For Livy this story is an index of Roman national character (Mucius exclaims at §9, *et facere et pati fortia Romanum est*); for S, Mucius' bravery shows what can be achieved even without philosophical training. Yet in taking Mucius as our model (even if our philosophical training renders us in some respects his superior) we also align ourselves with a particularly Roman kind of virtue, that death-defying courage which could terrorise neighbouring peoples and serve to bring them under Roman domination (see further §1on. on *multum . . . mortem*).

A climax of the letter (§§6–8) is the death of Cato, leader of the republican forces in the civil war, who, following their defeat in 46 BCE, killed himself in order not to live under Caesar's tyranny. The deaths of Socrates and Cato are also celebrated at 13.14 *cicuta magnum Socratem fecit; Catoni gladium adsertorem libertatis extorque: magnam partem detraxeris gloriae*, where they are balanced examples of men who have achieved glory through the manner in which they faced their ends (cf. 104.27–33, Isnardi Parente 2000). In 24, Cato is implicitly superior to Socrates, for Cato unites the themes of Roman military heroism (exemplified by Mucius) on the one hand and philosophical training (exemplified by Socrates) on the other. He thus instantiates the *uir fortis ac sapiens* who will be celebrated in §25. The *exempla* are not organised as a crescendo. With Scipio (Cato's contemporary, who also killed himself after defeat in the civil war) S next (§§9–10) offers a more accessible model. The letter then alludes briefly to the nameless, though numerous, *exempla* of more recent times (§11). S returns to the task of demystifying fear, addressing a rousing apostrophe to personified death and pain. Further examples of patient suffering are invoked, this time humble and ordinary (§14). S then (§§15–16) emphasises the pervasiveness of pain (often exacerbated by self-indulgence) as an intrinsic part of the human condition. The horrors, vividly evoked, of the Underworld, familiar from myth (§18), are of course illusory (though their inclusion in a letter which exhorts the reader to imagine real scenes of torture gives them a disturbing edge).

At §§19–20 S articulates a number of mental exercises for relating to death, returning to the preoccupation with time of a number of earlier (and later) letters (e.g. *Ep.* 1, 12.6, 13.11, 32.2). As Ker (2009a: 167) observes, the comments at §§20–1 work 'to deflate the importance of *final* death by revealing it to be little different from the steady passage of time throughout all of our life stages, and thus already familiar', while also inviting us 'to feel *now* the same urgency as final death will possess'. S then offers several quotations from Epicurus (§§22–3), highlighting the paradoxical hatred of life, which may be a consequence of the fear of death. The final part of the letter (§§24–6) warns against suicide for the wrong reasons. S observes that some choose death merely because they are bored of life.

The concern to achieve mental tranquillity by ridding oneself of the torments of both fear and hope is characteristic of Stoic philosophy from its inception (Diog. Laert. 7.118, Cic. *Tusc.* 3.13). It is also an important focus of Epicureanism; for Epicurus, most people fear death as 'the most terrifying of evils' (Diog. Laert. 10.125 = Epicurus, *Ep. Men.* 125, Nussbaum 1994: ch. 6, Warren 2004). S makes repeated reference to Epicurean thoughts and expressions in this letter (as in others in Books 1–4; see main intro. section 6). His crusade against the fear of death is in some ways reminiscent of Lucretius' Epicurean didactic poem *De rerum natura* (esp. 2.59–93, 3.1–93, 830–1094). The opening of Book 3 of the poem makes an explicit link between the hunger for public office and the fear of death; S in his Book 3 repeatedly encourages L to withdraw from the pursuit of office (*Ep.* 21, 22.9–11, 25.6). At 24.18, however, S is dismissive of the Epicurean concern to dispel fear of the Underworld, on the grounds that no one credits such stories.

S's emphasis on the contempt for death and pain as defining aspects of *uirtus* also echoes closely passages in Cicero's *Tusculanae disputationes*, composed in 45 BCE (though Cicero's authority in *Ep.* 24 is somewhat undercut by the implicit allusions, noted above, to his mental weakness in the face of exile). In the course of a discussion of Stoic strategies to rid humans of the suffering brought by the fear of pain and death, Cicero's characters A and M highlight the benefits to be derived from reinforcing Roman military bravery with the philosophical underpinning available within the Greek tradition (*Tusc.* 2.5). M stresses: *ratio, quae quibusdam quasi praeceptis confirmat uim fortitudinis* (2.11). The interlocutors also underline the importance of training (*exercitatio*, 2.38) and discuss how training and philosophy (*ratio, sapientia*) may supplement one another (2.40). In addition M highlights the need to dispel the false image of pain (*falsa eius uisione et specie*, 2.42). The consequent definition of *uirtus* resonates closely with the understanding of this quality in *Ep.* 24: *appellata est enim ex uiro uirtus; uiri autem propria maxime est fortitudo, cuius munera duo sunt maxima mortis dolorisque contemptio* (2.43) – though S does (unusually for him) allow some female examples (see §14n. below).

Although Socrates is discussed only briefly in *Ep.* 24, the arguments of Plato's *Phaedo*, recounting his death (a text with which S is well acquainted, Inwood: 110) are of some importance to this letter. While S does not share Plato's emphasis on the irrelevance of the senses to cognition, he often (as at 70.12) echoes the Platonic representation of embodied life as a burden. *Ep.* 24's engagement with the *Phaedo* highlights its celebration of the benefits of death; its critique of self-killing is not explicitly acknowledged (see Setaioli 1988: 117–18 and esp. Veyne 2003: 119–23 for key points of difference).

S himself is notorious for his advocacy of suicide as a positive option (Rist 1969: ch. 13, Griffin 1986). Certainly he often returns to the idea that the possibility of suicide constitutes a form of freedom (Inwood 2005: ch. 11; see e.g. *Ep.* 70). Life for the Stoics is itself an indifferent (Diog. Laert. 7.102, *SVF* III.117, Rist 1969: ch. 13). Yet while S's concern with suicide is particularly intense, his views are not at odds with those of other Stoics (cf. Cic. *Fin.* 3.60–2 reporting Cato's view). According to Diogenes Laertius (7.130), the Stoics considered self-killing to be an appropriate action if it would save a friend's life, if it would benefit one's country, or if it would allow one to escape from a painful or incurable disease. Esp. in *Ep.* 70 (see below) and *Ep.* 77 S pursues in detail the question of how to decide when it is right to kill oneself, what kind of factors should be included in the calculation.

For S, vision is the most powerful medium of communication: *exempla* (which play a critical role in *Ep.* 24), even when communicated verbally, have a visual impact. Indeed they may sometimes be reduced to an iconic phrase. In *Ep.* 66, S invokes *truncam illam et retorridam manum Mucii* (66.51), while elsewhere Cato's self-inflicted wound is made to stand for Cato's virtue, 67.7 *Catonis scissum manu sua uulnus*. S's invocation of Cato's death in his earlier treatise *De prouidentia* repeatedly underlines its spectacular nature, e.g. 2.9 imagining the gods themselves as the audience (indeed their enjoyment is such that a repeat performance is required). The mental training of the *proficiens* involves the frequent repetition of maxims (cf. e.g. §15) but also the frequent mental rehearsal of these vivid vignettes. The ultimate index of these exemplars' power is their emulation by others. The success of the transformation of the *proficiens* is demonstrated when he in turn becomes exemplary, a point S makes explicit in *Ep.* 98, which again lists the *exempla* of Mucius, Socrates, Rutilius and Cato, as well as that of Regulus. Terrible things have all been overcome by someone (§12–13) *et nos uincamus aliquid . . . nos quoque aliquid et ipsi faciamus animose; simus inter exempla*. On the role of *exempla* in Roman moral discourse see Langlands 2018: esp. chs. 7 and 10 on Mucius Scaevola.

Commentaries: Costa, Laudizi.
Further reading: Tandoi 1965, 1966, Mayer 1991, Hutchinson 1993: 273–87, Edwards 1999, Isnardi Parente 2000, Hill 2004, Inwood 2005: ch. 11, Edwards 2007: 75–7, 87–90, 100–10, Lampe 2008, Ker 2009a: 164–5.

1 sollicitum 'anxious' (*OLD* 2). This opening word picks up one of the concerns of the previous two letters. At 22.16 (with regard to the fear of death), S asks, *quid est turpius quam in ipso limine securitatis esse sollicitum?* At 23.2 he describes the condition of one who places his hopes in outside events rather than his own disposition towards them as *sollicitus* and *incertus sui* 'uncertain of himself'. *Sollicitus* also occurs frequently (thirty-seven times in *Ad Atticum* alone) in Cicero's correspondence, usually characterising Cicero himself. **de iudicî euentu:** while earlier letters, esp. *Ep.* 23, discuss L's hopes of securing further appointments, *Ep.* 24 appears to take its cue from one of the more hazardous experiences often accompanying a public career, litigation. S does not make clear its exact nature (though the penalty L might suffer if he loses is apparently exile, §3); this need not refer to any specific lawsuit; the threat functions as a useful point of departure (to which S returns fleetingly at §12 and §16), while adding further verisimilitude to L as a character. The lawsuit and its outcome are not referred to in later letters. **acquiescas spei blandae:** *acquiescere* 'find comfort in' with the dat. *blandus* 'pleasant', 'coaxing' (*OLD* 1) is almost always pejorative in S. **mala accersere** 'summon evils': the verb (see *OLD arcesso*, of which *accerso* is an alternative spelling, 5) is used elsewhere in relation to death (e.g. 69.6) and other ills (e.g. 11.6). **uenerint:** fut. pf. **praesumere** 'anticipate' (*OLD* 3); in this sense cf. 91.8, *Marc.* 7.4. **praesens tempus futuri metu perdere** 'lose the present through fear of the future'. S repeatedly advises his correspondent not to do this (e.g. 13.13 and, more elaborately, 98.6; also a central concern of *De breuitate uitae*). For S's ongoing preoccupation with time see esp. *Ep.* 1, 12.6. **stultum:** cf. the maxim of Epicurus cited at 15.9 *stulta uita ingrata est, trepida; tota in futurum fertur.* In Stoic thought, the *stulti* are often contrasted with the *sapiens* (e.g. 9.14, 37.3–4, *Ben.* 5.13.1); indeed apart from the *sapiens* all are *stulti* (Wildberger 2006: 308–9). **quia quandoque sis futurus miser:** subj. because the reason is in the mind of the subject of *esse . . . miserum* (*NLS* §240).

2 alia . . . uia: having made a commonplace consolatory move in his first section (reminiscent of the arguments offered in *Ep.* 13), S now offers an alternative and more demanding strategy, *praemeditatio*. This is one of the mental exercises by which the would-be *sapiens* fortifies his mind (cf. 18.6 *in ipsa securitate animus ad difficilia se praeparat et contra iniurias fortunae inter beneficia firmetur*). **securitatem** 'freedom from care', an important goal for Stoics, as well as Epicureans (see main intro. section 4); cf. §12 *securus*. **omnem sollicitudinem:** *praemeditatio* offers a way to alleviate all worries; cf. 76.34, 91.4–7, 104.4, *Tranq.* 11.6. **quidquid uereris ne eueniat** 'whatever you fear may happen'. **utique** 'for certain'. **propone:** here, as often elsewhere (e.g. 56.1, 70.17, 74.7), this imperative sets an exercise of the imagination of the kind which is crucial to effective *meditatio*. **tecum ipse metire ac timorem tuum taxa:** *taxa* 'rate' (*OLD* 2), not found before S. With emphatic alliteration, S advocates the reasoned assessment of emotion. **non magnum aut non longum:** this optimistic maxim of Epicurus (usually with specific reference to pain) was often quoted. See e.g. *Kuriai doxai* 4, Diog. Laert.10.133 = Epicurus, *Ep. Men.* fr. 447 Usener = 204 Arrighetti. S himself repeatedly invokes it (in this letter also at §14 *leuis es . . . non possum*); cf. 30.14 (explicitly attributed to Epicurus), 78.7, 94.7, *Prov.* 6.6. Marcus Aurelius makes a similar pronouncement without attributing it to Epicurus (7.33). This maxim is criticised at length by M in Cic. *Tusc.* 2.44-5.

3 exempla quibus confirmeris 'examples by which you may be given strength'. *confirmeris* generic subjunctive. Earlier letters have already stressed the potency of *exempla*. For *confirmare* used to characterise the development of the *proficiens* cf. 11.1 *cum se confirmauerit et omnibus uitiis exuerit, sapientem quoque sequitur.* **omnis . . . aetas:** the hyperbaton emphasises *omnis* (as is regular with words of quantity). **in quamcumque . . . memoriam miseris** 'To whichever phase of Roman or foreign history you direct your thoughts'. *miseris:* fut. pf. The construction is characteristic of familiar Latin (Bourgery 1922: 209 lists analogous uses of *mittere*). The paradigmatic assemblage of exemplars of particular virtues is in Valerius Maximus' work (organised into Romans and *exterae gentes*), though the practice is also characteristic of satire and featured in declamation. For S's use of such *exempla* see Mayer 1991. S provides in this letter only one non-Roman example (Socrates). **ingenia aut profectus aut impetus magni** 'characters of great achievement or endeavour'. The substantive *profectus* in the sense of philosophical or moral progress made by the *proficiens* (cf. e.g. 11.1, 33.7, 100.11, *Constant.* 17.3) is S's equivalent to the Greek προκοπή (which Cicero translates as *progressio*, e.g. *Off.* 3.14, and *progressus*, e.g. *Tusc.* 4.44). *impetus* 'effort' (*OLD* 4a). **numquid . . . carcerem?** 'If you are condemned, what worse fate can befall you than being sent into exile, than being led to prison?' **exilium:** here to be understood in a non-technical sense. There were a variety of forms of exile in Roman law. Under the republic, exile was an accepted means of avoiding a capital penalty (following conviction for e.g. *maiestas*); voluntary exile would be followed by an administrative decree outlawing the fugitive (see Kelly 2006). Under the principate, exile was increasingly formalised as a true penalty, permanent or temporary, which was statutory for certain crimes (such as adultery) tried by the standing jury courts and was also frequently imposed on elite defendants (such as S himself in 41 CE) by the emperor sitting as judge (see Berger 1953 s.v. *exilium*). Lucretius in his analysis of the fear of death also (3.48–58) takes exile as a particular test of an individual's moral strength. In the *Ad Helviam* 9.7, composed when he was in exile as a consolation to his mother, S argues that to the wise man exile is no hardship as he may flourish anywhere (Williams 2006; cf. *Ep.* 28.4). **carcerem:** imprisonment was not a specified penalty in Roman law, though individuals might spend time in prison awaiting trial or, subsequently, punishment (and owners frequently punished their slaves with imprisonment). The reference to prison also anticipates the example of Socrates in §4. **numquid . . . pereat?** the second rhetorical question, mimicking the syntactical form of the first and also introduced by *numquid*, recasts the prospect of death as paradoxically reassuring, since it brings a limit to all suffering. **non quaerendi sed eligendi** 'they are to be selected rather than hunted for'. This kind of distinction (*non . . . sed . . .*) is very characteristic of S (cf. e.g. 1.4, 2.6 *non acquisita sed acquirenda*, 6.1 *non emendari me tantum sed transfigurari*). Such examples are numerous and familiar, he suggests. He himself tends to reuse the same ones. Rutilius, Mucius, Socrates and Cato occur together at 98.12–13, *Prov.* 3.4, Rutilius, Socrates and Cato at *Marc.* 22.3, *Tranq.* 16.1.

4 Rutilius: Publius Rutilius Rufus studied with the Stoic Panaetius (Cic. *Brut.* 114), served as legate of the Metellus mentioned here and was consul in 105 BCE (Broughton 1953: 1.555, see also 11.9 n. 6). In 92 BCE (according to Dio Cass. 28, fr. 97.3–4) he was convicted of extortion, after serving in the province of Asia, where he offended the interests of some powerful Romans; his innocence was graphically demonstrated by his choice of Smyrna in Asia as his place of exile (on accounts of his exile see Kelly 2006: 89–91, 145–52). Rutilius is several times used as an example by S (cf. e.g. 67.7–13, 79.14, 98.12, *Ben.* 5.17.2, 6.37.2). S's references to Rutilius and to his other exemplars are highly allusive, assuming familiarity with the stories on the part of his reader. **Metellus:** Quintus Caecilius Metellus Numidicus, consul 109 BCE (Broughton 1953: 1.545), later attempted to expel from the senate Saturninus and Glaucia (associates of the powerful general Marius; Saturninus had introduced a grain law unpopular with the aristocracy) and, when he refused to swear to keep Saturninus' law, was forced into exile. Cicero also depicts him in a heroic light (*Fam.* 1.9.16 = 20 SB), terming him *summum uirum et ciuem* (*Off.* 3.79), while Valerius Maximus comments on the equaniminity with which he bore both exile and recall (4.1.13). On his exile see Kelly 2006: 143–5. **ut rediret rei publicae praestitit:** *praestitit* 'granted as a favour' (*OLD* 9a). *rei publicae:* dat. of advantage. For the construction with *ut* + subj. (frequent in S, in contrast to Ciceronian acc. and inf.) cf. *Ep.* 13.6 *illud praesta mihi ut . . .* (K–S 11.212). **Sullae:** Lucius Cornelius Sulla Felix, after two great victories in Greece, used his military power to dominate Roman

COMMENTARY: 24.5 139

politics, holding the dictatorship 82/81 BCE (Broughton 1953: II.66–7). At 11.4, S uses him as an example of the effects of anger. **Socrates:** as often, S includes a Greek example. Socrates was celebrated for, among other things, his principled acceptance of the death penalty imposed on him by the Athenian state after a conviction for impiety and for corrupting the young (see Pl. *Cri.* 48c–54e, Xen. *Ap.* 23). He also appears in e.g. 7.6, 13.14, 67.7–13, 70.9, 98.12. On his exemplary function in S see Döring 1979: 18–42; for the particular focus on his death cf. Epictetus, *Discourses* 4.1 'The remembrance of the death of Socrates is more useful to the world than that of the things which he did and said when alive.' The book of Plato Cato read on his last night (see §6n. below) is usually assumed to be the *Phaedo*. Wilson (2007: 130) comments on the relation between Cato's death and that of Socrates in *Ep.* 24, 'Cato's death is not only an example but an illustration of the need for examples.'

5 Mucius: Gaius Mucius Scaevola. According to some versions, Rome was under threat from the Etruscan leader Lars Porsenna (here 'Porsina' – though the form 'Porsenna' is predominant after Virgil, Citroni 1975: 78) in the late sixth century BCE (see Liv. 2.12–13 with Ogilvie 1965 *ad loc.*). Mucius made an unsuccessful attempt to kill the Etruscan leader. Caught in the enemy camp, he is alleged to have displayed his contempt for physical pain by holding his right hand in the fire brought to torture him. Proverbial for his endurance, he is the first exemplar of *patientia* in Valerius Maximus (3.3.1). S uses Mucius repeatedly (e.g. *Prov.* 3.5.1, *Ep.* 66.51, 98.12, and implicitly at 9.4 where he imagines how the would-be wise man will cope with the loss of a hand). Mucius is used to exemplify Roman contempt for death by Cic. *Sest.* 48.6 *cum eius essem ciuitatis, ex qua C. Mucius solus in castra Porsennae uenisset eumque interficere proposita sibi morte conatus esset*. As Langlands (2018: 207–10) notes, the specific detail of Mucius burning his hand, crucial to S's version, seems to have become central to the story only after Cicero's day. **acerbum est uri:** perhaps an echo of the discussion at Cic. *Tusc.* 2.17 as to whether pain is an evil, which is concerned with the Epicurean response *si uratur sapiens, si crucietur* . . . At *Dom.* 97, Cicero offers a reductive characterisation of the Stoic sage (significantly different from S's Mucius) who *cum uritur non sentit*. Narducci (1997: 60–2) stresses the association of the term *urere* in Cicero's writing with torture. Zeno (according to Clem. Al. *Strom.* 2.20.125 = *SVF* III.386) greatly admired the Indian sages who would undergo burning without complaint. **si id te faciente patiaris:** the reader is to put himself in the position of Mucius watching his own hand consumed by fire, his role as both agent and victim highlighted by the juxtaposition of *faciente patiaris*. This is a very active instance of the Stoic virtue of *patientia*, fleetingly referred to in §24 (on which see e.g.

Constant. 9.4).   **uides:** S describes the gruesome spectacle his reader is to visualise.   **non eruditum:** S uses *eruditus* to refer specifically to philosophical training. Cf. 68.9. There is a contrast here with Socrates, as well as with Cato.   **nec ullis praeceptis . . . subornatum:** if Mucius can show such bravery without any philosophical training, those who are armed with such training (*subornatum* has military overtones, *OLD* 1) should do even better (for the thought cf. Cic. *Tusc.* 2.41). Roman writers were frequently prepared to concede that the Greeks were their superiors in formulating precepts but claimed Roman supremacy in taking action and setting examples (cf. e.g. Quint. *Inst.* 12.2.29–30, contrasting the Greek practice of looking to *praecepta* with the Roman reliance on *exempla*). Several times elsewhere (e.g. 6.5), S. suggests that examples can be more persuasive than precepts, which, as he later stresses, require an *obsequens ingenium* to be effective (cf. 95.4 with Schafer 2009, who argues for a specific and technical sense of *praecepta* in *Epp.* 94 and 95).   **militari tantum robore instructum** 'equipped only with a soldier's courage'. S again stresses the value of military training. Elsewhere he explicitly advocates a military model for spiritual training, e.g. 18.6 (see further main intro. sections 6 and 9).   **spectator:** the visual is further emphasised, as S conjures up Mucius' experience observing the destruction of his own hand. The element of self-consciousness here is particular to S's version of the Mucius story, though Livy figures Porsenna as an internal spectator (see Fitzgerald 2007: 59). Several epigrams of Martial (1.21, 8.30, 10.25) respond to the torment of Mucius, apparently enacted as a mythologically themed punishment in the amphitheatre (see Fitzgerald 2007: 58–61, Citroni 1975: 76–7). Martial's *ipse sui spectator adest et nobile dextrae | funus amat* (8.30.5–6) surely echoes §5 *spectator destillantis in hostili foculo dexterae*. For S, less spectacular forms of suffering may also be validated by invoking the self as audience; 78.21 exhorts Lucilius on his sickbed: *ipse te specta! ipse te lauda!* See Edwards 1999.   **destillantis in hostili foculo dexterae** 'his right hand dripping off into the enemy's brazier', a graphic image reinforced by its counterpart *fluentem manum* in the same sentence. *foculo*: a type of brazier associated with sacrifice (e.g. Var. *L.* 6.14). S's evocation of Mucius at 67.51 is similarly vivid.   **facere aliquid . . . felicius potuit, nihil fortius:** the emphatic abbreviation of the second colon and the asyndetic antithesis are characteristic of S (Traina 1987: 31–2). The impression made on the enemy by this demonstration of Roman bravery is significant: Mucius turns practical defeat into symbolic victory. But S also emphasises the importance of intention rather than effect in evaluating the worth of an action (cf. Cic. *Parad.* 3.24, *Fin.* 3.32, *SVF* III.450–2, Long 1986: 197–9).   **uide . . . irroganda** 'see how much keener virtue is to make dangers its own [*OLD occupare* 5a], than cruelty to inflict them'.

An imperative (again the verb *uidere*) introduces the summation of the Mucius *exemplum*, structured through a series of antitheses.

6 decantatae . . . fabulae istae sunt 'Those stories are repeated in all the schools'. Ancient grammatical and rhetorical schools regularly had students give speeches in character (Quint. *Inst.* 9.2.29–37, Lausberg 1998: §§1131–6, Bloomer 2007). Persius seems to present Cato's deathbed speech as a standard schoolboy performance (3.45–6, see Tandoi 1965, 1966). **inquis:** the words S puts in another's mouth here are not necessarily to be attributed to Lucilius. **cum ad contemnendam mortem uentum fuerit:** impers. fut. pf. Contempt for death is a hackneyed theme, S concedes. **Catonem narrabis** 'you're going to tell me the story of Cato' (*OLD narro* 2). Marcus Porcius Cato (95–46 BCE) was a leading opponent of Julius Caesar, who committed suicide once Caesar's civil-war victory over Pompey at Thapsus in Africa gave Caesar control of Rome (Broughton 1953: II.298). He features more prominently than any other historical or mythological figure in the letters. For S, indeed, Cato perhaps instantiates the Stoic *sapiens* (*Constant.* 7.1). **quidni ego narrem . . .?** 'Why should I not tell . . .?' *quidni* + subj. (often used in comedy) is colloquial. The sentence offers a highly compressed vignette of Cato's last hours. **Platonis librum:** usually identified with the *Phaedo* (Plut. *Cat. Min.* 68, the most detailed account of Cato's death to have survived, mentions Plato's 'Dialogue on the immortality of the soul'), in which Socrates discusses his reasons for preferring to accept death rather than to escape from prison. Several passages in this letter implicitly evoke arguments in the *Phaedo*. See below, §§17, 20nn. 71.11 refers elliptically to Cato reading the night before his death. **posito ad caput gladio:** S gives equal weight to Plato's book, which sustains Cato's will to kill himself, and the sword, which provides the means to do it. His Cato combines the wisdom of Greek philosophy with a specifically Roman moral (and physical) fortitude; killing oneself with a sword came to be characterised as a distinctively Roman way of death (cf. e.g. Mart. 1.78.7). **prospexerat** 'had procured'. **ut uellet mori:** S's Cato (unlike most readers) seems to take the *Phaedo* as endorsing suicide. The version in Cic. *Tusc.* 1.74, in which Cato receives a sign from god sanctioning his departure from life, would be more in line with traditional readings of the *Phaedo*. **compositis . . . rebus:** the verb *componere*, here used in the general sense of 'arrange', 'put in order', is a significant term for S. At 30.12 S writes approvingly of the man who is able to welcome his own end because he has long since composed himself for death, *se ad illam diu composuerat* (cf. e.g. 2.1, 26.5). **ne cui Catonem . . . seruare contingeret** 'so that no one should have the chance to save Cato'. Julius Caesar allegedly intended to spare Cato. This would have been a humiliating display of *clementia*, which Cato claimed Caesar had no right to exercise (cf. Plut. *Cat. Min.* 66). On *clementia* see Dowling 2006, Braund: esp. 64–8.

7 quem . . . purum seruauerat: Cato, despite his leading role in the civil war, had not himself taken the life of any of his fellow citizens, it is implied. S makes the same point at *Prov.* 2.10 *ferrum istud etiam ciuili bello purum et innoxium.* Killing the 'enemy' (one's fellow citizens) in civil war is often characterised as impious; Lucan, in contrast to S, does not exonerate Cato (Luc. 2.264–6; see Edwards 2007: 31–3).   **'nihil' inquit '. . . in tutum':** while some have imagined that S here preserves Cato's own words, Tandoi (1965, 1966, esp. 1965: 329–36) argues convincingly that a deathbed speech did not feature in the earliest accounts of Cato's suicide (on which Thrasea Paetus, S's contemporary, drew in composing his biography of Cato) and that it was S himself who devised this part of the story.   **fortuna:** personification (Armisen-Marchetti 1989: 252–4, 258–9). For the idea of *fortuna* as an enemy with whom the *sapiens* is in conflict cf. 71.30, 82.5 *philosophia circumdanda est, inexpugnabilis murus, quem fortuna multis machinis lacessitum non transit, Prov.* 2.9, Asmis 2009.   **pro patriae libertate:** *libertas* was repeatedly invoked in the political debates of the late republic (see Wirzubski 1950, Roller 2001, Arena 2012). For the more specifically philosophical sense of the term (whose importance here is underlined by the echo in *liber* and *liberos*) see Inwood 2005: ch. 11, Edwards 2007: ch. 3, Degl'Innocenti Pierini 2014). If Cato cannot live *inter liberos* 'among free men' (in the sense of men participating in government of their own society), the goal he has been fighting for until now (*adhuc*), he is nevertheless himself achieving freedom of a more important kind, freedom from fear and hope, as well as from subservience to Caesar. Cf. *Prov.* 2.10, where Jupiter declares that Cato's sword can give him *libertatem quam patriae non potuit* (also *Ep.* 95.72). In *Constant.* 2.3, S treats Cato as synonymous with *libertas*: *neque enim Cato post libertatem uixit, nec libertas post Catonem.* For the idea cf. V. Max. 6.2.5 *libertas sine Catone? non magis quam Cato sine libertate.* On death as an escape route see further §11.   **deducatur** 'is led off' (*OLD* 8a).

8 non tantum . . . iratus: the self-destructive impulses of the Roman elite in civil war are internalised into Cato's own person (a conceit characteristic of Seneca's nephew Lucan, cf. e.g. Luc. 1.3). More often anger is viewed negatively by S; cf. e.g. 110.2 and *De ira passim.*   **nudas . . . egit:** according to many versions of the story, Cato only managed to kill himself by ripping open his wound after doctors had bound it up (see, most gruesomely, App. *B Civ.* 2.142). Elsewhere S comments, *non fuit dis immortalibus satis spectare Catonem semel* (*Prov.* 2.12). According to Plutarch (*Cat. Min.* 68–70), the reason Cato failed to kill himself with the first wound was that he had injured his hand hitting a slave whom he thought guilty of removing his sword from his tent.   **non emisit sed eiecit:** the violence of Cato's suicide is heightened. This self-correction is characteristic of S; cf. 70.19 (of Cato) *ferro non emiserat animam manu extraxit*, *Brev.* 11.1 *non tamquam exeant de uita, sed tamquam extrahantur.*

9 non . . . ut ingenium exerceam: for disapproval of displays of verbal ingenuity unconnected to important goals, cf. 113.1, *Ben.* 6.1.1 *quaedam . . . exercendi tantum ingenii causa queruntur*. Elsewhere (e.g. *Ep.* 80.2) S uses the phrase *exercere ingenium* positively in contrast to time and effort wasted on exercising the body.   **quod maxime terribile uidetur:** i.e. death.   **efflandae animae:** *OLD efflo* 1b. The expression occurs only here in S.   **quosdam ad alia ignauos:** those who do not aspire to emulate the matchless Cato are offered a more attainable model. Examples of those who, though otherwise cowardly and weak-willed, nevertheless rise to the occasion when faced with death are frequently invoked by Tacitus, e.g. Sempronius Gracchus, who had been convicted of adultery with Augustus' daughter Julia (*Ann.* 1.3.8): *constantia mortis haud indignus Sempronio nomine: uita degenerauerat*. Elsewhere (e.g. *Ep.* 70.19) S makes the rather different point that that even individuals of humble background may show great bravery in the face of death.   **Scipionem:** Q. Caecilius Metellus Pius Scipio Nasica, consul 52 BCE, died 46 BCE (Broughton 1953: II.234–5). His daughter Cornelia was married to Pompey. Prominent among the opponents of Caesar, he brought two legions to Thessaly in 48 and commanded the centre at the battle of Pharsalus, after which he became supreme commander in the African War. Defeated at Thapsus, he attempted to retreat to Spain but was driven by a storm onto the coast of Africa. Surrounded by the ships of Sittius, he killed himself to avoid falling into enemy hands (Flor. *Epit.* 2.13.68, Dio Cass. 43.9.5). For his dying words see Liv. *per.* 114 and V. Max. 3.2.13 (whose version S's resembles closely).   **ferro se transuerberauit:** the verb 'run through' (cf. *Ep.* 15.5) makes clear that Scipio used the same force against his own body as he had been deploying against the enemy troops. This is a suicide of the battlefield, not the bedroom.

10 uox 'pronouncement' (*OLD* 8); *uox* is often used in this sense by S (cf. 9.13, 19, 13.16, *De ira* 1.3.2). S encourages his reader to imagine hearing Scipio's words. On the potency of the spoken word see 6.5, 33.9, *Prov.* 3.3.   **parem maioribus:** a Roman aristocrat was supposed to live up to the achievements of his ancestors. See e.g. Liv. 7.10.3. Oakley (1998 *ad loc.*) cites the epitaph of Cn. Cornelius Scipio Hispanus (*ILLRP* 316), ll. 3–4 *maiorum optenui laudem ut sibei me esse creatum* | *laetentur; stirpem nobilitauit honor*. See further Flower 1996: 150–4, 220–1, Treggiari 2003: 155–7.

Although Metellus Scipio was defeated, the manner of his death allowed comparison with his distinguished forebears.   **fatalem Scipionibus in Africa gloriam:** P. Cornelius Scipio Africanus defeated Hannibal in 202 BCE (Broughton 1953: 1.317). P. Cornelius Scipio Aemilianus Africanus (his adoptive grandson) captured Carthage in the third Punic War in 146 BCE (Broughton 1953: 1.467). Suetonius (*Jul.* 59) refers to the prophecies current in the civil-war period that a Scipio could not be defeated in Africa (*felix et inuictum in ea prouincia fataliter Scipionum nomen*). Killing himself so courageously in Africa, the civil-war Scipio continues the family tradition of bravery (even if his valiant aggression is directed against himself). Cicero (*Brut.* 212–3) praises Scipio alongside his grandfathers and great-grandfathers, presenting his wisdom as a family trait.   **multum . . . mortem:** another epigrammatic formulation characteristic of S in which the verb of the first colon is to be understood in the brief second colon (cf. on §5 *facere aliquid . . .* Traina 1987: 34–5). Here as elsewhere S compares Rome's military conquests with victories over the passions, especially the fear of death, to the advantage of the latter (cf. 71.37, which concludes, *quem uicerim quaeris? . . . metum mortis, qui uictores gentium uicit*). For the imagery of fighting the fear of death see Armisen-Marchetti 1989: 95.

11 non reuoco te: that examples are to be found even in recent, less morally rigorous, times is an indication of how plentiful they are. Cicero and Livy regularly support older *exempla* with more recent ones, as Oakley (2005a) notes *ad* Liv. 9.34.14; cf. Cic. *Orat.* 169.   **contemptores mortis:** variants on *contemnere mortem* are repeated several times in this letter, cf. §3 *contemptores*, §6 *contemnendam mortem*, §8 *contemptorem*, §9 *hoc momentum . . . contempsisse*, §14 *mors . . . quam ancilla contempsit*; cf. Cic. *Tusc.* 2.43.   **respice ad haec nostra tempora:** S does not give particular recent examples of political suicides (there were many; see Plass 1995: 81–134, Hill 2004: ch. 8); his specific illustrations are almost all drawn from the safely distant past. For the idea that, with regard to facing death at least, Romans continue to show bravery cf. Tac. *Hist.* 1.3.1 commenting on the civil-war period, after the death of Nero: *supremae clarorum uirorum necessitates fortiter toleratae et laudatis temporum antiquorum mortibus pares exitus.*   **languore ac delicîs:** S repeatedly complains about the luxury and decadence of his contemporaries in comparison with Romans of earlier times (see e.g. 55.1, 86.7, 90.16, 95.18, 122.5–18, *Brev.* 12.7).   **omnis ordinis homines:** cf. §14. In 70.23, 26 and 77.14–15 S provides more detailed examples of brave individuals, the Spartan boy, the German condemned to fight in the arena (at 70.19 explicitly offering such humbler persons as a less daunting model than that of Cato). See further

70.1nn.   suggerent '[our own times] will pile up'.   **qui mala sua morte praeciderint** 'who have cut short their troubles with death'. *praeciderint*: generic subj.   **beneficio eius nihil timendum sit:** for death as a road to freedom (already introduced at 22.5–6, *libertas recedendi*) cf. most aggressively *De ira* 3.15.4, as well as e.g. *Prov.* 6.7, *Ep.* 26.10, 70.14, 24–5.

12 securus: cf. §2 *securitatem*. The verbal echoes (cf. §1 *inimici*, §12) underline the return to the initial topic of the letter.   **quamuis . . . faciat:** another reference to Lucilius' lawsuit; cf. §1.   **extra causam:** other factors may influence the outcome, beyond the case (*OLD causa* 4) considered on its merits.   **ad id te quod est iniquissimum compara** 'prepare yourself for that which is utterly unjust'.   **demere rebus tumultum** 'set aside from things the accompanying commotion'.   **quid in quaque re sit** 'the essence of each thing'.   **nihil . . . terribile nisi ipsum timorem:** picking up on §9 *quod maxime terribile uidetur*. On the vanity of fear see 13.7–13, 47.17.

13 quod uides accidere pueris 'the kind of thing which you might see happen to boys'.   **maiusculis pueris:** ironic diminutive (from *maior*), colloquial in flavour (Setaioli 1980: 23). At 110.6–7, a similar analogy with the fearfulness of children is credited to Lucretius (citing 2.55–6, verses which also appear at Lucr. 3.87–8, in relation to the fear of death, and 6.35–6). S there comments, picking up the imagery of light and darkness, which runs through Lucretius' poem: *non omni puero stultiores sumus qui in luce timemus? sed falsum est, Lucreti, non timemus in luce: omnia nobis fecimus tenebras*. S often compares adults to children to make the point that the former engage with life in an unreflective manner excusable only in the latter, while also allowing for the possibility of development; cf. e.g. 115.8 *simillimi pueris*, and, again invoking masked figures, *Constant.* 5.2, *uexemur more puerorum, quibus metum incutit umbra et personarum deformitas*.   **quos . . . quibus . . . cum quibus:** the triple anaphora of relative clauses is emphatic.   **personatos** 'wearing masks'. Cf. Lucr. who, discussing the fear of death, *metus . . . Acheruntis*, describes, in relation to identifying people's true feelings on this, the final test of an individual's character at 3.58 *eripitur persona, manet res* (this early correction of the problematic MS reading is defended by Kenney 2014). S himself several times uses the mask as metaphor, cf. e.g. 80.8, arguing that fortunate circumstances are incidental and must be stripped away to evaluate the true self, *omnium istorum personata felicitas est*.   **rebus persona demenda est:** echoes §12 *demere rebus tumultum*.   **reddenda facies sua:** the implication of the analogy is perhaps that death, too, once unmasked, is a familiar and even lovable figure.

14 quid mihi ... ferre non possum: change of addressee. An extended apostrophe first to death (*mors es* ...) and then to *dolor* 'pain' (*tu rursus* ...), named only after a long series of questions. The two are personified with considerable elaboration. Death brings swords and fire (the instruments used respectively by Cato in §7 and Mucius in §5) and is accompanied by a crowd of executioners. Pain brandishes a vast panoply of instruments of torture. This apostrophe is made up of series of rhetorical questions (*quid* ...? *quid* ...? *quid* ...?) interspersed with imperatives (*tolle* ... *pone* ... *iube* ...). **turbam carnificum circa te frementem:** the emphatic homoeoteleuton (*-am, -um, -em*) lends a deliberate pace to the parade of instruments of torture (Laudizi *ad loc.*). **pompam:** for a similar use of *pompa* 'procession' cf. 14.4, where S characterised evils inflicted by humans as coming in a procession: *ingens alterius mali pompa est.* **stultos:** those who fail to recognise the reality of death and pain (used in §1 of those who are needlessly preoccupied with what *may* happen). **seruus ... ancilla:** humble and nameless in contrast to the distinguished individuals invoked as *exempla* earlier. **flagella ... hominis:** S enumerates the instruments of torture; cf., even more graphically, 14.4–6. **quid singulis articulis ... particulatim hominis?** 'Why do you set out [sc. *explicas*] for each joint the individual instruments devised for their torment and the thousand other means by which a man may be butchered bit by bit?' *articulis* 'joints' (*OLD* 1a). Pain is presented as a torturer, whose ingenuity is bent on devising tailor-made sufferings for individual body parts. The polyptoton seems to multiply the instruments of torture, as Laudizi observes *ad loc.* **excarnificandi:** echoing the *turbam carnificum* accompanying death. For *excarnificare* paired with *extorquere* see *TLL* v.2.1203.1–10. *particulatim* echoes *articulis*. **gemitus ... acerbitatem** 'the groans and cries and anguish of the screams wrung out during torture'. *acerbitatem* echoes *acerbum* characterising Mucius' pain in §5. In ordering personified pain to silence the cries of the afflicted, S implies that the primary purpose of such sounds is to induce fear in others; they are a kind of theatre. After the primarily visual emphasis of earlier sections of the letter, S now focuses on sound, with a particular emphasis on *u, i, l, e, a*. **quem podagricus:** the triple anaphora of the relative pronoun *quem* introduces a tricolon. For *podagricus* 'a sufferer from gout' cf. 53.6, *De ira* 2.33.4. Celsus (4.31) presents *podagra* as a condition which can be controlled through a restricted diet; cf. Plin. *Ep.* 1.12.5. At 95.21 S associates the ailment specifically with a life of luxury and self-indulgence, taken to such an extreme that even women succumb to what is usually a masculine affliction. Both this and the following example present pain as comparatively trivial and the result of the sufferer's lack of self-restraint in eating and drinking. **stomachicus ... in ipsis**

delicîs 'the dyspeptic even as he feasts'. *stomachicus* is a Graecism first used by S, notes Bourgery (1922: 304), and subsequently by Pliny, e.g. *Nat.* 28.116.   **quem in puerperio puella perpetitur:** the alliteration echoes the panting of the woman giving birth. The term *puella* emphasises both her youth and perhaps also her low social status. The ability to endure pain is often presented as a specifically 'manly' quality and the failure to do so as effeminate (cf. 78.17 *muliebriter*, Cic. *Tusc.* 2.43 *uiri autem propria maxime est fortitudo, cuius munera duo sunt maxima: mortis dolorisque contemptio*). This female example is included with the sense of 'even a girl'. Cf. the inclusion of *seruus meus* and *ancilla* earlier in §14, as well as *omnis ordinis* §11 – even persons of lowly status are able to despise death.   **leuis es . . . non possum:** pain is either bearable or short-lived; cf. §2. For the form of expression, using the rhyme of *leuis/breuis* to underline the point, cf. Cic. *Tusc.* 2.22: *doloris medicamenta illa Epicurea tamquam de narthecio proment: 'si grauis, breuis; si longus, leuis'*.

15 haec in animo uoluta: S returns to addressing L. S uses a variety of terms in relation to the practice of *meditatio*; cf. e.g. 13.13 *hoc in animo uolue*, 42.9 *haec ergo tecum ipse uersa*.   **an uere . . . dixeris:** with the anaphora *an uere*, the same verbs are repeated, this time in the perf. subj. form. The process of repetition serves to internalise Stoic teaching; hearing (and reproducing) these words will protect L when he hears the threats of his enemy (*securus itaque inimici minas audi*, §12 above). On the relationship between precepts and habituation see also *Ep.* 95 (and compare Muson. frr. 5–6 Hense).   **effectu proba** 'prove by the result'. The learning process is put to the test when the time comes for the maxims to be put into practice (cf. 26.6, specifically in relation to facing death).   **uerba . . . non opera:** S refers frequently to the accusation of hypocrisy which was a standard charge against philosophers, particularly in the Roman world (e.g. 16.1, 20.1, 26.6, 34.4, 108.35, often opposing *uerba* and *res*, or *dicere* and *facere*). The serious danger posed by those whose lives do not follow their own teachings is underlined at 108.37. S himself regularly comes in for such criticism among both ancient and modern critics (see, for instance, Dio Cass. 61.10.3); this issue is addressed at length in *De uita beata* (Griffin 1992: ch. 9). For Jones (2014) the tension between Stoic precepts and the individual's necessarily flawed attempts to follow them in practice is deliberately foregrounded by S through his choice of letters as a literary form.   **quid?** 'Well?' This colloquial expostulation (*OLD* 10) is highly characteristic of S.   **mortem . . . scisti:** for the idea cf. e.g. 77.11 *nemo tam imperitus est, ut nesciat quandoque moriendum*.   **in haec natus es** 'you were born to these', i.e. they are part of the human condition. S often invokes this argument, e.g. 77.12 *ad hanc legem natus es*.   **quidquid fieri potest, quasi futurum cogitemus** 'Whatever can happen, let us imagine that it will happen!' S sums up *praemeditatio*, as first set out in §2.

16 quod facere te moneo scio certe fecisse: chiasmus with *te/certe* in assonance. S, confident of L's progress (cf. 16.2, 19.1), knows he will have already undertaken such mental exercises. The challenge now is to apply what he has learned.   **ut animum tuum non mergas in istam sollicitudinem** 'that you do not sink your spirit into that anxiety'. *sollicitudinem* returns us to the letter's starting point, L's impending lawsuit.   **hebetabitur** 'will be dulled' (*OLD* 4).   **exurgendum sit:** i.e. the human spirit must always be primed to respond to a challenge.   **abduc ... publicam** 'remove your mind from your own case to the general one', i.e. the common condition of humanity.   **corpusculum:** the diminutive further emphasises the body's weakness and vulnerability (*TLL* IV.1025–6, Setaioli 1980: 23 n. 1); cf. *Helv.* 11.7, *VB* 4.4, *Ep.* 23.6, 41.4.   **cui non ex iniuria tantum ... denuntiabitur dolor** 'to which pain will be a threat [*OLD denuntio* 2] not only through injury or the exercise of superior force'.   **ipsae uoluptates in tormenta uertuntur** 'our delights themselves become torments'. This assertion picks up particularly the example of the dyspeptic at the feast (§14).   **libidines pedum ... articulorum omnium deprauationes** 'our pleasures bring damage to the feet, the hands and all joints of the body'. This develops the idea introduced with the example of the pain suffered by the *podagricus* at §14. The personified *dolor* was imagined deliberately devising individually tailored torments. Driven by the pursuit of pleasure, it is humans who are often the agents of their own particular forms of suffering (*articulorum* echoes *articulis* at §14). Relevant here is the Epicurean concern with the pain brought by excessive pleasures (Diog. Laert. 10.129 = Epicurus, *Ep. Men.* 129, Cic. *Fin.* 1.32).

17 pauper fiam ... ero: the fear of poverty is often addressed in the letters (see main intro. section 7). S suggests we may be consoled by the knowledge that many suffer the same misfortunes as ourselves (see also e.g. *Helv.* 12.6–7). Elsewhere he advances the more positive view that poverty offers a form of *securitas*, for one has nothing further to lose, cf. e.g. *Ep.* 17. On S's attitude to wealth more generally see Griffin 1992: ch. 9.   **exul fiam ... mittar:** S suggests as a technique for dealing with exile that one should imagine oneself born in the place to which one has been exiled. In his address to his mother concerning his own exile, *Ad Heluiam*, S advances a variety of mental strategies for coming to terms with exile, e.g. at 4.2, 6.1. There was already an established philosophical tradition of *consolatio* (see Claassen 1999: 19–26, Williams 2006); cf. Cic. *Tusc.* 3.81 and *Fin.* 5.84 (where the view is attributed to Zeno that the wise man is happy even if an exile). Relevant here is the Stoic view that the *sapiens* is a citizen of the world: 28.4, *Helv.* 9.7.   **alligabor** 'I shall be put in chains'. For binding cf. *VB* 16.3 *ei . . . opus est aliqua fortunae indulgentia adhuc inter humana luctanti, dum nodum illum exsoluit et omne uinculum mortale.* In Plato's *Phaedo*, the soul at death is described by Socrates as freed from the body 'as from fetters' (ὥσπερ ἐκ δεσμῶν, 67d).   **graue . . . pondus:** the idea of the body as a burden to the soul is a regular concern of S's (see e.g. 23.6 and 26.2, on the experience of growing older, *uiget animus et gaudet non multum sibi esse cum corpore*, while *Ep.* 14 argues at length against becoming a slave to one's bodily needs). Compare the arguments against fearing death advanced by the character of Socrates in Plato's *Phaedo*, esp. 63e–65c. Socrates is made to contend: 'if we are ever to know anything absolutely, we must be free of the body' (66c–d).   **moriar** 'I shall die', the anxious subject exclaims, in response to which S offers the consolatory thought that death will bring an end to all other forms of sufferings.   **desinam . . . desinam . . . desinam:** the triple anaphora emphasises the release provided by death.

18 Epicuream cantilenam 'the refrain of the Epicureans': cf. fr. 341 Usener. An instance of *praeteritio*. Lucretius (3.978–1023), like S. seeking to dispel fears of what may happen after death, presents the stories associated with the Underworld as symbols of people's destructive passions in this world: (979) *in uita sunt omnia nobis*. S returns to this theme in 82.16, quoting with disapproval Virgil's depiction of the Underworld in the *Aeneid* (cf. *Marc.* 19.4). Cicero's characters M and A in *Tusc.* 1.10–11 dismiss such tales, observing that the energies philosophers devote to disproving them are misplaced (cf. *N.D.* 2.5).   **nec Ixionem . . . carpi:** S refers to a number of familiar myths associated with the Underworld: that of Ixion, king of the Lapiths, who revolved perpetually on a wheel as punishment for his attempt to seduce Juno (see e.g. Pind. *Pyth.* 2.31–2); that of Sisyphus, a king of Corinth proverbial for his trickery, condemned to roll uphill a stone which always rolled down again (see e.g. Hom. *Od.* 11.593–600); both Tityus and Prometheus were described as having their miraculously regrowing entrails plucked out daily by birds of prey, Tityus (*Od.* 11.576–81) in punishment for an attempt to rape Latona (mother of Apollo and Diana) and Prometheus (Aesch. *PV*) for stealing fire from heaven to give to humans. While S dismisses this description of the Underworld as something not even a child would credit, this evocation of a gruesome and familiar fantasy also echoes the more serious description in §14 of torments that may be suffered in this life.   **Cerberum:** Cerberus was the three-headed dog who guarded the entrance to the Underworld (Virg. *G.* 4.483, *A.* 6.417).   **larualem habitum nudis ossibus cohaerentium** 'the ghostly dress of those made up of bare bones', i.e. skeletons.   **aut consumit aut exuit** 'either destroys us or liberates us'.   **emissis meliora restant onere detracto:** for *onere detracto* cf. the baggage imagery in 26.2 *magnam partem oneris sui posuit* [sc. *animus*]. Stoics sometimes argued for the survival of the soul (cf. 57.7). On this see also 36.9–10, 71.16, 93.9–10, Setaioli 2000: 275–323. Busch (2009: esp. 262–5) argues that scholars have underestimated S's concern with the afterlife but, despite some passages stressing the liberated soul's freedom to engage with the sublime (e.g. 102.27), S himself acknowledges that this prospect may be no more than a comforting delusion (102.1–2). Epitaphs on Roman tombs exhibit a wide range of attitudes to post-mortem survival but many explicitly reject the possibility of any kind of life after death (Lattimore 1942: chs. 2 and 3, Hope 2009: 114–15).   **consumptis nihil restat:** the Epicurean view was firmly against the possibility of life after death (cf. Lucr. 3.323–49, 417–578, Warren 2004: 1).

19 permitte: with the infin., as always in S.   **uersum tuum:** S suggests that L already knows and has written about all this (on L's own writings see also 7.9, 19.3 *in medium te protulit ingenii uigor, scriptorum elegantia*, 46 (discussed below), 59.4, 79. Schönegg 1999: 179–94).   **te iudices non aliis scripsisse ista sed etiam tibi:** a reminder which might also apply self-referentially to S. He, too, is under a particular obligation to regulate his emotions in line with what he writes.   **turpe . . . sentire:** the double anaphora of *aliud* contrasts first speech and feeling (proverbial; cf. Hom. *Il.* 9.313), then writing and feeling, making the claim that hypocrisy in one's writing is the more shameful.   **non repente . . . procedere:** for the image of life as a journey, whose end is death, see Armisen-Marchetti 1989: 87–8, Chambert 2005: 157–65. At 26.4 S emphasises the benefits of the gradual withdrawal from life, which is a consequence of old age: *lenis haec est uia subduci*.

20 cotidie morimur 'every day we are dying'. *cotidie*, immediately repeated, stresses the reassuring ordinariness of death; S elaborates in 1.2 *se cotidie mori* (Gagliardi 1998: 72) but here, in contrast to *Ep.* 1, the idea is attributed to L himself. This same notion reappears also at 26.4 and elsewhere. Though dying is a gradual process rather than a repeated one, *cotidie* could also be read as echoing the daily tortures of Tityus or Prometheus in the Underworld alluded to earlier (the verb *carpi*, used of the plucked entrails at 18, is used of the incremental daily depredations of death at 120.18 *carpit nos illa non corripit*). On the significance of *cotidie* more generally see 1.2nn., 12.9nn. Augustine echoes this idea, *C.D.* 13.10.   **infantiam amisimus** 'we lost our infancy . . .': the choice of verb also implies people waste their lives in pointless activities; cf. *Ep.*

1, 58.22–3, *Brev.* 10.2.   **quidquid transit temporis perît:** pf. Past time is lost time; see further e.g. 49.2 *infinita est uelocitas temporis, quae magis apparet respicientibus.* At 74.73 S stresses that both past time and future time are *aliena*; only the present is ours.   **diem . . . diuidimus:** just as past years and days are lost to death, so too are the past hours of the current day.   **clepsydram:** a device used to measure the passage of time by the flow of a certain quantity of water (like an hourglass), from the Greek 'water-stealer' (esp. associated with the measurement of time in Athenian law courts; see e.g. Ar. *Ach.* 693).   **stilicidium:** a drop from the waterclock (cf. the metaphorical last drop at 70.5). For the dripping cf. Mucius' hand *destillantis* in §5.

21 haec cum descripsisses: S summarises the argument of L's poem before quoting a line.   **quo . . . ore:** 'in your usual style'.   **magnus:** S characterises L's writing style as lofty (*OLD* 14).   **malo te legas** 'I would rather you read yourself'. The *te* stands both for L's writing and for L himself. The importance of consistency between writing and action (§19) is further underlined.

22 uideo quo spectes 'I see what you're looking for'. S projects on to L the expectation that this letter, like all the letters so far (apart from *Ep.* 1), will conclude with a fitting citation from Epicurus or his followers (see 7.10–11nn).   **infulserim** 'I have crammed in' (cf. 106.5, 114.19).   **quod dictum . . . quod . . . utile:** sc. *sit* in both these indirect questions, expanding *quid* and *quod* as the objects of *infulserim*.   **animosum** 'spirited', cf. *animose* (98.13, cited in 33.7n.).   **ex hac ipsa materia quae in manibus fuit:** S implies he is himself currently reading Epicurus; cf. 8.7 *adhuc Epicurum complicamus, cuius hanc uocem hodierno die legi.*   **qui mortem concupiscent:** on desiring death as reprehensible see §25.   **ridiculum . . . effeceris:** Epicurus fr. 496 Usener (= 229 Arrighetti). This quotation and the two which follow explore the paradox of those who make their lives miserable with the fear of losing them, an issue discussed with particular pungency by Lucretius (3.1003–10).

23 alio loco: fr. 498 Usener (= 229 Arrighetti); cf. also Diog. Laert. 10.126, Lucr. 3.79–82 *et saepe adeo, mortis formidine, uitae | percipit humanos odium lucisque uidendae, | ut sibi consciscant maerenti pectore letum | obliti fontem curarum hunc esse timorem.*   **adicias:** subj. governed by *licet,* sc. *ut.* This appears to be the only time S chooses to cite an Epicurean *sententia* in indirect speech.   **et illud:** fr. 497 Usener = 229 Arrighetti.   **eiusdem notae** 'of the same stamp'. Literally a brand or mark (*OLD* 5c).   **quidam timore mortis cogantur ad mortem:** this apparently paradoxical Epicurean claim (which appears also at 70.8) is perhaps glossed by Lucretius when he contends that all human conflict is ultimately to be traced back to the fear of death (3.74–86); cf. Aeacus' description of pestilence in Athens, Ov. *Met.* 7.604–5 *animam laqueo claudunt mortisque timorem | morte fugant,* Luc. 7.105, Mart. 2.80.2.

24 confirmabis animum: see §3n. on *confirmeris*.   **uel ad mortis uel ad uitae patientiam:** this set of alternatives introduces the idea that sometimes it may be braver to choose to continue living rather than to die (see e.g. 78.1–2, where S describes his own decision in his youth to continue living despite the pain of illness, the phrase *ipse destillarem* there evoking the burning hand of Mucius at 24.5 *destillantis in hostili foculo dexterae*). We are to prepare ourselves to take either course.   **et ne nimis amemus uitam et ne nimis oderimus:** the right attitude to life (which we should neither love nor hate to excess) is the objective (the two substantival clauses introduced by *ne* explain *utrumque*) of the repeated mental exercises advocated in this letter.   **cum ratio suadet:** for the process of calculation by which one may come to a reasoned decision to take one's own life see 12.10, *Ep.* 70 and esp. *Ep.* 77.   **cum procursu:** the act of running forward, esp. in battle; cf. in relation to approaching death (perhaps influenced by this passage) Plin. *Ep.* 1.22.10 *nam impetu quodam et instinctu procurrere ad mortem commune cum multis, deliberare uero et causas eius expendere, utque suaserit ratio, uitae mortisque consilium uel suscipere uel ponere ingentis est animi.*

25 uir fortis ac sapiens: a pointed variant on the common phrase *uir fortis ac strenuus* (cf. e.g. 9.19, 22.7, Cic. *Phil.* 8.11.1, Liv. 4.3.16, 10.8.3), used to characterise individuals stalwart on the battlefield and in the forum. As in the example of Cato (§§6–8), strength and courage complement philosophical training. While *Epp.* 22 and 23 focused on the attitude of the foolish to death, here that of the wise man is foremost (for the technical Stoic sense of *sapiens* see main intro. section 4).   **non fugere debet e uita sed exire:** suicide should not be a cowardly retreat but a rational exit (for the characteristic form of this *sententia* see §8n. on *non emisit sed eiecit*). S does sometimes criticise individuals for taking the decision to kill themselves without proper thought (e.g. 4.4 *alius ante amicae fores laqueo pependit*). Socrates in the *Phaedo* characterises suicide as desertion (62b), while S comments at *Prov.* 6.7 with regard to the freedom offered by the possibility of suicide, *si pugnare non uultis, licet fugere.* Lavery (1980: 150) observes: 'the suicide would appear to be a deserter in battle and a soldier who surrenders to fortune'. There is perhaps some defensiveness in S's formulation in *Ep.* 24. For the Stoic focus on the rational exit cf. M. Aur. *Med.* 10.8.   **libido moriendi:** the term *libido*, normally associated with the desires of the flesh (as in §16), is rarely used in a positive sense by S.

For Stoic criticism of the desire for death cf. Epictetus 1.9.12 and 2.15.4–12 and the comments of Griffin 1986: 71–2.   **ad moriendum ... inclinatio:** the adjective *inconsulta* 'unthinking' makes clear that this *inclinatio* is reprehensible.   **quae saepe generosos ... iacentesque:** the anaphora of *saepe* links together these two very different categories of individual, those who are 'noble and of keenest spirit' and those who are 'inert and supine'. The term *acrior* (whose superlative *acerrimae* appears here) was used at §21 to characterise L's own writing; he too might be vulnerable to this sentiment.   **contemnunt:** despising death (what the would-be wise man should do) and despising life are related.   **grauantur:** sc. *uitam* 'are burdened by life' (passive + acc.: *OLD* 4b), echoing the imagery of being shackled to one's body (§17). See Armisen-Marchetti 1989: 116.

26 eadem faciendi uidendique satietas 'a surfeit of doing and of seeing the same things'.   **non odium sed fastidium** 'not hatred but disgust'. Here S, returning to the topic of *taedium uitae* (§22), qualifies the starkly characterised position (*uitam ... ne nimis oderimus*) of §24. While those who are tired of life are not presented as admirable, yet their attitude serves to reinforce the point that the end of life is not always unwelcome; cf. 12.7, 30.12, 77.6 *mori uelle non tantum prudens aut fortis aut miser, etiam fastidiosus potest*, *Tranq.* 2.15 *fastidio esse illis coepit uita et ipse mundus*, *Brev.* 17.3, Delatte 1950. On the *fastidiosi* see Hill 2004: 175–8 (stressing the influence of, as well as the contrast with, Lucr. 3.1060–7). For *taedium uitae* viewed as legitimate reason for taking one's own life in Roman law see *Dig.* 49.14.45.2. Elsewhere S presents *satietas* in relation to life as a desirable state, insofar as it constitutes an acceptance that any day may be one's last; the *sapiens* (98.15) is himself *uitae plenus* (Berno 2008: 556).   **prolabimur** 'slip into' (*OLD* 4). Use of the first person plural further suggests that S and L themselves may be the kind of people prone to feeling this contempt for life.   **ipsa impellente philosophia** 'with philosophy itself prompting'. The teachings of the Stoics on suicide are relevant here but also e.g. Plato's *Phaedo*, which insistently depreciates embodied life (see above). As Lampe (2008: 78–9) notes (referring aptly to *Ep.* 2.4, where S warns L against reading too many books: *fastidientis stomachi est multa degustare*), 'to say that "philosophy itself" contributes to ennui is not necessarily to imply that philosophy is being understood and applied correctly'.   **dum dicimus:** S and L are made to ventriloquise the complaints of the *fastidiosi*. Similar sentiments are elaborated at somewhat greater length at 77.6, 16–17 (as part of the argument to be addressed to the gravely ill Marcellinus for not setting too much store by living).   **quousque eadem?** 'How shall I endure the same old things?' This phrase also occurs at 89.19 as well as *Tranq.* 2.15, the latter a passage which explores people's inability to control their desires: *proposita* *saepe mutando in eadem reuoluebantur et non reliquerant nouitati locum, fastidio esse illis coepit et ipse mundus, et subiit illud tabidarum deliciarum: 'quo usque eadem?'* As Lampe (2008: 72–3) points out, the cause of these feelings is not an existential anxiety inevitably bound up with the human condition (as some have argued) but rather a moral or intellectual failing which the would-be wise man needs to address; cf. the similar comment at Lucr. 3.944 *eadem sunt omnia,* alluding to the Epicurean doctrine that pleasure does not increase with duration.   **nempe . . . aestuabo:** lack of balance in the list has prompted debate over the text here. Reynolds prints Gertz's conjecture *edam,* noting that other supplements are possible. For the list articulating the experience of the daily routine's repetitiveness cf. 77.6 (quoted below).   **in orbem nexa sunt omnia:** for the cyclical nature of human existence, linked to the circularity of day and night and of the seasons, see 12.6n. S often uses this topic for consolatory purposes; cf. e.g. 36.11 *obserua orbem rerum in se remeantium: uidebis nihil in hoc mundo extingui sed uicibus descendere ac surgere* (where, as Lampe 2008: 76 notes, the terms used are close to those of Lucr. 3.944–5) and 77.6 *cogita, quamdiu iam idem facias: cibus, somnus, libido, per hunc circulum curritur. mori uelle non tantum prudens aut fortis aut miser, etiam fastidiosus potest.*   **diem . . . dies:** the repetition underlines the relentlessness of the series.   **aestas . . . reuertantur:** the cloying repetitiveness of daily life is compared to the succession of the seasons. Bernardi Perini (2001: 270–1) reads S's vignette as a response to Hor. *Carm.* 4.7.9–16, where the cycle of the seasons is contrasted with the linear trajectory of the individual human life.   **compescitur** 'is subdued' (*OLD* 3).   **nihil noui facio:** cf. 77.12 *quid tibi noui est?* as consolation for imminent death (echoing Lucretius' personified nature at 3.944). The desire for novelty is often characterised as reprehensible (cf. 47.8, 122.5–18, *Brev.* 7.9; for hostility to novelty as distinctively Roman see Hor. *Ep.* 2.1.90–1). S's letter has highlighted the benefits of repetition, provided that the right things are repeated (§15).   **huius rei:** i.e. of this lack of novelty.   **nausia** 'sickness' (alternative spelling of *nausea*). While *nausia* is etymologically associated with seasickness (cf. 53.3n.), S invokes rather the idea of gluttony here (for the terms cf. *Helv.* 10.3). At 16.3, S insists that philosophy is not merely a diversion to take the boredom out of leisure: *nec in hoc adhibetur, ut cum aliqua oblectatione consumatur dies, ut dematur otio nausia.*   **acerbum:** cf. on Mucius' suffering §5 and on the cries of the tortured §14 (with an echo of *acrior* and *acerrimae*).   **superuacuum** 'pointless' (*OLD* 2).

LETTER 33

While the first three Books of letters are generally philosophical in approach, the fourth, comprising 12, relatively short, letters (*Epp.* 30–41;

COMMENTARY: 33

Ep. 33 at 614 words is one of the longer ones), is more distinctively Stoic (Stoic and Epicurean are explicitly contrasted at 33.4). S introduces (*Ep.* 31) the idea of indifferents – a key concept in Stoic philosophy (expressly postponed at 13.4); the divinity of the mind is a focus of several letters, particularly *Ep.* 41. This is also a notably unified book, the concern with how to read in *Ep.* 33 balanced by the concern with how to write in *Ep.* 40 (Maso 1999: 84). Yet while *Ep.* 33 (the fourth in Book 4) is closely linked particularly to the two letters immediately preceding it, which also focus on philosophical progress and self-sufficiency, there is an important sense in which this letter marks a significant and explicit shift of register, an important staging post on L's road to philosophical maturity (see Wilson 2001: 179–84). The change of approach concerns not only philosophical doctrine (the focus of Maurach 1970: esp. 128–9, 1975: 339–60 and Hachmann 1995: esp. 199–200). As Wilson (2001) and Davies have argued, in offering advice on how to read philosophical texts, S, characteristically self-reflexive, also invites his reader to scrutinise his or her own approach to the letters themselves.

Epp. 2 to 29 (the final letter of Book 3) close with quotations, almost all from Epicurus (that of 29 significantly described as *ultimam . . . pensionem*, 29.10); S has been presenting philosophy as inclusive, playing down distinctions between philosophical schools. At 6.5, S offers to mark up selected passages in the books he sends to L: *mittam itaque ipsos tibi libros, et ne multum operae impendas dum passim profutura sectaris, imponam notas, ut ad ipsa protinus quae probo et miror accedas*. In *Ep.* 33, however, S's earlier practice appears in a new light. Memorable one-liners, it seems, are an enticement for the neophyte (§§6–7). The more advanced student should engage with works in their entirety – and indeed it is characteristic of Stoic works (in contrast to Epicurean) that they offer a coherent system of consistent quality such that individual elements do not stand out as quotable (§§3, 5–6). Wilson (2001: 182) comments on 'the vehemence with which S repudiates the approach he previously advocated'. Books 1–3 now seem 'more purely preliminary and protreptic' than previously appeared. *Ep.* 33 thus needs to be read in the context of the structure of the collection overall.

Epicureanism, in this letter, though less effeminate than it appears (§2), is implicitly criticised (as the shopping image of §3 suggests) because the philosophical advice it offers, though superficially attractive, lacks substance. While S equivocates as to whether Epicureanism is really 'soft', the characterisation of Stoicism as manly, *uirilis* (§1; cf. *Ep.* 24) invokes the etymology of the key Stoic term *uirtus* (cf. Cic. *Tusc.* 2.43). A later letter in this book takes issue with those who term philosophy *mollem . . . militiam* (37.1), as S draws on the traditional military associations of *uirtus* to reinforce the appeal of the philosophical (see further main intro. section 9 on military imagery and on Stoic manliness more generally).

Individual Stoic thinkers now (§4) take a more prominent place (though Zeno and Cleanthes were first mentioned in *Ep.* 6). Yet at the same time S encourages L not to hold views simply because they have been articulated by Stoic authorities but to think for himself (§§7–10). The idea that books cannot offer all the answers is developed further in later letters, particularly in 64.8–9(nn.). S is, here as elsewhere, addressing himself as much as L, as is made clear in the shift to the first person plural (*fuerimus*) in §10 and the first person singular (*ibo, ego . . . utar, inuenero, muniam*) in the final section.

S is by no means the only writer to comment on the integrated and unified structure of Stoic thought (cf. Cic. *Fin.* 3.74). At the same time, *Ep.* 33 is also concerned with the unified structure of individual philosophical and literary texts. There is perhaps some slippage between the philosophical and the aesthetic here. At least in Cicero's time Stoic writers were associated with an unattractively dry and technical style of composition (Cic. *Fin.* 4.5–7; see Graver 2002: xxviii; on the significance of style see further *Ep.* 114(nn.)). For S, however, aesthetic unity seems to be important, to judge from §5 (*per lineamenta sua ingenii opus nectitur*) and, in particular, the analogy of the beautiful woman.

In this letter, S does himself offer one quotation (not, however, from a philosophical text), a half-line from Ovid's *Metamorphoses*. Commentators have struggled to see a larger significance in this but we might do well to recollect the opening lines of Ovid's poem:

> In noua fert animus mutatas dicere formas
> corpora; di, coeptis (nam uos mutastis et illas)
> adspirate meis primaque ab origine mundi
> ad mea perpetuum deducite tempora carmen!

S's epistolary project is no less ambitious in its scope than Ovid's epic (a work from which S quotes thirty times, though not always with approval, and to which L is said to be particularly partial, *Ouidium suum, Nat.* 4a.2.2; see Mazzoli 1970: 240, Setaioli 2000: 178–9). Both works, though in different ways, are profoundly concerned with transformation (for the attainment of Stoic perfection as a kind of transformation see, with verbal echoes of *Met.* 1.1, 118.17 *quaedam processu priorem exuunt formam et in nouam transeunt*). S asserts in this letter that the elements of Stoic philosophy should be seen as *perpetua* (§6). Relevant here is the association of the term with eternal glory (cf. Barchiesi 2005 *ad* Ov. *Met.* 1.4), an explicit preoccupation of 21.4–6. Moreover, the letter ends making a grand claim to novelty which invokes similar claims by earlier Roman (and Greek) writers, not least Ovid (*in noua . . .*). S's novelty is both literary and philosophical (for a similar articulation of the importance of scope for novelty, this time with regard to a literary project of L's, see 79.6). For a suggestive discussion of S's ideas of originality with regard to both literary style (on which see also *Ep.* 114) and philosophical content see Setaioli 2000: 197–215.

For Maso, it is precisely as a Stoic that S feels impelled to think independently, to add something new rather than be content with established doctrines (1999: 99; cf. Nussbaum 1994: 345–53). This ambition also serves as a riposte to Roman anxiety (e.g. Cic. *Tusc.* 1.1–8) that Greek pre-eminence in philosophy cannot be outdone. There is here a tension between the structural openness of Stoicism as a philosophical project (at least for S) – there is always something to be discovered (cf. 64.7–9) – and the desire to envisage it as a perfected whole. There is a paradox, too, in demanding that a series of letters, apparently one half of a continuing conversation, whose end point must, according to the fiction of correspondence, remain undetermined and whose course is subject to adjustment (cf. 38.1 *merito exigis, ut hoc inter nos epistularum commercium frequentemus*), should be treated as a unity, even if it is the case that groups of books were published together (see main intro. section 2).

S's concerns about the role of the *uox* (§§1–2), in the sense of memorable utterance (*OLD* 8), or *sententia* (§7), seem to correspond quite closely to those expressed by a number of other ancient critics in their analyses of literary style. Quintilian discusses *sententiae* at some length (*Inst.* 8.5.1–34); an excess of *sententiae* is liable to turn a speech into a series of fragments (§27) rather than a system of limbs. Such 'points of light', he emphasises (§29), would not be visible in a speech which shone (*lucet*) throughout. Petronius' Eumolpus is made to express similar concerns, 118.5 *curandum est ne sententiae emineant extra corpus orationis expressae, sed intexto uestibus colore niteant*. These 'quotable' highlights serve as an enticement to the listener, while lending themselves to excerption. But the quest for such 'highlights' runs the risk of distorting the overall dynamic of the whole. S himself, it should be noted, was widely criticised in antiquity and later for larding his own work with memorable one-liners, though even Quintilian admired some of them (*Inst.* 10.1.129 *multae . . . in eo claraeque sententiae*), while deploring S's influence on less talented authors (see main intro. section 11).

Commentaries: Summers, Davies.
Further reading: Maso 1999: 83–105, Wilson 2001: 179–86, Berno 2003.

1 Desideras his quoque implies (thus stressing the interactive nature of the correspondence) that L has read, found wanting and complained about *Epp.* 30–2 (cf. 113.1 *Desideras tibi scribi a me*).   **sicut prioribus:** *Epp.* 2–29 concluded with quotations from Epicurus and his associates;

a reminder that the letters are part of a sequence. **uoces** 'utterances' (*OLD* 8); cf. 2.4–5 on the role of *uoces*. **nostrorum procerum** 'our leaders'. It is clear from what follows that the phrase must refer to the Stoics (cf. *VB* 3.2 *Stoicis proceribus*). L has apparently requested choice Stoic morsels in parallel to the Epicurean material S offered in *Epp.* 2–29. **flosculos:** lit. 'little flowers' (pejorative diminutive), meaning quotable phrases or passages, an especially apt term in relation to Epicurus, known for his garden (cf. 4.10 *hoc quoque ex alienis hortulis sumptum est*). There is perhaps a hint here of the effeminacy with which Epicureans were often charged (see §2n.). **occupati** 'bothered with' (*OLD* 9). In this pejorative sense cf. *Brev.* 7.1 and Williams *ad loc.* **totus contextus illorum** 'the whole fabric of their work'. *contextus* (*OLD* 4) is a metaphor from weaving (continued in §5 *nectitur* and §6 *contexta*). S emphasises that Stoic thought is an integrated whole; cf. Cic. *Fin.* 5.83, where the character Cicero is made to comment, *mirabilis est apud istos* [sc. *Stoicos*] *contextus rerum*. At 106.1, S applies the term to his own work, explaining that he has not yet responded to L's query on a particular issue because he was working that matter *in contextum operis mei*. On the quotable *sententia* as a potential flaw in relation to integrated literary style see intro. above. **uirilis** 'forceful' (*OLD* 4); lit. 'manly'. S's emphasis on the manliness of Stoicism can be seen as a response to critics who see philosophy generally as a soft option (37.1 *mollis militia*; see Edwards 2005b). For a similar contrast between the *uirilitas* of the Stoics and the apparent *mollitia* of the Epicureans see *Constant.* 1.1. A story in Diogenes Laertius suggests that the Stoics represented themselves as masculine in comparison with the Epicureans even in the time of Arcesilaus (4.43). **inaequalitatem** 'unevenness'. Contrast the *aequalitas* S attributes to Stoic *constantia* at 31.8. **scias:** subj. 'you should know'. As Summers comments (xlii) it is often hard to distinguish between jussive and potential force. **ubi . . . sunt:** Fronto (pp. 153.11–154.13 van den Hout) makes very similar criticisms of S's own writing (see main intro. section 11); cf. the comments of Quint. *Inst.* 10.1.29, quoted in the intro. above. **non est . . . tota silua** 'the single tree does not excite admiration when the whole wood rises to the same height'. *admirationi*: predic. dat. *eandem* contrasts with *inaequalitatem*. This image of trees of equal and lofty height will take on added significance in the light of 41.3, where an ancient grove, characterised in the same terms, is a place for thinking of the transcendent: *si tibi occurrerit uetustis arboribus et solitam altitudinem egressis frequens lucus . . . illa proceritas siluae et secretum loci et admiratio umbrae in aperto tam densae atque continuae fidem tibi numinis faciet* (see further Hunt 2016: 186–7).

2 eiusmodi uocibus 'with sayings of that kind', i.e. *sententiae*. **referta** 'stuffed', often pejorative (e.g. *Constant.* 13.4), though it can be used neutrally (as in 59.6). The anaphora is emphatic. **carmina ... historiae:** the point is that not only philosophical writing offers material for pithy quotation (cf. 9.21). While *historiae* such as that of Velleius offered plentiful *sententiae*, S himself favours quotations from poetry, esp. Virgil (e.g. 12.9, 18.12, 70.2) and, significantly, in this letter (§4) Ovid, or cites historical examples (cf. e.g. 14.12–13, 86.1–12). **publicae sunt** 'they belong to everyone'. S repeats a point made before, notably in 12.11, 21.9, 29.11, the concluding letters of Books 1, 2 and 3 (Wilson 2001: 184). In *Ep*. 84, S develops this claim further, making clear that his conception goes beyond the traditional rhetorical idea of *publica materies*, common subject matter (Setaioli 2000: 201–15). **maxime nostrae** 'ours in particular', meaning 'we Stoics'. **in illo magis adnotantur** 'they are more noticeable in him'; cf. the backhanded compliment offered at *Constant*. 15.4 (*quam paene emisit uiri uocem!* 'How close he came to uttering a manly sentiment!'). For S the quotability of Epicurus turns out to be an indication of his limitations (though Epicurus' *Letter to Menoeceus*, Diog. Laert. 10.135, suggests his followers memorise passages from his work; see Clay 1983: 78–81). A more thoroughgoing critique of Epicurus' style (linked to a parallel critique of his morality) is perhaps attributable to Panaetius (Setaioli 2000: 191–2). **quia rarae ... homine mollitiam professo:** the anaphoric tricolon (*quia ... quia ... quia*) stresses the unexpectedly fortifying nature of Epicurean sayings, given the author's self-confessed softness. The alleged softness or effeminacy of Epicurus contrasts with the manliness of Stoic writing to which S has just referred (cf. *VB* 7.3). On *mollitia* see Edwards 1993: 63–97, Williams 2010: 139–53. In the next sentence, however, S goes on to distance himself from this assessment of Epicurus, whom he prefers to describe as strong, despite appearances (cf. the distinction drawn at *VB* 12.4–13.3 between Epicurus himself and some who claim to follow him). Nevertheless S has other criticisms to make of Epicurus' teaching (e.g. 67.15, 85.18, 97.15, in addition to his scathing comments at *VB* 7.3 about those who say virtue cannot be separated from pleasure). **plerique:** see e.g. Sen. *Con*. 2.6.2, where Epicureans are characterised as referring everything back to pleasure and the body. Cicero often attacks Epicureanism (particularly in his oratory, *Pis*. esp. 66–70, *Cael*. 41; cf. *Ac*. 1.5), while in his philosophical works sometimes conceding the propriety of Epicurus' life, in particular his bravery in the face of pain (*Off*. 3.117, *Tusc*. 3.46, *Fin*. 2.96–9). **apud me** 'in my view' (*OLD* 12). **et** 'even'. **manuleatus** 'wearing long sleeves', from *manuleus* 'long sleeve'. Often perceived as a sign of effeminacy (perhaps associated with the inability to endure cold); cf. Suet. *Cal*. 52, Gel. 6.12.1 *tunicis uti uirum prolixis ultra brachia et usque in primores manus ac prope in digitos, Romae atque in omni Latio indecorum fuit,* Corbeill 1996: 159–63, Richlin 1992: 92–3. At *VB* 13.3, S compares the Epicurean position to

that of a strong man in women's dress: *uir fortis stolam indutus.*   **fortitudo:** a characteristic esp. associated with manliness; cf. Cic. *Tusc.* 2.43
uiri autem propria est maxime fortitudo. The phrase *uir fortis ac strenuus* is
applied to the philosopher Demetrius at 9.18. and 77.6.   **Persas:** the
Persians wore long sleeves (cf. Fro. [*Ad M. Caes.* 4.3.7 =] p. 59 van den
Hout). But though their way of life could be characterised as in some ways
effeminate, they had been formidable enemies of the Greeks in the early
fifth century BCE.   **alte cinctos:** lit. 'fastened high', i.e. wearing a belted
tunic with the fabric pulled up for ease of movement (*OLD cingo* 1b).
Here this is a sign of energy and readiness for action (cf. Hor. *S.* 1.5.5,
2.8.10, as well as *Ep.* 92.35, applied to the words of Maecenas - though at
odds with his personal appearance, on which see further 114.4(nn.)). As
with *manuleatus*, dress is an index of moral disposition.

3 non est ergo quod exigas excerpta et repetita 'so it is not the case
that you should demand extracts and sayings'. *non est . . . quod:* see
7.9n.   **continuum:** echoing *contextus* in §1.   **ocliferia** 'things to
strike the eye', from *oculus* + *ferire*. Berno (2003) argues that this unparalleled term is colloquial (*ocli* is well attested as a colloquial abbreviation of
oculi) with the sense of 'window dressing' or decoy product rather than a
Senecan coinage; cf. Summers *ad loc.* S is alert elsewhere in the *EM* (e.g.
48.11, 88.22 *imperitorum feriuntur oculi*) to the risks posed by what is superficially attractive to the eye. On the privileged role of the visual more
generally in S see Solimano 1991.   **nec emptorem . . . sunt:** S uses a
homely image of the shopper drawn in by a tempting window display but
disappointed to find the shop contains nothing more than this.   **nihil
inuenturum:** as often, S uses a fut. partic. as equivalent to a relative clause
(cf. *NLS* §90).   **cum intrauerit:** fut. pf. S.'s emphasis on the virtues of
Stoic writing here must be seen as an implicit criticism of Epicurean failings. Once the few memorable phrases have been extracted, he implies,
nothing much remains. As Wilson (2001: 183 n. 35) notes, this commercial metaphor complements the characterisation of quotations as debts in
the earlier letters.   **ipsis** 'of their own accord' (*OLD* 7).

4 iam puta 'now suppose' (*OLD puto* 9a).   **sententias:** equivalent to
uoces in §1. The argument here is elliptical. S has been claiming that Stoic
teaching is a continuous whole from which elements should not be separated (cf. Maso 1999: 98–9). As Setaioli (2000: 160–2) notes, he is not
hostile to *sententiae* as such but rather making a claim for the sustained
force of Stoic works in contrast to the uneven quality of Epicurean. Now
he focuses rather on the link between reliance on *sententiae* and deference to authorities (anticipating the point in §7 that the *proficiens* should
develop his own thoughts rather than quoting those of others).   **turba:**

stressing the quantity. S uses this metaphor elsewhere also; cf. e.g. *De ira* 3.13.7. **Zenoni an Cleanthi an Chrysippo an Panaetio an Posidonio:** the leading thinkers of the Stoic school (see main intro.). **sub rege** 'under the rule of a king'. Epicureans, S suggests, are excessively deferential to Epicurus himself. The Epicureans' subservience to their founder is also stressed by other commentators (e.g. Cic. *N.D.* 1.72 *ista enim a uobis quasi dictata redduntur quae Epicurus oscitans halucinatus est*). Philodemus attributes to his students the view that 'we will obey the authority of Epicurus, according to whom we have chosen to live' (*On frank criticism* fr. 45; trs. Konstan *et al.*). On the hero cult of Epicurus see Clay 1986, Nussbaum 1994: 130–1. The dangers of rule by a *rex* are treated briefly at 47.20–1 (n.). **sibi quisque se uindicat** 'each is his own man'. Cf. 1.1 *uindica te tibi*. This echo signals that S is (Wilson 2001: 184) 'in some sense, starting afresh'; cf. Maurach 1970: 128–9. For S's stress on independence of mind as a Stoic trait cf. *De otio* 3.1, *Brev.* 2.4, *VB* 3.2, *Ep.* 113.23 (referring to a dispute between Cleanthes and his pupil Chrysippus) *ne putes autem primum me ex nostris non ex praescripto loqui sed meae sententiae esse*, 'lest you think I am first of our lot to give my own view rather than the party line'. Sedley (1989: 97–103), however, underlines the deference to Zeno, which characterised much Stoic thought. For S's dismissal of the request for authorities for particular doctrines cf. 39.1 *qui notorem dat, ignotus est*, 'he who cites an authority lacks knowledge'. **apud istos:** i.e. the Epicureans. **Hermarchus . . . Metrodorus:** Hermarchus succeeded Epicurus as head of the community in Athens (his close adherence to Epicurus is praised by S at 6.6 and 52.4). Metrodorus, apparently more highly regarded by S, was another committed follower of Epicurus (cf. 6.6, 14.17, 18.9 and 52.4, also *Epp.* 98–9 where S cites his correspondence). See further Clay 2009. **ad unum refertur** 'is referred back to one source', i.e. Epicurus himself. Even his most distinguished pupils are not given credit for their utterances. **omnia quae . . . dicta sunt** 'whatever anyone says in that fraternity is spoken under the leadership and commanding authority of one man'. *contubernium*, lit. 'tent-companionship' (see *OLD* 2 for the metaphorical use), is a military term which underlines S's point about the Epicureans' obedience to their founder, while also stressing their shared living arrangements (6.6 is the principal source for this; see Asmis 2004). *ductu et auspiciis* (a set phrase, *OLD auspicium* 4; cf. e.g. Liv. 8.31.1 with Oakley 1998 *ad loc.*) reinforces this with another military metaphor. The two terms are often coupled since it was also possible to win a battle under one's own leadership (*ductus*) but under the auspices of another (e.g. Tac. *Ann.* 2.41.1 *ob recepta signa cum Varo amissa ductu Germanici auspiciis Tiberii*). Military imagery is a (no doubt self-consciously) paradoxical choice to describe the peace-loving followers of Epicurus (*pace* Maso 1999: 97 n. 31), though it is also favoured by Lucretius (e.g. 3.642–56; see Kenney 2014: 32).   **licet temptemus** 'although we make the attempt'.   **aequalium:** picking up *inaequalitatem* in §1.   **pauperis . . . pecus:** Ov. *Met.* 13.824. The first of a number of quotations from or explicit references to this work (see 79.5, 90.20, 110.1, 115.13, Mazzoli 1970: 238–47). Though S has warned against taking quotations from philosophical works, it seems he is happy to cull a *flosculus* from what Ovid planned as a *carmen perpetuum* (*Met.* 1.4). Galatea is here reporting the speech made by the Cyclops Polyphemus in an attempt to woo her. Among the inducements he offers, besides his flocks, are his many trees from which she may gather various fruits (1.812–20). The quoted phrase (as Davies: 201 suggests) perhaps draws out herding metaphors latent in earlier phrases, *ex turba separare* and *educere ex*.   **miseris oculum** 'you shall have have directed your gaze'. *miseris:* fut. pf. (*OLD* 7b). The expression (which picks up *ocliferia* in §3) seems rare: see *TLL* VIII.1171.42–9.

5 quare depone istam spem: L should by now have been convinced to give up his hope for easily digestible quotations. S proposes a better approach to reading.   **degustare ingenia maximorum uirorum** 'dip into the thinking of the greatest men'. *degustare:* lit. 'take a taste of'. S often uses metaphors of eating and drinking to characterise people's engagement with philosophical literature (e.g. 2.4, 46.1 *tantum degustare uolui*, 84.3–8); see Armisen-Marchetti 1989: 143–4, Graver 2014. On *ingenia* cf. 21.5n. For the criticism of summary learning cf. 39.1. Implicitly Epicurus is not included among *maximorum uirorum*. S here stresses again the masculinity of the Stoics (cf. §1 *uirilis*).   **tota tibi inspicienda sunt, tota tractanda:** S now makes clear that philosophical works should be engaged with in their entirety, a point underlined through alliteration and the anaphora of *tota. inspicienda* here, as often, used of mental vision (*OLD* 4).   **<continuando> res geritur** 'by making connections is the plan carried out'. This refers to the ongoing work of the reader. Axelson's supplement of *continuando* (1939: 180–1, cf. *OLD* 1c) is generally accepted (*res geritur* normally has an additional modifier; see e.g. 7.4).   **per lineamenta sua ingenii opus nectitur** 'a work of the mind is being woven together in fulfilment of its own pattern'. *lineamenta* (*OLD* 2) 'outlines', 'blueprint' (e.g. in relation to *oratio*, Cic. *Orat.* 186, and in relation to painting, used as an analogy for rhetoric, *Brut.* 70); *sua* refers forward to *opus* (or perhaps, as Graver 1998: 627 argues, *ingenium*); *ingenii:* gen. of quality; *opus:* a term often used for a work of art (*OLD* 9c, e.g. Ov. *Tr.* 2.560 referring to the *Metamorphoses*); in the following letter (34.2), S refers to L himself as *meum opus*. See note *ad loc.* The weaving metaphor picks up *contextus* in §1. Graver (1998: 627) observes: 'The sentence must say that the writing or "work of the *ingenium*" is related to the structure of the *ingenium* itself as a building is related to its blueprint. That is, the cohesiveness of the Stoic text, the quality that makes it difficult to excerpt, is a kind of direct manifestation, even a sign, of the structured and systematic way these minds handle information.' The comments may be read as applying to S's own work as a whole, as well as to the writings of earlier Stoics (though this advice, given at a relatively early stage in the series of letters, is apparently offered before the work itself is complete).   **nec recuso quominus singula membra, dummodo in ipso homine, consideres** 'I do not forbid you to consider the individual elements, provided that it is in the context of the whole person'. As Davies notes (*ad loc.*, citing Wilson 1987: 107–8), this comment may be taken self-reflexively. S himself has often been treated as a collection of *sententiae* by ancient and modern readers (see main intro. section 11). There is slippage here between the person as visual object (an analogy for the literary work) comprised of individual elements (*membra* as limbs, *OLD* 2) and the person as author producing the elements (*membra* as parts of a written work, *OLD* 5b) encountered by the reader. Elsewhere (40.1, *Ep.* 46(intro.)) S explores writing as a means of access to the author (cf. Setaioli 2000: 165–71, linking S's position to the theories of Panaetius). At 100.8, in a discussion of the writing of the philosopher Fabianus, he urges L to consider the good effect of *totum corpus* rather than to regret the lack of striking *sententiae* (cf. 100.12, where he comments *sine commendatione partium singularum in uniuersum magnificus*).   **non est formonsa:** the choice of simile, comparing the serious work of philosophy to the attractions of a beautiful woman, takes the analogy of the previous sentence (*in ipso homine*) in a new direction, adding a further Ovidian touch (a few lines before the phrase S quotes in this letter, Polyphemus' praise of Galatea terms her 'more beautiful (*formosior*) than a well-watered garden', *Met.* 13.797). The contrast between a concern with individual beautiful elements and the beautiful whole also evokes the different approach set out in Cicero's version (*Inv.* 2.1–5) of the story of the painter Zeuxis, whose picture of Helen as an ideal of beauty was composed from individual elements, each modelled on that of a different woman: *uirgines formosas*. For Cicero, who relates the story in detail, this is a model for how one should compose a book on oratory, *artem dicendi*, in his case (in contrast to S) drawing elements from a range of authorities.   **cuius uniuersa facies admirationem partibus singulis abstulit** 'whose overall appearance pre-empts admiration for her individual parts'. Repetition of the word *admirationem* (cf. §1 *admirationi*) recalls the opening comparison between the single tree and the wood. For a comparison of two women in somewhat similar terms cf. Catul. 86.1–3: *Quintia formosa est multis . . . haec ego sic singula confiteor;* | *totum illud formosa nego*. As Davies notes, this is a paradoxical choice of simile given S's earlier stress on the virility of the Stoics (though cf. the personification of philosophy at 53.8).

6 si tamen exegeris 'If you still demand' (fut. pf.), despite the preceding advice.   **non tam mendice tecum agam** 'I will not treat you in such a niggardly way', *sc.* as the Epicureans (though Davies comments *ad loc.* 'the understood *quam* clause . . . is the modest quantity L has requested'). *fiet* suggests *agam* (*OLD* 37b) is fut. rather than subj.   **plena manu** 'generously' (*OLD plenus* 6).   **eorum:** i.e. *ingenia*, as the following neuters show.   **sumenda . . . non colligenda** 'to be embraced rather than collected' (cf. 24.3 *exempla . . . colligenda*), i.e. they are so plentiful there is no need to seek them out individually. For this use of *colligere* cf. Cic. *Tusc.* 4.3 *uestigia . . . Pythagoreorum . . . multa colligi possunt* (*OLD* 3a).   **excidunt** 'drip out' (*OLD* 1). The same contrast is used at 100.1 (it makes a difference *utrum exciderit an fluxerit*) and a similar one in the discussion of the style of Fabianus at 40.3 (on the correct style for a philosophical lecture, *aeque stillare illum nolo quam currere*).   **perpetua et inter se contexta:** the metaphor of a woven fabric (introduced in §1 *contextus* and continued in §5 *nectitur*) is sustained. For the pairing (though in this case of pleasures) cf. Cic. *Tusc.* 5.96 *perpetuas et contextas uoluptates*. Ovid described his *Metamorphoses*, from which S has just quoted an excerpt, as *carmen . . . perpetuum* (*Met.* 1.4). The analogy between literary text and woven artefact is relatively common but takes on a particular significance in the Arachne episode in Ov. *Met.* 6 (from which S quotes ll. 55–7 at 90.20; see note *ad loc.*).   **multum conferant rudibus** 'they are a great help to beginners'. For *rudibus* see *OLD* 5b (cf. *Ben.* 5.13.3 *non ex toto rudem, sed ad litteras altiores non perductum*). The sophistic tradition placed particular pedagogic value on *sententiae* (Hadot 2014a: 50–2). We might compare the contrast already drawn in antiquity between the esoteric works of Aristotle, aimed at his advanced students, and his exoteric works which were thought to be composed for a wider public (Cic. *Fin.* 5.11–12). Mature Stoics by contrast have no need of such an approach.   **extrinsecus auscultantibus** 'to those listening from outside', i.e. those who are not yet committed, the uninitiated. As Summers notes *ad loc.*, the image compares philosophy and religion (cf. 41.4, 52.14–15).   **circumscripta** 'abridged' (*OLD* 4b).   **carminis modo inclusa** 'sometimes confined in lines of verse' (*OLD includo* 7b). Davies cites as parallel Cic. *de Orat.* 3.184 *uerba uersu includere*.

7 sententias: memorable, pithy sayings (*OLD* 6b).   **chrias:** a collection of clever or witty sayings, so called for their usefulness (from the Greek χρεία, LSJ 5), often in the form of a question and answer attributed to specific speakers and context; cf. Quint. *Inst.* 1.9.3, Bloomer

2011: 119–28.   **quia ... potest:** this implies that *Epp.* 2–29, with their manageable quotations, treated L as a neophyte.   **adhuc** 'so far', repeated from the previous sentence, emphasises the provisionality of this stage.   **capit** 'has capacity for' (*OLD* 25). Maso (1999: 93) notes 52.2–4, where S stresses the need for the teacher to assess what the individual student is capable of grasping. The issue is pursued at length in *Epp.* 94 and 95 (see Schafer 2009).   **certi profectus uiro** 'for a man who has made marked progress'. On the Stoic significance of the verb *proficio* 'I make progress' (with which the noun *profectus* is cognate), particularly its present participle *proficiens*, see main intro. section 4.   *uiro* here contrasts with *pueris* and *puerilis* in the previous sentence, as well as evoking the earlier references to Stoic manliness. L's progress is celebrated in several letters in Book 4, esp. 31 and 34 (though 35 and 39 are more cautious).   **captare flosculos** 'to pluck little flowers'; cf. §1 (n.)   **turpe:** the tone shifts here to one of rebuke.   **fulcire se** 'prop himself up' (*OLD* 3).   **uocibus:** see §1n.   **sibi iam innitatur** 'let him now rely upon himself'. This reflexive use of *inniti* is not attested before S. The innovative and frequent use of such reflexive datives is especially characteristic of Senecan interiority (Traina 1987: 18, 60).   **dicat ista ... sapere** 'Let him [i.e. the *certi profectus uir*] be the pronouncer of such things, not their custodian; it is shameful for one who is an old man, or on the verge of old age, to look to his note-takings for his wisdom.' The two figures here may stand for S and L; L himself is presented (cf. 19.1, 96.3) as not much younger than S, who has repeatedly described himself as a *senex* (cf. *Ep.* 12, 26.1–2). *prospicienti*: the use of a singular participle as a substantive (where earlier prose writers such as Cicero would use a relative clause) serves brevity; cf. 26.1 for another visual metaphor for the approach of old age (*in conspectu esse me senectutis*). For the thought cf. 36.4 *turpis et ridicula res est elementarius senex. Ep.* 39 grudgingly agrees to supply *commentarios* for L, while urging him to take a more systematic approach (39.1). *sapere* is ironic.   **hoc Zenon ... Cleanthes:** on these philosophers see §4n. S (as elsewhere, e.g. 7.5(n.)) imagines a response, which is not necessarily to be attributed to L himself. He seems here (and note the repetition in §9) to criticise an approach to teaching Stoic philosophy reliant on commentaries and handbooks (cf. Hadot 2002: 149–53, Epictetus, *Enchiridion* §49).   **tu quid?** the tone becomes more urgent with the repeated second-person questions. Summers suggests a parallel with Epictetus, *Discourses* 2.19.5 'Cleanthes and Chrysippus hold these views. What is yours then?' As Davies comments *ad loc.*, as Epictetus is asked for an opinion but has none to offer, the differences are more significant.   **quousque sub alio moueris?** 'For how long do you act under another's command?' *sub alio* echoes *sub rege* in §4. Cf. *Nat.* 2.21.1 *dimissis praeceptoribus incipimus per nos moueri.* For the assertion of intellectual independence cf. *De otio* 3.1 *non quia mihi legem dixerim nihil contra dictum Zenonis Chrysippiue committere, sed quia res ipsa patitur me ire in illorum sententiam* 'not because I had made it a rule for myself to set up nothing against the pronouncements of Zeno or Chrysippus but because the matter itself allows me to go along with their view'. **impera ... memoriae tradatur:** *impera* 'give orders'; the military association evokes the imagery of the Epicurean chain of command (§4). *tradatur*, subj. of tendency (G–L §631). Just as elsewhere S advises L to act in ways which will make him an *exemplum* on a par with the historical figures to which S himself so often refers (e.g. 98.13 *simus inter exempla* 'let us be among the examples'), here L is urged to speak such words as will make him a philosophical authority. Finding a place in the memory of later generations is a goal (cf. 21.5–6(nn.)). **de tuo** 'from that which is your own'. S offered a definition of this at 23.6 *te ipso et tui optima parte* 'from your very self and the best part of you', having exhorted L *de tuo gaude*. For the importance of intellectual independence in the Stoic tradition see Nussbaum 1994: 345–53 (noting that S here may be seen as developing arguments put forward in Plato, *Phdr.* 275a–b). Cf. 45.4.

8 istos, numquam auctores, semper interpretes 'those people whose role is never that of originator but always that of interpreter'. Perhaps a legal metaphor: the *auctor* initiates legislation in the senate, the *interpres* merely explicates (Armisen-Marchetti 1989: 128–9): *OLD interpres* 3c. Setaioli (2000: 213–14) contrasts S's approach with that of Cicero (though at *Off.* 1.6 the latter, taking *interpres* in the more limited sense of those who cannot translate into good Latin, comments: *sequemur igitur hoc quidem tempore et hac in quaestione potissimum Stoicos non ut interpretes sed, ut solemus, e fontibus eorum iudicio arbitrioque nostro, quantum quoque modo uidebitur, hauriemus*). **sub aliena umbra latentes** 'lurking in another man's shadow'. *aliena* here contrasts with the possessive *tuo* in §7. In earlier letters, S presented himself as correcting those who referred to Epicurus' words of wisdom as *aliena* (cf. e.g. 2.5, 12.10). Here, however, the term *umbra*, traditionally associated with the life of retirement advocated by Epicurus, as well as his garden (cf. of the Epicureans, *Ben.* 4.2.1 *delicata et umbratica turba*; Bellincioni 1984: 99–100), suggests that we should see the comment as a criticism directed particularly at Epicurus' followers (elsewhere, e.g. 36.1, S can use *umbra* more positively to suggest philosophical retirement). Cf. the use of *aliena* to characterise philosophical ideas one has not yet made one's own through action at 108.38. **nihil ... generosi** 'nothing noble-spirited'. *generosi*: partitive gen. (G–L §369). S self-consciously redeploys an adjective associated with high birth (*OLD* 1), as well as nobility of character (*OLD* 2, cf. 24.25); philosophy offers the possibility of nobility to anyone (cf. 21.2(n.), 44.3). **numquam ausos**

aliquando facere quod diu didicerunt 'never having dared to put once into practice what they had taken a long time to learn'.   **aliud autem est meminisse, aliud scire** 'but it is one thing to remember, it is another thing to know': inf. as subject (G–L §422).   **et sua . . . ad magistrum** 'to make each [thought] one's own and not to hang upon [*OLD pendo* 13b] a model nor to look back so often to one's teacher'. A book, or even an adviser, cannot anticipate all eventualities (cf. 22.1–2, 64.8–9). For a more developed discussion of the process by which one makes ideas *sua* see *Ep.* 84, esp. §§5–6 (Setaioli 2000: 206–15, Graver 2014).

9 aliquid inter te intersit et librum 'Let there be some difference between you and a book.'   **iam et praecipe:** *et* is here equivalent to *etiam* (*OLD et* 6). Just as S sometimes characterises himself as a pupil (cf. e.g. 26.7, 27.1, 71.30), so here L is exhorted to be a teacher.   **quid est quare audiam quod legere possum?** 'Why should I listen to what I can read?' Here S, impersonating the potential recipient of L's precepts, makes clear that it is not enough to repeat the words of Stoic authorities.   **'multum' inquit 'uiua uox facit':** the comment, put in the mouth of a third person, repeats an assertion S made at 6.5. Thus S can now modify his own earlier position: the voice should be uttering its own words (*uox* here in a different sense from *uocibus* in §1). In line with other authors (e.g. Quint. *Inst.* 2.2.8, Plin. *Ep.* 2.3.9), S himself repeatedly stresses the value of the spoken word, the live presence, for reinforcing a message (cf. 38.1). Indeed part of the power of the letter form is that it is the closest writing gets to conversation (cf. 40.1). The key issue here, however, is the source of the words.   **quae alienis uerbis commodatur** 'which is the vehicle of the words of others'.   **actuari uice** 'the role of a shorthand writer'.

10 isti qui numquam tutelae suae fiunt 'those who never become their own guardians'. *tutelae suae:* gen. *tutela*, in Roman law, was the guardianship of a minor or other person not legally qualified to manage his or her own affairs (see Berger 1953 s.v. and *Dig.* 26.1.1.pr.: 'a right and power over a free person granted and allowed under *ius ciuile*, to protect him who, because of his age, is not able to defend himself'). *in tutelam suam uenisse* was commonly used to indicate coming of age (*OLD tutela* 3b). S continues the idea of philosophical development reflecting the passage from youth to adulthood.   **primum in ea re . . . desciuit** 'to begin with follow those who go before in matters in which no one has not deserted their predecessor'.   **in ea re sequuntur quae adhuc quaeritur** 'they follow them [sc. *priores*] in a matter where the truth is still being investigated'. *quaeritur* (*OLD* 9) is used in this sense several times by S (cf. e.g. 45.4, 76.4).   **numquam autem inuenietur, si contenti fuerimus inuentis** 'It will never be discovered, if we remain content with existing discoveries', i.e. philosophy will make no advances, if all we do is accept what others have already found out. **qui alium sequitur nihil inuenit, immo nec quaerit** 'one who follows another discovers nothing and is not even investigating'. Cf. 45.5 *inuenta* contrasted with *quaerenda*. The corrective *immo* is very common in S (Traina 1987: 32; cf. e.g. 7.3, 24.23). *nec* = *ne . . . quidem*, as often. See K–S II.44–5.

11 non ibo per priorum uestigia? 'Will I myself not follow in the footsteps of earlier men?': a response to an imagined critic. The metaphor of the well-trodden path was a common one, the claim to forge a new path often linked with bids for literary immortality. Lucretius (1.926–7) claims of his own work: *auia Pieridum peragro loca nullius ante | trita solo* (his allusion to Callim. *Aet.* 1.1.25 is noted by Kenney 1970). For the metaphor cf. too Virg. *G.* 3.1–11, esp. l. 8 *temptanda uia est* (with Mynors 1990 *ad loc.*), Hor. *Ars* 286–7 *uestigia Graeca | ausi deserere* (with Brink 1963–82 *ad loc.*) and *Ep.* 1.19.21–2 *libera per uacuum posui uestigia princeps | non aliena meo pressi pede*. As Setaioli (2000: 210) notes, with regard to content S's position differs significantly from that of Lucretius, who proposes, addressing Epicurus (3.3–4 *inque tuis nunc | ficta pedum pono pressis uestigia signis*) to reproduce faithfully his doctrines, even while innovating with regard to form.   **uero** 'Yes' with a reservation.   **si propiorem planioremque inuenero:** S here leaves open the possibility of innovation; he does not feel himself bound to follow existing paths.   **hanc muniam** 'I shall pave it as a new road': *OLD munio* 6. The phrase offers a Roman magistrate's gloss on the path-breaking of Greek poetics.   **non domini nostri sed duces sunt:** earlier philosophers are not our masters but our guides (cf. 80.1), although at §5 S used *dux* in the more strictly military sense of general (*OLD* 4) to criticise the Epicureans' excessive obedience to their founder, here the term contrasts with *dominus* and stresses their role as guides (*OLD* 1), thus continuing the road metaphor; cf. *De otio* 1.5 *non quo miserint illi, sed quo duxerint, ibo*, 'I shall go not where they have sent me but where they lead'.   **occupata** 'laid claim to' (*OLD* 3).   **multum . . . futuris relictum est:** in the final sentence of his letter S anticipates his own advice reaching a wider readership; cf. 64.7. As Maso (1999: 102) notes, the concluding reference to *futuris* balances §1's concern with the past authorities, *procerum*.

LETTER 34

The following letter (34), one of the briefest in the collection (185 words), complements *Ep.* 33 in a number of important respects. While *Ep.* 33 focused on the literary–philosophical work (§5 *opus*), *Ep.* 34 engages with the *proficiens* (L) as the work (§2 *opus*) of his teacher (S). The image of the farmer rejoicing in the flourishing of his fruit and the shepherd of his flock (34.1) subtly (and perhaps self-mockingly) echoes the voice of Ovid's Polyphemus, whose words were quoted at 33.4.

Several earlier letters focused expressly on L's progress, e.g. 13.1, 19.1. In particular, *Ep.* 34 resumes the opening of *Ep.* 31, *Agnosco Lucilium meum; incipit, quem promiserat, exhibere*. In identifying with his pupil (no matter that the pupil is, as the previous letter underlined, of mature years, 33.7) the teacher is rejuvenated, throwing off old age (the ageing process is repeatedly invoked to philosophic ends; see e.g. *Ep.* 12). Exhortations to the *proficiens* to work on himself, to transform himself feature frequently (e.g. 31.11 *te quoque dignum | finge deo*; 52.6 praise for one who *malignitatem naturae suae uicit et ad sapientiam se non perduxit, sed extraxit*: cf. Edwards 1997a, Long 2009). Yet, while *Ep.* 33 had urged him to independence, *Ep.* 34 celebrates L's role as S's creation.

The relationship between S and L in the *EM* is sometimes (as in *Ep.* 34) presented as that of teacher and pupil (an aspect stressed by e.g. Too 1994, Habinek 1998) but often rather as one of friendship. The role of the personal letter as a document of friendship was well established in Greco-Roman culture (see main intro. section 3). However, in S's letters, friendship, while reinforcing the epistolary effect, has a very particular significance (cf. Knoche 1975, Edwards 2018a). Parallels between *Ep.* 34 and *Ep.* 9 (and anticipation of *Ep.* 35) suggest slippage between the role of student, *alumnus*, in *Ep.* 34 and that of friend, *amicus*, in *Ep.* 9. *Ep.* 9 compares the *sapiens* to the sculptor Phidias, *faciendarum amicitiarum artifex* (§4), whose project in making a friend is likened to one of artistic creation, more rewarding in process than in completion (§7): *non aeque delectatur qui ab opere perfecto remouit manum. iam fructu artis suae fruitur: ipsa fruebatur arte cum pingeret*. In *Ep.* 34, however, L as pupil is the creation of S as teacher. Epictetus, though less starkly, also compares his relationship to his pupils with that of a craftsman to his work (*Discourses* 2.19.29–31).

S's preoccupation in *Ep.* 33 with the need for consistency in the literary–philosophical work (§5 *opus*), juxtaposed with his focus in *Ep.* 34 on consistency in L as S's creation (§2 *opus*), offers a suggestive parallel with the figure of the mistress in Roman love elegy, sometimes explicitly referred to as a *scripta puella* (Prop. 2.10.8). Recent scholarship, notably Wyke (1987), has highlighted the ways in which Propertius and Ovid, in particular, play on the conceit of the addressee as an authorial creation, whose role is to establish the author's position as 'lover' (see also e.g. Ov. *Ars* 3.538, Kennedy 1993: 89–90). References in the love poetry of Propertius or Ovid to 'Cynthia' or 'Corinna' resist attempts to generate a consistent picture of the poet's mistress (Is she a courtesan? Is she a married woman?). Attempts to assemble a consistent account of Lucilius' background and career have encountered some similar difficulties (in particular the uncertainty as to whether or not he has withdrawn from public life; see further main intro. section 2). On the multiple functions of L in the *EM* see Ker 2009a: 153–4.

There is a marked contrast between the apparent warmth and excitement of *Ep.* 34 (in part an effect of the sixteen first person singular verbs, mostly in the present tense) and the coolness of *Ep.* 35 which follows it (where S insists L is not yet sufficiently advanced to qualify as a friend, 35.1 *amicus non es*). In *Ep.* 35, S's affection for L appears wholly contingent on the latter's philosophical progress. Yet warmth of tone recurs in numerous later letters, such as *Ep.* 40, which stresses the power of L's letters (*uera amici absentis uestigia*) to make their writer present to S.

The latter part of *Ep.* 34 focuses on self-consistency, which is the goal both of the literary-philosophical work and the human individual (cf. 20.3 *unam semel ad quam uiuas regulam prende et ad hanc omnem uitam tuam exaequa*, 79.9 on the individual as a perfected opus, *quicumque fuerint sapientes, pares erunt et aequales*, 120.22, Long 2009: esp. 32–6, Bartsch 2009: 210–11). How is this goal to be achieved? In this letter (and elsewhere in Book 4, 35.4 *mutatio uoluntatis*, 36.5 *uoluntate*, 37.5 *qui sciat quomodo quod uult coeperit uelle*) S stresses the importance of the *desire* for self-improvement. Some scholars (esp. Pohlenz 1965; cf. Dihle 1982: esp. 134–5, Kahn 1988) have detected here (and in other passages such as 37.5, 71.36) an articulation of the will as a distinct faculty, without parallel in the work of earlier philosophers (others, e.g. Hadot 2014a: 299–312, argue that S's view does not differ significantly from that of earlier Stoics). Certainly S's thinking, in its emphasis (if not in its analysis), is often concerned with second-order desire, wanting to want, attending particularly to 'moments of causally efficacious judgement' (Inwood 2005: 155). For Inwood (2005: ch. 5), S's recurrent concern with self-directed commands as acts of will (alongside self-awareness, self-shaping and self-control) offers an alternative account of the phenomena associated by later thinkers, such as Augustine, with the operation of the will as a distinct faculty ('traditional will'). As he underlines, the passage from *Ep.* 34 cannot be pressed far in this regard.

Commentaries: Motto, Davies.

1 Cresco et exulto et discussa senectute recalesco: a tricolon of first person singular verbs conveys S's excitement; the opening of this letter is highly personal, a document of friendship. *cresco* (*OLD* 3c) 'I swell with pride'. L's letters have a revivifying effect (S claims) on their recipient. Old age (with whose symptoms Book 4 opened, observing Bassus *aetati obluctantem*, 30.1) is shaken off. *recalesco*: at 67.1 S complains that old age makes him susceptible to the cold (for the association cf. Liv.

6.23.7 with Oakley 1997 *ad loc.*, Virg. *A.* 5.394–6, Juv. 6.325–6 *frigidus aeuo | Laomedontiades*, Eyben 1972: 684). **quotiens:** the effect of L's correspondence is presented as cumulative, though, as Davies notes *ad loc.*, the excited tone suggests reaction to a particular letter. **quantum te ipse . . . superieceris** 'to what degree you have surpassed yourself'. A reprise of S's comment at 15.10 (*quid tibi cum ceteris? te ipse antecessisti*). *quantum:* adv. 'to what extent'. *turbam:* in the sense not only of others struggling towards self-improvement but also perhaps the distracting *sollicitantium turba* of 32.2. **si agricolam . . . iudicet:** the first two of the three protases are rustic in subject matter (vegetable, then animal), picking up on *cresco* in the first sentence (and perhaps recalling Ovid's figure of Polyphemus; see above): the fruit tree gives pleasure to the farmer (*uoluptatem* here, as occasionally elsewhere in S, in a positive sense, cf. e.g. 31.2), the young of his flock delight the shepherd. The third asserts rather the identification between teacher and pupil (*alumnus*, *OLD* 4, the philosopher's pupil), the former seeing his own youth in that of the latter as he develops. S frequently uses agricultural imagery (cf. Armisen-Marchetti 1989: 149–50, 235; arboricultural subject matter figures prominently at 86.17–21). **quid euenire credis . . . uident?** by implication, the teacher's pleasure will far surpass that of the farmer or shepherd. **ingenia:** see 21.5(n.). Here the process of education brings out innate potential. **tenera:** there is slippage between physical and mental immaturity. On the difficulty of moulding an older pupil see 25.1–2 and Laudizi *ad loc.* **formauerunt:** S uses several terms which emphasise the moulding of the student by the teacher; cf. 25.1 *tenera finguntur*. **subito:** S envisages the transformation as suddenly apparent, following a prolonged period of latent development (cf. the description of his own transformation, 6.2 *tam subitam mutationem mei*).

2 Two brisk and startlingly concrete assertions follow the lengthy rhetorical question. **assero te mihi; meum opus es** 'I claim you; you are my work'. *assero* (*OLD* 4a incl. *Ben.* 7.6.1), though the legal use, to claim a slave (or son) (*OLD* 2), is disconcertingly hinted at by the objectifying term *opus* which follows. For *opus* (*OLD* 9) as a work of art see intro. to *Ep.* 33 above (cf. Armisen-Marchetti 1989: 79). In §3 S uses *opus* to refer rather to the project of L's philosophical education. **cum uidissem indolem tuam** 'when I had noted your potential'. **inieci manum** 'I grabbed hold of you': the phrase *manum iniecere*, often used figuratively by S (e.g. *VB* 23.2, *Helv.* 11.7; cf. Ov. *Am.* 1.4.6, 40 of two men laying competing claims to a beloved), signifies in legal contexts seizing hold of property to which one has a claim (*OLD manus* 15). See Armisen-Marchetti 1989: 107. **incitaui:** L is compared to a horse, driven on by its rider (Armisen-Marchetti 1989: 91–2); S goaded him to philosophical excellence. This is a curious analogy for philosophical development but one whose urgency is in line with that of many other images in the letters (most notably the military, e.g. 36.7–9, and gladiatorial, e.g. 37.1–2).   **currentem . . . hortantem:** sc. *te* as subject of these participles. There has been a change of pace; L is now proceeding at speed. He in turn is also encouraging S (an outcome anticipated at 6.6). For the proverb of urging on a willing horse cf. Tosi 1991: §480, citing e.g. Plin. *Ep.* 1.8.1 *addidisti ergo calcaria sponte currenti*.

3 'quid aliud?' inquis, 'adhuc uolo' 'Why say more?' You ask, 'So far I am willing.' L's imagined interjection shifts the letter in a new direction, with the focus now on what remains to be achieved. The MS reading *quid aliud?* (also preferred by Graver and Long) is retained here (this is otherwise unattested in S and alternative readings have been proposed, with several scholars including Reynolds supporting Axelson's emendation *quid illud?* with *dicis* understood, though this is also without Senecan parallel).   **non sic quomodo . . . dicuntur:** it is not just 'well begun is half done'; rather, L's willingness means the greater part (*plurimum*) of the task is achieved. *totius operis dimidium* 'half the whole work'. The wording evokes the familiar Horatian version (*Ep.* 1.2.40 *dimidium facti, qui coepit, habet*). *occupare* 'to seize hold of' (*OLD* 3).   **ista res animo constat** 'this matter is based on the mind'.   **uelle fieri bonum:** the inf. *uelle* serves as predicate to the subj. *pars magna bonitatis*. *uelle* picks up on the *uolo* put in L's mouth. For this use of *uelle* cf. 71.36 *magna pars est profectus uelle proficere. huius rei conscius mihi sum: uolo et mente tota uolo*, 80.3–4 *quid tibi opus est ut sis bonus? uelle*; *Phaedra* 249 *pars sanitatis uelle sanari fuit*. See intro. above for the debate concerning the philosophical significance of the phrase.   **scis quem bonum dicam?** while 31.6 asked *quid est bonum?* the focus here is on defining the good man.   **perfectum, absolutum . . . possit:** S's definition of the good man is uncompromising. He is finished and complete. *perfectum* picks up the earlier concern with making (*meum opus es* §2). For the *sapiens* as thus characterised cf. Cic. *Fin.* 4.37 *qui sapientes sunt, absolutos et perfectos putamus* (though Cicero most often uses these terms in relation to fine oratory). The following letter further characterises the *sapiens perfectus* (35.4), acknowledging the difficulty of attaining such a state. S later terms such a one (the Stoic *sapiens*) as rare as a phoenix (42.1).

4 hunc te prospicio: for S, L has the potential to attain this perfection. As Davies notes *ad loc*., while earlier letters (e.g. 24.19) stressed the importance of consistency of words and deeds, here there is a further emphasis on consistency over time.   **si perseueraueris . . . percussa sint:** the conditional clause comprises a tricolon of verbs (fut. pf.) followed by a result clause with a further tricolon of verbs (pres. subj.). The six verbs underline the huge and sustained effort involved in this undertaking. *facta dictaque tua* echoes *quae agis ac scribes* in the opening sentence. *una forma percussa sint* picks up *formauerunt* and *discussa* in §1, the phrase evoking the minting of coinage (*OLD percutio* 5); character is often seen in terms of (base) coinage, on the analogy of the Greek χαρακτήρ: LSJ II.1 and 4; see e.g. Thgn. 1105–6. *una* balances *omnia*. Self-consistency is a key goal for S (see intro. above).   **animus:** S reiterates the paramount importance of the mind. Cf. §3 *animo*.   **in recto:** possibly a predicative phrase with neuter form of adjective, but we should perhaps understand *loco* here, thus 'the mind of someone whose actions are not consistent is not in its right place'. The same use of *in recto* also in relation to the mind occurs at *De ira* 1.5.2, *quo quid est mitius, dum in recto animi habitus est?*

LETTER 46

The brief and playful fifth letter of Book 5, *Ep.* 46, forms a contrast with the morally heavyweight preceding letter, in which S criticised at length those philosophers who focus on sophistical argument rather than how to live well (for the concerns of Book 5 more generally see intro. to *Ep.* 47 below). Earlier letters in the series often allude to L's letters, to which S claims to be replying. The literary interchange is not restricted to letters, it seems. *Ep.* 45 attributes to L a request that S should send some of his own books (*libros meos*), while *Ep.* 46 offers S's preliminary response to a piece of writing allegedly composed by L.

Ep. 46 'comes as close as any in the collection to a semblance of ordinary correspondence', suggests Wilson in his perceptive discussion (1987: 104). The first two paragraphs chart 'the dynamics of S's evolving response to L's work' (1987: 106). S focuses on the style rather than the subject, tracking its effects on himself as reader. The final paragraph, however, more distant in tone, advises that this is a provisional response (though L's piece is not referred to again) and goes on to warn teasingly against friends whose praise may be less than frank.

Ep. 46's praise of L's literary work offers a new perspective on his character. Relevant is Setaioli's contention (2000: esp. 174–5) that for S literary style expresses the particular individual character of the author (drawing on Panaetius' theory of the four *personae*; see further intro. to *Ep.* 114 below). S's addressee, almost a cipher in some letters, is vividly evoked by others (e.g. *Epp.* 19, 49). In particular, two other letters focus on L's writing: 59.4–6 on the style of his letters, 79.5–7 on his plans to write a poem, possibly on the subject of Etna (discussed by Schönegg 1999: 179–94, who argues that S uses the device of L's Etna project to explore issues relating both to S's own writing and also to his reputation more generally). On L's writings see also 24.21, *Nat.* 3.1.1.

At 45.3, S treats his own books as an analogy for his person, commenting that L's request for them is no more a testimony to his learning than a request for his picture would be to his good looks (a suggestive echo of the imagery of 33.5(n.)). *Ep.* 46 may be read as pursuing this analogy further; there are good grounds for seeing here an erotic dimension. On Habinek's reading (1998: 145–6), *Ep.* 46 initially positions S the reader as dominant; the active subject, he samples in pursuit of pleasure L's text, which is characterised as smooth – like a beardless boy (cf. 47.7n.). Yet soon this seductive text takes control of its reader. L's masculine writing (§2 *uirilis*) obliges his reader to adopt a subordinate position – but one that (shockingly in terms of Roman sexual morality) brings the reader pleasure (Habinek 1998: 145). One might compare the sexual model for the relationship between poet and reader as construed by Catullus, esp. poem 16; see Fitzgerald 1995: 50–3, 255 n. 38.

It is not just a question of S's succumbing to the charms of his far from boyish pupil (for the shame potentially associated with this see 47.7n.; the juxtaposition of these two letters adds bite). Since L is also a regular recipient of S's writing (and perhaps models his own virile style on that of his mentor), we should imagine him taking his turn as the one seduced. And while we, as readers, do not get to encounter L's seductive prose, we are perhaps invited to consider our own responses as we subordinate ourselves to the pleasure of reading S's letters.

This *jeu d'esprit* is, of course (like the reference to Nisus and Euryalus at 21.5, on which see note), not in itself support for the allegations Dio (61.10.4) reports that S himself had a sexual predilection for mature men (such claims are perhaps alluded to at *VB* 27.5, referring to comparisons with Alcibiades). Pedagogic pederasty seems explicitly rejected at 123.15. Bartsch (2005) discusses Roman responses to the emphasis on same-sex desire in the discourse of Platonic philosophy, where the teacher plays the role of a lover who appreciates and develops the moral beauty of his student, as this was received in first-century CE Rome. The association of philosophers with sexual submission is, she argues, to be related to the Stoic concern with *patientia*.

For an earlier instance of literary reciprocity characterised in terms of mutual sexual provocation cf. Catul. 50 (discussed by Fitzgerald 1995: 36–7, 46). While Cicero's letters make relatively infrequent reference to responses to his own literary works on the part of his correspondents (or vice versa), Pliny's correspondence often comments on the literary compositions of his friends (e.g. *Ep.* 8.7) or invites criticism of his own (e.g. 4.14) (see Marchesi 2008: ch. 2). Indeed, S's *Ep.* 46 seems (along with *Ep.* 21(intro.)) specifically echoed by Plin. 7.20 to Tacitus, whose opening

COMMENTARY: 46.1   175

words are *Librum tuum legi*; each, it appears, has been commenting on the other's work (cf. too Plin. *Ep.* 9.31 to Sardus).

Further reading: Wilson 1987: 104–7, Habinek 1998: 145–6.

1 Librum tuum balances *libros meos* which S grudgingly agreed in the previous letter (45.3) to send at L's request.   **tamquam lecturus ex commodo** 'as though I should read at my convenience'. *tamquam* is often used with the fut. partic. of thwarted intentions; see K–S 1.791. For *ex commodo* see *OLD commodum* 3.   **adaperui** 'unrolled' (*OLD* 1b).   **degustare** 'to taste'; cf. 33.5(n.).   **uolui:** the sequence of three active first person singular verbs underlines S's initial agency; his intentions are rapidly subverted.   **blanditus** 'beguiled' (*OLD* 6). S often uses words with this root pejoratively; cf. e.g. 45.7 *uenit ad me pro amico blandus inimicus*. It frequently has erotic associations; cf. Plin. *Ep.* 7.4.6 *fugaces blanditias* of the homoerotic flirtation between Cicero and his freedman Tiro.   **ut procederem longius:** consecutive, as often after *blandior* (see *OLD* 1b).   **qui quam disertus fuerit ex hoc intellegas licet** 'how skilfully expressed it was, you may understand from the following'. In the previous letter, S disclaimed this quality for himself, notwithstanding L's request to read his *libros* (45.3). The subject here is the book rather than L, a personification sustained in the succeeding sentences (cf. Wilson 1987: 105).   **leuis** 'smooth' (*OLD lēuis*² 3; *TLL* VII.2.1222–3, 1.B1b). *lēuis* is often used in descriptions of literary style, e.g. Cic. *de Orat.* 2.54 *Coelius . . . neque tractu orationis leui et aequabili perpoliuit illud opus*, Quint. *Inst.* 5.12.18, 9.4.116, Plin. *Ep.* 1.16.5; see also Fitzgerald 1995: 40–1 on the smoothness of Catullus' book (*pumice expolitum*, 1.2), and its complex erotic and Alexandrian associations. Fantham translates as 'light' (*OLD leuis*¹), thus a reference to scale; cf. Graver 1998: 617. But this is hardly a term to be applied to Livy or Epicurus, to whose work S will compare that of L.   **cum esset nec mei nec tui corporis** 'as if it were not of my work or of yours'. The circumstantial *cum* clause is part of the impression the work makes on S (following *uisus est*). For *corpus* in relation to a literary work (*TLL* IV.1020–1, IV.A) cf. e.g. 84.2, *Tranq.* 9.6, Ov. *Trist.* 2.535 (of the *Aeneid*), Plin. *Ep.* 2.10.3. The adjective *lēuis*, often used of skin (*TLL* VII.2.1222, 1.2, e.g. Ov. *Ars* 3.433 *uitate uiros cultum formamque professos, | femina quid faciet cum sit uir leuior ipsa?*), invites us to think in terms of actual as well as literary bodies; cf. the use of *membra* at 33.5(n.).   **Titi Liuii:** S was evidently familiar with Livy's work, engaging closely, for instance, with his treatment of Scipio (86.1–3). Quintilian writes of the *lactea ubertas* 'milky richness' of Livy's style (*Inst.* 10.1.32).   **Epicuri:** Epicurus' style is criticised for extravagance (ποικίλως διεφθορότα) by the astronomer Cleomedes, 2.1 pp. 166.1–168.10 Ziegler; Setaioli 2000:

191–2 argues that these comments derive from Posidonius. **dulcedine** 'charm'; cf. *OLD dulcis* 5a, often associated with the pleasures of the senses as well as of the mind. **sol . . . minabantur:** the anaphoric tricolon (extending the figure of personification further, as Wilson 1987: 105 notes) conveys the beguiled S's imperviousness to the passage of time and to his bodily needs. **exhausi** 'I drank it all in', returning to the tasting imagery introduced by *degustare* (§1). *ēxhaūsī tōtum* is an emphatically heavy *clausula*.

2 non tantum delectatus sed gauisus sum: *delectare* and the related noun, often used for pleasures of the senses (cf. *delectet* in the following letter, 47.8), frequently features in literary criticism; see e.g. Cic. *Inv.* 1.27 *quod delectationis causa non inutili cum exercitatione dicitur et scribitur*, Hor. *Ars* 333 *aut prodesse uolunt aut delectare poetae* with Brink 1963–82: II.352 on Hellenistic theories of poetry, 355. At 59.4 S examines the significance of the term, associating it with *uoluptas*; again it is L's writing (in this case a letter) which is the source (*me . . . delectauerit*). L's work is presented as a source also of *gaudium*, associated by S with only the most edifying of pleasures (cf. 23.4 *uerum gaudium res seuera est*, 27.3, 59.2). The previous letter, by contrast, chastised L for desiring the frivolous pleasure brought by varied reading matter; he should rather seek profit from reading the right books: *lectio certa prodest, uaria delectat* (45.1) (*uarietas* often features as a positive quality in literary criticism; see Fitzgerald 2016). **ingenii:** partitive gen. (G–L §369). For *ingenium* see 21.5n. **tenor** 'a sustained and even course' (*OLD* 1a). **compositio uirilis et sancta:** at 40.2 (in the course of a discussion of literary style), S advises that a philosopher's style, like his way of life, should be *composita*. Stoic philosophy is characterised as *uirilis* at 33.1; for *uirilitas* in relation to literary style cf. 114.22n. *sancta* 'pure' (*OLD* 4b). **dulce illud et loco lene:** cf. *dulcedine* in §1. The alliteration and assonance reproduce the smooth effect attributed to L's writing. *loco* 'in places', *TLL* VII.2.1599.40–64. **grandis, erectus:** here S shifts from third person (the book) to second person. Now L takes on the character of his writing. At 45.9, S used *erectus* to characterise the truly happy man, one who lives his life according to nature and can withstand any misfortune.

3 plura scribam: but the topic does not recur in the surviving letters. **parum . . . sedet** 'is not sufficiently settled'. **tamquam audierim illa, non legerim:** it was common for elite Romans to have things read to them, often by trained slave readers (Starr 1990–1; cf. *OLD audio* 6b, e.g. Plin. *Ep.* 4.23.1). S implies this is a more superficial way of engaging with a text. At 38.1, stressing rather the potency of the voice, S comments on the superiority of hearing over reading. **sine me et inquirere**

COMMENTARY: 47   177

'allow me to investigate it', i.e. L's book; *OLD inquiro* 2a.   **non est quod uererearis: uerum audies:** for *non est . . . quod* see 7.9n. *uererearis: uerum*: as often (see main intro. section 9), S juxtaposes similar sounding words with very different meanings.   **o te hominem felicem!** acc. of exclamation.   **quod nihil habes propter quod . . . mentiatur** 'because you have nothing on account of which anyone might lie to you for so long'; *OLD longe* 3a.   **nisi quod:** here a teasing correction.   **consuetudinis causa**: on the role of habit in instilling vices cf. *Ep.* 7.

LETTER 47

The first letter in the *EM* already invokes the idea of freedom – and its counterpart slavery – in the exhortation: *uindica te tibi!* (1.1n.). A key concern of Book 2 (see Soldo), freedom is an intermittent theme of Book 5. *Ep.* 42, the first in the book, criticises those who sacrifice their *libertas* in pursuit of the superfluous (42.7–8). *Ep.* 44, opening with L's alleged concern at his own lowly status, appropriates the vocabulary of Roman social distinction, the display of ancestral *imagines* as an advertisement of noble birth, to assert that only philosophy can confer true nobility, to which even an ex-slave may aspire (44.6). *Ep.* 47 (whose essay-like form contrasts with that of the highly epistolary 46) offers sharp insights into the complex relations between masters and slaves in Roman society, most particularly through S's vividly drawn picture of the wealthy master's morally dysfunctional relationship with his slaves. In *Ep.* 47, S returns to the satiric mode, which characterised particularly *Ep.* 18 (see above) and which is also to the fore later in Book 5 in *Ep.* 50 on Baiae (cf. *Ep.* 56, 86.6–13).

Ostensibly prompted by a report on L's relations with his own slaves (§1), the letter moves rapidly to a detailed critique of the failure on the part of many masters to appreciate their slaves' humanity and the cruelty with which they treat them. S develops at length (§§2–8) a satirically informed scene to illustrate this: the dinner (including a briefly sketched contrast with the fairer treatment of slaves in earlier times in §4). Yet such masters are willing to abase themselves to ex-slaves, once the latter are in positions of power (§9). S now develops a theme touched on in §1: the shared humanity of slaves (§10), stressing that anyone may chance to fall into slavery (§§10–13). Treat those inferior to you as you would wish to be treated by your own superior (§11). In urging that slaves should be included in the master's conversation and at his table, on the grounds that they too have the potential for virtue, S returns to the contrast with earlier times (§14) and stresses that there is no shame in sharing your table with your slaves, no matter how lowly. Furthermore, many freeborn individuals are themselves enslaved – to their passions (§17). At §18, S addresses himself to a different kind of objection: that this practice would undermine proper social hierarchy. Here emerge two intriguing analogies: the master who is revered (rather than feared) by his slaves is compared to a god (§18), while rage at minor annoyance is no more appropriate to a master than to a monarch (§20).

The letter has been regularly praised for its humanity and sometimes read as an attack on slavery as an institution (e.g. by Vogt 1975: 138–9, who argues that Stoic influence led to legislation mitigating cruelty against slaves). More recent scholars have read S as unconcerned with institutional change (Griffin 1992: ch. 8, Bradley 1986, 1994: 154–73, Garnsey 1996: ch. 9, esp. 150, Armisen-Marchetti 2013). Certainly S stresses the common condition of slave and free and underlines the capacity of slaves for virtue and for philosophical development (cf. *Ben.* 3.18). The letter portrays evocatively the suffering and humiliation experienced even (or especially?) by those 'privileged' slaves who are closest to their master. At the same time, in misusing his power over his slaves, the master may ultimately inflict greater damage on himself, S suggests.

It was, of course, prudent for masters to maintain the goodwill of their slaves. S vividly stresses the vulnerability of masters to their slaves at 4.8–9 *nemo non seruus habet in te uitae necisque arbitrium* (Bradley 1986: 168–9). At *Nat.* 1.16.2 S recounts that Hostius Quadra, notorious for his unbridled and perverse lusts (see 47.7n. below), was murdered by his slaves. Eigler (2005) argues that *Ep.* 47 should be seen against the background of the senatorial debate in 61 CE on the aftermath of the murder of Pedanius Secundus by one of his slaves (reported by Tac. *Ann.* 14.42–5; though see Griffin 1992: 400 on the chronology). A senatorial decree of 10 CE (*SC Silanianum*) had prescribed that if the master were killed by one of his slaves, all the slaves in the household would be executed (*Dig.* 29.5) – a chilling reflection of the anxiety of slave-owners. A similar case, though on a smaller scale, is the murder of the ex-praetor Larcius Macedo, notorious for his cruelty to his slaves, discussed by Pliny (*Ep.* 3.14; McKeown 2007b). For Finley (1980: 121), 'the *humanitas* of Seneca ... served to reinforce the institution [*sc.* slavery] not to weaken it', encouraging slaves to focus on their spiritual development instead of feeling indignant at their lot.

Indeed S exploits the symbolic potency of slavery as metaphor in ways which might ultimately work to reinforce distinctions between master and slave (cf. Bradley 1986: 170). Certainly the ideal in this letter is not the abolition of slavery but a situation where, as in earlier times (so S alleges), masters live on familiar terms with their slaves and are respected by them. Romans generally found slavery good to think with (Fitzgerald 2000: 11); metaphors of enslavement and liberation figure prominently in S's philosophical prose (Viansino 1979, Edwards 2009). Cicero (*Parad.* 33–41) records the well-known Stoic paradox: 'Only the sage is truly free, all others are slaves' (cf. e.g. *SVF* III.355, 364). A number of other passages in the *EM* offer variations on this, for instance *sapientia quae sola libertas est* (37.4). Those who have not attained *sapientia* remain enslaved by their attachment to externals, by the passions. Thus in §§2–9 the actual slave has an important role to play in servicing and stimulating those degrading appetites to which the master is metaphorically enslaved. S also invokes metaphors of slavery to characterise the relationship between mind and body; the body should be slave to the mind not, as all too often, vice versa (cf. *Ep.* 14). Habinek (2014: 21) comments: 'We might ... see the obsession with freedom on the part of Roman Stoics such as Seneca for what it is: a psychological and ideological response to the ubiquity of slavery and to the master class's dependence on it' (see further intros. to *Epp.* 24, 70).

The final part of *Ep.* 47 (§§19–21) sets up an analogy between the master–slave relationship and the relationship of monarch to subjects, which resonates significantly with S's treatise addressed to Nero, *De clementia* (composed soon after Nero's accession). *Clem.* 1.18.1–3 also criticised masters who ill-treat their slaves. Though a distinction is drawn between the relationship of a master to his slaves and that of a king to his subjects, they remain uncomfortably close, particularly when the hatred provoked by the cruel master is compared to that provoked by the unjust king. It is, then, tempting to read the final section of *Ep.* 47 as on one level a caution to Nero himself. Indeed Nero, like the bad master, is said to have boasted of the untrammelled power associated with his position (see §11n. below).

In *Ep.* 47 S also explores the suggestively paradoxical idea that those with the legal status of slaves may nevertheless be 'free' in the more important philosophical sense. While some individuals may have enslaved minds, despite being freeborn, others, despite being slaves, may be more truly free (§17). (Statements of this kind have some precedents in Greek tragedy, e.g. Eur. fr. 831 Kannicht; Richter 1958 associates such claims with the pre-Socratics.) Servitude, like *nobilitas*, is all in the mind. Joshel (2011: 234) comments: 'Seneca's pervasive use of slavery as a metaphor ... drains social realities of meaning.' Yet S's richly detailed account of the slave's experiences in *Ep.* 47 can work to draw the reader into identification with the slave. The reader, by imagining himself in the position of the real slave, feels the humiliation of his own metaphorical enslavement. In *Ep.* 80, similarly, S exhorts his reader to identify with the slave's consuming desire for freedom (e.g. 80.4).

S's vignette of the dinner party engages with a rich satiric tradition (already evident in the satirist Lucilius, Books 5 and 13; treatments of this theme by Horace and Juvenal are discussed by Gowers 1993: 109–219). There are notable resonances with Juvenal (esp. 5.120–4 on the ostentatious banquet of Virro) and numerous epigrams of Martial (e.g. 3.18). S himself returns to aspects of this topic in 78.23–4, 83.24, 95.23–9, *Ep.*

122, *Brev.* 12.5 (with many similarities of detail). A shared meal should symbolise (at least temporary) equality among the participants (an ideal which is graphically thwarted by the monstrous hosts depicted by Martial and Juvenal; cf. Plin. *Ep.* 2.6 and see D'Arms 1990, Gowers 1993: 211– 12), hence the particular resonance of the shared meal, which is the centrepiece of the Saturnalia (see §14n. below). The supposed etymology of *conuiuium* (from *cum* and *uiuere*, cf. Cic. *Fam.* 9.24.3 = 362 SB '*conuiuia*' *quod tum maxime simul uiuitur*, see Gowers 1993: 131–2) is played on in the opening sentence (cf. §11 *cum . . . uiuas*, §13 *uiue cum*). In focusing on the *conuiuium*, S chooses an especially charged scene, highlighting not the unequal treatment of guests (often themselves guilty of colluding in their humiliation, according to Martial and Juvenal) but rather the fundamental inequality between those who dine and those who are compelled to serve them. While other authors often treat the attendant slaves as mere symptoms of their master's vices (e.g. Hor. *S.* 2.8.10–15), S attempts to imagine what it feels like to service, mute and starving, a master's gluttonous excesses.

Satire was considered a vehicle for self-consciously free speech (see e.g. Hor. *S.* 1.4 with Gowers, 2.7 in which a slave addresses his master with Saturnalian licence). But this is a freedom conspicuously informed by the condition of slavery. In *Ep.* 18, S offered the slave's life as a model to be embraced (as a philosophical exercise) by the *proficiens* (18.9). Noting that the satirist Lucilius (he is perhaps deliberately evoked by the name of S's addressee; see Henderson 2004: 42, Gowers 2011) pictured himself as a freed slave (Lucil. 26), Freudenburg suggestively comments: 'To play the part of the satirist is to play the part of slave, parasite, lowlife' (1993: 214; cf. 211–23 on the Saturnalia more generally). We might link the strong satiric strand in S's letters with his appropriation of certain aspects of the slave's position as good to think with.

Scholars have long seen the comments Petronius puts in the mouth of Trimalchio at 71.11 as a parody of *Ep.* 47's advice on how to live with one's slaves (see e.g. Sullivan 1985: 174; whether the *Satyricon* is in fact Neronian in date has been recently disputed by Roth 2016). In terms of setting, there are numerous resemblances in the excessive dinner, at which a master (with inadequate control over his bodily orifices) presides, attended by numerous slaves, who have been trained in a wide range of specialisms to serve his luxurious appetites. Trimalchio himself observes (Petr. 71.11), *et serui homines sunt et aeque unum lactem biberunt, etiam si illos malus fatus oppresserit*. The assertion shares three common features with S's *Ep.* 47, the conceptual category *homines* (47.1), the adverb *aeque* (47.10), and *malus fatus* corresponding to S's *fortuna* (47.10); but in the clumsy and inaccurate Latin of Trimalchio (who uses the masculine forms *lactem* and *fatus* rather than the standard neuter) S's philosophically informed sentiment is a debased platitude (Armisen-Marchetti 2013: 3). Trimalchio makes clear his disdain for philosophy in his proposed epitaph (71.12 *nec umquam philosophum audiuit*); nevertheless Trimalchio (in line with S's advice) does live with his slaves *familiariter*. This is, however, in literal rather than moral terms, as Armisen-Marchetti (2013) underlines. Indeed, Trimalchio is all too close to his slaves; he invites some to join him at the table but his selection is not made, as S advises (47.15), on the basis of *boni mores*, and, when three are invited at Petr. 70.10, all rush in, causing the kind of chaos S's critics predict at *Ep.* 47.18. The slaves who join Trimalchio at the table are not edified by their master's outlook (the *sermo* is scarcely *honestior*) but rather share his base interests in gambling and the circus games (Petr. 70.10), just the kind of *sordida conuersatio* of which S disapproves (§15). At the same time, Trimalchio, once a slave himself, sympathises with his slaves' desire for legal rather than spiritual freedom, as he makes clear in announcing their manumission under the terms of his will (71.3, Armisen-Marchetti 2013; Roth 2016 notes the repeated plays on forms of manumission throughout the *cena*). Actual manumission does not apparently figure in S's plans for his own slaves or those of L. As Nussbaum (2000: 191) observes, insofar as the treatment of slaves is concerned, the shift in *Ep.* 47 from literal to metaphorical slavery is a manoeuvre which 'does too much work if it does any at all'.

Commentaries: Summers (bowdlerised), Costa.
Further reading: Viansino 1979, Bradley 1986, 1987, D'Arms 1990, 1991, Griffin 1992: ch. 8 and Appendix E, Garnsey 1996: 57–8, 128–52, Fitzgerald 2000: esp. 88–92, Nussbaum 2000: 189–91, Eigler 2005, McKeown 2007b, Edwards 2009, Joshel 2011, Armisen-Marchetti 2013.

1 Libenter ex iis ... cognoui: S several times claims to be hearing reports from others of how L lives (e.g. 32.1, 43.1), in this case from the messengers who bring L's letters. L himself returns to the fore at §16 and §19. The opening word *libenter* perhaps plays on *liber* 'free', while the first syllable also echoes the opening word of the previous letter, *librum*. **'serui sunt':** S imagines the interjection (truculently repeated four times) of one who thinks slaves should not be treated as fellow humans. S's responses by contrast increase in length (an expanding tetracolon) and intensity. **immo homines:** for S's frequent use of the corrective *immo* see Traina 1987: 32. On the common humanity of all cf. §5 and e.g. 48.3 *aliquod esse commune ius generis humani*, 95.52. **contubernales** 'share the same roof' (lit. 'tent-companions'). At 6.6, S praised the communal living (*contubernium*) associated with some Epicureans, which enabled them to learn from one another's example as well as from frequent conversation. At 47.15–16, S underlines the potential for shared daily interaction, particularly shared conversation over meals, in inculcating philosophical advice.   **humiles amici:** the nature of friendship (and its role in philosophical practice) is a recurrent concern in the *EM*; see intro. to *Ep.* 34 above. *humilis* 'of low social status' (*OLD* 3a) particularly when contrasted with *honestus* (at §15 S underlines the salutary effect of *honestiorum conuictus*); by the end of the second century CE, the contrast between *honestiores* and *humiliores* explicitly drove differential treatment in the law courts (Garnsey 1970: 221–4).   **conserui:** the retort evokes the Stoic doctrine that all but the wise man are slaves (see further above), thus dissolving the distinction between master and slave.   **si cogitaueris:** pf. subj. protasis of conditional (*NLS* §198), with apodosis 'as you would recognise' understood.   **tantundem in utrosque licere fortunae** 'fortune has the same power over either of you' (*utrosque* pl. agreeing with *seruos*). A notion expanded in §§10–13.

2 rideo flags the satiric flavour of the next section (cf. e.g. Hor. *S*. 1.1.24–5, 1.10.54 with Gowers).   **quare, nisi . . . circumdedit?** 'Why? Only because a most arrogant custom surrounds the master as he dines with a crowd of standing slaves.' On the *conuiuium* see D'Arms 1991.   **est ille** 'he eats'.   **capit** 'can hold' (*OLD* 25); cf. figuratively at 33.7.   **desuetum iam uentris officio** 'unaccustomed now to the proper role of a stomach'. The repetition *uentrem . . . uentris* stresses the master's unbecoming preoccupation with his appetite.   **ut maiore opera omnia egerat quam ingessit** 'so that he works harder to discharge all the food than he did to stuff it in'. *opera* f. 'effort'.

3 ne in hoc quidem, ut loquantur 'not even for this, that they should speak', i.e. let alone for eating. *in hoc: in* + acc. of goal aimed at. At *De ira* 3.35.1 S stresses the inconsistency of masters who complain at the curtailment of their own *libertas* even as they curtail the speech of their slaves and demand silence in the dining room. Plutarch (*De garr.* 511d–e) comments that slaves in Athens enjoyed greater freedom of speech than those in Rome.   **tussis, sternumenta, singultus** 'coughs, sneezes, hiccups'. Even involuntary noises are punished. There is a strong contrast between the extreme control exercised over the slaves' bodily orifices (cf. §4 *consuebatur*) and the total licence accorded to the master's.   **magno malo:** *malo* (here meaning punishment): abl. of instrument with *luitur*.   **ulla uoce:** abl. of agent with *interpellatum*.   **nocte tota:** the use of abl. rather than acc. to denote duration of time is common in S (found occasionally in republican Latin, this usage becomes more frequent from the Augustan period); see K–S 1.360.

4 isti de domino loquantur: concern is often expressed that slaves will talk about their masters behind their backs; cf. *De ira* 3.35.2, Mart. 2.82, Fitzgerald 2000: 59.   **cum ipsis:** i.e. 'with their masters'. The term *ipse* was often used by slaves to refer to the master of the household (*OLD* 12). For a similarly nostalgic vignette cf. Plin. *Nat.* 33.26 *apud antiquos singuli Marcipores Luciporesue dominorum gentiles omnem uictum in promiscuo habebant*, 'in olden times, a single servant for each master, as a member of his clan, Marcius' boy or Lucius' boy, took all his meals in common with the family'.   **sermo:** *sermo* was particularly associated with civilised dining (early in the letter quoted above, *Fam.* 9.24.3 = 352 SB, Cicero comments on the joy of shared meals so conducive to mental relaxation: *quae maxime sermone efficitur familiari, qui est in conuiuiis dulcissimus*). In S's letters, conversation serves as a privileged medium for philosophical instruction (cf. 38.1 *plurimum proficit sermo, quia minutatim irrepit animo, Ep.* 75, Traina 1987: 102, Setaioli 2000: 119–20). At least some slaves, as S makes clear at §§13–17, have the capacity for philosophical development through this means.   **quorum os non consuebatur** 'whose mouths were not sewn shut' (in a metaphorical sense). *consuebatur: OLD consuo* a.   **parati . . . porrigere ceruicem:** *ceruicem* balances *os*; cf. Ben. 3.19.2–4, 3.25. Stories of self-sacrificing slaves are collected in V. Max. 6.8 (under the rubric *De fide seruorum*), manifestations of a *fides*, which he characterises as 'the less to be expected, the more to be praised'. For a similar argument as to why monarchs should cultivate the love of their subjects (who will then be readier to lay down their lives to protect their ruler) see *Clem.* 3.5.4.   **in tormentis:** in Roman law, the evidence of slaves was normally extracted under torture (*Dig.* 48.18.1). The end of §4 is almost a terminal *sententia*, with the isocolon of *conuiuîs* and *tormentis* to underline sense.

5 deinde eiusdem arrogantiae prouerbium iactatur 'then a similarly arrogant proverb is thrown around'. *arrogantiae* is gen. of quality; cf. §2 *superbissma consuetudo.*   **totidem hostes esse quot seruos:** the proverb appears in the form *tot serui quot hostes* in Festus 314 Lindsay; for other instances, see Otto 1962: 319–20. At *Clem.* 1.24.1 S relates that proposals for slaves to be distinguished by a particular form of dress were rejected for fear that they would then realise the strength of their numbers. *De clementia* also explores the danger of revolt or conspiracy when monarchs treat their subjects with cruelty (1.8.7; cf. 1.11.4).   **non habemus . . . sed facimus:** masters are to blame for alienating their slaves. S makes clear that in being humane to his slaves the master will better ensure his own safety. On this kind of prudential reasoning see Griffin 1992: 262–3. Use of the first person plural implicates S, L and the reader (cf. *Tranq.* 8.8–9).   **alia . . . praetereo:** S's *praeteritio* allows him to allude to the more obviously cruel forms of treatment, such as corporal punishment, experienced by slaves (for examples see e.g. *De ira* 3.12.5–7). For Garnsey (1996: 57), S is pulling his punches here in choosing to focus on the dinner party, but this is to underestimate the pungency of S's satire.   **tamquam iumentis abutimur:** cf. the terms in which Plutarch criticises Cato the Elder (*Cat. Mai.* 5.1): 'I regard his treatment of his slaves like beasts of burden [ὑποζυγίοις], using them to the limit, then when they were aged, driving them away and selling them, as the mark of a very mean nature which recognises no bond between one human and another but that of necessity.'   **alius sputa deterget** 'one cleans up the master's saliva'; cf. §3. *alius* repeated five times stresses the number of specialised slave-roles deemed necessary to the dinners of the luxurious; for the high degree of specialisation among slaves of the very wealthy see Treggiari 1975: 51, 68 n. 74.   **reliquias temulentorum** 'what has been left by those who are drunk', presumably a periphrasis for vomit.   **subditus** 'positioned underneath'. It is not clear what the slave is underneath; Summers suggests that we should understand *mensae*, in nice contrast to S's proposal (§15) that some slaves be invited to join their master eating at the table (Reynolds, following Rossbach, supplies *toro* here).

6 alius pretiosas aues scindit: expensive fowl often constitute the *pièce de résistance* at the luxurious dinner party; cf. Juv. 5.114–24, Petr. 36, also putting a spotlight on the slave who carves.   **eruditam . . . excutit** 'flourishes his skilful hand pointlessly'. Cf. *VB* 17.2, where one of S's detractors, accusing him of hypocrisy, lists his luxurious habits, culminating in the use of such a specialist in his household, *obsonii scindendi magister*. The echo of *eruditionem decet* in §1 underlines the piquant contrast between the situation of the slave here and that of L, the educated Roman magistrate and *proficiens*.   **nisi quod . . . discit:** the situation of the master turns out to be worse than that of his slave. *causa* to be supplied with *necessitatis*. Emphatic homoeoteleuton sharpens the contrast between *uoluptatis* and *necessitatis*.

7 uini minister in muliebrem modum ornatus: in Plautus' *Menaechmi*, a character identifies himself as Ganymede (the desirable young cup-bearer of Jupiter) when wearing a woman's *palla* (*Men.* 143). For Ganymede-like slaves cf. Cic. *Fin.* 2.23, Mart. 10.98.1–2: *Addat cum mihi Caecubum minister | Idaeo resolutior cinaedo*, 'When an attendant more gorgeous than the catamite of Ida pours my Caecuban . . .'. The host Virro also has a beautiful boy to pour his wine (Juv. 5.56 *flos Asiae ante ipsum*). On the homoerotic associations of cup-bearers see further Hor. *Carm.* 1.29.7–8, 1.38, Dupont and Éloi 2001: 213–28, Williams 2010: 59–64). For handsome young slaves more generally as a paradigmatic symptom of luxury cf. the comment attributed to Cato the Elder (Polybius 31.25.5).   **cum aetate**

luctatur 'struggles against the signs of advancing years', thus maintaining the appearance of a sexually desirable adolescent. S elsewhere attacks those who engage voluntarily in such practices (122.7–8; cf. Mart. 3.74, 10.65, 12.38.4). **non potest effugere pueritiam** 'he is not allowed to escape boyhood'. **militari habitu:** his soldierly bearing emphasises his maturity (there may also be play on *pīlis*, hinting at *pīlis*). Only free men could serve in the Roman army; the jarring adjective *militari* highlights the contradictory nature of the role this slave is forced into. **glaber retritis pilis aut penitus euulsis** 'he is kept hairless by having his hair smoothed away or plucked out by the roots'. For *glaber* used of young male slaves cf. *Brev.* 12.5 *glabri ad ministeria discurrant.* The term is also found in descriptions of the positions of some slaves in the imperial household, as recorded in their epitaphs, e.g. *glaber ab cyatho* 'smooth boy who served wine' (*CIL* VI.8817 with Williams 2010: 35, 78–9). Beardlessness was often linked with the acme of desirability (see e.g. Quint. *Inst.* 5.12.18); facial hair, indicating the end of adolescence, might be taken as a sign that a male slave was no longer a suitable object of his master's sexual attentions (Mart. 4.7.1–3; cf. Tarán 1985 on the Greek epigram tradition). On male depilation see Richlin 1992: 168 (as a concern in Lucilian satire), 188–9; cf. below 114.14n. The small act of violence in *penitus euulsis* anticipates the more significant violations of the slave's person alluded to in what follows. **in cubiculo uir, in conuiuio puer est:** balancing the *libidinem* and the *ebrietatem* of his master. For similar antitheses cf. Caelius (quoted at Quint. *Inst.* 8.6.53) on Clodia *in triclinio coam, in cubiculo nolam* and Liv. 7.15.3 *in castris feroces, in acie pauidi.* Other letters, too, refer to slaves whose duties lie in the bedroom as well as at the banquet (95.24 *transeo puerorum infelicium greges, quos post transacta conuiuia aliae cubiculi contumeliae exspectant*, 122.7). Here it is made clear that the slave is to play an active sexual role. **uir**, adult male, a term normally only used of free men (Santoro L'Hoir 1992: 17–18, Walters 1997: 36–7), has a sexual dimension (cf. 122.7 on those who artificially prolong boyhood: *numquam uir erit, ut diu uirum pati possit?*). While it was generally found acceptable that masters used their young male slaves for sexual pleasure (the slave *puer* taking a receptive 'feminine' role, cf. Williams 2010: 31–40), the implication is that *this* master likes to be sexually penetrated by his slave, a much more perverse desire according to conventional Roman morality (cf. Hostius Quadra at *Nat.* 1.16.2, as well as, teasingly, Mart. 3.71; S himself was alleged to have taken pleasure in older youths and to have taught this vice to Nero, according to Dio Cass. 61.10.3–6, but see Bartsch 2005, esp. 78–83 on the complex associations of *patientia*, a key term in Stoic philosophy). At the same time the master is indicted for allowing himself to be penetrated by a person he would not deign to dine with.

8 censura: *OLD* 2. While the censors of old scrutinised the morals of the elite excluding those deemed unworthy to continue as members of the senate, this slave will rather weigh up and reward the vices of the dinner guests (invidious discrimination between the guests is a regular preoccupation of satire, e.g. Juv. 5). On the role of the *nomenclator* see D'Arms 1991: 172. **infelix:** cf. §3 *infelicibus*, §6 *infelix*. **expectat quos adulatio . . . reuocet in crastinum** 'must look out to see whose fawning and whose excesses whether of gullet or of tongue are to win them an invitation for the next day'. Cf. 122.12, where the impudent Varus secures invitations *improbitate linguae*. On the figure of the *scurra*, whose offensive wit secures him a place at the tables of wealthy hosts, see Hor. *S*. 1.5.52 with Gowers, *Ep*. 1.15.26–32 and Corbett 1986: 59–69. **obsonatores** 'caterers', apparently responsible for planning meals/laying in provisions (see e.g. Paulus, *Sent*. 3.6.72, including *opsonatores* among *urbana ministeria*). Augustus' widow Livia had a freed *obsonator* in her household (*CIL* vi.8945). **palati:** cf. the finicky hardened palate, *palato iam calloso*, of the luxurious individual at 78.23. **cuius nouitate nauseabundus erigi possit:** sc. *rei*, 'by the novelty of what thing he can be roused, when he is feeling like vomiting'. The terms used here recall the description of those suffering from *uitae . . . fastidium* at 24.26, *nihil noui facio, nihil noui uideo: fit aliquando et huius rei nausia* (see 24.26n.); cf. *Prov*. 3.6. *conchyliis . . . pigritiam stomachi nauseantis erigere* (on the stimulating delicacies absent from the wholesome life of Fabricius). For the luxurious master stuffed to the point of vomiting see also 89.22. **sustinet** 'tolerate' (*OLD* 7b). **maiestatis suae deminutionem . . . cum seruo suo accedere:** though he feels no compunction at submitting himself sexually to a slave. *maiestas* here in the sense of personal standing (*OLD* 1b). The phrase *maiestatis diminutio* (*OLD maiestas* 2b; cf. Cic. *Fam*. 12.15.2 = 406 SB) was particularly associated with infringements of the majesty of the Roman state, and, later, the person of the emperor (thus in both cases constituting treason, *Dig*. 48.4; Cic. *Inv*. 2.53 *maiestatem minuere est de dignitate aut amplitudine aut potestate populi . . . aliquid derogare*). This is mock heroic in relation to S's corrupt master but might also hint (esp. given the concerns of the final part of the letter) at the practices of the emperor Nero, notorious for flaunting his sexual relations with freedmen, most flagrantly in the consummation of his mock-marriage (to Doryphorus, Suet. *Nero* 28–9, or Pythagoras, Tac. *Ann*. 15.37) in which Nero noisily played the role of the deflowered bride. While these particular stories were associated with the latter part of Nero's reign, such interests on Nero's part may well have been evident earlier. **di melius!** we might supply e.g. *dent*; cf. Liv. 9.9.7, Ov. *Am*. 2.7.19. **quot ex istis dominos habet!** 'How many masters does he have from their ranks!' The figure of the powerful imperial freedman is a recurrent source of anxiety for elite Roman writers; see Tac. *Hist.* 2.57, *Ann.* 12.53, Suet. *Cl.* 28–9, Plin. *Ep.* 8.6; cf. Mouritsen 2011: 93–109.

9 Callisti: an influential freedman of the emperor Caligula, Callistus took part in the conspiracy to assassinate him and rose to still greater heights under Claudius, whom he served as *a libellis*, responsible for petitions (Tac. *Ann.* 11.29, 12.1). The splendour of his house provoked Pliny the Elder's disapproval (*Nat.* 36.60). S relates here that his erstwhile master, attempting to pay him a visit, was refused entry. There is a suggestive parallel in the story Epictetus tells (*Disc.* 1.19.19–23) about Felicio, sold by his master as useless, who eventually becomes a slave of Caesar and is sedulously cultivated by the same former master. **qui illi impegerat titulum** 'the one who had fastened a sales ticket on him'. *impegerat* from *impingo*. The ticket would presumably have listed his accomplishments. **reicula** 'discarded', 'worthless', dimin. cognate with *reicere* 'to throw away' (a plausible emendation suggested by Muretus of the MS *ridicula*). Anticipates §15 *reiecturum*. **in primam decuriam:** Callistus was not only sold but placed in the first lot, presumably reserved for slaves of low value (*TLL* v.1 *decuria* 223.l.84–224.i.3; cf. with regard to grouping slaves within the household Petr. 47). **apologauit:** unattested elsewhere, apparently a hybrid word derived from ἀπολέγω 'I reject' (LSJ ii). **sed domino quam multa Callistus** 'How much has Callistus cost his master!' To be supplied here *constitit* (*OLD* 11), as Costa suggests *ad loc.*

10 uis tu 'you really ought (to)', a colloquial periphrastic form of imperative, which occurs often in S (*OLD uolo* 8; see *Brev.* 19.2 with Williams, Setaioli 1980: 36). **ex eisdem seminibus ortum ... aeque mori:** *aeque* is emphasised by the threefold anaphora. This argument may be seen as an instance of the Stoic doctrine of *oikeiōsis* (see main intro. section 5); cf. *Ben.* 3.28.1 *eadem omnibus principia eademque origo*. Epictetus comments (*Discourses* 1.13): 'Don't you remember who you are and over whom you rule, that they are kinsmen, that they are brothers by nature, that they are the offspring of Zeus?' See intro. above for the similar sentiments expressed by Trimalchio at Petr. 71; cf. Juv. 14.16–17, with a Lucretian flavour, *animas seruorum et corpora nostra | materia constare putat paribusque elementis*, and the position rejected at Juv. 6.222 *'ita seruus homo est?'* **ingenuum:** while a man who had been a slave could become *liber* 'free', he could never be *ingenuus* 'freeborn' (unless through a rare imperial grant of *ingenuitas*, e.g. Suet. *Aug.* 74). **Variana clade:** in 9 CE the legate of the Rhine legions P. Quinctilius Varus suffered a devastating defeat at the hands of Arminius' forces in the German forest, regarded as the greatest disaster of Augustus' reign (Tac. *Ann.* 1.61–2, Suet. *Aug.* 23). Other accounts (e.g. Dio Cass. 56.18–22, Vell. 2.117–20) report that all the Romans – three legions – were killed, with none surviving to become slaves.   **senatorium per militiam auspicantes gradum:** *auspicari* 'make a beginning' (*OLD* 3). Under the principate only the sons of senators and men to whom the emperor had granted the *latus clauus* might aspire to become senators. This was almost invariably preceded by a period of service in the army as an officer (often as tribune of a legion; cf. Suet. *Aug.* 38 *liberis senatorum militiam auspicantibus*, Dio Cass. 67.11.4).   **fortuna** echoes §1 *fortunae*.   **nunc:** i.e. 'now you've heard this'. See *OLD* 10b.

11 locum 'commonplace', 'topic', often in a rhetorical context (*OLD* 23c); cf. 79.5.   **in quos superbissimi . . . sumus:** for the use of the first person plural see above on §5. The first superlative of the three echoes §2 *superbissima consuetudo*.   **uiuas** 'you should live'.   **quantum tibi in seruum tuum liceat** 'how much power you have over your slave'; cf. with contrasting emphasis the bon mot Suetonius attributes to Nero: *negauit quemquam principum scisse quid sibi liceret* (*Nero* 37.3).

12 bona aetas est! 'You're still young!' Cf. 76.1, Cic. *Cato Mai.* 48.   **habebis:** in verse and in prose after Livy, the subjunctive logically required by the indirect question inherent in *forsitan* is replaced by the indicative; see K–S 1.811.   **Hecuba:** in the aftermath of the sack of Troy, Hecuba, widow of King Priam, was said to have been enslaved by the victorious Greeks. Her plight was dramatised in Euripides' *Trojan women*. S himself reworked the theme in his *Troades*.   **Croesus:** the last king of Lydia, he was defeated and overthrown by the Persian leader Cyrus in 546 BCE. See *OCD*.   **Darei mater:** Curtius gives the name of Darius III's mother as Sisigambis, describing her as *aetate uenerabilis* (3.11.24). She was captured when Darius was defeated by Alexander at the battle of Issus in 333 BCE.   **Platon:** the philosopher was said to have been enslaved in Aegina when returning home from Sicily in 387 BCE but ransomed soon afterwards (Diod. Sic. 15.7, Diog. Laert. 3.19, Plut. *De tranq. an.* 471e, Jer. *Ep.* 53.1).   **Diogenes:** the Cynic philosopher (see 90.14n. below) was allegedly captured by pirates when sailing to Aegina and sold in Crete. Asked what his skills were, he replied he could rule men and pointed to a wealthy passer-by who, he said, needed a master. Sold to this man, Xeniades of Corinth, he became tutor to his sons and refused to be ransomed (Diog. Laert. 6.74).

13 uiue cum seruo clementer: the phrase echoes the opening sentence of the letter, *familiariter cum seruis tuis uiuere*. S's earlier treatise *De clementia*, whose title is perhaps alluded to here, several times draws analogies between the mercy of monarch to subject and that of master to slave (see intro. above) and is especially relevant to the final portion of the letter. On the significance of the term *clementia*, the self-restraint of the superior party (necessarily implying hierarchy), see Braund: 30–2. **comiter** 'in a friendly manner'. From the time of Augustus, emperors were praised for showing *comitas* in their interactions with (particularly senatorial) subjects (see Wallace-Hadrill 1982a). **et in sermonem ... in conuictum:** the tricolon (with alliteration of *c*) emphasises both social/philosophical communion (see §4(n.) for the philosophical flavour of *sermo*) and also shared eating, *conuictum* (tellingly it is the latter proposal which most immediately catches the attention of the luxurious). **delicatorum** 'of the fastidious' (*OLD* 4a); the term (much used by S; cf. e.g. 114.4 of Maecenas) also suggests self-indulgence (*OLD* 1b). **'nihil ... humilius, nihil turpius':** S has earlier described activities of the *delicati* which are of course far more degrading. **alienorum seruorum osculantes manum:** i.e. ingratiating oneself with the slave so as to secure the master's favour; cf. *Ben.* 3.28 *negas tibi a seruo tuo beneficium dari posse, cui osculum alieni serui beneficium est?* Epictetus, *Discourses* 4.1.148 makes the same point.

14 inuidiam 'odium', cf. *Ben.* 5.16.4 *potentiae suae detracturus inuidiam.* **maiores nostri:** the Romans of old (cf. 1.5n.), complementary to the philosophical *maiores* invoked at 44.3. To contrast the practices of earlier times with those of the present day is a ubiquitous move in satire. See e.g. Juv. 11.77–85 (Gowers 1993: 16–18). **dominum patrem familiae:** cf. *De ira* 3.35.2. **seruos ... familiares:** this usage is not attested in surviving fragments of mimes but cf. Pl. *Am.* 353–5. The phrase picks up *familiariter* in the opening sentence of the letter. **diem festum:** i.e. the Saturnalia. The festival involved feasting and the temporary suspension of social distinctions (see further intro. to *Ep.* 18); in earlier times, S claims, slaves often joined their masters at table (Bradley 1987: 40–5). This nostalgic vignette contrasts with *Ep.* 18's use of the Saturnalia as a negative model. **non quo solo ... sed quo utique** 'not as the only day but the one on which necessarily ...' **ius dicere permiserunt:** *ius dicere* 'to administer justice' (*OLD ius* 4b). This is perhaps a reference to the practice, associated with the Saturnalia, of appointing by lot a 'king' for the day, to direct the games and jokes (Epictetus, *Discourses* 1.25.8, Tac. *Ann.* 13.15, Lucian, *Saturnalia* 2, 4). **domum pusillam rem publicam:** for the idea of the household as miniature state cf. Plin. *Ep.* 8.16.2 *nam seruis res publica quaedam et quasi ciuitas domus est* (perhaps influenced by S).

15 'quid ergo ... mensae meae?' the luxurious interlocutor is still preoccupied with his table (and keen to insist on the size of his household). For *quid ergo* inviting a conclusion see *OLD ergo* 2b. **non magis ...**

liberos: S's response focuses particularly on *omnes*. The luxurious interlocutor is used to discriminating ruthlessly on the basis of status in issuing invitations (cf. the *conuiuarum censura* in §8).   **erras si ... reiecturum:** the criterion for discriminating will not be the kind of role performed by the slave.   **ut puta** 'as for example'. *puta* ('for example': *OLD* 9b) was probably colloquial in origin; *ut puta* 'as for example' is found first in S and Celsus, then in later writers of prose.   **illum** 'this particular'.   **mores, ministeria:** juxtaposition and alliteration highlight the contrast between character, under each individual's control, and role, a matter of chance (cf. §10 on the role of *fortuna* in determining slave status).   **honestiorum conuictus excutiet** reverses the more usual idea (see e.g. 7.3) that conversing with the bad corrupts the good. The dinner S proposes is the antithesis of the dinners given by arrogant hosts and attended by sycophantic guests where all are preoccupied with social position (which so often formed the subject of satire, e.g. Juv. 5 on Trebius; see above). On the slave's potential for virtue cf. *Ben.* 3.18.2 *nulli praeclusa uirtus est: omnibus patet, omnes admittit, omnes inuitat, et ingenuos et libertinos et seruos et reges et exules.*

16 non est, mi Lucili, quod: for *non est . . . quod* see 7.9n. After an exchange with the imagined *luxuriosus*, S now addresses L.   **cessat** 'lies idle' (*OLD* 4).   **sine artifice:** for the formation of the individual towards virtue compared to the moulding of an artwork at the hands of a craftsman, cf. *Ep.* 34.   **tempta et experire:** although the outrageous practices of others have been the focus of most of the letter, it is L who is now urged to implement S's advice to make his slaves, where they have the right potential, his friends.   **equum empturus:** cf. 80.9 *equum empturus solui iubes stratum, detrahis uestimenta uenalibus, ne qua uitia corporis lateant.*   **ex condicione, quae uestis modo nobis circumdata est:** social degree is as easily changed as a garment (cf. the focus on the mutability of fortune in §12). *circumdata:* in a metaphorical sense (*OLD* 3a), picking up *uestis modo* (cf. Liv. 21.43.3 *maiora uincula maioresque necessitates uobis . . . Fortuna circumdederit*).

17 'seruus est': the interjections echo those in §1.   **sed fortasse liber animo:** cf. 31.11 *hic animus tam in equitem Romanum quam in libertinum, quam in seruum potest cadere, Ben.* 3.18–20.   **ostende quis non sit:** for the idea that many are enslaved by the desire for externals which they should regard as *indifferentia* cf. 45.4, 80.4–5, *Ben.* 3.28.4 *seruum tu quemquam uocas, libidinis et gulae seruus et adulterae.*   **omnes spei:** Hense's supplement (adopted by Reynolds) on the analogy of Macr. 1.11.8 (which reproduces much of *Ep.* 47). Following the tricolon (*alius... alius... alius*), the phrase balances *omnes timori*.   **dabo** 'I shall give you as examples' (*OLD*

14); cf. 63.13, 82.20, 86.13.   **consularem aniculae seruientem** 'a consular at the beck and call of a little old woman', presumably in the expectation of a large legacy. The consular is enslaved by avarice. The practice of legacy hunting is a regular target in satirical literature; cf. e.g. Petr. 141, Juv. 12.94–126.   **ancillulae:** another derogatory diminutive (with a near-echo of *aniculae*). Here the passion is presumably *libido*.   **mancipia** 'creatures' (*OLD* 3b); cf. Sen. *Suas.* 7.6 *Lepidus . . . utriusque collegae mancipium*, Liv. 10.37.11 *mancipia nobilium, tribunos plebis*.   **pantomimorum:** the dancers in ballet-like versions of mythical stories, renowned for their licentiousness, are noted as conspicuously inappropriate objects of elite desire (cf. e.g. Suet. *Cal.* 36, 55, Tac. *Ann.* 1.77). The three examples of persons to whom men enslave themselves are in ascending order of shamefulness.   **nulla seruitus turpior est quam uoluntaria:** the paradox of voluntary servitude here diverts attention from the injustices which accompany the real thing (cf. Joshel 2011).   **non est quod:** see 7.9n.   **non superbe superiorem:** S plays on the etymology of *superbe* (from *super*). Contrast §11 *superbissimi*.   **colant potius te quam timeant:** Summers *ad loc.* aptly contrasts the praise of Appius which Cicero puts in the mouth of Cato the Elder (*Sen.* 37), *metuebant serui, uerebantur liberi*. In this case, too, similar concerns are expressed by S about the relations of monarchs and their subjects (*Clem.* 1.12.4 advises Nero against seeking as emperor to inspire fear).

18 dicet aliquis: another imagined interjection, this time expressing concern at the potential erosion of distinction between masters and slaves generally, which might be brought about by eating together. Such confusion could be considered an element of Trimalchio's dinner; at one point (Petr. 70) he invites the cook and other kitchen slaves to join him on his couch.   **uocare ad pilleum:** a technical phrase for manumission (Liv. 24.32.9, Suet. *Tib.* 4.2); the *pilleus* was a felt cap worn by freedpersons as a symbol of their liberation.   **de fastigio suo** 'from their position of superiority'.   **prorsus:** for *prorsus* as an intensifier see *OLD* 2.   **tamquam clientes . . . salutatores:** nom.; S's interlocutor asks whether he is proposing that slaves should behave with no more deference than *clientes* and those coming to pay their respects.   **quod deo sat est:** S responds that if gods are satisfied with deference, so should masters be. It is perhaps significant that the forms of *cultus* offered to the gods had much in common with those offered to the emperor (cf. Beard, North and Price 1998: 1.348–63, Gradel 2002). See further below on the emperor's presence in this letter.   **non potest amor cum timore misceri:** Cic. *Amic.* 53 observes that tyrants cannot have friends: *quis enim aut eum diligat quem metuat . . . ?* At 105.4 S observes that it is just as *molestum* to be feared by slaves as by free men.

19 rectissime ergo facere te iudico: a return to the letter's opening.   **uerborum . . . uerberibus:** a characteristic instance of wordplay involving a pair of words sharing the same first syllable but with contrasting meanings (see main intro. section 9). *uerberibus* echoes §3.   **muta** 'dumb creatures' (*OLD* 1a), i.e. not human (though note the enforced muteness of the slaves in §3).   **offendit** 'annoys'.   **ad rabiem:** the anger to which slaves so easily provoke their masters is a central preoccupation of *De ira,* e.g. 2.25.1. Strategies to inhibit oneself from taking offence are described at length in that treatise (see Harris 2001: 325–35).   **deliciae** 'refinement' in a negative sense; cf. §13 *delicatorum.* For the irritability generated by soft living cf. *De ira* 2.25.4 *nulla res magis iracundiam alit quam luxuria intemperans et impatiens.*   **non ex uoluntate respondit:** *respondere* 'to turn out as one wished' (*OLD* 10a) is reinforced by *ex uoluntate.*

20 regum nobis induimus animos: *induimus* continues the metaphor of clothing (§16 *uestis modo*). On the disposition of kings cf. *De ira* 2.31.3 *regis quisque intra se animum habet ut licentiam sibi dare uelit.* The term *rex* often had negative overtones (cf. e.g. Cic. *Att.* 14.11.1 = 365 SB *interfecto rege liberi non sumus,* referring to Julius Caesar), but S also uses this term to refer to monarchs generally in *De clementia* addressed to Nero. A parallel between household and state *res publica* is drawn in §14.   **fortunae suae magnitudo tutissimos praestat** 'the scale of their good fortune keeps them very safe'. The anger of the master and the powerlessness of the slave are to be understood on the analogy of the anger of the ruler and the powerlessness of the subject.   **acceperunt iniuriam ut facerent** 'they have treated something as an injury in order that they may themselves inflict one'.

21 leuis est malitia: cf. *De otio* 1.2 *uitia ipsa mutamus: . . . iudicia nostra non tantum praua sed etiam leuia sunt.*   **aliud** 'simply something different'.

LETTER 53

While Book 5 is full of advice, sometimes (e.g. *Ep.* 46) directed at L, sometimes (e.g. *Ep.* 47) at a more general readership, in this first letter (of ten) in Book 6, S turns the spotlight on himself. This is a notably unified book (Cancik 1967: 147). Here and in the four following letters (54–7), S subjects his own weaknesses and idiosyncracies to sharp scrutiny. A particular focus on place and travel in Campania characterises the first half of Book 6 (anticipated by 49.2 with its exclamation about the effect of seeing Naples and Pompeii and *Ep.* 51 with its satirical description of Baiae). *Ep.* 53 opens with a sea journey from Naples to Puteoli; the Bay of Naples also features in *Ep.* 55 (S describes Vatia's villa near lake Avernus), while *Ep.* 57, balancing *Ep.* 53, describes a journey by land back from Baiae to Naples, an ordeal deemed marginally preferable to the alternative by sea. *Ep.* 55 (like *Ep.* 49 and 45.2) also links Campanian topography to S's feelings for his correspondent L (originally from the region).

In *Ep.* 53, S describes his journey from Naples to Puteoli, as a storm gathers. Overcome by seasickness, he begs the pilot to put him ashore. Rough conditions do not permit this, so, despite the waves, S decides to swim back to land (§§1–4). Following this self-consciously comic opening, the letter moves on to explore the contrast between afflictions of the body (§§5–6) and those of the mind (§§7–8). While the former, when severe, receive our particular attention, the latter are often overlooked precisely when they are most serious (just as a light sleeper may be aware that he sleeps, while a heavy sleeper is oblivious). Only Philosophy, here personified (and compared to the figure of Alexander the Great, §10), can bring true health to the mind, raising her adherents to a level comparable to that of the gods (§11) and offering protection against every assault (§12).

The situational opening presents S in the self-examining mode characteristic of 'Stoic autobiography' (Ker 2009a: 151). Only in *Epp.* 53–7 does S open successive letters with such anecdotes (Berno: 29). Allusive and self-deprecating, these five letters give an initial impression of lightness (in notable contrast to the more technical character of *Epp.* 58 and 59 which follow; see Inwood *ad Ep.* 58) but suffering and mortality are present too, particularly in *Ep.* 54, where S describes himself experiencing an attack of asthma as a rehearsal for death (in poignant contrast to the end of *Ep.* 53, which stresses philosophy's potential to confer a kind of invulnerability). Death-like experiences recur at 58.33 and at the end of 60.

The relationship between travel and mental tranquillity is a frequent concern of earlier philosophical writers, notably Lucretius (e.g. 3.1054–75; *Tranq.* 13–15 cites l. 1068) and Horace (e.g. *Ep.* 1.11.27), and is a persistent preoccupation of the letters (Montiglio 2006: 553–4). S introduces the theme of travel, *peregrinatio*, in *Ep.* 2, as he praises L for staying in one place; scurrying about, he claims, is a sign of an ailing spirit (2.1): *non discurris nec locorum mutationibus inquietaris. aegri animi ista iactatio est* (see Henderson 2006: 125). The sea's turbulence as a metaphor for mental uncertainty in evoked in *Ep.* 52; §1 declares *fluctuamur inter uaria consilia*. Stückelberger *ad* 88.7 lists numerous instances in S of metaphorical storms. The subtle allusion (53.1) to Book 2 of Lucretius' Epicurean poem (detected by Ronnick 1995) adds a further irony. Lucretius there describes the mental calm of an Epicurean philosopher watching another's troubles from the shore. S here puts himself rather in the position of troubled seafarer.

More explicitly, the opening section of *Ep.* 53 (analysed by Berno 2015) casts the would-be philosopher as an epic anti-hero. Invoked at 53.4, the complex and ambivalent figure of Ulysses, the archetypal traveller, though appropriated by different philosophical schools in different ways, was particularly favoured by Cynics and Stoics (Montiglio 2011: 84–7). S values Ulysses for his spectacular powers of endurance (*Constant.* 2.1); he features in a number of other letters (31.2–3, where he takes action to prevent his shipmates being seduced by the songs of the sirens, 56.15, 66.26 Ulysses' love of Ithaca as an example of love of home, 88.7–8, 123.12; in *Troades* by contrast he is less than admirable). Exploring the philosophical value of the traditional liberal education, S writes contemptuously at 88.7 of those who, insensitive to the urgency of the Stoic philosophical project, fret over identifying the precise locations through which Ulysses travelled. 'We have no leisure to hear' *utrum inter Italiam et Siciliam iactatus sit an extra notum nobis orbem*. Rather: 'every day storms of the spirit (*tempestates . . . animi*) toss us and evil drives us towards all the troubles of Ulysses'. A model for human suffering, Ulysses is also a model for how to cope with adversity: 'Through him teach me, how I am to love my country, my wife, my father and how, though shipwrecked, I am to make for these honourable goals.' Ulysses, despite his wanderings, is homeward bound; his tortuous and long-drawn out course models for the centripetal nature of the journey to wisdom (Montiglio 2006: 563, 2011: ch. 5, Berno 2015). Particularly pertinent to *Ep.* 53 is the episode of the storm and shipwreck off Phaeacia (brought on by the sea-god's curse) and Odysseus' struggle, after two days and two nights in the water (Hom. *Od.* 5.388), to find a safe place to land on the rocky shore (*Od.* 5.405).

Ulysses' presence in the letters is also mediated through Virgil's *Aeneid*, a work alluded to or echoed on numerous occasions (see main intro. section 8). At 88.7, for instance, Ulysses is *iactatus*, evoking the hero of *A.* 1.3 *multum ille et terris iactatus et alto*. In *Ep.* 53, Seneca draws, too, on Virgil's portrayal of Aeneas, engaging with the Odyssean first half of the *Aeneid*, particularly Book 6 (cited twice in §3). 53 is the first letter of S's own Book 6, in which Campania's mythical topography is frequently alluded to (for the significance of his book numbers see intro. to *Ep.* 24, on Book 3 and its relationship to Book 3 of Cicero's *Letters to Atticus*). Aeneas approaches Virgil's Underworld through Cumae (*A.* 6.106–9); *Ep.* 55, notably, presents Vatia's villa near Cumae as a place of perdition (Henderson 2004: 71–7, Berno: 56). *Ep.* 57 offers a vignette of S's descent into a tunnel in order to avoid another journey by sea (Berno: 29). Having struggled to reach the shore of Italy after his difficult (if much shorter) journey in *Ep.* 53, S like Aeneas scrambles to find the right way to his goal.

In *Ep.* 53, S exploits the comic dimension of such epic parallels. Referring earlier to a slave woman, Harpaste, kept by his wife as a clown,

S insists that if he needs someone to laugh at he can laugh at himself
(50.2): *si quando fatuo delectari uolo, non est mihi longe quaerendus: me rideo.*
On *Ep.* 53, Motto and Clark (1971: 220) comment, 'perhaps nowhere in
the *EM* does Seneca appear more of a clown' (see also Hurka 2005). We
may detect a resemblance to the mythomaniac anti-hero of Petronius'
Satyricon Encolpius, who, in the course of his adventures around the Bay
of Naples, also compares himself to epic heroes, conscious of the comic
aspect of this comparison (Berno: 64–5, Conte 1996: 73–104).

From §5 the tone of the letter becomes more serious. As he pauses to
recover from his bout of seasickness, S is prompted to reflect on his experience. The comparison (§§5–8) between ills of the body and those of
the mind is a common move in Epicurean and Stoic writing; Chrysippus
in particular seems to have stressed the therapeutic role of philosophy
(*SVF* III.471, *ap.* Gal. *De placitis Hippocratis et Platonis* 5.2.22–8, 298–300
De Lacy, Nussbaum 1994: 328–9). S's rueful delineation of the all-too-
human tendency to deny the significance of physical symptoms until they
can no longer be ignored is here contrasted with our much more serious
inclination to overlook precisely the most severe disorders of the mind.

The strikingly spondaic first person plural imperative *expergiscamur*
(§8) marks a turning point in the letter, the remainder of which will be
concerned with the unique power of Philosophy (emphasised by the
anaphora of *sola*) to rouse us from this state of oblivion. Philosophy is
here personified (as often elsewhere in S and, earlier, by e.g. Cic. *Tusc.*
2.5; on the operation of personification in this letter see Dressler 2016:
83–5). First characterised as a worthy consort (§9), she goes on to play
the role of exigent mistress, whose peremptory demands are compared to
those made by Alexander the Great. Stories about Alexander often feature
confrontations with philosophers (frequently Diogenes the Cynic but also
others, Arr. *Anab.* 7.2, Moles 1995, 1996, Stoneman 2003). Comparisons
were also made between Alexander's achievements in creating a world-
state and those of the Stoic philosopher Zeno (to the advantage of
the former in Plut. *De Alex. fort.* 329a–b); indeed the cosmopolitanism
of the Cynics and Stoics was perhaps only conceptually possible in the
Hellenistic world Alexander created. For Dio of Prusa Alexander is a phi-
losopher-king (*Oration* 2). While for S Alexander occasionally exemplifies greatness of spirit (59.12, *De ira* 2.23.2–3), more often he serves as
an example of vices, particularly impulsiveness, cruelty, pride and indulgence of appetite (e.g. *De ira* 3.17.1, 3.23.1, *Clem.* 1.25.1, *Ben.* 1.13.1,
Spencer 2002). At 53.10, Alexander's urge to world-domination, once
channelled by Philosophy, becomes appropriate and benign.

While S seems to enjoin, with the tricolon of imperatives at the start
of §11, a single-minded devotion to Philosophy of a quasi-religious kind,
such devotion can, it seems, propel mortals themselves into a god-like

position. Although elsewhere in the *EM* (e.g. 42.1) S emphasises the extraordinary rarity of the *sapiens*, here he appears to encourage his correspondent to imagine himself achieving this exalted state. Indeed, after placing Lucilius as *sapiens* only a little below the gods (*non multo te di antecedent*), S goes on to underline the ways in which he is actually superior to them; the gods are naturally indifferent to death, while those who know they will die must go to superhuman lengths to attain this *securitas*.

The contrast which emerges between the mock heroism of S himself in the opening part of the letter and the true heroism of both the *sapiens* (§11) and Philosophy (who appears as a warrior figure in §12) may then prompt us to re-evaluate the opening anecdote, which comes to serve as a metaphor for the existential condition of the *proficiens* (as Berno: 31–2 suggests). The deep-seated *errores* (§8) which only Philosophy can help us to correct are foreshadowed by S's confusion on the rocky shore (§4): *uiam quaero* (elsewhere, *Constant.* 1.2, S presents the route to philosophy as itself a steep and rocky road, *ardua ... et confragosa*). Despite the apparently personal opening, this letter raises the issue of S's shifting *personae* (an explicit concern in 57.3 where S ventriloquises the Stoic sage, before confessing his own inadequacy; see Edwards 1997a, Henderson 2006, Jones 2014).

The lengthy letters in the latter part of Book 6 engage with more technical philosophical issues, such as the translation of philosophical terms from Greek to Latin. The substantial *Ep.* 58 explores at length the nature of existence and offers a sustained engagement with Platonic thought (see Inwood). Yet the images used also recall topics from the first half of the book. *Ep.* 58 includes a humorous reference to the deleterious effect of sea voyages on the health of Plato (58.30 *sed nauigationes ac pericula multum detraxerunt uiribus*). *Ep.* 59 revisits (§14) the theme of metaphorical wandering and twice cites Virg. *A.* 6 (6.278–9 at §3, 6.513–14 at §17).

Commentary: Motto, Berno.
Further reading: Hurka 2005, Armisen-Marchetti 2006, Berno 2015, Edwards 2018b.

1 Quid non potest mihi persuaderi . . .? 'What can I not be persuaded of . . .?' S often opens with a direct question (cf. e.g. *Epp.* 21, 42, 103). The tone is ironic.   **solui mari languido:** elevated vocabulary marks an abrupt shift of register; the phrase (Ronnick 1995) 'slurringly mimics' Lucr. 2.1 *suaue mari magno* (cf. Berno 2015). The adjective *languidus* is poetic when applied to water; cf. notably Hor. *Carm.* 2.14.17–18 *uisendus ater flumine languido | Cocytus errans*. S is apparently the first to apply it to the sea (cf. *Nat.* 2.6.4). In *Hercules furens*, echoing the Horace passage more closely, S applies it to the waters of the Underworld: *stat nigro* *pelagus gurgite languidum* (554). The calm before the storm has a sinister aspect.   **sine dubio:** used concessively.   **caelum graue:** cf. *Helv.* 7.8 *caeli grauitas* (cited in full in §4n. on *aspera ... et importuosa*).   **sordidis** 'dark' (*OLD* 3a). *exigua nubes sordido crescens globo* is the first sign of a terrible storm in *Ag.* 462. For clouds as moral metaphor in S see Armisen-Marchetti 1989: 93.   **in aquam aut in uentum resoluuntur:** the verb *resoluuntur* (echoing *solui*) maintains the elevated tone.   **tam pauca milia** 'so few miles': the distance is *c.* 12 km.   **Parthenope tua:** the poetic name for Naples (cf. e.g. Virg. *G.* 4.564, Ov. *Met.* 14.101; elsewhere, e.g. 49.1, S uses *Neapolis*) is an indication that we have moved here into a poetic world (alliteration and an equal number of syllables emphasise further the proximity to *Puteolos*); the term appears nowhere else in prose (with the exception of Plin. *Nat.* 3.62). L's Campanian origins are emphasised also at 49.1 (*ecce Campania et maxime Neapolis ac Pompeiorum tuorum conspectus*) and 70.1. Summers *ad loc.* reads the phrase as alluding to some treatment of Naples in Lucilius' poetry (on the analogy of *Aetna tua* in 79.10).   **Puteolos:** a major port and trading centre, Puteoli was also a fashionable resort at least until the time of Hadrian (*NP* x.606–7).   **surripi** 'be snatched', suggesting furtiveness, as if S might make the trip before the weather took notice (cf. 1.1(n.)). Note also *euaderem* in the next sentence. S is implicitly critical of his own attempt to evade difficulties rather than confront them.   **per altum:** poetic term for sea (*OLD* 1), echoing the third line of the *Aeneid* (the poem is quoted twice in §3), where Aeneas is *terris iactatus et alto* (Motto and Clark 1971). Berno *ad loc.* sees here an allusion to *in altum prouectum* in Livy's description of Cicero's last hours (*ap.* Sen. *Suas.* 6.17), one of a number of echoes of that episode.   **Nesida:** Gk acc. of Nesis (a small island near Puteoli). Cicero records his own visit there to see Brutus in 44 BCE (*Att.* 16.1.1 = 409 SB).   **derexi:** the role of the ship's captain is elided; S is in charge.

2 cum iam eo processissem ut mea nihil interesset utrum irem an redirem 'when I had gone so far that it made no difference to me whether I carried on or turned back'. *mea* is abl. (*OLD* 8b), with *re* understood, on the analogy of *refert* in which *re* was taken as abl.   **aequalitas:** this term, often used by S (as in e.g. 59.16) to characterise mental balance, here refers rather to physical composure (rarely used in relation to the sea, *TLL* I.1003.71–2, but there is perhaps a pun on *aequor*).   **subinde** 'continually'.   **gubernatorem:** only as the situation becomes critical does S refer to the boat's pilot. Elsewhere the figure of the *gubernator* has a metaphorical significance, representing the *animus* as a guide or standing for the figure of the *sapiens*; cf. esp. 30.3, 85.30–6, *Marc.* 6.3, Armisen-Marchetti 1989: 148.   **aspera ... et importuosa** sc. *litora*. The pilot's response is terse and practical. The term *importuosa* is used elsewhere by

S only to characterise his own place of exile, Corsica, at *Helv.* 7.8 *caeli grauitas an praepotentis Italiae conspectus an natura importuosi maris*. Note also the paradox of *nec quicquam se aeque in tempestate timere quam terram*, the unexpected object, *terram*, emphasised by its position.

3 peius autem uexabar quam ut mihi periculum succurreret 'but I was suffering too much to consider the possible danger'. S often uses *uexare* to characterise physical afflictions. For the comparative with the second term introduced by *quam ut* see 21.8n. **nausia** 'seasickness'. The etymology is played on by S in §4 (S elsewhere uses the term in the context of surfeit; see 24.26n). At *Tranq.* 1.17 Serenus is made to contrast the internally generated disturbance of *nausia* with the external affliction of a storm, *non tempestate uexor sed nausea*: he requests Seneca's help, *succurre in conspectu terrarum laboranti*. **sine exitu** 'without vomiting'; cf. *Thy.* 1041 of stomach contents. **torquebat:** the term might seem inflated in characterising a bout of seasickness but cf. 78.9 on gout. **uellet nollet:** the pairing of these two verbs in the subjunctive (though generally present tense) is common and colloquial (*OLD nolo* 1d). **coegi, peteret:** S often uses directly dependent subjunctive with verbs such as *adhortari, exigere, cogere*. **non expecto:** shift to vivid present from narrative in perfect tense. **ex praeceptis Vergilii:** rather than using technical vocabulary to describe the boat's manoeuvres, S jokily invokes two brief quotations from the *Aeneid*, reinforcing the mock epic tone of this letter. *Ep.* 28, also concerned with travel, quotes twice from the *Aeneid* (§1 *A.* 3.72, §3 *A.* 6.78–9). **obuertunt pelago proras:** from *A.* 6.3. Aeneas and his men approach Cumae, where he will meet the Sibyl, his future guide to the Underworld. Cumae is also the point of departure in *Ep.* 55. **ancora de prora iacitur:** this phrase occurs at *A.* 3.277 (as the Trojans take refuge in Leucas) but also (more significantly) in the final line of Book 6, where Aeneas, having returned from the Underworld, rejoins his companions and they make for Caieta. As Berno notes *ad loc.*, the last line of Book 6 marks the conclusion to the Odyssean half of the *Aeneid*, an apt point of reference in a letter which will explicitly invoke the figure of Ulysses. **memor artificii mei uetus frigidae cultor** 'mindful of my profession as a veteran devotee of cold water'. *artificium*: *OLD* 2; *frigidae*: sc. *aquae* (the ellipse is colloquial; cf. *OLD frigidus* 1a, citing Petr. 74.12). S several times refers to his austere physical regime, involving cold-water baths, exercise and a limited diet: 15.1–2, 83.3–5, 108.16. The moral superiority of cold baths is celebrated at 51.6 and 86.10–12. Cold-water baths are often recommended by ancient medical writers. Celsus prescribes *aqua egelida* for *podagra* (4.31.3) and *aqua frigida* for sleep disorders (3.20.2); both afflictions are mentioned in *Ep.* 53. Earlier Stoics were opposed to hot baths (*SVF* III.229 = Chalcidius *ad Timaeum* p. 165);

cf. Epictetus, *Discourses* 1.1.29. *Ep.* 45.2 proclaimed S's willingness to swim to Sicily to be with L (Gowers 2011).   **mitto me in mare:** alliteration suggests the chattering teeth of one who has plunged himself into cold water.   **psychrolutam** 'one who bathes in cold water' (from Greek). Not attested in Latin before S; at 83.5, S describes himself as a sometime *psychrolutes*. This may be a colloquialism (Setaioli 1983: 296); the contrast with the Virgilian citations in the first half of the same sentence would thus underline S's unheroic behaviour.   **gausapatus:** this rare term appears to have the literal meaning 'wearing a garment of *gausapa*', coarse woollen cloth with a nap on one side (cf. e.g. Strabo 5.1.12, Plin. *Nat.* 8.193). Here it is plausibly read by Armisen-Marchetti (2006) as a colloquial expression for 'naked' (on the analogy of the French *à poil*), with the suggestion of bristling body hair (cf. Pers. 4.37 *maxillis balanatum gausape pectas*). In contrast to suggestions that S jumped into the water wearing a heavy cloak, this reading fits *quomodo . . . decet*. It also reinforces the analogy with Ulysses (see §4), who, instructed by Ino to cast off his clothes, as he struggles in the water (Hom. *Od.* 5.343–4), finally arrives on Phaeacia quite naked (*Od.* 6.127–9).

4 dum per aspera erepo, dum uiam quaero, dum facio: sc. *uiam* with *facio*. S echoes the *gubernator*'s earlier characterisation of the shore as *aspera* (§2). The tricolon, describing S's scramble to safety, also sums up the would-be philosopher's mental challenge as he struggles through rough places, searches for a road, then makes one for himself (cf. 33.11). For *asper* of the difficulties faced by the would-be philosopher cf. 76.34 and 104.27, where Socrates is *per omnia aspera iactatum* (another echo of Aeneas). The final letter in Book 6 asserts, by contrast (62.3): *breuissima ad diuitias per contemptum diuitiarum uia est*. For *uiam facere* used metaphorically cf. on Cato's suicide (*Prov.* 2.10): *una manu libertati uiam faciet*. Also relevant here, particularly given the quotations in §3 from the same book, is Virg. *A.* 6.359–60, where the *gubernator* of Aeneas' ship, Palinurus, having fallen overboard, reaches the shore but is killed by hostile forces, as he is *madida cum ueste grauatum | prensantemque uncis manibus capita aspera montis*.   **nautis terram timeri:** echoing §2 *timere . . . terram*; *nautis*: dat. of agent. The phrase recalls *timent terram rates* (*Ag.* 576) used by S to characterise a terrible storm, which brought shipwreck to many, including Ulysses (*Ag.* 513). See §1n. on *sordidis*, citing *Ag.* 462. On echoes of Ovid and Virgil in the description of the storm in *Ag.* 456–78 see Tarrant *ad loc.*   **incredibilia sunt quae tulerim, cum me ferre non possem** 'the sort of things I endured, when I could not endure myself, are unbelievable'. Self-irony; for the thought, cf. 96.1 *non feram me, quo die aliquid ferre non potero*.   **illud scito:** formula used by S to introduce precepts (cf. e.g. 6.7, 110.2).   **Ulixem . . . nausiator erat** 'It was not so much because Ulysses was from birth the object of the sea's anger that he had shipwrecks all over the place; he suffered from seasickness'. S adapts the proverbial expression *diis iratis natus* (cf. e.g. Hor. *S.* 2.3.8), *mari* here representing the sea-god Neptune, whose anger against Odysseus is, in the *Odyssey*, the cause of his multiple shipwrecks (*Od.* 1.20–1, 5.286–90; though in Homer Neptune's anger is long-standing, it does not date from Odysseus' birth); cf. Stückelberger *ad* 88.7 on shipwreck as a favoured Stoic metaphor, Garbarino 1997 and Berno 2015 on the more general association of shipwreck with philosophers, including Zeno (*Tranq.* 14.3). *nausiator*: apparently a Senecan neologism; S flippantly suggests that the mythical Ulysses suffered badly from seasickness and would often swim ashore when conditions were poor – thus prolonging his journey home. At 108.37, S comments on the uselessness of a *gubernator in tempestate nauseabundus*.   **et ego . . . perueniam** 'I, too, wherever I must travel by boat, will take twenty years to get there'. Odysseus' journey home (according to the *Odyssey*) took ten years, though (having spent ten years waging the Trojan War) he was away from home for twenty in total.

5 After the playful literary comedy of the letter's first section, S moves on to explore the food for thought it may provide.   **ut primum . . . collegi** 'as soon as I calmed my stomach (which, as you know, does not escape sickness at the moment one leaves the sea)'. *stomachum*: see 12.2 *stomachandi* and note *ad loc.* on the comically self-deprecating flavour of this term in Cicero's letters.   **ut corpus unctione recreaui:** in other contexts (e.g. 51.10), S disapproves of this practice, often associated with luxury. Here it is apparently justified by the cold-water swim, and echoes the restorative treatment undergone by Homer's Odysseus, ashore after the shipwreck off Phaeacia (*Od.* 6.218–21).   **hoc coepi mecum cogitare:** following a common pattern in the letters, personal anecdote serves as a prompt for philosophical reflection (for *coepi . . . cogitare* introducing a philosophical reflection cf. Sulpicius' letter of consolation to Cicero, *Fam.* 4.5.4 = 248 SB). The term *cogitare* denotes the practice of repeated mental reflection, which is central to the Stoic way of life; cf. e.g. 3.2, 14.5, 47.10, 62.1, 70.5, 70.16.   **nos:** S shifts from the first person singular of the anecdotal opening to plural; others too can learn from his experience.   **quae subinde admonent sui** 'which repeatedly remind us of their existence'.

6 leuis aliquem motiuncula decipit 'a slight attack of shivering escapes someone's notice'. *motiuncula*: dimin. of *motio* 'ague' (*OLD* 2). *leuis* with the diminutive underlines the apparent insignificance of the symptom. S in the following letter claims to have suffered almost every kind of ill-health (54.1); implicitly he speaks here from his own experience.   **uera febris exarsit:** S recounts his own experience of fever, 104.1. Elsewhere (e.g. 18.15) S uses *exardesco* of the passions.   **perpessicio:** almost certainly a Senecan neologism, suggesting superlative powers of endurance, here employed inappropriately (when symptoms are ignored, the illness becomes worse). Elsewhere (104.27) S uses the term of Socrates.   **confessionem exprimit:** illness is figured as a torturer extracting confession (cf. S's *praemeditatio*, designed to steel the mind against the prospect of misfortunes, on the pains a torturer may inflict, compared with the symptoms of various illnesses, 14.5–6, 24.14, 78.19). The process is described in a concrete sense at 82.7 *exprimitur sera confessio: magna uerba excidunt cum tortor poposcit manum, cum mors propius accessit* (for *exprimo* in relation to torture cf. *Constant.* 4.1, *De ira* 1.9.1). S often uses the language of legal process (Armisen-Marchetti 1989: 106–8, 128–9, 155–7).   **pedes dolent:** cf. 24.14 *podagricus*.   **articuli punctiunculas sentiunt:** the assonance of the diminutives (*articuli* from *artus*, *punctiunculae* from *punctus*) works to echo the repeated sensation of pain. For the focus on pain in the extremities cf. 24.14.   **in exercitatione aliqua laborasse:** S elsewhere pokes fun at the excessive pursuit of physical fitness (15.1–3, 56.1); a litter-ride suffices for a man of his years (55.1).   **talaria:** a kind of apparatus for torture (cf. *De ira* 3.19.1), here in a figurative sense.   **distortos pedes fecit:** this use of *facio* with a past participle in a predicative sense is colloquial (Setaioli 2000: 19; cf. *NLS* §100 n. ii).   **podagram** 'gout'. We might sense anti-climactic bathos; cf. 24.14n. on *quem podagricus* (afflictions there, as here, are of stomach and foot), 67.3 *podagra distortus*, 78.8–9 on the severe pain associated with *podagra*, *De ira* 3.33.3 *distortis pedibus et manibus*.

7 contra euenit in his morbis quibus afficiuntur animi: S often compares or contrasts afflictions of the body with those of the mind (see main intro. section 9); cf. the parallel between physical and mental ills at 56.10. Here the opening adversative *contra* emphasises the antithesis; those who suffer more serious physical illness are all too aware of their affliction, while those who suffer the worst disorders of the soul are the more oblivious.   **non est quod:** a common Senecan construction; see 7.9n.   **Lucili carissime:** one of the few epistolary touches in this letter.   **species secundum quietem capit** 'has impressions in his sleep'.   **sopor ... animumque altius mergit:** *mergo* here in the sense of 'overwhelm' (*OLD* 9) but primarily of plunging into liquids, esp. the sea, while *altius* picks up *per altum* in §1.   **quam ut in ullo intellectu sui sit** 'so that he has no awareness of himself': balances *quae subinde admonent sui* §5.

8 uitia sua nemo confitetur: contrast the effects of serious physical illness expressed with a cognate term in §6, *etiam duro et perpessicio confessionem exprimit*.   **in illis est:** sc. *quisque*.   **somnium ... uitia:** the comparison between vice and dreaming is already to be found in Plato (*Resp.* 574e).   **expergiscamur:** the *clausula* is an emphatic double spondee.   **sola ... sola:** the exclusive claim of philosophy is underlined by the anaphora.   **philosophia:** here personified, as often in the *EM* (e.g. 4.2, 5.4, 8.7, Dressler 2016: esp. ch. 5).   **excutiet** 'will dispel' (*OLD* 2a). Rimell (2015a: 137–47) highlights the significance of this term, used to suggest both scrutiny, particularly self-scrutiny (*OLD* 9), and rigorous movement in the *EM* (e.g. 16.7, 72.1).   **illi te totum dedica:** S shifts from first person plural to second person singular. The relationship of the would-be philosopher to philosophy is cast in religious terms (*OLD dedico* 2); cf. 64.9–10.   **dignus illa es, illa digna te est:** philosophy here appears as a worthy partner; cf. *cum digno digna fuisse ferar*, Sulpicia [Tib.] 3.13.10 (Treggiari 1991: 122 on the association of this language with marriage). The conjugal image suggests an erotic attraction between the *proficiens* and philosophy, further reinforced by the imperative, *ite in complexum* 'embrace one another!' We might see here an implicit reference to Odysseus' encounter with Nausicaa, who (herself motivated by thoughts of marriage) comes to his rescue, goddess-like, immediately following his shipwreck off the coast of Phaeacia (Hom. *Od.* 6.244).   **precario** 'when other matters allow' (cf. Plin. *Ep.* 7.30.4 *precario studeo*).

9 si aeger esses: S returns to the metaphor of illness; when sick in body, one concentrates entirely on recovery, deferring all other business. The same should be true in the case of maladies of the soul.   **forensia:** in 28.6–7 the forum is described as a place deleterious to mental health. To enter it is analogous to setting out *in fluctus medios*.   **nec quemquam tanti putares cui aduocatus in remissione descenderes** 'nor would you consider anyone of such importance that, when called as legal assistant, you would attend to his business, though convalescent'. *tanti*: gen. of value. *remissione*: often used by S for a favourable turn in an illness (cf. 54.6). *descenderes*: sc. *in forum*.   **ut quam primum morbo liberareris:** the verb anticipates the association of freedom with philosophy.   **uaca bonae menti** 'free up your time for (the attainment of) a healthy mind'. while *mens* for S signifies intelligence, *mens bona*, a goal to be striven for (see e.g. 16.1, 17.1), signifies intelligence liberated from worldly concerns (Grimal 1992b: 149–50, Hachmann 1995: 194–211). At the same time, Mens Bona, also a traditional Roman divinity (Liv. 22.10.10, Ov. *Fast.* 6.241, Mello 1968), anticipates the characterisation of philosophy in divine terms in §11 (Berno: 92).   **occupatus:** a key term in *De breuitate uitae* for those who are too preoccupied with business or social duties to attend properly to their own mental and spiritual condition (see esp. *Brev.* 7.1–3, Williams *ad loc.*); cf. the concerns of *Ep.* 1.   **exercet philosophia regnum suum:** the imagery is now political. Philosophy is obliged by human weakness to exercise autocratic power. **subsiciua** 'spare' of time (*OLD* 2), also a relatively rare technical term denoting the land left over following the process of allotment (*OLD* 1, e.g. Var. *R.* 1.10.2). **ordinaria:** used as in *consul ordinarius* (one of the first pair appointed in the year, which takes its name from them) as opposed to the less prestigious suffect consul, appointed as a substitute to fill in for the remainder of the year, if e.g. a regular consul died.

10 Alexander: for the complex associations of the figure of Alexander the Great in the Roman period in general and in S's work in particular see intro. above. Here, as he coolly reminds the conquered that they are in no position to negotiate, Alexander serves as a stark model for Philosophy's unqualified dominion.   **partem agrorum:** the imagery of land allocation implicit in *subsiciua* (§9) comes to the fore.   **Asiam:** the conquest of Asia features elsewhere in the topos of human insatiability; cf. e.g. 94.65 on Pompey.   **non id acciperem:** cf. §9 *dat tempus, non accipit* (Philosophy). Personified Philosophy goes on in §10 to repeat the same imperious terms: '*non sum hoc tempus acceptura...*'

11 totam huc conuerte mentem, huic asside, hanc cole: following the emphatically positioned *totam*, a punchy descending tricolon, linked by the polyptoton of *hic. cole* 'worship' (*OLD* 6, cf. 90.3, 95.47, *VB* 26.7). Philosophy is now presented in divine terms (on the nature of the cult required by Virtue, which consists in *pia et recta uoluntate*, cf. 115.5). As Berno notes *ad loc.*, there is a subtle contrast here with the bathetic image of S as *cultor* of cold baths in §3.   **ingens interuallum:** total commitment to philosophy will bring superhuman powers.   **non multo te di antecedent:** cf. the views of the Stoic speaker in Cic. *N.D.* 2.153: through virtue, for the wise man, *uita beata existit par et similis deorum, nulla alia re nisi immortalitate, quae nihil ad bene uiuendum pertinent, cedens caelestibus*.   **diutius erunt:** the difference between human and divine is reduced to one of quantity of time lived. The same point is elaborated at 73.13 where S (developing an insight of Sextius, on whom see main intro. section 6) makes clear (comparing first Jupiter with the *sapiens*, then two *sapientes* of different lifespans) that a longer life is not superior; for virtue is the only thing that matters and *non est uirtus maior quae longior* (cf. *Prov.* 6.6).   **magni artificis est clusisse totum in exiguo** applies not only to the achievement of a properly philosophical life within the narrow span of human existence but also to the literary project of *Ep.* 53, which articulates an epic theme within the confines of a single, brief letter (Motto and Clark 1971: 225; cf. *Ep.* 58's concluding comparison (§37) between ending a letter and ending one's life). *artificis* here echoes *artificii mei* in §3, underlining S's own role. For *sapientia* as itself *artifex uitae* cf.

90.27n. **tantum sapienti sua quantum deo omnis aetas patet** 'his own life-time offers the wise man as much scope as the whole of time offers to god'. **ille naturae beneficio non timet, suo sapiens:** it is in the nature of the divine to be immortal and thus to be free of, in particular, the fear of death. The self-sufficiency of the *sapiens* is summed up in the last two words of the phrase. In this sense at least, the *sapiens* is superior to the god. There is a significant echo here of 24.11 (which refers particularly to the advantage of being able to end one's own life), *adeo mors timenda non est ut beneficio eius nihil timendum est.*

12 incredibilis philosophiae uis: having stressed Philosophy's divine aspect, S reverts to the military domain evoked by the Alexander analogy. In this final section, Philosophy is a mighty warrior, able to withstand any attack. The military imagery (often used by S, see main intro. section 9; here an 'Iliadic' coda to the earlier 'Odyssean' episode, on Berno's reading, 31) leads neatly into the following letter whose opening describes S's periods of ill-health and remission in military terms (54.1). **ad omnem fortuitam uim retundendam:** *uis* (of philosophy), the subject of the sentence, and *uim* (of fortune) here are pitted against one another (for the *uis* of philosophy cf. 94.24, 108.4). *retundere* 'destroy the force of an assailant' (*OLD* 1), but cf. also the use of *tundere* of waves of the sea, esp. in poetic contexts (*OLD* 1c), thus echoing the stormy setting of the letter's opening. The opening of the following letter (54.1) compares an attack of asthma to a brief squall at sea (*procellae similis est impetus*). **defetigat** 'breaks the force of' (*OLD defatigo* 1c). **laxo sinu eludit** 'deflects with the loose fold of a cloak' (*OLD sinus* 1). A soldier without a shield might defend himself by wrapping his left arm in his cloak (Caes. *Civ.* 1.75 *sinistras sagis inuoluunt*). **discutit:** cf. philosophy's power to dispel (*excutiet*) sleep in §8.

LETTER 64

This relatively brief letter, the second in Book 7, offers a light, upbeat contrast to *Ep.* 63's discussion of bereavement and its alleviation, with which the book opens. With the elegance of a Horatian ode, *Ep.* 64 modulates from intimate, fireside conversation (though presumably not in this case lubricated by wine; see 108.16) to bracing philosophical tonic, via a heady vision of philosophy's development across the centuries and a rejection of the empty formalities of Roman public life, to conclude with domestic birthday celebrations in honour of S's heroes.

Book 7 of the *EM* (*Epp.* 63–9) is dominated by the heavyweight *Epp.* 65 (on which see Inwood's commentary), which discusses causation, engaging in some detail with arguments of Plato, Aristotle and Epicurus, and 66 (on which see Inwood, Hachmann, who argues that *Ep.* 66 marks the start of a new phase in the letters, and Berno 2017a), and develops philosophically sophisticated reflections on the nature of the good. In both cases this is presented as the account of a day's debate among friends. Interwoven with these increasingly technical discussions, a number of letters in the book, notably the first, 63 (but see also 66.24–5), pursue a more general ethical concern with the philosophical issues raised by friendship. The concern of *Ep.* 63 (on which see Wilson 1997, Wilcox 2012: 165–72) is ostensibly the consolation of L, in the face of the recent loss of his friend Flaccus. With much reproof, S offers bracing Stoic advice (§11 you have lost a friend? Find another one) but concludes by highlighting his own weakness: unprepared, he was devastated by the death of his own friend Serenus. The challenges posed by ill-health are an insistent preoccupation of *Epp.* 65, 67 and 68, while 66 opens with reflections on the situation of a friend, the elderly Claranus, strong in spirit but wrestling with the afflictions of a feeble body; its concluding sections in particular (so Inwood: 178), celebrating the moral value of brave endurance, offer arguments especially appropriate to consoling one in Claranus' situation. The final, very brief, letter of Book 7, 69, finishes by offering advice on how to face one's own death, anticipating a dominant theme of *Epp.* 70 (see notes) and 77.

Ep. 64, which opens, like many others, with an incident or episode apparently taken from S's daily life, offers a subtle exploration of the relationship between the group of those present, sitting around the fire at S's house, and the wider circle of others, who also enjoy a kind of presence through the mental reflections of S and his companions (on the power of the imagination to overcome the distance separating friends see 55.8–9). These include L, whose absence is regretted (and who, through the letter itself, is made part of the occasion) but also the philosopher Sextius (on whom see main intro. section 6), from whose work a reading is made to the group (other philosophical authorities are remembered in the closing paragraph). A wider audience is also brought into play, both through L as proxy but also through S's reflections on the philosophical work which remains for future generations (see Edwards 2018a).

Rousing and emotive, readings from Sextius' book make its author almost corporeally present. S draws a contrast (§3) between the hortatory words of Sextius and the more technical and less inspiring writings of many other philosophers (elsewhere he criticises in more detail the emphasis on syllogistic reasoning to be found in the work of e.g. Zeno). Sextius' writing exemplifies for S a militant, hortatory approach to philosophy, whose potency he often celebrates (e.g. 65.18, 71.36–7, 82.20–4, 120.12; see main intro. section 6). Negative circumstances, the challenges of ill-fortune, are valuable for training one's character and to be embraced, indeed summoned. This anticipates the celebration in *Ep.* 67 of *fortitudo*, a quality which can only be manifested under adverse circumstances, where S initially (§§3–4) agrees he would not wish for torture, war or ill-health but goes on (§6) to celebrate the beauty of bravery, and to welcome challenges (§14, a life without them is a *mare mortuum*, in the memorable phrase of Demetrius) concluding (§15) with the rousing sentiments of the Stoic Attalus, *malo me fortuna in castris suis quam in deliciis habeat*.

At 66.49–53, also, S argues that, even though physical suffering is contrary to nature (cf. 66.37), under some circumstances one might actively prefer hardship to comfort, *si ulla bona maiora esse aliis possent, haec ego, quae tristia uidentur, mollibus illis et delicatis praetulissem, haec maiora dixissem. maius est enim difficilia perfringere quam laeta moderari*; Inwood *ad loc.* argues that the two scenarios given as examples are implicitly characterised as in accordance with nature (66.51, 53 Mucius sacrificing his hand, as he seeks to defend his country; cf. 24.5nn.) and against nature (66.53 having one's hands massaged by *exoleti* or a eunuch, whose gender has been subverted for the purposes of luxury; cf. 12.8, 47.7nn., 95.24). As Inwood concedes, the moral instinct, to feel admiration for bravery, also plays a significant role here (cf. 67.11–12).

Important too, however, is the issue of exemplarity (see *Ep.* 24(nn.), Langlands 2018). The heroic acts of Mucius, Cato and Socrates play a critical role in spurring others to virtue, just as Decius' bravery inspires his son to emulate him (67.9). As Newman (2008: 323–4) comments, '[t]he essence of *gloria* for the *sapiens* is providing *exempla*.' The value of engaging an audience makes the gladiatorial aspect of Sextius' challenge to fortune – a spectacle of virtue – particularly pertinent. In *De prouidentia*, S highlights the spectacle offered by the wise man pitted against ill fortune, suggesting at 2.9 that this is all the more thrilling when *et prouocauit* 'he has issued a challenge' (Edwards 2007: 75–7; cf. 64.4). This is a transcendent and edifying version of the visceral thrill of the amphitheatre.

Conuiuia among Rome's intellectual elite often seem to have involved readings (see further below), as did *symposia* among Greek intellectuals. Plutarch, in his account of the readings and philosophical conversation of a lengthy symposium, articulates a similarly nuanced model of interaction between participants, texts and later readers (*Quaest. conv.* 686c); the record of sympotic conversation allows those who are not present to benefit from the spiritual nourishment offered by the occasion, while the inclusion of quotations from earlier authors offers both symposium participants and later readers the vicarious experience of reclining at a table with, for instance, Socrates (König 2012: 31–2, 41).

After the deployment of the imagery of inheritance to characterise the transmission and enhancement of philosophical knowledge (an analogy which, given the religious obligations of heirs, also anticipates the religious imagery of the letter's concluding sections), the latter portion of the letter (§8) returns to the medical analogy which so frequently features in the letters (cf. 53.6n.) and here reflects Sextius' particular interest in medicine. It is not coincidental that S chooses diseases of the eye as his example; for the explicit analogy between intellectual and visual perception see 94.18–19 and 115.6–7. Here he returns to the critical issue articulated at 22.1: *non potest medicus per epistulas cibi aut balinei tempus eligere: uena tangenda est.* The concern now is not the difficulty of giving properly targeted advice at a distance but rather the need for the *proficiens* himself to learn how in particular cases to apply the remedies of philosophy; S stresses, in Schafer's words (2011: 33), that 'his contribution to moral education lies more in its modalities than its matter'.

In *Ep.* 62 (the final letter of Book 6), S contrasts at §3 the true reverence he feels for the philosopher Demetrius (who also features at 67.14) with the vain honours he is obliged to pay to powerful men in Rome (cf. *Brev.* 14.5 with Williams: 23). It is perhaps not irrelevant that Q. Sextius is elsewhere celebrated for turning down the offer of a *laticlauus* from Julius Caesar (98.13). Again contrasted with the florid rituals of deference habitually paid to magistrates, in *Ep.* 64, the homage proposed to other philosophers takes a more ceremonial form (venerating images, celebrating birthdays). Von Albrecht (2004: 66) notes S's use of familial metaphors in relation to earlier philosophers at 64.9–10 (a manifestation of Roman *pietas*) in contrast to the erotic imagery characteristic of Plato (the *Symposium* offers an apt contrast here).

The private sociability with which the letter begins opens out into an exhilarating conversation across the centuries, which serves to generate a philosophical community unbounded by place, time or mortality, but linked by a shared enterprise and celebrated through engagingly domestic rituals.

1 Fuisti here nobiscum: a poignantly playful opening, as S goes on to make clear that he and L have been apart for some time.   **potes . . . tantum:** S imagines L's teasing response to his opening; S often observes that L is in his mind (e.g. at 40.1, 55.8–11, 67.2).   **interuenerant quidam amici:** this phrase is echoed at 65.1 *interuenerunt amici.* In neither case are any of them identified. Such social gatherings rarely feature elsewhere in the letters as part of S's current life. At 67.2 Lucilius' letters *interuenerunt,* as proxy for their author with whom S imagines an amicable conversation (on the topic of whether every good is desirable). The pursuit of philosophy is an interactive, shared enterprise.   **propter quos maior fumus fieret:** subj. expressing result.   **ex lautorum culinis:** *lautorum* 'luxurious' (*OLD* 3). A satirical dig at the hazards associated with the culinary excesses of S's contemporaries (cf. 104.6, where foremost among the trials of urban life is *odorem culinarum fumantium*). **uigiles:** the *uigiles urbani* were established under Augustus in 6 CE with the aim of limiting the extensive damage regularly caused to the urban fabric by fire (Dio Cass. 55.26.4–5, Robinson 1992: 185).

2 uarius . . . sermo, ut in conuiuio: Macrobius, in his evocation of learned festivities at the house of Praetextatus, notes the *uariae doctrinae ubertas* (1.2.8; cf. 1.1.3–4); it was considered polite for conversation at such events to be learned but playful. Fitzgerald (2016: 171) comments in a discussion of the aesthetics of *uarietas*, 'the feast is both an image of and a prompt for the variety of the text'. Cf. Plin. *Ep.* 1.10.5 praising the varied conversation of Euphrates, 9.23.2 on a conversation at the games. Letters, too, might be praised for variety; Cicero praises the letters of Atticus, *Att.* 2.15.1 (= 35 SB) *ipsa me uarietas sermonum opinionumque delectat*. There is, though, an implicit contrast here with the more focused *sermo* through which a particular philosophical question might be pursued systematically (cf. 67.2). **lectus est:** it was common practice for more erudite dinner parties to include readings (cf. Nep. *Att.* 14, Plin. *Ep.* 1.15.2, 9.36.4, Gel. 2.22.1–2, Parker 2009: 203–4 and König 2012: 31–2, 41). **Quinti Sexti patris:** Quintus Sextius (on whom see main intro. section 6) the Elder, to distinguish him from his son Sextius (sometimes referred to as Sextius Niger; see e.g. Plin. *Nat.* 1.12b.5, where he is listed as a source *qui graece de medicina scripsit*), who was also a philosopher (Di Paola 2014). His writings are known only through references in S and a handful of other authors. **magni . . . uiri:** S focuses on the moral qualities of the individual as manifested through his work; this is masculine writing (cf. 46.2, where Lucilius' book is described as *uirilis*). Praising another of his teachers, Fabianus, S notes at 100.5 that his words are not *contra naturam suam posita et inuersa*, though in this case he concedes (100.8) that his style is not *fortis*. **licet neget Stoici:** first appearing only at 9.19, the term *Stoicus* is used rarely, though a number of letters in the latter part of the series focus on comparing specifically Stoic doctrines with the teachings of other schools (*Epp.* 58, 65, 117). *licet neget* 'though he may deny it': *NLS* §124 n. iii.

3 quantus . . . animi: S uses the different constructions, *quantus* + *uigor* and *quantum* + *animi* (by this point equivalent), for variation. *animi* 'spirit' (*OLD* 13b), as in the next but one sentence, *non faciunt animum*, and §4 *illius animum induo* (cf. also e.g. 11.1, 13.1 *multum tibi esse animi scio*). **quorundam . . . nomen:** S does not name names here but elsewhere criticises this aspect of the Stoic Zeno's teaching. **exanguia:** lit. 'bloodless', here 'lacking vitality' (*OLD exsanguis* 3b). **instituunt,**

disputant, cauillantur: S frequently criticises technical philosophical argument, esp. the use of syllogisms (cf. e.g. in Book 8, 82.19–24, discussed by Wilson 1987, 83.8–12, 85, 87.41, also 45.8–13, 48.4–12, 49.5–6, 102.20, 117.18–20). As Inwood (xvii–xviii, 218–19) notes, however, he is himself a master of technical argument (see further Barnes 1997: 12–23, Wildberger 2006: 133–46 esp. on *cauillationes*, σοφίσματα); it is his choice of the letter as literary form which leads him to undercut his own presentation of dialectic and metaphysics.   **uiuit, uiget, liber est:** as Wilcox (2012: 174) notes, S implies a parallel future for his own work.

4 prouocare 'issue a challenge to fight' (*OLD* 3a). Cf. 67.6 of *fortitudo*, who (personified) *pericula contemnit et prouocat*, 88.29, *Nat.* 6.32.3 *ingenti animo mors prouocanda est*, also *Prov.* 2.9, quoted in the intro. above. Leigh (1997: 274) compares Lucan's description of Cato at 9.884 *omni fortunam prouocat hora* with the 'Stoic athleticism' S advocates here.   **quid cessas...?** 'why do you hang back?' Fortune is personified as a gladiatorial/military opponent (as in *Prov.* 9.2) to whom the *proficiens* issues a challenge 'like a Homeric fighter' (Asmis 2009: 125). On the relationship of the *proficiens* to fortuna, one often characterised in adversarial terms, see also 99.32, 104.22.   **illius animi induo ... uirtutem suam ostendat** 'I take on the spirit of that man who asks where he may test himself, where he may display his virtue'.   **spumantem ... leonem:** Virg. *A.* 4.158–9, of the young Ascanius, who dashes ahead on a hunting expedition, longing for the appearance of a boar or a lion, so that his mettle may be tested.

5 libet ... exercear 'I want to have something I may conquer, through the endurance of which I may be trained.' On *patientia* in this sense see Kaster 2002: 133–8. For the analogy between philosophical education and military/athletic training see main intro. sections 6 and 9. The emphasis here is on the power of Sextius' words to stimulate the desire for such an experience.   **quod ... penetrabilem:** expanding on the outstanding quality, *hoc ... egregium*, of Sextius.   **tibi ... scies:** use of the second person singular underlines the intimate sense of personal interpellation felt by one who reads or hears Sextius' words.   **illam:** i.e. *beata uita*.   **uolenti penetrabilem** 'within the grasp of one who wants it'. Cf. *De ira* 2.12.3 and the teachings attributed to Fabianus at *Ep.* 100.12, which *ad imitationem sui euocarent sine desperatione uincendi*.

6 uirtus: the writings of Sextius (described in §2 as *uir magnus*) have an effect analogous to that of virtue itself, *idem ... praestabit.*   **multum auferre temporis solet contemplatio ipsa sapientiae** 'the very contemplation of wisdom tends to absorb [*OLD aufero* 14] much time'.   **obstupefactus** 'stunned'. Cf., also in a positive sense, 115.4, 120.5.   **mundum,**

quem saepe tamquam spectator nouus uideo 'the world which I often see as though through new eyes'. S repeatedly highlights the positive effects on one's mental disposition of scientific investigation of the natural world, e.g. at 65.16 (philosophy soothes the spirit, instructing *respirare rerum naturae spectaculo*), *Helv.* 8.4, 20.1–2 with Williams 2006, *De otio* 5.3–6 with Williams *ad loc.*, *Nat.* 3.pr.1.

7 ueneror . . . inuenta . . . inuentoresque: emphatic assonance. Cf. Lucretius on Epicurus, praised as (3.9) *rerum inuentor* in words which Kenney 2014 *ad loc.* terms characteristic of a hymn. Cicero, while praising the Stoics, describes Zeno (*Fin.* 3.5.3) as *non tam rerum inuentor . . . sed uerborum nouorum.* **multorum hereditatem** 'the inheritance of many', *sc.* ancestors, here in a figurative sense. At 44.3, L (despondent at his own lack of distinguished ancestry) is advised to regard earlier philosophers as his personal *maiores*, forebears (cf. *Brev.* 15.3). Heirs, *heredes*, (in contrast to legatees) were the principal beneficiaries of an estate. An heir was responsible for continuing the deceased's family *sacra* (religious observances) (Crook 1967: 118–23). **mihi . . . mihi:** the repetition highlights the role of the *proficiens*, here personalised by S, at the intersection between past and future generations. **laborata** 'toiled over' (*OLD* 8a). **agamus bonum patrem familiae** 'let us play the role of the good head of household'. Cf. 86.14 (in an agricultural context) and *Ben.* 4.39.2 with Griffin 2013: 257. The head of household's obligation to maintain and enhance the estate he was perceived to hold in trust for future generations is a preoccupation of a wide range of Roman texts from agricultural treatises to legal codes (Cato, *Agr.* esp. 2–3, Nep. *Att.* 13.1.1, *Dig.* 18.1.35.4, 40.4.22). The figure here is amplified, as S looks forward to the potential contribution to be made to this philosophical inheritance by generations in centuries far into the future. **multum adhuc restat operis multumque restabit** 'much still remains to be done and will remain to be done'. **nec ulli . . . adhuc adiciendi** 'the opportunity of adding something still further will not be denied to anyone, though born a thousand centuries hence'. S's writings are presented as having their own part to play in this process; he comments at 8.6, *cum posteris loquor* (cf. 21.5, 22.2).

8 hoc semper nouum erit 'this will always be a fresh task'. **dispositio** 'due ordering'. **medicamenta** 'curative remedies' (*OLD* 2). The analogy between physical and spiritual health is a recurrent one (cf. e.g. 22.1–2, 53.6–7nn.), pursued in more detail later in Book 7 at 68.8–9. At 8.2, S describes himself as writing health-giving advice (*salutares admonitiones*), which is comparable to *medicamentorum utilium compositiones*. Here the dispensing of medicine can also be seen as part of the remit of the *bonus pater* *familias*, listed among his duties by Columella (12.1.18; cf. Ker 2004: 230); prescriptions for numerous remedies are included in Cato's guidance for the *pater familias*, e.g. *Agr.* 94, 122–3, 156–60.   **oculi:** treatments for eye problems also feature at 85.5, 94.18–19 and 115.6–7. On ancient remedies for eye disease, a particular preoccupation of ancient medical writers, see Plin. *Nat.* 28.29, Cels. 6.6, Jackson 1993.   **teras . . . modum** 'it is necessary that you grind [*OLD tero* 3] these together, that you choose the right time, that you apply them only on an individual basis'.   **animi remedia** 'treatments for the spirit'. Corresponding to the eye treatments found over the centuries for a range of ailments, philosophers have discovered treatments for a range of spiritual disorders.   **quomodo . . . quaerere** 'how they are to be applied and when, it is our task to inquire'.

9 ritu deorum colendi: cf. the exhortation at 53.1 to pay reverence to (*cole*) philosophy. Religious responsibilities are also associated with the *pater familias* (cf. e.g. Cato, *Agr.* 134). But elsewhere S draws a contrast with traditional forms of worship; at 67.12 virtue is *non ture nec sertis sed sudore et sanguine colenda.*   **magnorum uirorum . . . imagines:** Romans of distinguished family kept portraits (*imagines*) of ancestors who had achieved higher magistracies in the *atria* of their homes (Flower 1996). Here S exhorts L to treat men distinguished for their moral virtue as virtual ancestors, to serve (as Roman ancestors were traditionally supposed to do; see Polyb. 6.54.1–4, Sal. *Jug.* 4.5 *cum maiorum imagines intuerentur, uehementissume sibi animum ad uirtutem accendi*) as both inspiration and model, with their *imagines* as a potent prompt. Cic. *Orat.* 110 records that Brutus had a bronze statue of Demosthenes among his ancestral *imagines* at his Tusculan villa. Pliny the Elder (*NH* 35.5), castigating the neglect of ancestral *imagines* in favour of expensive artworks among his contemporaries, criticises those who display portraits of Epicurus and celebrate his birthday.   **natales celebrem:** birthday celebrations (on which see *RE* VII.1.1142–9, Argetsinger 1992) of family and friends played an important role in Roman culture, particularly after Julius Caesar's reforms fixed the calendar (cf. Feeney 2007: 148–60). See Plin. *Ep.* 6.30.1 (to his wife's grandfather), 10.89.1 (Trajan acknowledges Pliny's birthday wishes), Fro. *Ant.*1.2.8.4 (= pp. 86–7 van den Hout), *Tab. Vindol.* II 291 (invitation to a birthday celebration). Birthdays appear as the occasion for numerous poems composed in the Augustan period (Hor. *Carm.* 4.11 celebrates Maecenas' birthday, Tib. 1.7, 2.2, Prop. 3.10, Ov. *Tr.* 3.13, Cairns 1971). Celebrations also marked the birthdays of members of the imperial family, with sacrifices offered by the Arval Brethren in Rome, as well as by army units, in some cases for centuries after the individual's death (Beard, North and Price 1998: 1.324–5, 348, Vout 2007: 12–13). The birthdays of great authors, particularly Virgil, were also celebrated; cf. Plin. *Ep.* 3.7.8

on Silius Italicus, *multum ubique librorum, multum statuarum, multum imaginum, quas non habebat modo, uerum etiam uenerabatur, Vergili ante omnes, cuius natalem religiosius quam suum celebrabat.* Stat. *Silv.* 2.7 celebrates the birthday of the poet Lucan (see Newlands 2011). **uenerationem praeceptoribus meis:** cf. 73.4 *praeceptores suos ueneratur ac suspicit, Ben.* 6.16. S also acknowledges his own teachers individually; cf. 49.2, 108.17–20 on Sotion, 9.7, 63.5, 108.23 on Attalus, 40.12, 100.2 on Fabianus and 20.9, 62.3, 91.19 on Demetrius. In the introductory section of his *Meditations* (1.5-15), Marcus Aurelius acknowledges at length his debt to his teachers.

10 consulem: S does not mention the emperor (to whom still greater deference was offered). **honor haberi honori solet** 'post of honour is used to being honoured'. The repetition *honor . . . honori* (the latter a predicative dative) mocks the excessive deference offered to magistrates. At 73.1, however, S disputes the characterisation of philosophers as *contemptores magistratuum aut regum eorumue per quos publica administrantur*. **equo desiliam:** this courtesy due to consuls is highlighted in Fabius Verrucosus' deference to his son (Quad. *hist.* F57 Cornell, Liv. 24.44.9–10) and that of Sulla, even when dictator, to Pompey (Sal. *Hist.* fr. v.20 Maurenbrecher, V. Max. 5.2.9 *dictator enim priuato Pompeio et caput adaperuit et sella assurrexit et equo descendit*). **Marcum ... Cleanthemque:** these philosophers constitute more worthy objects of deference, even if one does not encounter them in person. S does not to distinguish here between those who wrote philosophy and those known through the writings of others (cf. 6.6). The first two are exemplary Romans (they are also paired at 11.10). On Cato see 24.6–11(nn.), on Laelius, Edwards 2018a. Here explicitly linked to Plato (first mentioned in the letters at 6.6 as a moral exemplar; as Inwood underlines in his discussion of *Ep.* 58, S was very familiar with his writing), Socrates often appears in the letters, usually in relation to the circumstances of his death; he is also celebrated at 24.4(n.) and 70.9(n.). The last two, Zeno and Cleanthes, are among the foremost Stoics (see main intro. section 5). As Wildberger (2006: 146 n.) notes, we should not see significance in the omission of Chrysippus, who is warmly praised elsewhere; cf. 33.4 listing the Stoic authorities *Zenoni an Cleanthi an Chrysippo an Panaetio an Posidonio*. Lists of philosophers also feature e.g. at 7.6 (Socrates, Cato and Laelius, see note) and 104.21–2. **assurgo:** the act of rising up out of respect, as one would for e.g. a magistrate (see Cic. *Pis.* 26, Liv. 9.46.9 with Oakley 2005a, Suet. *Tib.* 31.2 *ipsum quoque eisdem* [the consuls] *et assurgere et decedere uia*, Mommsen 1887–8: 1.398); the imagery of §10 *honor* is continued, the conclusion reinforcing the letter's energetic and positive mood.

LETTER 70

The final paragraph of *Ep.* 69 (the last in Book 7) advises *hoc meditare et exerce, ut mortem et excipias et, si ita res suadet, accersas*. Pursuing this topic, *Ep.* 70 offers a lengthy exploration of how to determine when it might be appropriate to take one's own life (a topic S returns to repeatedly in the *EM*, both in general and in relation to individual examples) and what means might be used to achieve this. Yet the key concern of this relatively long letter, which moves from elegiac meditation on the inevitability of death to an insistence on the benefits of suicide, illustrated with examples from the senate house and, most graphically, the arena, could rather be described as freedom, with suicide serving as the sphere of action, where the individual, when most constrained, may still exercise significant agency.

The letter opens (§§1–4) with the sight of Pompeii, which triggers memories of youth, prompting reflection on the swiftness of time's passing, followed by an assertion of the greater importance of living well over a long life. Thus the wise man will at all times be ready to consider (§§5–6) whether it may be an appropriate moment to bring his own life to an end. The possibility of suicide offers an escape from any misfortune which prevents one from living well (§7), though only consideration of particular circumstances (as illustrated with the examples of Socrates, §9, and Libo, §10) can determine when this is the right decision. The means one chooses are ultimately insignificant, S argues (§§11–12); one should not be swayed by the views of others on the suitability of particular ways of dying (§13). Some contend that one should never take one's own life (§14), failing to appreciate the freedom offered by the possibility of suicide (§15), which can under some circumstances be seen as a therapeutic solution (§16). We must learn above all else to be ready for death (§§17–18). No matter how constrained one's situation, some instrument of death is at hand, so that freedom is always attainable. A series of vividly realised vignettes of ingenious self-killing from the games illustrates the bravery which may be shown in pursuit of this end, even by those without the benefit of philosophical training (§19–26).

Suicide and the question of the timing of death are also preoccupations of *Ep.* 4, 12.10(n. on *patent undique ad libertatem uiae multae, breues faciles*), *Ep.* 24(nn.), 66.13, *Epp.* 71 and 77, 98.15–16, 117.21–5, as well as *Prov.* 9–10, *Marc.* 20–2 and (an especially graphic passage) *De ira* 3.15.4. Many readers have found S's apparent enthusiasm for and interest in suicide disturbing, if not pathological (as noted in the intro. to *Ep.* 24); Nock (1933: 197) famously referred to the 'Stoic cult of suicide'. Rist (1969: 249), asserting rather the distinctiveness of S's position, comments, 'Seneca's wise man is in love with death'. Certainly Epictetus seems much less interested in suicide and does not treat it as the supreme test of Stoic freedom (cf. Long 2002: 203–4, Droge and Tabor 1992: 34–7). Yet S's position is not fundamentally at odds with that of other Stoics, who took the view that life itself was an indifferent (cf. Plut. *Mor.* 1076b, Cic. *Fin.* 3.60–2, Griffin 1992: 372–83). According to Diogenes Laertius (7.130 = *SVF* III.757), the Stoics held that one should calculate whether the natural advantages of living are outweighed by the natural disadvantages (cf. the words Cicero puts in the mouth of Cato at *Fin.* 3.60). Plutarch confirms that the Stoics advocated suicide under certain circumstances (*Mor.* 1069e).

Nevertheless, we may detect, as Hill (2004: 151) observes, 'a notable shift, not in the nature of suicidal ethics, but in the detail and urgency with which these are articulated'. Inwood's work (esp. 2005: ch. 11) has highlighted the crucial relationship between death and freedom in S's writing (cf. 95.72 on Cato's death). Of central importance here is S's emphasis on *possibility*. The essence of freedom lies in the availability of death as a way out; this does not constitute a *requirement* to take one's own life under any particular circumstances.

At the same time, the choice to give up one's life constitutes a recognition that life itself is an indifferent, that only virtue matters (Inwood 2005: 311). For Hill (2004: 151–7), S exploits the potential of suicide as an exercise in 'cognitive exemplarity', enabling detachment from one's social role and from other externals. Thus to appreciate suicide's value as a guarantee of freedom is also to make important progress in conquering the fear of death more generally; S's emphasis on suicide needs to be understood in this light (Griffin 1992: ch. 11, Edwards 2007: 98–107; cf. Ker 2009a: 252). Much of S's writing offers strategies for overcoming the fear of death, which he presents as the greatest obstacle to human happiness (see intro. to *Ep.* 24). While some letters (e.g. *Epp.* 54, 93, 101) address the prospect of death from natural causes, most of S's exemplars in *Ep.* 70 face the threat of violent death inflicted by an external agent, a particularly pressing concern, we should not forget, for prominent individuals living in the time of the emperor Nero.

It is important to see S's views in the context of Roman attitudes to self-killing more generally. In an era before effective pain relief, the choice to pre-empt a protracted and agonising end attracted little criticism and might even win praise (Plin. *Nat.* 25.23, Plin. *Ep.* 6.24, Hooff 1990: 123–6, Flemming 2005). Suicide was also viewed by many as a rational and honourable course of action to atone for wrongdoing or grievous error (Hooff 1990: 120–2); many aristocratic defendants killed themselves after being condemned, especially under the principate (e.g. Tac. *Ann.* 3.16, 11.31, 16.33). Some killed themselves before they were condemned, e.g. Cremutius Cordus, whose daughter is the addressee of S's consolatory *Ad Marciam*; his death is described at *Marc.* 22.6–7 and at Tac. *Ann.* 4.34–5 (cf. Gaius Silius, Tac. *Ann.* 4.19.4, Mamercus Aemilius Scaurus, Tac. *Ann.* 6.29.7). Such a move might be taken as an admission of guilt (though might also be taken as implying that the innocent could not expect justice). On the complexity of this phenomenon and Tacitus' dark treatment of it see Plass 1995: 81–138, Hill 2004: 183–212, Edwards 2007: 113–43. S's treatment of the circumstances of Drusus Libo's suicide (§10) verges on the Tacitean in its pointed and ironic ambiguities.

Virtue for the Stoics may be the only true good, but it is exercised in relation to choices among what are properly termed 'indifferents'. Some indifferents, such as health, or being of service to one's friends, are naturally preferable, while others, such as pain, are naturally dispreferred (Gill 2003: 40–1, Graver 2007: 48–51). The following letter, 71, offers a relatively technical account of how such choices are to be made, starting from an emphasis on the importance of particularity; Lucilius must learn for himself how, whatever the specific circumstances, to relate his choices to the *summum bonum* (see Inwood *ad loc.*). The process of weighing up whether or not life is worth living under particular circumstances is complex; 58.32–5 asks, with regard to extreme old age, whether, while still in command of one's senses, one should take one's own life, in case, when death is necessary (i.e. when one can no longer live an appropriately human life), one no longer has the capacity to procure it (cf. 22.5–6, 98.15–18, 104.21, 117.21). Inwood (commenting on 58.33–7) observes that S is 'outlining a framework for making choices about when and how to die rather than establishing a doctrine about the right time to die which could be applied to all cases'. A particular instance of this decision-making is adduced in relation to the failing health of Bassus in *Ep.* 30. Elsewhere S criticises those who take their own lives on impulse, without rational consideration of their circumstances (4.4, 24.23(n.), while 74.21 expresses disapproval of those who are pushed by *umbra uirtutis* towards *mors uoluntaria*). For a comprehensive account of S's comments on suicide see Tadic-Gilloteux 1963.

There might seem to be a tension between Seneca's emphasis elsewhere on the philosophical value of feats of endurance (e.g. *Epp.* 67, discussed briefly above in intro. to 64, and 78) and his contention at 70.24 that a more long-drawn out death is necessarily a worse one and that it is foolish not to choose a simple, quick death over a protracted one. At 58.36, S concludes that, while to choose death simply because of pain is a kind of defeat, one should not endure pain merely out of bravado: *imbecillus est et ignauus qui propter dolorem moritur, stultus qui doloris causa uiuit.* If one's life is so blighted by pain that one can no longer function as a human being should, then life is not worth living.

To overcome the fear of death, the would-be philosopher needs to contemplate the spectacle of his own death, a spectacle imagined in richly visual terms (70.8; cf. intro. to *Ep.* 24 on *praemeditatio*). But the examples of others also play a critical role. As S observes, underlining what he learned from repeated visits to his elderly friend Bassus, a man who, through prolonged reflection, had come to accept the prospect of imminent death with great calm (30.15): *libenter haec, mi Lucili, audio non tamquam noua, sed tamquam in rem praesentem perductus* 'I hear this message willingly, my dear Lucilius, not as something new but as if I were being made to confront reality fully' (for the phrase *in rem praesentem* cf. 59.6, Dressler 2012: esp. 152).

In *Ep.* 24 (describing the death of Cato) and elsewhere (e.g. 13.14), S celebrates the heroic nature of the sword as instrument of self-inflicted death. A poem of Martial (1.78) casts this as a quintessentially Roman way to procure one's end (*Romana mors*). Severing veins, which frequently features as a means of self-killing in S (and in Tacitus' *Annals*), seems also to have been seen generally as an honourable means of death, while Socratic associations could confer dignity on poison (in some cases, administered by doctors; see Flemming 2005). Other means of bringing about one's death, notably hanging, however, attracted particular stigma (on the hierarchy of forms of suicide see Hooff 1990: 166–72, Edwards 2007: 107–8). For S, such distinctions are ultimately insignificant (§§12–28). At *De ira* 3.15.3, S comments, *in omni seruitute apertam libertati uiam* 'in every situation of enslavement, the road lies open to freedom'. Sometimes it is right to choose death by any means rather than performing a slavish or degrading service (as in the example of the Spartan boy who, at 77.14–15, dashes his head against a wall in preference to carrying a chamber pot); even the most apparently degrading means of death is preferable to a life of indignity. §§19–26 feature a succession of individuals, at once in the public eye and in circumstances of the greatest wretchedness, who contrive to take their own lives rather than be the focus of the public spectacles of the amphitheatre. The manner of their deaths is squalid (in some cases) but bracingly virtuous.

While S's contemporary Petronius frequently exploits the potential of scatology for humour (for instance, at 47, where Trimalchio overshares details of his bowel movements with his guests; see Arrowsmith 1966), as indeed S does himself in describing the death of Claudius in his *Apoc.* 4.3 (see Eden *ad loc.*), in *Ep.* 70 (§20) he deploys disgust to more philosophical ends. The rehearsal in the mind of such memorably sordid detail can play an important part in the would-be philosopher's mental preparation for death. The spectacles of the games themselves (particularly beast-fighting in this case, though cf. *Ep.* 7) are subverted and translated into an alternative and far more edifying spectacle, as S replays for his reader the enterprising and ingenious deaths of individuals who have risen above their wretched circumstances to defy fortune and die with true bravery.

The politics of Neronian Rome are not explicitly foregrounded in the *EM* (Nero himself is never mentioned). But the range of examples used in *Ep.* 70, including a senator accused of conspiracy and enslaved prisoners of war, underlines the conceptual interdependence between freedom in the political sphere and freedom in relation to slavery (see Arena 2012: 73–8, Lavan 2011). S was eventually offered an opportunity to put into practice the techniques for banishing the fear of death, which he had been honing for so long, when he received the order to take his own life in 65 CE. Tacitus, in his *Annals* (15.60–4), gives a lengthy description of Seneca's final hours. Ker (2009a: 250–8) and Woodman (2010) analyse the ways in which Tacitus' account redeploys motifs drawn particularly from *Ep.* 70.

The ruler's power over life and death is his ultimate sanction. In highlighting the fundamental indifference of death, S challenges the ruler's power; *qui mori didicit, seruire dedidicit; supra omnem potentiam est* (26.10; cf. 58.34). The emperor may order a man's execution but he cannot stop him from pre-empting it; S's writing works to keep death under the control even of one who is condemned. At the same time, his emphasis on the role of specific circumstances means that the ruler can never assume that a particular condemned individual will necessarily commit suicide (Plass 1995: 102–3). The bravado of discussing which means of death *placet* may seem perverse but S's options must have felt increasingly limited.

Book 8 comprises five substantial letters, of which the dark and intense *Ep.* 70 is the first. While the fear of death is considered briefly at 74.3, 11 and 21, the three central letters of the book focus on other (though not unrelated) questions. Stoic value theory, the main concern of *Ep.* 71, where it is explored in relation to decision-making, is also pursued in *Ep.* 74 (and 76), while in its focus on the power of *fortuna*, *Ep.* 74 develops comments made at 70.7. *Ep.* 72 explores the practice of studying philosophy. *Ep.* 73 is one of the very few in the collection to reflect explicitly on the relationship between philosophers and rulers. S underlines the debt of gratitude owed by the philosopher to the ruler who makes his life of contemplative leisure possible. The implicit flattery here (which might also be characterised as protreptic in the manner of *De clementia*, on which see Braund: 23) is in interesting tension with the stark defiance of *Ep.* 70.

Commentary: Scarpat (c).
Further reading: Inwood 2005: 302–21, Ker 2009a: esp. 252–61.

1 Post longum interuallum: *interuallum* in a temporal rather than spatial sense (*OLD* 3); cf. Cic. *Fam.* 15.14.2 (= 106 SB) *ut te . . . tanto interuallo uiderem*.   **Pompeios tuos uidi:** see also 53.1 where Naples is *Parthenope tua* (see intro. to *Ep.* 53, Gowers 2011); at 49.1, the sight of Pompeii (*Pompeiorum tuorum*) apparently triggers an intense memory of the moment when S and L last saw one another (Edwards 2018a). As often (cf. e.g. 53), S opens the letter with a personal experience, here described in a single sentence, before he launches into the reflections thus stimulated.   **in conspectum adulescentiae meae:** while in *Ep.* 49 the sight of Pompeii prompts S to reflect on his relationship with L, here it provokes thoughts more particularly focused on S himself, as he is vividly transported back to his own youth. On the intertwined memories of S and L see Ker 2009a: 153–4.   **reductus sum:** *reducere* is often used of moments of nostalgia; Scarpat compares Cic. *Inv.* 1.98 *reducere in memoriam* and Plin. *Ep.* 3.10.2 *si in memoriam grauissimi luctus reduxissem*.   **quidquid . . . fecisse** 'whatever I did there as a young man, I seemed still capable of and to have just now been doing'. This experience, placed in the past tense, is presented as both intense and itself fleeting.

2 praenauigauimus 'we have sailed past'. S often compares life to a sea journey (e.g. *Marc.* 17.2–8, *De ira* 3.37.3, *Brev.* 7.10, Armisen-Marchetti 1989: 140–1, Garbarino 1996, Chambert 2005: 156–7, Montiglio 2006); cf. M. Aur. *Med.* 3.3.6.   **Vergilius noster:** cf. 21.5(n.).   **terrae urbesque recedunt:** Virg. *A.* 3.72. The same phrase (though altered to *recedant*) is quoted at 28.1 in the context of advice that travel can do nothing to alleviate mental ills (see intro. to *Ep.* 53). Here the Virgilian colouring (reinforced by *abscondimus*, see below), evoking Aeneas' sea journey towards his destined homeland, Italy, offers implicit reassurance.   **rapidissimi:** derived from *rapio* 'snatch', *rapidus* suggests not only swiftness (*OLD* 2) but also time's devouring force (*OLD* 1).   **abscondimus** 'we leave sight of' (*OLD* 1c), with the sense 'lose below the horizon'; cf. Virg. *A.* 3.291 *protinus aërias Phaeacum abscondimus arces*.   **ipsius senectutis optimos annos:** while S often details the physical afflictions of old age as reminders of mortality, or as points of comparison for spiritual weaknesses (12.1–3(nn.), 26), he also on occasion presents the experience of growing older in positive terms (developing further the arguments of Cicero's *De senectute*); he is, for instance, no longer subject to the prompting of sexual desire (12.4–5nn., 83.3, Edwards 2005b). For the succession of ages cf. 24.20 *infantiam amisimus, deinde pueritiam, deinde adulescentiam*, 49.3. A similar thought is expressed by Marc. Aur. *Med.* 9.2.1.   **publicus** 'universal' (*OLD* 5a).

3 scopulum . . . portus: continuing the image of life as a sea journey, S presents its end as, not a rock to be feared, but a harbour to be welcomed (at 77.3-4, by contrast, S comments rather that in life, in contrast to a journey, we can leave off at any point). For death as a harbour cf. *Polyb.* 9.6–7 *nullus portus nisi mortis est*, *Ag.* 592 *portus aeterna placidus quiete*, Armisen-Marchetti 1989: 153–4, Chambert 2005: 140–3 and, more generally, Bonner 1941.   **in quem . . . cito nauigauit:** a common thought in the consolatory tradition. See Manning (112) on *Marc.* 19.6–22.3. Here developed by S to present a brief life as, on the analogy of a speedy journey, potentially preferable (cf. 93.7, 99.12, *Marc.* 22.3). The metaphor of the speedy sea journey here anticipates the vignette of the rapid 'Alexandrian' ships' arrival, which opens *Ep.* 77 (also concerned with the ethics of suicide).   **uenti . . . lassant:** the terms in which the experience of the becalmed traveller is described also evoke the lives of the luxurious elsewhere castigated by S (*taedio*: e.g.18.7, 24.22, 59.15, *Tranq.* 2.6) or the experience of physical debility associated with illness or old age (cf. 74.33 *segnitia . . . lassitudo*, 26.1, 68.13, 83.3, 84.1, 101.4). We might also compare *Ben.* 4.6.4 *unde haec irritamenta lassae uoluptatis? unde ista quies, in qua putrescis ac marces?*   **pertinax flatus celerrime perfert:** assonance of *p* and *f* underlines the exhilarating rapidity.

4 idem euenire . . . puta: for the use of this phrase or variants of it to set up analogies cf. *Tranq.* 11.4 (invoking the attitude to death of gladiators as a comparison), *Ben.* 7.12.5, Dressler 2012: 162.   **macerauit** 'has vexed', *OLD* 4a (cf. 104.19), here figurative.   **coxit** 'has agitated' (*OLD* 6); also used by Virgil in a figurative sense, e.g. *A.* 7.345 *quam . . . femineae ardentem curaeque iraeque coquebant.*   **quae:** i.e. *uita.*

5 uidebit 'he will ascertain by consideration' (*OLD* 15).   **ubi uicturus sit, cum quibus, quomodo, quid acturus:** *uicturus sit* is to be understood following *cum quibus* and *quo modo*, while *sit* should be understood following *acturus*.   **qualis . . . non quanta:** an assertion often repeated by S (cf. e.g. 32.3, 74.27, 77.20, 93.2–4, 101.15) and also found in many other philosophical texts, e.g. Pl. *Cri.* 48b οὐ τὸ ζῆν περὶ πλείστου ποιητέον, ἀλλὰ τὸ εὖ ζῆν 'it is not living which is to be valued most but living well', [Plut.] *Apoll.* 111d.   **tranquillitatem:** the *tranquillitas* of the *sapiens* (quite different from the *tranquillitas* afflicting the becalmed traveller in §3) is immune to perturbation but such a state is not easily attained by the *proficiens* (see e.g. *Tranq.* 2.3, 14.10). *tranquillitas* already appears in this metaphorical sense at Cic. *Tusc.* 5.16, with the comment, *animi quietus et placatus status cernitur, cum perturbatio nulla est.*   **emittit se** 'he sends himself out', i.e. he brings about his own death; cf. of Cato at 24.8 *spiritum . . . emisit*, 71.16, 95.22 *libertas emisit animam*. As Scarpat notes *ad loc.*, *emittere manu* can mean to set free a slave (*OLD* 2b); *emittere* alone occasionally has this sense, e.g. at Pl. *Ps.* 994.   **in necessitate ultima** 'in extreme straits' (*OLD necessitas* 4b). While the phrase *ultima necessitas* is not uncommon in Livy, S is the first to apply it to death (cf. also *Brev.* 1.3, *Ep.* 17.9 *si necessitates ultimae inciderint, iamdudum exibit e uita et molestus sibi esse desinet*). Tacitus uses this distinctive phrase only once in this sense, of the message delivered by the centurion to S, instructing him to die (*Ann.* 15.61.4, Woodman 2010: 294–5).   **cum primum illi coepit suspecta esse fortuna** 'when first fortune begins to look troublesome [*OLD suspicio* 3]'.   **circumspicit** 'he considers' (*OLD* 5b).   **numquid illic desinendum sit**: *numquid* 'whether' (*OLD* 1b). *illic* (an adverb of location which would here have a temporal sense) is an emendation (in place of *illo* in some MSS) proposed by Beltrami, on the analogy of the passages in *TLL* VII.1.373.41–50, particularly Sen. *Ep.* 95.2. For *desinendum* in this sense, a relatively low-key expression of the appropriateness of death, cf. 23.11, 77.4 *uita . . . ubicumque desines, si bene desines, tota est*. At 26.8, ending a letter focused on death, S playfully comments on his writing: *desinere iam uolebam et manus spectabat ad clausulam* (a similar analogy concludes 58.37).   **nihil existimat sua referre** 'he considers that it makes no difference as regards him'; *refert* with abl. fem. of the possessive pronoun (*OLD* 1b), agreeing with the *re* of *refert* (an idiomatic usage).   **ex stilicidio**: from the drops (*OLD stillicidium* 1a), *sc.* of the waterclock (by which time was measured in Athenian law courts); cf. 24.20(n.) and 101.14 *per stilicidia emittere animam*.

6 citius . . . tardius: terms from the previous sentence are picked up but reversed (so emphasising their interchangeability in the great scheme of things).   **ad rem non pertinet** 'is not relevant to the point' (*OLD pertineo* 4b). A phrase common in Cicero; cf. e.g. *Div.* 2.46.   **bene . . . periculum:** paradoxically it is life (or rather living badly) not death which poses the true danger.   **effeminatissimam uocem** 'a most cowardly saying'; cf. 96.4 *effeminata uox uirum dedecet*, Cic. *Off.* 1.129, *Tusc.* 4.60. S (while prepared to concede that women may be capable of behaving bravely; cf. 24.14, *Helv.* 16.5, *Marc.* 16.1) presents bravery as a quintessentially masculine quality (cf. Cic. *Tusc.* 2.43, discussed in the intro. to *Ep.* 24) and cowardice as correspondingly effeminate. *uocem*: see *OLD* 7a; cf. 24.10.   **illius Rhodii:** his name is given as Telesphorus in *De ira* 3.17.3–4, where this episode is more fully developed, as an example of the excesses to which anger can propel even men with a philosophical education; cf. Plut. *De exil.* 606b, Ath. 616c.   **a tyranno:** in the *De ira* version, named as Lysimachus (an associate of Alexander), who first gives orders for his victim's ears and nose to be cut off. On his inhuman behaviour, S comments, at *De ira* 3.17.4, *cum dissimillimus esset homini qui illa patiebatur*, *dissimilior erat qui faciebat.*   **ut abstineret cibo:** frequently chosen as a means to end life by the terminally or very gravely ill (cf. e.g. 67.9–10, 77.9, Nep. *Att.* 21–2, Plin. *Ep.* 1.12.9 on Corellius Rufus) and sometimes by those anticipating judicial condemnation or execution (e.g. on Cremutius Cordus *Marc.* 22.6, Tac. *Ann.* 4.35.5 *uitam abstinentia finiuit*), this mode of suicide is especially appropriate here when the food on offer is not fit for a human being.   **'omnia . . . speranda sunt':** variants on this proverb are also found in Ter. *Haut.* 981 *modo liceat uiuere, est spes* and Cic. *Att.* 9.10.3 (= 177 SB) *aegroto, dum anima est, spes esse dicitur.* Contrast S's disapproval here with the advice he earlier offers L, seeking to allay his worries about the future, at 13.10–11 *quam multa expectata nusquam comparuerunt! . . . aliquis carnifici suo superstes fuit.*   **homini:** in piquant contrast to the *ferum . . . animal* to which he has just been compared.

7 ut sit hoc uerum 'though this may be the case'. *ut*: *OLD* 35.   **quaedam . . . non ueniam** 'some things may be great, may be guaranteed, yet I would not attain them by means of a shameful act [*OLD confessio* 3] of weakness'.   **ego cogitem . . . fortunam?** the shift from a positive conception of *fortuna* (as entertained by the Rhodian who considers that, where there is life, *omnia . . . speranda*) to a negative one underpins the contrasting formulations in this rhetorical question (for the negative sense, predominant in S, cf. e.g. 110.21 *liber est autem non in quem parum licet fortunae, sed in quem nihil*). The power of *fortuna* is a particular concern of *Ep.* 74, with which this book concludes (on *fortuna* in S see Asmis 2009). The repetition of *cogitem* underlines the importance of such reflections in informing virtuous behaviour (and picks up *cogitat semper* with the *sapiens* as subject in §5).   **qui scit mori:** S places great emphasis on the importance of knowing how to die; cf. 26.9 *egregia res est mortem condiscere,* 30 esp. §§4–6, 45.5, *Tranq.* 11.4 *male uiuit quisquis nesciet bene mori.* Such knowledge is to be acquired by the repeated rehearsing of *exempla,* a key feature of *praemeditatio* (Armisen-Marchetti 2008).

8 This section, reinforced by the example of Socrates (§9), explores situations where, while death is impending, suicide turns out not to be appropriate.   **aliquando:** the process of scrutinising the pros and cons of waiting for death (as opposed to anticipating it) is critical here; cf. 78.2 *aliquando enim et uiuere fortiter facere est.*   **sibi . . . sciet:** the subject here is the person who knows how to die. How this knowledge is put into effect will depend on the particular circumstances.   **non commodabit . . . manum** 'he will not lend a hand to his own punishment' (*OLD commodo* 2b w. *manum* 'help').   **sibi commodaret** 'he would lend a hand to himself'. The comment is potential of suppressed condition. S seems to mean 'he would <rather> help his own quest for virtue by staying unflinching in the face of the punishment'. The subjunctive is imperfect since its aspect is envisaged as present and not future. The following sentences are ones he might repeat to himself to steel his resolve. **stultitia est timore mortis mori:** cf. 24.23(n.) This paradox is also highlighted by Lucretius (3.79–82) and, to less philosophical ends, by Martial (2.80.2). **uenit . . . expecta:** a starkly concise command. **quid occupas . . . parcis?** a crescendo of three rhetorical questions. *occupas:* Scarpat notes as parallel Cic. *Tusc.* 5.27 *occupaui te, . . . fortuna.* **alienae crudelitatis procurationem** 'the responsibility for another man's cruelty'. A *procurator* in Roman legal texts is one who executes the business of another; cf. *Dig.* 3.3.1.pr. (Ulpian) *procurator est qui aliena negotia mandatu domini administrat.* **utrum . . . parcis:** envy of your executioner or the desire to spare him are equally absurd reasons to pre-empt his work.

9 Socrates: first appearing at 6.6, he is often chosen as an *exemplum* by S, frequently with regard to his behaviour in the face of death; cf. e.g. 13.14, 24.4(nn.), 71.17, 98.12, 104.21. Stressing rather Socrates' wish to demonstrate his own respect for the laws of Athens and to benefit his friends (as featured in Pl. *Cri.* 49e–50a; Socrates' refusal to escape is helpfully discussed by Nails 2006: esp. 15–16), S does not engage here with the arguments Socrates is made to articulate in the *Phaedo* (see intro. to *Ep.* 24) that suicide is only permissible when one has received a divine sign. **abstinentia:** see §6n. on *ut abstineret cibo.* **ueneno mori:** Socrates was condemned to die, after thirty days in prison, by drinking hemlock (Pl. *Phd.* 58a–c. The duration of the time in prison is inferred from Xen. *Mem.* 4.8.2; on the hemlock see 24.4(nn.).) At 13.14, S observes, *cicuta magnum Socratem fecit* (cf. 24.4(nn.), 98.12). A similar thought is expressed by Epictetus, *Discourses* 4.1. S himself is described (Tac. *Ann.* 15.64) as requesting from his doctor, when his attempt to bleed to death is too slow, a draft of the same poison as Socrates had taken (Griffin 1986: 66). **non hoc animo tamquam omnia fieri possent** 'not in the spirit that anything was possible'. **ut praeberet se legibus** 'so that he might submit himself to the laws'. An allusion to the *Crito,* argues Inwood (2005: 241–3), where the laws are personified. Socrates' appeal to 'rationality' and 'fairness' is used here by S to make clear 'our relationship to the laws of nature, in particular, the law of mortality.' **ut fruendum amicis extremum Socraten daret** 'so that he might give the last part [*OLD extremum* 3b] of Socrates for the use of his friends'. Cf. 98.15–18, where an elderly man, despite being in pain, is encouraged to live on to be of benefit, *utilis,* to his friends: *liberaliter facit quod uiuit.* At 78.2, S presents his own decision not to take his own life, when suffering from debilitating illness as a young man, as motivated by his desire not to cause grief which his father could not sustain. In Tacitus' account of S's own death, he is presented as seeking to aid his friends in his last hours (*Ann.* 15.62). For *fruor* in this sense cf. 63.8 *amicis ualide fruamur. Socraten*: Gk acc. form.

10 Scribonia: second wife of the emperor Augustus, she was the mother of his only child Julia, though they divorced on the day of Julia's birth in 39 BCE (Fantham 2006). Sister of L. Scribonius Libo (cos. 34 BCE), she was thus the paternal great-aunt of the Drusus Libo referred to here.   **grauis** 'serious' (*OLD* 13a). While Suetonius refers to her *morum peruersitas* (*Aug.* 62.2), Velleius Paterculus (2.100.5) implies praise in noting that she accompanied her daughter Julia into exile. Here her advice, plausible though it may seem, turns out to be misguided.   **Drusi Libonis:** Marcus Scribonius Libo Drusus (praetor or praetor designate in 16 CE), great-grandson of Pompey, was alleged to have plotted against the emperor Tiberius (the *fasti* of Amiternum refer to his *nefaria consilia* and confirm his praenomen as Marcus, *CIL* I², p. 244); having been questioned before the senate in September 16 CE, he killed himself (on the conspiracy: Vell. 2.129.2, Tac. *Ann.* 2.27–32, Suet. *Tib.* 25, Dio Cass. 57.15.4, Rutledge 2001: 158–61). For Tacitus (*Ann.* 2.31) the botched and chaotic manner of Drusus' death shows him in a poor light. On his family background see Syme 1986: 256–9.   **tam stolidi quam nobilis** 'as stupid as he was high born'. An ironic comment, as qualities linked by *tam* and *quam* are usually parallel rather than contrasting; cf. e.g. 12.6, 63.15, *Ben.* 4.28.2. Tacitus offers a similarly negative assessment of Drusus' character at *Ann.* 2.27 *iuuenem improuidum et facilem inanibus*. The reading *stolidi* was plausibly proposed by Torrentius (all the MSS read *solidi* but a negative term is clearly required by the context) on the analogy of Suet. *Tib.* 25.   **maiora . . . ullo** 'who hoped for greater things than anyone could have hoped for at that time, and than he himself could have hoped for at any time'. *ullo* sc. *saeculo*.   **aeger:** Dio, too, reports that Drusus Libo was ill (57.15.4), Tacitus that the illness was perhaps simulated (*Ann.* 2.29).   **non sane frequentibus exsequîs** 'with funeral laments, though not many'. *exsequiae* 'a funeral procession', as if Libo Drusus were already dead; his condemnation is a foregone conclusion. The contraction -*quîs* generates the *clausula* - ēntĭbŭs ēxsĕquīs.   **non reum sed funus** 'not a defendant but a corpse'. The use of *funus* in this sense is poetic; cf. Virg. *A.* 6.510, Prop. 1.178. In Tacitus' account of treason trials under Tiberius, the accused, and others too, regularly assume that an accusation of treason will be fatal and anticipate condemnation with suicide (see intro. above).   **consciceret mortem** 'he should inflict death on himself'. A phrase often used of suicide; cf. 77.10, Cic. *Brut.* 43 *ueneno sibi consciuisse mortem, Fam.* 7.3.3 (= 183 SB) *consciscenda mors uoluntaria,* Lucr. 3.81, Plin. *Nat.* 2.27, Hill 2004: 6.   **'quid te . . . delectat alienum negotium**

agere?': cf. the similarly diatribic question at 12.3 *quid te delectauit alienum mortuum tollere?* and the question at §8 *quare . . . alienae crudelitatis procurationem?* **manus sibi attulit** 'he laid violent hands on himself', *OLD affero* 9b. This low-key sentence, comprising three simple phrases each of three words, presents Drusus' suicide without drama. Tacitus' version is more atmospheric and detailed: *Ann.* 2.31 *feralibus iam sibi tenebris duos ictus in uiscera derexit.* Unlike numerous other self-inflicted deaths in the *Annals* (e.g. 1.53.8, 15.68.1, 16.9.2), that of Drusus Libo is not particularly noble. **nec sine causa:** S suggested in §8 that one who knows how to die might not choose to anticipate the work of his executioner but we may infer here that, in contrast to the case of Socrates, there is no real advantage in Drusus staying alive; *stolidus*, he is not capable of offering significant benefit to his friends. **nam . . . agit** 'for a man who is going to die in three or four days at his enemy's wish does another man's business if he lives' – the argument Drusus might have rehearsed to himself.

11 On the need to take account of particular circumstances see also 22.1, 64.8(n.), 71.1–3 (with Inwood *ad loc.*), 77.10, as well as Diog. Laert. 7.130. **in uniuersum:** for the adverbial use (relatively rare, as Scarpat notes) cf. Tac. *Ger.* 5.1. **cum mortem uis externa denuntiat** 'whenever an external force decrees death' (*OLD denuntio* 4a); cf. Cic. *Tusc.* 1.118 *ut a deo denuntiatum uideretur ut exeamus e uita.* Illness might constitute such a force (cf. e.g. 77.5), although the focus of this letter is rather violent death threatened by an external agent, in several cases specified as a ruler. **occupanda sit an expectanda:** indirect question (subject *mors*), following *pronuntiare*. The alternatives recall §8 *expecta. quid occupas?* **multa . . . possunt** 'for there are many factors which might push you in one direction or the other'. The phrase *in utramque partem* (see *OLD uterque* 1d) seems characteristic of philosophical exercises set in schools. Scarpat cites as instances Cic. *Off.* 2.19, Quint. *Inst.* 3.11.1. **quidni:** cf. 7.4(n.). **huic inicienda sit manus:** *huic*, i.e. the latter, simpler, death. *manum inicere* 'lay hands on', 'grasp' (*OLD inicio* 6), here in a figurative sense. Compare (in a more concrete sense) Liv. 2.12.13, where Mucius *dextram . . . accenso ad sacrificium foculo inicit* (on S's engagement with this episode in Livy see further *Ep.* 24.5(nn.)). S's phrase serves to convey the physical act of grasping e.g. a sword, by means of which death is to be attained. **quemadmodum . . . uita** 'In just the same way as I would select a ship, when I am going to travel by sea, or a house I am going to live in, so when I am going to cease living, I would select my death.' For the characteristic compression achieved by this use of the future participle (discussed by Traina 1987: 28–9) cf. 7.4. *nauigaturus*: this comparison returns us to §2's image of life as a sea voyage. *exiturus*: a verb S often uses of dying; cf. 17.9, 30.2, 54.10, 72.3, 93.2, Hill 2004: 6.

12 quemadmodum: here, in contrast to the previous sentence, the correspondence is one of opposites: 'just as a longer life is not necessarily better, so a longer death is necessarily worse'.   **utique** 'necessarily' (*OLD* 3).   **in morte morem:** paronomasia (cf. 7.4 *mortis morae*).   **morem animo gerere** 'to regulate one's conduct in accordance with one's spirit' (*OLD mos* 6).   **exeat** (subject *animus*) picks up §11 *exiturus*.   **impetum** 'impulse' (*OLD* 6); cf. Suet. *Otho* 9.4 *ac statim moriendi cepit impetum*.   **ferrum:** to die by the sword was often seen as a noble death, even when self-inflicted. Cato is the prime example (see 24.6–8nn.), but cf. also Mart. 1.78.7, praising as *Romana mors* the suicide by the sword of a man afflicted with cancer.   **appetit** 'desires' (*OLD* 3).   **laqueum:** hanging is frequently represented as a shameful way to die (Hooff 1990: 69–70). Those who have killed themselves in this manner are excluded, along with other degraded persons, from burial in the plot governed by regulations listed in *CIL* xi.6528 *Extra au[c] torateis et quei sibi [la] queo manu[m] attulissent et quei quaestum spurcum profecissent*; see Voisin 1979 and 1987.   **potionem:** the pre-eminent example of death by poison in the *EM* (even though not by choice) is Socrates, see §9(n.) *ueneno mori*.   **pergat et uincula seruitutis abrumpat:** the spirit is to be released from subjugation to the body; cf. 65.21 *maior sum . . . quam ut mancipium sim mei corporis* with Inwood (on metaphors of slavery in the letters see Armisen-Marchetti 1989: 113–15; Edwards 2009). For the idea of embodied life as a burden, implicit in *uincula*, cf. 24.17(nn.), 65.16 *corpus hoc animi pondus ac poena est*, Ben. 3.20, Polyb. 9.3.   **approbare** 'render acceptable' (*OLD* 2). With *mortem* as object, the only other occurrence, as Woodman (2010: 295) notes, is at *Ann.* 15.59, just preceding Tacitus' description of S's own death.   **optima . . . quae placet:** S challenges the hierarchy of modes of suicide. There remains a frisson of perversity, however, in presenting any death as excellent or pleasing.

13 stulte: the emphatically placed adverb dismisses any consideration of other people's opinions.   **'aliquis . . . animosius':** in diatribic mode, S ventriloquises the question posed by those anxious as to how others may judge their deaths. Three critics are imagined voicing similar objections (*temere, fortiter* and *animosius* are virtual equivalents).   **uis tu** 'you really ought (to)'; see 47.10n. The judgements of others are irrelevant; cf. 26.6 *remoue existimationem hominum.*   **in manibus** 'in your own hands', both figuratively (*OLD* 4 'in easy reach') and, given the means by which this goal is to be achieved, literally.   **fama** 'public opinion' (*OLD* 4).   **ut te fortunae quam celerrime eripias:** fortune here (cf. §7(n.) *fortunam*) is a negative force; cf. the terms in which a brief life well lived is presented as potentially preferable to a long but inert one at §§3–4 (see also 93.1–4).   **alioquin** 'otherwise'. Although S has just asserted that the opinions of others are irrelevant, he now underlines that failing to take one's own life when it is appropriate to do so will itself attract criticism.

14 S now turns to those claiming to be philosophers, who argue that it is wrong to take one's own life. This is the position taken by Aemilius Paulus in his advice to his son at Cic. *Rep.* 6.15. Epicureans were against suicide under most circumstances (Warren 2004: 199–212). A total prohibition seems to have been associated particularly with the Pythagoreans (Macr. *In Somn.* 1.12–13, Hooff 1990: 85, 192). A series of arguments for seeing suicide as ἀσέβεια is adduced at Joseph. *BJ* 3.376–9. For the ambivalent position of Plato's *Phaedo*, as interpreted in antiquity, see intro. to *Ep.* 24.   **professos sapientiam** 'who have laid claim to wisdom'. For *profiteri* in this sense (*OLD* 5b), cf. 71.30, *Constant.* 1.1, Cic. *Tusc.* 2.12 *artemque uitae professus*.   **qui uim afferendam uitae suae negent** 'who claim one should not inflict violence on one's own life'. *negent*: generic subj. Cf. Tac. *Ann.* 16.17 *uim sibi attulit.*   **nefas:** a strong prohibition with religious connotations (*OLD* 2b); cf. *De ira* 3.31.7 *nefas est nocere patriae.*   **ipsum interemptorem sui fieri** 'to become one's own killer'.   **expectandum esse exitum:** according to these self-proclaimed philosophers, the individual should wait for the death nature has prescribed. *expectandum*: contrast the alternatives given in §11 *occupanda . . . an expectanda.*   **libertatis uiam:** cf. 12.10(n.) *patet undique ad libertatem uiae multae, breues faciles*, *Prov.* 2.10, 6.7.   **nihil melius . . . exitus multos:** for the multiplicity of possible means by which death may be sought cf. 117.23 on *uiae mortis* and *De ira* 3.15.4. *aeterna lex*: cf. 77.12 on the inevitability of death, *ad hanc legem natus es*. For Pliny the Elder (*Nat.* 2.27), the possibility of suicide (*sibi mortem consciscere*) constitutes the greatest gift given to man amid life's sufferings, *optimum in tantis uitae poenis.*

15 ego . . . discutere? 'Should I wait for the cruelty of disease or of man, when I could in the midst of torments depart and shake off my troubles?' *expectem* challenges *expectandum*, the pronouncement of the *professos sapientiam* in §14. The word order *per media exire tormenta* reinforces the sense.   **hoc . . . queri** 'this is the sole ground on which we may not complain about life'.   **neminem tenet:** life obliges no one to stay; it is rather our own misguided attachment to life which makes it hard to let go. Cf. 26.10 *una est catena quae nos alligatos tenet, amor uitae*, 117.23.   **bono loco:** *locus* here in the sense of situation (*OLD* 22a).   **uitio suo** 'through his own fault'.   **placet? . . . non placet?** the decision as to whether or not one's life is still worth living is presented in coolly detached terms (*placet* usually used impersonally, *OLD* 4a), generating 'the kind of satisfaction produced by acting on one's own inclinations . . . rather than allowing oneself to be passively influenced by circumstances and the choices of others', Inwood (2005: 312). **eo reuerti unde uenisti:** cf. *Tranq.* 11.4 *reuerti unde ueneris quid graue est?*, Polyb. 9.2, *Ep.* 54.4, 77.11. The equivalence between time before birth and time before death (here imagined in spatial terms) is strongly emphasised in Epicurean arguments against the fear of death (Epicurus, *Ep. Men.* 124–5; see Warren 2004: 57–108 on symmetry arguments). This motif occurs in funerary inscriptions, e.g. *CIL* VIII.3463, as *non fui, fui, non sum, non desidero*; cf. *CIL* V.1813, 2893 NFFNSNC (the last two letters presumably standing for *non curo*). For the denial of immortality in funerary epigraphy more generally see Lattimore 1942: 78–86.

16 S proposes as parallels standard medical procedures for relieving discomfort. **ut dolorem ... misisti** 'you have often let blood to relieve a headache'. Blood-letting (*OLD sanguis* 1c + *mittere*) frequently appears as a remedy; cf. *Clem.* 1.5.1, Cels. 2.10, 4.2.5, Suet. *Cal.* 29.2. **extenuandum** 'to be reduced in bulk' (*OLD* 1b). **uena percutitur** 'a vein is cut through' (*OLD percutio* 6), apparently a technical medical phrase; cf. Scribonius Largus, *Compositiones* 84 *si quis super laqueum percusserit uenam*. Severing veins was often chosen as a means of suicide (sometimes through the agency of a doctor; see Flemming 2005), as in the case of S himself, according to Tac. *Ann.* 15.60–4, where an executioner is referred to as a *percussor* (15.63). Here the shift from perfect *misisti*, to present *percutitur*, paves the way for future possibilities, with suicide cast as (Ker 2009a: 270) 'an everyday therapeutic practice'. **uasto uulnere** 'a tremendous wound'. For *uastus* in this sense (*OLD* 3b) cf. *Nat.* 6.32.3 *ingenti itaque animo mors prouocanda est, siue nos saeuo uastoque impetu aggreditur, siue cotidiano et uulgari exitu*. **praecordia** 'the vitals' (*OLD* 1a), sometimes with the more precise sense of the diaphragm; Scarpat quotes Plin. *Nat.* 11.197 *exta homini ab inferiore uiscerum parte separantur membrana quam praecordia appellant, quia a corde praetenditur*. **scalpello aperitur ad illam magnam libertatem uia** 'by a scalpel is opened up the road to that great freedom', the opposite process to *libertatis uiam cludere* in §14; cf. *De ira* 3.15.4 *quaeris quod sit ad libertatem iter? quaelibet in corpore tuo uena*. **puncto** 'puncture' (*OLD* 1a), in contrast to the *uasto uulnere*. Ker (2009a: 270) observes: 'an aesthetics of the *punctum* matches the already minuscule temporal and spatial dimensions of human life'; cf. 49.3 *punctum est quod uiuimus*, *Nat.* 1.pr.11. **securitas:** a central goal of the *proficiens* is to achieve this state; cf. 92.3 *quid est beata uita? securitas et perpetua tranquillitas*. **pigros inertesque:** parallel to the situation of one who is becalmed in life in §3. **nemo nostrum cogitat** 'not one of us reflects'. **ex hoc domicilio exeundum:** while at §11 S compared choosing one's mode of death to choosing which house to move in to, here he reverts to the analogy of house and body developed in 12.1–4(nn.), 30.2, 65.21 *in hoc obnoxio domicilio animus liber habitat*. Once one's dwelling is no longer fit for purpose, it is time to think of leaving.   **sic ... detinet** 'thus a fondness for the place and familiarity keep hold of long-standing inhabitants despite the inconveniences'. *indulgentia loci*: for this use of the objective genitive with *indulgentia*, Scarpat adduces as parallel Stat. *Theb.* 4.252 *egregiae tanta indulgentia formae*. *detinet* picks up *neminem tenet* (of *uita*) in §14.

17 aduersus hoc corpus liber: cf. §12(n.)   *uincula*.   **tamquam migraturus habita**: the analogy of the house is continued. As Scarpat notes, the verb *migrare* evokes the articulation of the Epicurean position on how to approach death offered at Cic. *Fin.* 1.62 (of a *sapiens*) *non dubitat si ita melius sit, migrare de uita*.   **propone tibi**: here, as often elsewhere, this imperative sets an exercise of the imagination of the kind which is crucial to effective *meditatio*; cf. 24.2 *quidquid uereris ne eueniat euenturum utique propone*, 56.1, 74.7, *Marc.* 17.7, *Ben.* 6.30.1 *propone animo tuo carcerem, uincula, sordes, seruitutem, bellum, egestatem*, *Tro.* 582.   **contubernio**: a lodging, military accommodation or tent shared by a group of soldiers (*OLD* 4), a temporary kind of dwelling, in contrast to the *domus* of the previous section; cf. 102.24, 120.14 *nec domum esse hoc corpus sed hospitium, et quidem breue hospitium*. For the thought cf. *Tranq.* 11.1 and the words put in the aged Cato's mouth at Cic. *Sen.* 84, *e uita discedo tamquam hospitio non tamquam domo*.   **sed quemadmodum ... concupiscentibus?** *finis*: here, first in the sense of end (*OLD* 10a), then in the sense of limit (*OLD* 6a). For the thought cf. 77.18 *mortem times; at quomodo illam media boletatione contemnis?* The insatiable desire for more, be it food, drink, money, power or life itself (and all these desires are interlinked for S), is mankind's greatest affliction; cf. 58.22–37, 79.12, 89.20–2, 102.24, 120.14–16.

18 nullius rei meditatio tam necessaria est: of all the mental exercises S repeatedly advocates, the most important are concerned with overcoming the fear of death (cf. 26.8, 54.2, *Marc.* 22.2, *Nat.* 2.59.3, Newman 1989: 1487).   **alia**: n. pl., following the generic *nullius rei*, i.e. meditations on other things. A list follows of other perceived misfortunes, which the *proficiens* may prepare for. Of these, only his own death is certain to take place.   **exercentur** 'are practised', already in Cic. (e.g. *Tusc.* 2.41) with the sense of spiritual exercises.   **in superuacuum** 'unnecessarily' (*OLD superuacuus* 2c); cf. *Marc.* 1.6 *omnia in superuacuum temptata sunt*.   **aduersus paupertatem**: S offers various instances of exercises aimed at countering the fear of poverty, e.g. 18.6–12, 20.13, 24.17, 87.1–11, 95.54.   **ad contemptum ... doloris**: another common concern in the *EM*; cf. e.g. 14.4–6, 24.5, 78.10–21, Edwards 1999.   **armauimus**: military metaphors pervade the *EM* (see Lavery 1980, Galimberti

2001, Sommer 2001). For *armare* in this sense cf. 74.21 and Cic. *Fam.* 12.23.4 (= 347 SB) *philosophiae... quae me... contra omnis fortunae impetus armat.* **huius uirtutis experimentum:** for the testing of particular virtues cf. 18.7(nn.), 123.5, *VB* 25.8. **amissorum desideria:** *Epp.* 63 and 99 focus on how to prepare oneself for the experience of bereavement (as do *Ad Polybium* and *Ad Marciam*). See Wilson 1997. S concedes his own weakness in this respect at 63.14–15.

19 magnis tantum uiris: cf. 77.14 *exempla nunc magnorum uirorum me tibi iudicas relaturum? puerorum referam.* **seruitutis humanae claustra perrumperent** 'in order to break through the bonds of human servitude.' **non est ... non posse** 'you should not judge that this cannot be done unless by Cato'. Echoing and reinforcing, with the specific example of Cato, *non est quod existimes... perrumperent. non est quod*: see 7.9n. **quam ... extraxit** 'that spirit which he had not sent forth with the sword, he wrested out with his hand' (i.e. by tearing open the wound he had made earlier, which had been bound up by a doctor; see 24.8n.). For *emittere* cf. §5n. **uilissimae sortis homines:** their lowness will, by the manner of their deaths, be both graphically reinforced (on a physical level) and radically inverted (on a spiritual). *sors* 'condition' (*OLD* 9b). The examples which follow are of men compelled to perform in beast fights in the arena, presumably prisoners of war (Kyle 1998: 79–80). Arena performers of all kinds are systematically stigmatised in Roman law (Edwards 1997b) and often feature as conspicuous instances of degraded humanity; cf. e.g. Cic. *Mil.* 92 *infimi generis hominum* (on gladiators), *Tusc.* 2.41 *gladiatores, aut perditi homines aut barbari* (here, too, though, brought in as exemplars of bravery). **ingenti impetu** 'by a huge effort'; cf. §12(n.). **in tutum euaserunt:** death puts one safely beyond the reach of fortune; cf. the words put in the dying Cato's mouth at 24.7, *Cato deducatur in tutum.* At 32.3, the phrase is used simply of withdrawal: *perduc te in tutum.* **cumque ... fecerunt** 'and when they might not die comfortably nor choose their preferred means of death, they have seized upon whatever lay to hand and through their strength made weapons of things which were not by nature harmful'. *e commodo:* cf. 46.1 *librum... tamquam lecturus ex commodo.*

20 in ludo bestiariorum 'the training school for beast fighters'. On the history of beast-fighting in Rome see Wiedemann 1992: 55–101, Kyle 1998: 79–80. **Germanis:** presumably German prisoners of war, defeated enemies from tribes renowned (according to e.g. Tac. *Ger.* 4) for their physical prowess. **matutina spectacula:** there is some evidence that beast fights were customarily scheduled for the morning (cf. 7.4 *mane... leonibus*). But attempts to infer a standard programme are problematic (see 7.3n.).   **secessit:** in this sense cf. 82.12 *ad exonerandum uentrem secessit*, but this is a verb which often has a philosophical weight for S; cf. e.g. 8.2 *secessi non tantum ab hominibus sed a rebus*, 14.14, 19.11, 25.7, 68.6.   **ad exonerandum corpus** 'to relieve himself', lit. in the sense of defecation but elsewhere S frequently presents the body itself as a burden (cf. e.g. *De ira* 1.6.2 *abstinentia corpus exonerat*). It is this burden of which the German's arrestingly vile act of bravery will relieve him.   **lignum ... est** 'that stick which, with a sponge attached, is placed for the purpose of cleaning one's private parts'.   **totum:** i.e. the *lignum*.   **farsit** 'stuffed', a verb which S uses elsewhere of the eating habits of the luxurious, e.g. 108.17 *se ultra quam capiunt farcientibus*, 119.14, *Nat.* 1.pr.4; cf. Petr. 69.6. Here it intensifies the sense of disgust, with a strong contrast between *obscena* and *gulam*.   **interclusis faucibus** 'having obstructed his throat'.   **elisit** 'stifled' (*OLD* 1d); cf. 24.14 *uocum ... elisarum*.   **morti contumeliam facere** 'to give an affront to death'. At *Constant.* 11.2, S comments, *contumelia a contemptu dicta est*.   **ita prorsus** 'yes, indeed', looking forward; cf. *Ben.* 2.12.1.   **parum munde** 'not cleanly', picking up *emundanda*.

21 uirum fortem: thus, in his death the equal of the *magni uiri* of §19. Elsewhere, e.g. 104.29, *uirum fortem* is applied to Cato.   **dignum cui fati daretur electio** 'worthy to be given a choice of end'. For *dignus* with relative clause and subjunctive see *NLS* §158. *fati* 'death' (*OLD* 6).   **quam fortiter ... immisisset!** 'How bravely he would have used the sword, with what spirit he would have hurled himself into the depths of the sea or from the great height of a crag!' *in profundam altitudinem* to be understood with both *maris* and *abscisae rupis* (there is a tension between *profundam* 'extending a long way down' (*OLD* 1) and *altitudinem* signifying extension upward). S imagines three less unusual ways of finding death (on jumping to one's death see Hooff 1990: 73–7).   **undique** 'in every respect' (*OLD* 4).   **inuenit quemadmodum et mortem sibi deberet et telum:** perhaps 'he found the means by which he might be indebted to himself for death and a weapon'. The emphasis here is on *sibi*. As a *bestiarius* he was expected to inflict death on (or be killed by) a beast. Although the idea of dying as the repayment of a debt is not unusual in funerary epigraphy (see e.g. *CIL* VI.25617 *debitum reddidit*, Lattimore 1942: 170–1), *deberet* is awkward here where it must, following *quemadmodum*, mean payment of that debt; Hense conjectures *deferret*, which would have the sense of 'confer' (*OLD* 11a; cf. *Ben.* 4.9.1).   **in mora esse** 'is a source of delay' (playing on *moriendum*); cf. 7.4 *omnia ista mortis morae sunt*.   **uelle** 'the will', a term of great importance in S; see Inwood 2005: ch. 5.   **existimetur ... constet** 'let the deed of this most valiant man be judged as each thinks fit, so long as this is agreed'.   **spurcissimam ... mundissimae:**

superlatives frame the starkly juxtaposed nouns (while *mundissimae* looks back to §20 *emundanda*). The opposite paradox is evoked in relation to the over-nice bathing habits of S's contemporaries, at 86.12(n.) *postquam munda balnea inuenta sunt, spurciores sunt.*

22 sordidis exemplis: *sordidus* in the sense of 'humble' (*OLD* 4). Such examples are used elsewhere in S; cf. e.g. 24.9, 14, Hooff 1990: 20. **a contemptissimis . . . contemni:** Cicero invokes a similar argument at *Phil.* 3.35. Lowly examples constitute *ex maiore* proofs; cf. *Ben.* 3.19.2–3, *De ira* 2.12.4–6 and Quintilian (*Inst.* 5.11.9–10), who encourages the use of women as examples of *uirtus*, bravery, *ad moriendum non tam Cato et Scipio quam Lucretia*, Turpin 2008: 367. In Tacitus' account of deaths under Nero, the *clarius exemplum* (*Ann.* 15.57.3) of the lowly freedwoman Epicharis (an episode which Ker 2009a: 61–2 sees as influenced by this letter, noting particularly her suicide, contrived with a noose improvised from her breastband) puts to shame the more cowardly behaviour of elite males, such as S's nephew Lucan. **Catones Scipionesque:** in the case of both families, several individuals are regularly invoked as *exempla*; S himself has a preference for Cato the Younger (see 24.6–8(nn.)), but see intro. to *Ep.* 86 for instances of his use of Cato the Elder (with Maso 1999: 68–9). On Scipio Africanus see 86.1–13, while on Scipio Nasica see 24.9–10, 71.10. For the use of these names in the plural see also *Marc.* 25.1; cf. Cic. *Ver.* 2.3, 209.7, *Agr.* 2.64.7, *de Orat.* 3.56.4, *Amic.* 21.5, Langlands 2018, Henderson 2004: 104 on pairs of Scipios in Ennius and in Virgil. **audire** 'hear about' (*OLD* 8). **supra imitationem:** on the danger here implied that exalted exemplars may be discouraging cf. 24.9 and *Constant.* 2.71 (on Cato) *uereor ne supra nostrum exemplum sit*. **istam uirtutem:** i.e. preferring death to slavery. **in ducibus belli ciuilis:** alongside that of Cato, 24.9–10 also offers a vignette of the death of Scipio Nasica (see notes); cf. 71.10. **ostendam** 'let me show'. The visual vocabulary (cf. *uides* in §25) is particularly appropriate given that these exemplars are performers in *spectacula*, but S regularly prompts his readers to visualise *exempla*.

23 adueheretur 'was being transported'. **ad matutinum spectaculum:** cf. §20(n.) *matutina spectacula*. **missus** 'destined'. **tamquam somno premente** 'as if sleep were overpowering' (*OLD premo* 18); cf. *Phaed.* 520. **radiis** 'spokes' (*OLD* 2a). **circumactu rotae** 'the revolution of the wheel'. **ferebatur effugit:** the juxtaposition of passive and active verbs underlines the German's initiative in seizing his own destiny. *effugit* takes *poenam* as object.

24 erumpere: cf. §12 *abrumpat* and §19 *perrumperent*.   **cupienti:** it is the will which is critical here; cf. §21 *uelle*.   **in aperto:** sc. *loco*, a military phrase (cf. Caes. *Civ.* 1.71).   **circumspiciat:** in §5, when circumstances becomes difficult, he *circumspicit* whether it is appropriate to die; cf. 30.2 *circumspiciendum quomodo exeas*. The emphasis here is on considered choice.   **exitum mollem** 'an easy death'. S comments of death in old age at 30.4, *nullo genere homines mollius moriuntur*; cf. of the ailing Marcellinus (77.10), *mollissime excessit*.   **ad manum** 'to hand'.   **sese asserat** 'lays claim to himself' (*OLD* 2b), often in the context of a slave claiming freedom.   **is proximam quamque pro optima arripiat** 'let him lay hold of whatever is the nearest opportunity [sc. *occasionem*], to serve as the best'.   **inaudita . . . noua:** Roman interest in unusual means of procuring death is reflected in the substantial section 9.12 *de mortibus non uulgaribus* in Valerius Maximus, which includes such ingenious approaches as swallowing live coals.   **ad mortem:** death is the objective.   **ingenium** 'capacity to devise' (*OLD* 6a).   **cui non defuerit animus** 'for one who does not lack spirit', fut. pf.

25 extrema . . . mancipia 'the lowest slaves', the neuter term is a still more abjected variant on *uilissimae sortis homines* (§19).   **ubi illis stimulos adegit dolor** 'when suffering goads them on'. The terms *stimulos* and *adegit*, often used in relation to animals, highlight the scarcely human condition of these men. For the idea that extreme circumstances bring out the best, particularly in the untutored, cf. 30.8.   **ille uir magnus:** challenging the conventional use of the phrase at §19.   **sibi . . . imperauit:** on self-address as a strategy to alter one's own motivation see Star (2012: 49); at 113.31 S observes, *imperare sibi maximum imperium est*.   **inuenit** 'he has devised' (*OLD* 6a), a deliberately low-key verb.   **ex eodem tibi munere:** *munus* is a common term for a set of games in the arena, esp. gladiatorial shows (which had their origins in offerings made in memory of the recently deceased; see Tert. *De spect.* 12, Serv. *Aen.* 3.67 quoting Varro, Hopkins 1983: 2–12).

26 secundo naumachiae spectaculo: it appears (from §25 *ex eodem . . . munere*) that this set of games included two sea battles. Sea battles were occasionally staged in Roman arenas (the earliest attested is that of Julius Caesar in 46 BCE, Suet. *Iul.* 39); see Coleman 1993. Participants were usually condemned criminals, expected to fight until all were killed (Kyle 1998: 93–4). Nero is known to have given one (Suet. *Nero* 12, Dio Cass. 61.9.5) in 57 and another in 64 CE (Dio 62.15.1). Tacitus, commenting on a *naumachia* given by Claudius in 52 CE, notes (*Ann.* 12.56) the bravery of the contestants as something surprising in condemned criminals, though he does not mention suicides: *pugnatum quamquam inter sontis* *fortium uirorum animo.*   **totam iugulo suo mersit:** a variation on §20 *totum in gulam farsit. mergere* in this sense (*OLD* 6) is poetic.   **'quare . . .?'** S imagines the man's self-address. As Star (2012: 49) notes, 'his words mark the transition between knowing what he ought to do and actually doing it'.   **ludibrium** 'mockery', highlighting the humiliation inflicted on performers in the *ludi*.   **iamdudum** 'now, after all this time' (*OLD dudum* 3).   **'quare ego mortem armatus expecto?'** 'Why do I wait for death when I am armed?' *expecto* returns us to the alternatives given in §11, *occupanda . . . an expectanda*, while *armatus* echoes §18's metaphorical *armauimus*.   **speciosius spectaculum:** *speciosus*, often with the sense of 'showy' (*OLD* 6b) in contrast to inward qualities (cf. 90.28), is here paradoxically deployed to underline the authentic, rather than specious, honour of this performer, who shows not how to kill (the usual lesson of the arena display) but how to die.   **mori . . . quam occidere:** cf. 7.5 on the lessons of the amphitheatre. The ability of trained gladiators to face death bravely is treated as exemplary by Cicero; cf. e.g. *Phil.* 3.35, *Tusc.* 2.41.

27 quod . . . ratio? *quoque,* here in the sense of 'even' (*OLD* 4), is emphatically positioned before *noxiosi*. Again an *ex maiore* argument (see §22n. on *a contemptissimis . . . contemni*); cf. 24.5 (on the bravery of Mucius) *hominem non eruditum nec ullis praeceptis contra mortem aut dolorem subornatum*, 90.45–6.   **perditi** 'desperate' (*OLD* 2a); cf. Cic. *Tusc.* 2.41 on gladiators as *aut perditi homines aut barbari*, also arguing *ex maiore* from the gladiator to one who has strengthened his *animus* with *meditatio* and *ratio*.   **longa meditatio:** i.e. the practice of daily reflection carried out over many years, which is crucial to the progress of the *proficiens* (71.31, Newman 1989; see main intro. section 7); cf. §18 *nullius rei meditatio tam necesse est.*   **magistra . . . ratio:** reason, here synonymous with philosophy, is personified as a teacher; cf. Cic. *Tusc.* 5.5.   **fati uarios esse accessus** 'the approaches to death are varied'.

28 eadem illa ratio . . . tibi inuadas 'that same reason advises you, if it is possible, to die in the way that pleases you, if not, in the way you can, and to take hold of whatever has come to hand for the purpose of doing violence to yourself'. The text is problematic here. Reynolds, following Hense, supplies <*quemadmodum . . . minus*>. *obuenerit:* pf. subj. *uim afferendam:* cf. §10 *manus sibi attulit. inuadas* 'seize possession of' (OLD 6a).   **rapto** 'by robbery'; used of those who live by brigandage, e.g. Liv. 7.25.13 *quos rapto uiuere necessitas cogeret*, Virg. *A.* 7.749, 9.613. S ends the letter with a defiantly paradoxical *sententia:* while robbery is a degrading way to live, it can be a noble way to die. *rapere* and its cognates recur in this letter; cf. §2 *rapidissimi,* §13 *eripias,* §24 *arripiat.*

LETTER 86

In *Ep.* 84 (perhaps the first in Book 11), S highlighted the value of ethical examples from former ages (84.10); many letters feature heroic individuals from earlier periods in Roman history (cf. e.g. 24.5 Mucius Scaevola, 67.7, 71.17 Regulus, 95.72–3, 120.19 Tubero; see Mayer 1991, Maso 1999: 43–81), but the meditation on Scipio in *Ep.* 86 (briefly foreshadowed at 51.11) is much more developed than any of these other vignettes. Scipio Africanus (236–184/3 BCE), who led Roman forces to victory over Hannibal at Zama in 204 BCE, for which he was granted a triumph, was widely regarded as one of the greatest heroes of the republic. Scipio, as featured here, however, is not the great military hero at the height of his success but a man who, under attack from his political enemies in Rome, has withdrawn from public life to his modest country estate.

While *Ep.* 85 developed at length an abstract ideal of the *sapiens*, *Ep.* 86 offers an embodied, specific instance of a man who comes close to realising this ideal. As for the conditions in which virtue is exercised, one's own fatherland should offer proper scope, 85.40 suggested, while conceding that exile may sometimes be the better option: 'The wise man will develop virtue . . . if possible in his own country – if not, in exile'; Scipio's *exilium uoluntarium* offers a vivid illustration of exile put to good use. The potency of this bracingly austere *exemplum* as an inspiration is perhaps hinted at in *Ep.* 87's vignette of S and his friend Maximus, resolved to test themselves by journeying with only a minimal entourage (87.2–4, 9, Ker 2009a: 352). On this sequence of letters see Henderson 2004: 46–52. *Ep.* 84 probably opens Book 11 but book numbers are missing after *Ep.* 83 and the divisions between books are uncertain for this section of the MSS (some letters may be lost between 88 and 89, the first in Book 14; see Inwood: xiii, Cancik 1967: 8–12).

The use of a villa to spark reflection on the character of its owner features in *Ep.* 12 on S's own property, as well as *Ep.* 55 on that of Vatia (on *Epp.* 12, 55 and 86 see Henderson 2004). Though unusual in its sustained focus on this one location (Mazzoli 1991: 74–5), *Ep.* 86 nevertheless covers a lot of ground. Opening with an expression of reverence for Scipio (§1) and an account of the final stage of his career (§§2–3), S uses the villa's austerity, in particular its modest bathing arrangements (§§4–5), as the launchpad for a satirical attack on the luxury of his own age (§§6–13), interspersed with reflections on the admirable simplicity of Scipio's way of life. Ostensibly prompted by the activities of the estate's current proprietor Aegialus (§14), the letter then modulates, by way of suggestive comments on Virgil (§§15–16), into a meditation on techniques for transplanting olive trees (§§17–19) and vines (§§20–1).

Fabulous stories circulated about Scipio even in his own lifetime (on the early development of the Scipionic legend see Walbank 1967). Ennius' celebration (in epigrams, in his *Annales* and in a poem entitled *Scipio*, of which only fragments survive) brought Scipio more glory than any public inscription, claims Horace in his *Odes* (4.8.13–15). For Lucretius (3.1034–5, perhaps quoting Ennius; see §5n. on *Carthaginis horror*) Scipio serves as the paradigmatic great man. The most detailed account of Scipio's career, including his withdrawal from Rome when threatened with prosecution for a number of offences, is offered by Livy (Luce 1977: 92–104, Jaeger 1997: 161–72). His virtues feature at numerous points in Valerius Maximus (e.g. 3.7.1d–g, 4.1.6, 5.3.2b; see Del Giovane 2012, Rimell 2013: 1). The story, involving pirates eager to see the great man in his retirement (2.10.2), retrojects to Scipio's own day the idea of pilgrimage to the great man's residence (Bodel 1997: 5–6, 13). Certainly Pliny's comment on Aegialus (*Nat.* 14.49) suggests that the estate was a significant draw for visitors in the later first century CE (cf. the estate at Velitrae, where the emperor Augustus spent his early years, which was apparently still attracting crowds of visitors in the time of Hadrian, Suet. *Aug.* 6; see Bodel 1997: 13).

Scipio is described by Livy as (38.53.9) *uir memorabilis, bellicis tamen quam pacis artibus memorabilior*, the earlier part of his career on campaign outshining the later years back in Italy. S by contrast chooses to stress Scipio's *pietas* over his military achievements; it is precisely in leaving Rome that Scipio demonstrates his commitment to genuine Roman values (86.1–2). Even in the second century BCE, the 'real' Rome might be found not in Rome itself but in Campania, it seems (Ker 2009a: 350). At the same time, as Henderson (2004: 97) comments, the virtuous Scipio's austere and self-imposed exile from an ungrateful Rome models for that of S himself: 'The best of Rome had always, it could seem, taken themselves away on principle, and Seneca now follows suit' (cf. Gowing 2005: 80–1, Ker 2009a: 346–7, 352).

S's vividly evoked Scipio has precedents. In Cicero's *De re publica*, set in 129 BCE, P. Cornelius Scipio Aemilianus (the commander who defeated Carthage in 146 BCE) is made to recall a dream in which his adoptive grandfather, the Scipio of the Liternum villa, appears (6.10), causing an intense reaction in Aemilianus: *quem ubi agnoui, equidem cohorrui*. The figure of Africanus then predicts his grandson's future career and tells of the afterlife in store for those who bring great benefits to the state (6.13–25). S (100.9) is familiar with Cicero's philosophical works, though he rarely quotes from them directly (cf. Setaioli 2003: 65–6, Del Giovane 2012: 158, Armisen-Marchetti 2007). But while the first section of *Ep.* 86 evokes the Ciceronian epiphany of Scipio (Henderson 2004: 166–7, Del Giovane 2012), S does not summon forth a disembodied spirit to offer edifying comments on the afterlife. The Scipio of *Ep.* 86 utters a few terse words to his unappreciative contemporaries (§2), but the letter's main emphasis is on the physical presence of the living man, evoking the sight, but also the touch and smell, of him (Rimell 2013: 1).

Scipio's younger contemporary, Cato the Elder (234–149 BCE), features briefly in the following letter (87.9–10 with Inwood's commentary; see further Allegri 2004) as an exemplar of frugal living. Cato, a man known for his rigorous adherence to traditional Roman custom, his fierce hostility to luxury and his celebration of agriculture (Astin 1978), is also a significant, though largely occluded, presence in *Ep.* 86, in this case more directly mediated by Cicero. In *De senectute*, Cicero's Cato praises rustic labours (which he terms (§51) *uoluptates agricolarum*) as comparable to the existence of the Stoic sage (*mihi ad sapientis uitam proxime uidentur accedere*). He himself has been inspired, he asserts, by visiting the modest dwelling and industriously farmed estate of Manius Curius Dentatus (cos. 290 BCE), a triumphant general of outstanding virtue, who, despite his elevated position, chose to live a simple rustic life (*Sen.* 54–5): *uillam contemplans . . . admirari satis non possum uel hominis continentiam uel temporum disciplinam* (cf. Sen. *Ep.* 86.3, 5 *contemplantem*). This encounter has prompted Cato to devote himself to a frugal life, working his own land – and writing about agriculture (cf. Plut. *Cat. Mai.* 2.2, Del Giovane 2012: 159–60. As Del Giovane notes, the comments on Manius' farm in Cicero's *De senectute* may derive from Cato the Elder's own work; cf. Cic. *Rep.* 3.40). Insofar as S's own response to Scipio's villa mirrors Cato's to that of Manius Curius Dentatus (in Cicero's treatise), S may be read as offering, in Ker's words (2009a: 351), 'two archaic exempla for the price of one'.

Other aspects, too, of *Ep.* 86 could be characterised as Catonian; Cato the Elder was, to judge from his fragmentary writings, a ferocious critic of luxurious architecture. See e.g. *ORF*[4] VIII.185 = 139 Cugusi, *dicere possum, quibus uillae atque aedes aedificatae atque expolitae maximo opere citro atque ebore atque pauimentis Poenicis sient*, 'I can say this to those whose villas and houses are elaborately constructed and embellished with citrus wood, ivory and floors of Punic stone'; see Nichols 2010. The final third of *Ep.* 86, on the transplanting of olive trees and vines, evokes elements of Cato's only literary work to have survived largely intact, his treatise *De agricultura*.

Scipio himself is celebrated by Cicero (*Off.* 3.1, 4) as a model for contemplative retirement, who made proper use of *otium et solitudo* (Ker 2009a: 349–51). Cato (Cic. *Off.* 3.1 = Cato, *hist.* fr. 127 Leo = F130b Cornell) attributed to Scipio the paradoxical statement that *numquam se minus otiosum esse quam cum otiosus, nec minus solum quam cum solus esset*. Plutarch (*Apophthegmata regum et imperatorum* 1.196b) even suggests that writing figured among Scipio's retirement activities. The scholarly solitude S cultivates in the letters might itself be seen as Scipionic (Gross 1980: 127–8, Ker 2009a: 350). Yet even the military aspect of Scipio's career offers an analogy for the virtuous philosophical life; the frequency with which S uses military metaphors to characterise his Stoic project is noted above (see main intro. section 9). S's insistent attack on pleasures is explicitly presented at 51.6 as a kind of warfare (*nobis quoque militandum est*), where he compares his own campaigning (against, among other things, warm baths) to that of Hannibal (Scipio's arch-enemy) making war on Rome, while at 87.9 Scipio and Cato the Elder (there serving as S's proxy) render comparable service to the state: *alter enim cum hostibus nostris bellum, alter cum moribus gessit*. S's attack on the luxurious bathing habits of his contemporaries in *Ep*. 86, developing a recurrent concern of the letters (cf. *Ep*. 56 also on baths; see Rimell 2015a: ch. 4), is a bravura performance in particularly combative mode.

S's critique focuses both on architectural excess and on over-refined care of the body (cf. e.g. *De ira* 3.35 on the fastidiousness of S's contemporaries). The splendour of baths, with their coloured marbles and lavish use of water, is a frequent object of moralising criticism, e.g. Plin. *Nat.* 36.44. Although, not long after S wrote, the same terms are deployed to very different ends in praise of the private baths of Claudius Etruscus in Stat. *Silv.* 1.5 (Newlands 2002: 199–212; cf. Hardie 1983: 132–6 on Statius as an early exponent of the bathhouse ecphrasis), Statius also expresses a more conventional hostility to marble use in his *Thebaid* (1.144–6). On criticism of luxurious building in general see Edwards 1993: 137–72, esp. 139–40, Nichols 2010, 2017: ch. 3; on baths in particular, Dunbabin 1989.

The focus on corporeality in this letter takes us into the world of satire. While Horatian satire implicitly informs aspects of e.g. *Ep*. 18 (see above), *Ep*. 86 includes the *EM*'s first explicit reference to Horace and the first of three quotations from the *Satires* (the only Horatian text S quotes; see Mazzoli 1970, Berthet 1979, Henderson 2004: 115–18, Berno 2008, Del Giovane 2015a: 215–22, Edwards 2017a). Its concerns resonate also with those articulated by S's satirist contemporary, Persius, and in the *Satyricon* of another contemporary, Petronius (Rimell 2013).

The final third of *Ep*. 86, ostensibly shifting focus to the activities of the villa's current occupant, is marked by a significant change of gear. S offers a refreshing antidote to the dyspeptic tirade against luxury which dominates §§4–13. Summers, in his commentary, remarks: 'it is curious that the information as to the transplanting of olives and vines at the end of the letter is given apparently for itself, and not, as it might so easily have been, as the text of some moral lesson' (289). §14 proposes that any tree may be transplanted, no matter how old, *quamuis uetus arbustum posse transferri*; Cato the Elder similarly advises in his treatise on agriculture

(*Agr.* 49), 'You may transplant an old vine if you wish.' Channelling Cato the Elder, implicitly a model in the earlier portion of the letter, might constitute an invigorating moral exercise in itself. But the lesson of Scipio's exile is surely that, even if Scipio's age is not stressed, an old man, too (Liv. 38.53.4 refers to his *senectus*), can flourish in a new place (Henderson 2004: 139–41).

The concerns and indeed much of the vocabulary in the final third of this letter also evoke Book 2 of Virgil's *Georgics*, l. 58 of which is quoted in §15. Virgil is the author most cited in the *EM* (see intro. to *Ep.* 21 above) and the resonance of the *Georgics* is repeatedly exploited (Henderson 2004: 50–2, 129–38); *G*. 1.176–7, for instance (*possum multa tibi ueterum praecepta referre | ni refugis tenuisque piget cognoscere curas*), is quoted as the opening of *Ep.* 124 (the last of the series to survive intact), and the same book is quoted at 90.9, 11 and 37(nn.). Book 2 of the *Georgics* celebrates Italy as especially suited (2.143–4) to the cultivation of olives and vines, whose transplantation features in the latter part of *Ep.* 86, but also (2.170) to the production of heroic men, including the Scipios, *duros belli*, the most famous of whom features in the earlier part of S's letter. In Virgil's didactic poem (*G*. 2.458–74) the happy and fulfilled lives of hard-working farmers are contrasted with the worthless existence of those who dwell in luxurious mansions (cf. Sen. *Ep.* 86.4–13). As Henderson(2004: 121–2) underlines, S's comment on Virgil's project at §15, *qui non quid uerissime sed quid decentissime diceretur aspexit, nec agricolas docere uoluit sed legentes delectare*, is surely a prompt to his own readers; S, too, he assures us, is not primarily concerned to offer tips on farming.

The metapoetic concerns of the *Georgics* (suggestively drawn out e.g. in Thomas 1988, Nappa 2005) are also significant. At 112.2, S uses the varying suitability of vines for grafting as an analogy for the suitability of certain people for philosophical training (cf. 2.7). The term S uses for transplantation (§14 *transferri*), his focus in the final third of *Ep.* 86, often has the sense of metaphor (*OLD translatio* 4a), whose use in philosophical prose S (59.6–9) defends at length (analysed by Henderson 2004: 139–57; cf., on metaphor in S more generally, Armisen-Marchetti 1989, 2015, Bartsch 2009, Dressler 2012). *Ep.* 86 invites the reader to slip from literal to metaphorical transplantation, to see S's arboricultural principles, for all their vivid rustic detail, as applying more importantly to the subject of writing philosophical prose.

Ep. 86 grapples self-consciously with a succession of political – and literary – *maiores*. Despite his apparent deference to the Roman past, to an ideal of sweaty, earth-encrusted Roman manhood, S also stresses the infinite regress of any attempt to get back to the true Rome. Yearning for a bath like Scipio's might even be (as Henderson 2004: 155 points out) the imperial philosopher's equivalent of the jaded voluptuary procuring a special poor man's cell to divert him from his life of luxury (100.6; cf. 18.7(n.)). In its lessons on arboriculture, the final part of a letter poses more particularly the question of what is at stake when we quote or allude to great writers, and indeed great men, of the past.

Commentary: Summers.
Further reading: Henderson 2004, Ker 2009a: 346–58, Del Giovane 2012, 2015a: 215–22, Rimell 2013, 2015a: ch. 4.

1 In ipsa ... uilla: the preposition signals a notable contrast with S's visit to the villa of Vatia, which he chose not to enter at 55.6 (highlighting the contrast between these two villas, Henderson 2004: 115–16 charts verbal parallels). Scipio's villa is located at Liternum (see §3). This letter thus returns us to Campania (featured in *Epp.* 49 and 51, as well as many letters in Book 6, including 55; see above on *Ep.* 53). According to Livy (38.52.1), Scipio retreated there in 184 BCE to avoid the prosecution threatened by the Petilli. Livy later (38.56.3-4) reports on his own visit to Scipio's estate (D'Arms 1970: 2, Bodel 1997).   **Scipionis Africani:** P. Cornelius Scipio Africanus (236–184/3 BCE, cos. 205, *RE* 336). Scipio's military exploits culminated in the defeat of Hannibal at the battle of Zama in 204 BCE, in recognition of which he received the triumphal *cognomen* Africanus. See Liv. 30.45 with Briscoe 2008 *ad loc.* S refers to Scipio in seven of the letters (Maso 1999: 69–70). Scipios in the plural (the family's many distinguished individuals also included Scipio Aemilianus, a protagonist in Cicero's *De republica*, on which see intro. above) are invoked at 24.10(n.) and 70.22(n.).   **iacens:** as Ker comments (2009a: 347), the term 'evokes the epitaphic *hic iacet* ("here lies") and establishes a fleeting resemblance between S and the deceased Scipio'. On this see further Henderson, who also notes (2004: 53, 93, 103) the resonance with a formula equally common in funerary epigraphy, *hic situs est*, used ironically of Vatia's living death at 55.4, and in celebration of Scipio himself in an epigram of Ennius (cited by Cic. *Leg.* 2.57 = 43* Blänsdorf 2011), quoted in §2n. on *beneficio meo*.   **haec ... scribo:** S rarely calls attention to where he is writing from, in marked contrast to Cicero's practice. While epistolary markers in the remainder of this letter are few, S does note in §16 that he is writing in the month of June.   **manibus:** the shade of a particular person (*OLD manes* 1c).   **ara:** cf. V. Max. 2.10.2, where the pirates at Scipio's villa venerate *postes ianuae tamquam religiosissimam aram sanctumque templum*. The parallel suggests that *ara* is the more likely reading here (Henderson 2004: 95 n. 4). Bodel (1997: 5 n. 2) prefers the reading *arca* (offered by the ninth-century MS ς) on the grounds that it 'better accords with the burial practice of the Cornelii Scipiones'.   **quam ... suspicor:** Livy's account acknowledges (38.56.1–4) a number of conflicting traditions surrounding Scipio's downfall, retirement, death and burial. Although noting the existence of a statue and monument in Rome, Livy records ('the sole instance of a claim to autopsy in Livy', as Briscoe 2008 comments *ad loc.*) that he himself had seen a *monumentum* and a statue at Liternum. S makes no explicit mention of the alternative tradition. Valerius Maximus (5.3.2b) reports Scipio's epitaph: *ingrata patria, ne ossa quidem mea habes.* According to an earlier passage in Livy (38.53.8 with Briscoe 2008), when he was dying Scipio requested that he be buried on his estate and that no funeral should take place in his ungrateful fatherland.   **animum quidem:** the post-mortem survival of the *animus* is the subject of Cic. *Rep.* 6.29 (words put in the mouth of Scipio Africanus, as he appears in his grandson's dream). The quasi-divine nature of Scipio in particular is celebrated at V. Max. 2.10.2, where the pirates make offerings to the living Africanus, *quae deorum immortalium numini consecrari solent.*   **in caelum ... redisse:** at Cic. *Rep.* 6.13 Scipio reassures his grandson: *omnibus, qui patriam conseruauerint, adiuuerint, auxerint, certum esse in caelo definitum locum.* He goes on to insist (6.26) that only the body is mortal. Also pertinent is the fragment of Cic. *Rep.* (fr. 2 Powell = Lactant. *Div. inst.* 1.18), quoted by S at 108.33, in which Cic. cites lines of Ennius concerning Africanus: *si fas endo plagas caelestum ascendere cuiquam est, | mi soli caeli maxima porta patet* (44* Blänsdorf 2011). Skutsch reads this as part of an epigram of which Cicero quotes the first lines at *Tusc.* 5.49. S offers a range of different positions on post-mortem survival of the spirit (Busch 2009). Close to 86.1 (and also influenced by the Platonising/ Pythagorean flavour of Cicero's *De republica*) are *Marc.* 26.7 and (though proposing a different model of transcendence) *Nat.* 1.pr.8–13 (Setaioli 2000: 296–9, Armisen-Marchetti 2007, Del Giovane 2012: 166–8). In 102.1–2, by contrast, belief in the immortality of the soul is dismissed as a beautiful dream. Some earlier Stoics took the view that the souls of the virtuous live on after death until the time of the great conflagration (e.g. Chrysippus *SVF* 1.522, 11.811).   **persuadeo mihi:** S signals that this is a personal, intuitive interpretation (Henderson 2004: 96, Del Giovane 2012: 164–6); cf. Cicero's Cato at *Sen.* 78 on the immortality of the soul, *sic persuasi mihi* (also 80, *Tusc.* 1.29, 1.24).   **non quia ... duxit:** military success may be achieved even by very flawed men, as the example of Cambyses demonstrates. In privileging Scipio's peacetime virtues over his martial achievements, S differs from Livy (though in the following letter, 87.9, S pursues a rather different line, equating Cato the Elder's great achievement in policing Roman morals with that of Scipio in fighting Rome's enemies). For the relative depreciation of military success, on which Roman culture had traditionally placed high value, cf. e.g. 113.30, where *imperare sibi* is a greater achievement than conquering new territories.   **Cambyses:** son of King Cyrus, ruled Persia 530–522 BCE.

Herodotus (3.25) describes his military campaigns, including victories in Egypt (hence *feliciter* here), but presents him as frenzied. S uses him as an example in *De ira* 3.20–1. See Setaioli 1988: 485–503.   **furiosus** 'a madman' (*OLD* 1b).   **furore . . . usus** 'having exploited his frenzy'.   **moderationem pietatemque:** *pietas* (along with *iustitia*) is one of the qualities enjoined on Scipio Aemilianus following his grandfather Scipio Africanus as model in Cic. *Rep.* 6.16. On the celebrated *moderatio* of Scipio see Liv. 38.56.11, V. Max. 4.1.6, 5.3.2b.   **reliquit patriam:** in this instance what might look like abandonment is deemed a greater deed even than Scipio's stupendous victory over Hannibal.   **Romae:** Rome is named on only six occasions in the entire series of letters, with three instances in *Ep.* 86, a letter set not in the city but at a distance from it (Henderson 2004: 159). As Ker (2009a: 350) comments, 'Scipio is never less absent from Rome than when in exile'. See further Edwards 2018b.   **libertate:** in Livy's account, Scipio's critics assert that, for *libertas* to be equally shared, it is crucial that even the most powerful are answerable (38.50.8 *aequandae libertatis*). For *libertas* in this sense see Arena 2012: 47–8. It is not germane to S's purpose to go into the particular political and legal background to this story, familiar from Livy's version (the charges against Scipio are detailed at Liv. 38.51.1–4, though for problems with Livy's account see Briscoe 2008: 170–9).

2 The speech S puts in Scipio's mouth is composed of short and simple assertions and injunctions.   **institutis** 'established customs' (*OLD* 2).   **aequum . . . ius:** in Livy's account (38.50.9), it is Scipio's critics who, in justifying their attack, assert that Scipio cannot endure *ius aequum* (on *ius aequum* see 90.6(n.)).   **beneficio meo:** as Ker notes (2009a: 348–9), this recalls Ennius' epitaph (as reconstructed by Turnebus) from which S quotes at 108.33, referring to the debt owed to Scipio: *hic situs est, cui nemo ciuis neque hostis | quibit pro factis reddere opis pretium* (= 43* Blänsdorf 2011), the first part of which is quoted at Cic. *Leg.* 2.57. On the epitaph see Walbank 1967: 57, Henderson 2004: 102.   **causa . . . argumentum:** the chiastic sentence, juxtaposing *fui* and *ero*, encapsulates Scipio's career.

3 quidni ego admirer: the defiant first-person pronoun draws attention to the parallel with S's own situation, following his effective withdrawal from Nero's court (Henderson 2004: 97, Ker 2009a: 346–7, 352). *admirer* evokes the admiration for Manius Curius Dentatus, provoked in Cato the Elder by the contemplation of the former's villa in Cic. *Sen.* 55 *admirari satis non possum uel hominis ipsius continentiam uel temporum disciplinam.*   **exilium uoluntarium:** Livy reports (39.52.9) that Scipio imposed a voluntary exile (*uoluntarium . . . exilium*) not only on himself but also on his own funeral. Valerius Maximus (5.3.2b) writes of *eiusque uoluntarii exilii acerbitatem*. As a colony, Liternum could not serve as an official place of exile. The conclusion of the previous letter (85.41) lists exile among universal objects of fear: *ubique horrenda*. Yet even as an exile, the wise man can live virtuously (85.40).   **exonerauit:** cf. Liv. 2.2.7 *exonera ciuitatem . . . metu*.   **locum dedit legibus:** Scipio's withdrawal from Rome serves to reinforce the authority of Roman law. Valerius Maximus (3.7.1f) stresses Scipio's concern for the law's spirit, rather than its letter.   **Liternum:** Scipio was famously the first Roman to build a villa in Campania (D'Arms 1970: 1–2, 9). Scipio's choice of Liternum (established as a Roman colony in 194 BCE) as his place of retirement is praised by S (51.11) as far preferable to neighbouring Baiae (the satirical target of that letter), whose soft pleasures, including baths, unmanned even Hannibal (51.5 *uirum eneruauerunt*, Ker 2009a: 345–6). Liternum by contrast was known for its lack of attractiveness (Liv. 22.16.1 *Literni harenas stagnaque*, cf. V. Max 5.3.2b *uici ignobilis . . . ac desertae paludis*).   **tam . . . Hannibalis** 'in order to put the republic in his debt for his own exile as much as that of Hannibal'. *imputare* + acc. 'to enter as a debt' (*OLD* 1a); *imputaturus*: fut. partic. expressing purpose (*NLS* §92). The Carthaginian leader, famously defeated by Scipio at Zama in 204 BCE, was subsequently driven into exile (Liv. 33.47–9, 39.52.8, Nep. *Han*. 7).

4 uidi: several times repeated in this letter (§§14, 16, 17 and twice in §20). The importance of autopsy is underlined by the alliteration with *uillam* (cf. 55.8; see Del Giovane 2012: 156).   **lapide quadrato** 'dressed stone'. The adjective sometimes has military overtones; cf. the image of the *quadrato agmine* proposed by Sextius in 59.7 (on whom see intro. to *Ep*. 64 above). The defensive potential of the villa comes to the fore in Valerius Maximus' account of the unsuccessful assault on it by the band of pirates (2.10.2b). See §1n. on *ara*.   **murum circumdatum siluae** 'a wall surrounding the wood'. Henderson (2004: 105) describes this as 'the Roman army camp's circumvallation turned inside-out'. Even the villas built near Baiae by the great generals of the late republic are like military camps, *castra*, S asserts (51.11), compared to those of his own contemporaries.   **propugnaculum** 'bulwark'.   **surrectas** 'raised up' (*OLD subrigo* 1a).   **cisternam:** Varro (*R*. 1.11.2) and Columella (1.5.2) both recommend cisterns to collect rainwater, for villas lacking a natural water supply.   **uiridibus** 'vegetation' (*OLD* 1b) anticipates the focus on cultivation in the final third of the letter.   **uel:** *OLD* 5a.   **exercitus:** the military aspect of S's villa is explicitly underlined.   **balneolum angustum:** Setaioli, in his discussion of colloquial features, notes (1980: 24) S's use of the diminutive alongside an adjective indicating smallness (cf. e.g. 77.8, *De ira* 3.22.4). Henderson (2004: 107) reads the bath of the freedman Trimalchio (Petr. 73.2 *balneum . . . angustum scilicet et cisternae frigidariae simile*, following Courtney's reading, 2001: 117–18) as an iconoclastic parody of that of Scipio (cf. Rimell 2013: 7). See §7(n.) *libertinorum*.   **antiqua:** note alliteration with *angustum* (as well as *angulo* in §5).

5 magna . . . uoluptas: the pleasure might seem to lie in the vivid evocation of the exemplary Scipio. Yet the emphasis on the confrontation between the virtuous habits of earlier times and the decadent ones of S's own day (in which S himself seems to be implicated; cf. *nostros*) gives this 'pleasure' a curiously painful dimension. For *uoluptas* in this 'everyday' rather than Stoic sense (S is perhaps here echoing Cic. *Sen.* 51 *uoluptates agricolarum*) see 59.1.   **contemplantem** 'examining', 'gazing at'. Cf. Cic. *Sen.* 55, where Cato describes himself in relation to Manius, *cuius quidem ego uillam contemplans*.   **mores Scipionis ac nostros:** already in the *Ad Heluiam* (10.10), S contrasted cosmopolitan luxury with the simple life of *maiores nostri* (which exile paradoxically allows one to emulate). This is a particular concern also of the following letter, 87.9–10, 41 (with Inwood); see also 47.14. On the limitations of the *maiores* as a model see below, intro. to *Ep.* 90.   **in hoc angulo:** repeated demonstrative pronouns have a deictic force which gives this description particular vividness (Ker 2009a: 350). Varro (*L.* 6.41) understands *angulus* as derived from *angustum* (used to characterise the *balneolum* in §4); see Maltby 1991: 36, Henderson 2004: 107. On the metaphorical force of the *angulus* as a place of withdrawal see Henderson 2004: 106–7, Rimell 2015a: ch. 4.   **'Carthaginis horror':** the quotation is underlined (*ille*) but not attributed (Henderson 2004: 100). The phrase occurs in Lucretius (3.1034), who may have taken it from Ennius (Henderson 2004: 102–3; cf. Freudenburg 2001: 82–92, noting Ennius' predilection for the verb *horrere*), as indeed may S himself. On S's relationship with Lucretius see Mazzoli 1970: 206–9. In Lucretius, the invocation of Scipio underlines the fact that even the most renowned of men, like the most humble, will one day have their remains consigned to earth (3.1034–5): *Scipiadas, belli fulmen, Carthaginis horror, | ossa dedit terrae proinde ac famul infimus esset*. The quotation in S (if from Lucretius rather than directly from Ennius) also implicitly evokes death and burial.   **quod . . . capta est:** by the Gauls in 396 (as recounted by Liv. 5.43–50) – but not, thanks to Scipio, by Hannibal.   **corpus laboribus rusticis fessum:** as Rimell (2013: 8–10) emphasises, Scipio's physical presence is vividly evoked; the reader can almost smell him (cf. §12).   **exercebat . . . opere se:** *se exercere* is used in the previous letter (85.39) of the *sapiens'* mental exercises (Del Giovane 2012: 161).   **ut mos fuit priscis:** the term *priscus* (which recurs at §12) is one favoured by Cicero but rarely used by S (though cf. 108.35).

Moralising texts often emphasise the interrelationship of prowess in warfare and hands-on agriculture as exemplified in the practice of early Roman heroes such as Quinctius Cincinnatus, called from the plough in 458 BCE to serve as dictator in a time of crisis (Liv. 3.26.8, Cic. *Sen.* 55–6; cf. Sen. *Ep.* 51.10), as well as Manius, admired by Cicero's Cato. See, too, Xen. *Oec.* 4.20–5, reporting that King Cyrus regularly broke a sweat planting trees in his garden (on this cluster of concerns see Woodman 2014 on Tac. *Ag.* 1.1). We might also note the words spoken by Alfius in Hor. *Epod.* 2.1–3 (*Beatus ille qui procul negotiis | ut prisca gens mortalium | paterna rura bobus exercet suis*), rehearsing the clichés of wistful rustic fantasising by modern urbanites. Fowler (2000: 272–3) compares this epode's ironic conclusion with S's approach in the *EM*.   **subigebat:** a term for working the land frequently used in agricultural treatises; cf. e.g. Cato, *Agr.* 45.1 on preparing the ground for cuttings (*locus bipalio subactus siet*), Virg. *G.* 1.125. The kind of work entailed here is fleshed out in the account of Aegialus' activities (§§14–21).   **sordido** 'humble' (*OLD* 4); cf. 18.7 *panis durus ac sordidus*.

6 A bitingly satirical characterisation of the aficionados of luxury, drawing on a rich tradition of invective against luxurious private building (e.g. Sen. *Con.* 2.1.13, Plin. *Nat.* 36.1–3); S is similarly critical of marble use at 115.8–9, *Ben.* 4.6.2 (Pensabene Perez 2000). On the use of marble in Roman buildings see Schneider 1986: 139–60, Gnoli 1988.   **sordidus:** here in a more emphatically pejorative sense, focalised through one anxious that he may be falling behind his peers in sophistication and splendour.   **nisi . . . nisi . . . nisi . . . nisi:** anaphora piles up the oppressive weight of luxurious features.   **orbibus** 'mirrors' (as suggested at *OLD* 2g), perhaps, though possibly marble discs (for which cf. Juv. 11.175; Stat. *Silv.* 2.2.87–8 praises *ubi marmore picto | candida purpureo distinguitur area gyro*).   **Alexandrina marmora:** Gnoli (1988: 10) interprets these as marbles and alabasters quarried in Egypt and shipped from Alexandria (cf. 115.8).   **Numidicis crustis distincta** 'picked out with inlays of Numidian marble'. Also referred to as 'giallo antico', this marble is distinctively tawny in colour (Gnoli 1988: 166–8). Its use features at Plin. *Nat.* 5.22, Suet. *Jul.* 85.   **undique . . . praetexitur** 'elaborate and patterned borders are everywhere applied'. *circumlitio* 'paint' or similar substance. For *uariatio* as a feature of luxurious interiors see Purcell 1987. Cf. 100.6 *uarietas marmorum*, Stat. *Silv.* 1.5.35–6 *uario fastigia uitro* and 1.5.42; Pliny (*Ep.* 2.17.3) celebrates a less ostentatious kind of variety in his Laurentine villa.   **absconditur** 'is sheltered' (*OLD* 1b).   **Thasius lapis:** fine white marble from the Aegean island of Thasos. See Plin. *Nat.* 36.44, Gnoli 1988: 262–3. In Statius' *Siluae*, it is explicitly excluded from the hyper-refined baths of Claudius Etruscus (1.5.34–5) but features in the luxurious villa of Felix Pollio (2.2.92). See also Cic. *Pis.* 89, Vitr. 10.2.15.   **quondam ... templo:** for a similar complaint about precious materials, once reserved for sacred contexts, now used for private luxury, cf. Plin. *Nat.* 36.44. Moralists sometimes claim that luxury from the east first infected Rome via public buildings such as temples (see e.g. Vell. 1.11.3–5, 2.1.1-2, Plin. *Nat.* 33.13–15, 36.5), thereafter spreading more perniciously to private use (see Nichols 2017: ch. 3).   **nostras:** S slides from third person singular to first person plural, implicating himself and his readers in the desire for luxury.   **exsaniata** 'thoroughly cleansed'. Cf. *Helv.* 3.1.   **argentea epitonia:** for silver taps as a positive feature of luxury baths cf. Stat. *Silv.* 1.5.48–50.

7 plebeias 'of ordinary people', a sarcastic comment in relation to the luxury just described. We might note that in praising the baths of Claudius Etruscus (the son of an imperial freedman), Statius (*Silv.* 1.5.47) comments, *nil ibi plebeium.*   **fistulas** 'water pipes' (*OLD* 1a).   **libertinorum:** unexpected as the point of contrast with *plebeias* (whose standard antonym would be patrician). S is critical of the pretensions of wealthy freedmen, e.g. 27.5 *Caluisius Sabinus . . . et patrimonium habebat libertini et ingenium* (see Mouritsen 2011: esp. 113–14. Elsewhere, however, at 44.6, S invites L to consider that, even if he were a freedman, he might come to be the only free man among the *ingenui*; cf. 47.15–16, where S stresses that slaves, and therefore implicitly freedmen, too, may have as much capacity for virtue as anyone else). His disapproval relates not only to the alleged excesses of their establishments but also to the inappropriateness of such luxury in the case of those who had been of slave status (cf. Cic. *Leg.* 3.30–1, arguing that, while a grand villa may be appropriate to Lucullus, it is not right for his freedman neighbour to emulate him, Plin. *Nat.* 33.134, Edwards 1993: 150–60). The vividly realised freedman Trimalchio, whose grotesquely lavish dinner party features in Petronius' *Satyricon*, is merely the most flagrant example of a stereotype, as Mouritsen (2011: 115) notes. See §4n. on *balneolum angustum* for a suggestive parallel.   **nihil sustinentium:** in §5 a humble floor bore (*sustinuit*) Scipio, while S complains that none of his own contemporaries can bear (*sustineat*) to bathe in the old-fashioned way. For the concern about deceptive decorative features cf. Vitr. 7.5.4, Papirius Fabianus *ap.* Sen. *Con.* 2.1.13, Edwards 1993: 137–43, Nichols 2010 and 2017: ch. 4. See, too, Pliny the Elder's complaints (*Nat.* 36.59–60) about the thirty luxurious pillars of onyx in the house of Claudius' freedman, Callistus.   **impensae causa:** for the criticism of spending money as an end in itself cf. 122.14. Statius, by contrast, praises Polla (*Silv.* 2.2.151–4) for wisely putting her wealth on display (*expositi census*) in her splendid, marble-encrusted villa, rather than hoarding it in secret.   **ut nisi gemmas calcare nolimus:** S shifts back from his attack on freedmen, reverting to the first person plural, once more implicating himself and his reader in the seductions of luxury. **gemmas:** i.e. precious materials generally (rather than gemstones), which would include coloured marbles (cf. Stat. *Silv.* 1.5.12–13 *nitidis . . . gemmantia saxis | balnea*). At 16.8, S conjures up the lifestyle of the wealthy who may *calcare diuitias*. Cf. Lucan's description of Cleopatra's palace in which (10.117) *calcabatur onyx*.

8 S now launches into a second, amplified, exposition of the contrast between Scipio's bathing practice and that of his own contemporaries.   **rimae** 'slits'. In Petronius (26.4, 92.2) these are associated with voyeurism (Rimell 2013: 7).   **sine iniuria munimenti** 'without damage to the building's defences'.   **blattaria** 'dark crannies', from *blatta* 'moth'.   **ut totius diei . . . recipiant:** Statius praises this feature of Claudius Etruscus' baths at *Silv.* 1.5.45–6 *multus ubique dies, radiis ubi culmina totis | perforat*. For the concern of villa builders with light and aspect cf. 55.6 on Vatia's grottoes (as well as Vitr. 6.1.2, Plin. *Nat.* 18.33, Plin. *Ep.* 2.17.6, Sen. *Con.* 5.5; on aspect in relation to baths see Yegül 1992: 382–3).   **colorantur** 'they get a tan' (*OLD* 3). A tan derived from working outdoors rather than indolently lingering in the baths would be praiseworthy. Conversely, 122.4–6 criticises those pale from pursuing their luxurious lives by night (individuals who look down on the ways of *patres familiae rustici*).   **solio** 'bath tub' (*OLD* 3).   **agros ac maria prospiciunt:** such views are prized as a feature at Vitr. 6.4, Plin. *Ep.* 5.6.7–16, Stat. *Silv.* 2.2.74–82. See Purcell 1987: 196–200.   **in antiquorum numerum:** the term *antiquus* (used in §4 to refer to the reassuringly distant and virtuous past) is here relativised. For the endlessly shifting standards of luxury cf. Plin. *Nat.* 36.109–10.   **aliquid noui:** for luxury's reprehensible impulsion towards the new cf. 122.14, 17 (with Ker 2004).   **commenta est** 'has devised', usually with negative overtones (*OLD comminiscor* 1a); cf. 14.5, 78.23, 90.14, 23. As Mantovanelli (2001) notes, S regularly uses this term of novel vices.   **obrueret** 'overwhelm' (*OLD* 6), often used in the sense of bury (*OLD* 2). S assimilates a life of luxury to death; cf. 55.4, 60.3–4, 122.2–3, Henderson 2004, Ker 2004, Edwards 2007: 172–6.

9 quadrantaria: adj. from *quadrans*, coin of the value of quarter of an as, often used as token of minimal value (cf. 'farthing'), here presumably referring to the entrance fee to the baths.   **nec referre . . . deponerent** 'they did not consider it mattered whether the water, in which they were to deposit their dirt, was crystal clear'. The subject is 'the men of old'. *si aqua esset* is to be understood with *pellucida*. The point is reinforced by the juxtaposition of *pellucida* and *sordes* (here *sordes* in a literal sense, *OLD* 1a, as opposed to the figurative *sordidus* of §6). Statius (*Silv.* 1.5.52) praises the abundant clear water in the baths of Claudius Etruscus.

10 quam iuuat: cf. §5 *magna . . . me uoluptas.* This wholesome spiritual pleasure, prompted by the humble spot where Scipio bathed, is in marked contrast to the enervating corporeal pleasures associated with the lavish baths of S's contemporaries.   **obscura:** the darkness of the small bathhouse is an index of its virtue (Ker 2004), though in different circumstances, as Ker notes, S invokes living in darkness as a symptom of perversity (cf. e.g. 122.3–4).   **gregali** 'ordinary' (*OLD* 3a).   **inducta** 'covered' (*OLD* 16b).   **quae scires** 'of the kind which you know'.   **Catonem:** presumably Cato the Elder (*RE* 9, 234–149 BCE), on whom see intro. above.   **aedilem:** it is in the capacity of aedile (the magistrate responsible for the maintenance of public buildings, a position usually held early in one's senatorial career) that all of these individuals are imagined carrying out their inspections (cf. *VB* 7.3, also figuring aediles as guardians of morality). Henderson (2004: 114) notes the traditional etymology of the title, as it appears in Festus (Paulus *ap.* Fest. 13: '*aedilis' initio dictus est magistratus quia aedium non tantum sacrarum, sed etiam priuatarum curam gerebat*; cf. Maltby 1991: 10).   **Fabium Maximum:** presumably Q. Fabius Maximus Cunctator (*RE* 116, cos. 233 BCE), whose successes against the Carthaginians (also celebrated by Ennius, 370 Vahlens) laid the foundations for Scipio's victory at Zama. Valerius Maximus praises Fabius' *moderatio* at 4.1.5 immediately before his treatment of Scipio.   **ex Corneliis aliquem:** Scipio himself was a member of the Cornelian *gens*, one of the most prominent in Rome.   **manu sua:** magistrates of that era, S suggests, did not shrink from carrying out their duties with their own hands (just as they did not shrink from getting their hands dirty working their estates).   **temperasse** 'had regulated', in relation to temperature (*OLD* 5b).   **nobilissimi:** here in the sense of very well born (*OLD* 5b), though Cato at least was a *nouus homo*; the emphasis is on their dutiful willingness nevertheless to inspect the bathhouses used by the common people.   **utilem . . . temperaturam:** S repeatedly expresses his disapproval of very hot baths (51.6), preferring himself to bathe in cold water (see 53.3(n.) *uetus frigidae cultor*).   **quae nuper inuenta est** 'which has recently become the fashion'.   **adeo quidem . . . oportet** 'so much so indeed that a slave convicted of some crime ought to be made to wash alive'. *lauari* here, hinting at the idea of being boiled alive, aligns taking a bath with the physical torments commonly inflicted on slaves found guilty of a crime (on slave punishments see Bradley 1987: 113–37, Saller 1991, Hopkins 1993: 7–10). S elsewhere criticises masters who inflict extreme punishments on their slaves in anger (*De ira* 3.40).

11 rusticitatis: the term might connote the virtues of old-fashioned country life (*OLD* 3b) from S's point of view, but *damnant* makes clear the perspective here is that of the lovers of luxury, for whom it signifies reprehensible lack of sophistication (*OLD* 3a; cf. 90.19, Ov. *Ars* 3.128).   **specularibus:** the n. pl. form of the adj. *specularis*, meaning windows of transparent stone (often forms of mica or gypsum), on which see Plin. *Nat.* 36.160–2; cf. 90.25, *Prov.* 4.9, Plin. *Ep.* 2.17.21. On Roman use of windows see Verità 1999.   **decoquebatur** 'stewed' (*OLD* 2b); cf. 108.16 *decoquere corpus atque exsanire sudoribus*. See Gowers 1994.   **concoqueret** 'digest', *sc.* 'his dinner'. Traditionally a bath was taken before rather than after dinner. At 122.6, S lists among the offences of those in quest of novel luxuries the practice of bathing after drinking. The fashionable voluptuary of Pers. 3 dies in the bath after feasting (3.98 *turgidus hic epulis*). Trimalchio's topsy-turvy dinner party includes, following a profusion of elaborate dishes, an intermission in the bath (which, as noted above, bears an odd similarity to that of Scipio): Petr. 72 *coniciamus nos in balneum.*   **o hominem calamitosum!** exclamation and exaggeration characterise the protests of the advocates of luxury.   **nesciit uiuere:** at 55.3, S imagines (and protests at) praise of Vatia's life of idle withdrawal in similar terms: *'o Vatia, solus scis uiuere'*. At 122.3 he criticises those who sleep late: 'Surely you do not think they know how to live (*scire quemadmodum uiuendum*) when they do not know when?'   **saccata** 'filtered' (through a bag).   **lutulenta:** this relatively rare term is used by Horace (*S.* 1.4.11 *flueret lutulentus*) to characterise pejoratively the writing of his archaic predecessor, the satirist Lucilius; Del Giovane (2015a: 222) explores its possible metaliterary resonances in *Ep.* 86. For Rimell (2013: 2) the satirist 'subliminally "partners" S's homonymous interlocutor' (cf. Gowers 2011). The distinctively Horatian adjective anticipates the collection's first reference to Horace and first quotation from his *Satires* at §13.   **sudorem:** for the link between masculinity and the right kind of sweat see 31.7 '... *non est uiri timere sudorem'*. At 51.6, attacking (more briefly) the fashion for sweating rooms in baths, S asserts, *omnis sudor per laborem exeat*; sweat should only be generated, as in Scipio's case, through physical work.   **unguentum:** for S and other moralising writers the use of perfumed oils is synonymous with luxury and decadence; cf. 51.10 *in primo deficit puluere ille unctus et nitidus*, 122.3, *VB* 7.3 *uoluptatem ... unguento madentem*, *Ben.* 7.25.1, Petr. 47.1, Suet. *Nero* 31.2.

12 S sarcastically imagines the terms in which his contemporaries might criticise Scipio.   **quas ... credis?** 'What comments do you think certain people will make at this?'   **lauabatur:** cf. *Nat.* 1.17.7 *cum antiqui illi uiri incondite uiuerent, satis nitidi si squalorem opera collectum aduerso lumine eluerent.*   **si scias** 'if you knew'; *si scias* is used quite often after *immo* (e.g. Pl.

Ps. 749, Ter. *Eu.* 355). **ut ... tradiderunt:** a fragment of the antiquarian Varro's treatise on education *Catus* (cited by Nonius 108 Mueller = 155 Lindsay, s.v. *ephippium*) reports that in earlier times boys only owned one tunic and did not have *balneum cotidianum*. The statement may have been attributed to Cato the Elder (Fagan 1999: 47). **nundinis** 'on market days' (i.e. once every eight days), with 'only' understood. **quid ... oluisse?** S goads his urbane critic to comment on Scipio's smell. **militiam, laborem, uirum:** S pre-empts his critic's response with an acclamation of the traditional Roman ideal; military service and agricultural labour complement one another, together forging a true man (cf., of the Romans of old, 51.10 *nullum laborem recusant manus, quae ad arma ab aratro transferuntur*). Presenting it in olfactory terms, S revivifies this well-worn image. For Scipio as a model of antique virility even when dancing see *Tranq.* 17.4 *corpus mouebat ad numeros ... ut antiqui uiri solebant inter lusum ac festa tempora uirilem in modum tripudiare*. **munda balnea ... spurciores:** cf. Sen. *Con.* 1.pr 8 attacking the luxurious behaviour of his own contemporaries. For the opposite paradox see 70.21(n.) *spurcissimam ... mundissimae*.

13 infamem 'disgraceful' (*OLD* 3). **Horatius Flaccus:** S knows Horace's works well but the use of *nomen* and *cognomen* here contrasts with §15 *Vergilius noster* (Mazzoli 1970: 235). **pastillos Buccillus olet:** internal limiting accusative with *olet*, the *pastillos* (dimin. of *panis* 'bread') are to freshen breath (see Gowers 2012 *ad* Hor. *S.* 1.2.27). The phrase adapts the first part of Hor. *S.* 1.2.27 *pastillos Rufillus olet, Gargonius hircum*, a line which Horace himself repeats at 1.4.92, summing up his own practice; it thus, in Henderson's words, 'stands as a one-line essence of Horatian satire' (2004: 17). The name Rufillus is misquoted as Buccillus, evoking the *bucca*, loud-mouth or puffed cheek, associated with satire (Hor. *S.* 1.1.20–1, Henderson 2004: 117). Though Horace is implicitly present often in the letters (see e.g., engaging with Horace's *Odes, Epp.* 12 and 18(nn.)), only the *Satires* are quoted, here and on two other occasions, *Ep.* 119.13–14 (Hor. *S.* 1.2.114–16) and *Ep.* 120.20–1 (Hor. *S.* 1.3.11–17), each time with Horace named. See Mazzoli 1970: 233–8, Berthet 1979, Edwards 2017a. **dares** 'if you were to produce'. **proinde ac esset si hircum oleret** 'it would be as if he reeked of goat', thus taking on the role of the uncouth comparator occupied in the original Horace line by Gargonius (see above). Scipio himself may smell strongly but S underlines his virile dignity in contrast to the animal stink of the would-be man of fashion. **parum est** 'it's not enough'. **ne euanescat:** on the volatility of perfume see Plin. *Nat.* 13.7, 18.150. **tamquam suo gloriantur:** in contrast to the smell of the virile sweat produced by Scipio's own body.

14 tristia 'austere' (*OLD* 4a). We are given the rather disconcerting sense that S, in the spirit of his old-fashioned surroundings, has, with his diatribe against the bathing habits of his contemporaries, been impersonating moralists of earlier times, such as Cato the Elder. There may be an element of humour in this bracing tirade (in contrast to the solemn words of Scipio in Cicero's *De republica*), which resembles the speech of Appius, reprimanding the scandalous behaviour of his descendant Clodia, at Cic. *Cael.* 33–4. Cicero comments of Appius: *aliquis mihi ab inferis excitandus est ex barbatis illis . . . [barba] illa horrida, quam in statuis antiquis atque imaginibus uidemus* (33). According to Quint. *Inst.* 12.10.61 this was a textbook example of how to evoke the voices of dead (cf. Lausberg 1998: §§820–5). Cicero, with regard to Caelius' case, asks (33.2) whether he should advise in an old-fashioned manner *seuere et grauiter et prisce* or instead *remisse et leniter et urbane* (see Geffcken 1973: 18–19 on the comic elements). For *tristis* in a similar context see the words put in the mouth of the bon viveur at 123.11, disdaining the views of '*istos tristes et superciliosos alienae uitae censores*'. **uillae imputabis:** cf. §3 *imputaturus*. **didici:** cf. §14 *discere*. S, despite his years, often presents himself in the role of student, usually in a philosophical context (cf. e.g. 26.7, 27.1, 76.1–5). **Aegialo:** Pliny (*Nat.* 14.49) makes clear he was well known for his expertise: *magna fama et Vetuleno Aegialo, perinde libertino, fuit Campania rure Liternino, maiorque etiam fauore hominum, quoniam ipsum Africani colebat exilium.* Unsurprisingly (given his comments about freedmen in §7), S does not mention that Aegialus himself is a *libertinus*. See Henderson 2004: 160–3. **patre familiae:** the *diligens paterfamilias* is a central figure in Col. 1.1.3, 1.2, 1.8.18. See also *Ep.* 64.7–8(nn.), where S uses the *pater familias* as an explicit analogy for the philosopher who contributes to an inheritance, which is to be further amplified by future generations. **agri possessor:** Aegialus now occupies the estate. **quamuis . . . transferri** 'a tree can be transplanted no matter how old'. Cf. Cato, *Agr.* 49 (quoted in the intro. above). We might note that the old Corycian, whose fecund plot is celebrated in Virg. *G.* 4, also plants out mature trees (4.144–7). **nobis senibus:** here, as often elsewhere (see e.g. 12.1–6 and intro. to that letter), S draws attention to his own advanced age. *nobis* does not include Lucilius here; the age difference between them is implicitly stressed in the following sentence. **nemo non oliuetum alteri ponit:** as olive trees are slow to mature, an old man who plants them does so for the benefit only of his successors (cf. Cic. *Sen.* 24, citing a comedy of Caecilius). It is not evident why this would make the transplanting of old trees particularly pertinent. Pliny reports that Scipio's estate at Liternum boasted an olive tree planted by Scipio Africanus himself, as well as a spectacular myrtle, underneath which was a cave where a snake guarded Scipio's *manes* (*Nat.* 16.234). Given his emphasis on Scipio's agricultural labours, it is curious that S does not explicitly include a reference to this (Henderson 2004: 165–6). †quod . . . deponere†: the text is corrupt in the latter part of this sentence and scholars have struggled to come up with a reading which makes sense in the context. The general sense required is conveyed by Graver and Long: 'I've seen such a grove produce acceptable fruit in abundance in its third or fourth season.' At 34.1 S, delighted at L's intellectual progress, invokes as an analogy the feelings of a farmer whom *arbor ad fructum perducta delectat.*

15 te quoque proteget: Lucilius, as S's younger pupil, is imagined benefitting from a slow-growing tree planted by his older teacher. The figurative force of the apparently digressive discussion of arboriculture is underlined, as the letter's final analogy between the teacher–pupil relationship in farming and in philosophy is here anticipated (Henderson 2004: 121–2).   **tarda . . . umbram:** Virg. *G.* 2.58. Virgil's words, referring in the *Georgics* to trees which grow from seed, here serve a significantly different end, reinforcing S's point about planting olive trees for later generations; a few lines earlier (*G.* 2.49–52), Virgil stresses the benefits, for the fertility of trees, of grafting and transplanting, S's focus in §§17–21.   **Vergilius noster:** on S's use of Virgil in general see *Ep.* 21(nn.). On the significance of the didactic *Georgics* in the letters, 86 in particular, see Henderson 2004: 50–2, 129–38.   **decentissime** 'most gracefully'.   **nec agricolas . . . delectare:** Virgil's *Georgics* explicitly refers to its addressees as *agricolae* (2.35–6). Modern scholars usually see this as a fiction and S's judgement as unmasking Virgil's purpose (Thibodeau 2011: 18). Pliny (e.g. *Nat.* 18.120) and Columella (e.g. 2.10.11, 2.21.2), however, both defer to Virgil as an agricultural authority (Mazzoli 1970: 221–2). Thibodeau (2011: ch. 2) stresses the ambiguity of the addressee in Virgil's poem. Since no reference is made to the slave overseer (the *uilicus*, who plays a key role in Cato's *De agricultura*), the master's apparent engagement in manual labour is perhaps rather an instance of 'masterly extensibility' (see Reay 2005: 333–5 in relation to Cato the Elder's references to his own agricultural labour). How much manual labour, we might ask, was really undertaken by Scipio – or indeed S himself? On the lack of concern with truth among poets, S makes more explicitly critical comments, again referring to *decus*, at *Ben.* 1.3.10 *poetae non putant ad rem pertinere uerum dicere, sed aut necessitate coacti aut decore corrupti id quemque uocari iubent, quod belle facit ad uersum.*

16 ut . . . transeam: S's *praeteritio* implies there are many other such instances in the *Georgics*. Are we to contrast Virgil's alleged lack of interest in the 'truth' of agriculture with S's own expertise?   **quod . . . deprehendere** 'something I could not help noticing today'. S suggests that he is currently (re)reading the *Georgics*, a text from which he quotes sixteen times in the *EM* (first at 58.2, and three times in *Ep.* 90, §§9, 11 and 37, on which see below; see Henderson's table, 2004: 51–2).   **uere... cura:** Virg. *G.* 1.215–16. Henderson (2004: 133–4), noting the context of the Virgilian passage (in the course of instructions on synchronising ploughing and sowing with the stellar calendar), comments that S 'grossly misrepresents Virgil'. As Pliny (*Nat.* 18.120) more forgivingly suggests, Virgil's advice might better apply in the Po valley than in regions further south (on Pliny's and Columella's engagement with Virgil as an agricultural authority see Doody 2007).   **sulci** 'furrows' (*OLD* 1a).   **an... licet:** S poses two questions: are both these plants (beans and millet) to be sown at once? Should this be in the spring? Other ancient agricultural authorities offer more deferential qualifications to Virgil's advice. Columella (2.9.17–18) proposes sowing millet in the spring and suggests that, while beans are sown in autumn, under some conditions it may be better to sow them on a six-monthly cycle (2.10.8–9, 2.7.2); cf. Plin. *Nat.* 18.120, Henderson 2004: 135–8.   **Iunius... Iulium:** S rarely gives any indication of date or season in his letters (23.1; though cf. 18.1, 67.1), much to the frustration of modern scholars (see main intro. section 2). Virgil's *Georgics*, though composed fifteen years after Caesar's calendar reform (at which point months were reliably synched with seasons, as had not been the case earlier), makes no reference to months of the year (Feeney 2007: 206–8).   **procliuis** 'verging on'.   **eodem die:** another temporal marker, this time fixing S's observation of agricultural practice.   **uidi:** S's autopsy trumps the poetic authority of Virgil.

17 reuertar: following the digression on Virgil. S's explanation of the processes for transplanting trees goes into what looks like great technical detail.   **duobus modis:** S describes two approaches undertaken by Aegialus, one used for larger trees (the trunk, its roots and branches drastically cut back, is planted in a hole), the other (described in §19) for substantial branches, which do not require cutting back but are otherwise planted in the same way. Henderson (2004: 157) suggests that we may see the two approaches as offering analogies for S himself (the older tree) and his addressee Lucilius (the substantial branch, which takes longer to produce a crop).   **ad unum... pedem** 'to the length of one foot'.   **transtulit:** although he is not referred to by name again until the final sentence of the letter, Aegialus is the subject of a long string of active verbs.   **rapo** 'underground stock'.   **amputatis radicibus:** contrast Cato's advice at *Agr.* 28.1. On the violence of the procedure advocated here by S and its figurative force see Henderson 2004: 124–5.   **capite** 'central boss'.   **fimo** 'dung'. This procedure is also recommended by Cato, *Agr.* 28.2 *arbores... praecisas serito oblinitoque fimo summas*, while (at

Cic. *Sen.* 54) the character Cato also asserts the importance of manure, noting its omission by Hesiod. The strong rustic smell hinted at here resonates with S's celebration of the smell of Scipio's sweat in §12 (Rimell 2013: 12).   **scrobem** 'a hole in the ground', usually for planting; cf. Cato, *Agr.* 28.1 (also on olive trees), Virg. *G.* 2.50.   **calcauit:** this productive trampling of the earth (also recommended in relation to olive trees by Cato, *Agr.* 28.1, *calcato*) contrasts with §7 *gemmas calcare*.

18 ut ait: S reminds us that the lesson comes from Aegialus.   **pisatione** 'pounding'. The MS readings are problematic but the emphasis laid by the structure of the sentence on the word justifies Reynolds' preference for this unusual noun, derived from *pi(n)sere*.   **uidelicet** 'plainly' (*OLD* 2a).   **excludit:** subject *pisatio* understood.   **quas ... agitatio** 'which, while they are still pliable and only just grasping the earth, even a light disturbance would certainly rip out'. Semi-dependent jussive subj. *reuellat*, following *necesse est* (*NLS* §123.4 n. ii).   **radit:** another violent action.   **uestietur:** by foliage. Cf. Col. 3.10.11.   **nec magna pars ... arida et retorrida erit** 'nor will there be a large dry and withered section, as happens in old olive groves'. Cf. the superannuated trees on S's own estate, whose condition is lamented at 12.2 '*quam nodosi sunt et retorridi rami, quam tristes et squalidi trunci!*'

19 ramos fortes: the second method involves planting substantial branches (an approach discussed in similar terms in Cato, *Agr.* 45, 61.2, passages which Pliny, *Nat.* 19.124–5, cites in his own discussion of the topic).   **planta** 'cutting' (*OLD planta*² a), as in Virg. *G.* 2.23–4 *hic plantas tenero abscindens de corpore matrum | deposuit sulcis* (cf. 2.299–300, Cic. *Sen.* 52). Cf. with a figurative sense *Ep.* 2.3 *non conualescit planta, quae saepe transfertur* (though *OLD* translates *planta* here as a seedling rather than a cutting).   **abhorridum** 'repellent'.   **triste:** cf. §14 *tristia*. Should we infer that S's fresh and lithe philosophical writings are equally to be contrasted with the old-style ranting he performed in the earlier part of the letter?

20 If the lesson on olive trees came from Aegialus, S himself, known for his success in viticulture, is the authority on vines. See 112.2 *nostrum artificium* invoked as an analogy, while at *Nat.* 3.7.1, he pictures himself in retirement as *uinearum diligens fossor*. Columella (3.3.3) reports that S engaged in very profitable vine-growing on his estate at Nomentum, another facet of his *ingenium* and *doctrina* (Ker 2006: 24–5).   **etiamnunc** 'too'.   **arbusto:** here a plantation of trees on which vines were trained (*OLD* 2). For vines trained on trees cf. Plin. *Nat.* 17.207, 17.19, Cato, *Agr.* 1.7, Var. *R.* 1.4.2, Liv. 22.15.1.   **capillamenta** 'root hairs';

cf. Plin. *Nat.* 19.33. **Martio exacto** 'at the end of March'. **non suas ulmos:** i.e. different elms from those on which they were originally trained. Cf. Virg. *G.* 2.81–2 *arbos | miratur . . . nouas frondes et non sua poma* (where *non sua poma* are the fruit of slips from more fertile trees which have been grafted onto the original *arbos*); the final word of the following line, 2.83, is *ulmis*. The use of elms as support for vines is touched on at *G.* 2.221, 367–8.

21 grandiscapiae 'having a big trunk' (from *scapus*), a term not found elsewhere. **ait:** again Aegialus is deferred to as expert. **aqua . . . cisternina** looks back to the cistern ample enough for an army, which S noted in §4 as a feature of Scipio's villa. **pluuiam:** cf. the muddy water in which Scipio bathed in §11, *cum plueret uehementius* (Henderson 2004: 140–1). **ne . . . mihi:** the final sentence articulates a playful rivalry between S and his pupil Lucilius, while posing S as potentially in competition with Aegialus.

LETTER 90

Ep. 90 explores the scope of philosophy and its role in history, complementing 89, the opening letter of Book 14, in which S offered an account of philosophy's constitutive parts (apparently in a response to a request from L, 89.2). In particular, *Ep.* 90 tackles the question of why philosophy, rather than being inborn, must be learned. S offers a distinctive account of the development of human society, celebrating the simple way of life of the earliest generations but going on to make clear that these primitive individuals did not have the benefit of true philosophy. S takes issue at length with the Stoic Posidonius' claims about the role of philosophy in the development of technology. Technological advance, S argues, has always been in the service of luxury and avarice. Philosophy, however, is exclusively concerned with higher things. Since true virtue, S asserts, can only be achieved through arduous struggle and long reflection, there were no philosophers in the days when human life was simple and primitive.

The letter opens (§§1–2) with a distinction between living and, through the help of philosophy, living well, underlining that, while everyone has the capacity for philosophy, no one is born a philosopher. S briefly sets out (§3) philosophy's true nature and scope. In particular philosophy's teaching makes secure the social cohesion which, without it, is always liable to be subverted by corruption. S offers an initial summary of Posidonius' account of the history of human development in two stages, a 'golden age' (§§4–5), when people were uncorrupted by avarice and luxury and submitted to the leadership of the best men, followed by a decline into more troubled times with the advent of vice (§6). While S agrees with some features of Posidonius' account, the lengthy central section of the letter (§§7–35) disputes Posidonius' contention that philosophers invented various arts and crafts: architecture (§8), tool-making (§10), working metal and mining (§12), weaving (§20), ploughing (§21), baking bread (§§22-3), ship-making (§24) and the potter's wheel (§31), before withdrawing from such activities at a later stage (§30). S argues that Diogenes is more to be admired than Daedalus (§14); nature provides enough for human needs (§§16–18), while crafts pander to luxury (§19). These arts and crafts, S contends (§24), are the product of reason but not right reason (i.e. philosophy). Philosophy is concerned only with understanding the truth of nature, with grasping the divine, the soul and morality (§§27–8), as well as logic (§29). Thus the proper concerns of the philosopher (§§34–5) are the study of the heavens, natural law, the divine and morality. As Armisen-Marchetti (1998: 201) underlines, the section of the letter discussing natural *consortium* among humans and the lengthy polemic against Posidonius which follows together form a substantial digression, which serves as S's response to an implicit objection on the part of the reader to S's initial assertion that philosophy is not inborn but must be acquired: what about the golden age? The final section of the letter (§§36–46) returns to the fortunate circumstances of primitive man (§§36–8, 40–3), later subverted by the advent of vice (§§38–9) in order to make clear (§§44–6) that this pleasant and simple life did not allow scope for true (i.e. Stoic) philosophy, since nature does not make a gift of virtue itself – that is something which must be striven for.

Ep. 90 has attracted much attention but this has often focused on attempts to reconstruct from S's argument the views both of Posidonius and of earlier Stoic thinkers (Blankert, Boys-Stones 2001, Nikolaides 2002, Zago 2012: esp. chs. 1 and 2, Van Nuffelen and Van Hoof 2013). Posidonius (*c.* 135–*c.* 51/50 BCE) was a hugely influential Stoic philosopher and historian, who played a key role in modifying third-century Stoicism and in transmitting Stoic philosophy to a Roman audience; his writings have survived only in fragmentary form. S has particular sympathy with Posidonius on some issues, referring to him in very positive terms at e.g. 104.22–3, where he is named alongside Chrysippus as an authority on matters human and divine (S is more critical of the arguments discussed at 87.33–7; see Inwood *ad loc.* and, on S's engagement with Posidonius more generally, Setaioli 1988: 316–57). S is usually understood to be endorsing the theories of earlier Stoics (Frede 1989: 2088–9, Boys-Stones 2001: 18–22) when he challenges the claims of Posidonius in *Ep.* 90 (though for a different view see Van Nuffelen and Van Hoof 2013). Kidd's commentary (1988) on the relevant sections (§§5–13, 20–5, 30–2) of *Ep.* 90 (= Posidonius F284) offers a judicious analysis of the extent to which S may be misrepresenting Posidonius.

The account of the so-called 'golden age', which S attributes to Posidonius (§§4–7), focuses on government (other fragments of Posidonius' work also suggest a strong interest in the relationship between ruler and ruled, Kidd 1999: 27). According to S, Posidonius characterised the earliest phase of human society as one in which the best men, described as *sapientes*, were rulers, who maintained a just and peaceful community and ensured all were provided for. When the rulers themselves became corrupted (§6), laws were required; the lawgivers, too, are described as *sapientes* in Posidonius' schema. Also to Posidonius is attributed the view, with which S himself at §7 explicitly disagrees, that it was these early philosopher-rulers who taught their fellow men, hitherto living scattered in caves and hollow trees, to gather together and build houses.

The idea of a golden age is found as early as Hesiod (*Op.* 106–201, Lovejoy and Boas 1997 [1935], Gatz 1967), but Posidonius is unusual in locating in the distant past an ideal community ruled by philosophers. Plato, *Laws* Book 3 (677c–679d) offers an account of primitive humanity as uncorrupted but pre-philosophical (cf. the simple life associated with the rule of Kronos at *Plt.* 271d–274e); many other philosophers, following Aristotle (see e.g. *Pol.* 1269a48), rejected the view that mankind might have been in any way better off at the earliest stages of development. Closer to Book 3 of Plato's *Laws*, the historian Dicaearchus of Messene, though a follower of Aristotle, attributed to early humans an innocent, pre-philosophical happiness, distinct from the philosophical achievement of virtue (fr. 31, 19.15–17 Wehrli, Boys-Stones 2001: 14–17, Setaioli 1988: 324). Adapting elements from Hesiod, he seems to have focused on their simple way of life, particularly their diet (Zago 2012: 61–2). The Cynic tradition also seems to have celebrated as a model the simplicity of primitive human life (Griffin 1996, Boys-Stones 2001: 7–8).

As regards the relationship of philosophy with technology, the term *sophia* (regarded by S, 89.7, as equivalent to *sapientia*) is sometimes used of technical knowledge in earlier Greek philosophy (Zago 2012: 114–16). Academic and Peripatetic texts (e.g. Arist. *Metaph.* 981b13–15, Diog. Laert. 3.63) occasionally distinguish practical *sophia*, associated with invention, from theoretical *sophia*, in which human progress culminates. Posidonius, in his emphasis on the role of human ingenuity in the development of technology, was perhaps challenging the traditional mythological accounts, which attributed a key role in technological advance to Prometheus (Kidd 1988: 964 *ad* F284). The nub of the disagreement between S and Posidonius (as Kidd 1988: 968–9 argues *ad* Posidonius

F284) is that while S wishes to distinguish sharply between philosophy on the one hand and arts and sciences on the other, Posidonius, though he distinguishes between them, also emphasises their necessary relationship. True *sapientia* is for Posidonius the root of cultural progress.

Stoics certainly held that only the wise man is capable of exercising kingship properly (Stob. *SVF* III.613). According to Sextus Empiricus, perhaps referring to Posidonius, some Stoics took the view that there were early human beings who surpassed in intelligence (*synesis*) 'men of today' and apprehended divine nature (Sext. Emp. *Math.* 9.28, Boys-Stones 2001: 48). This need not entail (despite the arguments of Zago 2012: 114–16) that Posidonius saw early *reges* and lawmakers as true *sapientes* in the Stoic sense, though S, in arguing against such a position (as he does from §7), seems to impute this view to him. Hirzel (1882: 285–7) suggests, through inference from Diog. Laert. 7.91, that Posidonius, like some other Stoics, did not believe even Socrates to have been a true *sapiens*. Indeed whether Posidonius himself intended his account as properly historical remains unclear (as Kidd 1999: 971 notes).

A difficulty with *Ep.* 90 is the apparent contradiction between the account of the golden age featuring *sapientes* at §§4–7, which is attributed to Posidonius but with which S appears to agree (§7 *hactenus Posidonio adsentior*), and the claim made at §§36 and 44 that there were no true *sapientes* in those early times; people led blessedly simple lives because they knew no alternative, not because they had achieved true *uirtus* (Setaioli 1988: 326–33, Zago 2012: 49–108). One solution (following Boys-Stones 2001: 18–24) might be to see the comment at §5 as a parenthesis (expanding on Posidonius' view), with which S himself does not necessarily agree. Another solution (following Hirzel 1882: 286–8, Blankert: 89–96; cf. Mazzoli 1992: 350–1, Armisen-Marchetti 1998: 201–2) is to see the term *sapientes* as used in a weak sense at §§5–6 and a strong sense at §§36 and 44 (where S adds the gloss *quando hoc iam in opere maximo nomen est*). Hirzel (1882: 287) notes a parallel with Cic. *Off.* 3.16 *nec ii qui sapientes habiti et nominati M. Cato et C. Laelius sapientes fuerunt, ne illi quidem septem, sed ex mediorum officiorum frequentia similitudinem quondam gerebant speciemque sapientium* (a passage which he suggests may itself be drawn from Posidonius). The *sapientia* exhibited by these early *reges* would thus resemble the *antiqua sapientia* of 95.13–14 (termed by S *sapientia . . . rudis*) which people often associate, he says, with the *simplex . . . et aperta uirtus* of earlier simpler times but which is not true *sapientia* (just as the associated *uirtus* is not fully developed *uirtus*). For S *sapientia* is the culmination rather than the driver of human progress.

It may be better, however, to see S himself as ultimately less concerned with the detailed process of chronological development but rather, at §7, agreeing with Posidonius to the extent that government and lawmaking are *the sort of* arts (*artes*) a philosopher might properly engage in (for the philosopher's duty to participate in government see e.g. *De otio* 3.2, Cic. *Fin.* 3.68, Diog. Laert. 7. 121, Griffin 1992: 315–66), in contrast to those other, more materialist, arts which Posidonius (wrongly on S's view) also attributes to them. S is thus not necessarily agreeing that there was a particular time in the very distant past when philosophers as he would recognise them actually ruled (if this was indeed Posidonius' view; see Kidd 1988 *ad* F284).

S himself elsewhere (e.g. 95.52–3, *Clem.* 3.1.2, *Ben.* 4.18.1, *De ira* 1.15.2) underlines the value of the human impulse towards *societas* but, where Posidonius apparently regarded the construction of houses as a means to make possible larger human communities and attributed the invention of this practice to the same *sapientes* who governed these communities, S is violently opposed to the idea that a philosopher would ever be concerned with such mundane technical matters, particularly given the strong link he perceives between architecture and moral degradation in his own day (see intro. to *Ep.* 86). The gulf separating the ancient 'golden' age from the age in which S writes emerges graphically from his accounts of the simple dwellings of early humans, on the one hand, and the extraordinarily ingenious contrivances boasted by his contemporaries. The radical contrast between simple past (insistently associated with *securitas*, §§10, 16, 38, 41) and corrupt present bulks large in this letter, as Degl'Innocenti Pierini (2008: 108) underlines, placing S's comments in the context of the Roman tradition of moralising criticism of the present in relation to the past but, more particularly, the specific concerns of Neronian Rome (see Pani 1992).

The political organisation of the so-called golden age is not what most interests S here. When at §16 he equivocates *sapientes aut sapientibus similes*, he no longer refers to community leaders but rather to all primitive humans. Most of the references to the simple lives of primitive humans later in the letter make no mention of leadership or political structures but are concerned rather with the manner of life in this period, specifically with regard to food, clothing and shelter. S (in this respect like Dicaearchus, perhaps) is concerned to emphasise how their way of life is in accordance with nature. In describing primitive life, S focuses initially on Posidonius' account of human development but, particularly in the latter sections (Posidonius is not explicitly referred to after §33, though some scholars, e.g. Blankert, have argued for traces of his influence in the later paragraphs), he also draws (selectively) on the pictures of early human society offered by Lucretius (5.925–1457), Cicero (*Tusc.* 5.5, *Off.* 1.21), Virgil's *Georgics* (quoted at §§ 9, 11 and 37) and Ovid (particularly *Met.* 1.87–112), as Armisen-Marchetti (1998) and Degl'Innocenti Pierini (2008: 105–29) have emphasised.

Lucretius, Catullus and, fleetingly, Cicero celebrate some features of the primitive past but regard them as beyond recall. The 'golden age' acquired a new resonance in the triumviral and Augustan periods, with Virgil heralding its return, first in *Eclogue* 4, later (by implication) in the *Georgics*, where it takes a more agricultural form (Barker 1996: 441, Johnston 1980), and then, specifically with reference to Augustus' agency, at *A.* 6.792–4, where the emperor is proclaimed the *conditor* of renewed *aurea saecula* (see also 1.291, 8.324–5). Wallace-Hadrill (1982b: 25) comments on the golden age that 'for the Augustans, its function is to put Augustus at the centre of things' (though see the important qualifications of Galinsky 1981, Barker 1996).

The associations of gold were not unequivocally positive even in the Augustan period (on Horace's ambivalence to gold, cf. e.g. *Carm.* 2.18.1–2 rejecting gold and ivory ceilings, see Barker 1996: esp. 444). Reworking Propertius 3.13.49–50, Ovid exploits the tension between associations of the metal in its figurative and in its literal aspects; his own age is all too 'golden' in its venality (*Ars* 2.277–8): *aurea sunt uere nunc saecula: plurimus auro | uenit honos, auro conciliatur amor.* Conversely, at *Fast.* 1.191–226, Janus is made to comment that primitive Romans of Saturnian days would also have grabbed gold if they had had the chance; their 'virtue' was enforced by circumstance. At *Ars* 3.113, however, Ovid celebrates his own age as more truly golden thanks to its refinement and culture, the fruits of *artes*, and far removed from the simplicity of the age of Saturn: *simplicitas rudis ante fuit, nunc aurea Roma est* (Galinsky 1981).

Later emperors, too, seem to have exploited golden age imagery (Gatz 1967: 136-43, Wallace-Hadrill 1982b). Such imagery was insistently invoked in contemporary celebrations of Nero's rule, which linked him to Apollo, particularly as the sun god (Fabre-Serris 1999, Champlin 2003: 112–44). Indeed a passage in S's *Apocolocyntosis* (§4 with Eden's commentary) proclaims Nero's golden age, *aurea formoso descendunt saecula filo*, while his protreptic addressed to Nero celebrates a manifestation of Nero's clemency as worthy of *publica generis humani innocentia . . . cui redderetur antiquum illum saeculum* (*Clem.* 2.1.3–4 with Braund: 11–16). Though their Neronian date is not universally accepted, Calpurnius Siculus' *Eclogues* also celebrate a new ruler restoring the golden age: 1.42 *aurea renascitur aetas* (Townend 1980 and Mayer 1980 argue for a Neronian date, Champlin 1978 and Horsfall 1997 for a later one). The emperor himself christened his fabulous new palace, built in the wake of the great fire of 64 CE, the Domus Aurea (Tac. *Ann.* 15.42.1, Suet. *Nero* 31.1–2, Champlin 2003: 178–209). Even if this construction project postdates the writing of *Ep.* 90, the emperor's tastes (and plans) will surely have been known to S.

The evils of luxurious architecture are a theme prominent more generally in attacks on luxury (see *Ep.* 86 and intro.). Elaborate ceilings (*laqueata tecta*) are criticised by Cicero (*Leg.* 2.2, Degl'Innocenti Pierini 2008: 118–19). The Augustan moralist Papirius Fabianus is quoted at length in the *Controuersiae* of S's father (2.1.11–12), in a passage closely echoed by *Ep.* 90 (Degl'Innocenti Pierini 2008: 109–14 documents parallels in detail); at 100.12, S recalls Fabianus' lectures with approval. But such criticism was particularly pertinent in Nero's Rome. Suetonius comments on Nero (*Nero* 31.1): 'There was nothing in which he was more ruinously prodigal than building.' According to Tacitus (*Ann.* 15.42), Nero's architects Severus and Celer were celebrated for their ability to achieve through art what nature refused: *Seuero et Celere, quibus ingenium et audacia erat etiam quae natura denegauisset per artem temptare et uiribus principis illudere* (though Tacitus may himself have drawn inspiration from S; see intro. to *Ep.* 70 above).

Having noted the opulent decoration of the house (*cuncta auro lita, distincta gemmis*), Suetonius (*Nero* 31.2–3) attests the emperor's taste for ingenious and lavish ceilings in particular: *cenationes laqueatae tabulis eburneis uersatilibus, ut flores fistulatis, ut unguenta desuper spargerentur; praecipua cenationum rotunda, quae perpetua diebus ac noctibus uice mundi circumageretur*. Ceilings with moving panels are an architectural feature singled out for particular criticism at *Ep.* 90.15 and 42 (noted by Bradley 1978: 179–80 *ad* Suet. *Nero* 31). Nero's mechanism, with multiple moving parts to enable shifting celestial displays, was evidently complex; the cosmic motion in Suetonius' description elides the elaborate ceiling and the night sky, elements strongly contrasted in S's scheme (as to whether the comments in Suetonius relate to extant remains of the Golden House see Champlin 2003: 203–6; remains more recently discovered on the Palatine have also been identified with Nero's *cenatio*, Villedieu 2011). Another Neronian text features a strikingly similar device; at one point in Trimalchio's banquet (Petr. 60.1–3), *repente lacunaria sonare coeperunt totumque triclinium intremuit* and panels shift to reveal a hoop hung with golden crowns and perfume vessels; the mechanisms are described in terms evoking those used in the theatre (cf. Plin. *Nat.* 36.117; see Panayotakis 1995: 90–1). S himself associates ingenious contrivances of this kind with the stage (88.22). Degl'Innocenti Pierini (2008: 127–8) also notes a suggestive resonance with the false ceiling (*lacunaria . . . laxata machina*) of the boat through which Nero plotted to kill his mother (Suet. *Nero* 34.2); in Nero's Rome a fear of collapsing ceilings might be amply justified.

The manifestation of luxury in architecture is treated in *Ep.* 90 as emblematic of the moral failings of S's contemporaries and the existential dangers these failings entail (Degl'Innocenti Pierini 2008: 109). S frequently contrasts luxurious and simple architecture (cf. e.g. *Ep.* 86, *Helv.* 9.2–3; on S's sometimes schematic opposition of idealised past and immoral present see Citroni-Marchetti 1991: 133–4). The author of the pseudo-Senecan *Octavia* evidently regarded such sentiments as distinctively Senecan, putting a similar speech in the mouth of the philosopher himself ([Sen.] *Oct.* 397–406). The concerns of *Ep.* 90 find a close parallel in the speech S gives to Hippolytus in his *Phaedra* (484–564), praising life in the woods in contrast to the corruption of the city, and comparing it to the simple life of early man (here the primary points of comparison are spatially rather than temporally distinct; see Maxia 2000).

The excoriation of present-day luxury in *Ep.* 90 is, as noted above, balanced by a lyrical celebration of the life of primitive man (particularly at §§42–3; cf. §13). Not only do primitive people satisfy their needs without fuss, using only what nature makes readily available, they also engage more thoughtfully (although they may not be philosophers) with the world they live in, observing celestial movements with appropriate awe. A focus on the sublime movements of the heavens often functions for S as emblematic of philosophical contemplation more generally (cf. e.g. *Helv.* 20.2, *Ben.* 4.5.1–4.6.3, *De otio* 5.3–5 with Williams *ad loc.*); S at 89.1 compares the synoptic vision offered by philosophy to the spectacle of the universe, *simillimum mundo spectaculum.* There are notable echoes in *Ep.* 90 of Manilius' astronomical treatise (1.15–19). The claim that nature has created man erect precisely so that he might follow the stars as they glide from their rising to their setting (to which S returns at 92.30, 94.56, *Nat.* 5.15.3) has numerous precedents (Pl. *Resp.* 586a, Arist. *Parv. nat.* 468a, Nightingale 2004, Cic. *N.D.* 2.14, Ov. *Met.* 1.84–6; cf. Pers. 2.61). As Degl'Innocenti Pierini (2008: 123–4) argues, it is perhaps S's particular fascination with the sublime experience of gazing at the sky which gives such an edge to his obsessive critique of ornate ceilings whose ingenious design provokes more tawdry wonder (cf. *Ben.* 4.6.2, *Phaed.* 496–8).

While S is drawn to the idealisation of early human society which characterises so many Roman texts, his nostalgia for primitive living is significantly qualified. The true life of virtue is only to be secured through philosophy. Philosophy requires discipline and must be deliberately striven for (the final section of the letter thus returns to the claims asserted at its outset). Indeed this emphasis on the pre-eminent role of philosophy is the main point of the letter. Thus, as S makes clear, however salubrious the simple life led in primitive times, the conditions were not conducive to the development of philosophy. Paradoxically, it is the proliferation of vice which has made necessary the full development of philosophy, no longer just a matter of wise advice on how to live (*praecepta*), of the kind which those early kings may have dispensed, but a body of thought underpinned by theoretical doctrine (*decreta*) (cf. 95.32–4). Only when it is challenged by human corruption can philosophy develop to become fully *contemplatiua* (Zago 2012: 130). At 95.15–29, S develops at length an analogy between philosophy and medicine, which only becomes a complex, sophisticated and powerful set of practices in response to the complexities of human disease resulting from the unhealthy living associated with the flourishing of a multitude of colourful vices. Nostalgia for the so-called golden age can serve as a valuable prompt, encouraging us to emulate the material simplicity of a life in accordance with nature, but the knowledge and choices humanity has painfully acquired in making the transition to a more advanced existence are essential prerequisites for the practice of philosophy.

Ep. 90, though lengthy, is by no means the longest in the collection (longer letters increasingly predominate in the later books). The critique of liberal arts in *Ep.* 88 (on which see Stückelberger) has much in common with the attack on *artes* in *Ep.* 90, engaging specifically (§§21–3) with Posidonius' classification of crafts. The nature of the process by which virtue is acquired is examined in detail and at great length in *Epp.* 94 and 95 (on which see Schafer 2009), two of the three letters in Book 15. Other longer letters, also foregrounding more technical philosophical issues, are included in Inwood's collection.

Commentaries: Summers (omitting §§26–9), Blankert, Motto, Costa, Nikolaides.
Further reading: Novara 1988, Setaioli 1988: 322–57, Castagna 1991, Pani 1992, Armisen-Marchetti 1998, Maxia 2000, Panayotakis 2004, Degl'Innocenti Pierini 2008: 105–29, Zago 2012, Van Nuffelen and Van Hoof 2013.

1 Quis dubitare . . . uiuimus? the opening question is characteristic of the protreptic, an exhortation to philosophy which (to judge from that of Iamblichus) usually included an account of the benefits and advances philosophy had brought humankind. For the protreptic attributed to Posidonius see Kidd 1988 *ad* F1–3, Diog. Laert. 7.91. For Posidonius' *Protreptikos* as a source for *Ep.* 89 see Wildberger 2006: 674–7 nn. 685–7.   **uiuimus . . . bene uiuimus:** for the opposition between living and living well see 70.5(n.) *qualis . . . non quanta*, Ben. 3.31.4.   **philosophiae:** here used as equivalent to *sapientia* (at 89.4–8, by contrast, *philosophia* is rather *sapientiae amor*, the process by which one comes to *sapientia*).   **tanto . . . tribuissent** 'that we are by the same degree more in debt to this [i.e. philosophy] than to the gods, as a good life is a greater benefit than life, would be a certainty, if it were not the case that the gods had granted us philosophy itself'. The noun-clause *tanto . . . dis* and the clause *quanto . . . uita* which depends on it all forms the subject of *haberetur*.

For philosophy as a gift of the gods cf. Pl. *Ti.* 47b (a passage invoked at Cic. *Tusc.* 1.64). S's use of the plural (cf. e.g. *Prov.* 2.12, *Ep.* 95.36) need not be inconsistent with the Stoic belief in a single deity (Zago 2012: 14–15). For the nature of the divine in Seneca see 95.47–50, *Nat.* 1.pr.13 with Wildberger 2006: 3–48.   **cuius scientiam:** i.e. expert knowledge (*OLD* 2a) of philosophy.   **facultatem:** *sc.* of acquiring this knowledge. See Trapp 2007: 50.   **omnibus:** on the accessibility of philosophy to all cf. 44.1–2, 47 and *Marc.* 16.1, *Ben.* 3.18.2. At 95.36, however, S concedes that some people are more naturally inclined to good conduct than others. See further Wildberger 2006: 315–17.

2 hanc: i.e. *scientiam.*   **inter fortuita** 'among the gifts of chance'; cf. 89.1. The gifts of fortune are regarded by the Stoics as *externa* and therefore *indifferentia* (Armisen-Marchetti 1998: 199–200; see further 92.2). As Cotta notes at Cic. *N.D.* 3.87–8, we praise virtue by contrast, *quod non contingeret* (Zago 2012: 34). The acc. + inf. *inter . . . esse* is in explicative apposition to *quod . . . optimum* in the previous sentence.   **non obuenit:** contrast the simple necessities of life which, in the golden age at least, were *obuia* (§18).   **illam sibi quisque debet** 'each person has the right/ duty to procure it for himself'. Cf. the use of *debet* at 70.12.   **beneficiaria** 'given as a favour', i.e. with no effort on the recipient's part. This seems to be the sole use of the adjective in extant classical Latin (the masculine noun *beneficiarius* occurs in Caesar and Pliny the Younger of soldiers given privileges).

3 diuinis: philosophy's concern with the divine, which includes physics as well as theology, is particularly salient in this letter (the gods are presented in §1 as philosophy's ultimate source). See esp. §§28, 34. S's claim here corresponds with a Stoic formula at *SVF* II.35–6, where σοφία is defined as θείων τε καὶ ἀνθρωπίνων ἐπιστήμη; cf. 89.5, Cic. *Off.* 2.5 *rerum diuinarum et humanarum causarumque . . . scientia*, Maximus of Tyre, *Or.* 26.1.   **numquam recedit:** S stresses consistency. While these qualities may sometimes be present without the underpinning of philosophy, they are then precarious, liable to be undermined by vice (as happens with the descent into tyranny in §6). Accounts of the transitions from one age to another are frequently marked by the departure of virtues (e.g. Hes. *Op.* 197–201, Aratus, *Phaen.* 96–136, Ov. *Met.* 1.149, Juv. 6.1–20).   **religio . . . cohaerentium:** a similar list of qualities is presented as characteristic of the ideal state at *Clem.* 1.19.8, 2.1.4. On the *comitatus uirtutum* see Degl'Innocenti Pierini (2016).   **docuit:** S shifts here from an analysis of the nature of philosophy (in the present tense, e.g. *unum opus est*) to a discussion of the role of philosophy in human development.   **penes deos imperium esse** 'ruling is in the hands of the gods'.   **auaritia:** a corrupting force, whose toxic effects are repeatedly stressed; cf. §§8, 36, 38, 40, *Clem.* 2.1.4 *alieni cupidine, Phaed.* 540–1 *rupere foedus impius lucri furor | et ira praeceps.* Accounts of Rome's moral decline frequently stress the role of *auaritia*; cf. e.g. Sal. *Cat.* 10.4, Liv. 1.pr.11, Virg. *A.* 8.327 *amor successit habendi,* Ov. *Met.* 1.130 *amor sceleratus habendi.* **distraxit:** technical (*OLD* 7a), 'break up a partnership'. **paupertatis causa:** 'poverty' is essentially a mistaken perception of one's relationship to material goods (cf. §38, 2.6, 4.10, 17.2–5). **desierunt . . . propria** 'they ceased to be in possession of all things, as soon as they desired their own things'.

4 naturam . . . sequebantur: to follow nature as one's guide is a key tenet of Stoic thought. Nature is the standard from which luxury rebels at §19. The account here derives from Posidonius, as is made clear by §5 *ergo.* **eundem . . . ducem et legem:** S is rather vague on the process by which a leader emerges. Zago (2012: 51–2, 72, 79–85) notes parallels with Polybius 6.5.7–9, including the comparison with animal behaviour (one of Posidonius' projects was implicitly a continuation of Polybius' history; see Kidd 1999: 25–7). Later, less virtuous, rulers themselves have need of laws (§6). **potioribus deteriora summittere:** in the examples drawn from the animal world (bulls, elephants) size and physical strength determine pre-eminence. For articulations of the principle that worse men should submit to better cf. 65.24, Pl. *Grg.* 483 c–d (Callicles' proposal is robustly rejected), *Leg.* 3. 690b, Arist. *Pol.* 1252a30–4 and 1254a41–1254b2, Cic. *Rep.* 1.51. A key role is also played by the good ruler in the version of the golden age described at Virg. *A.* 8.324–7. **animo** 'on the strength of his mental capacity', abl. of cause. **summa felicitas:** *felicitas* (unlike *uirtus*) is the province of *fortuna.* **tuto . . . posse** 'for safely can that man do as much as he wishes, who does not think he can do other than he should'.

5 saeculo 'generation' (*OLD* 5) or 'race' (*OLD* 2). **quod aureum perhibent:** on the term *saeculum aureum* see Barker 1996: esp. 438. For earlier ideas of the golden age/race see intro. above. S distances himself from using the term *aureum* in a positive sense (Degl'Innocenti Pierini 2008: 109; Zago 2012: 59–61 suggests that this distancing may derive from Posidonius); cf. 115.13 *quod optimum uideri uolunt saeculum aureum appellant.* At 90.45 this happy primitive phase is characterised precisely by its lack of interest in gold. For an ironic application of the term 'golden age' to contemporaries obsessed with the metal itself see Porcius Latro *ap.* Sen. *Con.* 2.7.7: *o nos nimium felici et aureo, quod aiunt, saeculo natos!* **penes sapientes . . . iudicat:** S makes clear at §§35–6 and 44–6 that he does not believe there were any *sapientes* in the golden age. Yet at §7, S states that he agrees with Posidonius (on whom see intro. above) thus far. Scholars have offered different solutions to this apparent contradiction (see intro. above). While in §4 S writes of the ruler in the singular, the use of the plural here perhaps refers to a number of individual rulers, each in his respective community.   **regnum:** here in the sense of βασιλεία, as Zago (2012: 82) suggests; cf. Cic. *Rep.* 2.47 of Greek usage (contrasting the terms *tyrannus* and *rex*): *nam regem illum uolunt esse, qui consulit ut parens populo, conseruatque eos quibus est praepositus quam optima in condicione uiuendi*. See, too, S's protreptic *De clementia*, addressed to Nero (e.g. 1.3.4, 1.11.4 with Braund *ad locc.*), where *rex* is a positive term for an autocrat, in contrast to the negative *tyrannus*.   **manus** 'hands' (as an instrument of violence, *OLD manus*[1] 8). The impulses towards violence which the rulers are obliged to constrain may suggest elements of corruption are already present, notwithstanding §4 *incorrupti* (which Zago 2012: 59 sees as S's own supplement to Posidonius' account; cf. Boys-Stones 2001: 46–8, arguing that Posidonius saw humans as having the seeds of vice within them). Certainly there is a contrast here with §40.   **infirmiorem ... tuebantur:** cf. Cic. *Off.* 2.41–2, where people willingly submit to a *rex*, someone of outstanding *uirtus*, who *prohiberet iniuria tenuiores* (Posidonius may be Cicero's source; see Zago 2012: 74). At Lucr. 5.1019–23, by contrast, there is rather a general pact to take care of the weak.   **suadebant dissuadebantque:** at 95.65–7, S invokes Posidonius as an authority on the role of persuasion in philosophical education.   **monstrabant:** foreshadowing the role of philosophy itself on a more elevated level at §15 *monstrat*. Primitive people also get pleasure from sharing what they find with one another at §40 *inuentum monstrari alteri uoluptas erat*.   **prudentia:** in a weaker sense, we must assume, than §2 *prudentes* (and §46 *prudentia*).   **prouidebat:** S plays here on the equivalence between *prudentia* and *prouidentia* (*OLD prudens*).   **regnum:** here (in contrast to the first sentence of §5) in the negative sense of *OLD* 3 (much more common in Latin; cf. e.g. Cic. *Rep.* 2.52, Liv. 27.19.4, Suet. *Aug.* 94.3).   **nemo ... posse** 'no one tested the limits of his power against those who had granted him that power [as *rex*] to begin with'.   **nihilque ... e regno:** i.e. precisely because the community was so well ordered, to be exiled from it would be a dreadful punishment. *rex*: see *regnum* in the first sentence of §5(n.).

6 surrepentibus uitiis: the agency through which vices enter is not specified; given that their subjects already exhibited moral flaws (see §5n. on *manus*), it is presumably the rulers who are now affected. As Zago (2012: 109–10) notes, if Posidonius viewed these original rulers as *sapientes* in a strong Stoic sense and thus incorruptible, we might infer that these are their inferior descendants (cf. Polyb. 6.7.2–8). For the terminology cf. 7.2(n.) *uitia ... surrepunt*, *Nat.* 3.30.8 *cito nequitia surrepit*.   **in**

tyrannidem regna: as in *De Clementia* (see *regnum* in the first sentence of §5(n.)), the distinction is drawn between benevolent and self-interested autocracy.   **opus esse legibus:** in the earlier period, the ruler himself *was* the law (§4 *eundem . . . ducem et legem*); on the need for law following the collapse of kingly rule cf. Lucr. 5.1136–50. S's examples here are all Greek but Lactantius (*Div. inst.* 7.15.4) attributes to S an account of the history of Rome in terms of the six ages of man (on the authenticity of this see Griffin 1972: 19); infant innocence is educated in the time of Romulus, a legal system is imposed after the tyranny (Griffin 1992: 194–201). Cf. Tac. *Ann.* 3.26.   **inter initia** 'at this early stage'. Later on in Posidonius' schema, by implication, lawmakers were not necessarily *sapientes*.   **tulere:** *ferre* is quasi-technical of passing laws (*OLD* 28).   **sapientes:** either the term is meant in a weak sense here or this is a part of the summary of Posidonius' position which S does not fully endorse. See further intro. above.   **Solon:** probably during his archonship of 594/593 BCE, he introduced a series of reforms to Athens and is described by Herodotus as a sage lawgiver (1.29). By the fourth century BCE he was referred to by orators as the source of all Athenian law; cf. *Ath. Pol.* 2–13 (Raaflaub 2006). Lists of the Seven Sages (see below) always feature Solon.   **aequo iure:** S refers here to ἰσονομία, in the sense of equal participation and political equality (cf. 107.6), but this is a feature of Athenian political organisation which postdates Solon, though his legislation laid the foundations for later developments. His pronouncements stress rather *eunomia* 'good order' (Raaflaub 2006: 400). Cicero, too, praises the introduction of *ius aequabile* (*Off.* 2.40–1) in developing states.   **septem . . . sapientia notos:** Plato (*Prt.* 343a) lists Seven Sages of the seventh and sixth centuries BCE, whom he describes as 'emulators and disciples of the culture of the Spartans'; four of these (Thales, Pittacus, Bias, Solon) became canonical; the other three vary in later versions (Diog. Laert. 1.13). Although S does not explicitly disagree with the formulation here, later parts of the letter suggest his position is closer to that of Themistius (*Or.* 34.3–4), namely that Solon, Lycurgus and other lawgivers, though they were regarded by their own contemporaries as wise men, were not truly such; cf. Cic. *Off.* 3.16, quoted in intro. above, *Amic.* 7.   **Lycurgum:** according to Herodotus (1.65–6), responsible for establishing (in the time of King Leobotes in the ninth century) the laws and political institutions of classical Sparta, celebrated by some for its *eunomia* 'good order'. Plutarch's biography attributes to him a still wider range of measures (see also Cic. *Tusc.* 5.7). See Tigerstedt 1965: 70–3, Hölkeskamp 1999: 53–9. Diogenes Laertius (7.178) suggests that he was admired by the Stoic Sphaerus, who composed a treatise on Sparta and served as adviser to the Spartan king Cleomenes III. Schofield (1999: ch. 2, esp. 35–42) emphasises Spartan elements in Zeno's ideal state. This need not (as Zago 2012: 120 stresses) mean Zeno viewed Lycurgus as a true *sapiens*.   **si eadem aetas tulisset** 'if the same age had produced him'.   **Zaleuci:** referred to by Aristotle (*Pol.* 1274a) as the lawgiver of Locri in Magna Graecia of the seventh century BCE (cf. Diod. Sic. 12.19–21). His laws, reputed to be the earliest committed to writing, were noted for their severity (Polyb. 1.16, Gagarin 1986: 52, 64–5, 76).   **Charondaeque:** though somewhat later (probably late sixth century BCE), often associated with Zaleucus, and credited with giving laws to his native Catana and other Chalcidic colonies. See Arist. *Pol.* 1274a, Gagarin 1986: 64–5.   **in consultorum atrio:** in Rome, advice was sought from law-specialists (*OLD consultus* 1) in their homes (see e.g. Cic. *Brut.* 306).   **Pythagorae:** a hugely influential, if somewhat mysterious, figure, noted for his contributions to philosophy and science. Originating on Samos, he moved to Croton around 530 BCE, where he founded a sect characterised by initiation rites and special dietary restrictions. Already a legendary figure in his own lifetime, in later traditions he was revered as a benefactor of humanity (KRS 214–38, 322–50, Barnes 1979: 100–20) and sometimes included among the Seven Sages (Diog. Laert. 1.13). Aristoxenus (a pupil of the Pythagorean Xenophilus) composed a biography of Pythagoras, which (frr. 17, 43 Wehrli) associates him with the lawgivers Zaleucus and Charondas.   **tacito ... secessu:** Pythagoras prescribed a five-year period of silence for his disciples (see 52.10; cf. Porphyrius, *Life of Pythagoras* 19 = 14, 8a DK, Diog. Laert. 8.15). *sancto* indicates the religious awe associated with the Pythagorean sect. For the benefits that can be conferred by thinkers and teachers not directly involved in public life cf. *De otio* 6.5 with Williams *ad loc.*   **florenti ... Siciliae:** the Greek colonies of Sicily and southern Italy were at the height of their wealth and power in the seventh and sixth centuries BCE; cf. Cicero's description (*Tusc.* 4.2) of the period in which Pythagoras and his followers flourished.   **per Italiam Graeciae:** (sc. *florenti*) the Greek communities of South Italy.

7 hactenus ... adsentior: see intro. above and §5(n.) *penes sapientes ... iudicat* for a potential conflict between Posidonius' views even thus far and S's, as expressed later in the letter.   **artes ... inuentas:** on S's probably unjustified criticism of Posidonius see Kidd 1988: 936.   **fabricae ... gloriam:** for S it is absurd that glory should accrue to mere craftsmen.   **illa:** i.e. *philosophia*.   **sparsos:** sc. *homines*. For Zago (2012: 65–71), Posidonius must be referring here to the phase in human life prior to the well-ordered communities under the rule of *sapientes* (of §§4–5 earlier). For scattered living as a feature of the earliest phase of human life cf. Pl. *Prt.* 322a–b, Cic. *Tusc.* 1.62 (praising the man who *dissipatos homines congregauit et ad societatem uitae conuocauit*), Virg. *A.* 8.321–2 (where Saturn gathers together and gives laws to men who had been *dispersum* *montibus altis*). See also Aristotle (*Pol.* 1252b), who describes the life of scattered humans, before the formation of cities, as savage like that of the Cyclops (for whose way of life, including cave-dwelling, see Hom. *Od.* 9.112–15).   **et cauis tectos:** the text is corrupt here. I follow the reading proposed by Zago (2009); the phrase *aut aliqua . . . trunco* then serves in exegetical apposition. As Zago points out, Summers' conjecture (followed by Reynolds), *aut casis tectos*, suggests that some people are already living in houses, as well as caves and hollow trees, at the point when philosophy teaches them *tecta moliri*.   **aliqua . . . trunco:** for caves and hollow trees as the first human dwellings cf. *Phaed.* 539, Ov. *Met.* 1.121, Plin. *Nat.* 7.194 (Zago 2009).   **docuit . . . moliri:** a process which would seem to be contemporaneous, in Posidonius' account, with the political organisation described in §§4–5; cf. Cic. *Rep.* 1.41, *Tusc.* 1.62, Arist. *Pol.* 1285b. While S himself stresses the importance of *societas* to human life (see intro. above), he does not link this to the construction of the material fabric of towns and cities.   **machinationes:** Tacitus describes the architects of the Domus Aurea as *machinatores* (*Ann.* 15.42).   **tectorum supra tecta surgentium** 'storeys piled on top of storeys'.   **uiuaria piscium:** fish-reserves (whether to secure a constant food supply, as here, or to keep pet fish) are a frequent object of moralising criticism; cf. 55.6, *De ira* 3.40.2, V. Max. 9.1.1 (on Sergius Orata), Mart. 10.30, 19.20. Cicero labels some of his contemporaries *piscinarii*: *Att.* 1.19.6 (= 19 SB), 1.20.3 (= 20 SB), 2.1.7 (= 21 SB). His protreptic *Hortensius* fr. 68 Grilli (= 40a Straume-Zimmermann) observes, *primus balneola suspendit, inclusit pisces* (Zago 2012: 44). The grounds of the Domus Aurea also boasted lakes, *stagna* (Tac. *Ann.* 15.42.3, Suet. *Nero* 31).   **distinctos:** pointed emphasis on the quest for variety; cf. V. Max. 9.1.1 *piscium diuersos greges separatim molibus includendo*.

8 clauem et seram: cf. Tib. 1.3.43 *non domus ulla fores habuit*.   **signum dare:** to give the signal for action, often in a military context (*OLD signum* 8); cf. e.g. Caes. *Gal.* 2.21.3 *proelii committendi signum dedit*.   **tanto . . . periculo:** cf. Pap. Fab. *ap.* Sen. *Con.* 2.1.11, attacking the houses of his contemporaries: *periculo non praesidio* <*sint*>.   **suspendit** 'builds on arches or vaulting' (*OLD* 4b).   **parum:** sarcastically emphasising luxury's insatiability.

9 felix 'fortunate' (*OLD* 4b); cf. §4 *summa felicitas*. This characterisation is significantly qualified at §34.   **ista:** i.e. the following techniques.   **in quadratum** 'into a squared form'.   **tigna** 'wood for building' (*OLD* b); cf. Gaius, *Dig.* 41.1.7.10 *appellatione tigni omnes materiae significantur, ex quibus aedificia fiunt*.   **per designata** 'according to the marked out lines'.   **nam primi . . . lignum:** this line (Virg. *G.* 1.144) and those quoted at §§11 and 37 are taken from the section of *Georgics* Book 1 (121–59) where the idyllic pre-agricultural age, before the reign of Jupiter, when land was held in common and the earth was more generous, is contrasted with the subsequent period, when men were obliged to develop *artes*, including that of agriculture, in order to extract a living (Johnston 1980: 50, 69–71). On S's engagement with the *Georgics*, see also intro. to *Ep.* 86, 86.15(nn.).   **cenationi:** the term *cenatio* seems to have become current in the Neronian period. See Perrin 1987.   **pinus aut abies . . . uicis intrementibus:** cf. Juv. 3.254–6 (where *abies* and *pinus* judder menacingly through the streets), Plin. *Pan.* 51. Massive beams on the move signal the ominous beginning of ship-building (associated with the desire for imported goods), which is a key indicator of moral decline at Enn. *Medea* fr. 103 Jocelyn, Catul. 64.1 *Peliaco quondam prognatae uertice pinus*, Tib. 1.3.37, Ov. *Met.* 1.94–5, Sen. *Med.* 335–6 (Degl'Innocenti Pierini 2008: 111–12).   **auro:** gold (desire for which poses a moral danger in e.g. *Ep.* 115) here also poses a physical threat, adding dangerous weight to the ceiling (cf. *Phaed.* 497–8).

10 furcae . . . casam echoes Vitr. 2.1.3 on the early development of architecture: *primumque furcis erectis et uirgultis interpositis luto parietes texerunt.* [. . .] *posteaquam per hibernas tempestates tecta potuerunt imbres sustinere, fastigia facientes, luto inducto proclinatis tectis, stillicidia deducebant* (though Vitruvius' focus is on continuous improvement, *in dies melioribus iudiciis efficiebantur*; see Degl'Innocenti Pierini 2008: 113, Pani 1992). At *Helv.* 9.2–3, S associates living in a hut with virtuous simplicity, recalling the hut of Romulus still to be seen on the Capitol, and often taken as a symbol of the simple life of Rome's founder (cf. Vitr. 2.1.5, Liv. 5.53.8, Sen. *Con.* 1.6.4, Edwards 1996: 32–43).   **ramalibus** 'branches', a relatively rare term; cf. the humble dwelling of Philemon and Baucis (Ov. *Met.* 8.643–5), signal exponents of a simple and virtuous life, and serving no master (*Met.* 8.632–6, Degl'Innocenti Pierini 2008: 115).   **securi:** suggesting both safety (cf. §41 *tuti*) and lack of anxiety. *securitas* (repeatedly associated with primitive human society, §§16, 38, 41) is a key goal for the would-be wise man; cf. e.g. 18.7.   **culmus** 'straw thatch', a recurrent term in vignettes of primitive living; cf. 8.5 *scitote tam bene hominem culmo quam auro tegi, Prov.* 4.14 (of barbarians) and Virg. *A.* 8.654 *Romuleoque recens horrebat regia culmo*.   **seruitus:** on the metaphorical slavery of those in thrall to their material possessions see *Ep.* 47(nn.).

11 ferramenta fabrilia 'workmen's iron tools'. Manual work, S stresses, is of no concern to the *sapiens*.   **tunc . . . saltus:** Virg. *G.* 1.139–40. See §9(n.) *nam primi . . . lignum.*   **sagacitas . . . non sapientia:** cf. §24 *ratio* vs *recta ratio.*

12 incendio . . . fudisset: a similar but more detailed account is given in Lucr. 5.1252–80.   **ista tales inueniunt quales colunt** 'the same sort of people discovered these things as [now] practise them'. *colunt* 'attend to' (*OLD* 4a).

13 ne . . . tam subtilis . . . quaestio: the issue is too trivial, suggests S, to be worth the consideration Posidonius gives it.   **excitati ingenii, acuti:** corresponding to the *sagacitas* of §11.   **magni . . . elati:** sc. *ingenii*, corresponding to §11 *sapientia*.   **corpore . . . spectante** 'when the body is bent towards the earth and the spirit looks at the ground'. S frequently emphasises the importance of looking up towards the heavens as part of – but also a metonym for – philosophy; cf. §42 with intro. above.   **sapiens:** at §16 S describes people of these early times as at least *sapientibus similes*. Here the *sapiens* is rather a timeless figure whose wants would be the same in the present as in the distant past.   **facilis uictu:** the ability to be satisfied with the bare minimum as a goal to be striven for (thus freeing oneself from anxiety about provisions) is emphasised e.g. in *Epp.* 17 (see Soldo) and 18.   **expeditissimus** 'most unencumbered', 'most ready for action', often of troops. Travelling light literally and metaphorically is a preoccupation of *Ep.* 87, where S comments (§3) that the *animus* is never greater than when it has laid aside all superfluous things, *aliena*. The adjective anticipates Diogenes' behaviour in §14.

14 Diogenen: Diogenes the Cynic was known for the extreme simplicity of his mode of life (Diog. Laert. 6.32–7). S adduces his example at 29.1, *Ben.* 5.4.3–4, 5.6.1, *Tranq.* 8.4–7 (see also 47.12n. above); see Del Giovane 2015a: 60–1, 227. The Cynics, stressing the irrelevance of physical comfort to happiness, seem to have argued that early humans, content with their basic circumstances, knew how to live and should be taken as a model (Boys-Stones 2001: 7–8). Maximus of Tyre (*Or.* 36), praising the golden age of early humanity and contrasting it with the decadent present, goes on to celebrate Diogenes as superior to all other men (including Socrates) for achieving a life of primitive simplicity, though surrounded by the luxury of his contemporaries. On S's interest in Cynicism see further main intro. section 6. As Castagna (1991: 115) notes, the life according to nature celebrated for much of *Ep.* 90 is notably Cynic in character.   **Daedalum:** renowned as a great inventor, e.g. of the mechanical cow by means of which King Minos' wife Pasiphae had sex with a bull (thus conceiving the Minotaur, *Phaed.* 120–3; this is a key moment in the collapse of the golden age at Virg. *Ecl.* 6.45–7), the Cretan Labyrinth (*Phaed.* 1171) and the wax wings through which he disastrously sought a means of escape for himself and his son Icarus (Ov. *Met.* 8.159–235, Degl'Innocenti Pierini 2008: 131–8). Morally ambiguous, he often serves as archetype of the craftsman (Frontisi-Ducroux 1975: esp. 121–41). **serram:** Pliny (*Nat.* 7.198) also credits Daedalus with the invention of the saw (attributed to his nephew at Ov. *Met.* 8.244–6). Roman visual representations show Daedalus surrounded by tools (Frontisi-Ducroux 1975: 123). **commentus:** see 86.8(n.) *commenta est*, Suet. *Nero* 34.2 *nauem . . . commentus est*, on the ingenious collapsing boat Nero devised to kill his mother. **cum uidisset . . . habui:** for this story see also Diog. Laert. 6.37; cf. *Phaed.* 519–20 *quam iuuat nuda manu | captasse fontem.* **<cum>:** supplied by Baehrens, making clear that *obiurgatione* is not instrumental. **sarcinas:** literal and figurative baggage; cf. 25.4, 44.7, 65.16, 87.10, *Ben.* 6.35.3.1. **in dolio:** for the story that Diogenes slept in a large earthenware jar cf. Diog. Laert. 6.23.

15 hodie: emphatically placed. **crocum . . . exprimat:** *crocum*, a perfume prepared from crocus stigmas (saffron), which might be sprinkled on the stage in theatres (see e.g. Lucr. 2.416 *scena croco Cilici perfusa*). For the practice described here cf. Petr. 60, Suet. *Nero* 31.2 (on the dining room ceilings of the Golden House designed to scatter perfume and flowers on those beneath), Tac. *Ann.* 15.42, with intro. above. **euripos:** the name for the strait between Boeotia and Euboea came to be used for artificial, ornamental waterways; cf. e.g. 55.6, Cic. *Leg.* 2.2, where the character Atticus, celebrating nature, expresses his contempt for the artificiality of *ductus uero aquarum, quos isti Nilos et Euripos uocant*. **subito aquarum impetu:** cf. the criticism of elaborate water features at 86.6–7, 89.21 and 100.6. **uersatilia cenationum laquearia** 'dining-room ceilings with movable panels' (cf. Suet. *Nero* 31.2, quoted in intro. above). As Degl'Innocenti Pierini (2008: 125) notes, *uersatilis* is used by Lucretius (5.1436) to describe the sky, *mundi magnum . . . templum*, in his discussion of early human life. For S's recurrent concern with elaborate ceilings cf. intro. above, §42 and e.g. *Ben.* 4.6.2, *Phaed.* 496–8. **fericula:** cf. 95.18, 122.3. The *ferculum* (in the form of signs of the zodiac) served at Trimalchio's dinner (Petr. 35.1) astonishes the guests with its celestial novelty (his *ingeniosus cocus*, distinguished for his ability to craft anything out of pork, is named Daedalus, 70.3). **hoc monstrat:** *hoc* is the direct object of *monstrat*, and in explanatory apposition to *hoc* is the indirect question introduced by *quam* and the three indirect statements containing *posse*. The threefold repetition of *posse nos* underlines the capacity of every individual with the help of philosophy to reject luxury. **commercio sericorum:** see the complaint later at §20 *uestis nihil celatura*; cf. *Ben.* 7.9.5. Pliny (*Nat.* 12.84) complains at the vast cost of the trade with India. **cocum:** cf. 114.26. The prizing of cooks is a conspicuous symptom of moral decline for Livy (39.6.9), who dates the corrupting influx of eastern luxury to the time of Manlius Vulso's triumph in 187 BCE: *tum* *coquus, uilissimum antiquis mancipium et aestimatione et usu, in pretio esse, et quod ministerium fuerat, ars haberi coepta.* His complaint is capped by that of Plin. *Nat.* 9.67.   **militem:** S implies that the cause of war is human greed (cf. §41 *arma cessabant*). Thus, if we learned to be content with what we really needed, there would no longer be any wars and soldiers would be unnecessary. The absence of warfare is a common motif in accounts of the golden age; cf. Lucr. 5.999–1001, Virg. *A.* 1.291, Ov. *Met.* 1.98–9, *Phaed.* 533 *non arma saeua miles aptabat manu*, [Sen.] *Oct.* 400–1, Johnston 1980: 11.

16 sapientes . . . aut . . . sapientibus similes: S prepares to qualify his earlier use of *sapientes* (§§5–6). Focusing here on the admirable way of life of these people of earlier times, S turns later (§§27–9, 34–46) to the question of inner disposition, emphasising that, lacking the arduous mental discipline without which true *uirtus* cannot be achieved, they cannot in fact have been *sapientes* in the strong sense of the word.   **simplici cura:** abl. of price.   **in delicias laboratur** 'work is done to secure luxuries'. The passive makes for a pithier formulation.   **sequere naturam:** nature, here personified, is the key point of reference; cf. §43. Our lives should be *secundum naturam*, S repeatedly insists, e.g. 5.4, 41.8, 94.8, 118.12, 122.7, 124.7, *VB* 8.2.2, *De otio* 5.1.1.   **districtos** 'busy/preoccupied', *sc.* too busy for philosophy. *nos* is understood.   **quid ergo?** repeated four times in §§16–17, the hectoring formulation structures a torrent of evidence for nature's bounteous provision of means to ward off extremes of temperature, responding to imagined complaints against cold (§16) and heat (§17).   **conseruntur** 'join together' (*OLD consero*[2] 1).   **hodieque** 'even today'. See *OLD* 2c for this idiom.   **Scytharum:** often invoked as an example of quintessential barbarian simplicity (Lovejoy and Boas 1997: 315–44). See further below §31 n. on *Anacharsis*.   **tergis** 'pelts' (*OLD* 7a).   **murum:** here presumably marmots or similar; cf. Plin. *Nat.* 8.132 on the *mures alpini*, Amm. Marc. 31.2.5 on the skins of *siluestres mures*, worn by the Huns.   **uirgeam . . . luto:** cf. Plin. *Nat.* 35.169.   **pluuiis:** cf. §10 on the ability of primitive roofs to keep out rain.   **securi:** see §10(n.) *securi*.

17 defosso: the substantival use (= 'hole') is unusual; *OLD defodio* 3a cites only this passage.   **Syrticae gentes:** people dwelling near the North African coast, between Carthage and Cyrene, off whose shores lay the dangerous sand-banks called the *Syrtes* (Plin. *Nat.* 8.32).   **ipsa arens humus:** the earth itself, though hot, affords the most basic and readily available protection from the heat.

18 actum uitae 'method of life' (*OLD actus* 7c).   **parata** 'things easily obtained'.   **difficilia facilium fastidio fecimus:** alliteration underlines the paradox.   **fomenta** 'warm wraps'.   **obuia** 'ready to hand'.   **modus enim omnium prout necessitas erat** 'for the allocation of all things was in accordance with necessity', i.e. people only helped themselves to what they actually needed.   **sufficit ad id natura quod poscit** 'Nature supplies enough to meet her own demands.'

19 a natura luxuria desciuit: for *desciscere* in the sense of 'to turn away from' (*OLD* 2) cf. 122.9 'when men have begun to desire all things *contra naturae consuetudinem*, they end by abandoning nature's ways completely', *De otio* 2.1, Cic. *Fin.* 4.43. Similar complaints are articulated in Papirius Fabianus' attack on luxurious architecture (*ap.* Sen. *Con.* 2.1.13): *aduersum naturam alieno loco aut terra aut mare mentita aegris oblectamenta sunt.*   **ingenio** 'ingenuity'.   **animum ... iussit** for the figure of the mind enslaved to the body's pleasures cf. *Ep.* 47, esp. §17 and intro., 110.10, *Helv.* 11.6.   **addixit** 'handed over', a technical term for enslavement (*OLD* 6b); cf. 71.14 *mens hebes et quae se corpore addixerit.*   **circitatur** 'is thronged'. The verb, which occurs only here, is cognate with the more common *circitator* 'hawker'.   **textorum** 'of the weavers'.   **molles ... infractos** 'those who teach delicate dancing and delicate and effeminate singing'. For the pejorative associations of *mollis* see Edwards 1993: ch. 2, Williams 2010: 139–48. Seneca the Elder disapproves in similar terms of dancing and singing on the part of young men of his day (*Con.* 1.pr.8): *cantandi saltandique obscena studia effeminatos tenent*, which he links with their *mollitia corporis*. See further 114.7, 15nn.   **rusticitatis:** cf. 86.11(n.).

20 S takes issue with Posidonius' attribution of the invention of spinning and weaving to philosophers. Compare Lucr. 5.1350–60 on the role of the loom in the development of civilisation.   **mi Lucili:** the first epistolary marker since §1.   **dulcedo orationis:** similar comments on Posidonius are made by Strabo 3.2.9.   **ex iis** 'of those'.   **quemadmodum ... ducantur** 'how some threads are twisted and others are spun softly and loosely'. Threads twisted more tightly by the spinner, as they are pulled from the wool on the distaff, would be stronger, those twisted less tightly would be softer.   **quemadmodum ... extendat** 'how, with weights suspended, the warp [*OLD tela* 3: vertical threads] stretches its thread straight'. Each warp thread would be attached to the loom's crosspiece, with a weight attached at its lower end to make it hang straight. On the technology of weaving (with explanatory illustrations) see Wild 2008.   **quemadmodum ... iungi** 'how the weft [i.e. the horizontal/cross threads], inserted to soften the warp threads which press it on each side, is forced by the batten to come together and join up'. Weft threads are here of softer stuff than the more robust warp threads. **postea:** i.e. after the golden age. **hoc subtilius genus** 'this more sophisticated kind', i.e. of loom, which S asserts was invented after the time of Posidonius' *sapientes*. **tela ... dentes:** S quotes Ov. *Met.* 6.55–8, describing the weaving of Arachne. *harundo*: a rod threaded through the warp threads to make a passage for the weft (*OLD* 2e). Although most MSS of Ovid have *feriunt* in l. 58, modern editors of the *Metamorphoses* adopt the rare technical term *pauiunt* 'they tamp down' (on which *feriunt* may originally have been a gloss) from this passage in the *EM* (Jan Gruter conjectured *pauiunt* in 90.20 as a correction to the meaningless *pariunt* 'they give birth'). See Tarrant 2016: 8. **illi:** i.e. Posidonius. **uestis nihil celatura:** see §15n. on *commercio sericorum*. Horace associates clothing of revealing Coan silk with prostitutes (*S.* 1.2.101–4; cf. Ov. *Ars* 2.298). Transparent garments are a frequent focus of moralising disapproval; cf. e.g. 114.21, *Helv.* 16.4, *Ben.* 7.9.5, Plin. *Nat.* 11.76, Juv. 2.66–78, as well as S's description of Caligula (*Constant.* 18.3): *pellucidus, crepidatus, auratus*. **nullum pudori:** sc. *auxilium*.

21 iteratum: a technical farming term (*OLD* 6a) for the second ploughing; cf. Var. *R.* 1.32.1. **herbas** 'weeds' (*OLD* 1b). **cultores:** as opposed to *sapientes*.

22 pistrinum: lit. bakery (or mill) but also figuratively, signifying a place of drudgery to which slaves were sent as punishment (Pl. *Per.* 420, Cic. *Q. fr.* 1.2.14, Apul. *Met.* 9.10–11). **rerum naturam imitatus:** for nature as a pattern for the arts cf. Arist. *Protrepticus* 50.2–4 (Johnson and Hutchinson 2017), Cic. *Leg.* 1.26, Lucr. 5.1361–9, Vitr. 1.21. **concurrens ... dentium:** *concurrens* is transferred from the teeth to *duritia*. **aequali eius feruore** 'its [i.e. the stomach's] constant heat'.

23 utriusque attritu 'by the grinding of the one against the other'. **cinis ... percoxit:** sing. vb. agreeing with the nearer (of two) subjects. The dough would be cooked by warmth from the heated tile and the hot ash beneath it. **quorum feruor seruiret arbitrio** 'whose heat could be regulated'. **sutrinum:** *reductio ad absurdum* for S, since shoemaking is a proverbially lowly craft. Some ancient sources refer to Socrates' philosophical conversations with Simon the shoemaker; in the Cynic tradition particularly, the shoemaker-philosopher could be deemed a faithful follower of the Socratic model (Sellars 2003). S may be distancing himself here from the paradox associated with the Stoic Chrysippus that since the wise man was perfect he must be the perfect cobbler as well as the perfect king (see Hor. *S.* 1.3.124–8).

24 ratio . . . recta ratio: *ratio* is sometimes qualified as right reason, *recta ratio* (corresponding to the *orthos logos* of earlier Stoics), to distinguish it from more practical forms of understanding (Wildberger 2006: 249–52). At 89.6 philosophy is defined as *appetitio rectae rationis*. If Posidonius attributed such an aim to the philosophers of early times, this certainly suggests that he regarded them as true *sapientes* (Setaioli 1988: 327).   **commenta est:** see §14 *commentus* earlier.   **exemplum a piscibus:** the invention of rudders, inspired by the swimming of fish, is, like bread-making, an instance of technology imitating nature.

25 sed minora . . . dedit 'as they were too trivial for him to deal with he handed them over to more lowly operatives'. The activities referred to correspond to the *artes uulgares et sordidae*, described as 'belonging to workmen (*opifices*) and mere handwork' (88.21 attributes the definition to Posidonius; cf. the βάναυσοι τέχναι of Pl. *Resp.* 371e and Arist. *Pol.* 1337b14–15, Nightingale 2004: 123–7). At 88.21, these are contrasted with the *artes liberales*. The latter, while they are not part of philosophy, may nevertheless serve as preparation for it (88.20).   **hodieque:** see §16n.   **speculariorum usum:** cf. 86.11.   **testa** 'tile' of glass or other transparent material such as alabaster (*OLD* 3b).   **suspensuras balneorum** 'the raised floors of bathhouses' (*OLD suspendo* 4b). Baths often featured a hypocaust; cf. Plin. *Ep.* 2.17.9 on his bath complex, *suspensus et tubulatus*.   **tubos . . . aequaliter** 'the tubes fitted into the walls through which circulates warmth which heats evenly and simultaneously the lowest and highest parts'. Cf. *Nat.* 3.24.3, *Prov.* 4.9 *subditus et parietibus circumfusus calor temperauit*. Plin. *Nat.* 9.168 attributes the invention to Sergius Orata (on whom see §7n. on *uiuaria piscium*). On the technology see Yegül 1992: 356–95 and 2010: 80–100.   **marmora . . . fulgent:** for more detailed complaints about the use of marble see 86.6(nn.).   **lapideas . . . formatas:** a facetiously elaborate periphrasis for columns.   **leue** 'smooth' (*OLD leuis*² 1).   **capacia populorum tecta:** cf. 115.8 *capacem populi cenationem*.   **uerborum notas:** Suetonius (p. 135 Reifferscheid) attributes to Ennius, a grammarian of the Augustan period, the first use of shorthand on a large scale, though he also associates some use of shorthand with Cicero's freedman Tiro (cf. Plut. *Cat. Min.* 23).   **excipitur** 'is taken down'; cf. 108.6.   **uilissimorum mancipiorum:** cf. 70.25(n.) *extrema . . . mancipia*. The contempt for manual work expressed here has several parallels in Roman texts, notably Cic. *Off.* 1.150 *opifices . . . omnes in sordida arte uersantur* (Finley 1973: 41–5, Greene 2008; cf. Xen. *Oec.* 4.2, Arist. *Pol.* 1337b), though Cicero regards architecture as, like medicine and teaching, an art of significant value, characterised by *prudentia* and *utilitas* (*Off.* 1.151; cf. the celebration of technological developments, including house-building, at *Off.* 2.12–15, Vitr. 2.1.3, Pani 1992).

26 S now moves on to praise of philosophy, which is concerned with what affects the mind not the body.   **altius sedet** 'sits higher up', like a magistrate on a tribunal.   **eruerit** 'has brought to light' (*OLD* 2).   **tibiam:** a musical instrument made of a pipe with holes and a reed mouthpiece.   **in exitu:** from the horn.   **in transitu:** through the *tibia*.   **ad concordiam uocat:** the musical imagery here (echoing §3 *haec docuit . . . inter homines consortium*) balances the dissociation of philosophy from the practical business of music-making (as Zago 2012: 140–1 notes, there is no reason to suppose that Posidonius included music and dance among the discoveries of the *sapientes*). For musical harmony with a figurative sense cf. 84.9–10.

27 opifex: often disparaging; cf. Cic. *Flac.* 18 *opifices et tabernarios atque illam sordidam faecem ciuitatum, Off.* 1.150 (quoted at §25n.).   **artificem:** for *sapientia* as *artifex uitae* cf. 53.11, 95.7, 117.12, Cic. *Fin.* 3.4. For the grander connotations of *artifex* (in contrast to *opifex*) cf. the dying words attributed to Nero (Suet. *Nero* 49.1): *qualis artifex pereo!*   **beatum statum:** the goal of human life (= εὐδαιμονία).   **illo** 'thither'.

28 S offers a variety of formulations to express philosophy's concern to teach us to distinguish between what is truly bad or good and what merely seems so (on *indifferentia* see main intro. section 4).   **notitiam . . . sui** 'self-knowledge'.   **quid sint di:** cf. §3 on philosophy's concern with the nature of the gods.   **inferi** 'the gods of the Underworld'. At 24.18, S suggests that fear of the Underworld is unfounded.   **lares:** gods associated with the protection of certain places (frequently the household). The term is often used to translate the Greek δαίμων.   **genii:** cf. 12.2(n.) *iurat per genium meum.*   **perpetitae:** pf. partic. of *perpetere* perhaps (two MSS have *perpetuae*), thus 'souls brought through to a secondary form of divinity' (the only occurrence of this word in classical Latin). See the reference to gods of lesser rank (*inferioris notae*) at 110.1.   **initiamenta:** rites were associated with initiation into mystery religions such as at Eleusis (Cic. *N.D.* 1.119).   **reseratur** 'is opened up' (*OLD* 1b).   **cuius:** i.e. of the *mundus*.   **uera simulacra:** paradox.   **hebes:** i.e. too dull.   **uisus:** i.e. the vision of our eyes.

29 inditam 'implanted' (*OLD indo* 3a).   **uim . . . figurantem** 'the capacity of all seeds which gives shape to individual things according to their kind'. For these σπερματικοὶ λόγοι see Wildberger 2006: 205–8.   **animo** 'the soul'.   **a corporibus:** the Stoics took the view that the mind was wholly corporeal (Long 1996: 224–49).   **argumenta** 'evidence'.   **excussit** 'discovered by scrutiny' (*OLD* 9b), a term S often uses of self-examination (e.g. 72.1; Rimell 2015a: 137–47 explores S's deployment of this 'shaking out' metaphor).   **uitae aut uocis ambigua** 'uncertain matters in life or in language'; cf. *Nat.* 1.pr.2, where philosophy *lumen admouet quo discernantur ambigua uitae*.

30 ut Posidonio uidetur: according to S, Posidonius argued that philosophers were responsible for inventing various technologies but later withdrew from such concerns.   **illas:** i.e. those such as weaving and bread-making.   **ponenda non sumeret** 'he would not take up things which would have to be put aside'.

31 Anacharsis: a Scythian prince (according to Hdt. 4.76–7), noted for his wisdom, who travelled through Greece in the sixth century BCE (Diog. Laert. 1.101–5). He seems to have been included among the Seven Sages by Ephorus of Messene (Strabo 7.3.9). Sayings and fragments of letters attributed to him extol the simple life of the Scythians (Kindstrand 1981; cf. Cic. *Tusc.* 5.90). He is repeatedly invoked in Cynic texts (Martin 1996). S uses a Scythian example at §16.   **rotam figuli:** the potter's wheel (wheel-made pottery is attested on Crete from *c.* 1900 BCE).   **Homerum:** *Il.* 18.600–1. Strabo (7.3.9) also refers to this inconsistency, which may have been a well-known crux (see Kidd 1988 *ad* Posidonius F284).   **maluit:** Summers' emendation. Several MSS have *malunt*, which might be justified if this was indeed a topic widely debated among philosophers.   **puta:** see 33.4n.   **uitrearium:** specialist glass-workers in the Roman world produced sophisticated and complex objects, such as perfume bottles (Israeli 1991). The glass-worker's ability to form things into many shapes (echoing the potency of the seeds in §29) implicitly excites admiration, though the objects he produces might be thought a manifestation of luxurious variety (of which S disapproves).   **postquam sapientem inuenire desîmus** 'since we have ceased to discover the wise man', i.e. at a time when we no longer found there were *sapientes* (presumably here *sapiens* in the weak sense, as far as S is concerned). S plays on *inuenire*, a recurrent term in §§30–1. As in the case of the loom, S associates such inventions with a period later than the point at which Posidonius allegedly suggests 'philosophers' withdrew from such technical interests (§30 *abduxit ... se ... ab istis artibus sapiens*). Kidd (1988 *ad* Posidonius F284) argues S is misrepresenting Posidonius (see introd. above). The contracted form *desîmus* gives the common cretic spondee clausula – ∪ – – ×.

32 Democritus: see 7.10(n.). The latest chronologically of the figures invoked by Posidonius, he is not elsewhere associated with inventing the arch (he seems, however, to have taken a positive view of the role of technology in human progress, KRS 402–33, Boys-Stones 2001: 6). Pliny (*Nat.*

7.56) offers a list of such 'first inventors'.   **fornicem:** arches are indeed attested from much earlier periods.   **ut . . . alligaretur** 'with the effect that the curve of the gradually leaning stones is linked together by the keystone'; cf. the metaphorical use at 95.53, 118.16.

33 excidit: ironic. 'You have forgotten. . .' Cf. 27.5 on the ignorant Calvisius Sabinus: *illi nomen Ulixis exciderit*. For the attribution to Democritus see DK 68.300.14 (Diels and Kranz associate this kind of interest with a pseudo-Democritean author, Bolus of Mendes, rather than Democritus).   **porro** 'on top of that' (*OLD* 5).   **ebur molliretur:** Plutarch (*Mor.* 499e) suggests that ivory can be softened using beer.   **zmaragdum:** the term is used for a number of different green stones. Pliny (*Nat.* 37.197) refers to treatises describing how rock crystal may be made to resemble emeralds (see also 9.117 on the jewels of Lollia Paulina, 37.62–4).   **hodieque:** see §16n.

34 sapiens: this is the true Stoic wise man/philosopher.   **quaeris:** as in §1, S presents his account as a response to his interlocutor's inquiry.   **tardis ad diuina** 'slow to perceive the divine'; cf. §28.   **uitae legem** 'law of life'; cf. 120.12 with Inwood *ad loc.* and Inwood 2005: ch. 8.   **quam:** i.e. life.   **ad . . . derexit** 'made to conform with'; cf. Cic. *Leg.* 2.13 *naturam, ad quam leges hominum deriguntur*.   **sequi deos:** cf. *VB* 15.5 *illud uetus praeceptum: 'deum sequere'*, 107.9.   **accidentia . . . imperata:** an allusion to the Stoic doctrine that we should accept all that happens as fated; cf. 76.23, 107.9 *malus miles est qui imperatorem gemens sequitur* (going on to cite Cleanthes), 120.12 (Inwood links the last passage with the military imagery ascribed to Sextius at 59.7, on which see 64.2, with intro. to that letter).   **quanti quidque esset** 'what is the value of each thing'. *quanti*: gen. of value.   **mixtas paenitientia:** cf. 24.14, 27.2 *istas uoluptates turbidas, magno luendas*. Several philosophical schools stressed the subsequent sufferings often entailed by the pursuit of bodily pleasure; cf. e.g. Antisthenes (Ath. 12.6) and, notoriously, Epicurus (Diog. Laert. 10.129).   **felicitate non opus est:** all that is necessary is virtue (cf. the paradoxical formulation of 124.24, with Inwood *ad loc.*). This is a significant qualification to the emphasis on *felicitas* in S's earlier characterisation (§§4, 9) of the so-called golden age. On the intrinsic fragility of *felicitas* see e.g. 98.1.   **qui se habet in potestate:** cf. 94.61–7, 113.29–30, *Nat.* 3.pr.10.

35 de ea . . . uoluptati: a critical characterisation of Epicureanism (cf. at greater length *Ben.* 4.2 and 4.19), objecting to what were generally perceived as its three central features: the advice not to participate in politics (cf. Epicurus, *Sent. Vat.* 58), the claim that the gods have no involvement in the world (cf. Epicurus, *Ep. Men.* 123–4, Lucr. 5.146–55, Cic. *N.D.* 1.19.49), the proposal that pleasure should be the criterion by which all choices are made (cf. Epicurus, *Ep. Men.* 127–32, Cic. *Fin.* 1.29); see Schiesaro 2015. The contrast with S's more positive references to Epicurus in earlier letters (e.g. 7.11, 12.10) is marked (a shift introduced in *Ep.* 33; see intro. to that letter).   **hanc philosophiam . . . non credo:** philosophy in the Stoic sense was not in existence in primitive times – a key contention in this letter.   **rudi saeculo:** S now returns to his praise of primitive times. At 95.13–14, he terms the *sapientia* of such a period *rudis*.

36 †sicut aut†: the text is corrupt here. Haase's emendation *sint licet* makes better sense, though the sequence of tenses is awkward. As Boys-Stones (2001: 19; cf. Blankert: 71) notes, the sense of the letter requires something along the lines of *sic erant fortunata tempora*; S is here summing up the positive features of the 'golden age'.   **fortunata tempora:** S often stresses that the wise man should not be dependent on *fortuna* for his happiness (e.g. 25.6).   **<docuere>:** supplied by Hense, subject *auaritia atque luxuria*.   **non . . . sapientibus:** though not philosophers themselves, men of this time lived a simple, natural life of the kind appropriate to philosophers. S here corrects his equivocation at §16 *sapientes aut sapientibus similes*.

37 nec . . . apud quos 'nor, if god were to permit someone to shape earthly matters and give customs to the peoples, would he have approved anything other than that which was to be found among those, it is recorded, among whom'.   **nulli . . . ferebat:** Virg. *G.* 1.125–8. Again S quotes from Virgil's account of the transition from the age of Saturn to the beginnings of agriculture (cf. §§9 and 11). The passage quoted here is also closely echoed at *Phaed.* 528–9.

38 felicius: cf. §34(n.) *felicitate . . . est*.   **ut parens:** whereas in Posidonius' account human leaders exercised a parental concern for their subjects (§5), here it is rather Nature who occupies this role.   **secura:** because goods are held in common there is no anxiety that one may lose one's possessions. S revisits the idea articulated at §3, where private property is *paupertatis causa*.   **irrupit . . . auaritia:** as in §6(n.) (*surrepentibus uitiis*), agency is occluded as vices are personified.

39 licet 'no matter that', repeated three times, highlights the insatiable but pointless activity of those obsessed by property ownership.   **conetur:** subject *auaritia*.   **uicinum uel pretio pellens uel iniuria** 'pushing out a neighbour by buying him out or doing him wrong'. **in prouinciarum spatium:** cf. 89.20, *De ira* 1.21.2, *Ben.* 7.10.5, Petr. 48. **per sua longam peregrinationem:** Trimalchio is made to boast that he wants to add Sicily to his estates, so that *cum Africam libuerit ire, per meos fines nauigem* (Petr. 48.3). **propagatio** 'extension'. For the thought cf. 87.7. **unde discessimus:** shifting from a real to a figurative point of departure. **multum habebimus: uniuersum habebamus:** an instance of S's characteristically skilful use of adversative asyndeton, supported by the parallelism of *habeb-*... *habeb-*.

40 terra ipsa ... illaborata: a common topos in representations of pre-agricultural paradise; cf. Lucr. 5.933–44, Virg. *Ecl.* 4.18–30, Ov. *Met.* 1.102–6, *Phaed.* 537–8. **non minus ... erat:** the two elements of the comparison are inverted. **nondum ... nondum:** while in §5 primitive life was characterised in positive terms, here the use of anaphoric negation (cf. §45) creates a dual focus on the innocent past and on the corrupt times which will follow. Such repeated negations also feature in earlier vignettes of primitive innocence (e.g. Lucr. 5.932–6, 953–7, Ov. *Met.* 1.89–112; cf. Galinsky 1981) but the absent vices are realised in much more vivid detail by S (Novara 1988, Maxia 2000). **iaceret** 'lie idle' (*OLD* 9c). **par ... cura:** in this version of early human society, there is no need for a beneficent ruler or for laws (contrast the Posidonian accounts in §§4–5, Zago 2012: 72). The lack of greed in early human communities also features in Maximus of Tyre's Cynic account of early human life (*Dissertation* 36, Boys-Stones 2001: 8, 15).

41 arma cessabant 'weapons lay unused'; cf. §15(n.) *militem*. **incruentaeque ... sanguine:** the characterisation through negation confronts us with humanity's blood-stained future. **odium ... uerterant:** though at §45 S suggests, *parcebant adhuc etiam mutis animalibus*. Cf. *Phaed.* 502–3 *callidas tantum feris* | *struxisse fraudes nouit*. **tuti sub fronde:** cf. the optimistic account of the shelter afforded by branches at §§10 and 17. **placidas noctes:** cf. *Phaed.* 520–1 *certior somnus premit* | *secura duro membra laxantem toro*, Epicurus fr. 207 Usener (= 126 Arrighetti), Lucr. 2.34–6, Hor. *Carm.* 3.1.17–24. The use of a hard bed features as part of the rehearsal of poverty, which S advocates as a regular philosophical exercise at 18.7. **acerrimis ... stimulis:** the possession of riches causes mental torture.

42 caelata laquearia: cf. §15 *uersatilia cenationum laquearia* and intro. above on S's recurrent concern with oppressively elaborate ceilings. The pun *caelata ... caeli* highlights the contrast between artifice and nature. **superlabebantur:** see *OLD labor*¹ 2, poetical, of heavenly bodies (though this is the only attestation of this verb before Ausonius and Augustine); cf. also *De otio* 5.4. *ab ortu sidera in occasum labentia*.   **in praeceps agebatur** 'was being driven round at great speed'.   **opus:** cf. *Prov.* 1.2, *Nat.* 7.25.6, Ov. *Fast.* 5.12.   **domus** 'heavens' (*TLL* v.1978.2a); cf. Enn. *Ann.* 586 Skutsch *diuum domus altisonum cael*, Virg. *A.* 10.101 *deum domus alta*, Cic. *Rep.* 6.29. At 102.21 S asserts that the *patria* of the *humanus animus* is the whole space which encircles the land, sea and upper air.   **libebat:** on the pleasure of contemplating the sky see intro. above.   **signa** = *sidera* (Var. *L.* 7.14; cf. *OLD* 13).   **media caeli parte** 'the zenith'.   **quidni iuuaret:** this passage echoes Man. 1.13–19 on the joy of observing the heavens (Degl'Innocenti Pierini 2008: 119–20). Cf. also the words spoken by the character Seneca in [Sen.] *Oct.* 385–8 : *O quam iuuabat, quo nihil maius parens | natura genuit, operis immensi artifex, | caelum intueri, solis et cursus sacros | mundique motus*.   **sparsa miracula:** cf. the description of Phaethon's audacious (but ultimately fatal) journey through the heavens (Ov. *Met.* 2.193–4): *sparsa quoque in uario passim miracula caelo . . . uidet*. S quotes from the same episode at 115.13, *Prov.* 5.10–11, *Nat.* 7.10.1, *Phaed.* 1090–2 (Degl'Innocenti Pierini 2008: 120–1, Berno 2003: 261–3).

43 uos 'you' (of the present day).   **attoniti** 'terrified' (*OLD* 2a). On the fear provoked by the sounds of a grand residence cf. 96.1, 103.2 *crepant aedificia antequam corruant*, *Phaed.* 495, *Ben.* 4.6.2.   **instar urbium** 'the size of cities'. Cf. §7, *Ben.* 7.10.5. On this topos in moralising on luxurious architecture see Purcell 1987: 197–200, Edwards 1993: 158–60. Nero's Golden House was famously criticised for occupying the entire city of Rome (Suet. *Nero* 39, Plin. *Nat.* 36.111–12, Mart. 2.4 *unaque iam tota stabat in urbe domus*). Suetonius (*Nero* 31.1) describes its lake as *maris instar.*   **spiritus** 'breeze' (*OLD* 8a). Cf. *Tranq.* 17.8 on the refreshment brought by walking in the open air: *et in ambulationibus apertis uagandum ut caelo libero et multo spiritu augeat attollatque se animus*, Hor. *Ep.* 1.10.15–16.   **leuis umbra:** along with a gentle breeze, grassy banks and clear waters, refreshing shade is a frequent feature of idealised rustic scenes; cf. Ov. *Met.* 3.155–62 (including a *fons . . . pellucidus*); on the *locus amoenus* see further Schönbeck 1962.   **riuique . . . currentes:** naturally flowing streams, the opposite of the artificial *euripi* criticised at §15 (cf. Pap. Fab. *ap.* Sen. *Con.* 2.1.13 and the complaints at Juv. 3.17–20).   **rustica politum manu:** oxymoronic, given that *politus* means refined. Contrast the negative sense of *rusticitas* (from the perspective of the luxurious) at 86.11.   **secundum naturam domus:** see §16n. on *sequere naturam*.   **nec ipsam nec pro ipsa timentem:** for fear of being crushed by one's grand house, along with fear at its vulnerability to fire, cf. Pap. Fab. *ap.* Sen. *Con.* 2.1.12 *anxii et interdiu et nocte ruinam ignemque* *metuant.* See intro. above for the particular poignance of this motif in Nero's Rome.

44 non fuere sapientes: following a long sequence of negations to highlight positive features of primitive life, whose innocence is insistently contrasted with the corruption of the present, S now uses negation to address the limitations of this innocent existence, which lacks the potential for true virtue now available through philosophy (Novara 1988, Maxia 2000).   **quando ... est** 'when this term is now attached to the greatest achievement', i.e. of being a true *sapiens* as S defines it – 'now', that is, following the full manifestation of philosophy. See Armisen-Marchetti 1998: 203–4.   **a dis recentes:** S is in mythological mode here; cf. Pl. *Leg.* 948b5–7, Dicaearchus fr. 49 Wehrli, Cic. *Tusc.* 1.26, *Leg.* 2.27.   **nondum effetus** 'before it was exhausted' (cf. Lucr. 2.1150 *iam ... effeta tellus*).   **ad labores paratior:** though at §40 S comments that the earth was more fruitful, *illaborata*, in those times (while at §16 a contrast is drawn, *simplici ... laboratur*).   **ingenia ... consummata:** cf. 92.27, where S comments on the *ratio* shared by gods and humans: *in illis consummata est, in nobis consummabilis.*   **non ... uirtutem:** returning to the contention of §§1–2; cf. 123.16 *discenda uirtus est.*   **ars ... fieri:** cf. Chrysippus *SVF* III.214. While this process is the general concern of the letters, *Epp.* 94 and 95 offer a detailed and systematic analysis (see Schafer 2009). For S, this *ars* alone is to be celebrated (cf. §27 *sapientia* as *artifex uitae*), in contrast to the material *artes* whose development Posidonius (§7) attributed to philosophers.

45 non aurum: this primitive age may be termed *aureum* by some (cf. §5), but its people were quintessentially uninterested in gold (see further S's comment on their fabrics in the next sentence, *nondum texebatur aurum*); cf. Lucr. 5.1273, Man. 1.75 *tumque in desertis habitabit montibus aurum.* For this paradox see intro. above.   **pellucidos <lapides in>:** the two supplements (the first found in D and the second proposed by Schweigh) plausibly posit precious stones as an accompaniment to gold and silver (contrast the readily available *pellucidi fontes* of §43, which satisfy a natural want).   **ima ... faece:** the dross from which some eagerly pull forth treasure is an indicator of its true value. At 94.56–9, S argues that nature has deliberately concealed these potential incitements to avarice beneath the earth (cf. Hor. *Carm.* 3.3.49–50 *aurum irrepertum et sic melius situm | cum terra celat*).   **parcebantque ... animalibus:** in Virgil's age of *aureus ... Saturnus* (*G.* 2.537) people did not yet feast on *caesis ... iuuencis.* Pertinent here, too, may be Pythagorean doctrine (cf. the words of Pythagoras describing a golden age at Ov. *Met.* 15.103–10); S reports (108.17) that under the influence of his Pythagorean teacher Sotion he himself abstained from eating meat in his youth. **ut homo . . . occideret:** a substantive clause which serves as the subject of *aberat*. S returns to the concerns of *Ep.* 7(nn.); cf. 95.33. The juxtaposition *homo hominem* ironically highlights the inhumanity of such behaviour. **tantum spectaturus** 'just to achieve a spectacle'. The sense is compressed. Although it is the killer doing the looking here, the reproach extends to the spectators implicitly present in the amphitheatre. **nondum . . . nondum:** cf. §40(n.) *nondum.* **uestis . . . picta:** a garment embroidered or otherwise decorated with colours.

46 nolit an nesciat: for a similar characterisation of early human society see *Nat.* 3.30.8 *illis quoque innocentia non durabit, nisi dum noui sunt.* Cf. Janus' cynical characterisation of the men of the age of Saturn in Ov. *Fast.* 1.191–226 (on which see intro. above); their 'virtue' is merely the consequence of lack of opportunity (cf. 42.3–4). As S notes at 95.5, of those who have not absorbed good *praecepta, etiam si recte faciunt, nesciunt facere se recte.* S's position here is close to that of Plato in *Leg.* 678b (Boys-Stones 2001: 14). Gellius (7.1.1–13 = *SVF* II.1169) reports Chrysippus' argument that virtues cannot exist without their opposites. **deerat . . . deerat . . . deerat:** emphatic anaphora. **iustititia . . . prudentia . . . temperantia ac fortitudo:** these are the four virtues into which Cicero divides the *honestum* at *Off.* 1.15 (cf. *Fin.* 5.67); cf. S's argument at §2 that humans are not born *prudentes*, since this would make philosophy a gift of fortune. As Novara (1988: 133) notes, while *prudentia* usually leads the cardinal virtues (e.g. Pl. *Resp.* 427e σοφία, *SVF* I.200, 201, Gel. 7.1), here *iustitia* comes first, since it is this quality above all which philosophy must impart to compensate for the lost *consortium* enjoyed by early communities (§3). **rudis uita:** it is the lack of virtues rather than the lack of material *artes* which make this life primitive (cf. §36 *rude saeculum*). See Novara 1988: 134. **contingit:** cf. Cic. *N.D.* 3.87–8, quoted above in §2n. on *inter fortuita*. S here shifts from the past (*habebat*) to the timeless present, as he returns to the unchanging nature of philosophy (cf. the reverse shift in §3; see §3n. on *docuit*). **instituto . . . perducto:** this is a prolonged and challenging process which involves above all intellectual effort, the acquisition of a full reflective awareness of the nature of one's own virtue (see Trapp 2007: 42–5); cf. 89.8, where S observes, *nec philosophia sine uirtute est, nec sine philosophia uirtus.* **uirtutis materia:** cf. 108.8 *omnibus . . . natura fundamenta dedit semenque uirtutum,* 120.4, Diog. Laert. 7.89 (observing that nature gives humans uncorrupted inclinations to virtue).

LETTER 114

Ep. 114 returns to the issue of literary style, which S has discussed from a number of different perspectives in earlier letters (see *Epp.* 33 and 46nn.). Book 19, the penultimate of the surviving books, comprises eight letters (*Ep.* 114 is the fifth), most of which, unlike the majority of the letters in the later books of the collection, are relatively short and markedly epistolary in character, though *Ep.* 114 itself has few epistolary markers. The concerns of the more philosophically substantial *Epp.* 113 and 117 with the relationship of Stoic corporealism to ethics (see Inwood *ad locc.*) also manifest themselves, if in a rather different form, in *Ep.* 114, while the focus on style is pursued further in the opening of *Ep.* 115.

Starting from the question of why a corrupt literary style flourishes at certain times, *Ep.* 114 alludes to some of the different faults which style may exhibit (§1). While the maxim that a man's literary style corresponds to the way he lives is extended to apply to societies (§2), S focuses initially on the ways in which an individual's moral flaws are revealed in every detail of his bearing, dress and comportment (§3), his prime example being Maecenas, whose weaknesses of character (§4) are particularly reflected in his extraordinary literary style (§§5–8). Reprehensible style sometimes results from vices characteristic of society in general, which may reflect widespread moral laxity (§§9–11), but S returns to the literary faults of specific individuals, conceding that even the most admired have their failings, which may be an inextricable part of their greatness (§12). S now complicates his argument by making clear that what should count as proper style depends necessarily on the context; the language of the Twelve Tables sounds affectedly archaic deployed centuries later (§§13–14). Having explored infelicities of word order (§§15–16), S goes on to emphasise the influence of individual models (using the example of Arruntius imitating Sallust) in the transmission of particular practices (§§17–19). Where literary faults are due to imitation (rather than originating with the writer) they do not necessarily indicate flawed character (§20); deliberate literary faults, like excesses in personal grooming, are the result of reprehensible attention-seeking (§21) and indicate significant disturbance of the mind (§22). Developing a political analogy for the relationship between the mind and the body, S ends (§§23–7) describing the dreadful consequences when the mind rules not as a king but as a tyrant.

The question of why better or worse literary styles flourish at particular times was one to which many ancient literary critics gave attention, often focusing on a perceived decline in oratory; notable discussions include Cicero's *Brutus*, Seneca the Elder *Con.* 1.pr.7 and, among S's contemporaries, Petronius' *Satyricon* (1–5 and 118) and Persius' *Satire* 1. Among later analyses, Quintilian's *Institutio oratoria* (esp. 6.pr.3, 8.6.76) and Tacitus' *Dialogus* (25–35) engage with similar ideas (another treatise of Quintilian, *De causis corruptae eloquentiae*, is now lost). In certain respects, S's assessment concurs with these as to the criteria by which literary style (S, as his discussion of Maecenas underlines, is not concerned only with oratory) is to be judged. All these writers scrutinise particularly *compositio*, the choice and arrangement of words, and term *uirilis* features of style (as well as delivery) they regard as laudable (e.g. Quint. *Inst.* 1.8.9 on old Latin writers, 2.5.9, 5.12.18, 8.3.6, 12.10.79, Tac. *Dial.* 5.4). At the same time these critics differ as to exactly which styles are most praiseworthy; as we saw in the main intro. section 11, Quintilian is highly critical of S's own style (deploying against him some of the criticisms S offers of Maecenas; see Dominik 1997b: 58–9).

The use of strongly gendered terms to characterise good and bad literary style may perhaps be traced back to attacks on the approach of the so-called Asianist orators (*Rhet. Her.* 3.22, Sen. *Con.* 2.pr.1 criticising Arellius Fuscus, Leeman 1963: 137–67, Gleason 1995: 103–30, Richlin 1997). As Graver (1998: 608) notes, S, unlike these earlier writers, does not comment on mode of delivery but attaches gendered language specifically to the literary style of the works themselves. The culturally determined association of *uirtus* with masculinity (cf. Cic. *Tusc.* 2.43) plays a critical role in shaping S's language. Yet in S, as in earlier writers, it is not easy to pin down exactly what might constitute an ideal 'masculine' style (Graver 1998: 614–20; cf. Quint. *Inst.* 9.4.3); and indeed it seems this may vary depending on the context.

In *Ep.* 33 S had underlined that, since Stoic philosophy is manly (cf. *Constant.* 1.1, comparing the difference between Stoics and other philosophers to the difference between male and female), the style used to articulate it should be, too (33.5). S considers in *Epp.* 40 and 75 what style may be most appropriate to delivering a philosophical message. Lucilius' style is the concern of *Epp.* 46 (§2 praised as *uirilis*), 59 and 79. Style as a criterion for evaluating authors is explored further in *Ep.* 100, where S defends from criticism the works of the philosopher Papirius Fabianus, whose *compositio* Lucilius has found wanting (100.4): *oratio sollicita philosophum non decet*. At 115.1–2, S suggests that Lucilius should not be overly preoccupied with his own style; this is itself a stylistic fault.

Unsurprisingly S associates a fashion for perverse literary style with periods when morals more generally are corrupt, but he is more preoccupied in *Ep.* 114 with literary faults whose genesis is to be found in the moral character of the specific individual. His prime example here is Maecenas, confidant of the emperor Augustus. S is unremitting in his critique of Maecenas' character more generally, as well as his writing. In criticising Maecenas' literary style, S was not alone; Suetonius observes

(*Augustus* 86.2) that the emperor 'despised affected (*cacozelos*) writers . . . and sometimes took them to task, particularly his friend Maecenas whose "scented curls" (*myrobrechis . . . cincinnos*), as he called them, he attacked relentlessly, making fun of him through parody'. Quintilian (*Inst.* 9.4.28) criticises Maecenas' perverse ordering of words. Tacitus' Messalla (*Dial.* 26.1), like Augustus taking a metaphor from hairdressing, derides his *calamistros* 'crimping'. Macrobius (2.4.12) quotes a letter of Augustus to Maecenas, itself perhaps a parody of Maecenas' style, which Macrobius (influenced by S, suggests Graver 1998: 629–31) interprets as a teasing comment on his wealth and sexual behaviour, as well as his recherché prose.

Yet Velleius Paterculus, despite his comment (2.88.2) that Maecenas was *otio ac mollitiis paene ultra feminam fluens*, also praises (as does Cassius Dio) his firmness and vigilance in public business, qualities passed over by S. The celebration of Maecenas' generous support for literature, a prominent theme particularly in Horace's work (cf. Sen. *Suas.* 1.12, 2.20 on Maecenas' support for Virgil and others, *Laus Pisonis* 230–45, Labate 2012, Gowers forthcoming), finds no echo in S's analysis; conversely, many of S's hostile comments about Maecenas' behaviour are without precedent in earlier writers (Byrne 1999). Maecenas is also the object of criticism at 19.9, 92.35 (though here S contrasts a nice turn of phrase with the author's depraved character), 101.10–15 (where S denounces *carminis effeminati turpitudo*), 120.19. At *Prov.* 3.10–11, invoked as the antithesis of the noble Regulus, he serves as an emphatically negative *exemplum*, a figure for base self-indulgence; we should deem Regulus in his extreme sufferings for a virtuous cause more truly fortunate, S insists, than Maecenas amid his luxurious pleasures. Yet again Maecenas' masculinity is called into question; at *Prov.* 3.11 one who wishes to have been born Maecenas might just as well wish to have been Maecenas' wife Terentia, while, at *Ep.* 19.9, S comments on good fortune's effect on him: *eneruasset . . ., immo castrasset.*

Setaioli (2000: 191–2, 255–74) intriguingly suggests that S's critique of Maecenas' style echoes Posidonius' attack on that of Epicurus (as preserved by Cleomedes). The suggestion that Maecenas was Epicurean in his sympathies (for which inference from S is the main evidence) and that this is the reason for S's fierce hostility (André 1967: 15–61, Ferguson 1990: 2263–5) is rather tenuous (Graver 1998: 628, Setaioli 2000: 255–74), though certainly S discusses the differences between Stoic and Epicurean in strongly gendered terms (*VB* 13, Edwards 2005b), which might give some support to Mazzoli's

(1968) suggestion that S regarded him as the type of the superficial Epicurean.

Lunderstedt (1911: 8, followed by Mayer 1982: 315) diagnoses S's hostility to Maecenas' literary style as a response to literary fashion at Nero's court, where, in the latter years of his reign, Maecenas' work was in circulation and inspiring imitators (Morford 1972–3 argues that Lucan and Persius, along with S, were reacting against this). Certainly the literary politics of Nero's court were intense; Sullivan (1985: 17–6; see further Armisen-Marchetti 2013) traces complex rivalries played out through parody, persuasively suggesting that Petronius takes S's writing as his target in passages in the *Satyricon* (though on the dating of the *Satyricon* see intro. to *Ep.* 47 above). Byrne (2006: 92–3), noting that in S's earlier *De beneficiis* (4.36.2, 6.32.2–4) Maecenas is mentioned in neutral or positive terms, argues that S's critical remarks follow his withdrawal from Nero's inner circle in 62 CE (though on the difficulty of dating *De beneficiis* see Griffin 2013: 91–6). In S's demonisation of Maecenas, Byrne (2006: 95–111) traces a covert attack on Petronius, resented because he had recently come to exert a potent influence over Nero. Certainly there are some parallels between the character of Maecenas in S's *Ep.* 114 and Tacitus' (*Ann.* 16.18) portrait of Petronius (Byrne 2006). Yet the chief concern of S's attack on Maecenas is his literary style; as Byrne (2006: 104) concedes, parallels between Petronius' style and that of Maecenas are far from obvious.

For Graver (1998: 607), by contrast, S chooses to treat Maecenas reductively because 'his real object is . . . an abstract principle which Maecenas serves to illustrate'. S's concern in this letter is rather to emphasise how *uirtus*, as a condition of the human psyche, the *animus*, is to be outwardly recognised. Roman texts often suggest that character can be revealed by trivial details of gesture, dress, facial expression and movement (O'Sullivan 2011: 34–40). Such an assumption is pervasive in the satiric tradition (Degl'Innocenti Pierini 2013); the republican satirist Lucilius asserts, for instance (638 Marx = 662 Krenkel = 678 Loeb), *animo qui aegrotat, uidemus corpore hunc signum dare*.

That one's inner character was revealed in details of one's appearance, including one's gestures, was also a central contention of physiognomic writers, e.g. Polemo (Barton 1994: 95–131; cf. Gleason 1995). A story in Diogenes Laertius attributes an interest in such diagnoses to the Stoic Cleanthes (7.173). Stoic doctrines concerning the corporeal nature of virtue (Long 1996: 224–49, Inwood 1985: ch. 3, esp. 55–66) give particular potency to this perceived relationship. Just as the *ingenium* pervades the *animus* (114.3 *totum animo permixtum*), so the *animus* pervades the *corpus*. *Ep.* 113 discusses the corporeal nature of the soul and the bodily nature of virtue, particularly as these bear on the relationship between wisdom and being wise (see Inwood *ad loc.*). Elsewhere (106.4–6), S underlines that emotions are bodily things (*bonum agitat animum et quodammodo format et continet, quae propria sunt corporis*), while diseases of the spirit (*uitia*) are also corporeal. S often insists that a virtuous mind can dwell in a feeble or mutilated body (e.g. *Epp.* 15, 66, 78, 115.6); it is rather the body's gestures and expressions which betray the *animus* within (52.12; cf. 114.22).

Just as the *incessus* of the *sapiens* will be modest (40.14), so his *oratio* will be *pressa, non audax*. Given the close relationship between the mind and language, linguistic expression constitutes an even more reliable index of moral character than do movement and gesture (Graver 1998: 612–14). At 114.22 a healthy *animus* is reflected in an *oratio*, which is *robusta, fortis* and, of course, *uirilis*. The correctly composed *animus* (whose ideal state §3 is *sanus, compositus, temperans*) will reveal itself in perfectly balanced literary *compositio* (though this may, paradoxically, in its avoidance of excessive ornament appear *incomposita*, 40.4). Yet the vividly physical terms in which S describes features of literary style return us insistently to the realm of the body. At 100.8, S comments on Fabianus' writings: *totum corpus uideris quam sit comptum*, a not uncommon figurative use of *corpus* (cf. *Rhet. Her.* 4.58, Petr. 118.5; see Bramble 1974: 36-7). At 84.2, S likens reading (an essential counterpart to writing) to the process of digestion; one's own work, though it is the product of one's individual *ingenium*, grows out of and is nourished, like one's body, by that of others (see Graver 2014). This figure reinforces the link on which S dwells between loose clothing and loose writing, his striking and graphic metaphors drawn from personal grooming. Like Persius (see Bramble 1974: preface, Bartsch 2015), S takes the concepts and metaphors of literary criticism back to their physical origins. The invitation to picture Maecenas' grotesque appearance as he moves around the city grounds characterisation of his literary style in vividly imagined comic detail (Degl'Innocenti Pierini 2013: 55 notes S's masterly deployment of the orator's trope of *euidentia*).

As noted above, Stoic literary style is itself repeatedly characterised by S as *uirilis*; the link with *uirtus* is paramount. A virile style may not be exactly the same at different times but a virtuous style, like virtuous character (cf. 120.19–22), should always be consistent and clear (Graver 1998: 618–19). Maecenas is criticised for his excessive metaphors, for his contrived neologisms, but above all for being hard to understand (so much so that he sounds drunk; cf. 19.9 *ebrius sermo*). Reason, *ratio*, is the key concern. Cicero uses *uirilis* in praising particularly the logical rigour of Stoic writing (*Tusc.* 3.22 *qui maxime forti et . . . uirili utuntur ratione*; as Graver notes,

Aristotle uses μαλακός, for which *mollis* is usually seen as equivalent, to criticise feeble reasoning; see LSJ III.2g). For S, too, clarity is critical.

Yet the custom of the time also plays a role in determining what style is right. In his *De officiis* (1.107–21), Cicero gives an account of the Stoic Panaetius' four *personae* theory (see main intro. section 4). Each individual should take account of four aspects or 'roles' in determining how he ought to behave: the demands of universal human nature, his own individual strengths and weaknesses, the lot in life allocated by chance (health, wealth) and the career path chosen by himself. The idea of the fourth *persona* entails a recognition that different ways of behaving are appropriate to different occupations; the emphasis on what is 'proper' (*decorum* features in the account of Panaetius' schema offered by Cicero, e.g. *Off.* 1.110) as a standard also allows scope for different behaviour to be appropriate at different times. As Setaioli (2000: 162–89) suggests, this principle can be readily extended to literary style. At the same time (as Setaioli 2000: esp. 174–5 persuasively proposes), for S literary style expresses the particular individual character of the author, on the analogy of the second *persona* in Panaetius' theory. An individual's *ingenium* may develop through the imitation of other writers (cf. 84.8) but the nature of the *ingenium* for S is specific and personal (Graver 2014: 281–4). In this way a style which is fitting for one individual will not be right for another. Nevertheless we may detect a tension in this letter between the moral sphere and the aesthetic. Remarkably (and in this S is unparalleled among ancient commentators on style, as Setaioli 2000: 174–5 underlines; cf. Leeman 1963: 272), at §12 he observes that the very best writers will have intrinsic faults whose removal would undermine their genius. In an aesthetic context at least, *uitium* can have a positive value.

The final three paragraphs of the letter appear to take us in a new direction (indeed Summers' edition omits them). S explores the proper relationship between mind and body in terms of analogies with different styles of autocracy, contrasting kingship (to which corresponds the rule of the healthy *animus*) and tyranny (the domain of an *animus* which is disordered). Nero himself (a gaping absence in the *EM*; see intro. to *Ep.* 47 above) is never explicitly mentioned. Yet the analogy, underlining the dreadful consequences of disordered autocratic rule, recalls S's earlier treatise on clemency, whose addressee was the young emperor.

Nero's passion for literature was notorious; Tacitus (*Ann.* 14.16.1 *carminum quoque studium affectauit*) highlights the emperor's enthusiasm for composing poetry. Some fragments survive (on which see Bardon 1936: 337–49, Courtney 1993: 357–9, Baldwin 2005); S himself (*Nat.* 1.5.6) quotes and praises a line, *ut ait Nero Caesar disertissime*. A scholiast on Pers. 1.99–102 quotes lines purporting to be from Nero's *Attis* (Griffin 1984:

275 and Courtney 1993: 357–8 doubt their authenticity). Dio also reports (61.20.2) that Nero delivered an *Attis* or *Bacchae* at the Juvenalia of 59 CE. Dio does not make clear whether this was his own composition (Griffin 1984: 150). But it seems hardly coincidental (Sullivan 1985: 102–4) that Persius chooses to attack what he terms 'groinless' (*delumbe*) compositions such as *Maenas* and *Attis* (another instance of marking a literary style one does not approve of in terms of an effeminised body; this tendency finds its most graphic expression in Quintilian's extended comparison of faulty writing to a castrated youth, *Inst.* 5.12.18). As for Nero's prose, while S himself ghostwrote Nero's speeches in the earlier part of his reign (Tac. *Ann.* 13.3, 11, 14.11), a lengthy inscription (*IG* VII.2713) records a showy speech in Greek from 67 CE in which experimental, Asianist features have been diagnosed (Jones 2000: 58–62 argues that his Greek teacher may have been Niketes, whose florid, 'bacchic' style and daring phraseology are noted by Philostratus, *VS* 1.19.1).

Maecenas himself was the author of a poem in galliambics, entitled *Cybele* (Courtney 1993: 5–6; for a comparison with Cat. 63 on the subject of the self-castrated priest Attis, also in galliambics, see Avallone 1962: 305–7), a circumstance giving particular point to S's comment at 19.9 that good fortune had castrated Maecenas (see above). Several parallels have been noted between Nero's own work and that of Maecenas (Byrne 2006: 104–5). S's Maecenas may not be a plausible Petronius (contra Byrne 2006, 2007). Yet the parallels between Petronius' Trimalchio and S's Maecenas are nevertheless suggestive, given that a case has been made for interpreting Petronius' portrait of Trimalchio as refracting features of Nero as viewed by his court circle (Walsh 1970: 137–9, Rose 1971: 77–9, 82–6, Edwards 2007: 167–71). If we read S's attention-seeking, pleasure-loving, gender-subverting Maecenas as figuring for Nero (a possibility raised briefly by Degl'Innocenti Pierini 2013: 61–2), writing in a manner which deliberately scorns his old tutor's wise advice (Tac. *Ann.* 14.52), the ferocity of S's critique becomes more understandable.

Commentary: Summers (omitting §§5, 24–7).
Further reading: Lunderstedt 1911, Leeman 1963, Graver 1998, Byrne 1999, 2006, Laudizi 2004, Möller 2004: 167–240, Degl'Innocenti Pierini 2013, Gowers forthcoming.

1 Quare ... quaeris: emphatic alliteration. *Ep.* 114 has few epistolary markers, though for this kind of opening prompt cf. 7.1n., 22.1, 72.1. Degl'Innocenti Pierini (2013: 46 n. 2; cf. Möller 2004: 169) notes the parallel with the first words of Tac. *Dial.* 1, *saepe ex me requiris, Iuste Fabi, cur...*, also concerned with literary decline. See Lausberg 1998: §§767, 771.   **quibusdam temporibus** 'in certain times'. S does not here suggest a straightforward trajectory of decline (cf. 97.1 on *uitia* which flourished in the time of Cato the Elder).   **corrupti generis:** gen. of quality.   **oratio** 'literary style' of prose in general, not only, since Maecenas' works are not speeches, of oratory (Graver 1998: 608). As §6 *legeris* makes clear, S envisages the response of the reader to the written text.   **uitia:** a term with strong moral overtones, often the counterpart to *uirtus* (cf. e.g. Cic. *Tusc.* 4.34) but which is well established in discussions of style (Möller 2004: 170–1); cf. *Rhet. Her.* 2.31 *uitia argumentationis*, 4.17–18 *uitia in compositione*.   **inclinatio** 'decline' (*OLD* 1d).   **ingeniorum** 'literary talents', 'linguistic ability as demonstrated in speech or writing' (*OLD* 5a); cf. 21.5, 24.3, 33.5. On the potential slipperiness of this term in *Ep.* 114 see Graver 1998: esp. 612–14; cf. Graver 2014: 281–6.   **inflata:** pejorative; cf. 90.28 *uanitatem . . . inflatam*. Specifically a negative characteristic in oratory in *Rhet. Her.* 4.15, Cic. *Brut.* 202, Sen. *Suas.* 1.12, Quint. *Inst.* 12.10.16 (a feature of the *Asiani*, contrasted with the *Attici*; see Leeman 1963: 95), Plin. *Ep.* 9.26.5. Lucilius' style by contrast is praised (59.5) for having *nihil tumidi*.   **explicatio** 'style of exposition' (*OLD* 4a); cf. Cic. *Brut.* 144, Sen. *Con.* 2.pr.1.   **infracta:** cf. 90.19(n.) *infractos*, 115.1, Sen. *Con.* 7.4.8. The use of 'broken' imagery to denote the effeminate is also common in Greek analysis of style (e.g. Demetr. *Eloc.* 189; see Gleason 1995: 112). Elsewhere S uses *fractus* of one who is in thrall to pleasure and whose masculinity is compromised (*VB* 13.4): *eneruis, fractus, degenerans uiro, peruenturus in turpia*.   **in morem cantici:** cf. Cic. *Orat.* 57 *hic e Phrygia et Caria rhetorum epilogus paene canticum*. Summers *ad loc.* argues that the reference is to rhythm; elsewhere (1908b: 173–4), noting the plethora of cretics (— ◡ —) in the fragments of Maecenas quoted in §5, he observes that this metre is especially characteristic of the *cantica* in Plautus. Quintilian (*Inst.* 9.4.142) uses *saltare* of what he terms *compositio effeminata* (though he does allow, at *Inst.* 11.3.167, that *quiddam cantici* is desirable in certain contexts). On the perception of verse rhythms as strongly gendered see Demetr. *Eloc.* 189; Morgan (2010: 40–8) notes that the Ionic metres sotadean and galliambic (see above on Maecenas' poetry) were particularly associated with *cinaedi* (at Petr. 23.2–3 a *cinaedus* performs a poem in sotadeans).   **ducta** 'drawn out' (*OLD* 23).   **sensus** 'expressions'. Cf. 100.5 on the *sensus honestos et magnificos* of Fabianus. See §11 in this letter.   **abruptae . . . suspiciosae** 'phrases that are broken off short and full of innuendo'. Cf. Suet. *Dom.* 10.2 *suspiciosos . . . iocos*. See further §11 *suspicionem*.   **translationis** 'metaphor' (*OLD* 4a); cf. §10, 59.6, 108.35, Henderson 2002: 151–3.   **inuerecunde:** cf. Cic. *de Orat.* 3.156 *uerecunda debet esse translatio*; see also Quint. *Inst.* 8.6.14.   **hoc:** abl. of cause in response to *quare*.   **talis . . . uita:** gnomic aor. Compare the injunction at 75.4 *concordet sermo cum uita*. Cic. *Tusc.* 5.47 attributes a similar saying to Socrates (cf. Pl. *Resp.* 400d, Quint. *Inst.*

11.1.30 *Graeci prodiderunt ut uiuat quemque etiam dicere,* Tosi 1991 : §158). Contrast the claims conspicuously made by a number of Roman writers that their literary works are not to be taken as a reflection of their character; cf. e.g. Cat. 16, Ov. *Tr.* 2.323–60, Sen. *Con.* 6.8.

2 uniuscuiusque actio †dicendi† similis est: the text is corrupt. A supplement such as that of Russell (*dicendi <generi>*) would clarify what must, from the context, be the general sense: 'just as each individual's actions resemble his manner of speaking'. **genus . . . mores** 'thus the style of speaking sometimes reflects the general standards of the time'. For the phrase *publicos mores* cf. 103.5. The two clauses are not strictly parallel but such a reversal of elements can also be found at e.g. 90.40 *non minus . . . erat.* **disciplina** 'moral instruction'. Cf. Cic. *Ver.* 3.161 *erudire ad maiorum instituta, ad ciuitatis disciplinam.* **laborauit:** cf. *Prov.* 3.10 *felicitate nimia laborantem.* The causal relationship is complex; at 94.54 S observes that individuals are corrupted by the society they live in but that the converse is also true. **argumentum . . . luxuriae publicae:** for Seneca the Elder (*Con.* 1.pr.7) *luxus temporum* is a significant cause of the decline in oratory. **orationis lasciuia:** the fashion for a corrupt literary style itself indicates a corrupt society, given over to pleasure (the sexual overtones in this context are not specific to S; cf. Quint. *Inst.* 12.10.73, Plin. *Ep.* 9.26.5). Petronius' characters place significant blame on the teachers of oratory (Petr. 1–5; see Leeman 1963: 283).

3 animo: used in the sense of 'mind' (the relation between mind and body is a concern throughout the letter) but with an emphasis on moral constitution (cf. *OLD* 14). See intro. above. **color** 'quality' (*OLD* 5); cf. 20.2 *unus sit omnium actionum color* (thought the text here is problematic). **sanus:** imagery of health (and sickness) plays an important role in this letter (cf. also 40.5, 75.6–7). See further §25n. on *morbus.* Imagery of disease also features in the literary polemic of Persius, *Satire* 1 (see Bartsch 2015: 64–75). **compositus:** cf. 2.1 *primum argumentum compositae mentis existimo posse consistere et secum morari.* **siccum ac sobrium:** conversely drunkenness (§§4, 22) serves to illustrate the connection between a disordered mind and disordered speech; cf. 18.4, where S suggests that the would-be wise man might strive to remain *siccus et sobrius* even during the Saturnalia, when licence is given to *luxuria publica* and the *populus* is *ebrius et uomitans* (Degl'Innocenti Pierini 2013: 49). Cicero (*Brut.* 202) characterises Cotta's speech, with approval, as *siccus et sanus.* **afflatur** 'is infected' (*OLD* 4); cf. *Nat.* 2.53.2, Petr. 2 (on the influence of 'Asian' style) *ueluti pestilenti sidere afflauit.* **effeminatus:** the use of gendered terms to mark laudable and reprehensible practice is especially prominent in this letter. See intro. above. On the vocabulary of gender variance more generally, see Williams 2010: ch. 4. **incessu:** cf. 52.12 *impudicum et incessus ostendit*, Petr. 119 *fracti enerui corpore gressus*, Quint. *Inst.* 5.9.14 *fortasse corpus uulsum, fractum incessum, uestem muliebrem dixerit mollis et parum uiri signa*, Juv. 2.17 of the *cinaedus, qui uultu morbum incessuque fatetur*. On the perceived capacity of gait to reveal moral character see Edwards 1993: 88–90, Corbeill 2004: 107–38, O'Sullivan 2011: 20–2; cf. Gleason 1995: 55–61, stressing the link to physiognomic writings. **apparere mollitiam ... concitari gradum ... turbatum ... ferri:** governed by *uides* in the preceding sentence. **mollitiam** 'softness', antithetical to *uirtus*. See further 33.2(n.) *quia rarae ... homine mollitiam professo*. **furori simile:** cf. 18.15(n. on *furor*). **nec ire sed ferri:** cf. *De ira* 3.3.3 *uelut tempestate correptus non it sed agitur*. **ingenio ... permixtum:** as Graver (1998: 613–14) argues, rather than taking *ingenium* here in the more general sense of character, we should interpret this claim in the light of Stoic emphasis on the correlation between the capacity for rational, logical language (connected to *ingenium* in the sense of literary talent; cf. §1, 33.5n.) and the possession of a healthy *animus* (Sext. Emp. *Math.* 8.275, Gal. *De placitis Hippocratis et Platonis* 2.5.11–12). This interrelationship is stressed below at §22. At 115.1, S comments, *oratio cultus animi est*.

4 quomodo: the first indirect question (cf. §1) is expanded by four further ones, the last three each introduced by *quam*. **Maecenas:** an equestrian of distinguished family, Gaius Maecenas (d. 8 BCE) never held public office but was a trusted associate of Octavian/Augustus, serving as his diplomatic agent on numerous occasions and as his deputy in Italy during Octavian's absences of 36–33 BCE and 31–29 BCE (*RE* XIV.1 cols. 207–29). He is reported to have written several works in verse, including a *Cybele*, and prose (André 1967, Byrne 1999, 2006). Other ancient sources for Maecenas include Tac. *Ann.* 1.54, Dio Cass. 54.17.5, 19.3, 30.4, Vell. 2.88.2 and, an elaborate defence of Maecenas' character, the two *Elegiae in Maecenatem*, esp. 1.21–6, 59 (while their date cannot be determined with certainty, Schoonhoven 1983 suggests that they may be a response to S's *EM*). See Schanz–Hosius II.20–1, §214. **quomodo ambulauerit:** see above §3 *incessu*. On walking's capacity to reveal character and mood, particularly in satire, see Degl'Innocenti Pierini 2013: 56–8. At Hor. *S.* 1.2.25 (S quotes 1.2.27 at 86.13) Maltinus (apparently a *cognomen* denoting effeminacy, comments Gowers *ad loc.*) *tunicis demissis ambulat*. Porphyrio observes in his commentary on Horace: *sub Malthini nomine quidam Maecenatem suspicantur significari*. The comment may itself, of course, have been influenced by S's description of Maecenas. **quam cupierit uideri:** S highlights Maecenas' attention-seeking; cf. §21 *uolunt ... conspici*. Mazzoli (1968: 325) sees this as a pointed comment on Maecenas' conspicuous failure, despite his professed Epicureanism, to live up to the Epicurean maxim λάθε βιώσας, 'live without drawing attention to yourself'. See intro. above on the question of Maecenas' Epicureanism. **oratio . . . soluta:** lack of order is a common criticism of style; cf. e.g. Quint. *Inst.* 8.5.27 (expressing the concern that an excess of *sententiae* undermines the coherence of a speech). Macr. 2.4.12 characterises Maecenas as *dissolutus*. While Cicero sometimes uses the term *solutus* to refer to prose in contrast to verse (e.g. *de Orat.* 3.184, *Brut.* 32), he also uses it positively of free-flowing, relaxed style; cf. *Orat.* 64, 228, *Brut.* 173 (see Möller 2004: 184). The focus has now shifted to the connection between Maecenas' way of life and his literary style. **discinctus:** here literal but the metaphorical sense is also relevant; see Edwards 1993: 90, Corbeill 1996: 159–61. At 92.35, where he concedes merit in a line of Maecenas' poetry, S comments *alte cinctum putes dixisse. habuit enim ingenium grande et uirile nisi illud secundis discinxisset* (see 33.2, for *alte cinctos* used metaphorically). S is the first extant source to comment on Maecenas' dress (Byrne 1999: 29–30) and may have influenced Mart. 10.73.4, Juv. 12.38–9, while *Elegiae in Maecenatem* 1.21 apparently echoes S's remark, *quod discinctus eras, animo quoque, carpitur unum.* **insignita** 'noteworthy' (*OLD* 3), here in a negative sense (cf. Tac. *Ann.* 4.51). **cultus** 'grooming' (*OLD* 4a). **comitatus:** specified later (§6) as *spadones duo.* **uxor:** Terentia, sister of Varro Murena (Dio Cass. 54.3.5, Suet. *Aug.* 66.3), is alleged to have had an affair with Augustus (Dio Cass. 54.19, 55.7.5). A riposte addressed to Augustus (then Octavian) by Antony (Suet. *Aug.* 69) links his name with that of a number of women including a Terentilla, identified by some with Maecenas' wife. S comments on Maecenas' relationship with her in more detail at *Prov.* 3.10–11. **magni . . . fuerat:** cf. 19.9 *ingeniosus ille uir fuit . . . nisi . . .*, 92.35. For *magni ingenii* cf. *De ira* 1.20.6, quoting a phrase attributed to Livy (fr. 66.1), *uir ingenii magni magis quam boni.* S often uses a vivid indicative in the apodosis of an unreal conditional; cf. 55.11, *De ira* 1.11.5. **diffluueret:** cf. 78.25, *Tranq.* 17.4, Cic. *Amic.* 52.1 *deliciis diffluentes.* Velleius Paterculus (2.88.2) comments on Maecenas' leisure pursuits, *ultra feminam fluens.* **ebrii hominis:** at 19.9, a phrase from Maecenas' *Prometheus* is described as *ebrius sermo.* S repeatedly expresses disapproval of drunkenness, which often serves as a figure for mental imbalance, esp. at 83.17–27 (see Richardson-Hay 2001). Chrysippus is said to have argued that drunkenness can imperil virtue (Diog. Laert. 7.127; cf. *SVF* III.238, intoxication undermines both rationality and virtue). Zeno is alleged to have criticised a loquacious pupil with the comment that his father must have been drunk when he was conceived (Diog. Laert. 7.18, Moretti 1995: 53–4). See §22 *ebrietas.* **inuolutam:** convoluted word order is a feature of the quotations from Maecenas in §5. At 100.5 S praises Fabianus' word order for not being *huius saeculi more contra naturam suam posita et inuersa*, suggesting that in Neronian Rome contrived word order was once again in fashion (see further intro. above). *Maecenas de cultu suo* is almost certainly an interpolation, perhaps by a scribe desiring a title for the work from which S quotes (Lunderstedt 1911: 85–6, following Hirzel 1882, Summers 1908b: 172), which has been interpreted as Maecenas' attempt to defend himself from those criticising his lifestyle (see e.g. André 1967: 105, Bardon 1956: 17) but, as Byrne (1999: 24) notes, there is nothing in the lines quoted by S to suggest a defence against critics and no other evidence for the existence of such a work. Lunderstedt (1911: 86–7) suggests that they more likely formed part of e.g. a Menippean satire.

5 Problems of textual transmission compound the difficulty of interpreting the quotations from Maecenas (S also quotes him at 19.9, 92.35, 101.11). The fragments are edited by Lunderstedt (1911) and Costa (2014); all of §5 appears as fr. 11 Lunderstedt and fr. 2 Costa and it is likely that the series of quotations comes from a single work. See the discussions by Summers 1908b, Bardon 1956: 13–19, Avallone 1962, André 1967: 104–14, 1983: 1768, Möller 2004: 189–95. S highlights the syntactical weakness of Maecenas' writing, his florid neologisms and excessive use of metaphor.   **quid turpius** opens a polemical rhetorical question.   **'amne siluisque ripa comantibus'** 'the river and the woods in leaf on the bank', with *amne* and *siluisque* coordinate and *ripa* as ablative dependent on *comantibus*. The liquid opening example is particularly apt given the terms S has been used to characterise Maecenas' style (§4 *soluta, difflueret, ebrii hominis*).   **uide ut** 'see how': treated as part of the quotation from Maecenas (thus Haase 1852–3, Summers 1908b, Lunderstedt 1911 and Graver 1998, though Harder 1889 and Reynolds attribute them to S), these words explain the subjunctives which follow.   **alueum . . . hortos:** *alueum* is the navigable channel of a river (poetic when used in this sense; cf. e.g. Virg. *G.* 1.203, Hor. *Carm.* 3.7.28). The metaphor of 'ploughing' the water (*arent uersoque uado*) is not uncommon in poetry (*OLD aro* 3b; cf. e.g. Virg. *A.* 2.780). Passengers in a boat are presumably the subject of the two verbs; their movement appears to push back (*remittant*) the gardens bordering the river (Avallone 1962: 238 compares Ov. *Met.* 6.512 *tellusque repulsa est*).   **'feminae . . . tyranni'** 'he puckers up with a feminine pout and coos with his lips and, sighing, begins, like lords of the forest who writhe with drooping neck'. *cinno* 'a grimace' or 'pout' perhaps (otherwise unknown). *crispat* 'becomes puckered' (cf. Pers. 3.87 *ingeminat tremulos naso crispante cachinnos*). *columbatur*: a neologism derived from *columba* 'pigeon'. Gellius (20.9.2) quotes a phrase of Matius (*columbatim labra conserens labris*) which may have inspired Maecenas. *suspirans*: cf. Tib. 1.6.35 *amorem suspirans. fanantur*: apparently derived from *fanaticus* but there is no parallel for this sense. *nemoris tyranni*: i.e. wild beasts. Cf. Virg. *A.* 12.719 *quis nemori imperitet, quem tota armenta sequantur*. **'irremediabilis ... exigunt'** 'An unregenerate crew, they probe with feasts, make trial of households with a goblet of wine and, exploiting hope, extract death.' *irremediabilis* is not found earlier. Lunderstedt (1911: 81) suggests that it is a coinage modelled on ἀνήκεστος. Lunderstedt (1911 *ad loc.*) and Costa (2014 *ad loc.*) interpret this as a reference to the use of banquets to extract compromising testimony (cf. *Ben.* 3.26–7). **'genium festo uix suo testem':** Graver and Long, taking *testem* as a predicate of *genium*, translate 'a genius that scarce attests to its own festal day'. For the *genius* see 12.2n. on *iurat per genium meum*. Some scholars see the words from *genium* to *inuestiunt* as a single quotation, conveying a scene of domestic festivity (with a Grecising use of the accusative: *fila* and *molam*). **crepacem:** a neologism from *crepare* 'to creak'. **inuestiunt** 'clothe', presumably with garlands or similar.

6 solutis tunicis: i.e. *discinctus* as in §4 above, where his writing is described as *oratio ... soluta*. **in urbe ... incesserit:** such dress would have been more excusable within a private house. **Caesaris partibus:** Maecenas served as Augustus' deputy (see intro. above). **signum ... petebatur:** the phrase *signum petere* is regularly used of asking someone in authority for the password. See *Constant.* 18.3, Liv. 28.24.10, Suet. *Gai.* 56.2, Tac. *Ann.* 13.2.3. **pallio ... auribus:** with his cloak drawn up like a hood but leaving his ears exposed; cf. the disapproving comment on Pompey's freedman Demetrius (Plut. *Pomp.* 40.4) that he wore the hood of his toga drawn down behind his ears. Petronius' Trimalchio (32.2) wears a purple cloak, which leaves his head exposed, *pallio enim coccineo adrasum excluserat caput*. On parallels between S's Maecenas and Trimalchio see Byrne 2006: 99–100, Labate 2012. **quam in mimo fugitiui diuitis solent** 'as the rich man's slaves do when they are running away in the mime'. The stock characters of Roman mime, including the *diues* (cf. e.g. Petr. 80.9) and the runaway slave (Juv. 13.110–11 *mimum agit ille | urbani qualem fugitiuus scurra Catulli*), were immediately recognisable. **spadones duo:** eunuch attendants (associated with eastern autocracies; cf. Hor. *Epod.* 9.13, *Carm.* 1.37.9–10 on Cleopatra's attendants) were relatively rare in Rome (though cf. Suet. *Cl.* 28 on Claudius' regard for his eunuch freedman Posides). Nero is said to have gone through a marriage ceremony with a eunuch called Sporus (see Suet. *Nero* 28.1; Dio Cass. 62.28 places this in the later years of his reign). No other source associates them with Maecenas. Trimalchio (Petr 27.3) is also attended by *duo spadones*. On the literary critical associations of castration see Möller 2004: 205–6 (and further §8nn.). **magis ... uiri:** a paradox which nevertheless underlines the limited contribution made to Roman ideas of virility by sex organs.   **uxorem milliens duxit:** the phrase *uxorem ducere* is commonly used of a male subject to mean 'get married' (*OLD duco* 5a). At *Prov.* 3.10, S describes Maecenas as complaining about Terentia's *cotidiana repudia* 'daily petitions for divorce'. Her repeated rejections of her husband, S implies, obliged him to woo her back on a daily basis. In surviving fragments of his treatise *De matrimonio*, S warns (F27 Vottero) against excessive devotion to one's wife.

7 tam: the tricolon of words introduced by *tam* is answered by *nouos et prauos et singulares*.   **neglegenter abiecta** 'carelessly tossed off'; cf. 75.2, Cic. *Brut.* 227 *uerbis non ... quidem ornatis ... sed tamen non abiectis*. At 100.4 S defends the philosopher Fabianus from such criticism: *non erat neglegens in oratione, sed securus*. Carelessness is sometimes associated with a 'masculine' style (§14 *plus iusto neglegit*), mistakenly, says S. Yet at 115.2 he himself advises that excessive care in style is *non ornamentum uirile*.   **nouos:** in a pejorative sense (cf. *OLD* 3); cf. §10 criticising those who in their style seek out what is *nouum*.   **mansuetudinis:** Dio praises Maecenas' leniency (55.7.2–4), though, according to Velleius Paterculus (2.88.3), he repressed the conspiracy of Lepidus' son against Octavian with speed and firmness; the young man was swiftly executed. S's earlier treatise *De clementia* (1.8.6, 1.16.1, 2.5.1) celebrates *mansuetudo* as a notable characteristic of Nero (1.11.1, 2.2.1).   **delicîs** 'refinements' (pejorative); cf., also on Maecenas, 120.19. The juxtaposition of this seductively slippery word with the unusual and remarkably heavyweight *portentosissimae* perhaps echoes the contrived effects of Maecenas' own prose.   **mollem ... non mitem:** S draws a striking distinction between terms more usually aligned (cf. e.g. Cels. 5.26.23c, Col. 8.17.13, Hor. *Carm.* 3.10.17–18, Man. 2.189).

8 hoc ... hoc ... hoc: the emphatically placed object of *facient*, with *motum ... caput* in explanatory apposition.   **ambages** 'obscurities' of arrangement (*OLD* 2).   **compositionis** 'arrangement of words' (*OLD* 6), one of the aspects of style regularly discussed by rhetorical theorists; cf. e.g. Quint. *Inst.* 9.4. *Rhet. Her.* 4.18 defines it as 'the arrangement of words that makes all parts of the speech equally polished'. At the beginning of the following letter (115.1), S advises Lucilius not to be too particular about *compositio*.   **uerba trauersa:** an expression otherwise unattested. The term *trauersus* 'lying across the line of the direct way' is often contrasted with *rectus*; cf. Quint. *Inst.* 2.5.11 on *sermo rectus* and its opposite.   **sensus miri** 'bizarre thoughts'.   **eneruati** 'lacking virility' (cf. *OLD neruus* 1b 'penis'). See §1n. on *infracta*.   **dum exeunt** 'when they are spoken' (*OLD exeo* 2d).   **felicitate nimia:** cf. *Prov.* 3.9–11 on Maecenas *felicitate nimia laborantem*. Elsewhere S stresses in explicitly gendered language the negative effects on Maecenas of too much good fortune (19.9 *eneruasset felicitas*, 92.35 *habuit . . . ingenium et grande et uirile, nisi illud secundis discinxisset*; cf. *Prov.* 4.9 on good fortune's potential to inebriate and emasculate).   **uitium hominis:** as Möller (2004: 201) underlines, though he does suggest that failings of the individual and of society are mutually reinforcing, S does not pursue further the degree to which Maecenas might be thought personally responsible for his failings.

9 S now returns to the dynamic of vices within society.   **cultus . . . corporum:** excessive concern with this is a target of 86.10–11 (on which see above), though as §14's analogy makes clear, S does not advocate neglecting personal grooming altogether.   **supellectili laboratur** 'a fuss is made over household paraphernalia' (dat.).   **in ipsas domos:** a recurrent concern in the letters. See *Epp.* 55, 86(nn.), and esp. 90.   **in laxitatem ruris excurrant** 'so that they spread into country-house spaciousness' (on the luxurious aspect of *rus in urbe* cf. Plin. *Nat.* 19.50).   **parietes . . . fulgeant:** cf. 86.6, 90.25.   **tecta . . . auro:** cf. 90.9nn.   **lacunaribus . . . nitor:** S here combines fulminations against elaborate ceilings (cf. 90.9 and 15) and marble floors (cf. 86.7).   **commendatio . . . captatur:** luxury's quest for novelty in banqueting is explored several times elsewhere, particularly at 78.23–4, 95.23–9, 119.14, 122.3–4. See Richardson-Hay 2009.   **ex nouitate:** S criticises those who are driven by the quest for the new (see §7 *nouum*).   **quae . . . ponantur:** for the inversion of 'normal' practice as a key preoccupation of the luxurious cf. 122.14, Mart. 13.14 *cludere quae cenas latuca solebat auorum, | dic mihi, cur nostras inchoat illa dapes?*

10 fastidire: cf. 24.26 *non odium sed fastidium*.   **illi:** the *animus*.   **pro sordidis solita** 'customary treated as commonplace'.   **antiqua uerba atque exoleta** 'archaic and obsolete words'. See further §13 *ex alieno . . . uerba*.   **fingit et nota deflectit** 'invents words or twists familiar ones to a new use'. *deflecto:* OLD 5b. There is a textual problem here. Reynolds obelises *et ignota ac deflectit*. Winterbottom (1972: 11) plausibly suggests *modo fingit et nota deflectit*. Cf. 108.35 *non ut uerba prisca aut ficta captemus et translationes improbas figurasque dicendi*.   **pro cultu habetur** 'is regarded as elegant'.   **translatio:** see §1n. on *translationis*.

11 praecidant 'cut short' (*OLD* 3b); cf. Quintilian's criticism (*Inst.* 10.2.17) of those who emulate the obscurity of Sallust and Thucydides, *praecisis conclusionibus*.   **pependerit** 'is left hanging' (*OLD* 10b).   **suspicionem sui:** i.e. the hearer fears he has failed to understand; cf. §1n. on *abruptae . . . suspiciosae*.   **illos detineant et porrigant** 'prolong them [i.e. *sensus*] and draw them out'.   **sunt qui non accedant . . . ament** 'there are those who not only come (*accedant*) very (*usque*) close to <the

committing of> a stylistic flaw (it is necessary for anyone trying to write in the grand style to do this) but who love the flaw itself'. *necesse . . . temptanti*: cf. Quint. *Inst.* 2.4.9. For *grande* in this sense (*OLD* 6a and b), cf. 79.7. *ament*: cf. 39.6 *mala sua, quod malorum ultimum est, et amant.* **uestium:** sc. *luxuria.* **procidisse** 'have suffered a moral collapse' (*OLD* 1c); cf. Tac. *Ann.* 4.18.

12 corona 'the bystanders', e.g. at a trial (*OLD* 4a).   **togis . . . distant:** the grubby attire of the poor often serves as a metonym for their vulgar manners and taste, in contrast to that of those who can afford clean, white togas; cf. e.g. Var. *L.* 9.33 *pullus sermo.* For S such differences mask essential similarity. At 102.16–18, S stresses the corrupting effect of popular approval in particular (§16): *nihil enim aeque et eloquentiam et omne aliud studium auribus deditum uitiauit quam popularis assensio.* Cf. Hor. *Ep.* 2.1.187–8 on the corrupted taste even of the educated: *uerum equitis quoque iam migrauit ab aure uoluptas | omnis ad incertos oculos et gaudia uana.*   **nullum . . . ingenium:** i.e. every author whose work achieves recognition has some fault which must be forgiven.   **maximae famae:** sc. *uiros.* A characteristic use of the genitive of quality without a governing noun (Setaioli 2000: 47, Summers: lvi).   **uitia uirtutibus immixta:** as Leeman (1963: 273–4; cf. Setaioli 2000: 174–5) notes, S's acknowledgement that vice may be an intrinsic part of virtue (at least when it comes to literary style) has no parallel in the writings of other ancient literary critics (though some others do recognise that those who aim for true greatness run great risks).

13 At this point the letter takes another disconcerting turn, as S appears unwilling to identify one single way of writing as intrinsically superior (cf. 100.6, where S concedes that opinions differ as to the ideal for *compositio*). Seneca the Elder makes a similar concession at *Con.* 9.6.11 *eloquentia cuius regula incerta est.*   **consuetudo . . . ciuitatis:** this insight (not developed here) is explored more fully in Aper's account of the development of oratory at Tac. *Dial.* 19 (Leeman 1963: 274). Instead S returns to the range of faults which may be exemplified in choice of words. The cultural variation of *consuetudo* here contrasts with universal *consuetudo* in the criticism of Maecenas at §5.   **ex alieno . . . uerba:** cf. §10 *antiqua . . . exoleta.* Sallust was criticised for this (Suet. *Gram.* 10, *Aug.* 86). S suggests that what was acceptable as common practice in one era will often seem perverse and affected in the context of the altered norms of a later period. S criticises Cicero for his borrowings from Ennius in the section of Book 22 of the *EM* preserved by Gel. 12.2.8. Cf. Quint. *Inst.* 2.5.21 *elocutione, quae tum sine dubio erat optima, sed nostris temporibus aliena est* and Tac. *Dial.* 23.   **duodecim tabulas:** the archaic (and often obscure) language of the original Twelve Tables, the earliest Roman law code (conventionally dated to the fifth century BCE), survives in only a few fragments (for what survives of their text see Crawford 1996: no. 40). On the resonance of this language see Cic. *Leg.* 2.18.   **Gracchus:** presumably C. Gracchus, the populist tribune of 122 BCE (cf. Tac. *Dial.* 18, 26). Cicero thought his oratorical style too *durus* (reports Quint. *Inst.* 9.4.15).   **Crassus:** presumably L. Licinius Crassus (cos. 95 BCE); Cicero was his student (Cic. *de Orat.* 3.78). Cf. Cic. *Brut.* 143–5, noting his *grauitas*, Tac. *Dial.* 26.   **Curio:** C. Scribonius Curio (cos. 76 BCE), a contemporary of Cicero, was known for the purity of his Latin (Cic. *Brut.* 213 *puro sermone*), despite his lack of formal training.   **Appium:** Appius Claudius Caecus (cos. I 307 BCE), known for his speech against Pyrrhus (Quint. *Inst.* 2.16.7), invoked as the type of archaic oratory at Tac. *Dial.* 18.4.   **Coruncanium:** Tiberius Coruncanius, a prominent jurist and orator, cos. 280 BCE (Broughton 1953: 190–1). He too spoke against the peace proposals of Pyrrhus. The philosopher Favorinus (quoted by Gel. 1.10.1) cites Coruncanius as an instance of archaic eloquence, clear in its own day but not to be imitated.   **in sordes** 'into banality'. At 100.5 S defends Fabianus from this charge: *nihil . . . sordidum.*   **nolle . . . poeticis:** S mentions a third kind of fault, using excessively poetic language. Arist. *Rh.* 3.3 criticises Alcidamas for poetic vocabulary in prose.

14 The illustration relates to the first two kinds of fault, i.e. excessive archaism and excessive colloquialism.   **crura:** on depilation cf. 47.7. Ovid (*Ars* 1.506) also warns men against depilating their legs; this practice, like hair-curling, is associated with eunuchs, such as the priests of Cybele: *Ars* 1.507–8 *ista iube faciant, quorum Cybeleïa mater* | *concinitur Phrygiis exululata modis*; for men a *forma neglecta* is more appropriate.   **alas:** S implies that respectable men of his day had their armpit hair removed. An *alipilus* features in S's vignette of the baths (56.2); cf. Juv. 11.157 *nec uellendas iam praebuit alas*. The advice to avoid extremes in personal grooming echoes *Ep.* 5.2's warning that *intonsum caput* and *barba neglegentior* are to be avoided by the would-be philosopher; cf. also Sen. *Con.* 1.pr.9–10, linking the decay of oratory to the decay of manliness, evidenced, *inter alia*, by *uulsis . . . uiris.*

15 S now turns his attention to the arrangement of words.   **compositionem:** the argument here is close to that of 100.6.   **salebra** 'roughness', regularly of style (*OLD* 1b). Cf. 100.7 *Pollionis Asinii salebrosa* [*sc. compositio*] *et exiliens*, Cic. *Orat.* 39 *sine ullis salebris . . . fluit.*   **iuncturam:** for Quintilian (*Inst.* 9.4.32–4), one of the three subdivisions of *compositio* (the others being *ordo* and *numerus*, rhythm). A significant factor here, as Quintilian makes clear, is the degree to which hiatus (i.e. where, one word ending in a vowel and the next beginning with one, they are pronounced distinctly) is avoided (some types are more offensive than others for Quintilian). On Roman attitudes to hiatus in prose see Riggsby 1991.   **uirilem ... fortem:** cf. the praise of Lucilius' style at 46.2. Here, however, S suggests that some people mistakenly equate a virile style with a deliberate roughness. As Graver (1998: 615) notes, 'by implication the truly "masculine" stylist will pay at least some attention to the aural qualities of his prose'.   **modulatio** 'inflection of tone'. See above §1n. on *in morem cantici*. On this discussion of *clausulae* and aphorisms see Leeman 1963: 275–6.   **adeo blanditur et molliter labitur:** for the associations of *molliter* see §3 and 33.2 *mollitiam* with notes. Some degree of sweetness or charm is presumably acceptable since at 46.1 S praises the *dulcedo* of Lucilius' writing.

16 quid de illa 'What of that . . .?' *sc. compositione*.   **uerba ... redeunt** 'words are postponed and, long anticipated, barely appear at the very end of the sentence', i.e. prolonged hyperbaton; cf. §11 on those who hold back and extend their *sensus*.   **Ciceronis:** Cicero's style (which is characterised by lengthy and heavily subordinated periods) is also discussed at 40.11, 100.7 and in the fragment of Book 22 preserved in Gel. 12.2.4–9.   **deuexa et molliter detinens** 'gradually sloping and gently holding [the reader] back'. While at 100.7, contrasting Cicero's *compositio* with that of Pollio, S comments *una est, pedem seruat, lenta et sine infamia mollis*, here he seems more critical (while the focus of 100.7 is indeed Cicero's philosophical works, as Leeman 1963: 276 notes, it is not clear that *Ep.* 114 is aimed particularly at his oratory).   **pedemque** 'prose rhythm' (*OLD* 11b); cf. Quint. *Inst.* 9.4.60, 134.   **tantum uno in genere** 'only of one kind'. Reynolds posits a lacuna between *tantum* and *in* (though Graver and Long see no need for this). If we supply *uno* then the comment here about *sententiae* balances the question about *compositio* (*quot genera . . . quibus peccetur?*) at the start of §15.   **sententiarum:** see 33.4, 7nn. on *sententias*. At 100.8 S admits that Fabianus' work lacks the *subiti ictus sententiarum* (a characteristic apparently associated with potency) but maintains its evenness to be a positive feature (cf. Quint. *Inst.* 8.5.27, associating an excess of *sententiae* with uneven texture).   **pusillae ... et pueriles:** cf. Sen. *Suas.* 2.16.11, criticising *pueriles sententias*, Quint. *Inst.* 12.10.73 *puerilibus sententiolis*.   **improbae:** cf. §1 *inuerecunde*, §7 *improbe*.   **floridae:** cf. 33.1n. on *flosculos*. Quintilian (12.10.73) also reproves a style which *casuris ... flosculis nitet*.   **nimis dulces:** Seneca the Elder frequently uses *dulcis* of *sententiae* (e.g. *Con.* 2. Pr. 1) but warns this can be taken to excess (*Suas.* 7.12). S himself is criticised by Quintilian (*Inst.* 10.1.129) for seducing the young with his *dulcia uitia*.   **nihil amplius quam sonant:** S similarly criticises at 40.5 the empty words used by some philosophers.

17 S now examines the role of fashion in transmitting a style modelled on that of an influential individual; cf. Cic. *de Orat.* 2.91–8.   **sub quo** 'under whose direction' (*OLD sub* 15b)   **Sallustio:** the historian Sallust (probably 86–35 BCE; *RE* I.A2 cols. 1913–55), author of *Bellum Catilinae* and *Bellum Iugurthinum*. His *Historiae*, from which the passages quoted here are presumably taken, survive only in fragments.   **cadentia:** cf. 100.7, contrasting Cicero and Pollio: *omnia apud Ciceronem desinunt, apud Pollionem cadunt*.   **fuere pro cultu:** see §10 *pro cultu habetur*.   **L. Arruntius:** presumed to be the veteran of the civil wars, cos. 22 BCE (a younger contemporary of Sallust), though his writing is not otherwise attested (Cornell 2013: 448–50).   **rarae frugalitatis** 'of unusual temperance'. Cf. Velleius Paterculus' characterisation (2.86.2), *prisca grauitate celeberrimus*. In this case, S implies, faults of style are not a reflection of the author's faulty character (for *frugalitas* as characteristic of the *uir bonus* cf. 115.3).   **historias belli Punici:** the fragments of this work, evidently an account of the First Punic War, are discussed in Cornell 2013: 870–3.   **'exercitum . . . fecit':** Sall. *Hist.* fr. 1.27* Maurenbrecher = frr. of uncertain reference 5 McGushin.   **'fugam . . . fecere':** = Arruntius fr. 1 Cornell. Arruntius' mannerism is to replace a verb with a noun (usually cognate) + *facere*, thus *fugam facere* for *fugare* (though this is not uncommon; cf. e.g. Cic. *Dom.* 67).   **'Hiero . . . fecit':** = Arruntius fr. 2 Cornell. Hiero II (270–215 BCE), tyrant of Syracuse, played a key role in the First Punic War.   **'quae audita Panhormitanos dedere Romanis fecere':** = Arruntius fr. 3 Cornell. *facere* + inf., found in many authors (e.g. Cic. *Brut.* 142), is perhaps a colloquial usage. *Panhormitanos:* the inhabitants of Panhormus (modern Palermo).

18 contexitur: cf. 33.1n. on *totus contextus illorum*.   **in haec incidebat** 'chanced upon them' (cf. §13 *in sordes incidunt*).   **quaerebat:** cf. Cicero's complaint that Fufius in imitating Gaius Fimbria (*de Orat.* 2.91), *imitari etiam uitia uoluit*.   **uitium pro exemplo:** Quintilian echoes this in his complaint about S's own followers (*Inst.* 10.1.25).

19 hiemantibus: the passage from Sallust (missed by Maurenbrecher and McGushin) does not otherwise survive. Derived from *hiems* 'winter', this verb occasionally appears in a military context meaning 'to pass the winter' (*OLD* 1) and rarely, as here, to mean 'be wintry, stormy' (*OLD* 2; *TLL* VI.2.2773.46–51).   **'repente . . . tempestas':** = Arruntius fr. 4 Cornell.   **'totus . . . annus':** Arruntius fr. 5 Cornell.   **'inde . . . misit':** Arruntius fr. 6 Cornell.   **infulcire** 'to ram in'.   **aequi bonique famas:** fr. 1. 90* Maurenbrecher = fr. 1.79* McGushin (who interprets this as a reference to the conduct of Quintus Sertorius in the civil war of 87–83 BCE). *fama* normally occurs only in the singular.   **'famas':** Arruntius fr.

7 Cornell. The plural of *fama* is very rare (aside from Pl. *Trin.* 186, the instances quoted here are the only ones before late antiquity).

20 alicui impressit imitatio: the process of imitation is itself given agency; it remains unclear what makes the imitator liable to follow a faulty model. Elsewhere S places greater emphasis on personal responsibility in choosing one's literary/intellectual models; see esp. *Epp.* 33 and 84. **propria... nata:** i.e. faults must be intrinsic to the individual, if they are to count as *indicia ... corrupti*. This does not seem to be the case with e.g. Arruntius, whom S describes at §17 as *uir rarae frugalitatis*. **ex quibus ... affectus** 'from which you may infer a person's corruption'. **delicati** 'addicted to pleasure' (*OLD* 1a); cf. §7 on Maecenas. **fluxa** 'unstable'; the liquid connotations (cf. §4 *difflueret*, §23 *fluido*) reinforce the contrast with the *siccus* and *sobrius* (§3) ideal style.

21 quod ... sequi 'you will see that those men follow this pattern'. **interuellunt:** cf., of depilating armpits, Pl. *Am.* 326. Here presumably of plucking out some hair in order e.g. to create a goatee or an overall thinning out. **labra ... parte:** those who depilate the upper lip, while allowing the rest of the beard to grow freely. Cf. 115.2, where over-refined oratory is *circumtonsa*. **coloris improbi:** coloured cloaks are objectionable for S but the sense of *color* as rhetorical quality (cf. §3 above) is perhaps also present (cf. Petr. 118.5, where Eumolpus advises that the brilliancy of *sententiae* should be woven into the fabric of one's writing, *intexto uestibus colore niteant*). Coloured clothing is used as a metaphor for attention-seeking style at Tac. *Dial.* 26.1 *melius est orationem uel hirta toga induere quam fucatis et meretriciis uestibus insignire*, Quint. *Inst.* 8.pr.20, 8.3.6, 10.1.33, Lucian, *Rhetorum praeceptor* 15. See, too, 115.2, decrying *oratio ... fucata*. **pellucentem togam:** presumably one of translucent fabric. See 90.20(n.) *uestis nihil celatura*. **quod ... liceat** 'which could escape people's attention'. **uolunt uel reprehendi dum conspici** 'they are happy even to be criticised, so long as they are noticed'. S comments on Maecenas (§4), *quam cupierit uideri, quam uitia sua latere noluerit*. **talis ... oratio:** echoing §1 but now with a more specific focus. **scientes uolentesque:** those who self-consciously seek after what they know to be wrong and take pleasure precisely in rejecting the good; cf. 90.19, 122.9–14.

22 animi: see intro. above for the Stoic correlation between rationality (a characteristic of the *animus*) and the capacity to produce meaningful utterance. **quomodo in uino:** S uses wine-drinking as an illustration, suggesting that the drinker's speech is not slurred until his mind is affected by the wine. **ista orationis quid aliud quam ebrietas** 'that condition of style which is nothing other than intoxication'. **uirilis:** cf. 115.3 *non est ornamentum uirile concinnitas.*

23 rege ... fidem: Virg. *G.* 4.212–13, describing the behaviour of bees (on S's engagement with the *Georgics* particularly in the later letters in the series see intro. to *Ep.* 86 and 86.15n.). The same passage is cited at *Clem.* 1.4.1 to illustrate the importance of the ruler as the mind of the state, *mens imperii* (while the bees' devotion to their ruler exceeds that of eastern people to their kings; see Braund: 214 *ad loc.*). **rex ... animus:** *rex* here is a positive term, as in S's treatise on clemency addressed to Nero (e.g. *Clem.* 1.3.4, 1.11.4, with Braund *ad locc.*; cf. *Ep.* 90.4). At 47.20 by contrast, where the *reges* are literal rather than metaphorical, it is a source of reproach that *regum induimus animos* (see note *ad loc.*). **in officio:** i.e. all elements observe their proper function. **cessit uoluptati** 'has given in to pleasure'. **omnis ex languido fluidoque conatus est** 'every undertaking derives from something feeble and unsteady'.

24 modo ... tyrannus: for the contrast king/tyrant cf. *Clem.* 1.3.4, 1.11.4, *Ep.* 90.5(n.) *regnum.* Given the extensive use of the contrast in *De clementia,* addressing Nero on the subject of how an autocrat should behave, it may not be far-fetched to detect here an allusion to Nero's own notoriously uncontrolled and pleasure-oriented behaviour, which might be readily characterised (see e.g. Tac. *Ann.* 13.46–7, 15.37, Suet. *Nero* 26–31) as *impotens, cupidus, delicatus* (cf. 47.21 with intro. to that letter). **salute ... curat:** conversely, in *De clementia* the relationship between ruler and ruled is discussed in terms of the analogy between mind and body (Braund: 205–6). **affectus:** the emotions are characterised, in the same terms as the tyrant, as *impotentes*; it is through being ruled by emotions that the *animus* becomes a tyrant rather than a just ruler. **ut ... contrectans:** the emotion-driven *animus* is compared to the common people, initially pleased at the largesse it receives, despite the physical harm this largesse will bring. Nero is reported to have been very popular with the dregs of Rome's population because of his generosity (Tac. *Hist.* 1.4 describes those who mourned Nero's death as *plebs sordida et circo ac theatris sueta, simul deterrimi seruorum aut qui adesis bonis per dedecus Neronis alebantur*). **frustra plenus:** since, though they wish to, they have no capacity to consume more (insatiable desires are a frequent theme in S's analysis of the human condition; cf. 70.17(n.) *sed quemadmodum ... concupiscentibus?*).

25 morbus: now invoking a medical analogy, S returns to the body, whose grooming and gait serve as an index of the effeminate *animus* at §§3, 6, 22. Comparable is the vivid account of physical afflictions brought on by luxury at 95.15–29, where the highly developed procedures consequently required of the medical profession serve as an analogy for the sophisticated approach needed by philosophy in attempting to cure the complex and proliferating vices of the *animus* in S's day.   **neruosque:** cf. *eneruati* in §8.   **descendere:** subject *deliciae*.   **conspectu . . . laetus:** 'happy [i.e. the *animus*] at the sight of those things for which, through excessive greed, it has rendered itself useless'.   **pro suis . . . spectaculum** 'it treats the sight of other people's pleasures as substitutes for its own'. S perhaps hints at voyeuristic sexual pleasures; cf. *Nat.* 1.16.1 on Hostius Quadra (Bartsch 2006: 106–14).   **ingerendo** 'through drinking to excess' (*OLD* 1c).   **nec illi . . . transmittit** 'to abound in pleasurable things is for it [i.e. the *animus*] not so sweet as it is bitter because it does not consume through its gullet and belly its entire store'.   **exoletorum:** see 12.8(n.).   **corporis angustiis:** i.e. the physical limitations of the individual human body prevent the tyrannical *animus* from fully indulging its unlimited desire for pleasures.

26 nemo . . . cogitat: death sets the ultimate limit to all human desires; cf. 70.17.   **unum esse se:** i.e. that the needs of one human individual are necessarily very limited.   **unum . . . uentrem:** cf. the heavily sarcastic critique of luxury at 95.24 *quantum hominum unus uenter exercet!*   **ueteraria:** wine cellars.   **tot consulum. . . uina:** vintages were identified by the names of the ordinary consuls for that year (cf. e.g. Hor. *Carm.* 3.21.1, 3.28.8, Plin. *Nat.* 14.55).   **colonorum:** share-cropping tenants.   **in Sicilia et in Africa:** the wealthiest Romans of this period typically owned estates in a number of different provinces (Garnsey 2000: 695–8); Sicily and Africa were among the most fertile. Pliny (*Nat.* 18.35) refers to six senators who 'owned half of Africa' (their land was confiscated by Nero); cf. the extensive estates of which Trimalchio boasts at Petr. 48.2–3 (discussed at 90.39n.). Maecenas may have owned estates in Egypt (Rostovtzeff 1957: 293).

27 sani erimus: a return to the *animus sanus* and *temperans* of §3, made personal with the first person plural verb.   **si unusquisque se numeret** 'if each person counts himself' and realises he has only the capacity of one.   **tibi:** concluding the letter, S at last reverts to his addressee.   **frequens . . . incerti:** this practice is repeatedly advocated; cf. e.g. 12.9(n.).

BIBLIOGRAPHY

SENECA: EDITIONS, TRANSLATIONS AND COMMENTARIES

Works included in this section are cited by author's name only.

Berno, F. R. 2006. *L. Anneo Seneca. Lettere a Lucilio, libro VI: le lettere 53–57*, Bologna
Blankert, S. 1940. *Seneca (Epist. 90) over natuur en kultuur en Posidonius als zijn bron*, Amsterdam
Braund, S. M., ed. 2009. *Seneca: De clementia*, Oxford
Costa, C. D. N., ed. 1988. *Seneca: selected letters*, Warminster
Davies, M. 2010. 'A commentary on Seneca's *Epistulae morales* book IV (*Epistles* 30–41)', PhD diss., University of Auckland
Eden, P. 1984. *Seneca: Apocolocyntosis*, Cambridge
Fantham, E., trs. 2010. *Seneca: selected letters*, Oxford
Graver, M., and A. A. Long, trs. 2015. *Lucius Annaeus Seneca: Letters on ethics*. Chicago
Gummere, R., trs. 1918–25. *Seneca ad Lucilium epistulae morales*, 3 vols., Cambridge, MA
Haase, F. 1852–3. *L. Annaei Seneca opera quae supersunt*, 4 vols. in 5, Leipzig
Hachmann, E. 2006. *Seneca: Epistulae morales Brief 66. Einleitung, Text und Kommentar*, Frankfurt
Inwood, B. 2007. *Seneca: selected philosophical letters*, Oxford
Laudizi, G. 2003. *Seneca Lettere a Lucilio: libro terzo, Epp. xxii–xxix*, Naples
Manning, C. E. 1981. *On Seneca's Ad Marciam* (Mnemosyne suppl. 69), Leiden
Motto, A. L. 1985. *Seneca: Moral epistles*, Chico, CA
Nikolaides, T. 2002. *Epistolē 90: Senecas enantion Posidōniou*, Athens
Reynolds, L. 1965. *L. Annaei Senecae epistulae morales*, 2 vols., Oxford
Richardson-Hay, C. 2006. *First lessons: book 1 of Seneca's Epistulae morales. A commentary*, Bern
Scarpat, G. (a). 1970. *La lettera 65 di Seneca*, Brescia
  (b).1975. *Seneca: Lettere a Lucilio. Libro primo*, Brescia
  (c).2007. *Lucio Anneo Seneca: anticipare la morte o attenderla. La lettera 70 a Lucilio* (Antichità classica e christiana 35), Brescia
Soldo, J. 2018. 'A commentary on Seneca's *Epistulae morales* book 2 (Epp. 13–21)', PhD diss., Munich
Stückelberger, A. ed. 1965. *Senecas 88. Brief: über Wert und Unwert der freien Künste*, Heidelberg
Summers, W. 1910. *Selected letters of Seneca*, London
Vottero, D. 1998. *Lucio Anneo Seneca: i frammenti*, Bologna
Williams, G. 2003. *Seneca: De otio, De brevitate vitae*, Cambridge

OTHER WORKS

Adams, J. N. 2016. *An anthology of informal Latin, 200 BC – AD 900: an anthology of fifty texts*, Cambridge

Albertini, E. 1923. *La Composition dans les ouvrages philosophique de Sénèque*, Paris

Allegri, G. 2004. *Progresso verso la virtus: il programma della Lettera 87 di Seneca*. Quaderni di Paideia 2, Cesena

Altman, J. 1982. *Epistolarity: approaches to a form*, Columbus, OH

André, J. M. 1967. *Mécène: essai de biographie spirituelle* (Annales Litteraires de l'Université de Besançon 86), Paris

1983. 'Mécène écrivain (avec, en appendice, les fragments de Mécène)', in *ANRW* II.30.3: 1765–87

Andria, G. 1999. *Le figure rhetoriche nel primo libro delle Epistule a Lucili*, Salerno

Arena, V. 2012. *Libertas and the practice of politics in the late Roman Republic*, Cambridge

Argetsinger, K. 1992. 'Birthday rituals: friends and patrons in Roman poetry and cult', *ClAnt* 11: 175–93

Armisen-Marchetti, M. 1989. *Sapientiae facies: étude sur les images de Sénèque*, Paris

1995. 'Sénèque et l'appropriation du temps', *Latomus* 54: 547–64

1998. 'Le statut morale de l'homme primitif chez Sénèque: anthropologie, éthique, théâtre', in *Les Origines de l'homme* (Publications de la Faculté des Lettres, Arts et Sciences humaines de Nice) (Nice) 197–208

2006. 'Un terme argotique chez Sénèque? À propos de *gausapatus* (*Ep.* 53.3)', in C. Santini, L. Zurli and L. Cardinali, eds. *Concentus ex dissonis. Scritti in onore di Aldo Setaioli*, vol. 1 (Naples) 35–47

2007. 'Échos du songe de Scipion chez Sénèque: la géographie de la Consolation à Marcia 26.6 et des Questions naturelles I praef. 8–13', in G. Hinojo Andrès and J. C. Fernández Corte, eds. *Munus quaesitum meritis: homenaje a Carmen Codoñer* (Salamanca) 71–9

2008. 'Imagination and meditation in Seneca: the example of *praemeditatio*', in Fitch 2008: 102–13 [= 'L'imagination et méditation chez Sénèque. L'exemple de la *praemeditatio*', *REL* 64 (1986) 185–95]

2013. '*Conservi*: à propos encore une fois de Pétrone, *Sat.* 70.10–71.1 et Sénèque *Ep.* 47', in F. Gasti, ed. *Seneca e la letteratura greca e latina* (Pavia) 67–82

2015. 'Seneca's images and metaphors', in Bartsch and Schiesaro 2015: 150–60

Arrighetti, G. 1973. *Epicuro: opere*, 2nd edn, Turin

Arrowsmith, W. 1966. 'Luxury and death in the Satyricon', *Arion* 5: 304–31
Ascoli, A. R. 2015. 'Epistolary Plutarch', in Ascoli and Falkeid 2015: 120–37
Ascoli, A. R., and U. Falkeid, eds. 2015. *The Cambridge companion to Petrarch*, Cambridge
Asmis, E. 2004. 'Epicurean economics', in J. Fitzgerald, D. Obbink and G. S. Holland, eds. *Philodemus and the New Testament world* (Leiden) 133–77
  2009. 'Seneca on fortune and the kingdom of god', in Bartsch and Wray 2009: 115–38
  2015. 'Seneca's originality', in Bartsch and Schiesaro 2015: 224–38
Astin, A. 1978. *Cato the Censor*, Oxford
Auvray, C. 1987. 'La citation virgilienne dans les *Lettres à Lucilius* de Sénèque: des *praecepta* aux *decreta* du Stoicisme', *Bulletin de la Faculté des Lettres de Mulhouse* 15: 29–34
Avallone, R. 1962. *Mecenate*, Naples
Avotins, I. 1977. 'Training in frugality in Epicurus and Seneca', *Phoenix* 31: 214–17
Axelson, B. 1933. *Senecastudien*, Lund and Leipzig
  1939. *Neue Senecastudien*, Lund and Leipzig
Baier, T., G. Manuwald, and B. Zimmermann, eds. 2005. *Seneca: philosophus et magister. Festschrift für Eckard Lefèvre zum 70. Geburtstag*, Freiburg-i-Br.
Baldwin, B. 2005. 'Nero the poet', in C. Deroux, ed. *Studies in Latin literature and Roman history* XII (Brussels) 307–18
Barchiesi, A., ed. 2005. *Ovidio: Metamorfosi*, vol. I: *Libri* I–II, Milan
Bardon, H. 1936. 'Les poésies de Néron', *REL* 14: 337–49
  1956. *La Littérature latine inconnue*, vol. II, Paris
Barker, D. 1996. '"The golden age is proclaimed?" The *Carmen saeculare* and the renascence of the golden race', *CQ* 46: 434–46
Barnes, J. 1979. *The pre-Socratic philosophers*, London
  1997. *Logic in the imperial stoa*, Leiden
Barton, C. 1993. *The sorrows of the ancient Romans: the gladiator and the monster*, Princeton
Barton, T. 1994. *Power and knowledge: astrology, physiognomics and medicine under the Roman empire*, Ann Arbor
Bartsch, S. 1994. *Actors in the audience: theatricality and doublespeak from Nero to Hadrian*, Cambridge, MA
  2005. 'Eros and the Roman philosopher', in S. Bartsch and T. Bartscherer, eds. *Erotikon: essays on eros ancient and modern* (Chicago) 59–83
  2006. *The mirror of the self: sexuality, self-knowledge, and the gaze in the early Roman empire*, Chicago

2007. 'Wait a moment, Phantasia! Ekphrastic interference in Seneca and Epictetus', *CPh* 102: 83–95

2009. 'Senecan metaphor and Stoic self-instruction', in Bartsch and Wray 2009: 188–217

2015. *Persius: a study in food, philosophy and the figural*, Chicago

2017. 'Philosophers and the state under Nero', in Bartsch, Freudenburg and Littlewood 2017: 151–63

Bartsch, S., K. Freudenburg, and C. Littlewood, eds. 2017. *The Cambridge companion to the age of Nero*, Cambridge

Bartsch, S., and A. Schiesaro, eds. 2015. *The Cambridge companion to Seneca*, Cambridge

Bartsch, S., and D. Wray, eds. 2009. *Seneca and the self*, Cambridge

Beagon, M. 2005. '*Mors repentina* and the Roman art of dying', *SyllClass* 16: 85–137

Beard, M. 2002. 'Ciceronian correspondences: making a book out of letters', in T. P. Wiseman, ed. *Classics in progress* (Oxford) 103–44

2014. *Laughter in ancient Rome: on joking, tickling and cracking up*, Berkeley

Beard, M., J. North, and S. Price. 1998. *Religions of Rome*, 2 vols., Cambridge

Bellincioni, M. 1984. *Potere ed etica in Seneca: clementia e voluntas amica*, Brescia

Berger, A. 1953. *Encyclopaedic dictionary of Roman law*, Philadephia

Bernardi Perini, G. 2001. *Il Mincio in Arcadia: scritti di filologia e letteratura latina*, Bologna

Berno, F. R. 2003. '*Ocliferia* (Sen. *Ep.* 33.3): la filosofia in vetrina', *Paedeia* 58: 40–6

2004. 'Enea *pius inperitus*: nota a Sen. *Epist.* 56.12–13', in L. de Finis, ed. *Colloquio su Seneca* (Trent) 7–24

2008. 'Seneca e la pienezza', *BStudLat* 38: 549–66

2011. '*Epistulae morales ad Lucilium*', in *The literary encyclopedia*, www.litencyc.com/php/sworks.php?rec=true&UID=32192, accessed 18/1/2016.

2014. 'Il saggio destino di Didone: *Aen.* 4.653 in Seneca', *Maia* 66: 123–36

2015. '"Naufragar m'è dolce in questo mare": filosofi e naufraghi da Lucrezio a Seneca (e Petronio)', *Maia* 67: 282–97

2017a. 'Claranus, Héraclès, Mucius Scaevola: paradigmes de persuasion dans la lettre 66 de Sénèque', in E. Gavoille and F. Guillaumont, eds. *Conseiller, diriger par lettre* (Tours) 265–81

2017b. 'Nurses' prayers, philosophical *otium*, and fat pigs: Seneca *Ep.* 60 versus Horace *Ep.* 1.4', in Stöckinger, Winter and Zanker 2017: 53–72

Berthet, J. F. 1979. 'Sénèque lecteur d'Horace d'après les lettres à Lucilius', *Latomus* 38: 940–54

Blänsdorf, J. 2011. *Fragmenta poetarum Latinorum*, 4th edn, Berlin
Bloomer, W. M. 2007. 'Roman declamation: the elder Seneca and Quintilian', in W. Dominik and J. Hall, eds. *A companion to Roman rhetoric* (Oxford) 297–306
  2011. *The school of Rome: Latin studies and the origins of liberal education*, Berkeley
Bodel, J. 1997. 'Monumental villas and villa monuments', *JRA* 10: 5–35
Bonner, C. 1941. 'Desired haven', *HThR* 34: 49–67
Bourgery, A. 1910. 'Sur la prose métrique de Sénèque le Philosophe', *RPh* 34: 167–72
  1911. 'Les lettres à Lucilius, sont-elles de vraies lettres?', *RPh* 35: 40–55
  1922. *Sénèque prosateur: études littéraires et grammaticales sur la prose de Sénèque le philosophe*, Paris
Boys-Stones, G. R. 2001. *Post-Hellenistic philosophy: a study of its development from the Stoics to Origen*, Oxford
  2007. '*Fallere sollers*: the ethical pedagogy of the Stoic Cornutus', in Sorabji and Sharples 2007: 77–88
  2013. 'Seneca against Plato: Letters 58 and 65', 128–46 in A. G. Long, ed. *Plato and the Stoics*, Cambridge
Bracke, E., S. Hodkinson, and P. Rosenmeyer, eds. 2013. *Epistolary narratives in ancient Greek literature* (Mnemosyne suppl. 359), Leiden
Bradley, K. 1978. *Suetonius' Life of Nero: an historical commentary*, Brussels
  1986. 'Seneca and slavery', *C&M* 37: 161–72 [= Fitch 2008: 335–47]
  1987. *Slaves and masters in the Roman empire: a study in social control*, Oxford
  1994. *Slavery and society at Rome*, Cambridge
Bradley, K., and P. Cartledge, eds. 2011. *The Cambridge world history of slavery*, vol. I: *The ancient Mediterranean world*, Cambridge
Bramble, J. 1974. *Persius and the programmatic satire*, Cambridge
Branham, R. B., and M.-O. Goulet-Cazé, eds. 1996. *The Cynics: the Cynic movement in antiquity and its legacy*, Berkeley
Braund, S. M. 2015. 'Seneca *multiplex*: the phases (and phrases) of Seneca's life and works', in Bartsch and Schiesaro 2015: 15–28
Brink, C. O. 1963–82. *Horace on poetry*, 3 vols., Cambridge
Briscoe, J. 2008. *A commentary on Livy Books 38–40*, Oxford
Brooke, C. 2012. *Philosophic pride: Stoicism and political thought from Lipsius to Rousseau*, Princeton
Broughton, T. R. S. 1953. *The magistrates of the Roman republic*, vol. I, New York
Brouwer, R. 2014. *The Stoic sage: the early Stoics on wisdom, sagehood and Socrates*, Cambridge
Brunt, P. A. 2013. *Studies in Stoicism*, ed. M. Griffin and A. Samuels, with M. H. Crawford, Oxford

Busch, A. 2009. 'Dissolution of the self in the Senecan corpus', in Bartsch and Wray 2009: 255–82
Butrica, J. L. 2005. 'Some myths and anomalies in the study of Roman sexuality', *Journal of Homosexuality* 49: 209–69
Byrne, S. 1999. 'Maecenas in Seneca and other post-Augustan authors', in S. Byrne and E. Cueva, eds. *Veritatis amicitiaeque causa: essays in honor of Anna Lydia Motto and John R. Clark* (Wauconda) 21–40
  2004. 'Martial's fiction: Domitius Marsus and Maecenas', *CQ* 54: 255–65.
  2006. 'Petronius and Maecenas: Seneca's calculated criticism', in S. Byrne, E. Cueva and J. Alvares, eds. *Authors, authority and interpreters in the ancient novel.* (Groningen) 83–111
  2007. 'Maecenas and Petronius' Trimalchio Maecenatianus', in *Ancient Narrative*, vol. VI (Groningen) 31–49
Cairns, F. 1971. 'Propertius 3.10 and Roman birthdays', *Hermes* 99: 149–55
Cancik, H. 1967. *Untersuchungen zu Senecas Epistulae morales* (Spudasmata 18), Hildesheim
Castagna, L. 1991. 'Storia e storiografia nel pensiero di Seneca', in Setaioli 1991: 91–117
Cermatori, L. 2010. 'L'*epistula* come *monumentum*: Seneca e l'autocoscienza della filosofia (*epist.* 21.3–6)', *Athenaeum* 98.2: 445–66
Chambert, R. 2002. 'Voyage et santé dans les lettres de Sénèque', *BAGB* 61: 63–82
  2005. *Rome: le mouvement et l'ancrage. Morale et philosophie du voyage au début du Principat*, Brussels
Champlin, E. 1978. 'The life and times of Calpurnius Siculus: technique and date', *JRS* 68: 95–110
  2003. *Nero*, Cambridge, MA
Chaumartin, F.-R. 1985. *Le De beneficiis de Sénèque: sa signification philosophique, politique et sociale*, Lille and Paris
Citroni, M. 1975. *M. Valerii Martialis Epigrammaton liber primus*, Florence
Citroni Marchetti, S. 1991. *Plinio il vecchio e la tradizione del moralismo romano*, Pisa
Citti, F. 2015. 'Seneca and the moderns', in Bartsch and Schiesaro 2015: 303–17
Claassen, J.-M. 1999. *Displaced persons: the literature of exile from Cicero to Boethius*, London
Clay, D. 1983. *Lucretius and Epicurus*, Ithaca
  1986. 'The cults of Epicurus', *Cronache Ercolanesi* 16: 11–28
  2009. 'The Athenian garden', in Warren 2009: 9–28
Coleman, K. 1990. 'Fatal charades: Roman executions staged as mythological enactments', *JRS* 80: 44–73

1993. 'Launching into history: aquatic displays in the early Empire', *JRS* 83: 48–74
Coleman, R. 1974. 'The artful moralist: a study in Seneca's epistolary style', *CQ* 24: 276–89
Colish, M. 1985. *The Stoic tradition from antiquity to the early Middle Ages*, Leiden
Conte, G. 1996. *The hidden author: an interpretation of Petronius' Satyricon*, Berkeley
Cooper, J. M. 2004. 'Moral theory and moral improvement: Seneca', in *Knowledge, nature and the good: essays on ancient philosophy* (Princeton) 309–24
Corbeill, A. 1996. *Controlling laughter: political humour in the late Roman Republic*, Princeton
2004. *Nature embodied: gesture in ancient Rome*, Princeton
Corbett, P. 1986. *The scurra*, Edinburgh
Cornell, T. 2013. ed. *The fragments of the Roman historians*, 3 vols., Oxford
Costa, C. D. N. 1974. ed. *Seneca*, London
Costa, S. 2014. ed. *Maecenas: frammenti e testimonianze latine*, Milan
Courtney, E. 1993. *The fragmentary Latin poets*, Oxford
2001. *A companion to Petronius*, Oxford
Courtouil, J. 2014. 'Torture in Seneca's philosophical works: between justification and condemnation', in Wildberger and Colish 2014: 189–207
2015. *Sapientia contemptrix doloris: le corps souffrant dans l'oeuvre philosophique de Sénèque*, Brussels
Crawford, M. H. 1996. ed. *Roman statutes*, London
Crook, J. 1967. *Law and life of Rome*, London
Cucchiarelli, A. 2005. 'Speaking from silence: the Stoic paradoxes of Persius', in Freudenburg 2005: 62–80
Cugusi, P. 1983. *Evoluzione e forme dell'epistolografia Latina nella tarda repubblica e nei due primi secoli dell'impero*, Rome
1989. 'L'epistolografia: modelli e tipologie', in G. Cavallo *et al.*, eds., *Lo spazio letterario di Roma antica*, vol. II: *La circolazione del testo* (Rome) 379–419
Damschen, G., and A. Heil, eds. 2014. *A companion to Seneca*, Leiden
D'Arms, J. 1970. *Romans on the bay of Naples: a social and cultural study of the villas and their owners from 150 BC to AD 400*, Cambridge, MA
1990. 'The Roman *convivium* and the idea of equality', in O. Murray, ed. *Sympotica* (Oxford) 308–20
1991. 'Slaves and Roman *convivia*', in W. Slater, ed. *Dining in a classical context* (Ann Arbor) 171–83
De Pretis, A. 2002. *Epistolarity in first book of Horace's Epistles*, Piscataway

2003. '"Insincerity", "facts" and "epistolarity": approaches to Pliny's Epistles to Calpurnia', *Arethusa* 36.2: 127–46
De Robertis, T., and G. Resta, eds. 2004. *Seneca: una vicenda testuale*, Florence
De Vivo, A., and E. Lo Cascio. 2003. *Seneca uomo politico e l'età di Claudio e di Nerone*, Bari
Degl'Innocenti Pierini, R. 2003. 'Cicerone nella prima età imperiale: luci ed ombre su un martire della repubblica', in E. Narducci, ed. *Aspetti della fortuna di Cicerone nella cultura Latina* (Florence) 3–54
  2008. *Il parto dell' orsa: studi sull'Virgilio, Ovidio e Seneca*, Bologna
  2013. 'Seneca, Mecenate e il ritratto in movimento', in F. Gasti, ed. *Seneca e la letteratura greca e latina: per i settant'anni di Giancarlo Mazzoli* (Pavia) 45–66
  2014. 'Freedom in Seneca: some reflections on the relationship between philosophy and politics, public and private life', in Wildberger and Colish 2014: 167–87
  2016. 'La virtù come compagna e la "compagnia" delle virtù in Seneca e nella tradizione filosofica', *Prometheus* 42: 123–43
Del Giovane, B. 2012. 'Seneca, Scipione e l'ombra di Cicerone: a proposito dell'Epistola 86', *Prometheus* 38: 155–74
  2015a. *Seneca, la diatriba e la ricerca di una morale austera*, Florence
  2015b. 'Attalus and the others: diatribic morality, Cynicism and rhetoric in Seneca's teachers', *Maia* 67: 3–24
  2017. 'Dressing philosophy with *sal niger*: Horace's role in Seneca's approach to the diatribic tradition', in Stöckinger, Winter and Zanker 2017: 27–52
Delatte, A. 1950. 'Le case de Pacuvius', *BAB* 36: 91–119
Delpeyroux, M.-F. 2002. 'Temps, philosophie et amitié dans les *Lettres à Lucilius*', in L. Nadjo and E. Gavoille, eds. *Epistulae antiquae*, vol. II (Tours) 203–21
Di Paola, O. 2014. 'The philosophical thought of the school of the Sextii', *Epekeina* 4.1–2: 327–39
Dickey, E. 2002. *Latin forms of address: from Plato to Apuleius*, Oxford
Dickison, S. 1977. 'Claudius: *Saturnalicius princeps*', *Latomus* 36: 634–47
Dihle, A. 1982. *The theory of the will in classical antiquity*, Berkeley
Dillon, J. M., and A. A. Long, eds. 1988. *The question of 'eclecticism': studies in later Greek philosophy*, Berkeley and Los Angeles
Dinter, M. 2014. 'Seneca's *Sententiae*', in Wildberger and Colish 2014: 319–41
Dominik, W., ed. 1997a. *Roman eloquence: rhetoric in society and literature*, London
  1997b. 'The style is the man: Seneca, Tacitus and Quintilian's canon', in Dominik 1997a: 50–68

Doody, A. 2007. 'Virgil the farmer? Critiques of the *Georgics* in Columella and Pliny', *CPh* 102: 180–97
Döring, K. 1979. *Exemplum Socratis: Studien zur Sokrates Nachwirkung in der Kynish-Stoischen Popularphilosophie der frühen Kaiserzeit und in frühen Christentum*, Wiesbaden
Dowling, M. 2006. *Clemency and cruelty in the Roman world*, Ann Arbor
Dressler, A. 2012. '"You must change your life": theory and practice, metaphor and *exemplum* in Seneca's prose', *Helios* 39: 145–92
  2016. *Personification and the feminine in Roman philosophy*, Cambridge
Droge, A., and J. Tabor. 1992. *A noble death: suicide and martyrdom among Christians and Jews in antiquity*, San Francisco
Dueck, D. 2009. 'Poetic quotations in Latin prose works of philosophy', *Hermes* 137: 314–34
Dunbabin, K. 1989. 'Pleasures and dangers of the baths', *PBSR* 57: 7–46
  2003. *The Roman banquet: images of conviviality*, Cambridge
Dupont, F., and T. Éloi. 2001. *L'Érotisme masculin dans la Rome antique*, Paris
Dyck, A. 1996. *A commentary on Cicero: De officiis*, Ann Arbor
Earl, D. 1967. *The moral and political tradition of Rome*, London
Ebner, P. 1970. 'Nuove iscrizioni di Velia', in *Nuovi studi su Velia* (Parola del Passato 25) (Naples) 266–7
Edelstein, L., and I. Kidd, eds. 1989. *Posidonius*, vol. I: *The fragments*, 2nd edn, Cambridge
Edmondson, J. 1996. 'Dynamic arenas: gladiatorial presentations in the city of Rome and the construction of Roman society in the early empire', in W. Slater, ed. *Roman theater and society* (Ann Arbor) 69–112
  2008. 'Public dress and social control in Rome', in J. Edmondson and A. Keith, eds. *Roman dress and the fabrics of Roman culture* (Toronto) 21–46
Edwards, C. 1993. *The politics of immorality in ancient Rome*, Cambridge
  1994. 'Beware of imitations: theatre and the subversion of imperial identity', in Elsner and Masters 1994: 83–97
  1996. *Writing Rome: textual approaches to the city*, Cambridge
  1997a. 'Self-scrutiny and self-transformation in Seneca's letters', *G&R* 44: 23–38 [repr. in Fitch 2008]
  1997b. 'Unspeakable professions', in Hallett and Skinner 1997: 66–95
  1999. 'The suffering body: philosophy and pain in Seneca's letters', in J. Porter, ed. *Constructions of the classical body* (Ann Arbor) 252–68
  2005a. 'Epistolography', in S. Harrison, ed. *Blackwell companion to Latin literature* (Oxford) 270–83
  2005b. 'Response to Shadi Bartsch', in S. Bartsch and T. Bartsherer, eds. *Erotikon: essays on eros ancient and modern* (Chicago) 84–90
  2005c. 'Archetypally Roman? Representing Seneca's aging body', in A. Hopkins and M. Wyke, eds. *Roman bodies* (London) 13–22

2007. *Death in ancient Rome*, London and New Haven
2009. 'Free yourself! Slavery, freedom and the self in Seneca's *Letters*', in Bartsch and Wray 2009: 139–59
2014. 'Death and time', in Damschen and Heil 2014: 323–41
2017a. 'Saturnalian exchanges: Seneca, Horace, and satiric advice', in Stöckinger, Winter and Zanker 2017: 73–89
2017b. 'Seneca and the quest for glory in Nero's golden age', in Bartsch, Freudenburg and Littlewood 2017: 164–76
2018a. 'Conversing with the absent, corresponding with the dead: friendship and philosophical community in Seneca's Letters', in P. Ceccarelli, L. Doering, T. Fogen and I. Gildenhard, eds. *Letters and communities: studies in the socio-political dimensions of ancient epistolography* (Oxford) 325–51
2018b. 'On not being in Rome: exile and displacement in Seneca's prose', in W. Fitzgerald and E. Spentzou, eds. *The production of space in Latin literature* (Oxford) 169–94
Eigler, U. 2005. '*Familiariter cum servis vivere*: eigene Überlegungen zu Inhalt und Hintergrund von Senecas Epistel 47', in Baier, Manuwald and Zimmermann 2005: 63–79
Elsner, J., and J. Masters, eds. 1994. *Reflections of Nero: culture, history and representation*, London
Engberg-Pedersen, T. 1986. 'Discovering the good: *oikeiosis* and *kathekonta* in Stoic ethics', in M. Schofield and G. Striker, eds. *The norms of nature: studies in Hellenistic ethics* (Cambridge) 145–83
Evenepoel, W. 2004. 'Seneca on suicide', *AncSoc* 34: 214–43
Eyben, E. 1972. 'Antiquity's view of puberty', *Latomus* 31: 677–97
Fabre-Serris, J. 1999. 'Néron et les traditions latines de l'âge d'or', in *Neronia v: Néron. Histoire et légende* (Brussels) 187–200
Fagan, G. 1999. *Bathing in public in the Roman world*, Ann Arbor
2011. *The lure of the arena: social psychology and the crowd at the Roman games*, Cambridge
Fantham, E. 2006. *Julia Augusti: the emperor's daughter*, London
Fedeli, P. 2004. 'Le lettere a Lucilio: introduzione', in De Robertis and Resta 2004: 203–9
Feeney, D. 2007. *Caesar's calendar: ancient time and the beginnings of history*, Oxford
Ferguson, J. 1990. 'Epicureanism under the Roman empire', in *ANRW* II.36.4: 2257–2327
Finley, M. 1973. *The ancient economy*, London
Fitch, J. 1981. 'Sense-pauses and relative dating in Seneca, Sophocles and Shakespeare', *AJP* 102: 289–307
ed. 2008. *Oxford readings in classical studies: Seneca*, Oxford

Fitzgerald, W. 1995. *Catullan provocations: lyric poetry and the drama of position*, Berkeley
  2000. *Slavery and the Roman literary imagination*, Cambridge
  2007. *Martial: the world of the epigram*, Chicago
  2015. 'The epistolary tradition', in P. Cheney and P. Hardie, eds. *Oxford history of Classical reception in English literature*, vol. II (Oxford) 273–90
  2016. *Variety: the life of a Roman concept*, Chicago
Flemming, R. 2005. 'Suicide, euthanasia and medicine', *Economy and Society* 34.2: 295–321
Flower, H. 1996. *Ancestor masks and aristocratic power in Roman culture*, Oxford
Fohlen, J. 2000. 'La tradition manuscrite des *Epistulae ad Lucilium*', *GIF* 52: 113–62
Foucault, M. 1986. *The history of sexuality*, vol. III: *The care of the self*, trs. R. Hurley, London
  1997. *Ethics, subjectivity and truth*, trs. R. Hurley and others, New York
Fowler, D. 2000. *Roman constructions: readings in postmodern Latin*, Oxford
Frede, M. 1989. 'Chaeremon der Stoiker', in *ANRW* II.36.3: 2067–2103
Fredrick, D. 2002. *The Roman gaze: vision, power and the body*, Baltimore and London
Freudenburg, K. 1993. *The walking muse: Horace on the theory of satire*, Cambridge
  2001. *Satires of Rome: threatening poses from Lucilius to Juvenal*, Cambridge
  ed. 2005. *The Cambridge companion to Roman satire*, Cambridge
Frontisi-Ducroux, F. 1975. *Dédale: mythologie de l'artisan en Grèce ancienne*, Paris
Futrell, A. 2006. *The Roman games: historical sources in translation*, Oxford
Gagarin, M. 1986. *Early Greek law*, Berkeley
Gagliardi, D. 1998. *Il tempo in Seneca filosofo*, Naples
Gagliardi, P. 1988. 'Lingua e stile nell'epistola 12 di Seneca', *Vichiana* 17: 163–73
Galimberti, A. 2001. 'Seneca e la guerra', in M. Sordi, ed. *Il pensiero sulla guerra nel mondo antico* (Milan) 195–207
Galinsky, K. 1972. *The Herakles theme: the adaptations of the hero in literature from Homer to the twentieth century*, Oxford
  1981. 'Some aspects of Ovid's Golden Age', *GB* 10: 193–205
Garbarino, G. 1996. '*Secum peregrinari*: il tema del viaggio in Seneca', in *De tuo tibi: omaggio degli allievi a Italo Lana* (Bologna) 263–85
  1997. 'Naufragi e filosofi: *Ep.* 87', *Paideia* 52: 146–56
Garnsey, P. 1970. *Social status and legal privilege in the Roman empire*, Oxford
  1996. *Ideas of slavery from Aristotle to Augustine*, Cambridge
  2000. 'The land', in *The Cambridge Ancient History*, 2nd edn, vol. XI (Cambridge) 679–709

Gatz, B. 1967. *Weltalter, goldene Zeit und sinnverwandte Vorstellungen*, Hildesheim
Geffcken, K. 1973. *Comedy in the Pro Caelio*, Leiden
Gelzer, M. 1969. *The Roman nobility*, trs. R. Seager, Oxford
Gibbon, G. 1994. *The history of the decline and fall of the Roman Empire*, ed. D. Womersley, 3 vols., London
Gibson, R. K., and R. Morello. 2012. *Reading the letters of Pliny the Younger: an introduction*, Cambridge
Gigante, M. 2000. 'Seneca, ein Nachfolger Philodems?', in M. Erler, ed. *Epikureismus in der späten Republik und der Kaiserzeit* (Stuttgart) 32–41
Gill, C. 1988. 'Personhood and personality: the four-*personae* theory in Cicero's *De officiis* 1', *OSAPh* 6: 169–99
  2003. 'The school in the Roman imperial period', in B. Inwood, ed. *Cambridge companion to the Stoics* (Cambridge) 33–58
  2006. *The structured self in Hellenistic and Roman thought*, Oxford
  2008. 'The ancient self: issues and approaches', in P. Remes and J. Sihvola, eds. *Ancient philosophy of the self* (Dordrecht) 35–56
  2009. 'Seneca and selfhood: integration and disintegration', in Bartsch and Wray 2009: 65–83
  ed. 2013. *Marcus Aurelius: Meditations books 1–6*, Oxford
Gleason, M. 1995. *Making men: sophists and self-presentation in ancient Rome*, Princeton
Gloyn, L. 2017. *The ethics of the family in Seneca*, Cambridge
Gnoli, R. 1988. *Marmora romana*, 2nd edn, Rome
Goldschmidt, V. 1977. *Le système stoicien et l'idée de temps*, 3rd edn, Paris
Gordon, P. 2012. *The invention and gendering of Epicurus*, Ann Arbor
  2013. 'Epistolary Epicureans', in Bracke, Hodkinson and Rosenmeyer 2013: 133–51
Görler, W. 1996. 'Seneca über Glück und Vollendung', *Museum Helveticum* 53: 160–9
Gosling, J., and C. Taylor. 1982. *The Greeks on pleasure*, Oxford
Goulet-Cazé, M.-O. 1990. 'Le cynisme à l'époque impériale', in *ANRW* II.36.4: 2730–2833
Gowers, E. 1993. *The loaded table: representations of food in Roman literature*, Oxford
  1994. 'Persius and the decoction of Nero', in Elsner and Masters 1994: 131–50
  2011. 'The road to Sicily: Lucilius to Seneca', *Ramus* 40.2: 168–97
  ed. 2012. *Horace: Satires*, Cambridge
  forthcoming. *Maecenas: transformations of an Augustan patron*, Princeton
Gowing, A. 2005. *Empire and memory: the representation of the Roman republic in imperial culture*, Cambridge
Gradel, I. 2002. *Emperor worship and Roman religion*, Oxford

Grant, M. 2000. 'Humour in Seneca's *Letters to Lucilius*', *AncSoc* 30: 319–29
Graver, M. 1998. 'The manhandling of Maecenas: Senecan abstractions of masculinity', *AJPh* 119: 607–32
  2002. *Cicero on the emotions: Tusculan disputations 3 and 4*, Chicago
  2007. *Stoicism and Emotion*, Chicago
  2009. 'The weeping wise: Stoic and Epicurean consolations in Seneca's 99th epistle', in T. Fögen, ed. *Tears in the Graeco-Roman world* (Berlin and New York) 235–52
  2014. 'Honeybee reading and self-scripting: *Epistulae morales* 84', in Wildberger and Colish 2014: 269–93
  2016a. 'The emotional intelligence of Epicureans: doctrinalism and adaptation in Seneca's *Epistles*', in Williams and Volk 2016: 192–210
  2016b. 'Seneca the Younger's philosophical works', *Oxford bibliographies*, www.oxfordbibliographies.com/view/document/obo-9780195389661/obo-9780195389661-0224.xml
Greene, K. 2008. 'Inventors, invention, and attitudes towards innovation', in Oleson 2008: 800–18
Griffin, M. 1968. 'Seneca on Cato's politics: *Ep.* 14.12–3', *CQ* 18: 373–5
  1972. 'The Elder Seneca and Spain', *JRS* 62: 1–19
  1984. *Nero: the end of a dynasty*, London
  1986. 'Philosophy, Cato and Roman suicide', *G&R* 33: 65–77 and 192–202
  1988. 'Philosophy for statesmen: Cicero and Seneca', in H. W. Schmidt and P. Wülting, eds. *Antikes Denken- moderne Schule* (Heidelberg) 133–50
  1989. 'Philosophy, politics, and politicians at Rome', in Griffin and Barnes 1989: 1–37
  1992 [1976]. *Seneca: a philosopher in politics*, 2nd edn, Oxford
  1995. 'Philosophical badinage in Cicero's letters to his friends', in Powell 1995: 325–46
  1996. 'Cynicism and the Romans: attraction and repulsion', in Branham and Goulet-Cazé 1996: 190–204
  2005. 'Seneca and Pliny', in C. Rowe and M. Schofield, eds. *Cambridge history of Greek and Roman political thought* (Cambridge) 532–58
  2007. 'Seneca's pedagogic strategy: *Letters* and *De Beneficiis*', in Sorabji and Sharples 2007: 89–113
  2008. '*Imago uitae suae*', in Fitch 2008: 23–58
  2013. *Seneca on society: a guide to De beneficiis*, Oxford
Griffin, M., and J. Barnes, eds. 1989. *Philosophia togata: essays on philosophy and Roman society*, Oxford
Grimal, P. 1978. *Sénèque ou la conscience de l'empire*, Paris.
  ed. 1991. *Sénèque et la prose latine* (Entretiens Fondation Hardt), Geneva

ed. 1992a. *La Langue latine: langue de la philosophie*, Rome
1992b. 'Le vocabulaire de l'intériorité dans l'oeuvre de Sénèque', in Grimal 1992a: 151–9
Gross, K. 1980. '*Numquam minus otiosus quam cum otiosus*: das Weiterleben eines antiken Sprichwortes im Abendland', *AA* 26: 122–37
Guillemin, A.-M. 1957. 'Sénèque, second fondateur de la prose latine', *REL* 35: 265–84
Gunderson, E. 1996. 'The ideology of the arena', *ClAnt* 15: 113–51
2015. *The sublime Seneca: ethics, literature, metaphysics*, Cambridge
Habinek, T. 1982. 'Seneca's circles: *Ep*.12.6–9', *ClAnt* 1: 66–9
1992. 'An aristocracy of virtue: Seneca on the beginnings of wisdom', in F. M. Dunn and T. Cole, eds. *Beginnings in classical literature* (Cambridge) 187–203
1998. *The politics of Latin literature: writing, identity and empire in ancient Rome*, Princeton
2000. 'Seneca's renown: *gloria*, *claritudo*, and the replication of the Roman elite', *ClAnt* 19: 264–303
2014. '*Imago suae uitae*: Seneca's life and career', in Damschen and Heil 2014: 3–31
Hachmann, E. 1995. *Die Fuhrung des Lesers in Senecas Epistulae morales*, Münster
Hadot, I. 1969. *Seneca und die griechisch-römische Tradition der Seelenleitung*, Berlin
2007. 'Versuch einer doktrinalen Neueinordnung der Schule der Sextier', *RhM* 150: 179–210
2014a. *Sénèque: direction spirituelle et pratique de la philosophie*, Paris
2014b. 'Getting to goodness: reflections on Ch. 10 of Brad Inwood *Reading Seneca*', in Wildberger and Colish 2014: 9–41
Hadot, P. 1995. *Philosophy as a way of life: spiritual exercises from Socrates to Foucault*, ed. A. I. Davidson, trs. M. Chase, London
2002. *What is ancient philosophy?*, Cambridge, MA
Hall, J. 2009. *Politeness and politics in Cicero's letters*, Oxford
Hallett, J., and M. Skinner, eds. 1997. *Roman sexualities*, Princeton
Harder, A. 2004. 'Catullus 63: a Hellenistic poem?', in R. Nauta and A. Harder, eds. *Catullus' poem on Attis: text and context* (Leiden) 574–95
Harder, F. 1889. *Über die Fragmente des Maecenas*, Berlin
Hardie, A. 1983. *Statius and the Silvae: poets, patrons and epideixis in the Graeco-Roman world*, Liverpool
Harris, W. V. 2001. *Restraining rage: the ideology of anger control in classical antiquity*, Cambridge, MA
Hellegouarc'h, J. ed. 1972. Sallust: *De Catilinae conspiratione*, Paris
Henderson, J. 1997. *Figuring out Roman nobility: Juvenal's eighth satire*, Exeter
2002. *Pliny's statue: the letters, self-portraiture and classical art*, Exeter

2004. *Morals and villas in Seneca's Letters*, Cambridge
2006. 'Journey of a lifetime: Seneca *Epistle* 57 in Book VI in *EM*', in Volk and Williams 2006: 123–46
Hijmans, B. L. 1966. 'Drama in Seneca's Stoicism', *TAPhA* 97: 237–51
1976. *Inlaboratus et facilis: aspects of structure in some letters of Seneca* (Mnemosyne suppl. 38), Leiden
1991. 'Stylistic splendour, failure to persuade', in Grimal 1991: 1–37
Hill, T. D. 2004. *Ambitiosa mors: suicide and the self in Roman thought and literature*, London
Hine, H. M. 2005. 'Poetic influence on prose: the case of the Younger Seneca', in T. Reinhardt, M. Lapidge, and J. N. Adams, eds. *Aspects of the language of Latin prose* (Oxford) 211–238
2006. 'Rome, the cosmos and the emperor in Seneca's *Natural questions*', *JRS* 96: 42–72
Hirzel, R. 1882. *Untersuchungen zu Cicero's philosophischen Schriften*, vol. II, Leipzig
Hodkinson, O., P. Rosenmeyer, and E. Bracke, eds. 2013. *Epistolary narratives in ancient Greek literature*, Leiden
Hölkeskamp, K.-J. 1999. *Schiedsrichter, Gesetzgeber und Gesetzgebung in archaischen Griechenland*, Stuttgart
Hoffer, S. 2007. 'Cicero's stomach', in Morello and Morrison 2007: 87–106
Hooff, A. Van. 1990. *From autothanasia to suicide: self-killing in classical antiquity*, London
Hope, V. 2009. *Roman death: dying and the dead in ancient Rome*, London
Hopkins, K. 1983. *Death and renewal*, Cambridge
1993. 'Novel evidence for Roman slavery', *P&P* 138: 3–27
Hopkins, K., and M. Beard. 2005. *The Colosseum*, London
Horsfall, N. 1997. 'Criteria for the dating of Calpurnius Siculus', *RFIC* 125: 166–96
Hunt, A. 2016. *Reviving Roman religion: sacred trees in the Roman world*, Cambridge
Hurka, F. 2005. 'Seneca und die Didaktik des Lachens: Spiel und Ernst in der Briefgruppe epist. 49–57' in Baier, Manuwald and Zimmermann 2005: 117–38
Hutchinson, G. 1993. *Latin literature from Seneca to Juvenal*, Oxford.
1998. *Cicero's correspondence: a literary study*, Oxford
Inwood, B. 1985. *Ethics and human action in early Stoicism*, Oxford
ed. 2003. *The Cambridge companion to the Stoics*, Cambridge
2005. *Reading Seneca: Stoic philosophy at Rome*, Oxford
2007. 'The importance of form in Seneca's philosophical letters', in Morello and Morrison 2007: 133–48
Isnardi Parente, M. 2000. 'Socrate e Catone', in Parroni 2000: 215–25

Israeli, Y. 1991. 'The invention of blowing', in M. Newby and K. Painter, eds. *Roman glass: two centuries of art and invention* (London) 46–55
Jackson, R. 1993. 'Eye medicine in the Roman empire', in *ANRW* II.37.3: 2228–51
Jaeger, M. 1997. *Livy's written Rome*, Ann Arbor
Johnson, M., and D. Hutchinson, eds. and trs. 2017. *Aristotle: Protrepticus or exhortation to philosophy*, www.protrepticus.info
Johnson, W., and H. Parker, eds. 2009. *Ancient literacies: the culture of reading in Greece and Rome*, Oxford
Johnston, P. A. 1980. *Vergil's agricultural Golden Age: a study of the Georgics*, Leiden
Jones, C. P. 2000. 'Nero speaking', *HSPh* 100: 453–62
Jones, M. 2014. 'Seneca's Letters to Lucilius: hypocrisy as a way of life', in Wildberger and Colish 2014: 393–430
Joshel, S. 2011. 'Slavery and Roman literary culture', in Bradley and Cartledge 2011: 214–40
Kahn, C. H. 1988. 'Discovering the will: from Aristotle to Augustine', in Dillon and Long 1988: 234–59
Kaster, R. 2002. 'The taxonomy of patience, or when is *patientia* not a virtue?', *CPh* 97: 133–44
  2007. Review of McDonnell, *Roman manliness*, *BMCR* 2007.02.08
Kelly, G. 2006. *A history of exile in the Roman Republic*, Cambridge
Kennedy, D. 1993. *The arts of love*, Cambridge
Kenney, E. J. 1970. 'Doctus Lucretius', *Mnemosyne* 4.23: 373–80
  ed. 2014. *Lucretius: De rerum natura* III, 2nd edn, Cambridge
Ker, J. 2004. 'Nocturnal writers in imperial Rome', *CPh* 99: 209–42
  2006. 'Seneca, man of many genres', in Volk and Williams 2006: 19–41
  2009a. *The deaths of Seneca*, Oxford
  2009b. 'Seneca on self-examination: reading *On anger* 3.36', in Bartsch and Wray 2009: 160–87
  2010. 'Socrates speaks in Seneca *De uita beata* 24–8', in A. Nightingale and D. Sedley, eds. *Ancient models of mind: studies in human and divine rationality* (Cambridge) 180–95
  ed. 2011. *A Seneca reader: selections from prose and tragedy*, Mundelein, IL
  2015. 'Seneca and Augustan culture', in Bartsch and Schiesaro 2015: 109–21
Kidd, I. G. 1988. *Posidonius*, vol. II: *The commentary*, Cambridge
  1999. *Posidonius*, vol. III: *The translation of the fragments*, Cambridge
Kindstrand, J. F. 1976. *Bion of Borysthenes: a collection of the fragments with introduction and commentary*, Uppsala
  1981. *Anacharsis: the legend and the apothegmata*, Uppsala
Knoche, U. 1975. 'Der Gedanke der Freundschaft in Senecas Briefe an Lucilius', in Maurach 1975: 149–66

König, J. 2012. *Saints and symposiasts: the literature of food and the symposium in Greco-Roman and early Christian culture*, Cambridge
Konstan, D. 2015. 'Senecan emotions', in Bartsch and Schiesaro 2015: 174–86
Konstan, D. et al., eds. 1998. *Philodemus: On frank criticism*, Atlanta, GE
Kraye, J. 2007. 'Senecanismus', in G. Ueding, ed. *Historisches Wörterbuch der Rhetorik*, vol. VIII (Tübingen) cols. 826–41
Kyle, D. 1998. *Spectacles of death in ancient Rome*, London
Labate, M. 2012. 'Mecenate senza poeti, poeti senza Mecenate', in G. Bastianini, W. Lapini and M.Tulli, eds. *Harmonia: scritti di filologia classica in onore di Angelo Casanova*, vol. I (Florence) 404–24
Lakoff, G., and M. Johnson. 1980. *Metaphors we live by*, Chicago
Lampe, K. 2008. 'Seneca's nausea: "existential" experiences and Julio-Claudian literature', *Helios* 35.1: 67–88
  2014. *The birth of hedonism: the Cyrenaic philosophers and pleasure as a way of life*, Princeton
Lana, I. 1973. *Studi sul pensiero politico classico*, Naples
  1991. 'Le lettere a Lucilio nella letteratura epistolare', in Grimal 1991: 253–302
  1992. 'La scuola dei Sestii', in Grimal 1992a: 109–24
Langlands, R. 2018. *Exemplary ethics in ancient Rome*, Cambridge
Lattimore, R. 1942. *Themes in Greek and Latin epitaphs*, Urbana
Laudizi, G. 2004. 'Seneca (ep. 114)', *BStudLat* 34: 39–56
Lausberg, G. 1998. *Handbook of literary rhetoric: a foundation for literary study*, Leiden
Lavan, M. 2011. 'Slavishness in Britain and Rome in Tacitus' *Agricola*', *CQ* 61: 294–305
Lavery, G. B. 1980. 'Metaphors of war and travel in Seneca's prose works', *G&R* 27: 147–57
Leach, E. W. 1993. 'Horace's Sabine topography in lyric and hexameter verse', *AJPh* 114: 271–302
  2017. 'Roman literary letters', *Oxford bibliographies*, www.oxfordbibliographies.com/view/document/obo-9780195389661/obo-9780195389661-0265.xml
Leeman, A. D. 1953. 'Seneca's plans for a work "moralis philosophia" and their influence on his later Epistles', *Mnemosyne* 6: 307–11
  1963. *Orationis ratio: the stylistic theories and practice of the Roman orators, historians and philosophers*, 2 vols., Amsterdam
Leigh, M. 1997. *Lucan: spectacle and engagement*, Oxford
Lendon, J. 1997. *Empire of honour: the art of government in the Roman world*, Oxford
Lévy, C. 2003. 'Sénèque et la circularité du temps', in B. Bakhouche, ed. *L'Ancienneté chez les anciens*, vol. II (Montpellier) 491–509

Lintott, A. 1999. *The constitution of the Roman Republic*, Oxford
Long, A. A. 1986. *Hellenistic philosophy*, 2nd edn, London
  1996. 'Soul and body in Stoicism', in *Stoic studies* (Cambridge) 224–49
  1999. 'Stoic psychology', in K. Algra, J. Barnes *et al.*, *The Cambridge history of Hellenistic philosophy* (Cambridge) 560–84
  2002. *Epictetus: a Stoic and Socratic guide to life*, Oxford
  2006. *From Epicurus to Epictetus*, Oxford
  2009. 'Seneca on the self: why now?', in Bartsch and Wray 2009: 20–36
Long, A. A., and D. Sedley. 1987. *The Hellenistic philosophers*, 2 vols., Cambridge
Lotito, G. 2001. *Suum esse: forme dell'interiorità senecana*, Bologna
Lovejoy, A., and G. Boas. 1997 [1935]. *Primitivism and related ideas in antiquity*, Baltimore
Luce, T. 1977. *Livy: the composition of his history*, Princeton
Lunderstedt, P. 1911. *De Maecenatis fragmentis* (Commentarii Philologici Ienenses 9.1), Iena
Macaulay, T. B. 1976. *The letters of Thomas Babington Macaulay*, ed. T. Pinney, vol. III, Cambridge
McConnell, S. 2014. *Philosophical life in Cicero's letters*, Cambridge
McKeown, N. 2007a. *Inventing ancient slavery?*, London
  2007b. 'The sound of John Henderson laughing: Pliny 3.14 and Roman slaveowners' fear of their slaves', in A. Serghidou, ed. *Fear of Slaves – Fear of Enslavement* (Besançon) 265–79
Malaspina, E. 2018. 'Sénèque, *Lettres à Lucilius* Livres I–II: petit vadémécum philologique entre *CUF*, *OCT* et aujourd'hui', *VL* 197–8: 77–98
Maltby, R. 1991. *A lexicon of ancient Latin etymologies*, Leeds
Mann, W.-R. 2006. 'Learning how to die: Seneca's use of *Aeneid* 4.653 at *Ep. Mor.* 12.9', in Volk and Williams 2006: 103–22
Manning, C. E. 1974. 'The consolatory tradition and Seneca's attitude to the emotions', *G&R* 21: 71–81
Mantovanelli, P. 2001. '"Perversioni" morali e letterarie in Seneca', in P. Fedeli, ed. *Scienza, cultura, morale in Seneca* (Bari) 53–86
Marchesi, I. 2008. *The art of Pliny's letters: a poetics of allusion in the private correspondence*, Cambridge
Marshall, C. W. 2014. 'The works of Seneca the Younger and their dates', in Damschen and Heil 2014: 33–44
Martelli, F., ed. 2016. *Envois: new readings in Cicero's letters* (Arethusa special issue 49.3), Baltimore
Martin, R. P. 1996. 'The Scythian accent: Anacharsis and the cynics', in Branham and Goulet-Cazé 1996: 136–55
Maso, S. 1999. *Lo sguardo della Verità: cinque studi su Seneca*, Padua
Maurach, G. 1970. *Der Bau von Senecas Epistulae morales*, Heidelberg
  ed. 1975. *Seneca als Philosoph*, Darmstadt

2000. *Seneca: Leben und Werk*, Darmstadt
Maxia, C. 2000. 'Seneca e l'età dell'oro: negazione, eterocronie e eterotopie', *BStudLat* 30: 87–105
Mayer, R. 1980. 'Calpurnius Siculus: technique and date', *JRS* 70: 175–6
    1982. 'Neronian classicism', *AJPh* 103: 305–18
    1991. 'Roman historical *exempla* in Seneca', in Grimal 1991: 141–69
    2005. 'Sleeping with the enemy: satire and philosophy', in K. Freudenburg, ed. *The Cambridge companion to Roman satire* (Cambridge) 146–59
    2015. 'Seneca *redivivus*: Seneca in the medieval and Renaissance world', in Bartsch and Schiesaro 2015: 277–88
Mazzoli, G. 1968. L'epicureismo di Mecenate e il Prometheus', *Athenaeum* 46: 300–26
    1970. *Seneca e la poesia*, Milan
    1989. 'Le *Epistulae morales ad Lucilium* di Seneca: valore lettarario e filosofico', in *ANRW* II.36.3: 1823–77
    1991. 'Effetti di cornice nell'epistolario di Seneca e Lucilio' in Setaioli 1991: 67–88
    1992. Review of A. Setaioli, *Seneca e i greci: citazioni e traduzioni nelle opere filosofiche* (1988), *RFIC* 120: 341–52
Mello, M. 1968. *Mens bona*, Naples
Meritt, B. 1957. 'Greek inscriptions', *Hesperia* 26: 51–97
Mindt, N. 2017. 'Horace, Seneca, and Martial: "sententious style" across genres', in Stöckinger, Winter and Zanker 2017: 315–43
Moles, J. 1995. 'The Cynics and politics', in A. Laks and M. Schofield, eds. *Justice and generosity: studies in Hellenistic social and political philosophy* (Cambridge) 129–58
    1996. 'Cynic cosmopolitanism', in Branham and Goulet-Cazé 1996: 105–20
Möller, M. 2004. *'Talis oratio qualis uita': zu Theorie und Praxis mimetischer Verfahren in der griechischen-römischen Literaturkritik*, Heidelberg
Mommsen, T. 1887–8. *Römisches Staatsrecht*, 2 vols., Leipzig
Montiglio, S. 2006. 'Should the wise man travel? A conflict in Seneca's thought', *AJPh* 127: 553–86
    2011. *From villain to hero: Odysseus in ancient thought*, Ann Arbor
Morello, R., and A. Morrison, eds. 2007. *Ancient letters: classical and late antique epistolography*, Oxford
Moretti, G. 1995. *Acutum dicendi genus: brevità, oscurità, sottigliezze e paradossi nelle tradizioni retoriche degli Stoici*, Bologna
Morford, M. 1972–3. 'The Neronian literary revolution', *CJ* 68: 210–15
    1991. *Stoics and neo-Stoics: Rubens and the circle of Lipsius*, Princeton
Morgan, L. 2010. *Musa pedestris: metre and meaning in Roman verse*, Oxford

Morrison, A. 2007. 'Didacticism and epistolarity in Horace's *Epistles* 1', in Morello and Morrison 2007: 107–31
　2013. 'Narrative and Epistolarity in the "Platonic" Epistles', in Bracke, Hodkinson and Rosenmeyer 2013: 107–32
Motto, A. L., and J. R. Clark. 1971. '*Et terris iactatus et alto*: the art of Seneca's Epistle LIII', *AJP* 102: 217–25
　1993. *Essays on Seneca*, Frankfurt
Mynors, R., ed. 1990. *Virgil: Georgics*, Oxford
Mouritsen, H. 2011. *The freedman in the Roman world*, Cambridge
Nails, D. 2006. 'The trial and death of Socrates', in S. Ahbel-Rappe and R. Kamtekar, eds. *A companion to Socrates* (Oxford) 5–20
Nappa, C. 2005. *Reading after Actium: Vergil's Georgics, Octavian, and Rome*, Ann Arbor
Narducci, E. 1997. 'Perceptions of exile in Cicero: the philosophical interpretation of real experience', *AJPh* 118: 55–73
Newlands, C. 2002. *Statius' Silvae and the poetics of empire*, Cambridge
　ed. 2011. *Statius: Silvae book* II, Cambridge
Newman, R. J. 1989. '*Cotidie meditari*: theory and practice of meditation in imperial stoicism', in *ANRW* II.36.3: 1473–1517
　2008. '*In umbra virtutis*: *gloria* in the thought of Seneca the philosopher', in Fitch 2008: 316–34
Nichols, M. 2010. 'Contemporary perspectives on luxury building in second-century BC Rome', *PBSR* 78: 39–61
　2017. *Author and audience in Vitruvius' De architectura*, Cambridge
Nightingale, A. W. 2004. *Spectacles of truth in classical Greek philosophy: theoria in its cultural context*, Cambridge
Nisbet, R. 1995. *Collected papers on Latin literature*, Oxford
Nock, A. 1933. *Conversion: the old and the new in religion from Alexander the Great to Augustine of Hippo*, Oxford
Novara, A. 1988. '*Rude saeculum* que l'âge d'or selon Sénèque', *BAGB* 5: 129–39
Nussbaum, M. C. 1994. *The therapy of desire: theory and practice in Hellenistic ethics*, Princeton
　2000. 'Duties of justice, duties of material aid: Cicero's problematic legacy', *Journal of Political Philosophy* 8.2: 176–206
　2002. 'The incomplete feminism of Musonius Rufus, Platonist, Stoic, and Roman', in M. C. Nussbaum and J. Sihvola, eds. *The sleep of reason: erotic experience and sexual ethics in ancient Greece and Rome* (Chicago) 283–326
Oakley, S. 1997. *A commentary on Livy: books vi–x*, vol. I: *Introduction and Book* VI, Oxford
　1998. *A commentary on Livy: books vi–x*, vol. II: *Books* VII–VIII, Oxford
　2005a. *A commentary on Livy: books vi–x*, vol. III: *Book* IX, Oxford

2005b. *A commentary on Livy: books VI–X*, vol. IV: *Book X*, Oxford
Ogilvie, R. M. 1965. *A commentary on Livy: books 1–5*, Oxford
Oleson, J. P., ed. 2008. *The Oxford handbook of engineering and technology in the classical world*, Oxford
O'Sullivan, T. 2011. *Walking in Roman culture*, Cambridge
Otto, A. 1962. *Sprichwörter und sprichwörtlichen Redensarten der Römer*, Hildesheim
Pani, M. 1992. 'La polemica di Seneca contro le artes (Ep. 90): un caso di sconcerto', in *Potere e valori a Roma fra Augusto a Traiano* (Bari) 99–112
Panizza, L. 1983. 'Textual interpretation in Italy, 1350–1450: Seneca's Letter 1 to Lucilius', *Journal of the Warburg and Courtauld Institutes* 46: 40–62
 1987. 'Erasmus' 1515 and 1529 editions of Seneca and Gasparino Barzizza', *CML* 7: 319–32
Panayotakis, C. 1995. *Theatrum Arbitri: theatrical elements in the Satyrica of Petronius*, Leiden
 2004. review of T. Nikolaides, *Seneca's ninetieth letter*, *CR* 53: 103–4
Parker, H. 2009. 'Books and reading Latin poetry', in Johnson and Parker 2009: 186–231
Parkin, T. 2003. *Old age in the Roman world: a cultural and social history*, Baltimore
Parroni, P. ed. 2000. *Seneca e il suo tempo*, Rome
Pensabene Perez, P. 2000. 'I marmi in Seneca: residenze fastose ed esecrazione del lusso', in Parroni 2000: 91–109
Perrin, Y. 1987. 'La *domus aurea* et l'idéologie néronienne', in E. Lévy, ed. *Le système palatial en Orient, en Grèce et à Rome* (Leiden) 359–91
Pflaum, H. 1960–1. *Les carrières procuratoriennes équestres sous le Haut-Empire romain*, 3 vols., Paris
Plass, P. 1995. *The game of death in ancient Rome: arena sport and political suicide*, Madison, WI
Pohlenz, V. 1965. 'Philosophie und Erlebnis in Senecas Dialogen', Anhang, 'Ein römischer Zug in Senecas Denken', *Kleine Schriften*, 2 vols. (Hildesheim) 1.440–6
Powell, J. 1995. *Cicero the philosopher*, Oxford
Protopapas-Marneli, M. 2002. *La Rhétorique des Stoïciens*, Paris
Purcell, N. 1987. 'Town in country and country in town', in E. B. MacDougall, ed. *Ancient Roman villa gardens* (Dumbarton Oaks) 187–203
Raaflaub, K. 2006. 'Athenian and Spartan *eunomia*, or: what to do with Solon's timocracy', in J. Blok and A. Lardinois, eds. *Solon of Athens: new historical and philological approaches* (Leiden) 39–428
Rawson, E. 1976. 'The Ciceronian aristocracy and its properties', in M. I. Finley, ed. *Studies in Roman property* (Cambridge) 85–102

1985. *Intellectual life in the late Republic*, London
1989. 'Roman rulers and the philosophic adviser', in Griffin and Barnes 1989: 233–57
Reay, B. 2005. 'Agriculture, writing, and Cato's aristocratic self-fashioning', *ClAnt* 24: 331–61
Reydams-Schils, G. 2005. *The Roman Stoics: self, responsibility and affection*, Chicago
  2010. 'Seneca's Platonism: the soul and its divine origin', in A. Nightingale and D. Sedley, eds. *Ancient models of mind* (Cambridge) 196–215
Reynolds, L. 1983. *Texts and transmission: a survey of the Latin classics*, Oxford
Richardson-Hay, C. 2001. 'Drunk on false argument: Seneca's *Epistulae morales*, Epistle 83', *Prudentia* 33: 12–40
  2009. 'Dinner at Seneca's table: the philosophy of food', *G&R* 56: 71–96
Richlin, A. 1997. 'Gender and rhetoric: producing manhood in the schools', in Dominik 1997a: 90–110
Richter, W. 1958. 'Seneca und die Sklaven', *Gymnasium* 65: 196–218
Riggsby, A. 1991. 'Elision and hiatus in Latin prose', *ClAnt* 10: 328–43
  2003. 'Pliny in space (and time)', *Arethusa* 36: 167–86
  2016. 'Tyrants, fire and dangerous things', in Williams and Volk 2016: 111–28
Rimell, V. 2013. 'The best a man can get: grooming Scipio in Seneca *Epistle* 86', *CPh* 108: 1–20
  2015a. *The closure of space in Roman poetics: empire's inward turn*, Cambridge
  2015b. 'Seneca and Neronian Rome: in the mirror of time', in Bartsch and Schiesaro 2015: 122–34
Rist, J. M. 1969. *Stoic philosophy*, Cambridge
Roberts, M. 1989. *The jewelled style: poetry and poetics in late antiquity*, Ithaca
Robinson, O. 1992. *Ancient Rome: city planning and administration*, London
Roller, M. 2001. *Constructing autocracy: autocrats and emperors in Julio-Claudian Rome*, Princeton
  2004. 'Exemplarity in Roman culture: the cases of Horatius Cocles and Cloelia', *CPh* 99: 1–56
  2016. 'Praecept(or) and example in Seneca', in Williams and Volk 2016: 129–56
Ronnick, M. V. 1995. '*Suave mari magno*', *AJPh* 116: 653–4
  1999. 'Concerning the plane trees in Seneca's twelfth epistle', in S. Byrne and E. Cueva, eds. *Veritatis amicitiaeque cause: essays in honor of Anna Lydia Motto and John R. Clark* (Wauconda) 219–29
Rose, K. 1971. *The date and author of the Satyricon*, Leiden
Rosenmeyer, T. G. 1989. *Senecan drama and stoic cosmology*, Berkeley

Rostovtzeff, M. 1957. *Social and economic history of the Roman empire*, Oxford
Roth, U. 2016. 'Liberating the Cena', *CQ* 66: 614–34
Rudich, V. 1997. *Dissidence and literature under Nero: the price of rhetoricization*, London
Russell, D. 1974. 'Letters to Lucilius', in Costa 1974: 70–95
Russell, D., and M. Winterbottom. 1972. *Ancient literary criticism: the principal texts in new translations*, Oxford
Rutherford, R. 1989. *The Meditations of Marcus Aurelius: a study*, Oxford
Rutledge, S. H. 2001. *Imperial inquisitions: prosecutors and informants from Tiberius to Domitian*, London
Saller, R. 1991. 'Corporal punishment, authority and obedience in the Roman household', in B. Rawson, ed. *Marriage, divorce and children in ancient Rome* (Oxford) 144–65
Sangalli, E. 1988. 'Tempo narrato e tempo vissuto nelle *Epistulae ad Lucilium* di Seneca', *Athenaeum* 78: 53–67
Santoro L'Hoir, F. 1992. *The rhetoric of gender terms: 'man', 'woman' and the portrayal of character in Latin prose*, Leiden
Schafer, J. 2009. *Ars didactica: Seneca's 94th and 95th letters*, Göttingen
  2011. 'Seneca's *Epistulae Morales* as dramatized education', *CPh* 106: 32–52
Schiesaro, A. 2003. *The passions in play: Thyestes and the dynamics of Senecan drama*, Cambridge
  2015. 'Seneca and Epicurus: the allure of the other', in Bartsch and Schiesaro 2015: 239–51
Schneider, R. 1986. *Bunte Barbaren*, Worms
Schofield, M. 1999. *The Stoic idea of the city*, Chicago
Schönbeck, G. 1962. *Der Locus amoenus vom Homer bis Horaz*, Heidelberg
Schönegg, B. 1999. *Senecas Epistulae morales als philosophisches Kunstwerk*, Bern
Schoonhoven, H. 1983. 'The *Elegiae in Maecenatem*', in *ANRW* II.30.3: 1788–1811
Scullard, H. 1981. *Festivals and ceremonies of the Roman Republic*, London
Sedley, D. 1989. 'Philosophical allegiance in the Greco-Roman world', in Griffin and Barnes 1989: 97–119
  1999. 'The Stoic–Platonist debate on *kathekonta*', in K. Ierodiakonou, ed. *Topics in Stoic philosophy* (Oxford) 128–52
  2003. 'The school, from Zeno to Arius Didymus', in Inwood 2003: 7–32
  2005. 'Stoic metaphysics at Rome', in R. Salles, ed. *Metaphysics, soul and ethics in ancient thought* (Oxford) 117–42
Sellars, J. 2003. 'Simon the shoe-maker and the problem of Socrates', *CPh* 98: 207–16
  2014. 'Seneca's philosophical predecessors and contemporaries', in Damschen and Heil 2014: 97–112

Setaioli, A. 1965. 'Esegesi virgiliana in Seneca', *SIFC* 37: 133–56
  1976. 'On the date of publication of Cicero's letters to Atticus' *Symbolae Osloenses* 51: 105–20
  1980. 'Elementi di *sermo cotidianus* nella lingua di Seneca prosatore', *SIFC* 52: 5–47
  1981. 'Elementi di *sermo cotidianus* nella lingua di Seneca prosatore (continuazione)', *SIFC* 53: 5–49
  1983. 'Seneca e il greco della medicina', *Vichiana* 12: 293–303
  1988. *Seneca e i Greci: citazioni e traduzioni nelle opere filosofiche*, Bologna
  ed. 1991. *Seneca e la cultura*, Perugia
  2000. *Facundus Seneca: aspetti della lingua e dell'ideologia senecana*, Bologna
  2003. 'Seneca e Cicerone', in E. Narducci, ed. *Aspetti della fortuna di Cicerone nella cultura latina* (Florence) 55–78
  2007. 'Seneca and the divine: Stoic tradition and personal developments', *IJCT* 13: 333–68
  2014a. '*Epistulae morales*', in Damschen and Heil 2014: 191–200
  2014b. 'Theology', in Damschen and Heil 2014: 379–403
  2015. 'Seneca and the ancient world', in Bartsch and Schiesaro 2015: 255–65
Shackleton Bailey, D. R., ed. 1965. *Cicero's Letters to Atticus*, vol. I, Cambridge
  ed. 1966. *Cicero's Letters to Atticus*, vol. v, Cambridge
Shaw, B.D. 1985. 'The divine economy: stoicism as ideology', *Latomus* 44: 16–54
Sherman, N. 2005. 'The look and feel of virtue', in C. Gill, ed. *Virtue, norms and objectivity: issues in ancient and modern ethics* (Oxford) 59–82.
Sinclair, P. 1995. *Tacitus the sententious historian: a sociology of rhetoric in Annales 1–6*, University Park, PA
Sjöblad, A. 2015. *Metaphorical Coherence: Studies in Seneca's Epistulae Morales* (Studia Graeca et Latina Ludensia 20), Lund
Solin, H. 1996. *Die Stadtrömischen Sklavennamen: eine Namenbuch*, 3 vols., Stuttgart
Solimano, G. 1991. *La prepotenza dell'occhio: reflezzioni sull'opera di Seneca*, Genoa
Sommer, A. 2001. '*Vivere militare est*: die Funktion und philosophische Tragweite militärischer Metaphern bei Seneca und Lipsius', *ABG* 43: 59–82
Sorabji, R., and R. Sharples, eds. 2007. *Greek and Roman philosophy 100 BC – 200 AD*, vol. I (BICS suppl. 94), London
Sørensen, V. 1984. *Seneca: the humanist at the court of Nero*, trs. W. Glyn Jones, London
Soubiran, J. 1991. 'Sénèque prosateur et poète: convergences métriques' in Grimal 1991: 347–77

Spallone, M. 1995. '"Edizioni" tardoantiche e tradizione medievale dei testi: il caso delle *Epistulae ad Lucilium* di Seneca', in O. Pecere and M. D. Reeve, eds. *Formative stages of classical traditions: Latin texts from antiquity to the Renaissance* (Spoleto) 149–96
Spencer, D. 2002. *The Roman Alexander: reading a cultural myth*, Exeter
Star, C. 2012. *The empire of the self: self-command and political speech in Seneca and Petronius*, Baltimore
Starr, R. 1990–1. '*Lectores* and book-reading', *CJ* 86: 337–43
Stégen, G. 1972. '*Unus dies par omni est*', *Latomus* 31: 829–32
Stöckinger, M., K. Winter, and A. Zanker, eds. 2017. *Horace and Seneca: interactions, intertexts, interpretations*, Berlin
Stoneman, R. 2003. 'The legacy of Alexander in ancient philosophy', in J. Roisman, ed. *Brill's companion to Alexander the Great* (Leiden) 325–45
Sullivan, J. P. 1985. *Literature and politics in the age of Nero*, Ithaca and London
Summers, W. C. 1908a. 'Notes and emendations to Seneca's letters', *CQ* 2: 22–30
  1908b. 'On some fragments of Maecenas', *CQ* 2: 170–4
Syme, R. 1986. *The Augustan aristocracy*, Oxford
Tadic-Gilloteux, N. 1963. 'Sénèque, face au suicide', *AC* 32: 541–51
Talbert, R. 1984. *The senate of imperial Rome*, Princeton
Tandoi, V. 1965. '*Morituri verba Catonis* (1)', *Maia* 17: 315–39
  1966. '*Morituri verba Catonis* (2)', *Maia* 18: 20–41
Tarán, S. 1985. 'ΕΙΣΙ ΤΡΙΧΕΣ: an erotic motif in the *Greek Anthology*', *JHS* 105: 90–107
Tarrant, R. 2016. *Texts, editors and readers*, Cambridge
Thibodeau, P. 2011. *Playing the farmer: representations of rural life in Vergil's Georgics*, Berkeley
Thomas, R. 1988. *Virgil: Georgics*, 2 vols., Cambridge
Tigerstedt, E. N. 1965. *The legend of Sparta in classical antiquity*, vol. 1, Stockholm
Tischer, U. 2017. '*Nostra faciamus*: quoting in Horace and Seneca', in Stöckinger, Winter and Zanker 2017: 289–313
Too, Y. L. 1994. 'Educating Nero: a reading of Seneca's *Moral Epistles*', in Elsner and Masters 1994: 211–24
Torre, C. 2015. 'Seneca and the Christian tradition', in Bartsch and Schiesaro 2015: 266–76
Tosi, R. 1991. *Dizionario delle sentenze latine e greche*, Milan
Townend, G. 1980. 'Calpurnius Siculus and the *munus Neronis*', *JRS* 70: 166–74
Traina, A. 1987. *Lo stile 'drammatico' del filosofo Seneca*, 4th edn, Bologna
Trapp, M., ed. 2003. *Greek and Latin letters: an anthology, with translation*, Cambridge

2007. *Philosophy in the Roman empire: ethics, politics and society*, Farnham
Treggiari, S. 1975. 'Jobs in the household of Livia', *PBSR* n.s. 30: 48–77
  1991. *Roman marriage: iusti coniuges from the time of Cicero to the time of Ulpian*, Oxford
  2003. 'Ancestral virtues and vices: Cicero on nature, nurture and presentation', in D. Braund and C. Gill, eds. *Myth, history and culture in republican Rome: studies in honour of T.P. Wiseman* (Exeter) 139–64
Trillitzsch, W. 1971. *Seneca im literarischen Urteil der Antike: Darstellung und Sammlung der Zeugnisse*, Amsterdam
Trinacty, C. 2014. *Senecan tragedy and the reception of Augustan poetry*, Oxford
Turpin, W. 2008. 'Tacitus, Stoic *exempla* and the *praecipuum munus annalium*', *ClAnt* 27: 359–404
Van Nuffelen, P., and L. Van Hoof. 2013. 'Posidonius and the Golden Age: a note on Sen. *Ep.* 90', *Latomus* 73: 186–95
Verità, M. 1999. 'La sabbia e il vetro' in A. Ciarallo and E. De Carolis, eds., *Homo Faber: natura, scienza e tecnica* (Milan) 108–10
Versnel, H. 1993. *Inconsistencies in Roman religion*, Leiden
Veyne, P. 2003. *Seneca: the life of a Stoic*, trs. D. Sullivan [original French 1993], London
Viansino, G. 1979. '*Studia Annaeana* II', *Vichiana* 8: 168–96
Ville, G. 1981. *La Gladiature en occident des origines à la mort de Domitien*, Rome
Villedieu, F. 2011. 'Une construction néronienne mise au jour sur le site de la Vigna Barberini: la cenatio rotunda de la Domus Aurea?', *Neronia Electronica* 1: 37–52
Viparelli, V. 2000. *Il senso e il non senso del tempo in Seneca*, Naples
Vogt, J. 1975. *Ancient slavery and the ideal of man*, Cambridge, MA
Vogt-Spira, G. 2017. 'Time in Horace and Seneca', in Stöckinger, Winter and Zanker 2017: 185–209
Voisin, J. L. 1979. 'Pendus, crucifies, *oscilla* dans la Rome païenne', *Latomus* 38: 422–50
  1987. 'Apicata, Antinoüs et quelques autres: notes d'épigraphie sur la mort volontaire à Rome', *MEFRA* 99: 257–80
Volk, K. 2016. 'Roman Pythagoras', in Williams and Volk 2016: 33–49
Volk, K., and G. Williams, eds. 2006. *Seeing Seneca whole: perspectives on philosophy, poetry and politics*, Leiden
von Albrecht, M. 1989. *Masters of Roman prose*, trs. N. Adkin, Liverpool
  2004. *Wort und Wandlung: Senecas Lebenskunst*, Leiden
  2014. 'Seneca's language and style', in Damschen and Heil 2014: 699–744
Vout, C. 2009. 'The *Satyrica* and Neronian culture', in J. Prag and I. Redpath, eds. *Petronius: a handbook* (Chichester) 101–13
  2007. *Power and eroticism in imperial Rome*, Cambridge

Walbank, F. 1967. 'The Scipionic legend', *PCPhS* 13: 54–69
Wallace-Hadrill, A. 1982a. '*Civilis princeps*: between citizen and king', *JRS* 72: 32–48
  1982b. 'The golden age and sin in Augustan ideology', *P&P* 95: 19–36
Walsh, P. 1970. *The Roman novel: the Satyricon of Petronius and the Metamorphoses of Apuleius*, Cambridge
Walters, J. 1997. 'Invading the Roman body: manliness and impenetrability in Roman thought' in Hallett and Skinner 1997: 29–43
Warren, J. 2001. 'Socratic suicide', *JHS* 121: 91–106
  2004. *Facing death: Epicurus and his critics*, Oxford
  ed. 2009. *The Cambridge companion to Epicureanism*, Cambridge
Watson, A. 1987. *Roman slave law*, Baltimore
Watson, P., and L. Watson. 2009. 'Seneca and Felicio: imagery and purpose', *CQ* 59: 212–25
White, P. 2010. *Cicero in letters: epistolary relations of the late republic*. Oxford
Whitmarsh, T. 2001. *Greek literature and the Roman empire: the politics of imitation*, Oxford
Whitton, C., ed. 2013. *Pliny the Younger: Epistles book 2*, Cambridge
Wiedemann, T. 1992. *Emperors and gladiators*, London
Wilcox, A. 2012. *The gift of correspondence in classical Rome: friendship in Cicero's Ad familiares and Seneca's Moral Epistles*, Madison, WI
Wild, J. P. 2008. 'Textile production', in Oleson 2008: 465–82
Wildberger, J. 2006. *Seneca und die Stoa: der Platz des Menschen in der Welt*, 2 vols., Berlin and New York
  2010. '*Praebebam enim me facilem opinionibus magnorum uirorum*: the reception of Plato in Seneca, "Epistulae Morales 102"', in V. Harte, M. M. McCabe, R. A. Sharples and A. Sheppard, eds. *Aristotle and the Stoics Reading Plato* (BICS suppl. 107) (London) 205–32
  2014. 'The Epicurus trope and the construction of a "letter writer" in Seneca's *Epistulae Morales*', in Wildberger and Colish 2014: 431–65
Wildberger, J., and M. Colish, eds. 2014. *Seneca Philosophus*, Berlin
Williams, C. 2010. *Roman homosexuality*, 2nd edn, Oxford
Williams, G. D. 2006. 'States of exile, states of mind: paradox and reversal in Seneca's *consolatio ad Helviam matrem*', in Volk and Williams 2006: 147-73
  2012. *The cosmic viewpoint: a study of Seneca's Natural questions*, Oxford
  2015. 'Style and form in Seneca's writing', in Bartsch and Schiesaro 2015: 135–49
  2016. 'Minding the gap: Seneca, the self and the sublime', in Williams and Volk 2016: 172–91
Williams, G. D., and K. Volk, eds. 2016. *Roman reflections: studies in Latin philosophy*, Oxford

Williamson, G. 1951. *The Senecan amble: a study in prose form from Bacon to Collier*, London
Wilson, E. 2007. *The death of Socrates: hero, villain, chatterbox, saint*, London
 2014. *The greatest empire: a life of Seneca*, New York
Wilson, M. 1987. 'Seneca's Epistles to Lucilius: a reevaluation', *Ramus* 16: 102–21 [= Fitch 2008]
 1997. 'The subjugation of grief in Seneca's Epistles', in S. M. Braund and C. Gill, eds. *The passions in Roman thought and literature* (Cambridge) 48–67
 2001. 'Seneca's Epistles reclassified', in S. J. Harrison, ed. *Texts, ideas and classical literature* (Oxford) 164–88
 2015. '*Quae quis fugit damnat*: outspoken silence in Seneca's *Epistles*', in H. Baltussen and P. J. Davis, eds. *The art of veiled speech: from Aristotle to Hobbes* (Philadephia) 137–56
Winterbottom, M. 1972. 'Six conjectures', *CR* 86: 11–12
Wirzubski, C. 1950. *Libertas as a political ideal at Rome during the late Republic and early principate*, Cambridge
Wistrand, M. 1990. 'Violence and entertainment in Seneca the Younger', *Eranos* 88: 31–46
Woodman, A. 2010. '*Aliena facundia*: Seneca in Tacitus', in D. H. Berry and A. Erskine, eds. *Form and function in Roman oratory* (Cambridge) 294–308
 ed. with C. S. Kraus. 2014. *Tacitus: Agricola*, Cambridge
Woolf, R. 2009. 'Pleasure and desire', in Warren 2009: 158–78
Wyke, M. 1987. 'Written women: Propertius' *scripta puella*', *JRS* 77: 47–61
Yegül, F. 1992. *Baths and bathing in classical antiquity*, Cambridge, MA
 2010. *Bathing in the Roman world*, Cambridge
Zago, G. 2009. 'Posidonio e le origini dell'architettura: contributi al testo e a l'esegesi di Sen. *Ep.* 90.7 e di Isid. *Orig.* 15.2.6', *Hermes* 137: 45–59
 2012. *Sapienza filosofica e cultura materiale: Posidonio e le altre fonti dell'Epistola 90 di Seneca*, Bologna
Zak, G. 2015. 'Petrarch and the ancients', in Ascoli and Falkeid 2015: 141–53

INDEX OF LATIN WORDS

Note: References in roman type are to letter and section in the text and/or commentary. Numbers in *italics* refer to page numbers in the main introduction and introductions to individual letters.

abstinentia 70.6, 70.9, 70.20
accerso 24.1, *213*
acerbus 24.5, 24.26, 114.25
admiror 86.3
aedilis 86.10
aeger 7.1, 53.9, 70.10
aetas 12.1, 12.6, 90.6
affectus *10–11*, 18.15, 114.24
ago 7.5
alienus 1.3, 12.3, 12.10, 33.8–9, 47.13, 70.8, 70.10, 90.13, 90.38, 114.13
allino 7.2
altitudo 21.4
amicus 21.5, 47.1, 64.1, 70.9
angulus 86.5
anima 24.9
animus *10*, 7.6, 18.3–5, 18.11, 21.2, 24.15–6, 24.24, 34.4, 47.17, 47.20, 53.7, 64.3–4, 64.8, 70.12, 70.24, 86.1, 90.5, 90.19, 90.29, 114.3, 114.22–3
antiquus 86.8, 114.10
apparatus 18.1
ars 7.4, 90.7, 90.25, 90.44
artifex 47.16, 53.11, 64.11, 90.16, 90.27
articulum 24.14, 24.16, 53.6
assensio 7.12
auaritia 7.7, 47.17, 90.3, 90.8, 90.36, 90.38
auarus 7.3, 90.40
auctor 7.11, 33.8

beatus *10*, 12.9, 18.13, 21.1, 64.5, 70.16, 90.27, *109*
beneficium 24.11, 53.11, 86.2, 90.1
blandior 46.1, 114.15
blandus 18.3, 24.1, 46.1
bonus *10*, 1.5, 7.2, 7.12, 12.9, 21.10, 24.18, 34.3, 47.12, 47.16, 53.9, 64.7, 70.4, 90.1, 90.34, 90.44, *108, 206, 215*

calco 86.7, 86.17
capio 33.7, 47.2
carmen 33.6
cella 18.7

cenatio 90.9, 90.15, *260*
censeo 21.9
censura 47.8
census 12.6
certus 33.7
cinctus 33.2
circumfodio 12.2
ciuitas 18.1, 47.14, 53.10, 86.3, 90.19, 114.2, 114.13
chriae 33.7
clarus 21.2
clausula *9*, 70.5, 114.16
clementia 24.6
clementer 47.13
cliens 47.18
cludo 53.11
cogito 24.15, 53.5, 70.7, 70.16, 114.26
comiter 47.13
comminiscor 86.8, 90.14, 90.23
communis 12.10
complector 12.4
compono 7.1, 12.6, 24.6, 114.3, *288*
compositio 46.2, 114.8, 114.15, *285*
concordia 90.26
concupisco 24.22
condo 7.12
confirmo 24.3, 24.24
conscientia 12.9
consors 7.11
consuetudo 7.7, 18.2, 46.3, 114.13
consummo 12.8, 90.44
contemno 7.12, 18.13, 24.25, 70.22
contexo 33.1, 114.18
contextus 33.1, 33.6
continuus 33.3
contubernalis 47.1
conturbernium 33.4, 70.17
contumelia 70.20
conuersatio 7.2
conuictus 47.13, 47.15
conuiuium 47.7, 64.2, 114.11, *180*
corpus 46.1, 53.5, 70.17, 70.20, 86.5, 90.13, 90.20, 90.29, 114.10, 114.25
corpusculum 24.16
cotidie *19*, 1.2, 12.9, 24.28, 24.20, *94*
cresco 12.1, 34.1

INDEX OF LATIN WORDS 335

crudelior 7.3
crudelis 7.5
cultus 86.8, 114.4, 114.9–10, 114.17
cura 86.16

debeo 1.3, 12.4, 18.14, 21.11, 24.10, 24.25, 64.9, 70.12, 70.21, 86.1, 90.1–2, 114.20
debitum 7.10
decrepitus 12.3
degusto 33.5, 46.1
delecto 12.3, 46.2, 70.10, 86.15
delicatus 47.13, 114.20
deliciae 24.11, 24.14, 47.19, 90.16, 114.2, 114.7
deliciolum 12.3
desido 7.2
desiderium 21.10
destillo 24.5
deus 12.10, 18.12, 47.18, 53.11, 90.1, 90.28
dies 1.4, 12.6–7, 12.9, 18.1, 18.5, 18.9, 24.20, 24.26, 70.19, *94*
dignatio 21.6
dignus 53.8, 70.21
discinctus 70.6, 114.4, 114.6
disciplina 86.3, 114.2, *236*
disco 7.5, 7.8, 7.9, 7.10, 18.6, 33.8, 47.6, 86.14
disputo 7.9
distinctus 86.6, 90.7
diues 12.7, 18.8, 114.6
doceo 7.5, 7.8, 47.6, 70.27, 86.15, 86.21, 90.19
doleo 24.14, 53.6
dolor 24.5, 24.14, 24.16, 70.16, 70.18, 70.25, 70.27, *132, 134, 215*
dominus 34.11, 47.4, 47.8–9, 47.14
dulcedo 46.1
dux 33.5, 33.11, 90.4

ebrius 18.4, 114.4
educo 21.5
effeminatus 70.6, 114.3, *286*
emitto 24.8, 70.5, 70.19
eneruo 7.7, 86.3, 114.8, 114.25, *286*
epistula 3, 7.10, 12.10, 18.9, 18.14, 21.3, 24.21, 33.1, *157, 207*
erro 18.1, 21.2, 47.15, 114.4, 114.21
erudio 7.4, 24.5, 47.6, 70.27, 90.46, 114.2, *84*
eruditio 47.1
erumpo 64.1, 70.24
excerptus 33.3
excludo 12.6, 86.17

excutio 7.6, 47.6, 53.8, 90.29
exemplum 3, 7.5–7, 21.3, 12.9, 24.3, 24.5, 24.9, 70.22, 70.25, 90.24, 114.18, *93, 132–3, 135*
exerceo 18.6, 18.8, 24.9, 64.5, 70.18, 86.5, *213*
exercitatio 53.6, 90.46
exire 24.25, 70.15–16
existimo 7.1, 7.3, 12.2, 18.2, 18.7, 21.1, 21.8–9, 24.1, 33.2, 33.8, 47.15, 70.5–6, 70.13, 70.19, 70.21, 114.3
exitus 70.14, 70.24
exoletus 12.8, 114.10, 114.25
experimentum 18.7, 70.18
expleo 12.8

facio 21.2
fama 114.12
fames 18.9
familiaris 18.8, 18.12, 47.4, 47.14, 53.9
fastidium 24.26
fatum 12.9
felicitas 90.4, 90.9, 90.34, 114.8
finis 70.17
firmitas 18.5
flosculus 33.1, 33.7
formo 7.9, 34.1
fortitudo 33.2
fortis 24.5, 24.25
fortuitus 47.3, 53.12 90.2, 90.8, 90.21
fortuna 11, 12.9, 18.6–7, 18.10, 24.7, 47.1, 47.10–11, 47.20, 64.4, 70.5, 70.7, 70.13, 90.4, 90.35, *180, 206, 217*
frustra 7.3, 114.24
fugax 1.3, 18.10
fulgor 21.1
furor 18.15, 114.3

gausapatus 53.3
generosus 24.8, 24.25, 33.8
genius 12.2, 90.28, 114.5
gloria 7.9, 21.3,
gradus 12.6
grauis 18.8, 24.4, 24.17, 53.1, 53.8, 70.10, 90.9, 114.3, *84*

hodie 7.10, 86.16, 90.15–16, 90.25, 90.33
homo 7.3, 7.8, 24.11, 33.2, 33.5, 47.1, 70.6, 70.19, 86.11, 90.45
honor 21.6, 21.8, 47.14, 64.9–10, *121*
hospes 18.12, 21.10
hostis 47.5
humilis 47.1, 47.13

INDEX OF LATIN WORDS

iacio 86.1
imago 21.2, 64.9, *177*
imbecillitas 7.1
imitatio 70.22, 114.40
immo 7.3, 47.1, 86.12
imperator 24.10
imperium 90.3
impero 18.3, 33.7, 70.25
impetus *10*, 7.6, 24.3, 24.24, 46.2, 70.12, 70.19
impleo 21.8
incipio 1.5, 18.12, 18.14, 70.27, 75, *169*
includo 12.10, 33.6
infamis 86.13
infractus 90.19, 114.1
ingenium 7.6, 7.9, 18.4, 21.5–6, 24.3, 24.9, 33.5, 34.1, 46.2, 70.24, 90.13, 90.19, 90.44, 114.1, 114.3, 114.12
ingenuus 47.10, 86.7
inhumanus 25, 7.3, 47.5
iniuria 18.6, 24.16, 47.20, 70.16, 86.8, 90.5, 90.39
interfector 7.4
interpres 33.8
inuenio 33.10–11, 64.7, 70.21, 70.25, 86.10, 90.7, 90.12, 90.20, 90.31
inuidia 47.14, *122*
ira 18.14, 47.19
iratus 12.2, 18.7, 24.8, 53.4, 90.45
istunc 12.3
iugulo 7.5
iuro 12.2, 12.11
ius 86.2, 90.6, 114.1

labor 86.12, 90.44
laetus 12.9
languor 24.11
laquearium 90.15, 90.42
lateo 33.8
leuis 24.14, 47.21
lēuis 46.1
liber (n.) 24.6, 33.9, 46.1, 114.18, *173–5*
liber (adj.) 24.7, 47.1, 47.15, 47.17, 64.3, 70.7, 70.17, 90.10, 90.37, 90.43
libertas 1.1, 12.10, 24.7, 53.4, 70.5, 70.14, 70.16, 86.1, *133*, *177*, *179*, *213*, *216*
libertinus 86.9
libido 24.16, 24.25, 47.7, 47.17, 90.19, 114.25
locus 47.11
lucrum 12.9

lusus 7.3, 18.15
luxuria 7.7, 18.1, 18.4, 18.7, 86.8, 90.7, 90.19, 90.36, 114.2, 114.9, 114.20, *110*

maiestas 47.8
magister 18.9, 33.8
magnitudo 18.11
maiores 1.5, 24.10, 47.14, 64.7, 86.5
mancipium 70.25
manus 1.2, 7.3, 12.4, 24.5, 34.2, 47.13, 70.8, 70.10–11, 70.13, 70.24, 86.10, 90.5
meditatio *19*, 24.2, 24.15, 70.18, 70.26
membrum 33.5
memoria 21.5–6, 24.3, 33.7
mens *10*, *23*, 33.2, 53.9, 53.11, 90.19, *108*
mensis 12.6, 18.1, 18.6, 86.16, 114.22
merces 7.9
mereo 7.5
mergo 12.4, 24.16, 53.7, 70.26
metus 24.1, 24.4, 24.18, 24.23, 90.43
misericordia 7.3
moderatio 18.15, 86.1
molestus 12.6, 21.1, 21.11, 70.5, 114.22
mollis *30*, 33.1, 70.24, 90.16, 90.19, 90.41, 114.3, 114.7, *206*, *289*.
mollitia 33.2, 114.3, *286*
molliter 114.15–16
mollio 7.7, 90.33
morbus 53.7, 53.9, 114.24
morior 7.5, 24.17, 24.20, 24.25, 70.7–9, 70.26
mors 7.4, 24.11, 24.14–5, 24.22–4, 70.8, 70.10, 70.12, 70.21, 70.24, 70.26
mortalis 1.3, 24.16, 53.11, 90.36, 114.26
mos 7.1, 7.2, 18.2, 47.15, 70.12, 86.5, 114.1–2
muliebris 47.6–7
mundus (n.) 12.7, 64.6, 90.28, 90.35, 90.42, 90.44, *260*
mundus (adj.) 70.20–1, 86.12
mutuus 7.5, 7.8

natura 1.3, 53.11, 90.4, 90.16, 90.18–19, 90.38, 90.43–4
naturalis 21.11
nausia 24.26, 53.3
necessarius 18.6, 21.11, 70.18, 86.14, 90.15, 90.19, 90.27, 90.40, 114.14
necessitas 12.10, 34.3, 47.6, 70.5, 70.17
negotium *9*, 21.1, 53.9, 70.10, 90.18–19

INDEX OF LATIN WORDS 337

neruus 24.16, 114.25
nescio 21.1, 47.12, 86.11, 90.46
nobilis 21.2, 21.7, 47.17, 70.10, 86.10, *123*
nodosus 12.2
nosco 18.3
noster 22, *30*, 21.5, 70.2, 86.15, 114.23
nota 24.23
notus 21.3, 114.10
nouitas 24.26, 47.8, 114.9, *109*
nouus 24.26, 64.6, 64.8, 70.24, 86.8, 114.7
noxius 7.4, *83–4*

obliuio 21.4, 53.5
obscurus 21.1, 86.4, 86.10, 114.17
obsto 21.2, 24.7, 70.24
occupatus 33.1, 33.11, 53.9, *76*
odium 24.26, 90.41
officium 47.2, 114.23
onus 24.18
opes 18.13
opus 33.5, 34.2, 64.7, 86.5, 90.42
oratio 23, 12.7, 33.5, 46.1, 90.20, 90.25, 114.1–4, 114.7, 114.10–11, 114.13, 114.20–2, *157*, *285*, *288*
orbis 12.6, 24.26, 86.6

parento 12.8
patientia 24.5, 24.24, 47.7, 64.4–5, *174*
patria 24.7, 86.1, 90.35, 90.42
pauper 24.17, 18.7, 33.4, 86.6, 90.38, *108*
paupertas 1.4, 18.6, 18.8, 18.12, 18.15, 70.18, 90.3
peculium 12.10
pecunia 21.7
perago 12.9
percutio 34.4, 70.16, 114.15, *84*
perfectus 34.3, *169*
perpetuus 21.8, 33.6, *156*, *260*
permitto 24.19, 33.3, 47.8, 47.14, 70.24, 90.37
persona *11–12*, 18.15, 24.13, *173*, *289*
personatus 24.13
philosophia *10*, *14*, 7.3, 21.9, 24.7, 24.26, 53.8–9, 53.12, 70.18, 90.1–2, 90.7–8, 90.20, 90.35, 90.46, *110*
pietas 86.1, 90.3, *207*, *235*
pilleatus 18.3
pompa 24.14
pomum 12.4
populus 7.2, 7.5–6, 7.9, 18.4, 86.10, 90.5, 90.40, 114.24
possessio 1.3, 18.13, 90.38, *75*

posterus 9, 21.5, 64.7, *122*
praeceptor 33.7, 64.9
praeceptum 18.5, 21.11, 24.5, 47.11, 53.3, 90.34, 90.46, *134*, *238*, *261*
praecipio 1.4, 18.5, 33.9
praeoccupare 18.11
prior 33.1, 33.10–11, *156*
priscus 86.5, 86.12, 86.14, 114.10
proceres 33.1, 33.11
produco 7.9, 90.18
profectus 24.3, 33.7, 34.3
proficiens *11*, *168–9*
proficio 18.9
profundus 21.5, 70.21
promitto *14*, 21.5
propono 7.6, 21.1, 24.1–2, 70.17, 114.12
proprius 90.3, 114.20
prouoco 64.4, *206*
prudens 24.26, 90.2
prudentia 47.1, 90.5, 90.25, 90.46
publicus 18.1–2, 21.7, 21.9, 24.4, 24.16, 33.2, 47.14, 64.10, 70.3, 86.3, 90.38, 114.2, 114.6
puella 24.14
puer 24.13, 33.7, 47.7, 70.19, 90.14
puerilis 33.7, 114.16
pueritia 12.4, 12.6, 24.20, 47.7, 70.2
punctum 70.16
putris 12.1

reparabilis 1.3
ratio 2, *10*, 1.4, 24.11, 24.24, 70.27, 90.11, 90.24, *75*, *134*
recedo 7.8, 24.11, 70.2, 90.3, *111*
recito 7.9
rectus *10*, 7.6, 18.12, 21.2, 34.4, 53.11, 90.20, 90.24, 114.4, 114.11, 114.8
reduco 70.1, 90.39
regius 21.3, 90.10
regnum 53.9, 90.5–6
retorridus 12.2, 86.18, *135*
rex 21.4, 33.4, 47.20, 90.5, 114.23–4
rideo 47.2, *195*
Romanus 21.5, 47.17, *133*
rubigo 7.7
rudis 33.6, 90.35, 90.46, *257*, *259*
rusticitas 86.11, 90.19
rusticus 86.5, 86.8, 90.43

saeculum 24.11, 70.10, 90.5, 90.9, 90.19, 90.35, 114.4, 114.26, *259*
sanctus 46.2, 90.6,
sanguis 24.8, 64.9, 70.16, 90.41, 114.7
sanitas 18.15, 34.3, 53.8, *110*

sanus 114.3, 114.27, *288*
sapere 33.7
sapiens *11*, *14*, *18*, 24, 7.1, 7.6, 7.12, 12.9, 18.6, 18.8, 24.5–7, 24.17, 24.25, 34.3, 53.11, 70.4–5, 90.2, 90.5–6, 90.11, 90.14–16, 90.20–5, 90.30–1, 90.33–4, 90.36, 90.44, *111*, *122*, *133*, *170*, *196*, *206*, *234*, *236*, *256–8*, *288*
sapientia 1.1, 64.6, 70.14, 90.1–2, 90.6, 90.11, 90.26, *134*, *169*, *179*, *256–7*
satietas 24.26, 47.8
satur 18.7, *111*
saturitas 18.10
Saturnalia 12.3, 18.1–2, 18.7, 18.9, 47.14, *108–11*, *180*
secedo 18.12, 70.20, 86.3, *122*
secessus 90.6
securitas *10*, *20*, 12.10, 18.6, 21.1, 24.1–2, 24.17, 70.16, 90.10, *75*, *93*, *109*, *111*, *196*, *258*
securus 24, 12.9, 18.8, 24.12, 24.15, 90.10, 90.16, 90.38, 90.41, 114.7, *108*, *111*
senectus 12.1, 33.7, 34.1, 70.2, *238*
senex 12.2, 12.6, 21.8, 33.7, 86.14
sententia 25, 7.9–10, 21.7, 21.9, 33.2, 33.4–5, 33.7, 70.28, 114.1, 114.11, 114.16, *157*
sequor 18.12, 21.1, 21.9, 24.3, 24.26, 33.8, 33.10, 53.5, 90.4, 90.16, 90.25, 90.34, 114.18, 114.21–2
seruitus 47.17, 70.12, 70.17, 70.19, 90.10, *216*
seruio 25, 47.12, 47.17, 90.23, 90.27, *217*
seruus 24, 1.3, 18.8, 18.14, 24.14, 47 passim, 86.10, 90.19, 114.24, *108*, *110*, *178*, *180*
sermo 8, *21*, *23–4*, 18.7, 47.4, 47.13, 64.2, 114.1, 114.4, 114.8, 114.12–3, *108–9*, *181*, *288*
siccus 18.4, 114.3, *110*
sigillarium 12.3
silentium 21.5, 47.3, 90.42, *122*
sobrius 18.4, 114.3, *110*
sollicitudo 12.9, 24.2, 24.16, 90.41
sollicitus 24.1, 114.6
sono 18.1, 114.14, *260*
sordidus 18.7, 21.1, 47.15, 53.1, 70.22, 86.5–6, 90.25, 90.27, 114.10, 114.13, 114.24, *111*, *181*
spectaculum 7.2–3, 7.5, 64.6, 70.20, 70.23, 70.26, 86.6, 90.28, 90.42, 114.25, *261*

spectator 7.4, 24.5, 64.6, *83*
specto 7.11, 12.3, 12.9, 24.8, 24.22, 90.13, 90.45, *83*
spes 24.1, 33.5, 47.17, 70.6, 70.9
spurcus 70.12, 70.21, 86.12
stomachicus 24.14
stomachor 12.2
stomachus 53.5, 12.2, 18.10, 24.26, 47.8
studium 7.11, 21.2, 90.19, 114.12, *123*, *289*
stultitia 1.3, 70.8
stultus 12.10, 24.1, 24.13–14, 47.16, 70.9, 70.13, 70.20, 90.14, *215*
subduco 1.1, 7.6, 24.19, 33.5
suburbanus 12.1
sudo 18.1
sudor 64.9, 86.11
superuacuus 18.1, 18.6, 24.26, 70.18, 90.14
surrepo 7.2, 90.6
surripio 1.1, 53.1
sustineo 47.8, 86.5, 86.7

taedium 18.7, 24.22, 24.26, 70.3
temperans 18.4, 90.46, 114.3, *288*
temperantia 21.15, 90.46, 114.27, *109*
tempus 29, 1.1–3, 1.5, 12.4, 12.6–7, 12.9, 18.2, 21.5, 24.1, 24.11, 24.20, 33.8, 53.9, 64.6, 64.8, 70.2, 70.9, 86.3, 86.12, 86.16, 90.17, 90.20, 90.36, 114.1–2, 114.8, 114.13, *94*, *132*, *156*, *207*, *236*
tenax 7.6
tener 7.6, 34.1, 114.20
terribilis 24.9, 24.12
theatrum 7.11, 114.24, *83*
timeo 7.9, 12.10, 18.5, 18.11, 24.3, 24.11, 24.18, 24.21–2, 47.17–9, 53.2, 53.4, 53.11, 70.5, 70.9, 90.43, 90.45
timor 24.2, 24.12, 24.23, 47.17–18, 70.8
titulus 21.4, 47.9
tormentum 24.16, 47.4, 70.11, 70.15, 70.26
tranquillitas 12.5, 70.5, 70.16
transfero 21.8, 86.12, 86.14, 86.17, 86.19, 90.29, 114.9, *237–8*
translatio 114.10, *238*
transuerbero 24.9
tristis 7.5, 12.2, 18.2, 86.14, 86.19, *206*
tumultus 18.2, 24.12, 114.26
turba 7.1, 18.3, 24.14, 33.4, 33.6, 34.1, 47.2, 114.12, 114.25, *83*

INDEX OF LATIN WORDS 339

turbo 7.1, 70.5, 114.3
turpis 1.1, 24.1, 24.15, 24.19, 33.7, 47.2, 47.13, 47.17, 70.7, 114.5, 114.24
tutela 33.10, 90.16, 90.38
tyrannus 70.6, 90.5, 114.5, 114.24

uaco 7.4, 53.9, 77
uarius 18.1, 46.2, 64.2, 70.27, 86.6, 90.26, *193*
uenter 21.11, 47.2, 90.22, 114.25–6
uerto 12.1, 24.16, 90.38, 90.41, 114.26
uetulus 12.2
uia 12.10, 21.7, 24.2, 24.19, 33.11, 53.4, 70.14, 70.16, 90.27, 114.4, *196, 213, 216*
uideo 12.1, 24.5, 24.9, 24.22, 34.2, 47.9, 64.6, 70.1, 86.4, 86.14, 86.16–17, 86.20, 90.14
uilicus 12.1–3, 86.15, *96*
uindico 1.1, 12.9, 21.5, 33.4, *75, 177*
uinculum 24.17, 47.16, 70.12
uinum 12.4, 12.8, 47.7, 114.22, 114.26
uir *17*, 7.6, 18.1, 18.5, 24.4, 24.9, 24.11, 24.14, 24.25, 33.2, 33.5, 33.7, 47.7, 64.2, 64.9, 70.6, 70.19, 70.21, 70.25, 86.1, 86.3, 86.11–12, 90.12, 90.20, 90.36, 90.44, 114.4, 114.6, 114.12, 114.17, *133–4, 235*
uirtus *6, 10, 26*, 21.2, 24.5, 47.15, 64.4, 64.6, 64.9, 70.18, 70.22, 90.3, 90.16, 90.35, 90.44–6, 114.12, *75, 96, 123, 134, 155, 215, 257, 285, 287*
uirilis 33.1, 46.2, 114.4, 114.7–8, 114.15, 114.22, *155, 174, 285, 288*

uis 24.8, 24.16, 47.20, 114.25
uita *10, 24*, 1.1–2, 12.6–10, 21.1–3, 21.8, 24.8, 24.20, 24.22–6, 53.11, 64.5, 70.2, 70.4–5, 70.7, 70.9, 70.11–12, 70.14–15, 90.1, 90.7, 90.18, 90.27, 90.29, 90.34, 90.44, 90.46, 114.1, *94, 109, 111, 122, 170*
uitium 25, 1.4, 7.2, 7.6, 12.1, 21.9, 47.21, 53.5, 53.8, 70.15, 90.6, 90.19, 114.1, 114.4, 114.8, 114.11–12, 114.16, 114.18, 114.20, *82–3, 110, 288–9*
uito 7.1, 18.15, 114.4, 114.14
uiuo 12.10, 21.9, 24.7, 24.26, 47.1, 47.6, 47.10–11, 47.13, 64.3, 70.4, 70.6–7, 70.10, 70.15, 70.28. 86.11, 90.1, 90.18, 90.41
uiuus 33.9, 86.10
umbra 12.2, 21.2, 33.8, 86.15, 90.17, 90.43, *122, 215*
uolo 1.3, 7.9, 18.3, 18.13, 24.5–6, 24.18, 34.2–3, 46.1–2, 47.10, 47.19, 53.3, 64.5, 70.13, 70.21, 86.2, 86.15, 90.3–4, 90.15, 90.19, 90.26, 90.29, 114.12–13, 114.18–19, 114.21, *170, 195*
uoluntas 47.19, 53.11, *170*
uoluntarius 47.17, 70.10, 86.3, *108, 215, 234*
uoluo 24.15
uoluptas 7.2, 7.12, 12.4–5, 18.2–3, 18.9–10, 21.8, 21.10–11, 24.16, 34.1, 46.2, 47.6, 86.5, 90.34–5, 90.40, 114.23, 114.25, *82, 84, 94, 110, 236*
uox 12.10, 24.10, 33.1–2, 33.7, 33.9, 70.6, *157*

GENERAL INDEX

Note: References in roman type are to letter and section in the text and/or commentary. Numbers in *italics* refer to page numbers in the main introduction and introductions to individual letters.

Abelard, Peter *30*
absence 18.2, 64.1, 86.1, *82*, *205*, *289*
Academic philosophy 18.4
addressee *2–5*, *8–9*, *19*, 7.9, *75–6*, *131*, *169*, *173*, *180*
Aegialus 86.14
Aelius Aristides *27*
Aeneas 12.9, 18.12, 53.1, 53.3–4, 70.2, *110*, *194*
afterlife (see also 'underworld') 24.18, *235–6*
Agrippa, Marcus 21.4
Agrippina *1*, 21.6
Alexander 7, 53.10
anger *11*, 7.5, 12.2, 18.14–15, 24.8, 47.19–20, 53.4, 70.6, *110*
appetite *16*, *20*, 12.5, 18.9, 18.15, 24.10, 47.2, 47.17, 70.2, *110–11*, *179–80*, *195*
architecture 86.6–8, 90.7–10, 90.42, 114.9
arena shows *27*, *Ep.* 7 *passim*, 24.5, 70.19–28, 90.45 *82–4*
Ariston of Chios *25–6*
Aristotle *7*, 7.7, *204*, *256*, *289*
asceticism *16*, *20*, *Ep.* 18 *passim*, *110*
Attalus (Stoic philosopher) *1*, *23*, *206*
Atticus 21.4
Aurelius, Marcus *14*, 24.2, 64.9, 70.2
Augustine *30*, 7.3, 24.20, *84*, *170*
Augustus 18.1, 114.4, 114.6, *235*, *259*, *285–6*
authorities (philosophical) *Ep.* 33 *passim*, 64.10
avarice 7.7 47.17, 90.3, 90.38–9, *254*

Bacon, Francis *31*
Baiae 86.3–4, *177*, *192–3*
Bassus 12.1, 12.9, 34.1, *215–16*
baths *23*, 53.3, 86.4, 86.6–10, 90.25, 114.14, *82*, *234*, *237–8*
Bion of Borysthenes *23*
birthday celebrations 64.9, *207*
body, the *10*, *17*, *27*, 12.1, 18.11, 24.16–18, 24.25–6, 53.5–6, 70.12, 70.21, 86.10, 114.24, *94*, *110*, *179*, *195*, *205*, *237*, *284*, *288–90*
book divisions *3–4*, *6*, *234*

Caligula (Gaius) *1*, *29*, 47.9, 90.20
Callistus 47.9, 86.7
Calvisius Sabinus *21–3*, 86.7, 90.33
Cambyses 86.1
Campania *5*, 53.1, 86.1–3, *192–4*, *235*
Capitol 21.5
Cato the Elder *21*, 7.6, 47.5, 47.7, 64.7, 64.10, 70.17, 70.22, 86.3, 86.5, 86.10, 86.12, 86.14–15, *93–5*, *236–8*
Cato the Younger *11*, *13*, 7.6, 24.3–4, 6–8, 64.10, 70.19, 70.22, *133*, *135*
Catullus 18.14, 33.5, 46.1, 90.9, *174–5*, *259*
Celsus *17*, 24.24, 47.15, 53.3
Cicero *5–8*, *11*, *13*, *21*, *27–8*, *30*, 1.1, 7.6, 12.1–2, 12.8, 18.14, 21.4, 24.1, 24.4, 33.1–2, 33.5, 34.3, 33.8, 47.4, 47.17, 53.5, 64.2, 70.2, 70.14, 86.1, 86.14, 90.2, 90.7, 90.25, 90.46, 114.4, 114.16, *84*, *94–5*, *121*, *123*, *132*, *134*, *156*, *174*, *178–9*, *194*, *235–6*, *260*, *284–5*, *288–9*
Christians *30*, 7.4–5, *84*
Chrysippus *12*, *15*, *22*, *24*, 33.4, 33.7, 64.10, 86.1, 90. 23, 90.46, 114.5, *122*, *195*, *255*
civil war 24.6–7, *133*
Claudius 7.3, 47.9, 70.26
clausulae (metrical) *27–9*, 1.1, 1.2, 46.1, 53.8, 70.10, 90.31
Cleanthes *12*, 1.5, 33.4, 33.7, 64.10, *156*, *287*
cold 34.1, 53.3, 86.10
Columella 12.1–2, 64.8, 86.4, 86.15–16, 86.20
comedy *23*, 12.3, 53.1–4, *94*
community *10*, *12–14*, 33.4, 90.5, *82*, *207*, *256*

340

consistency *18*, 24.19, 24.21, 33.5, 34.3–4, 90.3, *169–70*
consolation 24.3, 70.3, *205*
conversation *8*, *19*, *21*, *23–4*, 18.2, 33.9, 47.1, 47.4, 64.1–2, *96*, *108–9*, *157*, *177*, *204*, *206–7*
Cornutus *14*, *21*
Corsica *1*, 53.2
crowd *Ep.* 7 *passim*, 18.9, *82–4*, *109*
Curtius Rufus *27–8*
cyclical time 12.6, 12.8, 12.10, 24.26, *95*
Cynicism *12*, *17*, *23*, 47.12, 90.14, 90.23, 90.31, *109*, *194–5*, *256*
Cyrus 86.1, 86.5

Daedalus 90.14–5
dating 18.1, 86.16
day (as a unit of time) 12.6–7, 12.10, *94–5*
daily routine *16*, *19*, 18.2, 47.15–16
death *3*, *9*, *20*, 1.2–3, 7.4–5, 12.3, 12.8–9, 18.11, *Ep.* 24 *passim*, 53.11, *Ep.* 70 *passim*, 86.1, 86.8, 114.26, *76*, *82*, *84*, *93–5*, *193*, *205*
debt 1.3, 7.9–10, 18.14, 21.11, 33.3, 70.21, 86.2–3, 90.1, *75*, *217*
December 18.1
Democritus 7.10
diatribe *11*, *23*, *27*, 7.3, 7.5, 70.10, 70.13
Dido 12.9, *96*
diet *17*, 18.5, 18.7, 18.9–11, 21.10, 53.3, 90.13
Dio, Cassius 24.15, *174*
Diogenes (Cynic) *17*, *20*, 12.5, 47.12, 90.14
Diogenes Laertius 7
disease 7.7, 53.6, 64.8, *83*
Domus aurea 90.7, 90.15, 90.43
dress 18.2, 18.5, 18.7, 33.2, 47.16, 47.20, 53.3, 90.15, 90.20, 90.45, 114.4, 114.6, 114.11, 114.21
duty *11–12*, 64.7, 90.2, *215*, *258*

effeminacy 70.6, 114.6–8
emotions *4*, *10–11*, *20*, 12.2, 12.9, 18.14–15, 24.2, 24.10, 114.24
emperors 24.3, 47.8, 47.13
endurance 24.5, 24.24, 53.6, 64.5
Ennius 86.1–2, 86.5
epic 22, 12.9, 53.1–4, *96*

Epictetus *14*, 12.3, 33.7, 47.9–10, 70.9, *169*
Epicureanism *9*, *15–16*, *21*, 12.8–10, 21.4, 24.5, 24.16, 24.18, 24.26, 33.2–4, 33.7–8, 47.1, 70.14–15, 90.34–5, 114.4, *96*, *110*, *134*, *155–6*, *193*, *195*, *204–5*, *287*
Epicurus *4*, *7*, *9*, *15–16*, 1.1, 7.11, 12.11, 18.4, 18.8–10, 18.14, 21.3, 21.5, 21.7–11, 24.2, 24.14, 24.16, 24.22–3, 33.1–4, 33.8, 33.11, 46.1, 64.9, *76*, *110*, *121–2*, *134*, *286–7*
 quotations from, *4*, *7*, 7.11, 12.11, 18.9, 18.14, 21.7, 24.22–3, 33.1–2, *174–5*
epistolary form *6–8*, *19–20*, *28*, 21.3–4
Erasmus *30*, 1.1
eunuchs 114.6, 114.13
exemplarity *3*, *20–21*, 7.6–7, 21.3, 21.11, 24.3
exile *1*, 24.3–4, 24.17, 53.2, 86.1, 86.3

Fabius Maximus 86.10
fame 18.9, 21.11
farming 34.1, 86.5, 86.12, 86.14–21, *96*
fate (see also *fatum*) *11*, 12.9, 70.27, 90.34
Felicio 12.3, *94*
fiction, letters as *5–6*
financial imagery 2, 1.2, 1.4–5, 7.9–10, 12.9, 18.14, 21.7, 21.11, 33.3, 86.3, 90.1, *75–6*
fortune *11*, *25–6*, 12.9, 18.6, 18.10, 24.7, 47.1, 47.10–13, 53.12, 64.4, 70.5, 70.7, 70.13, 70.18, 90.2, 90.4, 90.36, 90.46, 114.8, *180*, *206*, *217*, *290*
freedom *20*, 1.1, 12.10, 24.7, *Ep.* 47 *passim*, 53.4, 53.9, 70.5, 70.14, 70.16, 86.1, *133*, *135*, *177*, *179*, *213*, *216*
freedmen 47.9, 47.18, 86.7, 86.14
friendship 2, *5*, *8–9*, *14*, *16*, 1.1, 12.2, 18.5, 18.9, 21.5, 34.1, 47.1 64.1, 70.9, *75*, *123*, *135*, *168–70*, *174*, *205*, *215*
Foucault, M. *19*, *32*
Fronto *27*, *30*, 33.1
funerary inscriptions 12.3, 47.7, 70.15, 86.1–2
future participle, use of *24*, 12.1, 21.1, 33.3, 70.11

GENERAL INDEX

future *9*, 1.2–3, 12.1, 18.11, 21.11, 24.1, 24.20, 33.11, 64.7, 70.6, *111*, *121–2*, *132*, *205*

Ganymede 47.7
Gellius, Aulus *3–4*, *30*
Gibbon, Edward *83*
gladiators 7.3, 7.4, 70.26–7, *82–4*
gods 47.18, 53.11, 90.1–3, 90.28, 90.35, 90.37, *135*, *178*, *193*, *195–6*
gold 18.13, 90.5, 90.9, 90.15, 90.45, 114.9
Greek terms, S's use of *13*, 12.8, 18.9, 24.3, *196*
greeting 1.1

habit *16*, *19*, 7.7, 18.2, 18.8, 46.3
hair 47.7, 114.14
Hannibal 86.1–3, 86.5
Hecuba 47.12
Helvia (mother of S) *1*, 24.3
Heraclitus 12.7
Hercules 18.12
Hermarchus 33.4
history-writing 33.2
Homer 53.3–5, 53.8, 90.30
Horace *6–7*, *22–3*, 1.1, 1.5, 7.6, 12.8–10, 18.4, 24.26, 34.3, 86.5, 86.11, 86.13, 114.4, *77*, *95–6*, *108–9*, *111*, *179–80*, *193*, *235*, *237*, *259*, *286*
hypocrisy *2*, 24.15, 24.19, 47.6

Idomeneus 21.3, 21.7
illness *10*, *27*, 7.1, 24.24, 53.6–9, 70.9–11, *83*
imagery, S's use of *25–6*
imperative, use of *24*, 1.1, 24.2, 24.5
indifferents, Stoic concept of *10*
innovation, philosophical *13–14*, 64.11
interjections, imagined *24*, 1.4, 12.6, 24.6, 33.7, 47.1, 47.18, 70.13

journey (as metaphor) 12.6, 24.19, 53.3, 70.2–3
Julius Caesar 24.6, *133*, *207*
Juvenal *1*, 47.7–8, 47.10, 47.15, 86.6

Lactantius 7.4–5
Laelius *21*, 7.6, 64.10
legal terminology and procedure 1.1–2, 12.8, 18.3, 24.1, 24.3, 24.12, 24.26, 33.8, 33.10, 34.2, 64.7, 70.8, 114.13
Lipsius, Justus *31*
Liternum 86.1–3
Livy 24.5, 24.10–11, 46.1, 90.15
literary ambition *22–3*, *Ep.* 21 *passim*, *Ep.* 46 *passim*
logic *9*, *13*, 64.3, *255*
Lucan 24.7–8, 70.22, 86.7
Lucilius (S's addressee) *2–5*, *9*, 7.9, 21.1, 34 *passim*, 46 *passim*, 47.1, 47.16, 47.19, 114.1
Lucilius (satirist) 47.7, 86.11, *287*
Lucretius *22*, 24.3, 24.13, 24.18, 24.22, 24.26, 33.4, 53.1, 86.5, 90.12, 90.20
luxury *23*, *25*, 7.7, 12.2, 18.1, 18.4, 21.10, 24.11, 47.2–8, 47.17, 47.19, 70.3, 86.5–13, 90.15, 90.19, 90.41–3, 114.2, 114.9, 114.26

Macaulay, T.B. *31–2*
Macrobius *30*, 64.2
Maecenas 33.2, 64.9, 114.4–8, 114.21, 114.26, *77*, *284–90*
maiores (earlier generations) *21*, 1.5, 18.6, 24.10, 47.14, 86.5, *238*
manliness *26*, 33.1, 33.5, 33.7, 46.2, 47.7, 64.2, 114.14–5, 114.22, *156*, *173–4*, *285*, *288*
manuscript tradition *3–4*, *32–3*
Martial 24.5, 47.7
marriage 53.8
Maximus of Tyre 90.14, 90.40
medicine *17–18*, *27*, 53.3, 64.8, 70.16
Mela *27*
Mens Bona (divinity) 53.9
mental exercises *18–22*, 24.15, 24.17, 70.18, 70.27
Metrodorus *16*, *18*, 18.9, 33.4
military imagery *16*, *18*, *26*, 7.6–7, 12.8, 18.6, 18.8, 18.11, 24.5, 24.10, 24.24, 33.4, 33.7, 47.7, 53.12, 64.4, 70.18, 86.12, 90.34, *155–6*, *237*
Montaigne, Michel de *30*
Mucius Scaevola *21*, 24.3, 24.5

Naples 53.1, 70.1
natural world, contemplation of *10*, *12*, 12.7, 64.6, 90.28, 90.35, 90.42, 90.44, *260*
nature *11*, *14–5*, *17*, 1.3, 21.10, 24.17, 53.11, 70.14, 86.19, 90.4, 90.8,

90.15, 90.19, 90.28, 90.38, 114.4, 76, *111*, *206*, *214–15*, *255*, *258*, *260–2*, *289*
Nero *1–2*, *9*, 18.3, 21.6, 24.11, 47.7–8, 47.11, 47.20, 70.22, 70.26, 86.3, 90.7, 90.14, 90.27, 90.43, 114.6–7, 114.23–4, *121*, *123*, *179–80*, *214*, *217*, *258–60*, *287–90*
Nietzsche, F. *31*
nobility 33.8, *123*, *177*
normative self *18*, 90.34

occurrent self *18*
oikeiosis 14, 47.10
old age *Ep.* 12 *passim*, 33.7, 34.1, 70.2, 70.9, 86.14, *93–6*, *216*
oratory *1*, *23*, 114.14
Ovid 22, 12.4, 21.5, 33.4, 33.6, 34.1, 46.1, 90.20, 114.14, *156*, *169*, *258–9*

Pacuvius 12.8–9, 18.7, *95*
pain *10*, *16*, *20*, *27*, 18.10, 21.11, 24.2, 24.5, 24.14–16, 24.24, 53.6, 70.9, 70.18, *132–5*, *214–15*
Panaetius *11–13*, 24.4, 33.4, *173*
Papirius Fabianus *1*, *23*, *25*, 64.2, 64.5, 90.19, 114.4, 114.7, 114.16
Parentalia 12.8–9
pater familias 47.14, 64.7–8, 86.14
perfume 86.13
Persius 7.11, 24.6, 53.3, 86.11
personification 24.7, 24.26, 53.8–12, 70.27
Petrarch *30*
Petronius *27*, 12.9, 86.7–8, 86.11, 90.15, 90.39, 114.2, 114.6, *157*, *180–1*, *195*, *216*, *237*, *284*, *287*, *290*
Philodemus *15*, 33.4
Philositus 12.3
physics *3*, *9*, *17*
Plato 7, *13*, *16–18*, *27*, 1.5, 7.6, 12.2, 21.2, 24.4, 24.6, 24.17, 24.26, 47.12, 64.10, 70.9, 90.1, 90.6, *94*, *134–5*, *174*, *196*, *204*, *122*
pleasure *10*, *16*, 7.12, 12.4–5, 18.9–10, 21.8–10, 24.16, 86.3, 86.5, 86.10, 90.35, 114.23, *82–4*, *94*, *110*, *237*, *286*
Pliny the Elder 12.2, 47.4, 47.9, 64.9, 70.14, 86.7–8, 86.14–15, 114.26
Pliny the Younger *5–6*, *8*, *28*, 12.1, 24.24, 64.2, 64.9, 77, *94*, *108*, *123*, *174–5*, *178*
Plutarch 7, 24.8, 47.3, 47.5, *206*, *214*

poetry 33.2, 33.4, 33.6, 46.2, 86.15–16, 114.13
political life *11*, *26*, 21.3, 21.6, 21.9, 33.11, 53.9, 90.35, 114.23–7, *83*, *122*, *217*, *234*
Polyaenus 18.9
Pompeii 70.1
Posidonius *13*, 46.1, 90.1, 90.5–13, 90.20–23, 90.30–1
possessions *11*, *20*, *25*, 18.13, 90.38
posterity *Ep.* 21 *passim*, 33.11, 64.7–8, 86.14–15
poverty, fear of *17*, *20*, 18.6, 24.17, 70.18
praemeditatio (anticipation of future challenges) *20*, 18.11, 24.2, 24.15, 70.7, *216*
prison 18.11, 24.3, 24.6, 70.9, *132–3*
progress, philosophical *4*, *11–12*, *21–2*, 1.4, 7.1, 12.2, 18.5, 18.9, 21.1, 24.3, 33.7, *Ep.* 34 *passim*, 70.27, 77, *93*, *155*, *168–70*
Propertius *169*, *259*
protreptic 90.1, 90.7
public office *2*, *20*, 21.1, 21.3, 21.8, 64.10
Pythagoreanism *17*, 90.6
Pythocles 21.7–8

questions, use of *24*
Quintilian 2, *25*, *28–9*, 7.7, 24.5, 33.7, 46.1, 86.14, 114.1, 114.15, *157*, *285–6*
quotations, use of *3*, *7*, *17–18*, 22, 7.10–11, 12.9, 18.12, 21.5, 21.7, 21.9, 24.21–2, 33.3–4, 33.7, 53.3, 70.2, 86.5, 86.11, 86.13, 90.20, 114.5, 114.23, *96*, *110*, *134*, *155–7*, *206*, *237*

reading *21*, 33.5, 33.9, 46.1–3, 64.2
reason 2, *10*, 24.24, 70.27–8, 90.24
reception of the letters *29–32*
religion *10–11*, 21.5, 33.6, 47.18, 53.8–11, 64.9, 86.6, 90.1–2, 90.28, 90.31
repetition 24.25, 24.26, 70.8
Rome *1*, *5*, *12*, *15*, *17*, 18.12, 21.5, 86.1, *82*
Rutilius Rufus 24.3–4

Sallust 7.3, 64.9, 114.13, 114.17
satire *23*, 12.9, 18.4, 18.10, 47.2–9, 64.1, 86.6, 86.11, 86.13, *96*, *108–11*, *177–81*, *237*, *284*

GENERAL INDEX

Saturn 18.1, 90.7, 90.37, 90.45–6, *259*
Scipio Africanus *21*, 21.5, 24.10, 70.22, 86.1–14, *234–8*
Scipio Nasica 24.9–10, 70.22
Scribonius Drusus Libo, M. 70.10
securitas (mental calm) *10*, *20*, 12.9–10, 18.6, 18.8, 21.1, 24.1–2, 24.12, 70.16, 90.10, 90.16, 90.41, *75*, *93*, *109*, *121*, *132*, *196*, *258*
self-directed commands 18.3, 70.8, 70.25 *170*
self-scrutiny *17–20*, 1.1–4, 12.6, 21.1, *Ep.* 53 *passim*, *75*, *192–6*
self-sufficiency 18.9
senate 21.9
Seneca the Elder *1*, 90.19, 114.16
Seneca, *Ad Helviam 1*, 90.10
   Apocolocyntosis 18.1, *108*
   De brevitate vitae 76
   De clementia 1, 47.20, 114.23–4
   De ira 19, 70.6, *216*
   Libri moralis philosophiae 2
   Naturales quaestiones 2, *5*
   Phoenissae 2
   De providentia 5
   Thyestes 2
sententiae (maxims) *25*, *30*, 7.10, 24.25, 70.28, 114.16
sex 21.11, 47.7, 70.2, *174–5*
Sextius, Quintus *17–18*, 64.2, 64.6
shipwreck (as metaphor) 53.4, 53.8, *194*
Sicily *5*, 53.3, 90.6, 114.26, *120*, *194*
slaves and slavery *13*, *21*, *26–7*, 1.1, 1.3, 12.2–3, 12.8, 12.10, 18.3, 18.8, 18.14, 24.8, 24.14, 46.3, *Ep.* 47 *passim*, 70.12, 70.19, 86.10, 86.15, 90.10, 90.19, *75*, *94*, *110*, *177–81*, *216*
smell 86.12–13, 86.17, *236*
social status 21.2, 24.11, 24.14, 47.10, 47.15–16, 70.19, 90.25, 114.12, *84*
Socrates *16*, *20*, 1.5, 7.6, 12.2, 24.3–4, 24.17, 24.25, 53.4, 64.10, 70.9, 70.12, 90.14, 90.23, *82–3*, *133–5*, *206*, *213*, *257*
Sotion *1*, *17*
starvation 70.6
Statius 86.6–9
Stoicism, key teachings of, *9–12*; history of *12–15*
style, literary *23–9*, 33.6, *Ep.* 46 *passim*, *Ep.* 114 *passim*, *156–7*

sublime *12*, *25*, 24.18, 64.6
Suetonius *28*
suicide *3*, 12.9–10, 24.6–11, 24.25–6, 70.5, 70.9–28, *132*, *134–5*, *213–7*
Sulla 24.4
Sulpicia 53.8
syllogisms *13*, 64.3, *205*

Tacitus *1*, *3*, *5*, *29*, 21.6, 24.9, 24.11, 70.5–6, 70.10, 70.12, 70.16, 70.22, 70.26, 90.7, *108*, *123*, *174*, *215–17*, *260*, *285–7*, *289*
Terentia 114.4, 114.6
Tertullian *30*, 7.3, *84*
Thrasea Paetus 24.7
Tiberius 21.4
time *9*, *19*, *Ep.* 1 *passim*, *Ep.* 12 *passim*, 18.7, 24.20, 46.4, 53.9, 64.8, 70.1–4, 70.16, *122*, *207*, *213*, *215*
Timon 18.7
torture 24.5, 24.14, 24.20, 47.4, 53.6, 86.10
tragedy 2, *22*, *179*
trees 33.1; (olive) 86.14–21; (plane) 12.2
Trimalchio 12.3, 12.9, 47.10, 86.4, 86.7, 86.11, 90.15, 90.39, 114.26, *180–1*, *216*, *260*, *290*

Ulysses 53.3–4
underworld 24.18, 24.20, 90.28

Valerius Maximus 24.3–5, 70.24, 86.1
Varro 86.12
Vatia 86.1, 86.8, 86.11, *96*, *193–4*, *234*
villas *5*, 12.1–4, 86.1–14
Virgil *18*, *22*, 12.9, 18.12, 21.5, 24.18, 53.1–3, 64.4, 64.9, 70.2, 86.14–16, 86.20, 90.4, 90.9, 90.11, 90.37, 114.23, *96*
virtue *10–11*, 47.15, 90.2–3, 90.16, 90.44–6, 114.12, *75*
visualisation *21*, 24.5, *135*, *216*
Vitruvius 90.10
vocative address 1.1

wealth *1–2*, *12*, *20*, 18.8–9, 21.8, 24.17, 86.7
weaving 33.5, 90.19–20
wife (Seneca's) *15*
will, the 34.3, *70*
wise man (*sapiens*) *10–12*, *14*, *18*, 7.6, 7.12, 12.9, 18.6, 18.8, 24.1,

24.5–7, 24.17, 24.25–6, 34.3,
47.1, 53.11, 70.4–5, 90.5, 90.13,
90.16, 90.23, 90.31, 90.34–6,
90.44–6, *122*, *132–3*, *169*, *196*,
206, *234*, *288*
withdrawal *14*, *20*, *22*, 7.8, 33.8,
86.1, 86.3, 86.20, *108*, *120*,
235–6
witness *20*, *93*

women 24.14, 33.2, 33.5, 47.17, 70.6,
70.22, 114.4

youth 12.4, 47.7, 70.1

Zeno *12*, *25*, 24.5, 33.4, 33.7, 53.4,
64.7, 64.10, 114.4, *82*, *122*, *156*,
195, *205*
Zeuxis 33.5